Praise for *The Last Tycoons*, an *Economist* and *Evening Standard* (UK) Book of the Year

"A tour de force . . . a tale of mistresses, betrayal, and Cuban cigars."
—Bloomberg News

"Meticulously researched and titillatingly provocative . . . packed with juicy tidbits."
—*Fortune*

"An exciting insider's account of Wall Street infighting."
—*Publishers Weekly*

"Cohan, who once worked at Lazard, tells a sprawling, gossip-filled tale about the firm, the careful cultivation of its lustrous reputation and, in the last decade or so, that reputation's apparent undoing. It is far from an epic tragedy—the story is, after all, about money and its most avid pursuers . . . But Cohan's portrayal of the firm's dominant partners—whose gargantuan appetites and mercurial habits provide the unifying force behind the book's operatic melodramas—makes this an epic in its own way. In fact, *The Last Tycoons* bears a striking resemblance to F. Scott Fitzgerald's *The Last Tycoon*."
—*New York Times Book Review*

"Detailing the firm's founding and establishment in America and parallel development in Europe, Cohan proves an amiable and intelligent tour guide. In addition to his ample knowledge of business, finance, and human nature, he also places events in their historical context, a clear by-product of his research."
—*Columbia Daily Tribune*

"In *The Last Tycoons*, William Cohan pulls back the curtain to reveal a den of infighting, back-stabbing, and greed no different from the rest of Wall Street."
—*Boston Globe*

"A fascinating, if somewhat tangled, tale of power, ego, and lots and lots of money."
—*Enterprise*

"The most comprehensive primary-source history available."
—*Library Journal*

"William D. Cohan's *The Last Tycoons* has already become this decade's required reading in the dealmaking community."
—*Dealmaker*

"An intriguing mixture of *The Bonfire of the Vanities, Barbarians at the Gate,* and *Suite Francaise,* the revelatory novel about the first years of the Nazi occupation of France . . . If you want an understanding of today's capitalism, read this, but be warned, it is not a pretty sight."
—*Guardian* (UK)

Anchor Books
A Division of Random House, Inc.
New York

THE LAST TYCOONS

THE SECRET HISTORY OF LAZARD FRÈRES & CO.

WILLIAM D. COHAN

FIRST ANCHOR BOOKS (BROADWAY BOOKS) EDITION, 2008

Title page photograph courtesy of Inmagine

Library of Congress Cataloging-in-Publication Data
Cohan, William D.
The last tycoons : the secret history of Lazard Frères & Co. / William D. Cohan.
p. cm.
1. Lazard Frères & Co.—History. 2. Banks and banking—New York (State)—New York—History. 3. Bankers—New York (State)—New York—Biography. 4. Banks and banking—France—History. 5. Bankers—France—Biography. I. Title.
HG2613.N54L39 2007
332.660944—dc22 2006025303

Anchor ISBN: 978-0-7679-1979-1

Book design by Maria Carella

www.anchorbooks.com

PRINTED IN THE UNITED STATES OF AMERICA
10 9 8 7 6 5

Contents

To Deb, Teddy, and Quentin

CHAPTER 1

"GREAT MEN"

Even among the great Wall Street firms—Goldman Sachs, Morgan Stanley, and Merrill Lynch—Lazard Frères & Co. stood apart, explicitly priding itself on being different from, and superior to, its competitors. For 157 years, Lazard had punched above its weight. Unlike other Wall Street banks, it competed with intellectual rather than financial capital and through a hard-won tradition of privacy and independence. Its strategy, put simply, was to offer clients the wisdom of its Great Men, the finest and most experienced collection of investment bankers the world had ever known. They risked no capital, offering only the raw Darwinian power of their ideas. The better the idea, and the insights and tactics required to achieve the result contemplated by it, the greater was Lazard's currency as a valued and trusted adviser—and the larger were the piles of money the Great Men hauled out of the firm and into their swelling bank accounts. The lucky few men—yes, always men—at Wall Street's summit have always been portrayed as ambitious and brilliant on the one hand and unscrupulous and ruthless on the other. But the secret history of Lazard Frères & Co., the world's most elite and enigmatic investment bank, twists parts of this conventional wisdom into knots of unfathomable complexity. The Great Men chronicled herein amassed huge fortunes—to be sure—but they refused to admit to anyone, least of all to themselves, that their pursuit of these riches led to relentless infighting. Instead they spoke, without irony, of being part of a Florentine guild and of advice whispered to heads of state and to CEOs of the world's most powerful corporations, while all the time attempting to preserve the mythical *special idea* that was Lazard. They also, to a person, craved an equally elusive chimera: the assurance that somehow, despite everything, they alone had remained *virtuous*.

But starting in the mid-1980s, the wisdom of Lazard's Great Men strategy began to show its considerable age, especially when Lazard was compared with its better capitalized and more powerful and nimble foes. The firm's numerous strategic missteps were exacerbated by the increasingly titanic generational struggle inside Lazard between the likes of Felix Rohatyn and Steve Rattner—superstar investment bankers and pillars of New York society—as well as by the bizarre behavior of the increasingly isolated and bitter Michel David-Weill, the French billionaire who controlled Lazard and fomented the struggle from his imperial lair. And at the climactic moment, Bruce Wasserstein, the supreme opportunist, came along to pick Michel's considerable pockets. The decades of internal turmoil and paternalistic management led ultimately to the once-unthinkable: a Lazard Frères free from its founders, as a publicly traded company just like any other, its operational flaws and obscene profitability open to the world—its special cachet lost forever.

The story of Lazard has always been one of internecine warfare, calamity, and resurrection, proving definitively that the forces of "creative destruction"—in the Austrian economist Joseph Schumpeter's famous observation—are alive and well to this day in American capitalism.

OF ALL LAZARD'S Great Men, none was greater than Felix George Rohatyn. Felix was considered by many to be the world's preeminent investment banker. He was the man who saved, first, Wall Street and then New York City from financial ruin in the early 1970s. For some thirty years at the end of the twentieth century, he had unofficially presided over Lazard Frères, helping to transform it into Wall Street's most prestigious, enigmatic, and mysterious investment banking partnership. But on one of those impossibly close days in our nation's capital, in the summer of 1997, Rohatyn found himself at the end of his tenure at Lazard, testifying before a Senate subcommittee in hopes of obtaining ratification of his appointment to a position he had long maintained was beneath him.

"It is a great honor for me to appear before you today to seek your consent to President Clinton's nomination of me to serve as the next American Ambassador to France," the sixty-nine-year-old Felix told the Subcommittee on European Affairs of the Senate Foreign Relations Committee. "It is also a very emotional experience, for many reasons. . . . I am, as you know, a refugee who came to this country from Nazi-occupied Europe in 1942. As long as I can remember, going back to those very dark days, being an American was my dream. I was fortunate to achieve that dream, and America has more than fulfilled all of my expectations. To represent, at this time, my adopted country as her Ambassador would be the culmination of my career; to have been nominated to

represent my country in France, a country where I spent part of r childhood and with which I have had a lifelong relationship, both profe sional and personal, seems to me more than I could ever have hoped for.

In truth, the thick-browed, beaver-toothed Felix had for more thar twenty years campaigned relentlessly for more, much more. With absolute clarity of mind, he knew he deserved better than an ambassadorship, a position he once likened to that of butler. Felix was *the* Great Man of Lazard, Le Corbusier of the most important mergers and acquisitions, or M&A, deals of the second half of the twentieth century, the ultimate rainmaker and corporate confidant, who year after year single-handedly generated hundreds of millions of dollars in fees for himself and his partners, thereby controlling his colleagues through a delicious combination of fear and greed.

After all, who could possibly afford to disobey a man who put so much money into his partners' pockets while taking far less than he was entitled to? When Felix called or wandered through Lazard's spartan offices in One Rockefeller Center, his partners snapped to attention, dropped whatever they might be doing, and acceded to his every wish. As his deal-making prowess continued unabated over the years, he had somehow also found the energy to volunteer his precious time and incomparable insights to solve two of this country's major financial crises of the second half of the twentieth century.

First, in the early 1970s, he worked round the clock to cobble together solutions that stanched the bleeding caused by the "back-office crisis" afflicting many of the largest old-line Wall Street brokerages. Through a series of nail-biting and courageously conceived mergers, Felix prevented the meltdown of a large part of the securities industry. Second, he is credited with almost single-handedly devising the financial rescue package that saved New York City from bankruptcy in 1975, standing tall against President Gerald Ford and his incendiary refusal to help. With these matters resolved satisfactorily, Felix became Hamlet, the lone voice, *the* Democrat in exile during the fallow years of Ronald Reagan and George H. W. Bush, exhorting the party faithful to action through his regular dispatches in the tony pages of the *New York Review of Books*, creating what became nothing less than the Rohatyn Manifesto. He courted the great intellectuals and leaders of the day in his genteel salon on Fifth Avenue and at his annual Easter egg hunts at his Southampton manse. He was the epitome of the Great Man.

By the time of Bill Clinton's election in 1992, he not only wanted desperately to be secretary of the Treasury but believed he had earned it. Maybe he even was owed it. Indeed, some believe he had wanted the

post as early as the Carter administration. Had Jimmy Carter been able to win another presidential election and had Felix been less critical of Carter in his writings, speeches, and interviews, he might have had a shot. But in 1980, Carter lost in a landslide to Ronald Reagan. So Felix had waited stoically through the two Reagan terms and that of the first Bush for the return of a Democrat to the White House. His moment had finally arrived, along with Clinton's, in November 1992. Felix vigorously lobbied for the Treasury secretary post, through the clandestine channels that exist for such genteel advocacy and by manipulating the levers he had pulled for years with the dexterity of a maestro: his legendary orchestration of the notoriously fickle troika of corporate chieftains, New York society, and the press was the envy of every investment banker and corporate lawyer on the planet.

And yet Felix's considerable efforts had fallen short, for reasons that begin to reveal the many nuances and contradictions of one of America's most powerful—and least scrutinized—men. When Clinton came to see Felix in his diminutive, picture-lined Lazard office during the election season of 1992, the Napoleonic Rohatyn received him coolly and enigmatically, having for some reason failed to fully perceive the Clinton juggernaut. He chose instead to lend his considerable prestige to the third-party candidate H. Ross Perot, the Texas billionaire and founder of EDS Corporation, who was his former client.

Felix had first met Perot in the early 1970s at the urging of John Mitchell, Richard Nixon's first attorney general. Mitchell thought Perot would be helpful to Felix in solving the New York Stock Exchange crisis. Felix then brokered a deal whereby Perot invested what turned out to be close to $100 million in DuPont Glore, a failing old-line brokerage. Perot's investment at the time represented the largest amount of money ever invested by a single individual in a Wall Street firm. DuPont Glore failed anyway, and Perot lost his investment. Yet his friendship with Felix blossomed. Felix served on EDS's board of directors and advised Perot on the sale of EDS to General Motors. He rewarded Perot's loyalty by supporting him through much of the 1992 presidential campaign—a point Felix tries to parse today, in hindsight. But Perot's presidential aspirations were predictably unsuccessful, as were, not surprisingly, Felix's own to become secretary of the Treasury after Clinton's election.

Even though many important and influential people believed Felix to be immensely deserving, through a combination of hubris, bad luck, and political miscalculation he didn't get the prize. Clinton turned first to Senator Lloyd Bentsen and then to Robert Rubin, the former co-CEO of Goldman Sachs—a man nine years Rohatyn's junior with nary a trace

of his civic accomplishments or reputation. But Rubin had been doing something that Felix had not been willing to do, that Felix had felt uncomfortable doing: Rubin had raised millions of dollars for Clinton and for the Democratic Party. There are rewards for that kind of thing.

In his memoir, *In an Uncertain World,* Rubin makes no mention of perceiving any competition with Felix for the Treasury job. But he does recount, with some frustration, Felix's Great Man status and his preeminence as a banker. Rubin had hurt his back just prior to a board of directors meeting for one of his clients, Studebaker-Worthington, at which Rubin and Goldman were to play the dual role of board members and investment bankers. Rubin recounted how he attended the Saturday board meeting, at the request of the CEO, Derald Ruttenberg, lying flat on his back, as the board met to consider whether to sell the company.

"I thought," Rubin recalled, "If I don't go, he'll hire Felix Rohatyn—the renowned investment banker from Lazard whom Ruttenberg had also mentioned. I couldn't walk for more than a few yards at the time, or even sit, but I went to Ruttenberg's office and lay on his window seat. We got the business, though much to my dismay, Ruttenberg gave Felix part of the fee. (It's more than twenty-five years later, but I still remember the amount.) Ruttenberg said he wanted Felix to be satisfied, given his importance in the world."

His importance in the world. Rubin, as capable of flattery as the next monumentally successful investment banker, was simply and matter-of-factly acknowledging Felix's canonical position among the power elite of merger advisers, a rare breed of peacock the brightness of whose plumage had been known to fade from year to year.

Regardless of the decade, Felix has been a constant atop the leaderboard of M&A advisers. Even today, at seventy-eight, his diplomatic career complete, he still advises powerful CEOs on their most important deals and receives millions of dollars in fees for his work.

At Lazard, Felix had come to personify the firm's unique—and uniquely successful—business strategy of employing the smartest and most experienced investment bankers to offer ambitious corporate CEOs sagacious insight on how to do deals, and nothing more. No loans. No underwriting of debt or equity (or barely any). No published research. No questionable off-balance-sheet financing "vehicles." Only Great Men offering advice to the world's business leaders. There was a good deal of myth to this legend, of course, since as with any large group of people, the 80-20 rule applied to Lazard as well—with Felix among the 20 percent of the partners who produced 80 percent of the revenues.

But unlike his mentor, the tyrannical and legendary André Meyer,

Felix found offering advice to clients exhilarating—and he was bored by management responsibilities. He often described Lazard as simply "a group of important people, giving important people advice." Felix was proud to be solely an adviser whose wisdom was sought out internationally for cogent, insightful advice on mergers and acquisitions: nothing more, nothing less—and not a trace of apology for not being the top underwriter of junk bonds (a product he railed against) or equity offerings. No frustration with not being a private-equity investor. *The Big Boys*, a 1986 book by Ralph Nader and William Taylor, referred to Felix as "the interstitial man," someone who gets in the middle of things. Raymond Troubh, a former Lazard partner, was one of many people quoted by Nader and Taylor about Felix.

"Felix is enveloping the world," Troubh confided. "He is sort of the Henry Kissinger of the financial arena. He is stepping into politics as Kissinger is stepping into finance. . . . But I don't think his [public role] was a calculated decision. He never said, 'I'm going to be prominent on the public scene.' He wanted to be a great investment banker. That brought him into the eyes of the kingmakers in different arenas, in New York and Washington, and from then on his ability pushed him. . . . I equate him with Kissinger, who I think is an outstanding example of a combination of brilliance, power and will to win. I put Felix in the same basket, exactly the same basket." In his own interviews with Nader, Felix deflected the Kissinger comparison in a way that betrayed his hidden insecurities. "Oh, because we are foreign born," Felix allowed. "Because we are negotiators. Also, we are friends. But Henry has wielded levers of power that I haven't come close to." In his response to Nader, Felix conveniently overlooked one important trait he shared—and shares—with Kissinger: an insatiable desire to control all that is written about him. Accordingly, Nader also dubbed Felix "the Teflon investment banker" for his ability to generate impressive amounts of fawning publicity that ignored some of his more questionable judgments.

For years, Felix preferred to think of himself more in the mold of his hero, Jean Monnet, today a relatively obscure French economist, but essential to the creation of the European Common Market. Monnet never held a post in any French government. "But he accomplished a great deal," Felix told William Serrin of the *New York Times* in 1981. "I don't flatter myself into thinking I'm Jean Monnet. But I believe that ideas in themselves have great power, if you have a platform that has legitimacy."

Felix made the Monnet comparison often during the 1980s, the basic message being that one does not need to hold a powerful public office to introduce powerful ideas into the public debate. In 1982 he gave the commencement address at Middlebury College, his alma mater, and made Monnet the subject of his speech. "Monnet played the roles of negotiator, agitator, propagandist, tactician and strategist, which are needed to effect fundamental political change in a democratic society," he told the graduates. Four years later, Nader asked Felix whether his 1982 description of Monnet was equally applicable to himself. "Sure, absolutely," Felix replied. "It is the only role I can play. It is the only role a private citizen can play as long as you have some sort of platform. That's why Monnet was always my role model. He was never a member of government. He never held a cabinet position. He never ran for office."

Such an extraordinary comparison of an investment banker to a man of great political and economic accomplishment is simply not conceivable today (with the possible, ironic exception of Bob Rubin). Felix alone compares favorably. The aftereffects of the collapsing stock market bubble and the plethora of corporate scandals have left many observers believing that bankers are self-interested and greedy rather than purveyors of independent advice. "Investment bankers, as a class, are the Ernest Hemingways of bullshit," explained one well-known private-equity investor. Felix had few peers in the days when offering CEOs strategic wisdom was the métier of a select handful; he has none now that it is the medium of the many.

❦

But those who knew Felix best would recognize, for all the sincerity in his voice, the irony of the moment on the eve of his confirmation as the ambassador to France. Seated before the senators was indeed a remarkable man, whose life had resulted from the alchemy of mid-twentieth-century European history—complete with a wild dash across Europe, North Africa, and South America to escape the Nazis—and the American Dream. Felix may have come as close as any man—certainly any Jewish man—in the past century to replicating, in his own, less ostentatious way, the extraordinary financial, political, and social influence that J. P. Morgan had wielded in the previous one.

But unlike Morgan, who seemed satisfied with both his incredibly great wealth and the great power attached to it, Felix desperately wanted political influence on the world stage. But he was also an accomplished enough spinmeister to claim not to seek power overtly, either. "I think power is something you can't run after," he told Nader and Taylor. But when it came to politics, Felix would have to content himself with following Thomas Jefferson's footsteps along the Rue du Faubourg Saint-Honoré, in Paris, without having a prayer of following his path farther to Washington. His inability to achieve his political ambition is one of the very few failures in his otherwise charmed life. In a way, Felix had succeeded in becoming his hero, Jean Monnet.

To be sure, Felix's investment banking accomplishments are legendary. He alone can claim to have advised corporate executives on transformational deals in each of the last five decades across disparate industries. One could argue, quite rightly, that Felix invented the persona of investment banker as trusted corporate M&A adviser. Although he might find the comparison indelicate because he abhorred junk bonds, in the 1960s Felix divined the business of providing independent M&A advice to corporate chieftains in much the same way as the infamous Michael Milken conjured up the high-yield junk-bond market in the 1980s. In an utterly typical week in January 1969, for instance, Felix had many meetings, including those with Howmet, a French aerospace company where he was on the board of directors, and with Harold Geneen (CEO of ITT), Nicholas Brady (then a banker at Dillon Read and later the U.S. Treasury secretary), and the CEO of National Cash Register. On another day that week, he had meetings with both Herb Allen, the billionaire patriarch of Allen & Co., a media investment bank, and Pete Peterson, the newly appointed secretary of commerce in the Nixon administration and his former client when Peterson was CEO of Bell & Howell. The next day, after two internal meetings, he had meetings with the chairman of General Signal Corporation, the chairman of the Continental Insurance Companies, and ITT executives. Finally, there was again a meeting with the chairman of General Signal and with the CEO of Martin Marietta. His weekly schedule also noted that his son, Nicholas, had his tonsils removed.

Felix's tale is very much the affirmation of a refugee's idealized version of the American Dream. Felix's family is from the town of Rohatyn in the Ukraine, part of a region that has been conquered and reconquered for centuries. Before World War II, Rohatyn was somewhat of a Jewish enclave, especially after 1867, when Jews were granted full rights as citizens of Austria-Hungary. The 1900 census for the town shows a population of 7,201 people, with 3,217 of them Jewish. By 1939, Rohatyn still had 2,233 Jews. Today there are no Jews in the town of ten thousand, although the decrepit remains of a Jewish cemetery are still evident. A number of organizations in New York and Israel are dedicated to preserving the history of the Jewish families of Rohatyn. According to Felix, not only was his great-grandfather "the grand rabbi of the region" but "he was also a reasonably able capitalist, since, according to the stories, he owned some stables and rented them to the Polish cavalry."

At the turn of the twentieth century, his forebears moved to

Vienna—probably having taken the name Rohatyn from their town of origin—where his grandfather became a member of the Vienna Stock Exchange and the proprietor of a small bank, Rohatyn & Company. He also owned several breweries. Felix's father, Alexander, worked in the breweries, and over time he managed them for his father. In 1927, Alexander married Edith Knoll, an accomplished pianist "who came from a family of wealthy Viennese merchants." Felix was their only child, born in Vienna on May 29, 1928. Although circumstances prevented him from staying in Vienna long, something of the city's musical gestalt seeped into his bloodstream. He failed to develop any musical skills but appreciates classical music and still listens to it for hours at his Fifth Avenue home, while reading or writing. His favorite composers are Beethoven, Schumann, and Brahms. And the one piece of music he "would take to a desert island, if I could only take one," would be Mozart's Mass in C Minor. "It is the music I sort of take refuge with . . . no matter what I'm doing and I have some time and I'm home," he said. "I find it touching. I find it remarkable."

Economic reality quickly overtook the Rohatyns. Felix's grandfather was a bit of a speculator, and in the hangover from the Great Depression that swept across Europe in the early 1930s, he "rapidly lost all of his money," causing the failure of his bank. Thus began the small family's quasi-nomadic existence in Eastern Europe as Alexander moved from one of his father's remaining breweries to another. The first stop was Romania, where the family moved shortly after Felix was born so that his father could manage a brewery there. They returned briefly to Vienna in 1935, but in the wake of the July 1934 assassination of Chancellor Engelbert Dollfuss by the Austrian Nazis the growing specter of anti-Semitism was palpable. "I mean, the Austrians were Nazis themselves," Felix explained some seventy years later. The family quickly moved again, this time to France and in particular to Orléans, a city south of Paris on the Loire River. Alexander became the manager of another of his father's breweries.

Once there, though, Felix's parents divorced. "A very traumatic thing for me," Felix told *The New Yorker.* And when he was eight, his mother sent him to a French-speaking boarding school in Switzerland. "I remember that at the time I was so unathletic and overweight that I had great difficulty in tying my shoelaces," he said. "It took me so long to get dressed in the morning that I would go to bed with my pajamas over most of my clothes in order to save time. It was not a very glorious exercise." While Felix was away at school, his mother married Henry Plessner, a prosperous scion of a Polish Jewish family that owned a precious-metals trading business. The Plessners moved to Paris, where Henry ran the family operation. Plessner, a devoted Zionist, developed significant business relationships with both Lazard Frères et Cie in Paris and Les Fils Dreyfus, a small Swiss bank founded in Basel in 1813. Although Felix didn't get along with his stepfather at first, Plessner's relationships would prove to be very valuable to Felix.

The story of Felix's escape from the Nazis is intense and personal, and says much about his outlook on the world—especially when the multiple layers of veneer that he has applied to it over the years are stripped away. In 1938, Felix left his Swiss boarding school and returned to Paris. He remembered the continuous droning of the air raid sirens in the streets of Paris following the German invasion of Poland, and France and England's declaration of war. He carried a gas mask with him to school. There were big posters all over Paris declaring that the French would defeat the Germans. In May 1940, as the German armies were approaching the outskirts of Paris, he mistook for thunder the artillery outside the window of his luxurious Sixteenth Arrondissement apartment. His mother, Plessner's mother, and the family's longtime Polish cook fled Paris and headed south in their car. Strapped to the roof were mattresses. They also took with them as many gas coupons as they could find. In what is now one of the legendary Felix stories—whether apocryphal or true is not clear—his mother had him open the end of several tubes of Kolynos toothpaste and fill them with gold coins from a collection his stepfather had assembled. His stepfather, meanwhile, who remained a Polish citizen, had already been taken to an internment camp in Brittany for Jewish refugees. His outspoken Zionism had landed him on a Gestapo list. Thus began Felix's well-documented two-year odyssey across three continents, which took him and his family to Biarritz, Cannes, Marseille, Oran, Casablanca, Lisbon, Rio de Janeiro, and then finally to New York City—"the classic route, false papers, the whole bit," he told the *Wall Street Journal* in a 1975 profile. His harrowing escape across war-torn Europe couldn't have been more different from that of his future Lazard partners André Meyer and Pierre David-Weill, although in a way it was probably every bit as harrowing as the clandestine existence in the French countryside of Michel David-Weill—Pierre's only son.

At the outset, Felix's mother decided the family would be safe if it could get to Spain. So they set out to get across the Spanish border before France fell to the Germans. "We started driving down with thousands of other cars and trucks and bicycles and people walking along the roads," he explained more than sixty years later. "The roads were jammed, and every now and then German planes were coming over and strafing a little bit here and there. We kept going down [toward Spain], and we had to bribe people at gas stations to sell us coupons." Felix was eleven years old, and the Germans were sweeping through France. The family managed to get to Biarritz, the glamorous French city on the Atlantic coast adjacent to the Spanish border. Just before the Germans arrived in Biarritz—and even though they did not have Spanish visas—the family went to the closest town on the French-Spanish border, Saint-Jean-de-Luz, a picturesque fishing port, where guides were known to help refugees navigate the border crossing. But Plessner's elderly mother wasn't strong enough for a hike across the Pyrenees. So just as the Germans were occupying Biarritz and marching past the optimistic French posters—"something I will never forget," Felix said—the family set off again, this time for Cannes, on the Mediterranean.

The armistice had just been signed in June 1940, creating a divided France: German-occupied France and Vichy France. For a family of Jews from Vienna, there were not many good options. Biarritz was in German-occupied France. Cannes was in Vichy France, although still unoccupied by the Germans. "And we thought, clearly it's not good either way, but we'll be better off in Vichy France than in German-occupied France," Felix explained. "So we decided to try to drive down to Vichy France and to go south in order to ultimately try to get visas to go someplace. But we didn't really have any papers to get across these demarcation lines. And my mother talked to a guy in a hotel or something about some back roads that we could use to get across there, where there wouldn't be any German checkpoints. It was very early in the occupation. And so we took a secondary road out of Biarritz and we came around, out of the woods, and there was this long line of cars because there's a German checkpoint. And I didn't know much, but I knew enough to know this was bad news. And so we were there in this line and we couldn't turn, so we were inching along. And the car was getting closer and closer. I knew there was a young German soldier checking something. And finally we got there, and he decided to light a cigarette. And he waved the car ahead of us through, and my mother took her driver's license and waved it at him and he motioned us through. I don't think he stopped the car behind us or two cars behind us, but I mean it was very close. It was very close." Felix told *The New Yorker* that ever since this life-or-death incident, "I have felt that I had a great debt to somebody somewhere." Of this same incident, he told the *New York Times* columnist Bob Herbert in 2005, "It was a miracle." Somehow his mother was able to get messages to his stepfather, who had managed to escape, along with some others, from the internment camp. "As the Germans were coming in one side of the camp, they jumped over the other side and four of them stole a car and drove south," Felix explained. "And because they were always just a few miles ahead of the German columns, everybody thought they were Germans, so they got gasoline and stuff like that." Felix and the women kept driving south to the Mediterranean and stopped at a *pension de famille*—a small hotel—between Cannes and Marseille, where at last Plessner joined them. They stayed at the pension for nearly a year.

The Rohatyns' next objective was to try to secure visas to get out of Vichy France into a safer country, preferably America, which to Felix represented freedom and opportunity. "There were always hidden radios wherever we were going—because you weren't supposed to listen to overseas broadcasts—but I had managed to listen to Roosevelt and Churchill speaking, even though I didn't speak the language very well," he explained. Roosevelt inspired him. But visas to America were extremely difficult, if not impossible, for Jews to obtain. Visas to South America were slightly more plentiful, but only on the express condition that once they were obtained, the holders would make no effort to actually immigrate to the specified country. "Securing these visas was a dangerous and agonizingly difficult process," Herbert wrote in the *Times*. Exacerbating Felix's parents' overall concern was the deal the Vichy government made with the Germans, in April 1941, authorizing the roundup of all foreign-born Jews for deportation to the concentration camps. In all, some seventy-six thousand foreign-born Jews were deported from France with the help of the Vichy government. Some twenty-five hundred returned. The Rohatyns had to get out, fast. Felix's parents sought to get Brazilian visas but found themselves far down the list—number 447, to be exact—and their prospects for escape were growing dimmer.

Then another miracle occurred. This one, which Felix discovered the details of only recently and by serendipity, involved the courageous intervention of a relatively unknown Brazilian diplomat named Luiz Martins de Souza Dantas, the wartime Brazilian ambassador to France. Souza Dantas helped at least eight hundred Jews escape the Nazis and has since been dubbed "the Schindler of Brazil." He died in 1954. A recent book about him is titled *Quixote in the Darkness*. Souza Dantas, who was related by marriage to Katharine Graham (who in turn was related to André Meyer and to George Blumenthal, another Great Man of Lazard in the early twentieth century), helped Felix and his family obtain Brazilian diplomatic visas. They "looked very elegant," Felix said of the documents.

The Brazilian visas appeared to give Felix and his family a safety net, but they still hadn't given up the hope of obtaining the coveted safe passage to America. In pursuit of that dream, the family purchased tickets on a ship going from Marseille to Oran, a bustling port city in northwestern Algeria. The idea was to go from North Africa to Lisbon, one of the few places where it was still possible to secure visas to America. But the passage to Oran did not go smoothly, either. "As a last step, you had to go see somebody that was on an Italian commission because the Italians had taken over that part of France," Felix explained. "And they didn't like our papers, so they took us off the boat. And we didn't really know what was going to happen to us." But two weeks later, they tried again to take the ship to Oran. This time they were not taken off the boat.

They made it to Oran just as it appeared the Germans were set to invade Algeria, too. So they quickly took a train to Casablanca, Morocco. Felix has seen the movie *Casablanca* so many times that the reality of his experience in the city is utterly intertwined with Bogart's portrayal of it, and he has difficulty separating fact from fiction. He remembered, though, regularly visiting the docks in Casablanca to figure out when they could get a boat to Lisbon. He also recalled meeting and befriending Leo Castelli, who after arriving in New York became one of the world's foremost dealers of contemporary art. Castelli, it turned out, had also secured safe passage through the use of a Brazilian visa. For months, the Rohatyns attempted to get passage on a boat to Lisbon. "There were not that many ships going to Lisbon, and it was hard to get on them," he explained. But eventually, around the beginning of 1941, they did get on a boat bound for Lisbon, which must have seemed like paradise because the electricity was still plentiful and the city was ablaze at night. "I think that was probably the best moment, where I felt really that we had crossed over from one side to another," he said about arriving in Lisbon. Felix enrolled in a French-Portuguese school. But within months, the Germans looked like they might go through Spain, invade Portugal, and close off access to the Mediterranean.

The time had come to finally leave Europe. Still hoping to get to America, "we went to the American Consulate and got in line on the quota," Felix told *The New Yorker.* "It was very much like Menotti's opera 'The Consul.' There was a wait of eighty-seven years or something." Part of the problem, Felix said, was there were "people at the State Department . . . who really didn't want any more Jewish refugees in America. So the visas were very hard to get and [required] a very long, long wait."

With time running out, the family decided to use their unusual Brazilian diplomatic visas and get on a ship to Rio. The cross-Atlantic passage, beginning on March 17, 1941, took some two and a half weeks. They had no idea whether, when they arrived in Rio, they would be shipped back to Europe, as had happened to other Jewish refugees who thought they were safely on their way to Panama or Cuba or even America. But in Rio, the family was welcomed with open arms. "They thought this was a great visa and rolled out the red carpet," Felix said. It was yet another miracle.

Once again, they set about trying to obtain visas to America. This time it was a fifteen-month wait. In the meantime, Felix enrolled in school, played soccer, and developed a love for horseback riding and the samba. "I became enamored of the samba, as music, as culture, as rhythm," the socially conservative Rohatyn explained somewhat improbably. "And as a reflection of what Brazil was all about, which at that time was the country that gave us refuge." Stan Getz and João Gilberto's version of "The Girl from Ipanema" is still one of his favorite songs. Finally, in June 1942, Felix and his family were able to get the American visas and boarded a DC-3 from Rio to Miami. The plane, though, made an unexpected stop on the Caribbean island of Trinidad, because of "military priorities" or some such reason, Felix remembered. "We thought, 'My God! Are we gonna get stuck here or sent back or what?' " Finally, after a few weeks on the island, they got on another plane to Miami. They had made it.

NATURALLY, FELIX'S DESPERATE effort to escape, which began in Vienna in 1935 and ended in New York City in 1942, seared into him an inviolate worldview. He is at once preternaturally pessimistic about the outcome of events, extremely conservative financially, and far less prone to excessive ostentation than most of his extremely wealthy investment banking peers. "My most basic feelings about money go back to 1942, in France, when my family had to smuggle itself over the Spanish border one step ahead of the Nazis," he told the *New York Times* in 1976, recalling one of his favorite stories. "I spent our last night in a hotel room stuffing gold coins into toothpaste tubes. We had been well off, but that was all we got out. Ever since, I've had the feeling that the only permanent wealth is what you carry around in your head." By the time of his *New Yorker* profile in 1983, this tenet had been condensed to: "That experience has left me with a theory of wealth which is that of a refugee. The only things that count, basically, are things you can put in a toothpaste tube or carry in your head." For European Jewish families of means, such a lengthy and complex voyage was not unprecedented, but far more typical, of course, was the journey to the Nazi concentration camps.

What set Felix apart from the many thousands of other immigrants to these shores was how quickly he took the place by storm once he arrived in New York, at the end of June 1942. His stepfather had been able to transfer some money out of France to a bank in New York, and part of that money was used to buy a small apartment. Felix wasted no time making up for all the interruptions in his education. He enrolled in the McBurney School, then on West Sixty-third Street, because it was one of the few high schools in Manhattan to offer a summer program. He also convinced his mother that another way for him to learn English more quickly—Felix has always had an enviable facility with languages—would be to go to the movies, "because they had these sing-alongs—you know, follow the bouncing ball," he said. He excelled at McBurney, graduating in two years at the age of sixteen. He had a particular aptitude for math, science, and tennis and played on the varsity tennis team his last year at the school. A college counselor recommended to Felix, though, that he attend a small college because of his relative youth. His mother concurred. After a little investigation, he discovered that Middlebury College, in Vermont, offered a "cooperative program" with the Massachusetts Institute of Technology whereby he could study physics and engineering for three years at Middlebury and then for two years at MIT. He also liked to ski. He applied to Middlebury and was accepted.

He may have been one of the only Jewish students in the school at that time. During his sophomore year, he joined the Alpha Sigma Phi fraternity, whose national chapter had a policy against admitting Jews and blacks. Alpha Sigma Phi was founded in 1845 by three Yale freshmen. One day, the national organization sent a corporate executive—Felix thinks he was a vice president from AT&T—"to try to talk us out of this heinous thing of pledging a Jew and a Black." Felix sat through the meeting. The man had brought with him a couple of cases of beer to try to appease the fraternity members. Felix explained: "And this guy kept saying, 'You know, don't misunderstand me. Some of my best friends are Jewish.' " Soon after, "we gave him the beer back, and we took him to the railroad station and we sent him on his way." The local chapter got kicked out of the national fraternity for allowing a Jew and a black to join.

Felix diligently pursued his studies in physics, but soon it became clear to both him and his favorite professor, Benjamin Wissler—the chairman of the Middlebury physics department—that he was reaching his limit of aptitude in the subject. Wissler recommended not only that he pass on the MIT curriculum but also that he take a semester off.

Since he had not seen his father since 1941, Felix decided to go visit him in France in the summer of 1947. He took a ship across the Atlantic, and his father picked him up in the French port city of Le Havre. His father had remarried and was still managing the brewery, which had been relocated near Paris. They spent the summer in the south of France.

His father then asked him to spend the year working at the brewery. So Felix went to work in the Karcher brewery cleaning out the beer vats, having slimmed down sufficiently to be able to climb inside them. He also helped out in the bottling operation. He worked twelve hours a day, beginning at six in the morning. "I just stank from this stuff," he said. "And it was still a pretty hairy period where—I mean, here I was an American in a part of the city that was totally Communist, and all the unions working in the factory were Communist unions, and there were a lot of Algerians, too. So a couple of times a barrel came rolling by pretty close"—and here he chuckled to himself with the memory of an American Jew surrounded by Algerian Communists—"and I was never quite sure what it was. But I also remember when I would go back to the apartment and I was in the subway just stinking of this beer, people would look. I decided quickly this was not for me."

He returned to Middlebury for the second semester of 1948. He completed his degree in physics and graduated in 1949, thinking he might want to work at the nuclear laboratory in Oak Ridge, Tennessee.

Fortunately, though, with the help of his mother and stepfather, he also had been exposed to Wall Street. During the summers of 1945 and 1946, Felix was a runner and a stock transfer clerk at Jack Coe & Co., a small brokerage. He remembered celebrating VJ Day at the firm. He was paid about $20 a week and would occasionally be rewarded with baseball tickets to the Polo Grounds, on 155th Street. But to Felix, it was nothing more than a way to earn a few extra bucks, not unlike his previous summer jobs working in a drugstore and teaching English to Édith Piaf, the glamorous Parisian chanteuse. When he graduated from Middlebury, his stepfather helped again, this time getting Felix a job at Lazard Frères & Co. in New York. Plessner and Felix's mother had returned to live in Paris after the war. Plessner knew André Meyer through a foreign exchange and bullion trading operation that the two men had created somewhere between Les Fils Dreyfus, in Basel, and Lazard Frères et Cie, in Paris.

Patrick Gerschel, André Meyer's grandson, believed another reason that Felix was given a coveted spot at Lazard was that André was having an affair with Felix's mother. "It was about money and sex," Gerschel observed. "When has it ever been any different?"

CHAPTER 2

"Tomorrow, the Lazard House Will Go Down"

After two days of eerie silence following the earthquakes and fires that devastated San Francisco in the early morning of April 18, 1906, an unnamed bank officer of the London, Paris, and American Bank—the California outpost of Lazard Frères & Co.—was able to make his way through the rubble to a Western Union office and cable a staccato and desperate message back to his Lazard partners, three thousand miles away in New York City: "Entire business totally destroyed. Calamity cannot be exaggerated. Banks practically all destroyed. Our building completely destroyed. Vaults apparently intact. All records and securities safely in vaults. No lives lost among friends. Will wire fully upon . . ." The message ended tantalizingly. For the next few days, similar pleas for succor were sent to New York and the other two Lazard offices, in Paris and in London. These appeals met their own, inexplicable stony silence from the Lazard brethren, even though the capital needed to open these three offices had come from the ongoing success of the San Francisco operation.

A week after the initial calamity, on April 25, another, most emphatic missive was sent: "It is hardly necessary for us to say to you that this is the time for the London, Paris and American Bank, Ltd. to show all the strength that it may be able to command." Finally, the Lazard partners in New York responded and wired $500,000 to San Francisco and arranged for an additional $1.5 million line of credit to help resurrect their sister firm. The rescue financing allowed the San Francisco bank, operating from the basement of one of the partner's homes, to survive the disaster. This was not the first time—or the last—that the bank came close to collapse.

By the time of the great earthquake of 1906, Lazard had been around, in one form or another, for fifty-eight years. The story of the firm's humble origins as a dry goods store in New Orleans in 1848 has been buffed to such a high gloss it is no longer possible to determine if the tale is true. As a literal translation of the firm's name suggests, though, at least two Lazard brothers—Alexander, twenty-five years old, and Simon, then all of eighteen—likely in search of both a refuge from certain military conscription and better opportunities for Jews in America, moved to New Orleans in the early 1840s to be with an uncle, who had already been "making money in commerce" in the Big Easy. Once this beachhead had been established, the two brothers sent for their eldest sibling—Lazare Lazard—and he soon joined them. Together, on July 12, 1848, the three brothers founded Lazard Frères & Co. as a retail outpost for the sale of fine French clothing.

These three Jewish brothers had emigrated from Frauenberg, three miles from Sarreguemines, in the Alsace-Lorraine region of France. Their grandfather Abraham had probably walked to France through Germany, from Prague, in 1792, with the hope of seeking greater political freedom. At that time, France appeared momentarily more progressive in its treatment of Jews than did the surrounding countries: there were some forty thousand Jews in all of France then, with twenty-five thousand of them in Alsace-Lorraine (but only five hundred in Paris). Abraham became a farmer. His son Élie was born in Frauenberg. In 1820, Élie married Esther Aron, a banker's daughter who brought to the marriage a considerable dowry. Together they had seven children, among them five sons, including Lazare, Alexander, and Simon, the founders of the New Orleans store. When Élie Lazard died, Esther married Moïse Cahn. Together they had another four children, including Julie Cahn, who later married Alexander Weill, the Lazards' cousin and Michel David-Weill's great-grandfather.

WHILE REVOLUTION WAS sweeping across their homeland and reaching into other parts of Europe, the Lazards' New Orleans store was an immediate hit. Some of the profits were sent home to France—beginning a long Lazard tradition of sending the firm's profits around the globe.

Sadly, great calamities were not atypical in New Orleans, either. Fires destroyed huge swaths of the city in both 1788 and 1794. When a fire struck the city again in 1849, the Lazards' storefront was destroyed, only a year after the partnership started. The family was able to salvage much of the inventory, though, and in an act of prescience, the brothers moved the whole operation to San Francisco and set up a new store in the Wild West, selling their imported goods. The journey to California was arduous and took many months; Lazare and Simon nearly died from malnutrition. They survived to find San Francisco a bustling if somewhat disappointing frontier city where the prices of land, housing, and food were rising precipitously, along with the population. They realized quickly, though, that there was money to be made catering to the new arrivals, among them a wave of gold miners and speculators that had descended upon the city soon after a sustained vein of gold was found, also in 1848, on the edge of the Sierra Nevada. The Lazards' California operation (they were now joined by a fourth brother, Elie, named after his father) became the leading wholesale dry goods concern on the Pacific coast, and an increasingly important exporter of the gold coming out of the mines.

By 1855, "business was so brisk" that the Lazard brothers sent for their twenty-two-year-old cousin, Alexander Weill, to come from France to join the firm as the fifth employee. Weill served as the bookkeeper for his cousins' operation. "Gradually, the business became involved in financial transactions, first with its retail clients and then increasingly with others," according to a limited edition—only 750 copies were printed—of Lazard's 1998 self-published 150-year history. "Most often these dealings involved the sale of gold and the arbitrage of the different dollar currencies then in use, one backed by gold and the other by silver. Weill was the driving force taking the enterprise further and further into finance."

As the French were the chief trading partners for the Lazards, on or around July 20, 1858, the prospering firm opened an office in Paris under the name of Lazard Frères et Cie. With the Paris office up and running at 10 Rue Sainte-Cécile, the Lazard brothers returned to France. Alexander Weill remained in San Francisco in charge of the American outpost. Twelve years later, in the midst of the Franco-Prussian War of 1870–71, the family opened a third office, in London—christened Lazard Brothers & Co.—as a way to continue the importing and exporting of gold bullion after the French government curtailed all payments of foreign debts by domestic firms. The London office was considered a branch of the Paris office, but by enabling Lazard to continue to pay its bills as they came due, the London office added immeasurably to the firm's overall reputation at a time when other financial firms were defaulting on their debts.

By 1874, the firm was doing sufficiently well to be included in an article about the new breed of San Francisco millionaires.

In 1876, the partners made the "momentous" decision to sell their dry goods inventory at auction and refocus their business entirely on banking. On July 27, 1876, a new fourteen-year partnership agreement was drawn up between the four Lazard brothers, Alexander Weill, and the Lazards' half brother David Cahn, creating the Banking House of

Lazard Frères, to be known as Lazard Frères et Compagnie in Paris and as Lazard Frères in San Francisco. (London remained a branch of the Paris office.)

IN 1880, ALEXANDER Weill left San Francisco for New York with the intention of opening an office that would be a leader in the exporting of gold to Europe and spent four years in New York building the business there. In 1881, Lazard was named the treasurer of the Sutro Tunnel Company, a California gold mining concern that controlled the Comstock Lode, the Brunswick Lode, and a tunnel into Mount Davidson. Soon thereafter, Lazard vastly increased its export of gold to Europe. In March 1884, Lazard exported $500,000 of gold, some in bars, some in double eagle coins. Only Kidder Peabody, a once venerable old-line investment bank, at $1 million, exported more.

On August 30, 1888, Lazard Frères & Co. joined the New York Stock Exchange, with seven partners. While non–family members started to join Lazard at this time as "partners," ownership of the firm remained within the founding families.

The three Lazard houses, in New York, Paris, and London, continued to grow and thrive, mostly from successful foreign exchange and trading. The fact that by the turn of the twentieth century there were indigenous houses in the world's three most important financial centers made Lazard absolutely unique. No other fledgling banking partnership had a presence much beyond its country of origin, with the possible exception of the powerful J. P. Morgan & Co., which was developing pockets of influence across continental Europe and in England. Still, Lazard had something that even the omnipotent J. P. Morgan did not have: Lazard was an American firm in the United States, a French firm in France, and a British firm in the U.K. "The intellectual horizon at Lazard was, what do we make of the world," Michel explained at the time of the firm's 150th anniversary. "How do we understand it with the great privilege of being able to try to understand it from several points of view?"

One of the key ways Lazard maintained this aura of indigenousness was to engage in a form of loose primogeniture, with fathers passing to sons their coveted partnership seats. This occurred at each house. There was also, at least among the French families, a proclivity for arranged marriages and intermarriages. "The great strength of this family," observed the late writer Arnaud Chaffanjon, "is to have married between cousins, in the same clan. The Weill, Lazard, Cahn and Aron have married their first cousins. It's the best way to keep money within the family." This decision kept the growing fortune from getting dispersed. By the time Simon Lazard died, his son André and his nephew Michel were "already learning the business of banking in the Paris house." Alexander Weill brought his San Francisco–born, Paris-educated son, David Weill, into the firm, and he became a partner in 1900. In the late 1920s, David Weill would officially change the family name to David-Weill—he became David David-Weill—in an utterly successful effort to establish the family in French aristocracy, not the easiest thing to do at that time for immigrant Jews in socially stratified France. Pierre David-Weill would follow his father and assume the position of senior partner. And in due course, Michel David-Weill took over from Pierre as senior partner.

In London, the office was muddling along rather ineffectually as a bank or "bill office," regulated by the Bank of England. All of the partners in Paris were partners of the London branch, which accepted deposits, but mostly from other immigrant banking houses, such as the Rothschilds' and the Barings'. By 1905, Lazard Brothers wanted to develop more of a commercial and corporate business rather than simply being a bank to other banks. To that end, a year before his death, Alexander Weill searched for a well-regarded Englishman to bring into the firm, eventually enlisting Robert Kindersley, a highly successful and well-known City stockbroker—the City being London's equivalent of Wall Street—as a full partner in Lazard Brothers with the French. Kindersley joined Lazard Brothers in 1905 and quickly brought it to prominence. He was the first Lazard partner to focus on the business of advising corporations, not only in foreign exchange and commercial loans but also in the little-known world of mergers and acquisitions.

Kindersley helped to recruit badly needed new blood to the London house. Lazard Brothers' reputation had advanced sufficiently that by 1914, at the outbreak of World War I, the firm was named one of England's accepting houses and served on the Accepting Houses Committee, one of about seventeen such financial institutions so honored, an indication of how far Lazard Brothers had come from its origins as a lowly outpost of the French firm. In London's financial circles, this was a big deal.

Kindersley also had more than a passing business relationship with Weetman Pearson, a major British international financier and industrialist. At some point between 1910 and the dawning of World War I, Kindersley introduced Pearson to David Weill, and Pearson made a small investment in Lazard Brothers. After World War I, the Bank of England developed strict new regulations about the degree of foreign ownership it would permit in the English banking system. As a result, Pearson, now known as Lord Cowdray, and S. Pearson & Son Ltd. increased its stake in Lazard Brothers to 50 percent, with the other half being owned by Lazard Frères et Cie. The consequences of the Pearsons' stake in Lazard Brothers would reverberate through the three houses for years, finally coming to a head some ninety years later.

❦

As had been preordained, Frank Altschul, whose father, Charles, had emigrated from London to San Francisco during the gold rush and become one of the first nonfamily partners of Lazard, joined the New York office after graduating from Yale. He became a partner the same day his father retired—July 1, 1916. Except in the case of the descendants of Alexander Weill and, for a time, some of the Lazard family, the passing on of the partnership seat was not the same as passing along an ownership interest in the firm.

Still, the profitability of the Lazard partnership was even then an invitation to vast riches, and Lazard partners became among the wealthiest men in their respective countries, regardless of whether they had an ownership stake in the firm. Frank Altschul became fabulously wealthy at Lazard, too. During his lifetime, which spanned ninety-four years, he donated millions of dollars to Yale, his beloved alma mater. In 1913, Altschul had cemented his position in the upper reaches of the Jewish financial hierarchy of New York by marrying Helen Lehman Goodhart of the Lehman Brothers banking fortune. His sister married Herbert Lehman, the former Lehman Brothers partner who would later serve as the governor of New York and its U.S. senator. Over time, Altschul also contributed $500,000 to Williams College and $1 million to Mount Sinai Hospital. He also donated hundreds of thousands for the legal defense of Sacco and Vanzetti, an effort being led by Felix Frankfurter, then a Harvard law professor and eventually a Supreme Court justice. One day Frankfurter showed up at Altschul's office at Lazard, eager "to see what kind of man in Wall Street could be sending money for Sacco and Vanzetti." Thereafter, Frankfurter and Altschul remained lifelong friends. Altschul lived at 550 Park Avenue, at the southwest corner of East Sixty-second Street, and owned a 450-acre estate—named Overbrook Farm—outside Stamford, Connecticut, where in 1934, in an abandoned pigpen, he started Overbrook Press, known for the graphic and technical excellence of its elegant publications.

❦

One of the first issues Altschul confronted after he became a Lazard partner, as early as October 1917, was the growing possibility that the French families would decide to liquidate and shutter either Lazard Brothers in London or Lazard Frères in New York. This was yet another life-threatening crisis for the fledgling firm. During a multiweek visit to Paris in October 1918 (as part of his war service in the U.S. Army), where these matters were discussed "in some detail," Altschul became well versed in the views of the French. In a three-page, single-spaced letter to George Blumenthal, the New York office's senior partner, Altschul was happy to report that the French partners were now far more sanguine about the prospects for a three-house firm: "There is a very real desire to continue both L.F. and L.B. & Co., and a very strong belief that the Trio is in an excellent position because of their name, their connections, and their general lay-out, to play an increasingly important part, in the after-war development." He continued, "As they say, the firm had a first rate name before the war; the reputation of the house has if anything been enhanced during the war; and it should be possible to use our name and credit to greater advantage." Crisis averted.

When he returned to New York after the war, Altschul began to assume, from Blumenthal, more and more of the day-to-day responsibility of running the firm. But Altschul's authority extended only so far, as he still regularly deferred to the more powerful Blumenthal about matters such as negotiating annual partnership percentages, the reprimanding of partners who were deemed to be lazy or underperforming, and the proper accounting of costs among the three houses. Like his father, Altschul had numerous interests outside of Lazard, one of which was international affairs. In 1920, he helped to found the Council on Foreign Relations in New York, and from the start he hoped the council would be able to influence U.S. foreign policy—one of the organization's continuing goals.

AN INDICATION OF how important Lazard and Altschul had become in the world financial markets arose in 1923, when the French occupation of the Ruhr, Adolf Hitler's failed Beer Hall Putsch, and the resultant international uncertainty led to havoc in the market. France found itself in a full-blown financial crisis. The value of the French franc fell by some 50 percent. In January 1924, the French Ministry of Finance summoned Altschul to Paris to hear his views on solving the French currency crisis. In a carefully prepared speech, which Altschul delivered in Paris on January 24, he called for the French government to undertake what he called an "experiment" designed to stabilize the plunging currency. "This would involve arranging credits for the government in the United States and perhaps in England, in round amounts," he told the French. "It is felt that a banking group could readily be formed in New York to extend the necessary facilities under appropriate guarantees on reasonable terms. The present ease in the New York money market and the fundamental friendship for and confidence in France make this appear likely." He averred that with the cooperation of the media—and without being able to judge its political feasibility—"the experiment could be made to succeed." Altschul, though, was adamant about one thing: that Lazard Frères & Co. be kept out of the press. "As we do not desire publicity for ourselves, it must be understood that our name is not to be mentioned under any circumstances in connection with the following," he said. "If you care to, you may say that you have been informed by an influential banking house that they have advices from abroad to the effect that steps have been taken in Paris which seem adequate to restore confidence in France and to protect the French exchange, and the situation appears well in hand."

The French government quickly adopted Altschul's plan and constructed a classic "short squeeze" of the speculators who had been betting against the value of the franc. Due to "the sensitivities of the French government," Altschul's partners in Paris were given the job of implementing his ideas. According to a discussion of Lazard's role in the 1924 franc crisis in *The Fortune Encyclopedia of Economics,* "Using a $100 million loan from J. P. Morgan, [the French government] bid the franc from 124 to 61 per dollar in a few weeks. Speculators who had sold the franc short in the expectation that its value would fall were hit by big losses." A month after Altschul's speech, with the Lazard-designed intervention looking successful, Christian Lazard, a partner in Paris and a son of one of the founding brothers, wrote him: "Things are looking better in Paris although the bears on francs will no doubt renew their attacks more than once. But I still feel that there is a great change in the situation now that the truth has been told. The people here are ready to pay their taxes, even the peasants."

In March 1924, Altschul wrote Christian Lazard, taking a bit of a victory lap. "My heartiest congratulations on the success of the experiment, which I consider no longer at all in doubt," he wrote. "The situation has been dealt with in admirable manner." In a postscript to the letter, Altschul confided a twinge of regret that the house of Morgan, instead of the house of Lazard, seemed to be garnering the lion's share of the accolades for the success of the rescue plan. "Of course it is a matter of keen regret to me personally that we were not associated with Morgans in name in an operation the seed of which would seem to have originated with L.F.," he wrote, actually crossing out the typewritten words "me personally" and inserting, in his own hand, the words "all of us" instead. "We take for granted, however, that we will receive some adequate compensation through Joint Account or otherwise for the accommodation extended through Loan Account No. 2 and for the not inconsiderable services rendered." He also suggested that someone should be awarded the French Legion of Honor for the accomplishment—which is exactly what Altschul and Blumenthal received two years later from the French government, beginning another long tradition of Lazard partners so honored.

Eventually the truth came out about how the franc crisis was solved, and Lazard Frères et Cie in Paris received many a tribute in the press and from the French government. "You can imagine what thrilling hours we have gone through," Christian Lazard wrote Altschul. "I do not think the Firm of L.F. & Cie, Paris had ever known a period like that one before." But he recognized that perhaps the real acclaim belonged with Altschul in New York. "All the time, I missed your presence here, because I remembered all our conversations and our visits [on the] Rue de Rivoli and I was sincerely sorry that L.F.N.Y. could not play, on your side, the prominent part to which they were entitled considering that the first idea of the whole scheme came from you." He also confided to Altschul *"a secret"* about how he had sold part of his equity portfolio to have plenty of francs around for the upcoming June 1924 sale of the highbrow art collection of Arthur Meyer, the Jewish owner of *Le Gaulois,* an important French newspaper. Included in the sale was a sublime haystack painting Meyer commissioned from Claude Monet in 1909. "I hope you won't be against me in the market," Christian wrote.

A subsequent, handwritten letter a few days later from Christian reiterated his thanks to the "sister firms" for the "brave manner in which they have fought the battle with us." He also answered Altschul's postscript about how Lazard in New York would be compensated for its role by explaining, "We have placed all our staff and all our brains at the disposal of the B. of Fr. without accepting any remunerization whatsoever and . . . all our own business has been practically stopped since that first day of the fight. We feel sure you understand our point of view. We believe that in cases like that one, when public interest is at stake, it is not only patriotic but also wise policy to refuse any remuneration. We firmly believe that our firms will sooner or later get their reward for their present attitude. I might add that our London house has spontaneously offered the Bank of France to return the commission they have received from the English banks."

While in Paris to work his magic in the franc crisis, Altschul seized the opportunity to introduce to the French partners his idea to move Lazard in New York into a wholly new business: a closed-end investment fund. At the outset, David David-Weill agreed to put $1 million "at the disposal of the Trust." But David-Weill's other French partners were more cautious and wanted to know both George Blumenthal's opinion of the venture and how Altschul intended to divide the profits of the fund between Paris and New York. Altschul and Christian Lazard had some correspondence on the subject, but Altschul believed that Christian was pushing the idea too far, too quickly in Paris.

AT THE END of December 1925, the feared and venerated George Blumenthal retired from Lazard, after twenty-one years as the senior partner, to pursue a life devoted to philanthropy and art collecting. The news made the *New York Times.* Two years earlier, Blumenthal had transferred—by a vote of "13 white, no black"—his New York Stock Exchange seat to Frank Altschul, who was then thirty-six years old.

Blumenthal's departure coincided with—or perhaps facilitated—two major turning points in the turbulent history of Lazard to that time: Altschul's now unfettered pursuit of his desire to create the investment trust; and David David-Weill's now unfettered pursuit of a short, stocky powerhouse currency trader, André Meyer, later known as the "Picasso of banking." Although Meyer grew up in the Marais—Paris's old Jewish quarter—both of his parents were from Strasbourg, the Alsatian city hard on the German border. Jules Meyer, André's father, was said to be "some sort of printing salesman" or "small businessman."

André Meyer attended school in Paris but was an indifferent student and left his secondary school, Collège Rollin, in July 1913, before graduating. He needed to earn money for his struggling family, as his itinerant father spent more time gambling than working. André had always shown a keen interest in the Paris Bourse, the French stock exchange, and was said to know, by heart, the prices of all the stocks listed there. He quickly found a job as a messenger at the Bourse, and soon thereafter a position at a small French bank, Baur & Sons. André was exempted from military service in World War I because of a "weak heart" and because of his important role in supporting his family.

At Baur, he quickly learned the art and science of trading currencies as well as of government and corporate obligations. "It called for a quick mind, which the teenager certainly had," his biographer, Cary Reich, wrote in *Financier,* "a hardheaded sense of values, which he was fast acquiring; and boundless energy, a prerequisite that the nervous, fidgety boy had no problem fulfilling. Already as a youth he was awakening daily at four in the morning to study the financial tables of the newspaper and plot out his moves of the day. During family meals in the cramped apartment, he put his telephone on the dinner table and chattered away about the market between bites."

Like other traders at the time, André would dutifully report to the Bourse during the trading hours of one to three-fifteen every business day to conduct Baur's trading. "So it is with a clear head, alertness and quick action that a foreign exchange broker in Paris can, by the manipulation of a very few million francs routed via London and America, drop the Paris currency several points," the *New York Times Magazine* reported. "He can as quickly in a few short rounds jack it up to his eventual profit." André's success as a trader at the Bourse during and after the franc crisis of 1924 brought him to the attention of David David-Weill, who asked him in 1925 to come to Lazard's Paris office, at Rue Pillet-Will, for a job interview. "He just took everybody to the cleaners," his grandson Patrick Gerschel said of André's trading ability. But the exacting André, then twenty-seven, drove a hard bargain with David-Weill. He wanted to know when, precisely, he would become a Lazard partner. But at first David-Weill would not commit to a timetable. André walked out and returned to Baur. (Other accounts have David-Weill "dismissing" André.)

A year later, David-Weill tried to get André again, and this time he succeeded by promising him that if his performance was up to David-Weill's considerable expectations, André would be made a partner of the French firm. André joined Lazard as an associate in 1926, in part because he had been so impressed by the gutsy trading positions Lazard had taken during the franc crisis. Within a year, David-Weill kept his promise and promoted André to a partner of Lazard Frères et Cie, at the same time he named his son Pierre David-Weill to be a partner as well. André, with his financial genius and forceful personality, would dominate Lazard for the next fifty years.

AT THE START of 1927, Altschul turned his attention to establishing General American Investors Company as the nation's first closed-end mutual fund. And in May 1927, with Lazard and Lehman Brothers as its principal investors and owners, the fund opened for business to "acquire, hold, sell and underwrite securities of any nature, both foreign and domestic." Another fund, the Second General American Investors Company, was started on October 15, 1928. On September 5, 1929—a month before the Crash—the first and second General American funds were merged into one fund, which at the end of 1929 had $33 million in assets. General American would remain one of Altschul's passions for the remainder of his long life, but would lead to a permanent and irrevocable rupture of his relationship with André Meyer.

In New York, it is clear from Altschul's correspondence with his new partner Albert Forsch, there was increasing concern in Lazard's offices during the summer leading up to the stock market crash of 1929. "It seems to me that the cycle through which we are passing has not run its course, and aside from a slight change in the sentiment I fail to detect any indications of any betterment," Forsch wrote Altschul, who was in Paris. "The construction figures are certainly most discouraging. The automobile business if anything is worse, commodity prices have not changed their trend, and unemployment shows not only no signs of improvement but seems to be on the increase, and I think we shall see real distress this winter for the first time in many years."

Forsch was prescient, of course. The stock market slide, which began in September 1929 and ended in July 1932, sliced an astonishing 89.2 percent off the Dow Jones Industrial Average. Much of the industrialized world was thrown into a near-decade-long depression. The three Lazard houses survived the Crash and its aftermath—just barely—but the firm's latest brush with death ironically had nothing to do with the momentous macroeconomic events and everything to do with serious mismanagement.

A series of unexpected events, beginning in March 1931, almost led to the total liquidation of Lazard. First came the sudden death of André Lazard, son of Simon and brother of Christian, who had only three years earlier taken over as senior partner upon the death of his cousin Michel. André had died, at age sixty-two, in Nice after a short illness. He was the last Lazard family member to be a part of the firm. The impression has been given over the years that the reason for this was the lack of male issue in the Lazard family lineage following André Lazard's untimely death. And to some degree that is accurate. But the descendants of Elie Lazard did have several sons in their lineage. Whether they were ever part of the firm is not known. It is likely that the David-Weills used the occasion of the deaths of André and Michel Lazard to consolidate their control over the firm.

On the other hand, in the late spring and summer of 1931, as a result of an untimely combination of world events and a rogue Czech trader sitting in a Lazard Brothers office in Brussels, the David-Weills almost lost everything—yet again—that they had so carefully constructed during the previous eighty years. Financial trouble had been brewing for some time in Europe by 1931, for any number of reasons, among them the exporting of the U.S. and German Depressions, the chronic U.K. budget deficits, the unfavorable balance of trade payments, and the overvaluation of the pound versus the dollar. All of these factors combined to leave the London economy with liabilities far in excess of the gold and foreign exchange reserves then held in the Bank of England. When, on May 11, the Creditanstalt failed, due in part to the French government's refusal to continue to provide it with short-term credit, financial panic spread across Europe. The Austrian branch of the powerful Rothschild banking family controlled Creditanstalt, Austria's largest private bank. The bank's failure revealed how poorly the family had been managing the bank. "An immediate consequence was the freezing of London's claims, first those in Vienna and then in Berlin," R. S. Sayers wrote in his definitive history of the Bank of England. Lazard Brothers was one of the creditors of Creditanstalt. The London firm had an exposure estimated at around £40,000, equivalent to about £10 million today. Not an excessive amount, for sure, but given that the entire capital of the firm was just over £3 million, it was not an amount anyone was comfortable losing.

Lazard Brothers dispatched one of its most senior partners and a close friend of Altschul's, Robert Brand, to Vienna to negotiate, along with the other hundred or so creditors of the failed Austrian bank, how Lazard would get its money back. After days of negotiation, Brand took the train from Vienna to Brussels, and from there he was to make his way back to London to inform his partners about the status of their loan. On the train platform, as steam and smoke billowed through the glass-covered station, Brand saw Joe Macartney-Filgate, his junior partner, in the distance. When Macartney-Filgate saw Brand on the platform, he rushed over to him with shocking news he knew Brand did not have. But Brand spoke first. "There'll be a terrible time," he told Macartney-Filgate. "We're not going to get our money back. We're going to lose £40,000." Then the junior partner blurted out, "Well, I really have something to tell you. We are bust. We have lost £4 million." The loss was more than the entire capital of Lazard Brothers; the firm was technically bankrupt. The two partners then boarded the last night train for London, and over an entire bottle of scotch Macartney-Filgate proceeded to tell Brand the saga of the shocking overnight demise of Lazard Brothers.

Thanks to the cash infusion from Pearson, Robert Kindersley had decided after World War I to open a Lazard office in the quaint Belgian port city of Antwerp to conduct a business in foreign exchange. The office was successful, but the firm apparently felt "handicapped" without an additional office in Brussels, the capital of Belgium. An even smaller office was opened there, and a man of Czech nationality—whose last name has alternately been said to be "Vithek," "Wilcek," and "Cireak"—was put in charge. The Brussels office "developed quite a business" in foreign exchange. What Macartney-Filgate told Brand on the evening train to London on that July 1931 night was that he had been dispatched that day to Brussels to investigate reports that the Czech had made a massively bad bet against the French franc and had covered up the error by issuing unsecured promissory notes across Europe in the name of Lazard Brothers. Several holders of the promissory notes had called the firm to demand repayment, thus setting off a series of events that led to Macartney-Filgate's shocking discovery. When Macartney-Filgate confronted the banker with the rumor of malfeasance, the Czech confessed to his mistake.

Later that evening, though, as the magnitude of the capital loss became known and a full-scale investigation had begun, the Czech pulled out a gun and shot himself. He was found dead, in a pool of blood, underneath his desk. Kindersley had been increasingly suspicious of the Czech's behavior in the months leading up to his suicide. He had been getting odd reports that the Brussels office had been borrowing money on the Continent at above-market rates, a sign of financial distress. An immediate investigation revealed that the Czech had been engaged in an unsupervised series of catastrophic bets using the firm's capital. It is not clear whether these aggressive trades were limited to foreign exchange or whether he had also made several poorly timed major investments in the Brussels stock market. A subsequent, secret report by the Bank of England found that "the irregularities to which this state of affairs was due had been going on for some years but had not been discovered by the Company's Brussels auditors (Whinney, Smith & Whinney) owing to the facts that—1. All the senior members of the staff were implicated, 2. A secret set of books had been kept by the bookkeeper in addition to the ordinary books produced to the auditors, and 3. The office had been able to borrow large sums on the Company's credit without having to pledge security. . . . The Company has now to consider whether to suspend business at once and liquidate or, provided the necessary funds can be obtained, to reconstruct and carry on." The Czech was the classic rogue trader who doubled down on bad bets and hid his deception from the firm's auditors by keeping a duplicate set of accounting records. His suicide, combined with the confession of "another member of the staff," revealed a loss of some £5.85 million, some 50 percent more than Macartney-Filgate had thought originally and almost twice as much as the stated capital of Lazard Brothers. There was said to be a posthumous note from the Czech sent to the David-Weills in Paris: "Tomorrow, the Lazard House will go down."

A full-blown crisis engulfed the firm, one even more serious in its way than that caused by the great earthquake twenty-five years earlier. David David-Weill was summoned immediately from Paris to London. Pierre, his son, had been traveling in Egypt with his fiancée. He returned, too. On the night of July 14, 1931, Kindersley asked for—and received—a secret meeting with Montagu Collet "Archie" Norman, the governor of the Bank of England. Kindersley told Norman about the huge loss Lazard Brothers had suffered and said the firm needed, immediately, £5 million (estimated today to be equivalent to £250 million, or $450 million) to "put matters straight" or the firm would go under. Coming on the heels of the failure of Creditanstalt and the debt repayment moratorium declared soon thereafter by banks throughout Germany and Hungary, the Lazard disaster proved to be a major test of the Bank of England's role in rescuing one of its prized Accepting Houses.

At first, Kindersley told Norman he needed £3 million from the Bank of England, with the balance of £2 million to come evenly from Pearson and from Lazard Frères et Cie. On July 17, a Friday, a special meeting of the Committee of Treasury—made up of the most senior executives of the central bank—agreed to try to rescue Lazard after concluding that the Bank of England could not allow "an Accepting House of the standing of" Lazard to fail because that "would probably give rise to a state of panic in the City and create serious difficulties for other important Houses." The proposed rescue plan called for the Bank of England to make a secured £3 million loan to S. Pearson & Son, which then owned 50 percent of Lazard Brothers, proceeds of which Pearson could use only to help resurrect Lazard. Another £1 million would come from Inland Revenue (the U.K. equivalent of the IRS) in the form of a tax refund of Lazard Brothers' previous several years of tax payments. The balance of £1 million, the deputy governor of the Bank of England "had reason to believe," would come from Lazard in Paris and in New York. The committee further agreed that "the matter should be kept secret from everybody and that the advance should not be reported to the Committee of Daily Waiting or be included in the list of advances audited at annual audits."

On Saturday, at another special meeting of the Treasury Committee, the deputy governor reported that "late the previous evening" he had met with Clive Pearson, chairman of Pearson, who told the deputy governor that Lazard in Paris could no longer pony up its £1 million obligation because it "might unduly weaken their position" and requested that

Lazard in Paris only be required "to find" £500,000. The Bank of England was now asked for £3.5 million and told that, absent the infusion, the firm would not open for business on the following Monday morning. Pearson also asked that the bank charge a lower rate of interest on the proposed loan. "Mr. Pearson feared that unless the Bank could agree not to allow some concession on these points his Board would decide not to proceed further with the matter but would accept their existing loss and allow Messrs. Lazard to suspend payment on Monday," the deputy reported to the full committee.

The Bank of England, though, was not inclined toward compromise. Negotiations continued all day Saturday and concluded with a deal to save Lazard at Kindersley's house that night. Along the lines as originally proposed, the bank lent £3 million to S. Pearson & Son, Ltd., which in turn made the money available to Lazard. The Bank of England loan to Pearson was secured by all of Pearson's assets; in effect, the Pearsons had pledged their company as collateral to save Lazard. The central bank charged "penal rates" for the loan, which increased over time, and required the money to be repaid over seven years. Lazard, in both Paris and New York, invested a combined £1 million for the rescue of its sister firm. This money came from the owners of the French firm themselves, among them the David-Weills, André Meyer, and several of the heiresses of the recently deceased male Lazards. "For a long time," Michel David-Weill said later, "André Meyer and my father had a negative capital. It lasted at least until 1938." Help also came from the U.K. Office of Inland Revenue after Norman asked it to refund the taxes that the Lazard partners had paid on the firm's earnings for the previous five years. Somehow over that fateful weekend, Inland Revenue managed to refund to Lazard some £1 million.

The cost of the rescue was high in other ways as well. First, the remaining Lazard Brothers partners were no longer partners of the firm, and so no longer were entitled to both a sliver of ownership and profits. From then on, the U.K. working partners became employees—and not particularly well compensated ones at that. Since the Bank of England had determined that mismanagement had caused the near disaster, it forced Lazard Brothers to shutter its branch offices in Brussels, Antwerp, and Madrid, where yet another rogue trader had also done some misguided foreign exchange speculating.

When the rescue financing was completed, Pearson had increased its ownership in Lazard Brothers to 80 percent, with the balance still owned by Lazard Frères et Cie. But within eight months even that would change. The first inkling of further trouble at Lazard, this time in Paris, came at the end of a late April meeting of the Bank of England's Committee of Treasury when Archie Norman excused three members of the committee from the meeting and "then gave to the other Members of the Committee information, which cannot be disclosed to the Committee of Daily Waiting or to the Court, concerning certain Advances made by the Bank in support of their policy of maintaining the credit of the City." A month later, this oblique reference to "maintaining the credit of the City" became clarified when Lazard Brothers informed the Bank of England that now *Lazard Frères et Cie,* in Paris, was in financial distress, with a desperate need for £2 million. "The Paris House are now in trouble and need £2,000,000 to enable them to continue, but they cannot borrow in Paris without affecting their credit," according to the once secret notes of the Bank of England's Committee of Treasury. Once again, the Bank of England stepped in, giving Lazard Brothers a new £1 million loan, secured by "French Securities" sent to London from Paris. Lazard Brothers, in turn, used the £1 million "to support the Paris House." National Provincial Bank provided the balance of £1 million to Lazard Brothers, for the benefit of Lazard in Paris, after examining "their Balance Sheet and the list of Shareholders." The badly needed £2 million was made available to Lazard in Paris.

No word of how close Lazard once again came to total liquidation leaked to the press or to its competitors. At the time, there were no articles about the crisis, which also happened to be the precise strategy devised by the Bank of England to prevent a widespread financial panic. Hugo Kindersley, grandson of Robert Kindersley and himself a longtime Lazard Brothers partner, said he remained stunned the news never leaked but also explained that this was how his grandfather wanted it to be. "The most remarkable part of the whole affair was that there was no press coverage and no rumors about any problems with Lazard London," he explained. "My grandfather insisted that partners continue to live their lives as before with all their servants and all their houses and not show by the blink of an eyelid that anything was wrong. I don't know how they got away with it because they were wiped out."

FOLLOWING THE UNEXPECTED death, at age fifty-one, of the second Viscount Cowdray—also known as Weetman Harold Miller Pearson, the son of Weetman Pearson—on October 5, 1933, the executors of his estate commissioned a valuation from Deloittes (the accounting firm) of Lazard Brothers & Co. The remarkable fourteen-page document makes clear, at the time of the second Viscount Cowdray's death anyway, that S. Pearson & Son owned *100 percent* of the 337,500 then issued and outstanding shares of Lazard Brothers, not just *80 percent* of the firm. Understandably, resolving the May 1932 crisis in Paris must have wiped out, for a time anyway, the 20 percent stake in Lazard Brothers held by Lazard Frères et Cie. Also, the accounting states that Lazard Brothers' exposure to Creditanstalt was actually £200,000, not £40,000, and that the firm could reasonably expect to recover only 20 percent of the amount owed.

The document also revealed just how minuscule was Lazard Brothers' valuation at that time. Deloittes set £931,250 as the "fair valuation for probate" of the holding of 337,500 shares, the total number of Lazard Brothers' outstanding shares. The conclusion was unmistakable: the events of the previous two years had fully wiped out the ownership stake in Lazard Brothers previously held by Lazard Frères et Cie and by the English working partners. Lazard Brothers did get back on its feet during the mid-1930s, thanks in large part to a slow but steady increase in the number of the firm's corporate bond underwritings and the general slow improvement of the European economy. Over time, the obligation to the Bank of England was repaid.

What role, if any, Lazard Frères in New York played in rescuing Lazard Brothers is difficult to discern. There is no public mention of its involvement, other than that contained in the "secret" Bank of England minutes suggesting that some of the £1 million contribution to the rescue effort was to come from New York. Michel David-Weill said he believes Frank Altschul and his fellow New York partners were asked to support the rescue mission but that any contribution from them would have been small given the perilous economic environment at that time. "And the people of New York were furious," he explained. "Having successfully survived the Depression, they were now being asked, without explanation, to send money to Europe. This did not create a very happy atmosphere between Paris and New York." Altschul's many letters are devoid of any reference to what happened in London and Paris in 1931 and 1932. Indeed, there is no correspondence between Altschul and his partners in Paris and London between March 30, 1931, and April 13, 1934.

There was one very cryptic cablegram, dated August 10, 1931, between New York and London addressed to Altschul that seemed to relate to the London crisis. The original cable was written in a secret code, where each nonsensical word was ten letters long. The translation of the cable, a few weeks after London's rescue by the Bank of England, conveys an air of desperation: "In view of what we must be prepared to do here not for sake of prestige but as a matter of necessity in the event of those extremely unfavorable developments which appear every day more likely[,] we feel it might be serious and fundamental mistake to disturb our present position which though comfortable is no better than it really should be. [M]oreover it seems to us Paris would be in far better position if they borrowed entire amount from Banque de France at the beginning when skies are clear than if they borrowed a lesser amount and then filled their line under stress of circumstances at a time when doing so might create most unfavorable impression."

AT THIS TIME, Altschul appeared to be far more preoccupied with what the consequences of the recently passed Banking Act of 1933, also known as the Glass-Steagall Act after its main congressional sponsors, would mean for Lazard. The act, which rose out of the bank failures of the Depression, sought to separate commercial banking—the taking of deposits—from investment banking, that is, the underwriting of securities. Wall Street firms were given a year to decide which business line to choose. For Altschul and Lazard the decision was simple, considering it had long before withdrawn from its commercial banking roots in San Francisco.

Pursuant to the decision to focus on investment banking, at the end of September 1934 Lazard opened Lazard Frères & Co. Inc., at 15 Nassau Street, to underwrite and distribute corporate and municipal securities. Altschul was named chairman of the board of the new company, and Stanley Russell was recruited from National City Company (today's Citigroup) to be the president. "In the development of such business, it is our hope that Lazard Frères & Co., Inc., may play an appropriate part," Russell said at the time. The new business started with $5 million of capital. *Newsweek* lauded the firm at the time, without even the slightest hint that it had almost been dissolved: "While investment bankers complained that the Securities Act of 1933 was stifling their business, Lazard Frères boldly formed Lazard Frères & Co. to underwrite and sell corporate and municipal bonds. Although a smaller star in the financial firmament than J. P. Morgan & Co., Kuhn Loeb & Co., and Dillon Read & Co., Lazard Frères is no less brilliant. Its prestige is enhanced by its affiliated firms in Paris and London."

While the near-disastrous events were unfolding in London and New York was focused on complying with Glass-Steagall, André Meyer was busy in Paris transforming himself from a currency trader into the then far more prestigious and respected role of investment banker and a man who provides counsel to governments and to corporate clients. The first opportunity he had to showcase his skills as a financial alchemist came in cooperation with Citroën, the French automobile manufacturer in which Lazard had previously bought an important stake, no doubt in part because André Citroën was the father-in-law of Pierre David-Weill's sister Antoinette. (André Citroën first met David David-Weill at his home in Neuilly, a wealthy suburb of Paris, where, after showing off his impressive art collection, David-Weill told the industrialist he must reorganize his company to make it more profitable.) André Meyer, in turn, also befriended Citroën and convinced him to sell to Lazard ownership of Citroën's finance subsidiary, known as Société pour la Vente à Crédit d'Automobile, or SOVAC. André's idea was to turn SOVAC into a broad-based finance company. With the help of his two financial partners, J. P. Morgan & Co. and Commercial Investment Trust, now known as CIT, Lazard bought SOVAC and turned it into a finance giant before selling it for a huge profit many years later to GE Capital, the finance subsidiary of GE. André's next astonishing performance was to rescue Citroën itself from sure bankruptcy during the depths of the Depression. At first, André Citroën had asked Pierre David-Weill to assist him, but the situation was so dire that Pierre turned the assignment over to André Meyer, who in short order went on the board of the company and negotiated a deal with the tire maker Michelin, Citroën's largest creditor, to exchange Michelin's debt for equity. Overnight, as this sophisticated alchemy had never been seen before, André had become a sensation in France, sought out by corporate executives throughout the industrialized world.

Despite Meyer's rapidly growing stature, a pall continued to envelop the three Lazard houses during the mid-1930s. London and Paris were still struggling to pay off the debts incurred to stave off the firm's near collapse. And New York was just muddling along in the ongoing Depression. New York had developed its underwriting business, but it was not all that profitable, given the intense competition. Most of the firm's profits seemed to be coming from its investment in General American, Altschul's pet project. A July 1936 letter from Pierre David-Weill to Altschul reflected the French partners' increasing concern about the poor financial performance of New York, and specifically the ongoing lack of the 4 percent interest payments on their invested capital, an eerie foreshadowing of the same problem Michel would have seventy years later with Bruce Wasserstein. "As you remember," Pierre wrote, "nothing has been paid for the year 1935, and the full interest has not been paid since 1931. Now that these amounts have been earned there is no longer any reason to postpone the payments. Perhaps you will be good enough to look into the matter and let us have your views. We have noticed for sometime the increase of the item 'Partners' Withdrawals' which stands at a rather big figure. I imagine there is some fiscal explanation to it. The whole fiscal problem of L.F., N.Y. seems to me worthwhile reconsidering in the light of the provisions of the new tax law concerning foreigners." When Altschul wrote back nine days later, he told Pierre he was working on the answers but was reluctant to write them down, as "some of the questions involved are of such a nature that they had better not be dealt with by correspondence."

Altschul asked his partner Albert Forsch to study the matter raised by Pierre's letter. Forsch reported back that the 4 percent annual payment on capital had been split into two tranches, a 2.5 percent piece and a 1.5 percent piece. "The method was employed for fiscal reasons and comes from the first profits earned," he wrote. He further elaborated that his understanding of the contract was such that the 2.5 percent piece "does not become payable until the contract has terminated and it is determined that profits remain from which this 2.5 percent can be paid."

No doubt the news that their payments would not be made anytime soon did not please the David-Weills and likely exacerbated the family's ongoing cash needs. After David David-Weill's 1898 marriage to Flora Raphael, herself the heir to a sizable London banking fortune, the couple settled in Neuilly, where they built a huge mansion, complete with separate servants' quarters, horse stables, tennis courts, and formal gardens. David David-Weill also pursued the passion for art he had discovered during his transatlantic move to Paris as a teenager. He bought his first painting—a portrait of the French playwright Marie-Joseph Chénier by Adélaïde Labille-Guiard—when he was eighteen. His grandson Michel said that except during the war years, he bought or sold one piece of art, either for himself or for a museum, every day of his life. First thing every day, he would stroll through art galleries or arrange to meet an art dealer at the office, often postponing the day's business until the dealer's departure. While eighteenth-century painting was David-Weill's first love, his increasingly eclectic tastes also extended to medieval sculpture, enamels, Asian art, antiquities, textiles, tapestries, and oversized books of birds by the French counterpart of Audubon. He also indulged his love for silver; at one point he had amassed a world-class collection of nine hundred pieces. His wealth and artistic sensibility were such that by 1923, David Weill—no hyphen yet—had become one of the major benefactors of the Louvre Museum in Paris. His name, in gold-leaf lettering, remains sculpted into the marble walls of the museum. He was fifty-two years old.

In 1926, David Weill was named president of the Council of National Museums and announced a major gift of art to the Louvre to take place at his death. In 1927, Gabriel Henriot, the head of the French Library Association, undertook—with Weill's financial support—a luxurious two-volume catalog of David Weill's extraordinary art collection. Some 155 of Weill's paintings, watercolors, pastels, and gouaches were lovingly reproduced in the volumes, in black and white, and were accompanied by Henriot's descriptions. Included were works by Boucher, Chardin, David, de La Tour, Fragonard, Goya, Ingres, Prud'hon, Reynolds, and Watteau from the eighteenth century, and among the *tableaux modernes* were works by Corot, Daumier, Degas, Delacroix, Monet, and Renoir.

It had become nothing less than one of the world's finest art collections in private hands. The catalog showed photographs of David Weill's extraordinary home in Neuilly with nearly every inch of wall space covered with beautifully framed and valuable art. Indeed, the house was like a museum itself. A rarely seen painting of David David-Weill, by Édouard Vuillard, a family friend, shows the nattily dressed banker standing in one of the rooms of his Neuilly home surrounded by his many paintings, sculptures, and candelabras. Not many of these expensive catalogs were printed, probably fewer than a hundred, and David Weill gave them to his friends and a few public libraries. He gave number sixty-one to one of his favorite art dealers, Nathan Wildenstein, the patriarch of the Wildenstein clan, with the handwritten inscription "In remembrance of our so agreeable and friendly relationship—July 7, 1927." David-Weill's art acquisitions continued through the 1930s despite the near-death experiences of the Lazard partnerships in London and Paris. The curator of his collection, Marcelle Minet, became a full-time David-Weill employee. "David Weill was—what you would call in America—a compulsive buyer, yes," said Guy Wildenstein, the scion of the famous art-dealing family.

But the events of the early 1930s at Lazard and the ongoing lack of dividends from New York began to put the financial squeeze on David David-Weill. In 1936, David-Weill sold half of his "famous" collection of miniatures and enamels—"paintings delicately executed and small in size"—to Nathan Wildenstein, and the other half he donated to the Louvre. This was done after a commission of experts had divided the collection—described at the time as "probably the finest and most complete that exists to this day"—into two parts of equal value. Then, without warning, came the stunning announcement in February 1937 that David-Weill had also sold "a large part" of his "noted" collection of *paintings, drawings, and sculptures* to the Wildensteins, for $5 million. At the time, the $5 million payment was one of the largest ever in the art world—around $70 million today—and a fitting sum it was, too, for the collection was considered one of the world's best of eighteenth-century art. The sale comprised 60 paintings, 150 drawings, 50 sculptures, and several pastels, and was described as "one of the most important collections of French eighteenth century art in private hands." In the *New York Times* article about the announcement, no reason was given for the sale. In his memoir about his family, Daniel Wildenstein said David David-Weill sold the collection because he had simply run out of space in his Neuilly home and wanted to start over collecting more modern works. "He had liberated his walls," Wildenstein wrote, "and he started collecting again."

The truth, Michel David-Weill confirmed, was far less romantic. By 1937, the financial situation of the Lazard houses in Europe had once again become dire, and the David-Weills had lost control of their remaining 20 percent stake in Lazard Brothers to Pearson. The price to buy back 20 percent of the firm turned out to be very close to the $5 million David-Weill received from the Wildensteins. Although no doubt an extraordinary sacrifice at the time, David-Weill's $5 million investment in the London partnership was vital to Michel's 1984 deal to regain control of all three houses and then to merge them in 2000, creating the global Lazard that exists today. The reacquisition of the stake in Lazard Brothers also turned out to be very valuable in its own right.

AS OF January 1, 1938, Lazard in New York announced it would merge its separate three-year-old securities underwriting affiliate back into the main firm to create a new partnership, to be known thereafter as Lazard Frères & Co. This combination was said to be "a logical development to meet more effectively the existing conditions in the securities business." The firm's offices would be consolidated on the second floor of 120 Broadway, the Equitable Building, and would have three branches in Chicago, Boston, and Philadelphia. There were seven partners, led by Altschul, who was said to have a large mahogany desk "weighted with four telephones" and to enjoy a pipe, the smoke from which "floats past rare prints hanging on the walls." But Pierre David-Weill's concerns about the performance of the New York office under Altschul did not abate. In June 1938, Pierre sailed to New York to discuss the firm's performance with Altschul. "We all agreed the partners' room was top heavy and that something would have to be done to reduce its burden," Pierre wrote about the June meeting. "Notwithstanding that, you and I, and I think Stanley [Russell], felt that the team had to be strengthened. The more we have been thinking about it, the more certain we are that this is essential if we want to succeed in making a success of the new firm." In a November 10 letter of that year, Pierre told Altschul he was coming to New York again on November 26 on the *Queen Mary.* "The object of my trip is to confront our views on these questions and to take our decisions accordingly," he wrote. "That is, I think, in accord with what Stanley, you and I had in mind when I left in June, and it seems to me that nothing has happened since, either in results or otherwise, which makes it wise to postpone these matters further."

CHAPTER 3

ORIGINAL SIN

By 1938, everything in Europe seemed to be happening against the backdrop of increasing German military aggression. On March 13, 1938, Hitler announced the Anschluss, the annexation of Austria by the German Reich. Then, on November 9, more than two hundred synagogues across Germany and Austria were set aflame and destroyed in a devastation known as Kristallnacht, the first major orchestrated attack on the Jewish populations of those countries. Stores and businesses owned by Jews were ransacked and gutted. Some ninety-one Jews were murdered and another thirty thousand sent to concentration camps, in Dachau and Buchenwald. Hitler and the Nazis were seeking to make their country *Judenfrei,* and much of their original focus was on getting rid of the approximately fifty thousand Polish Jews then living in Germany. The Germans rounded up the Polish Jews and transported them to near Posen, on the Polish side of the border with Germany. Poland shunned these refugees as well, and many of them died of starvation and exposure during the harsh winter.

With a war in Europe looking more and more inevitable by Christmas 1938, the David-Weills and André Meyer took the opportunity to rewrite the Lazard New York partnership agreement. The estate of André Lazard had been settled by this time, and there must have been some recalibration of his family's ownership stake in the firm. The ostensible reason for the change, according to Michel, was the need to legally separate the French partnership from the New York partnership in the event that the Germans took control of Lazard in Paris—which they eventually did—and endeavored to run the New York firm (which they did not). The change in the agreement was designed to prevent such an event. But the main reason for the rewrite was to create a highly authoritarian management and governance structure—found in section 4.1 of the agreement—that would endow one person alone with the absolute power to unilaterally hire and fire partners and other employees and to unilaterally set annual compensation. In investment banking, as in most businesses, there is no more absolute power over employees than the authority to set their compensation and determine if they will still have a job.

The December 31, 1938, partnership agreement became the firm's Rosetta stone, and the "partner under section 4.1" became the firm's absolute monarch. As of the new year, 1939, André Meyer was not only the creator of the concept of Lazard's "partner under section 4.1," he *was* that partner. "He wanted the power of the firm in New York in granite," Michel said of the brilliant, mercurial, and impossible André Meyer.

Although the rewriting of the partnership agreement could not have been welcome news to Frank Altschul in New York, he did his best to ignore its implications. Instead, in the following stressful years of World War II, he performed for both André and Pierre David-Weill—and their families—any number of the most selfless acts of partnership, only to be betrayed by them in return. Regardless of the help he would later provide, it was clear with the new partnership agreement that considerable tension had developed in the relationship between André and Altschul.

"I suppose by now it will have occurred to you that your tone on the telephone this morning was highly offensive," Altschul wrote to André in August 1939. The two had been speaking and cabling about André's involvement in the just-announced bankruptcy of Mendelssohn & Company, a small but well-regarded Berlin-based investment bank. Dr. Fritz Mannheimer, a friend of André's and one of the leading financiers and art collectors of his day, ran Mendelssohn & Company from a branch in Amsterdam. Virulently anti-Nazi, Mannheimer, a Jew, had fled his home in Stuttgart, Germany, for obvious reasons and reestablished the bank in Amsterdam. On June 1, 1939, at his château just outside Paris, Mannheimer married Jane Pinto Reiss, another friend of André's.

On his wedding day, the 250-pound Mannheimer suffered a heart attack. Eight weeks later, on August 9, he suffered another heart attack, and died at his château after he discovered his bank was insolvent (although there remained the serious suspicion he committed suicide by gunshot). Eventually, it came out that Fritz Mannheimer had borrowed heavily from his own bank to buy his extraordinary art collection, which included works by Vermeer, Rembrandt, and Fragonard. When he died, the loans could not be repaid, and the bank failed.

A week after Mannheimer's death, Altschul wanted to determine the extent of André's personal involvement in the German banker's financial distress. "I dislike hearing from newspapers *and from others* that you have $1,000,000 unsecured credit, and I still cannot make out whether your secured liabilities amount to $2,500,000 or Fr. francs 2,500,000 or guilders 2,500,000; nor have I a clear idea as to whether there are any other further contingent liabilities of Mendelssohn toward you," he wrote. "It is quite clear from what you told me that whatever these figures may be, they are in no sense a matter of concern to you. Accordingly, they are not a matter of concern to me, but merely a matter of perfectly natural interest in view of the position that I occupy vis-à-vis all of you in Paris. And I object, once again, and most strenuously, to your tone on the telephone this morning." How long these hard feelings lingered is not clear. André did help put Altschul in touch with the trustee of Mannheimer's personal estate so that he could inquire about his French château—Villa Monte Cristo, in Vaucresson, seven kilometers west of Paris—as Altschul was thinking of purchasing it. "I am wondering whether it can be bought at a terrific bargain?" Altschul wrote André. "If so, I would like an opportunity to consider it, because I am sure happier days are coming again in your country, when it will be a delight to have a little place like that nearby."

ON SEPTEMBER 1, 1939, Germany invaded Poland without warning. Two days later, France and England joined together in announcing they were at war with Germany. These ominous world events did not take long to light on the doorstep of Lazard Frères et Cie; Lazard now faced a new life-threatening crisis. On September 13, 1939, David David-Weill wrote Altschul from Paris thanking him for his "friendly cable" sent on the "eve of the outbreak of war." He reported that his son Pierre, who had been drafted into the French army at the start of the war, had been gone from Paris for a "relatively long time" but was "far from the dangerous zone." He said his son Jean, who had received the coveted Croix de Guerre in World War I, was awaiting his "mobilization order" and his two sons-in-law had been mobilized. He explained that the Lazard Paris "staff" was "really very reduced" but "fortunately, André is here, but his task is tremendous, and it is in times like those we are going through that I realize how handicapped I am by the years and to what extent my age prevents my giving a continued effort."

And here David-Weill tugged at Altschul's emotions:

> I therefore turn to younger men to ask them to give this effort, of which, unfortunately, I feel myself incapable, and I am counting on you as head of the one of our houses the least affected by the world cataclysm. I know so well the noble traditions which your father transmitted to you, and to which you have always shown a faithful attachment, that I cannot but be confident that you will always do everything in your power so

that the name of Lazard Frères, in New York, as well as in Paris and London, will retain its full prestige, and so that, after the war is over, the magnificent working medium constituted by our three houses, will find again in the world the incomparable standing which they have enjoyed for so long. In the present circumstances, it is for me a great source of comfort to feel that, if need be, I can rely on your faithful and traditional cooperation.

Twelve days later, David David-Weill wrote Altschul again, to follow up his previous missive. This one was slightly cryptic and therefore somewhat mysterious. "Supplementing my letter of September 13 . . . I want to tell you that we all rely on you and that I personally rely on you to give our interests in the United States the most complete and friendly attention," he wrote. "If you are willing to do so, we shall ask you to follow very closely anything in your possession which belongs to us, and to make such changes and take such steps as circumstances may require or your judgment and faithful friendship may suggest to you." He added, by way of a postscript: "André sends you all his friendly greetings." Two days later, Altschul wrote directly to André asking him to write about "all the matters of common interest," because "you can't imagine how remote and isolated we feel from you and all of your cares." He concluded: "There are many matters about which we should speak and on this account it would be highly desirable if you sent Moser or some other homme de confiance on a flying visit to New York."

The outbreak of war across Europe was of particular concern, understandably, to the partners of Lazard Frères et Cie and to all those people associated with the Paris firm. Kristallnacht had definitively proved Hitler's determination to rid Europe of Jews as quickly as possible. Lazard was one of the best-known Jewish banks in Europe. The David-Weills and André Meyer were among the most famous bankers in Europe. So it was not long after the German invasion of Poland that many French Jews began to consider an escape. In the face of the Nazi war machine, survival was now the focus of the Lazard partners—for the firm and for themselves—on both sides of the Atlantic. Three days after the German invasion of France had started, Altschul wrote to David David-Weill about his concern for Pierre's safety. "I cannot tell you how much distressed we are by the happenings of the last few days, and I hope that you can still report as you did three weeks ago"—on April 23—"about Pierre's relative security," he wrote. "Our thoughts are constantly with you." After the German invasion of Poland in September 1939, André Meyer sent his wife, Bella, and their two children, Philippe and Francine, out of Paris to Bordeaux, in western France. He remained at Lazard in Paris. He knew, though, it was just a matter of time before he would have to abandon Paris and, together with his family, leave France. "Meyer had no illusions about his situation," Cary Reich wrote. "He was a prominent Jewish banker working for a prominent Jewish bank." He had also been outspoken in his efforts to help German Jews escape Germany. And André had contributed money to finance a plot to assassinate Hitler.

By the last week of May 1940, André decided the time had come to leave the City of Light. He locked his apartment on the Cours Albert Premier and hired a car and driver to take him to Bordeaux. After a few days there, he packed up his family, and together they headed to the Spanish border. Before leaving Bordeaux, André was able to obtain incredibly valuable and hard-to-come-by visas for entry into—and passage through—Spain. At the border, while other refugees from France were standing in interminable lines, often without success—a scene André's son, Philippe, remembered vividly as one of complete "havoc"—the Meyer family was whisked past the hoi polloi and into the country. They took a train to Santander, and then, a few days later, moved on to the relative safety of Lisbon, in Portugal, to begin the arduous task of obtaining an even more coveted visa for entry into the United States.

By the end of June 1940, less than a week after Paris fell to the Germans and an armistice was signed, the Lazard business in France, such as it was, had been moved to Lyon from Paris. Altschul's June 27, 1940, letter to André included a power of attorney, as André had requested, plus a copy of a message taken from "Mr. Harrington—Secretary of State" (perhaps a code name for, or an assistant to, Cordell Hull, the actual secretary of state) about the status of the Meyers' visa applications. Said the message: "It is understood that André Meyer is an active member of Lazard Frères & Co. and that his presence is urgently needed in the United States. Prompt consideration of cases should be given."

On July 2, Altschul wrote André again. "It is good to know that you, Bella and the children are safely out of France, and I cannot begin to tell you how glad I will be to welcome you all in New York," he said. "This morning I received your message that the State Department communication went through." He told André he was looking into getting the family on a flight from Lisbon to New York or, failing that, four seats on the American Export Lines ship. In closing, he wrote that it "must be frightful" for David David-Weill "to have no word about Pierre." By the end of July, André and his family were on a Pan Am Clipper, a large seaplane, on a direct flight from Lisbon to New York (with a refueling stop in the

Azores)—in retrospect one of the calmer passages out of war-torn Europe to freedom. There remains to this day resentment about the relative ease of André's exit. "There are people today, whom I met in Paris," said Felix Rohatyn, "who were related to André and who will never forgive him for leaving and leaving them behind, because they went through Spain, which others were not able to do."

Not unlike Felix, the David-Weills were not nearly as fortunate as André and his family. As the Germans continued their march across Europe in 1939 and their forward progress seemed unstoppable, at David-Weill's behest Minet began to pack up her boss's art collection. She carefully inventoried and crated the work—some 130 crates in all, with the initials "DW" marked on each—and shipped it to a huge château in Sourches along with much of the vast collection from the Louvre. Another twenty-two crates, containing rugs, rare Japanese prints, and some paintings, were sent to another château at Mareil-le-Guyon in northern France. Some of his paintings by Corot, Renoir, and Goya were sent to the United States, and the balance, including furniture, sculptures, and some paintings, remained at his house in Neuilly.

At the outbreak of the war in Paris, David David-Weill first went to Évian, in the French Alps, and obtained visas that would have allowed him and his family to immigrate to Switzerland. But he opted not to go to Switzerland and instead decided to try to get to the United States, via Portugal. He left France for Spain during the night of June 19 with a visa granted by the new Pétain government, in Vichy, and his passport in order. He then moved on to Portugal. On July 9, while he was away, the Germans looted his home in Neuilly of most of what remained of his priceless collection of art and antiques, although in recognition of their high value they were careful to preserve most of them. They also decided to use the mansion itself as a local headquarters.

David David-Weill returned to France on July 17 at the behest of Pierre, who had informed his father that following the signing of the armistice, there was now a "free zone" in France. Then thirty-nine, Pierre had been an officer in the French army. He had returned to civilian life and to worrying about the future of the firm. A week later, the Vichy government promulgated a decree saying that all Frenchmen who had fled France between May 10 and June 30—the pendency of the war in France—would be summarily stripped of their French citizenship. Michel has since mythicized his grandfather's crucial trip to Portugal. "We are very patriotic in our family and very French," he once said. "He was an old man. And he came back saying, 'I am too old. I want to die in my own country.' "

Meanwhile, the Nazis also descended upon the château in Sourches, where much of David-Weill's priceless art collection had been sent. Their information about where the great collections were hidden away was nearly perfect. "When you have the run of the country," the art dealer Guy Wildenstein explained, "and obviously mouths open and I think people are so avid to make money that they sort of are ready to—to betray." On April 11, 1941, the ERR (short for Einsatzstab Reichsleiter Rosenberg—Hitler's art confiscation apparatus), making sure to target the collections of France's Jews, began to abscond with the David-Weill collection.

On August 14, David David-Weill was staying at the Thermal Hotel in the town of Châtel-Guyon, about thirty miles southwest of Vichy, where all the Parisian banks had been ordered to move. He had then gone into the city of Vichy to see Pierre and his wife, and also to spend the day with another Lazard partner. After the rendezvous with Pierre, and despite the considerable disruption to his country, his firm, and his family, David David-Weill found time to correspond with Altschul about his partner's increasing concern about what André's arrival in New York—after even less than one month—would mean to Altschul's stewardship of the New York firm, now that André was in a position, physically, to exercise his absolute authority. David-Weill did his best to try to assuage Altschul's belief that André would soon replace him. Regarding his visit with the Lazard partner in Vichy, David wrote somewhat cryptically but with a sense of foreboding:

> I unfortunately had not the time to go with him over all the details of the important questions that you are actually studying in New York, but I am glad to have this occasion of letting you know my feeling which applies to all the relations which you or myself may have with the firm concerning questions of vital importance for the future of the firm. I sincerely believe that whatever you or I, or both of our fathers, may have done in the past for the benefit of the firm we are still both of us morally and materially indebted towards the firm whose high and undoubted standing contributed largely to our own personal standing and welfare. I am sure that on all such subjects you feel exactly as I do and that you will always do your utmost to help us bring about a continuous and sound development of the New York firm.

On September 8, David David-Weill heard over French radio that he had lost his French citizenship and that all of his property had been confiscated. At the end of October 1940, the Vichy government published the names of twenty-three well-known Frenchmen who had been stripped of their citizenship. The order to do so had been signed by Paul Baudoin, a longtime friend of André Meyer's and Vichy's new minister of foreign affairs. Nevertheless, among those people stripped of citizenship by Baudoin were both André Meyer and David David-Weill—a very bitter and very public humiliation. Even though he regained it after the war, David-Weill was devastated.

On February 22, 1941, the Finance Ministry in Vichy, following an order from the Germans, placed twenty-nine Jewish banking firms under "Aryan" control, after the confiscation in previous days of small shops and department stores owned by Jews. Actually, the Nazis had started the process of taking control of Lazard eight months earlier, when the firm was moved to Lyon and placed under the control of "provisional managers" because Lazard was within the category of "Jewish or part Jewish undertakings."

By 1941, Lazard Frères et Cie, one of the largest banks in France, had been taken over by the Nazis and effectively shuttered. The partners and the employees dispersed to worry about survival, and even the firm's office building, at 5 Rue Pillet-Will, was sold to a French insurance company. David David-Weill and his wife were in constant fear of being rounded up by the Germans. They fled Lyon and hid for a time in the Roquegauthier castle in Cancon, in southwest France. The castle was the home of a leader of the French Resistance. But by the end of 1942, this location was too dangerous, and they moved again, to Agen, in the Tarn department, and stayed in the home of a friend under the assumed name of Warnier. They survived the war, and David David-Weill got his wish to die in France, which he did at his home in Neuilly in July 1952.

AFTER HELPING TO get André out of Lisbon, in October 1941 Altschul turned his attention and his considerable political influence toward getting Pierre David-Weill and his family out of France, where it was obviously still very dangerous to be a Jew, let alone a prominent one from a powerful banking family. Unlike David David-Weill, who was now elderly and had no day-to-day responsibilities at Lazard, Pierre was a crucial part of the business. On Pierre's behalf, Altschul began an assiduous letter-writing campaign to high government officials in Washington. "When you are so busy with questions of first-rate importance, I dislike exceedingly bothering you in Washington with a personal matter," he wrote to Wallace B. Phillips, then director of special information services for the OSS, the precursor of the CIA. "However, in view of our short chat the other day about the case of Pierre David-Weill, I am taking the liberty of writing to you because I have this whole question so much at heart." Altschul was hoping to enlist Phillips's help to reverse the decision a few days earlier that had denied Pierre a visitor's visa into the United States. "It is hard for me to imagine what the reason for the disapproval could have been," he continued. "I have known Pierre all of his life, and have been intimately associated with him, as well as with his distinguished father, David David-Weill. Pierre is a fellow of splendid character, high intelligence, and great courage. The most recent evidence of the last named quality is the fact that he received two citations for bravery in the last war." Altschul informed Phillips that Pierre's presence in New York was needed "merely for business discussions, after which he was planning to return home." In closing, he pleaded: "If without too much trouble you can get at the facts, I should be grateful; and if you find there has been a miscarriage of justice, I should appreciate exceedingly anything you can do to have this situation set right."

Two weeks later, Altschul wrote Henry Styles Bridges, then a first-term Republican senator from New Hampshire and former governor of the state. He wanted the senator's help in cutting the "Gordian knot" keeping Pierre out of the country. He explained he had not spoken to Pierre since the war began and that the ongoing lack of communication had started to affect the ability of Lazard in New York to function. "It is not only a matter of his interest, but a matter of mine, and our firm's interest, that he should be allowed to come here," he said. He explained he had known Pierre ever since he was "a child in the house of his father who was a partner of my father's." Altschul also addressed the apparently unstated—but real—concern of U.S. government officials that Pierre may have, at some point, socialized in Paris with the French who were now running the collaborationist Vichy regime. "Pierre always moved around in the best Parisian society and in this society were to be found, of course, the leading Fascists, and today, no doubt, the leading adherents of the Pétain government," he wrote.

Altschul suggested that Pierre did not in any way share their political views. "I would vouch before anybody in the highest terms for his character and his completely loyal behavior during any visit to us," he continued. He offered to appear before any "person" in Washington in hopes of resolving the "great miscarriage of justice" that occurred by denying Pierre's visa application. He further explained that the Nazis had closed Lazard Frères et Cie in Paris and that "this firm is one in which his whole life, and the life of his father before him, centered, and it has had an honorable career from its start in the United States 100 years ago.

If there were any general reasons, and there are many, to justify one's belief that Pierre's cause must be our cause, this personal reason should offer convincing proof."

That same day Altschul also wrote Adolph A. Berle Jr., a longtime assistant secretary of state. Once again, he raved about Pierre's accomplishments and those of his father. He added to the previous litany that Pierre had also been awarded the Croix de Guerre with palm for his acts of bravery during the war. With Berle, he addressed the rumor that the State Department "may not like his friends" in high French society, where "so many Fascists, appeasers and Pétainists are to be found." But the crux of the matter was that the war had interrupted the ability of the Lazard partners to meet in person to discuss the changing needs of the firms. "He desires to come for a short visit for this purpose and I, and my partners, have very persuasive reasons for wishing to see him here," he concluded. "It is difficult for me to know where to turn in a matter of this sort and I could not help wondering whether it would not be possible for you to get to the roots of this matter without too much difficulty and to advise me whether there is a step which I can take to remove whatever obstacle stands in his way."

Finally, the Gordian knot appeared to be cut. Four days later, an assistant to Berle wrote back to Altschul that according to State Department records, the American consul in Marseille reported by telegraph on September 10, 1941—more than a month earlier—that a visa had been issued to "Pierre Weil" ("I believe this is same individual to whom your letter refers," according to the State Department missive). But it was a different man. Altschul wrote again that same day to the visa division of the State Department, renewing his by-now-familiar plea on behalf of Pierre, who was said to be in Lyon, not Marseille. Finally, on November 1, the chief of the visa division wrote Altschul that "after careful consideration" the State Department had given "advisory approval to the appropriate American Officer in Lyon" to issue Pierre a "nonimmigrant visa." Altschul quickly wrote a short letter of deep appreciation to Washington for the visa approval for "my good friend, Pierre David-Weill." But a visa, alas, as coveted as it was, was only the first step in the arduous process of Pierre actually arriving in New York. And there still was no word from him.

Finally, Pierre emerged from the shadows. By April 6, 1942, he had somehow made it from Lyon to Lisbon. At 11:30 at night, he sent Altschul a cable, typos and all, at his Lazard office: "Awaiting news from you. Look foreward seeing your very soon. Love to all. Pierre David Weil." But weeks went by, and Pierre was still having trouble getting a seat on the

Pan Am Clipper from Lisbon to New York. Pan Am executives in Lisbon had told him that "priorities" could be granted for "urgent business trips." Pierre asked Altschul to "keep after your friends" in Washington to get him a seat as "passenger list established each time in Washington." But the priority lists kept growing, and Pierre kept getting bumped. Altschul cabled him in Lisbon, at the elegant Hotel Aviz, to suggest that he deal directly with the agent at the airport to get a higher priority. "Distressed at all these delays," he wrote.

Finally, after almost two months in Lisbon, Pierre arrived in New York on May 17 under a temporary visitor's visa. Almost immediately, Altschul set about trying to secure permanent, *immigration* visas not only for Pierre but also for his wife, the former Berthe Haardt, then forty-three; their two children, Michel, then ten, and Éliane, then seven; and for Berthe's mother, Madame Gaston Haardt, then seventy-one. Pierre was in New York, staying at the Ritz Tower hotel on Park Avenue and Fifty-seventh Street; the rest of his family was still in France.

To help get the highly coveted immigration visas, Altschul enlisted the services not only of Arthur Ballantine, one of the founders of the law firm Dewey Ballantine, but also of his brother-in-law, Herbert Lehman, then in his ninth year as governor of New York. He asked Lehman to write a letter to Breckinridge Long, the State Department's head of the immigrant visa section, on Pierre's behalf. The letter to Long, whom many criticized afterward for thwarting the immigration of Jews into the United States, "should merely try to interest him in having the case dug out of the ordinary channels and expedited," Altschul wrote to Lehman after having already sung Pierre's praises to his brother-in-law.

But even Lehman's involvement didn't help. On August 22, 1942, the chief of the State Department's visa division wrote both Pierre and Altschul, informing them that a "preliminary examination" of the requested visa "has not resulted in a favorable recommendation." But the matter had been sent for further review to the Interdepartmental Visa Review Committee, and Pierre was invited to appear before this committee, if he desired, on September 18. Pierre's personal appearance in Washington, accompanied by Altschul and Ballantine, did the trick. The official word from the State Department came to Altschul on October 10 from the chief of the visa division. The immigration visas had been approved for the entire family, with the appropriate American officials being so notified in Nice and Montreal. Altschul had pulled off the near impossible. Pierre was free to stay in the United States, and his wife and children were free to immigrate.

Four days later, though, it had all gone off the rails for Pierre's wife and children. Berthe David-Weill had cabled her husband that the French authorities had blocked the family's departure from Nice. Berthe had consciously missed the deadline to leave France because she wanted to see if she could help her son—Michel's half brother—who although not Jewish had been captured by the Nazis for his role in the French Resistance. Altschul shot off a letter to the State Department to see if the unfortunate decision preventing the rest of the family from leaving France could be reversed. But it was of no use. Pierre's wife and children were out of viable options, despite their considerable wealth and having actually obtained the coveted visas. They spent the remainder of the war in hiding. A few months after being denied the chance to leave France, Berthe and her two stepchildren left Cannes "in a huff," Michel explained, after Michel's grandmother, who was Belgian, "was on the list to be arrested as a foreign Jew." He left Cannes by train, alone with his governess, and sat silently while listening to the other passengers engage in anti-Semitic conversation. "I was not completely foolish," he said. Using falsified papers given to them by sympathizers in Nice and under the assumed named Wattel—chosen because the name started with a *W*, like Weill—the family then moved to stay with a friend, the countess of Villy, in Aveyron, a small town in the Massif Central. The Weills stayed with the countess for a few months until she found them the castlelike Château de Béduer to rent. While plenty nice, the château had no running water. They stayed there for two years, from Easter 1943 until Easter 1945. Michel's official papers explained that he was now "Michel Wattel," born in Amiens (not Paris) and in a year different from his actual birth.

Even in hiding, the family kept their maids and butler. Michel rarely went to school during the war years. "It was wonderful," he said years later. "We had a great time. It was like being on holidays and I read a lot," including the literature of Flaubert, Stendhal, and Gide. But clearly this is the perspective of a child eager to keep the horror at a distance. In reality, there was constant danger. His father was away in New York. And his stepmother worried ceaselessly that the family's Jewish roots would be discovered and their fate sealed, as happened to other family members. Michel would never forget the implications of the whispered conversations on the train leaving Cannes. In an attempt to avoid detection as Jews, Michel and his sister were baptized in the middle of the night and raised from then on as French Catholics. Michel recalled: "My father told me, 'Look, you're French. It's more practical to be Catholic. France is a Catholic country. I will get you baptized.' " (Pierre David-Weill himself converted to Catholicism in 1965.) Michel said this nighttime conversion was of no great import to him as none of his family members were particularly religious. "It was perfectly ordinary," he said. "Frankly, I had no idea I was Jewish, either. I learned I was Jewish because of the war." (To this day, Michel provides financial support worldwide to both Catholic and Jewish charities.) Hubert Heilbronn, a Lazard partner who became acquainted with Michel during this time, believed that it was in hiding, during the war, that Michel developed his legendary "indifference" to other people. Michel's half brother Jean Gaillard—Berthe's son by a first marriage—was less fortunate. As a result of his membership in the France Libre resistance movement, Gaillard was captured by the Nazis and sent first to Dora and then to Ravensbrück, where he died. Berthe never recovered from the loss of her son.

WHILE ALTSCHUL WAS devoting himself to helping Pierre and his family, André was slowly but surely stirring up trouble for Altschul in Lazard's offices at 120 Broadway. At first, though, André and his family were struggling to adjust to the New World. Upon arriving in New York, the Meyers stayed at the Stanhope Hotel on Fifth Avenue. Then they moved on to the Delmonico on Park Avenue, and then on to a few others before settling, finally, at the ultraluxurious Carlyle Hotel on Madison Avenue, where they took up residence in a two-bedroom suite on the thirty-third floor. All this meandering around the Upper East Side was evidence of just how out of sorts André felt beyond the world he had created for himself in Paris. He had been misdiagnosed as having cancer. He had trouble speaking English. He had no clients. Worse, nobody knew who he was or what he had accomplished at Lazard in Paris. He was no longer important to anyone. "It was all a great shock for him—Nazism, the war, France's defeat," his son Philippe explained. "On the personal side, he had been a great, great success, and suddenly everything collapsed, and he had to start all over again. And he didn't know if he had the strength or courage to do it."

Finally, sometime around May 1, 1941, André recovered from this malaise and headed back into the fray. He hired a new assistant, Simone Rosen, a Belgian woman who had brought her mother to the interview with André at the Hampshire House hotel on Central Park South. Once hired, mother and daughter Rosen set up André's office at 120 Broadway—not in the Lazard offices on the second floor, but rather thirty floors above. Rosen would remain André's assistant for the rest of his life. Indeed the press of business surrounding André was such that over time he hired a second assistant, Annik Percival, the daughter of his Swiss accountant.

Typically, André—in his efforts to regain his previous form—set his sights on the grandest prize of all: wooing as a client the much-admired David Sarnoff, the chairman of RCA. For starters, André donated the unheard-of sum of $100,000 to the United Jewish Appeal, one of Sarnoff's favorite charities. Sarnoff, somewhat baffled by such largesse from a man he had neither heard of nor met, sought out André, as André hoped he would, much the same way that Felix Frankfurter had sought out Frank Altschul. The two hit it off famously; RCA remained a Lazard client for decades. "Getting the RCA account then was the equivalent of getting the Microsoft account today," explained Patrick Gerschel, André's grandson.

Finally, two days after the Japanese bombed Pearl Harbor, André began to stir up the New York partners on the second floor. Although he was not then one of the five partners of the New York firm, he still had the ability to get his way, thanks to his power under section 4.1 of the rewritten partnership agreement. He sent a most provocative memorandum, on his 120 Broadway letterhead, to the New York Lazard partners that could only be interpreted as a startling preview of an inevitable showdown. It was classic André: at once firm and authoritative but with a touch of deference and flattery.

"Dear Friends," he wrote, in surprisingly articulate English,

> At the time when we are about to sign a new contract, I wish to state, as representative of Lazard Paris, how much I am satisfied to see that harmonious relations exist among the partners, on the second floor. I do not doubt that in their mind, as in mine, all the questions are entirely clarified. I add, that I want them to know they have my entire confidence and that I wish to collaborate with them as fully as possible. By reason of the interests which I represent and the material and moral responsibilities which I bear, my intention is to be present, as often as possible, at the daily meetings which take place on the second floor at which the different problems concerning the House are discussed. I propose to continue to express my opinion freely there, whenever I consider that there is occasion to do so, and also to make any suggestion which seems to me useful in the interest of the House. I am sure that every one will agree to make, in the present circumstances, a very serious effort in order to reduce the overhead expenses, and that in this respect the study prepared by Singer, at the request of Altschul and Russell, will be specially taken into consideration. It is entirely understood that the final decisions concerning the management of the firm, as well as the responsibility for these decisions, remain in the hands of

the New York partners as, indeed, has never failed to be the case in the course of recent years.

Although he was somewhat cryptic, André had made it abundantly clear that as the sole representative in New York of the Lazard ownership interests in the New York and Paris firms, and given his power under the new partnership agreement, he intended to freely exercise his authority regarding how the New York firm should be managed and operated. Exacerbating this decision were, no doubt, the obvious facts that the British firm was controlled by Pearson, the Paris firm was basically defunct, André was now living in New York, and he had no choice—given his drive to succeed and to be relevant—but to seek to resurrect the firm as a whole from its New York base.

If André's December 9 memo was essentially a signal of intent, a month later he unloaded both barrels on Altschul. In a three-page, single-spaced letter, written this time in French, he told Altschul in no uncertain terms that the time had come to liquidate General American, Altschul's baby. He reminded Altschul that "for more than a year" he tried to convince him that General American had to go. "On a practical level, unfortunately, the facts have proven that I wasn't wrong," he wrote. He referred to a September 1941 General American board meeting where he had hoped Altschul would push for a winding up of the fund. "Purely out of a spirit of conciliation and friendship, that day, I made the mistake of not insisting any further," he continued. "Since then, at the end of last October, we have resumed that conversation without any specific decision being taken." The outbreak of war, André wrote, provided him with any number of additional, new reasons to push now for the "immediate liquidation" of the fund. "My wish would be that, with your quick mind, you would take yourself the initiative of the liquidation, you who are the Corporation's dominant personality," he wrote. "In all sincerity, I would like to convince you, as I have tried to do so in the past, of the necessity of such action. To face events straight on, to not nurture vain and often thwarted hopes, has never diminished anyone, on the contrary. To refuse, in 1942, to take unjustified risks with others' money in a firm which has outlived its economic necessity doesn't seem to me to incur the slightest loss of prestige for anyone. On the contrary, it's evidence of common sense and also evidence of strength." André explained he had been thinking about this decision "for a long time" and was sharing his views out of his loyalty as Altschul's "friend" and because of his "duty" as a "Paris associate."

On the small chance that somehow Altschul had missed the message, in the closing André smacked him with a two-by-four. "I hope that this time I will have succeeded in convincing you, and that it's out of conviction that you will act," he concluded. "I also believe that, due to my personal obligations, you ought to know my point of view, black on white. It is very painful for me, I must tell you in all honesty, to be constantly associated with the responsibilities of a firm whose difficulties and dangers I have witnessed for so long."

The upshot of André's missive was that Altschul was no longer in charge. This was a bitter pill that the dignified Altschul had no choice but to swallow. Yes, he had helped André get to the United States, and helped get him settled. And Altschul invited André, once here, to Overbrook Farm for weekends, where he met such socialites as Marietta Tree, the first woman to serve as U.S. ambassador to the United Nations. He also helped get André's son Philippe into both Deerfield Academy and Harvard. And he wrote to the State Department in January 1943 to see if he could obtain an emergency visa for André's nephew Michel Weill, then stuck in a Spanish prison.

But professionally, by the beginning of 1942 Altschul was under siege. André was hurling thunderbolts at him from the thirty-second floor. He still had no word from Pierre David-Weill, a potential counterbalance to André. He then received, in February 1942, a surprisingly sharp rebuke, out of the blue, from his friend Sir Robert Kindersley, head of Lazard Brothers. As a matter of courtesy, he had sent Kindersley an announcement of the end-of-year personnel changes in the New York partnership. For some reason, Kindersley became offended and wrote Altschul that he would have preferred to receive a "private letter" from one of the New York partners rather than to "have been treated merely as an ordinary member of the public." Altschul waited six weeks to reply, no doubt to allow time for things to cool down. He responded cordially, thanking "Bob" for his "very appropriate reproof." He added: "I suppose that our failure to advise you of the changes in the New York firm was due in the first instance to our feeling that with so many major problems confronting you in this war-torn world, minor matters of this sort would have lost temporarily much of their interest. Beyond this, the change in personnel has in itself been less important than the gradual shrinking of our sphere of activity. This raised, and continues to raise, major questions having to do with the future which can hardly be dealt with satisfactorily at this distance, at this time." He told Kindersley he hoped that a visit from "Pierre before long" would allow for "an opportunity to take common counsel with him" and help clear up the outlook for the future.

Pierre's arrival in New York, though, in May 1942, did not moderate André's increasingly aggressive behavior toward Altschul. True, Pierre David-Weill and Altschul were friendly and shared a certain air of sophistication and aristocracy, especially in contrast to the more cerebral and scrappy André. "Pierre used to refer to André always very correctly," Marietta Tree once said. "But I had a feeling that although he admired him, he trusted him and he counted on him, I'm not sure he liked him." Nevertheless, Pierre and André were united as owners; in their eyes, Altschul was nothing more than a well-compensated employee. For André's part, while assimilating as best he could into New York society—he would wear a three-piece suit on visits to Overbrook Farm—he also started confiding to his friends among the other European émigrés, "In one year, I will be the boss."

And that is precisely what happened. Altschul had devoted himself to the firm for close to thirty-five years—acting selflessly in the face of the possible liquidation of New York and London in 1919, anonymously leading it through the franc crisis of 1924, sticking with it during the near bankruptcies in 1931 and 1932, shepherding it through the choice between investment banking and commercial banking, and staying resolute after the Nazi seizure of Lazard in Paris. He had gone far beyond mere loyalty to use his substantial familial and political connections to secure safe passage to the United States from war-ravaged France for both of his powerful senior partners, Pierre David-Weill and André Meyer—two prominent Jews, no less. He had even done the impossible and secured immigration visas for Pierre's family. But despite this, Pierre and André, together, put the dagger in Altschul's back.

On December 16, 1943, a little more than a year after Pierre's arrival in New York, Lazard Frères & Co. announced that Altschul would be "retiring," effective December 31. The announcement also said that both Pierre and André would become individual partners in New York and that Lazard Frères et Cie would remain a partner in New York. As a parting gift, Altschul remained president of his beloved General American Investors. Per André's dictum, Lazard completely divested its interest in General American soon after Altschul's departure from the firm. After the split, Altschul moved his office to 40 Wall Street and spent a considerable amount of time at the Council on Foreign Relations trying to change the world. Lazard moved to 44 Wall Street.

The reasons for the coup are easy to conjecture about but difficult to know for certain, as all parties to the dispute have long since passed. Patrick Gerschel, a former Lazard partner himself, said the matter of André and Pierre taking over from Altschul was put to a vote of the partnership. Altschul was voted out, even though only one of the New York partners voted against him. The highly truncated official history of Lazard, published in 1998—on the occasion of the firm's 150th anniversary—makes only a passing unkind reference to the incident, stating that when André and Pierre arrived in New York they found a firm "that had become, in a word, pedestrian. But within a few years the two partners from France had begun to remake the Firm, bringing in new partners and new alliances on Wall Street and in business."

Altschul's late son Arthur, a longtime partner at Goldman Sachs, spoke at least once publicly about his father's fate in practical terms. "I don't think the control was *ever* in my father's hands," he said. "I believe it was always in the hands of the French partners. And anytime the French wanted to take control, they had it in their power to do so all along." Privately, though, Arthur Altschul was positively livid about how André and Pierre had treated his father. In the 1980s, when on vacation at a luxurious estate in Italy, he ran into the future Lazard partner Robert Agostinelli, who knew Arthur when they were both at Goldman Sachs. Agostinelli remembered the chance encounter, around the time he had announced he was leaving Goldman for Lazard:

> He looks at me, and he says, "How dare you go to work at that place? Don't you know what they did to my family?" And he said, "My father was there, he was loyal, my family was loyal to these people, we had understandings with them. We had no legal obligation to take them in when the war started. And they were rude. They left their firm in the hands of caretakers. We brought them in because we're decent people, and the next thing I know is that they're submitting papers to my father, and he's out on the street. We were big members of the Brahmin Jewish families in New York. We were proud people. We had made their name better than it was. And those guys just came in—and Pierre David-Weill just was under the thumb of André, a tricky, sneaky bad guy. You're a Goldman guy. How could you go to these people?"—I didn't know any of it.

Frank Altschul obviously felt betrayed by his partners. But somehow, in public, he managed a stiff upper lip. Four days after the official announcement of his departure, he cabled Robert Kindersley in London: "Many thanks for your friendly message transmitted through Pierre. Stop. Feel sure new set up is most sound and promising New York firm has had in many years. Friendliest seasons greetings to partners and families." In January 1944, Altschul recommended Pierre for membership in the Recess, an exclusive Wall Street social club on the twenty-first floor of 60 Broadway, with a dining room overlooking New York harbor. He also recommended André for the same club in March 1945. In October 1944 he wrote a four-paragraph letter to David David-Weill, then in his seventies, wishing the firm's patriarch well and telling him he had thought of him often during the war. He also spoke of his own departure from the firm, putting the best possible spin on it under the trying circumstances. "You no doubt are fully informed about the termination of my long relationship with the firm," he wrote. "As you know, this represented the realization of a desire that circumstances had implanted in my mind almost seven years ago. My only regret is that, as I suppose was inevitable, misunderstandings have arisen which have clouded friendships that I valued." He never received a reply.

In May 1945, Altschul went to Paris. From there, he wrote a gut-wrenching two-page letter in French to André about what he had come to learn about the weeks leading up to the death of Jean Gaillard, Michel's half brother. The facts are gruesome: The Nazis captured Jean and sent him to Dora in 1943. Once there, he was immediately forced to work, for between twelve and eighteen hours a day, digging an underground tunnel for seven months without being allowed to come to the surface. The Nazi guards brutalized him and forced him to sleep inside the tunnel. Around May 1944, many of the prisoners, including Jean, were allowed to come aboveground for the first time in many months. But Jean soon developed a heart ailment, which left him feeble. He was given a new job having something to do with electrical work. In this role, he occasionally had the chance to play chess and work out mathematical problems with his fellow prisoners, many of whom, like Jean, were professors and intellectuals. On April 6, 1945, Jean was forced to go by train from Dora to Ravensbrück, another concentration camp, northeast of Berlin. En route, he developed dysentery. Altschul wrote: "The trip was abominable, with 130 men squished together in each car of the train like animals, with nothing to eat, and forced to stand for nine straight days. Few made it to the destination. I don't need to tell you about atrocities that occurred on this train but, suffice it to say, that about 80% of the passengers on the train died before reaching Ravensbrück." Although he almost died, Jean somehow survived and was dumped on the steps of the infirmary at Ravensbrück. He was said to have died in the infirmary on April 15 or 16. A fellow prisoner who escaped Ravensbrück and returned to Paris conveyed these awful—but still officially unconfirmed—details to Pierre David-Weill. But there remained a "very, very tiny glimmer of hope" that Jean had somehow made it to a hospital in an area away from Ravensbrück that the Russian army controlled.

Naturally, this tragic accounting devastated Pierre and Berthe. Altschul, though, asked André not to communicate to Pierre or Berthe, or to those close to them, any inkling that Jean was likely dead since they still clung to the faint hope that he was safely in the hospital. Finally, sometime in late June 1945, Pierre and Berthe received confirmation that Gaillard had died in the Ravensbrück concentration camp. Altschul cabled his and his wife's "deepest sympathy in heartbreaking news which you have now confirmed." Pierre cabled back, from the temporary Lazard offices on 5 Rue Drouot, in Paris: "Berthe deeply touched by Helens and yours sympathy. Affectionately, Pierre David Weill."

But clearly—and understandably—the events of the war years had taken their toll on the relationship between Altschul and the David-Weills and between Altschul and André. While this may be hard to discern from the direct correspondence between them, the substance of the rift is clear from Altschul's letters to others. For many years after he left Lazard, he wrote often to Ginette Lazard, André Lazard's widow, who lived in Neuilly. The depth of Altschul's lifelong hurt at the hands of André and the David-Weills fairly leaps off the page of a letter he wrote to Ginette in July 1952, ten days after David David-Weill's death. "It is such a long time since I have heard from you and I think of you so often with affection," he wrote. "I was saddened the other day to hear of the death of David David-Weill, whom I had known since childhood and had been associated with in the friendliest manner until Pierre poisoned his mind against me with his colored story of our late unpleasantness. I should have liked to send a word of condolence to Flora"—David David-Weill's wife of fifty-four years—"which I feel now would only be an intrusion on my part. But enough of this!"

Not surprisingly, André gave no thought whatsoever to Altschul's hurt feelings. First, such a sentiment was utterly alien to André's persona; and second, there simply was no time to dwell on the past. With the war quickly coming to a close, André foresaw in both America and Europe the need to revitalize badly wounded economies and physical infrastructures. Lazard desperately needed to be in a position to help the future leaders of America and American businesses accomplish these goals. To that end, he quickly jettisoned *all* of the old partners under Altschul. And he assembled a new team: Albert Hettinger from Altschul's General American; George Murnane, a former top partner and deal maker at Lee, Higginson & Company and then with the French financier Jean Monnet at Monnet & Murnane; and Edwin Herzog, a former army officer and employee at Shields & Company, a small brokerage. "What André Meyer had in mind, from the start, was the total gutting and rebuilding of Lazard Frères," Cary Reich wrote in *Financier*. "Lazard's mix of business—which was typical for a firm of its size—he regarded as an unstructured, unprofitable hodgepodge. And Lazard's partners and staff, as far as he was concerned, were largely a bunch of lazy mediocrities. In both areas, he wasted no time in forcing through major upheavals." After dumping the old Altschul partners, he closed the three regional brokerage offices in Boston, Chicago, and Philadelphia. New York, specifically the shabby confines of 44 Wall Street, would be the only Lazard office in the United States. Costs would be reduced drastically, in keeping with André's refugee mentality. The firm would no longer spend any of its precious time or capital on retail customers.

In its first hundred years, Lazard had faced repeated brushes with financial disaster, only to barely survive each time. André hoped to change that unfortunate pattern now that he was finally and fully in charge. André wanted to transform Lazard into a firm focused on rebuilding and growing corporations around the world. "He wanted to make this *the* leading firm in the business, not in terms of size, but in terms of excellence," the partner Fred Wilson, who began at the firm in 1946, remembered. "He said this many times, that this was his ambition for Lazard."

CHAPTER 4

"You Are Dealing with Greed and Power"

The Great Men strategy emerged at Lazard after World War II under the leadership of the cigar-smoking André Meyer, following his evisceration of Frank Altschul. The peripatetic Meyer chose to live in an elegant suite of rooms at the Carlyle Hotel. "He wanted to be able to go downstairs on any day and check out and leave—to just shut the door, turn in the key, pick up his airplane ticket, and go," Felix Rohatyn said of André. André's preference for living in a luxurious hotel on the Upper East Side seemed to infect his New York partners. Bizarrely, many of them lived in hotels, too: for about five years in the early 1970s, Felix lived at the Alrae, Simon Alderweld lived at the Stanhope, Engelbert Grommers lived at the Hyde Park, Albert Hettinger kept an apartment at the Westbury, and Howard Kniffin had one at the Berkshire. Lazard itself had an apartment at the Waldorf. As with his partners the David-Weills, fine art was one of Meyer's few indulgences, and his Carlyle rooms were filled with priceless paintings.

André began collecting art modestly for his apartment on the Cours Albert Premier, overlooking the Seine. "André was not a rich man then," said his friend Francis Fabre, who helped to keep Lazard together during the war, "but he was a man in a very good situation." He put together a "respectable collection" before the war, but when he fled Paris before the invasion, he did not take the time to protect the art. What the Germans confiscated has not resurfaced. Undaunted, André started collecting anew for his apartment at the Carlyle, but this time with far more passion—not necessarily for the art itself, but for the *idea* that a man in his position, as head of Lazard Frères & Co. in New York, should have a world-class art collection. André was well aware of the admiration, status, and respect that George Blumenthal's passion for art had bestowed upon him in New York, where he was the first Jewish board member of the Metropolitan Museum of Art and had made one of the largest contributions ever of both money and art. After his death, Blumenthal even donated to the Met (where it remains) the magnificent, enclosed, two-story balcony from a sixteenth-century Spanish castle that he had imported and reassembled in his own Park Avenue mansion. André's friendly rival Bobbie Lehman—who had taken Blumenthal's seat on the board of the Met to become the second Jewish director—had a world-class art collection, too, as of course did the David-Weills. "The difference between Bobbie Lehman and André," a former Lehman partner once said, "was that Bobbie was truly interested in art. For André, it was like hunters hanging antlers on the wall." Still, when Lehman would visit Meyer at the Carlyle, he would rarely fail to mention his admiration for André's collection. "You know, André," Lehman would say, "you have a beautiful collection." Engaged in his own dance with Lehman, André would deflect the compliment. "It's *nothing,*" he would reply. "It's *nothing* compared to yours." Actually, according to the many Lazard partners who would be summoned daily to André's lair, his art collection was quite something to behold. There was Manet's *Woman in a Fur Coat,* Rembrandt's portrait of Petronella Buys, and Picasso's *Boy with a White Collar.* There were priceless works by Renoir, Cézanne, Degas, Bonnard, and van Gogh. He once paid $62,000 for a Pissarro landscape, at the time a record price for the artist.

He also collected sculptures by Henry Moore, Picasso, and Rodin. He had Greco-Roman bronzes and ancient Chinese wine vessels and six bronze Buddhas. The apartment's furniture was a seemingly endless collection of Louis XV and Louis XVI pieces, as were the various ephemera he displayed.

Like David David-Weill, André would often stop by galleries and auctions to look for his latest acquisition. He did not have David-Weill's insatiable appetite for art, and he was more inclined to haggle, but he was always on the lookout nonetheless, in keeping with his attitude that collecting priceless art made an important statement. He also encouraged his partners, on occasion, to buy art for their homes as well (but never for their offices).

André's art-filled Carlyle apartment was in perfect keeping with the Lazard credo that all evidence of partners' increasing wealth should be reserved for their private homes and never revealed at the offices, which were considered ratty at best. "The Lazard offices are the last word in facelessness," the *Times* observed in 1976. "The conference room, the lobby and most of the other rooms are painted beige, with beige carpeting, beige wallpaper and beige leather chairs (or are they vinyl?). Except for Meyer's office, there is no great art on the walls, no minor art, no art at all. Just a lot of beige. At 12 feet by 15 feet, Rohatyn's office is about as big as they come."

André Meyer became the confidant of kings and presidents and of the late Jackie Kennedy Onassis. According to the *New York Times,* "in some rarefied social circles" Jackie Kennedy's marriage to Aristotle Onassis was "jokingly" referred to "as a Lazard Frères marriage" because of the rumor, denied by Meyer but believed by most everyone else, that he had authored the marriage contract between the two. "In many ways, he is the most creative financial genius of our time in the investment banking field," said David Rockefeller, his longtime friend. "He's really a very extraordinary man. He has an enormous sense of integrity and honor, and great pride in the reputation of the firm." Rockefeller hired André often to advise him and his bank, Chase Manhattan, on potential deals. André in turn invited Rockefeller into his venture capital deals.

Ralph Waldo Emerson once observed that "an institution is the lengthened shadow of one man." Emerson's insight is especially true in the case of André Meyer and Lazard. "He had kind of a crazy passion for Lazard," remembered François Voss, who was related to André by marriage and whom André invited to join the Paris firm in 1958. "Lazard for him was his god. A kind of statue to be worshipped. The name of Lazard was more important to him than anything. For him, it was everything, everything, everything." But André was also a complex personality: he possessed the angst of a refugee and, when it suited him, the skills of a diplomat on the world stage. "He works at the top of Rockefeller Plaza, a wizened brown nut of a man," the British writer Anthony Sampson once observed about Meyer, "with a pulled-in mouth which can suddenly turn to a grin; he switches suddenly from apparent passivity to bursts of energy, striding across the room or picking up a telephone, gripping it like a gun, muttering 'yes' or 'no' and plonking it down. He rules by the telephone; he gets up at five in the morning, and does his business with Europe before reaching the office; bankers complain that if they ring him up at 5:30 a.m. the number is likely to be engaged." But like many a successful investment banker, his charm with clients and the powerful could evaporate instantly around his partners and subordinates. He often referred to them as "clerks" in his quest to get "the ultimate buck." Felix explained André's volatile behavior as a symptom of his insecurity. "Behind that stern, forbidding, and sometimes theatrical facade lay a man who was really yearning for affection," he once said. He added years later: "André carried with him the complexes of a Jewish refugee in the face of French aristocrats."

André was also a control freak and had his finger in nearly every aspect of Lazard. For instance, every Christmas he ordered up a bushel of same-sized Brooks Brothers shirts and handed them out as gifts to the firm's employees, regardless of their size. The task then fell to Mel Heineman, the firm's longtime general counsel, to obtain a list, right before Christmas, of all the employees who had written a thank-you note to André. Failing to write a note of thanks could be grounds for dismissal. André also had no patience for anything but hard work. He hated it when anyone took a vacation, something he himself did rarely. When George Ames, a partner who worked at Lazard for more than sixty years, refused to curtail a family vacation in the late 1960s to California and Hawaii, Meyer appeared to have fired him over the telephone. When he was back in New York, Ames returned to his desk at Lazard. André "chewed me out for things I hadn't done," Ames recalled. "But he never fired me, and I never paid any attention to it." From this experience, Ames concluded that the only way to achieve long-term success at Lazard was "to fly a half-inch below the radar screen." In keeping with Ames's observation, the onetime Lazard partner Frank Zarb recalled being invited to lunch with André and the international financier Siegmund Warburg, perhaps as a reward for using Zarb's Washington connections (he had been President Ford's energy czar) to extricate the son of the Paris Lazard partner Antoine Bernheim from Nicaragua to the United States when the younger Bernheim did not have a U.S. visa. Zarb just sat and listened—"I wasn't dare gonna say a word, not a damn word," he said—while the two banker warriors lamented the professional failings of their younger partners. Warburg and Meyer were also known to sit around Meyer's apartment at the Carlyle and engage in mutual admiration. "André, you are the most brilliant man in Wall Street," Warburg said. To which André replied: "Siegmund, you are without question the most brilliant man in London." André Meyer was said to be the only man Siegmund Warburg actively feared.

André alone made the decisions about who would become a partner at Lazard, and when, knowing full well that a partnership at the firm was highly coveted for its ability to bestow prestige and vast wealth. There were no known criteria for his selection process, other than the anecdotal preference André seemed to show for matching established industrialists with young deal executors.

The experience of the longtime partner David Supino seemed to be illustrative of André's idiosyncratic approach. Supino credits his own spunk as the key to being elevated—after seven years as an associate—to the Lazard partnership ranks. For a few years after Harvard Law

School, he worked at the Wall Street law firm Shearman & Sterling, slogging through tedious loan agreements day after day. But the ponderous life of a legal associate proved unbearable.

One day in June 1968, Supino had lunch with the Lazard partner E. Peter Corcoran. At the end of the lunch, Corcoran asked him to join Lazard. Not knowing much about the firm, but having a vague sense from being a Wall Street lawyer that it was "a dangerous place to work," Supino told Corcoran he wasn't interested. "Also," Supino said, "I told Corcoran that I had heard Felix Rohatyn was a shit. Those were my exact words. So, 'thank you,' I told Peter, 'but no thank you.' " Corcoran went back to the office after lunch and reported the conversation to André, including Supino's characterization of Felix. André's response: "You must hire him."

A month later, Supino agreed to go to Lazard, with compensation three times what he had made as a lawyer. On his first day at 44 Wall Street, which he described as a "very serious place" but also "very dismal, bare with drab walls," he wondered to himself, "Now what? What am I going to do?" He quickly figured out "you had to invent what you were going to do." One of his first assignments was to write a white paper on why synergy was good for corporate America, in effect a massive justification for the merger activity that Lazard was facilitating and dominating.

A few years later, André asked Supino to go help fix a company, Republic Intermodal Corporation, in Lake Success, New York, in which Lazard had an investment. Supino was "seconded" to Republic for two years, turned the company around, and arranged for its successful sale. Before the sale closed, André summoned him to the Carlyle.

"I went to the Carlyle and up to André's suite," Supino recalled. "I walk into one of the libraries and see partners Frank Pizzitola, Tom Mullarkey, Peter Corcoran, and André. I walk in and see all these faces facing me, and André says, 'So, David, tell me what you are going to do now that we are selling Republic?' And I said, 'Mr. Meyer, I've given that no thought at all. Mr. Meyer, I am just trying to get this deal closed.' 'Well,' he said, 'why don't you come back to Lazard and we will pay you some thousands of dollars plus a bonus?' And I said, 'Well, I don't think I can do that, Mr. Meyer. I am sorry but I've been associated with Lazard for six years, and if you don't know by now whether I'm partner material or not, you'll never know.' And, anyway, I told him, 'Who knows? The deal may not close, so I may have to stay at Republic.' And he got furious at me, absolutely furious in front of all these other people. So he started shouting at me. 'You are an arrogant, brash young man!' And he said,

'Look, you go talk to my partners. I did not decide this. My partners decided this.' "

About a week later, Supino remembered, André called him up and asked him to come to the Carlyle at 10:00 the next morning. One "always had fear and trembling going to see him," Supino said, but he duly appeared at the appointed hour. "I went back to the Carlyle, and this time there was nobody there but André," he recalled.

"It is good to see you, David," André said. "How are you?"

"Very well, Mr. Meyer," Supino responded.

"David, I have decided I would like you to come back to Lazard as a partner," André said.

"Oh, Mr. Meyer," Supino recalled saying. "Enormous honor, Mr. Meyer. Enormous honor."

"Yes, I would like to give you a 1 percent interest," André continued.

"I said, 'Mr. Meyer, whatever you say is perfectly acceptable,' " Supino recalled. " 'You could give me a quarter of a percent. It is a great honor to become a partner of Lazard.' " Supino got his 1 percent share of the profits.

FELIX WAS UNQUESTIONABLY André's protégé, a mantle he assumed with less and less angst as André's health deteriorated throughout the 1970s and as it benefited Felix more and more in the marketplace. They spoke French to each other, even in New York. No one else at Lazard ever came close to achieving the level of intimacy Felix had with André—and those who tried quickly came to regret the attempt. "In some sense, Felix *was* André's son," explained one partner. "They had a very close and very frank relationship." André's obituary mentioned Felix—and Felix alone—as his heir apparent. What Felix was able to accomplish as an adviser requires the proper homage to André. André was said to have loved three things only: stunning women, priceless art, and complex deals. When asked about this, André told a reporter, "The first two are really one and the third is not always the case." The sort of service Meyer provided to his clients differed from that of Felix. Meyer saw himself as much more of a principal than as an adviser. True, he was the ultimate confidant, of David Rockefeller, William Paley, David Sarnoff, and Jackie Kennedy among others, but he saw them as peers, and they saw him as charming, effervescent, and exotic.

Meyer's introduction to the First Lady came through Stéphane Boudin, the diminutive Parisian interior designer and head of Jansen, who worked with them both. "He was a great womanizer," said Paul

Manno, Boudin's New York representative. "Boudin and I went to see him and said, 'How would you like to meet Jacqueline Kennedy?' His eyes popped out of his head. I said, 'It will cost you $50,000.' He said, 'For what?' I said, 'For a rug.' " At Manno's instruction, Meyer bought for the White House a nineteenth-century Savonnerie rug for the Blue Room. The introduction was made, and later André would become Jackie's financial adviser and close friend. In 1967, he accompanied the former First Lady to a gala at the Wildenstein gallery to raise money to help restore Italian art damaged in a flood in Florence. Arm in arm they made a grand entrance to the gallery as the paparazzi surged.

André was a notorious ladies' man, despite being married throughout his adult life to Bella Lehman. "Oh yes, André had a wandering eye," explained one of his friends. "And he made no secret of it. Even to his wife. They were almost members of the family. It was taken for granted. If the women wanted it and he wanted it, and Bella didn't object—who could make a big deal out of it." Soon after arriving in New York during World War II, he began a long romance with Claude Alphand, the wife of the French diplomat Hervé Alphand. Alphand had been assigned to the French embassy in Washington at the time France fell to the Nazis and immediately left for London to join the Free French. Claude was left behind in New York, where she began a career as a chanteuse at nightclubs such as the Blue Angel. She was said to resemble Marlene Dietrich. Their affair was "*very* common knowledge," one New York socialite recalled. After the war, the Alphands got back together, and then divorced. But Hervé, by now the French ambassador to Washington during the Kennedy administration, never blamed André. Claude moved back to New York and became a fixture at the Carlyle. "She would get away with it because he adored her," André's granddaughter Marianne Gerschel explained. "Absolutely adored her. She was just bohemian enough to appeal to his own sense of creativity. He enjoyed that in a woman."

André also had a long relationship with Henriette Bloch, another French émigrée, who was the wife of Maurice Bloch. Like Alphand before him, Bloch accepted his wife's affair with André. "I think my grandfather was the one true man in her life," Marianne Gerschel said. "As far as she was concerned, he could do no wrong." She also became one of Bella's closest friends. And, according to André's grandson Patrick Gerschel, André had an affair with Felix's mother, which may in part explain how André came to know Felix. "It's very possible because André Meyer was quite a flirt and so it's quite possible," Michel explained. "But it's also quite possible that it's not true."

Then, of course, there was Jackie O. André and Jackie were together constantly during the years after President Kennedy's death and before her marriage to Aristotle Onassis. "Jackie opened up his life," Gianni Agnelli once said. "She was part of those aspects of life that he didn't really know. And he absolutely *adored* being with someone that important." She seemed taken with him, too, for a time. "His name constantly came up in conversations with her," a friend of Jackie's said. "It was always, 'I'm going to talk to André about this, see André about that.' But she never actually talked about the relationship. You just sort of knew it was there." André was said to have advised Jackie on the $200,000 purchase of her penthouse apartment at 1040 Fifth Avenue. And she was a frequent guest, along with Caroline and John, at André's suite at the Carlyle. (When the Kennedys came to New York from the White House, they stayed in the Carlyle, one floor above André.) The Kennedy men were also quite taken with André, and thanks to Sargent Shriver, he became one of the trustees of the family's vast fortune. André became close not only with Sargent Shriver but also with Bobby and Teddy Kennedy. "These Kennedys," he once told his friend David Lilienthal, "are difficult people to do things for. Bobby has such energy, is moving about constantly. The other evening we had dinner together on Third Avenue in a small restaurant. During the meal he had to go to put in appearances at three dinner meetings; three times."

André was disappointed that Jackie married Onassis, even though, in the end, he helped her negotiate their financial arrangement. "I think he was probably upset because she had really played the little girl to the hilt, OK?" Marianne Gerschel said. "And, you know, no man wants his little girl to get married—it's that sort of feeling. If you're going to play the little girl, you will always be the little girl, and therefore you're not allowed to get married. You're *not* allowed. And there's also this feeling, 'If she's going to marry somebody, why can't she marry me?' I mean it's totally illogical, but it's totally the way fathers behave." Despite Jackie's marriage to Onassis, André remained close to her and would often go to her parties at 1040 Fifth. But it seems unlikely he ever had an affair with Jackie. Jackie attended André's memorial service at Temple Emanu-El on Fifth Avenue, in October 1979. Afterward, walking home up Fifth Avenue, "she was very sad," remembered Roswell Gilpatric, a longtime Kennedy aide and friend of Jackie's. "She felt that in her life there was nobody else to take his place."

André also liked to mix it up with the likes of William Zeckendorf, whom he bankrolled whenever the developer was desperate for cash. Meyer and Lazard made a bundle backing Zeckendorf in the purchase and relatively quick sale of both the Chrysler Building and the Graybar

Building in Manhattan. Zeckendorf and Lazard bought a 75 percent interest in the buildings for $52 million, in 1953, and sold the interest, in 1957, for $66 million, making the deal the largest in New York real estate history at that time.

André was also behind one of the greatest deals in the Lazard lore. In 1950, he fell in love with the complexity of trying to wrangle a massive windfall from Matador Ranch, some 800,000 acres of land in the Texas Panhandle between Fort Worth and Amarillo, on which grazed some forty-seven thousand head of cattle. A publicly traded Scottish company had owned Matador since 1882. André decided he wanted the whole operation, including its potential for finding oil and gas. With the Matador stock then trading at $6 per share on the London Stock Exchange, Lazard offered the Matador shareholders a whopping $23.70 per share, or just under $19 million, a premium of astronomical proportions. The massive Matador Ranch, second in size only to the King Ranch (at 950,000 acres), was some fifty-six miles across. André decided to divide it into fifteen separate "cattle and ranch" corporations and sell them off individually during the next nine years. Lazard even outlasted a three-year drought in the mid-1950s that almost killed off all the cattle. But in the end, after some clever tax arrangements, the for-once-patient André persevered, and Lazard and its investment group made between $10 and $15 million on their original investment. Remembered George Ames: "It was a monster of its kind. It started in Edinburgh, kept going in New York, and wound up in Amarillo."

In 1948, Lazard observed the firm's one hundredth anniversary, with André doing as little as possible to celebrate. He refused to pose for newspaper photographers and shunned all press coverage. He was simply too busy focusing on his deals to worry about anniversaries. On October 23, 1948, André had arranged for Lazard in New York to buy 20 percent of Les Fils Dreyfus for $153,300 directly from the founding Dreyfus family. When Henry Plessner, Felix's stepfather, then working with Les Fils Dreyfus, saw André in Paris at the start of the summer of 1949, he said to him, "I have this stepson who's really not very smart, but he's looking for a summer job, and it would help me if you could [help him out]."

The job, dealing with brokerage confirmation slips, paid $37.50 a week. Felix recalled, "I said to myself, 'Sure, why not? It will give me a chance to think about what I would like to do with myself.' " He worked the whole summer in the dingy offices at 44 Wall Street. André was not there; he spent much of each summer working from his chalet high in the Swiss Alps at Crans-sur-Sierre. The Lazard partners appreciated Felix's work and raised his salary to $50 per week, and his responsibilities shifted to valuing the accounts of the firm's rich customers every month. When André returned from Switzerland after Labor Day, Felix was ushered in to meet him, finally. But, as advised, he made no mention of his increase in pay. "André yanked me in [to his office] and said, 'I understand your pay has been increased, and I would've thought you would have had the good manners to thank me.' And I said, 'Well, Mr. Meyer, I was told not to say anything to anyone.' I thought, 'Here's the end of my career, before it starts.' "

Felix told the *The New Yorker* about this incident with André:

> He made it crystal clear to me that nothing in the firm, however small, happened without his approval, and that he expected both recognition and gratitude. Anyway, he was an extraordinary man, a powerhouse; he had just gigantic energy, power and will. André could make people do things. He had volcanic, towering temper tantrums. He was very complicated. He had enormous complexes. He wanted to be loved. He had a great sense of buying and selling—things and people. He was the most ruthless realistic analyst of human character I have ever met. He could peel people and find their strengths and weaknesses. He was absolutely merciless in criticizing sloppy work. I fought him every day for twenty years. You had to. If you didn't fight him, you were finished. I am sure this is the only reason we got along. He destroyed a lot of people. But he could also be exceedingly generous. He made the fortune and the career of as many people as he destroyed—sometimes they were the same people. On balance, I owe him a great debt of gratitude, although I bear many scars.

Years later, Felix elaborated on his mentor: "André also had a Great Idea about Lazard. He looked at Lazard the same way de Gaulle looked at France. De Gaulle once said, 'I have a special idea of France.' And André had a special idea of Lazard as a kind of unique firm with unique qualities. And even if those qualities were not always as real as he thought they were, or as he wanted them to be, creating that image was certainly very good business."

But at this initial confrontation with André in 1949, Felix said he didn't care all that much what André thought, since he was thinking about leaving Lazard anyway in search of his coveted job in Oak Ridge or some other technology haven. He thought the Lazard job was a temporary one. Felix explained what happened then: "André said to me, 'Well, you know you're doing good work. Why don't you think about this business?' And I said, 'Well, Mr. Meyer, I know nothing about this business, you know.' 'Well,' he said, 'we'll send you to Paris and we'll send you to London and we'll send you to Basel, then you can see whether you like it.' So I thought, 'A free trip to Europe, why not?' "

In 1950, he essentially took an all-expense-paid odyssey through western Europe, using André's and his stepfather's relationships as touchstones. In London, he was assigned to Samuel Montagu's daily money market operation, where short-term loans were made and collected. His job was to go around and see who needed money or who had too much. He remembered that everyone wore a black homburg and that he never even owned a hat. "This was summer and I only had this vanilla-ice-cream-colored suit," he said. "And I went out to buy this black hat. It looked totally ludicrous." He met the well-known international banker Louis Frank, then head of Montagu. But he decided the experience in London was not for him. Next up was the newly resurrected Lazard in Paris. He met Pierre David-Weill and his partner Jean Guyot. But the chemistry wasn't right there, either. He found Lazard in Paris very social and not the right fit for a Jewish-Polish refugee. "Well, this was a time when social status was very important," Felix explained. "Paris was very much of a club." Then, a few months after André had bought for Lazard a minority stake in Les Fils Dreyfus, Felix went off to Basel to work in that firm's foreign exchange and precious-metals trading operations.

In 1949, Felix achieved his lifelong dream—to that point anyway—of becoming a U.S. citizen. His first act of citizenship was to be drafted, in the winter of 1951, and he was sent overseas to Göppingen, Germany, near Stuttgart. The good news was that on the weekends, he was able to take the Orient Express from Stuttgart to Paris to spend time with his father. He served his two years in the military, without incident, and when he got out in 1953, he worked for Cantrade, a new private bank in Zurich. While Felix remembered that his various whirlwind apprenticeships were not the norm at Lazard, he didn't think they were unprecedented. "It was done—maybe I flatter myself—partly to keep me in the firm and show me broader horizons and opportunities," he said. "At the time I was seriously thinking of going back to Europe and living there."

Instead, he returned to Lazard in New York in 1955 and became a legend. At first, he continued working at Lazard in foreign exchange. And he might very well have stayed doing just that had it not been for a chance weekend invitation from Phyllis Bronfman, the daughter of Samuel Bronfman, to come to the family's estate in Tarrytown, New York. Upon being introduced to Felix, Samuel, a great friend of André's and the patriarch of the Seagram fortune, asked him what he did. When Felix told Bronfman he worked at Lazard in foreign exchange, he received the invaluable advice to forgo foreign exchange altogether and focus on mergers and corporate finance, since these were the only aspects of the investment banking business that truly interested André. At first, Felix resisted making the change, in part because it would likely mean a pay cut and because he had no training in finance, economics, or accounting and could not read a corporate balance sheet. "Take the pay cut and do it," Bronfman insisted. Felix talked to André about making the switch. André didn't like the idea. "You don't know anything about it," he said. Felix told André he would go to business school at night if need be. André relented but, as Felix feared, his pay was cut to $15,000 a year, from $22,000.

"I went to work for a man named Howard Kniffin, who was head of corporate finance," Felix told the author of his 1983 profile in *The New Yorker.*

> I also went to night school to learn accounting, and to read Graham and Dodd on security analysis—dreadful, dreadful stuff. In addition, I was doing all the dog work that goes with running numbers on work sheets when one is trying to put companies together. I had a good sense of numbers, and quickly became very, very interested in how to put two companies together. I think that the reason I became quite good at working out mergers—at how to structure them—was that I had a feeling for the symmetry and the dynamics involved; when you get all through, the entity coming out should be stronger and better than what you had before, and the merger should be as seamless as possible. When it comes down to the essentials, you are dealing with greed and power. The greed has to be handled by the financial way that you put these companies together, so that, in the last analysis, everyone's interests are served. The power is a different matter. That requires as much negotiation as the financial side, maybe more. More deals break down on the power side than on the financial. There are valid issues of face, of authority, and of appearance. Of course, when I started under Kniffin I was simply given the task of analysing balance sheets, to determine statistically how best to make a merger or an acquisition. I used to sit through endless meetings of lawyers and accountants and read through contracts and work sheets to understand what was involved. I was kept with the drones and the paper shufflers and would, from afar, watch the principals disappear into André's office, and then I'd wait for the outcome to go back to my number shuffling. But that process taught me a very im-

> portant thing; namely the nitty-gritty of what goes into making one of those deals. I can read a contract. I know what a tax ruling is about. I know what accounting is. I know what accountants can do and what they can't do. I know what is baloney and what isn't baloney. I know what lawyers will tell you and what you can believe and what you shouldn't believe, and I know where to press them. It is very important, at this point, that no technician can frighten me by talking about things I don't understand. I may have to rely on him or her for facts, but I don't have to rely on him for concepts. Too many high-level executives are prisoners of their staffs. They have never really done the nitty-gritty stuff, which is not terribly mysterious once you tackle it. And if you haven't seen these things the technicians can absolutely wrap you up in details, and you never find your way out. There are banking firms that are so big that the staff does all these things, but at Lazard we are so small that's out of the question.

Felix, much more risk averse than André, perceived great honor and prestige in being the middleman, the enabler. He was also able to convince corporate chieftains to pay him millions in fees for his advice, without the firm putting up a dime. "Firms used to do M&A for nothing," Felix explained. "Rohatyn is in total contrast to Meyer," Anthony Sampson wrote in the early 1970s, "with none of the traditional bankers' smoothness and deep camouflage, and a stimulating openness of manner. He has crew-cut hair, a piercing expression, talks fast in a high voice, drives a small Toyota, wears an old raincoat, seems oblivious to surroundings." Felix had "total mastery of figures" and "enormous drive." And like Meyer, he hated to lose and was a fierce negotiator, "like a terrier with a rat," one observer noted to Sampson.

IN MANY WAYS, Felix was the perfect man at the perfect time. Corporate America was on the precipice of creating conglomerate America, and Felix had the wisdom, experience, and gravitas to become the era's midwife—and to get paid handsomely for his services. The world got a peek at this revolutionary alchemy as early as 1962, one year after Felix became a partner of Lazard in New York, when Lazard advised Pechiney, a large French aluminum producer, to buy 40 percent of Howmet, an American manufacturer of aluminum castings for aircraft, for $18 million, some 36 percent above Howmet's then trading price in the market. The deal was a huge financial success for Pechiney—and for Lazard, which won most of Pechiney's follow-on M&A and financing business for years to come.

Felix and Lazard came to dominate the M&A business. While Lazard continues to be among the leaders globally in providing clients M&A advice, there has been a virtual explosion of purveyors during the past twenty-five years. It is hard to conceive in 2006 how inchoate—even quaint—the specialized and clubby world of M&A advisers was forty years ago when Felix pioneered it.

The key to Felix and Lazard's early success in the world of mergers was ITT—the International Telephone and Telegraph Corporation. Felix counseled the infamous Harold Geneen in the 1960s and 1970s as Geneen transformed ITT away from its roots in international telecommunications to become the symbol of corporate conglomeration—a journey that ensnared Felix in a political and legal maelstrom in the early 1970s and almost ended his career.

CHAPTER 5

Felix the Fixer

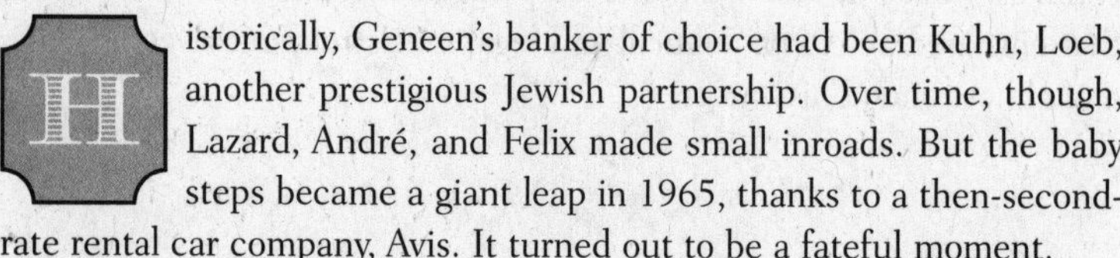

Historically, Geneen's banker of choice had been Kuhn, Loeb, another prestigious Jewish partnership. Over time, though, Lazard, André, and Felix made small inroads. But the baby steps became a giant leap in 1965, thanks to a then-second-rate rental car company, Avis. It turned out to be a fateful moment.

Meyer and Lazard first came across Avis in the summer of 1961. At that time, Hertz and Avis were battling for supremacy in the relatively insignificant business of renting cars, but the competition between them really wasn't even close: Hertz had revenues of $138 million, and Avis, with $24 million in revenue, was continuously unprofitable and struggling for its life. At the same time, Edward Rosenthal, the head of Kinney System Inc., was looking to expand his own tiny New York rental car business to complement his growing parking lot and funeral home businesses. Rosenthal and his son-in-law Steve Ross—who would later turn Kinney into what is now Time Warner—approached Hertz about buying the company, but Hertz had no interest. When they approached the struggling Avis, though, they were encouraged in their quest. As Kinney had never bought a business of the size or type of Avis before, the two partners sought the advice of David Sarnoff, then head of RCA. Sarnoff's nephew worked for Kinney. "Get in the car," Sarnoff told the Kinney executives. "I will take you down to see André Meyer." André and his "flunky," as Felix was then thought of—whom André brought along to meetings because "he knows how to use a slide rule"—together tried to broker a deal for Kinney to acquire the struggling Avis. But Ross ultimately declined, believing the risks too great.

Sensing a financial opportunity, André and Felix pursued the deal on their own, after their client passed, and won a ninety-day exclusive period from the company, then publicly traded, to see if it could pull the opportunity together. Somewhat out of character for the fiscally conservative Felix, he became the deal's champion. The two Lazard partners quickly ran into the problem perennially faced by financial buyers: to wit, who will run the company? They had nobody, could barely understand the nuances of the business themselves, and realized the current management was doing a lousy job. They needed to find someone who understood the car rental business and who could give them an honest and quick assessment of the Avis deal.

So challenged, Felix came up with the idea of asking a man named Donald Petrie to help. The imposing Petrie, with a face not dissimilar to a gargoyle on the facade of the Notre Dame Cathedral, was the former president of an international car rental joint venture between Hertz and American Express. In early 1962, he had just left the Hertz venture to return to practicing law, at a small firm on Long Island. "I get a call one day," Petrie recalled. "It was from Felix Rohatyn. I had never heard of Felix Rohatyn. The firm is Lazard Frères. I never heard of Lazard Frères. He says, 'Mr. André Meyer would like to meet you.' Well, I never heard of André Meyer, either. So I said fine, how do I do that? 'You come to the Carlyle,' Felix says.

"So I go to the Carlyle," Petrie continued. "And since I'd never heard of him and I'd never heard of Lazard, I thought he was a guest, and I went and asked for his room number. And they said, 'No, no, no, you go up to the thirty-third floor.' So I went up and a man in a white coat took me into one room, sat me down, and I waited there for a while. And I looked on the wall, and there was a Manet and a Monet and a Corot and a Seurat. And I thought, 'Gee, this guy's a print nut. He's got beautiful prints.' Then they took me out and put me in another room, and there was a Picasso and a Renoir. And so I went up and I felt one of them. I remember saying, 'Holy Christ, these things are real. Whoever this guy is, he's not kidding.' "

Petrie signed on for the due diligence phase of the exercise but declined André's offer to run Avis. Instead, he suggested for the job Robert Townsend, another executive at American Express, who was a year older than Petrie. Townsend was interested, primarily for the opportunity to run his own company and to be a significant shareholder. As for his salary, Meyer offered him $50,000 a year. Townsend turned him down. He wanted only $36,000. "That is the top salary for a company that has never earned a nickel for its shareholders," Townsend told André, who consented immediately and knew he had found the right man for the job. With Townsend on board, Lazard did the deal, as both André and Felix were convinced of its wisdom.

In March 1962, Lazard, acting through a newly created affiliate, the Silver Gate Corporation, purchased for $5.5 million a controlling stake in Avis. The Avis deal was purely a venture capital transaction for Lazard, the idea being to fix the company and sell it as quickly as possible. Under the stewardship of Felix, Townsend, and Petrie, Avis became a fabulous success story. In three years, these three men turned a company that had an operating loss of $600,000 in 1962 into one gushing profits of $5 million by the end of 1965. The first step for Townsend was to eschew unnecessary overhead by slashing bureaucracy, cutting memos, and eliminating corporate secretaries. André also moved Avis's "world headquarters" to the Roosevelt Field Mall, on Long Island, from Boston. André had developed Roosevelt Field, a former airstrip, with Zeckendorf in 1953. "These people felt they were losers," Petrie later recalled. "They were people who were consistently beaten every time they tried to get their heads above water. They were beaten by Hertz, and they needed a lot of attention." Under Townsend and Petrie, whom André convinced to spend more and more time at Avis, the company's morale blossomed in part because they had the prescience to pursue the famous "We're Number Two. We Try Harder" ad campaign. Soon, "We Try Harder" buttons and red jackets were everywhere, making Avis, almost overnight, one of the most easily recognizable names in American business. The improved marketing turned into higher revenues, and the lower cost base turned the revenues into profits.

With the turnaround firmly in place and proposed budgets easily surpassed, Townsend began to lose interest in Avis, spending more and more time away from the office, infuriating Meyer, who preferred to be kept informed on a daily basis about the most minute details of the business and wanted his partners to work hard. "Townsend would torture Meyer," one partner remembered. "André would carry on about something and Bob would say, 'OK, André, have it your way. I'll be out on Monday. You send someone over to run the company.' And André would just go through the roof."

Townsend explained his thinking to Petrie: "I'm ahead of your plan, Donald. I'm ahead of my plan. I'm ahead of any plan André could possibly have had. I'm not only on budget, I am ahead of budget. I'm ahead of our objectives on revenue, growth, return on assets, return on equity, and return on revenue. So what the hell do I need to be in the office for?" The relationship would soon become irreparable when Townsend and Petrie insisted on promoting a man André disdained to be the company's president. "You insist on this?" André asked Petrie. When Petrie responded affirmatively, André shot back, "All right, now I sell the company." And that is precisely what Meyer set out to do. First he tried to sell Avis to the

Mobil Corporation, but Townsend's meddling caused the oil company to lose interest.

Then André turned to ITT, this time without the involvement of either Townsend or Petrie. The negotiations between ITT and Avis began in December 1964 and proceeded quickly: the deal was completed less than a month later.

For Lazard, the ITT-Avis deal was momentous. Not only did Felix and André turn a $5.5 million investment in three years into a $20.3 million bonanza for Lazard and its well-heeled investors, who all became large shareholders of ITT, but the deal was also an incredible windfall for Avis's long-suffering public shareholders, who owned the remaining 60 percent of the company (for which they received almost $32 million of ITT stock) when it had been on the verge of bankruptcy—which surely would have occurred had André and Felix not come to the rescue. And of course, Lazard was now the acknowledged "expert" in the car rental business, and so it was no surprise that the firm advised David Sarnoff when RCA bought Hertz, Avis's longtime rival, in 1966. Lazard received a fee of $750,000 for its advice to RCA, one of the largest M&A fees at that time. After the Avis deal closed, André pocketed about one-third of the Lazard windfall, about $7 million, and turned around and donated the astounding sum, at the time, of $2.5 million to New York University. He had hoped to make the donation anonymously, and at first did, but then the university beseeched him to allow for a public announcement. He yielded, and soon followed a "Man in the News" profile of André, a first, in the *New York Times*. "I'm terribly allergic to any kind of article about me," he said. "Maybe it's an excess of humility."

For Felix, the Avis payoff was far more modest, stunningly so. After the deal closed on July 22, 1965, and all the outstanding Avis shares were converted into ITT shares, Felix received 454.1375 shares of ITT common stock and 330.1 shares of ITT preferred stock. Felix's first wife, Jeannette Streit, was also an investor in Avis, and she received 648.725 shares of ITT common stock and 471.8 shares of ITT preferred stock. Together, the Rohatyns' stock that day was worth all of $135,571.47.

Not everyone was thrilled by the Avis deal. Petrie told André, "You have been screwed" by ITT on the price, because he figured the company's best growth was ahead of it still. But since one of André's mantras was "Nobody ever got poor taking a profit," it was difficult for him to see Petrie's point. Then there was Robert Townsend, the true architect of Avis's turnaround. It is likely he never forgave André for selling the company, and to a conglomerate no less. His experience at Avis led him to write *Up the Organization,* a *New York Times* best seller for seven months, where he laid bare many of his experiences. In the chapter "Mergers, Conglobulations, and Joint Failures," he wrote presciently about a coming era, with some passion: "If you have a good company don't sell out to a conglomerate. I sold out once but resigned. Conglomerates will promise anything for your people (if your stock sells for a lower multiple of earnings and has a faster earnings growth than theirs), but once in the fold your company goes through the homogenizer along with their other acquisitions of the week, and all the zeal and most of the good people leave."

For ITT, the $53.1 million deal for Avis was its first successful diversification. In 1965, some 54 percent of ITT's revenue and 60 percent of its consolidated net income derived from overseas, with the bulk of its European sales being telecommunications equipment. With Avis, ITT had taken the important first step toward becoming the more U.S.-focused conglomerate Geneen envisioned. He was the Jack Welch of his day. "Even those who hate the man admit he's a genius," *Forbes* explained in 1968. And there were plenty who hated him. Who could love a man that told his senior executives one day, "Gentlemen, I have been thinking. Bull times zero is zero bull. Bull divided by zero is infinity bull. And I'm sick and tired of the bull you've been feeding me." He was a sponge for executive talent, though, paid top dollar for it, and was unabashed about pilfering.

He also was an extremely aggressive—and successful—acquirer of businesses. From 1960 through 1968, ITT acquired 110 companies, about evenly split between foreign and domestic. In the first ten months of 1969, it completed an additional forty-eight mergers and had thirteen pending. In 1968, thanks to Geneen, ITT ranked eleventh on the Fortune 500 list, up from fifty-first in 1960, and its revenues increased 400 percent during that time period to just above $4 billion.

ITT was the first corporate deal machine, and soon after the Avis deal closed, Felix became the grease. The Avis deal brought Lazard and Felix infinitely closer to the most aggressive corporate deal maker of his era, Harold Geneen, and led directly to the creation of the M&A advisory business and Lazard's domination of it. This was the real payoff for Felix from the Avis deal, not the $100,000 or so he pocketed. If Felix was not the architect of Geneen's acquisition strategies, he certainly was cognizant of them. He was able to charm Geneen when Meyer, Lazard's famous senior partner, could not, and became "practically an employee" of ITT by meeting the CEO at his office nearly every night at six o'clock.

After the Avis deal closed, André all but insisted that he be given a seat on the ITT board of directors, a demand to which the strong-willed Geneen, a Brit, objected mightily. (André never had much respect for the British.) Felix's solicitous approach with Geneen proved far more felicitous. That Felix was "the best man always to placate" Geneen was the view of Stanley Luke, an ITT senior vice president. The return on Felix's investment of time began in 1966, when ITT hired Lazard to advise ITT Consumer Services Corporation (the new division created with the Avis deal) on its acquisition of Airport Parking Company of America. ITT paid Lazard a fee of $150,000 for that assignment. In 1967, ITT hired Lazard again to advise it on the acquisition of Claude Paz & Visseaux, a French audio equipment manufacturer, and paid a fee of $125,000. "Geneen is a very difficult person," Felix said in the early 1980s. "A *very* difficult person. But I always knew where he was going." The two of them together started a revolution in corporate deal making that continues, with the occasional bump along the way, to this day.

Also in 1967, Lazard advised the Douglas Aircraft Company on its sale to the McDonnell Company, creating McDonnell Douglas (now part of Boeing). Douglas hired Lazard in late 1966, when the company was near bankruptcy, and Lazard put together a SWAT team of six partners to work diligently between Thanksgiving and New Year's to find a buyer for the company. Six bids for Douglas were solicited, and McDonnell was chosen the winner. Lazard asked for, and received, the first $1 million merger advisory fee for the McDonnell Douglas deal. "Actually," recalled Stanley de Jongh Osborne, the Lazard partner in charge of the deal, "we were entitled to *twice* that, under the terms of the contract. But we thought a million dollars was enough. Even so, Mr. McDonnell wasn't particularly pleased." (As a practical matter, buyers end up paying M&A fees.)

On at least one occasion—in advising Levitt and Sons, the Long Island–based tract-home builder and suburban scourge—Felix found himself on the other side of ITT. Lazard's part in the sale of Levitt to ITT, which began in 1966 and closed in 1968, illustrates the nuanced role an M&A adviser often plays in a CEO's most important decisions. It was then especially true, and remains so, a world of social salons and clubby relationships where the best bankers are as much armchair psychiatrists as financial engineers. No one was better at mixing and serving as fine a cocktail of these subtleties than Felix Rohatyn.

Equally fascinating, though, was how little Felix appeared to know about what Levitt actually did before going into the assignment's kickoff meeting with Joel Carr, the general counsel of Levitt, even though, because it was a public company, any number of financial reports would have been available to him. "Apparently Levitt's forte is his ability to undertake the construction of large agglomerations of single family dwellings and shopping centers at low cost," Felix later wrote André. "What the company needs for future expansion is the ability to bank sizable amounts of land for future operations." That lack of detailed knowledge of Levitt's business was entirely consistent with an era where M&A bankers were generalists and tacticians; Lazard, more than any other firm, worshipped at that particular altar. And Felix was its high priest. The thinking was that management knew its industries; the Lazard bankers were specialists in the art of M&A regardless of industry. (Now, of course, bankers, even at Lazard, must be both industry and product experts.)

Felix was very enthusiastic about the Levitt assignment, even though at $40 million it was a small deal, made even smaller because Felix agreed to split the fee with Wertheim & Company, Levitt's longtime banker. Then there was the matter of Levitt's personality, which Carr must have given Felix enough of a sense of for Felix to warn André. "Mr. Levitt is apparently a rather mercurial individual with a highly developed sense of his own importance and requiring a somewhat highly personalized approach. He knows you by reputation and Carr believes that at the appropriate point a meeting between you and Levitt should be arranged." Felix went on in the memo to muse about potential acquirers of Levitt, including large oil companies, because "they are already active in the real estate business . . . plus the fact that they have the cash resources required in any kind of a land banking operation," or "companies like Alcoa, Kaiser, or eventually, Georgia Pacific." Felix concluded, "In any case, I believe that, from everything I have been told, in its field Levitt & Sons is the number one company; its current business seems to be profitable and growing and if proper safeguards can be taken for retention of management it should be a saleable property. The problem will undoubtedly be Mr. Levitt's personal ambitions and requirements for continued unquestioned control over the operation once the company is owned by somebody else, and possibly an overly inflated idea of value. This, however, seems to be a proposition worth pursuing." There is no recorded response from André, which was his style. The best one could hope for in that regard was that he would return the memo, whether read or not, to its writer with a big *A* scrawled on it, indicating not a praiseworthy analysis but rather that he had seen it.

In any event, less than a week later, Levitt had signed an engagement letter with both Lazard and Wertheim agreeing to pay them together the lower of $500,000 ($250,000 each) or 1 percent of the total consideration received to advise on the sale of the company. (This agreement ended up giving Levitt a 45 percent discount on the fee.) This was at a time when one of Levitt's homes cost less than $20,000. Within a month of the signed engagement letter, Lazard had created one of the first "selling memoranda" used to solicit bids for a public company. The twenty-seven page document was unremarkable in every way, except for the fact that it was done at all—becoming most likely the first such document ever produced.

When the selling memorandum was complete, Lazard began calling potential buyers of Levitt. Felix quickly focused on his wonderful client ITT. But the initial response from Geneen was negative, in large part, Felix believed, because ITT was preoccupied with shepherding its bold attempted acquisition of the ABC television network through the increasingly sticky thicket of Washington regulators, who were starting to worry about ITT's M&A campaign.

On April 11, 1966, Peter Lewis, a Lazard associate working on the Levitt deal, wrote Felix a memo about other potential buyers of Levitt; it is highly unlikely Lewis would have written the memo voluntarily and showed one indication of what working for Felix was like. This analysis led Lewis to suggest to Felix that Lazard consider both electric utilities and, rather improbably, aircraft frame manufacturers, such as Lockheed, Boeing, and Douglas. When asked about Lewis's memo during his later congressional testimony, Felix disavowed its relevance: "This is an internal memorandum setting forth some ideas and views. They are just that. They are one man's ideas and views. We were having discussions with I.T. & T. at that point, and from that point on we didn't have any discussions with anybody else."

Felix's willingness to undercut his subordinates, as evidenced by his decision to distance himself from Lewis's memorandum, would become an unfortunate trademark and create much resentment toward him from other Lazard professionals. Felix had a nasty habit of cozying up to younger partners and senior vice presidents and seducing them into working for him on his deals. These unsuspecting men, and the occasional woman, would slave away for Felix, and bask in his enormous spotlight, before being summarily dismissed or undermined. Then some other poor soul would suffer the same fate. Despite his deal-making prowess, many partners over time came to view Felix as more of a liability to the firm than an asset. "The thing that strikes me about working for Felix is that he always wanted to be in control of the plane," one partner recalled, disapprovingly. The irony, of course, was that since Felix was so good at what he did, he always found himself in the midst of the most important or interesting deals. So, naturally, young ambitious bankers wanted to work for him and be part of that excitement. Unfortunately, he was well aware of that attraction and took advantage. He became the third rail of investment banking. "Working for Felix was very difficult because it was so unrewarding," said one longtime partner. "He never wanted you to get any credit with the client or, for that matter, within the firm." Lamented one banker, "Working for Felix was a death sentence." Partners often complained that Felix had no loyalty to them. Once, David Supino was discussing this aspect of Felix's personality with Percie du Sert, the CFO of Renault, a longtime Lazard client. "No, David," du Sert said, "you are wrong. Felix is loyal, but his loyalties are successive loyalties."

Lewis's thoughts on other buyers for Levitt aside, Lazard continued to push for a deal with ITT, which, in May 1966, was suddenly smitten with the prospect of owning Levitt. ITT made an offer of $16.50 per Levitt share, all in ITT stock. The offer valued Levitt at about $51 million, about 50 percent premium to the then trading price of $11 for each Levitt share. Lazard recommended that Levitt pursue a deal with ITT. The two sides continued to negotiate, though, and conducted due diligence sessions at Levitt's Lake Success headquarters. Soon, ITT revised its offer for Levitt to $17.50 per share, or $54 million, a 59 percent premium. Levitt continued to hold out, and on August 8, 1966, Felix sent Geneen a letter with "a small list of questions" that Levitt still had along with Felix's answers to the questions "based on my prior knowledge of ITT and the way it operates." He suggested to Geneen that he, Levitt, and Felix "have lunch" in the middle of September to "clarify these points." The two sides did meet on September 15, 1966, and Geneen's notes from the meeting are on a slip of paper with the headline "Important Concepts," in his own hand. Geneen noted, "L. is *unique*. When housing was declining, they're 30% above budget." The deal trudged on. It was still not done by early 1967, and Levitt's stock price kept going up based, in part, on a series of marketing meetings Bill Levitt had arranged with Wall Street research analysts.

Apparently, Levitt's "educational campaign" with Wall Street had begun to pay off as the Levitt stock was then at $19 per share, a big move up. On February 28, 1967, in response to a request from André for an update, Felix produced a three-page memo. Because no deal had been achieved with ITT, Levitt returned to the idea of doing a secondary stock offering and wanted his bankers' view of that option, given that the stock had risen materially. "The Levitt stock is undoubtedly not cheap at this price," Felix wrote to André. "A considerable amount of glamour has been generated over the last few months because of the potential recovery of the housing market, the Company's 'New Cities' program, and the

Company's unique record in the industry." Felix further explained that he had had a conversation that day with the Wertheim banker Al Kleinbaum, who also thought the Levitt stock "too high," and described how Kleinbaum thought a public stock offering at this price "would be undesirable until such time as the earning power foreseen for the coming year actually becomes apparent." But since Levitt wanted to sell an additional 450,000 shares, which together with the existing 550,000 shares already public would give the company 1 million shares traded publicly and qualify for a coveted New York Stock Exchange listing, Lazard and Wertheim were faced with having to give their professional opinion to the CEO.

Felix sought cover. First, he spoke with his old classmate Joel Carr, the general counsel at Levitt, and discovered that Levitt had agreed not to receive dividends on his stock until the end of 1967, an agreement that could not be changed. Selling the Levitt shares without the capability of receiving the same dividend paid to the other public shareholders was a nonstarter. Therefore, given this restriction, a secondary was not practical at least until the end of 1967. "This is probably just as well," Felix wrote, "since, in my judgment, telling Bill Levitt at this point that his stock is overpriced for purposes of making a public offering would be psychologically most undesirable and I would hope that this question could be avoided altogether or," and here Felix conceived of a classic investment banker ploy, "if Wertheim is somewhat cautious on the current level of Bill Levitt's stock that, since it will not cost us anything we can be somewhat more bullish." Felix went on to recommend that as an alternative to the ITT deal, a secondary stock offering be considered for early 1968 plus an acquisition program of other troubled builders, suppliers, or companies "whose activities could be brought to bear, such as insurance, mortgage servicing, title guarantee, etc." All of these options would, of course, be moneymakers for Lazard.

Still, Felix preferred the ITT deal. "It may be that alternatives to ITT should be discussed, although I believe that we should make a strong pitch that ITT is probably the best ultimate answer to Bill's problems and that during the next few months everything should be done to try to consummate that transaction on the most favorable terms possible," he wrote.

Finally, on July 11, 1967, there was a little movement from ITT. In the face of an unanticipated antitrust challenge from the Justice Department on its ABC deal, ITT decided to abandon that increasingly controversial merger and turned its attention back to the long-simmering Levitt deal. On July 22, ITT and Levitt announced the two companies had agreed to acquisition terms, valuing Levitt at about $91.3 million, more than double the value of the company when Felix attended the first meeting with Carr in January 1966. The Levitt stock had been soaring throughout the first half of 1967 and closed at $28.75 the day the merger was announced, just below the $29.07 per share the ITT deal was worth to Levitt shareholders. While the process of the Levitt deal for Lazard must have been extremely cumbersome and required much hand-holding, especially as ITT delayed repeatedly and there were clearly no other buyers around, the outcome for Levitt shareholders was better than could possibly have been anticipated.

Ironically, the loser in the deal was Lazard, which benefited not at all from the stupendous increase in Levitt's market value. The terms of Lazard's fee agreement called for the fee to be the lower of $500,000 or 1 percent of the total consideration received by Levitt. At $91.3 million, 1 percent was $913,000. Unfortunately, with $500,000 being lower than $913,000, $500,000 became the operative fee, which, when split with Wertheim, amounted to $250,000 for Lazard for almost two years of work. After "advertising" expenses of $24,310.76 (half of which Wertheim absorbed), Lazard pocketed $237,844.62 when the deal closed in February 1968.

Once again, though, as with his relatively inconsequential take on the Avis deal, Felix turned Lazard's small payday on the Levitt deal into something far more meaningful: a December 13, 1967, appointment to a coveted seat on ITT's board of directors and on its executive committee. The so-called Lazard ITT board seat, which André had demanded of Geneen two years earlier, would be occupied by Felix until 1981, and after that by Michel, until he relinquished it in May 2001. In the decades before the passage of the Sarbanes-Oxley Act, in 2002, made it untenable for an investment banker to sit on his client's board, such board seats were much sought after by bankers as a way to garner the most insight into their client's strategic thinking and, of course, to make sure the banker's firm walked away with the lion's share of the investment banking business.

With the Levitt deal finally concluded and Felix on the board, Lazard resumed its representation of ITT on the company's increasingly aggressive acquisition campaign. In 1968 alone, Lazard represented ITT in its $293 million acquisition of Rayonier, the nation's largest cellulose manufacturer and a large owner of tracts of timber (a $600,000 fee); its $280 million acquisition of Continental Baking, the nation's largest baker (a $400,000 fee); and its acquisition of Pennsylvania Glass Sand Corporation, then the country's biggest producer of silica and clay for glass and ceramics (a $250,000 fee). In 1969, Lazard represented ITT on the acquisition of Canteen Corporation (a $250,000 fee) and United Homes (a $50,000 fee). In 1968, Canteen had been a client of Lazard when Lazard sold Canteen's Rowe Division for a $75,000 fee. The only large deal during these years that Lazard seems to have missed out on was ITT's $193 million acquisition of the Sheraton hotel chain. Still, Lazard had nearly a monopoly on ITT's advisory business. This fact, while well hidden from the general public, was most likely of no interest to the greater populace, either.

It is tempting today to shrug with indifference at these relatively small deals and smaller fees. But in the late 1960s, these deals and fees were considered *enormous*, and portentous of significant change, so much so that Congress began an unprecedented—if utterly unheralded and all but ignored—investigation into what were then known as "conglomerate corporations," companies such as ITT and Gulf & Western that, with wild abandon, seemed to be acquiring companies far beyond their traditional lines of business. Under the auspices of the then-long-tenured Jewish Brooklyn congressman Emanuel Celler, the House Judiciary Committee began, in October 1968, a "comprehensive" study into the economic and political significance of the merger activity of conglomerates.

Celler's subcommittee decided the best way to get a handle on the wave of merger activity would be to select six conglomerates, study their acquisition strategies, and interview their CEOs. These companies—ITT among them—were abetted in their acquisition activities by "the assistance of a few advisers," who also came under congressional scrutiny. Lazard was singled out by the subcommittee for close examination because of its role advising ITT, which quickly took center stage in the hearings.

On December 3, 1969, Felix testified for two hours and twenty minutes before the subcommittee, with partner Ray Troubh and associate Mel Heineman at his side. Neither of these men uttered a word. Felix later claimed he couldn't even recall making the appearance before the Celler commission. For the intensely secretive house of Lazard, these hearings were an unprecedented public bloodletting. Not only did Felix's testimony lay bare for all to see for the first time the inner workings of the firm, but Congress forced Lazard to turn over thousands of pages of documents to the subcommittee about everything from who worked for the firm, by name, to the intricacies of the Avis sale to ITT. The documents revealed that Lazard earned more than $16 million in fees advising on seventy-two transactions during this time period. More important, though, these pages provided a prism through which to peer into Lazard's DNA.

Felix's testimony offered listeners a remarkable blueprint for understanding the nascent world of advising corporations on mergers, acquisitions, and divestitures. It was really quite a simple insight, Felix explained. "Our corporate clients should get advice on acquisitions in the same manner that they get advice raising money," he said. "A company, or the owner of a company, wishing to sell should seek professional representation of the same caliber as when he wishes to refinance a loan or go public." Simple, but before André and Felix came up with the idea, the business of advising corporations on their M&A activity did not exist. Felix then codified for the committee in layman's terms the four distinct roles an M&A adviser plays: initiation, analysis, negotiation, and coordination. These are the same roles played by advisers today. In the first phase, "Lazard will, from time to time, initiate or originate an idea for an acquisition at the request of a company wishing to expand or to diversify into a given area of activity," he said. "Conversely, it may be retained as an exclusive agent of a corporation if we can recommend an association which is both feasible and economically sound. Lazard's assistance has also been requested in past instances to assist a corporate client desirous of disposing of a segment of its business, such as a particular division or subsidiary." During the analytical phase, the Lazard bankers "would look into businesses and prospects of potential acquisition candidates, as well as of a company or companies which might consummate the acquisition. Such analysis may encompass the background of the industry involved, particularly with a view toward trends and industry direction and a detailed picture of the companies under study. Upon the conclusion of this phase, we are in a position to make a judgment whether a given combination will be in the best economic interests of the participants."

Assuming the decision is made to proceed with a transaction, the next task is one of valuation, for the purpose of divining the buy or sell price or of determining an exchange ratio if stock is involved. "In this connection, we may analyze the securities and debt instruments of both companies in order to protect the security holders of the company to be acquired and the existing securities of the acquiring company, as well as the integrity of its balance sheet. We would surely be asked to advise our client on the optimum structure for the acquisition, whether it should be an exchange of stock, tender or exchange offer or a purchase of assets. This judgment can be made only after financial, legal, accounting and tax considerations are brought to bear on the information previously developed." Felix then conveyed the bane of every investment banker's existence: "It should be obvious that for every transaction that is actually consummated, many times that number never see the light of day, for a variety of reasons, after considerable efforts."

Felix said that negotiating a deal is Lazard's "major function" on behalf of a client.

> Typically, we are asked to participate in discussions with the management of a prospective acquisition candidate to explain the background of the proposed acquisition and the nature of the business of our client. It may be our job to sit down with the investment bankers or financial advisers of the other company involved to discuss the merits of the acquisition and to arrive at mutually acceptable terms which are inevitably the result of arm's-length bargaining and arduous negotiations. What emerges from this process, if it is successful, is an agreement in principle which all parties in good conscience recommend to their respective clients and on which Lazard will often be asked to opine as to fairness. The skill in performing this function, however long or short the time period over which it is performed is one of the fundamental contributions of an investment banking firm in the merger and acquisition area.

Once an agreement is reached, the bankers would review drafts of the various legal documents required to be executed depending on the type of transaction. Bankers might also give advice about publicity for a deal, the preferred exchange for listing securities to be issued, or the solicitation of shareholder proxies, if needed. In his closing thought, Felix said insightfully, "The only generalization that can be made with respect to mergers and acquisitions is that no two are similar. Consequently, our activities from case to case will be different but in each case some or all of the above will be included. We believe it is in the public interest that the mechanism for the acquisition or sale of a business be handled as professionally, ethically and soundly as the investments of individuals or the financing of companies. We attempt to provide this service in this fashion."

The first series of questions for Felix from the committee went to the heart of the most proprietary of investment banking information: how Lazard decides what to charge corporate clients for its advisory services. Felix was appropriately evasive. When asked whether the size of the deal had an impact on the size of the fee, he acknowledged that it did. "As I tried to indicate before, philosophically we think of an acquisition as not being a terribly dissimilar service to raising money for a company," he said. "If we negotiate a private placement for $3 million, our fee to the client will be different than if we negotiate a loan of $300 million. Actually, the analogy is not too dissimilar to an acquisition."

Today, every M&A group on Wall Street has an approved "fee grid" where, depending on the size of the deal, a percentage fee is derived. For every $100 million increase in deal size, a new percentage kicks in. The smaller the deal, the higher the percentage fee; the larger the deal, the smaller the percentage fee. Obviously, bigger deals generate larger fees. But as Felix suggested, even these printed and approved fee grids are subject to negotiation, a fact well known by clients. Managers of M&A groups are constantly urging bankers to stick to the grid, but the reality of investment banking is that that rarely occurs, especially in the era of the financial supermarkets, such as Citigroup and JPMorgan Chase, where to win ancillary financing business, or even to capture "league table" credit (the constantly updated list of which banks have advised on the most deals), bankers constantly cut fees.

The other historically revealing aspect of Felix's testimony is his equating M&A fees with financing fees. Thirty-five years ago, investment bankers raised capital privately, both debt and equity, for their corporate clients and got paid for it. So, for instance, on behalf of ITT, Lazard might negotiate a bank facility from a money-center bank and some private subordinated debt from a few insurance companies and charge a fee based on the amount of capital raised, with lower fees for debt and higher fees for equity. There was no syndicated loan market. There was no public high-yield market. Now, aside from raising private equity, investment bankers are rarely paid for raising capital for clients. What they are paid for, rather, is *underwriting* the loan, high-yield deal, or equity offering. Using their own balance sheets, the banks agree to provide their corporate clients the money they are seeking and take the risk *themselves* of syndicating the loan, bond, or equity to the world of investors, be they other banks, hedge funds, insurance companies, mutual funds, or the public. Usually the risks for underwriters are minimal and the fees disproportionately generous, but when markets crash—after September 11, or upon the collapse of Long Term Capital Management—these same underwriters can get stuck with major capital losses. Lazard, with a tiny balance sheet, has never been very interested in making loans or underwriting junk bonds, which require large amounts of capital.

The subcommittee then zeroed in on another of Lazard's secret competitive advantages: its so-called interlocking directors, where Lazard partners also sit on their clients' boards of directors. Felix produced a list for the subcommittee showing that he served on two boards, ITT and

Howmet, the manufacturer of aircraft parts. Stanley Osborne served on three boards. André served on six boards, including Fiat and RCA, to which he was appointed in 1957, the payoff for years of courting David Sarnoff. And Albert Hettinger, the former professor and economist, served on eight boards, among them Harcourt, Brace & World, the book publisher, and Owens-Illinois, the glass manufacturer. Kenneth Harkins, the chief counsel on the committee, pointed out to Felix that in nearly 40 percent of the deals Lazard gave M&A advice on between 1964 and the end of 1969, a Lazard partner served on the board of one of the companies involved in the deal. "Does having a member of your firm on the board of directors of other corporations assist your organization in its merger activities?" Harkins asked. Felix replied, "I would say that in general having one of your partners on the board of a company would certainly enable us to serve that company better by being more intelligent about what the company is doing and what it needs. Whether it would give us a competitive advantage, vis-à-vis other investment banking firms who give that service, I would say no, because corporations today are pretty sophisticated and they will go to whomever can perform the service for them."

Harkins later walked Felix through a year-by-year analysis of the percentage of Lazard's M&A fees that derived from companies where Lazard had a board seat. In 1965, it was 85 percent. In 1966, it was 63 percent. In 1967, it was 29 percent. In 1968, it was 58 percent, and through Labor Day 1969, it was 42 percent. Harkins then tried again. "Do you find that having a director on these various corporations increases the business of your firm?" he asked.

"No, sir," Felix responded, sticking to his guns, "but I find that generally corporate clients sooner or later will invite one of our partners on the board, because really this is the way it happens. We can't force our way on a board of directors. If we had dealings with a company and have performed services, by and large, at some point or another we will be invited on the board, and the relationship will become close."

"What you are saying is that obtaining director positions is a natural evolution in the business community as a result of the relationship of investment bankers or marriage brokers, with their clients?" Harkins asked.

Clearly offended at the reference to "marriage brokers," Felix replied: "We don't view ourselves as marriage brokers. But in terms of what we render, it is a very personal service." The concept of Lazard as a marriage broker would come up again. Five weeks after his testimony, Felix sent to the subcommittee a list of all the deals its clients did from 1964 to Labor Day 1969 where Lazard did *not* get a fee and where Lazard had a board seat. The list included ten deals ITT did in 1968 and 1969, including Sheraton and Yellow Cab Co. (Kansas City), where Lazard had not been hired. It also showed five deals "done away" by Howmet, Felix's other board seat, during the time period.

The subcommittee then turned the spotlight on Lazard's arbitrage business, the then-little-known strategy of simultaneously buying and selling the securities of companies involved in a merger in the hope of profiting from discrepancies in their prices over time. Felix read aloud for the committee a surprisingly succinct and understandable overview of the arbitrage concept as it applies to the securities industry. "While it is highly technical, it is age-old in concept and execution and represents essentially the hedged short-term investment of funds at fairly high risk with commensurate rewards," he explained. "The classic example in present day markets is the arbitrage of a merger between two publicly traded companies after the exchange values have been announced. Theoretically, since one security is soon to be exchanged at a specific ratio for other securities, the two values should be identical but for reasons enumerated later they are not." Among these reasons, Felix explained, were "abrupt changes in securities and money markets," "various warranties and other 'outs' in the merger agreement," "governmental opposition," and "shareholder opposition." He continued, "The arbitrageur is willing to take the risk that the transaction will go through and to profit by the difference between the present market and the ultimate realized value." While Celler commended Felix for providing an "excellent" definition of arbitrage, his general counsel wanted to dig into whether Lazard partners were profiting improperly from mergers on which Lazard was advising.

"Do you have a rule that prohibits dealing in securities of companies to which Lazard Frères is providing merger services or where Lazard Frères has a director on one of the companies involved?" Harkins asked.

"Yes, sir," Felix responded. "With respect to our arbitrage department we have two rules. We have a rule which has been in effect since our inception in the arbitrage business, which goes back maybe three to four years only, actually, and that is that we have never arbitraged securities involving transactions where one of our partners is a director. We have, last year, or at the beginning of this year, extended that rule to exclude transactions involving companies where we do not have a director, but in one way or another we act in an advisory capacity. In addition, we obviously have rules throughout the firm of not getting involved in securities transactions on the basis of any inside information we may have."

When the chairman pressed Felix to explain Lazard's self-restraint in this regard, he continued,

> First of all, we don't feel that we should in any way be involved in short sales of any securities of any company where we have a director because we feel that is a philosophical contradiction to begin with. Secondly, when we excluded transactions involving our firm in any advisory capacity in arbitrage transactions, we became concerned, Mr. Chairman, as we became involved in more and more of these transactions, with the internal security problems within our firm. Although we have always managed to be absolutely purer than Caesar's wife, and been able to limit the information within the firm to the people who really need to know, we felt that we might make a little less money in the arbitrage department, but we would sleep a great deal better if we just simply excluded them from any of these transactions.

In perhaps the first recorded instance of a congressman trying to come to grips with the massive problem soon to be known as insider trading, the Illinois Representative Robert McClory asked Felix what he would think if an M&A banker told his clients to buy the stock of a company targeted for purchase before the deal had been announced.

"It would be illegal," Felix said.

"What is the illegality involved?" asked McClory, trying to follow.

"The situation as you describe it, sir, would be if we, for instance, were retained by a corporation to act as their adviser in the acquisition of another company, and prior to the announcement of any transaction we went around to our clients and said, 'Buy this stock,' that would be the use of inside information," Felix said. "The arbitrage as I tried to underline, only begins—"

"Does that violate the SEC rules?" McClory interjected.

"Yes, sir," Felix continued. "But the arbitrage transaction only begins after the announcement of the terms of the transaction, so there is no use of inside information involved here, because the terms are out in the open. But the situation as you describe it, Congressman, would be an out-and-out illegality, as least as far as my understanding of the law."

Celler then stepped in. "Let me ask you this question," he said. "This restriction that you have placed on yourselves, has that restriction been followed by other houses on Wall Street who are competitors of yours?"

"I don't know, Mr. Chairman," Felix answered. "We don't talk to our competitors."

"You don't know?" Celler continued.

"No," Felix replied.

"They know about your restrictions, don't they?" Celler asked.

"No, sir," Felix answered. "They would not."

"It is not secret, is it?" Celler wondered.

"Well," Felix replied, the irony of the situation apparent, "the way we operate our firm, Mr. Chairman, is not something that we—let me say we are very jealous of our privacy."

"What you have adopted is credible," the chairman concluded. "Would it be to your advantage to spread that good gospel around the street?"

"I think, Mr. Chairman, people might think that we were being a little presumptuous," Felix answered.

"Maybe they would think you are fools," Celler followed.

"Maybe," Felix said.

After this pleasant exchange, the subcommittee moved on to Lazard's role as a paid strategic adviser to corporations. Celler said, "Can you tell us, roughly, how many concerns, and for want of a better term I use the words 'marriage brokers'—how many so-called marriage brokers effecting these mergers there are, say, in New York City, of the size and consequence of Lazard Frères?"

"I would hope that you would add moral caliber, Mr. Chairman, as another of our characteristics," Felix responded. "I would say, Mr. Chairman, that of the major, reputable investment banking firms that perform functions in this area, you would find most of the major investment banking firms in this business, I would say, being 10 or 15 firms of a major character." Felix would return often to this public obsession with the moral and ethical conduct of his fellow investment bankers—seemingly so fraught with cognitive dissonance—even as recently as July 2004, some thirty-five years after his testimony before the Celler commission. In a *New York Times* interview, he opined, "You should come to the business with a moral code. You're certainly not going to learn it later on. If people conduct themselves in ways that could be deemed immoral, I really wouldn't blame Wall Street, I would blame the individuals themselves who by and large should know better."

BETWEEN 1966 AND 1969, investment banking fees soared, mirroring the merger boom across Wall Street. The year 1970 would be very different. On Wall Street a full-fledged crisis was brewing, with brokerages becoming overwhelmed by an explosion in the volume of equities traded, without having the back-office capability to handle the increased paperwork.

While the problem sounds mundane in the computer age, it was anything but boring for those involved. Even the most prescient firms suffered. The New York Stock Exchange quickly figured out it had a major problem. To get a handle on how to solve the crisis of failing firms and to salvage as many of them as possible, the exchange created the Surveillance Committee of the New York Stock Exchange, loosely referred to as the Crisis Committee. The exchange appointed Felix to head up the Crisis Committee in June 1970. He had been appointed to the stock exchange's board of governors in May 1968. Among his five partners in the effort were Bernard "Bunny" Lasker, then chairman of the board of governors. These wise men were very concerned that the collapse of one big firm would start dominoes falling, badly undermining confidence in the markets and potentially destroying the country's position as the center of global finance.

The crux of the problem, which Wall Street historians have dubbed the "back-office crisis," was that during 1967 trading volumes on the major stock exchanges exploded, and the private, poorly capitalized Wall Street partnerships were ill equipped to handle the extensive paperwork of settling trades occasioned by the "sudden and unexpected upsurge" in volumes. Many firms were slow to add the back-office personnel required to handle the new flow. Unfortunately, when the personnel were eventually hired—in a rush, of course—talent suffered. Some firms were drowning in a sea of unprocessed, and inaccurately accounted for, paper. But by the end of 1969, "the worst of the paperwork problems had been surmounted," according to Lee Arning, then a New York Stock Exchange executive. The crisis, though, had just begun, for at the very moment that many brokerages had increased their personnel costs to scale the mountain of paper, the volume of business fell off a cliff.

There was a feeling that 1970 was capitalism's most acute test since 1929. "We were looking at the world from a 650 Dow Jones, the Penn Central bankruptcy, a credit crisis, Cambodia, Kent State—and we didn't know where anything was going and it was a pretty grim world at this time," Felix told the *New York Times.* By midsummer 1970, Felix had a full-fledged crisis to resolve as head of the Crisis Committee: the near dissolution of the old-line, blue-blood retail brokerage Hayden, Stone & Co., where Joseph P. Kennedy had begun to build the fortune that would be used to propel his second son to the presidency. Hayden, Stone had sixty-two offices nationwide, but its back-office systems were a mess. Compounding its problems, the firm's older partners, upon retiring, were withdrawing their capital from the firm. This, combined with the failing fortunes on Wall Street in general, created operating losses that together pushed Hayden, Stone dangerously close to defaulting on a $17.5 million loan made in the spring of 1970 to the firm by a few of its clients in Oklahoma. When a lawyer for the Oklahomans discovered that Hayden, Stone couldn't account for some $7 million in securities, Felix and the exchange began searching for a buyer.

Although the Street would be aghast, Felix quickly found a savior for Hayden, Stone in Sandy Weill, the wunderkind financier who had presciently built a state-of-the-art securities clearing operation at his firm, Cogan, Berlind, Weill & Levitt (known as "Corned Beef with Lettuce" among Wall Street wags). Felix decided that Weill, who would go on to create the financial behemoth Citigroup, was one of the few people able to grapple quickly with Hayden's accounting deficiencies. According to *Tearing Down the Walls*, Monica Langley's authoritative account of Weill's Wall Street career, Hayden, Stone's scion, Hardwick Simmons, was dispatched to meet with Weill to see whether "a bunch of blue bloods would work for these scrappy Brooklyn Jews." Simmons, who later would head Prudential Securities and become chairman and CEO of the Nasdaq Stock Market Inc., recalled that he had "never heard of them, or 'Corned Beef and Mustard' or whatever it is. They're not even on our radar screen." On the three days leading up to the September 11 deadline, Felix alternated between meetings at the stock exchange, with Lasker and Robert Haack, the president of the exchange, and those with Harold Geneen, up at ITT. For his part, Simmons, the great-grandson of the founder Galen Stone, had no choice but to acquiesce, of course, and on September 11, 1970, CBWL purchased what it wanted of Hayden, Stone, especially the tony name, and became the new Hayden, Stone with, voilà, instant prestige and history.

It was a real nail-biter, though, as the September 11 deadline loomed—either to approve the CBWL deal or to shutter Hayden, Stone. Felix recalled:

> At 9:15 that morning, Lasker and I were talking to Golsen [Jack Golsen, the last holdout against the deal and one of the Oklahoma investors] and he said why shouldn't Hayden Stone go broke? Why should this be any different from Penn Central or Lockheed? He was mad. Somebody told him the financial community would never forget it if he failed to go along and he felt this was a threat. I think he also felt he was going to lose everything either way. The Cogan people had flown out there the night before and were working on him from 4 a.m. on. Golsen wanted to talk to Bunny and to me. . . . Bunny and I talked to him for over an

> hour. We talked national interest. We talked self-interest. Bunny was extremely effective. He's an enormously sincere man and in the clutch this was important because it came through. Finally, he said how much time can you give me and we said 15 minutes is all we have because we have to close the firm down before the opening of trading. Larry Hartzog [a lawyer for Mr. Golsen] got back to us and said, "Felix, you've got a deal." I went into the next room and told all these people they had a deal and then I took a very deep breath and walked out. It was five minutes to the opening.

On behalf of the New York Stock Exchange, Felix cut a deal with Weill that required the exchange to contribute $7.6 million in cash to the new company and to assume $10 million of Hayden's liabilities. The deal was a brilliant one for Weill and set him on his extraordinary path.

❦

TWO MONTHS LATER, Felix and the Crisis Committee had another near disaster on their hands. This time, one of the Street's largest brokerages, F. I. DuPont, Glore Forgan & Co. started to fail barely six months after the shotgun merger that had brought F. I. DuPont & Co., Glore Forgan Staats, and Hirsch & Co. together in the first place. According to the *Times,* "The brokerage firm found itself in deep distress . . . its back office an insoluble snarl of paperwork and its account ledgers mired in red ink." Felix had had doubts about the three-way merger from the outset. "Figures from firms with huge back-office problems are meaningless," he told *Fortune,* "because you can't really know their position."

Once again, nothing less than the future of Wall Street was at stake with the potential failure of DuPont Glore. At the same time as DuPont was imploding, Felix and Co. had corralled the venerable Merrill Lynch into saving yet another firm, Goodbody & Co., a firm similar in size to DuPont. Felix remembered a particularly poignant moment when James Hogle, the principal investor in Goodbody, appeared before the Crisis Committee but refused to divulge the extent of the firm's capital shortage. "If you don't tell me the facts, you are not leaving here," Felix told Hogle. "And he looked at me and two tears rolled down his cheeks. It was a terrible, terrible moment."

But the deals had a house-of-cards aspect to them; Merrill agreed to take over Goodbody—after a $20 million indemnification from the New York Stock Exchange—but only if no other firm failed before Merrill could complete the deal. Recalled Lasker: "If DuPont had failed, Merrill Lynch would not have taken over Goodbody, and if both of these leading firms had gone down at once, there's no question that the effect on the country, on the industry, on investors, on the economy would have been severe, if not disastrous."

Riding in from Texas to rescue DuPont, sporting a three-piece suit and a crew cut, was H. Ross Perot, the founder, in 1962, with all of $1,000 in his pocket, of Electronic Data Systems Corporation, a computer services company. At that time, Perot was "one of the few men who ever made a billion dollars on paper," after EDS went public in 1968, at $16.50 per share, before soaring to as high as $161 per share in 1970. DuPont was also one of EDS's largest customers, a fact that had no doubt drawn Perot's attention since he owned, at that time, 80 percent of EDS's stock and the loss of a major customer would surely affect EDS's stock price. Perot claimed that EDS's stock price was not what motivated his interest in DuPont. "At *any* price per share, I am worth more than I ever dreamed I'd be," he said.

Felix initially considered Perot a potential Wall Street savior when he went to the White House for his friend William Casey's swearing in as SEC chairman and met President Nixon for the first time, as well as—more significantly for Felix's future—Attorney General John Mitchell. He also saw at the ceremony Peter Flanigan, Nixon's close adviser and a former investment banker at Dillon Read. "I'm sort of going through the line, and I get to Nixon," Felix said. "And Flanigan introduces me to Nixon, and says, 'Felix Rohatyn. He's head of the Crisis Committee of the exchange.' Nixon says, 'Oh, I hear you're doing such a great job and I hear that everything's gonna be all right.' I said, 'Well, Mr. President, I don't know where you hear that because we're up to here with Goodbody.' At that point, it looked really bad for Glore DuPont." The president pulled Felix aside. " 'Does Flanigan know all this?' " he asked. Felix said they talked every day. " 'Good,' Nixon said. He calls John Mitchell over, and he said, 'John, I want Felix to call you every night to tell you what's happening and what they need because I don't want anything to go wrong here.' So I said, 'Fine.' And I started calling Mitchell every night at 10:00, and half the time Mrs. Mitchell answered the phone, and she was absolutely, totally drunk." Felix further explained that in one of those late-night conversations with Mitchell, the attorney general suggested that if DuPont Glore needs "five million or ten million, why don't you talk to Perot, who wants to be helpful. So that's how he got involved. That's how I met him."

It turned out, though, that the deal Perot made for DuPont was not one of his smarter ones. "We just threw money in," Perot said at the time. "It took more guts than brains." On May 14, when DuPont had been saved, Perot became the largest single individual investor in a Wall Street firm at that time. He had his work cut out for him and quickly installed EDS managers to run the brokerage. "I've been told," Perot said, "that you can't expect people on Wall Street to be as disciplined as they are in the computer business. But until DuPont has the same position in the brokerage business that EDS has in the computer service industry, I won't be able to rest." Despite Perot's determination, it didn't work out. Felix said that Perot eventually lost more than *$100 million* in his ill-fated Wall Street adventure when even the newly reconstituted DuPont could not be saved. "And nobody ever said thank you [to Perot] for actually saving Wall Street," Felix concluded. In 1974, lawyers hired by Perot liquidated DuPont Glore, despite the last-ditch decision to second Mort Myerson, Perot's partner at EDS, to run the brokerage.

Despite this deal's terrible outcome, Perot harbored no ill will toward Felix—he was just the agent after all—and their relationship flourished for the next thirty-five years. Perot put Felix on the EDS board. Felix would later represent Perot in the $2.5 billion sale of EDS to General Motors, in 1984, for a new class of GM stock. More fatefully for Felix, he supported Perot for president in 1992 and more than likely, as a result, lost his chance to be secretary of the Treasury. Felix's loyalty had cost him.

Three months after striking the deal between Perot and DuPont and a year after he took on the assignment, Felix quit his position as chairman of the Crisis Committee. In the end, about one hundred New York Stock Exchange member firms, one-sixth of the total, either had failed or had been merged out of existence during the crisis. In his three-page letter of resignation to Haack and Ralph DeNunzio, distributed to the thirty-three members of the New York Stock Exchange board, Felix suggested his task was complete. He continued to worry, though, about Wall Street's self-regulating ability. "The questions raised by the not infrequent inaccuracy of both internal and audited reports will have to be studied by the Exchange," he wrote. "In my opinion, they involve the entire concept of self-regulation since, if our tools are inadequate we either have to get new tools or someone else should do the job. I think we have, at enormous cost and with little public recognition, paid for the sins of the past and have stopped the current bleeding. I am not convinced that we have adequate early warning and adequate measuring to prevent recurrence if industry conditions should change again." In closing, he wrote, "I don't believe we can take the position that it has been a success over the last few years. Hopefully, we may convince our critics, which will include the Congress, the SEC, and the public, that very costly lessons"—estimated by Felix later at more than $140 million, at the time a considerable sum—"have been learned and will result in greater effectiveness. The proof of the pudding will obviously be in the eating."

Subsequently, the House of Representatives convened a series of hearings to study the securities industry to determine just what occurred during the crisis and what additional legislation, if any, was required to prevent a recurrence. Felix testified, as did his friend Bill Casey. "We had a house on fire," Felix at one point told the congressmen, "and we could not change the fire regulations at the time; we had to put the fire out and then start to work on these things, and I think that is being done." It would not be the last time Felix would combine prescience with a sky-is-falling doom and gloom.

FELIX'S JUNE 1971 resignation from his prominent role at the stock exchange to return full-time to Lazard coincided with the release of the Celler commission's final report. In a matter-of-fact way, the report definitively linked Felix and Lazard to ITT's aggressive acquisition program. "Felix Rohatyn, a [Lazard] partner on ITT's board of directors and a member of its executive committee, was in a position to play a major role in shaping ITT's acquisition program," the report concluded.

> Information on companies available for acquisition came through Lazard Frères investment banking activities. With an intimate knowledge of ITT operations, Lazard Frères stimulated its own income and facilitated ITT's acquisition program. . . . Further, the major thrust in ITT's acquisition program came after Mr. Rohatyn's appointment and election to the ITT board. ITT's acquisition activity greatly accelerated both in terms of numbers and size of companies acquired. A total of 24 acquisitions were made in 1968, as compared with the totals of 13 in 1967, and 11 in 1966. Such acquisitions included Continental Baking Company (for a total consideration of $279.5 million); Rayonier ($293.1 million); Sheraton ($193.2 million)—all the largest firms in their industries.

Left basically unexplored by the subcommittee (since Lazard was asked to produce a list of *closed* deals through September 5, 1969, and so this deal was mentioned only in passing by Felix) was to that time the largest ever merger in corporate history and, accordingly, Lazard's biggest assignment for ITT: the proposed $1.5 billion acquisition of the Hartford Fire Insurance Company. At the time of Felix's Celler commission testimony, December 1969, ITT was awaiting the approval of the insurance commissioner in Connecticut in order to close the deal. It would be a long wait. And the deal, first announced two days before Christmas 1968, would over the course of the next thirteen years of controversy become, according to André Meyer, a "cause célèbre," and change the lives of all of those involved in it, especially that of Felix Rohatyn, ITT's principal investment banker.

"The Extraordinary ITT Affair," as the *New York Times* dubbed it, was a jambalaya of exceptionally intricate international financial shenanigans and political influence peddling that at times devolved to the level of opera buffa. It became nothing less than the overture to the Watergate drama that followed it directly. Three highly entertaining and informative accounts of the scandal are *Inside Story,* by Brit Hume, who made his bones as a reporter covering it for Jack Anderson's column; Anderson's own *Anderson Papers;* and Anthony Sampson's authoritative *Sovereign State: The Secret History of ITT.* There is also a treasure trove of information about what transpired in the records of the Senate Judiciary Committee and thirty-two boxes of documents at the SEC. It is the unusual role in the affair played by Felix—who told the Celler commission that he wanted Lazard to be "purer than Caesar's wife"—that concerns us here.

A PREREQUISITE FOR a better understanding of what transpired—from late 1968 until the matter was once and for all resolved in 1981—is a brief overview of Lazard's by then almost fifteen-year relationship with Mediobanca, an equally secretive and enigmatic Italian investment bank run with absolute authority by Enrico Cuccia. "Very shy but very clever" is how Lazard partner François Voss described him. If an Italian analog to Lazard were to be conjured cosmically out of "star stuff" and plunked down in the heart of Milan, Mediobanca would be it. Like Lazard, Mediobanca in Italy had its fingers in every important deal and its hand in every important politician's pocket. If possible, Cuccia was more elusive than even the tight-lipped André. "If any banker could be said to cast no shadow, it was Enrico Cuccia," Cary Reich said of him in *Financier.* "The standard shot of him," according to the *Financial Times,* "conveys a man in a homburg hat, coat tightly wrapped around him, giving a hasty backward glance down a foggy Milan street." But Cuccia and Meyer were said to be birds of a feather. "Their relationship was exceptional," recalled Jean Guyot, a longtime Lazard partner who knew both men well. "There was a fundamental confidence between them, which was relatively astonishing, because the two were so different. But they had something in common—the exclusive love for work." They spoke on the telephone nearly every day. "They were intimates," Voss remembered. André was one of the few men in the world of finance whom Cuccia respected, and he kept a picture of André in his office throughout his long career at the Italian bank. For his part, André described Cuccia as "on top of everybody in the banking fraternity. . . . I have the highest regard for his character and his decency and his loyalty and everybody feels the same way as I do."

They also had in common a relatively simple business arrangement. In 1955, Lazard in New York and Lehman Brothers each bought 10 percent stakes in the Italian investment bank for an undisclosed amount and with a vague understanding that they all would attempt to do business together. In April 1958, Lazard Brothers in London also bought an unspecified block of shares in Mediobanca, along with two other European banks—Sofina, of Brussels, and Berliner-Handelgesellschaft, of Berlin. In 1963, Lazard represented the Agnellis in the sale of the Ferrania film company to what is now 3M.

By the end of 1963—December 18, 1963, to be exact—the three firms felt a need to get a little bit more specific about their ongoing relationship and so drew up a "memorandum of understanding concerning cooperation between Mediobanca, Lazard Frères & Co., and Lehman Bros. respecting Italian business." Cuccia was the signatory of the agreement for Mediobanca, and André signed for Lazard. It is a crude document, reflective perhaps of a less litigious and more trusting time. The gist of the agreement was that the firms would split the fees received for M&A deals and equity underwritings involving Italian companies in the United States and American companies in Italy. How the publicity for the assignments would work was also agreed.

The history of successful joint ventures among investment banks is mercifully short, because they typically devolve rather quickly into petty jealousies and arguments over the proper allocation of fees and publicity—the two hot buttons these three firms were clever enough to try to address up front. With this agreement, there were three high-strung, fiercely proud partnerships trying to work together, a sure recipe for disaster. The irony, of course, is that the three houses of Lazard, where there was much common ownership, had never shown even the slightest aptitude for working together. Nevertheless, there is evidence that Lazard in New York sought to shuffle business toward Mediobanca and vice versa. And there were at least two deals where the three firms did in fact work together and split fees: the aforementioned Ferrania film company deal and Royal Dutch Shell's acquisition of the petrochemical business of Montecatini.

Nowhere was that more evident than in the case of ITT, perhaps Lazard's most important client. ITT was constantly looking at deals all over the globe. And Geneen and his team kept the Lazard bankers hopping. Just as ITT was in the midst of its full-fledged assault on the Hartford, it was also pursuing, albeit less aggressively, the acquisition of a small, family-owned Italian manufacturer, Necchi. Necchi was best known for its newfangled sewing machine, with a rotating bobbin, but the sewing machine division, faced with heavy Japanese competition, was a money loser.

With the pace of activity on the Necchi deal having slowed considerably during the early spring of 1969, André and Cuccia turned their attention to another matter. Thinking that Lehman had been operating outside the parameters of their agreement, the two blood brothers decided to jettison Lehman Brothers from the five-year-old working arrangement. On March 19, 1969, André wrote a letter to a Mr. Joseph Thomas—and in a quaint touch addressed it "c/o Messrs. Lehman Brothers"—summarizing the meeting the two of them had had the day before. "I refer to our meeting of yesterday relating to the Memorandum of Understanding of December 18, 1963 among Mediobanca and our respective firms," André wrote. "I advised Mediobanca of our discussion, and they have concurred with our conclusions. Accordingly, on behalf of Mediobanca and ourselves, this is to confirm that the Memorandum of Understanding is terminated as of this date." Thomas signed on behalf of Lehman and returned the letter to André. Apparently, André would later explain, "behind the back of Mediobanca," a Lehman Brothers partner went to see an Italian company to suggest a deal, "which was absolutely contrary to the spirit of the agreement, and it is on that basis that the agreement was cancelled." For Lazard, with Lehman out of the picture, there was now a new arrangement with Mediobanca, where any and all applicable fees were split fifty-fifty. The timing was propitious. For his part, though, Felix would testify in 1973, he never saw the document at the time André negotiated it but was aware that Lazard "did have and do have a continuing relationship with Mediobanca."

Meanwhile, back on November 2, 1968, ITT's management had completed a report about the opportunities that might derive from an ITT-Hartford combination. The code name for the Hartford was "Tobacco," and the so-called Tobacco Memorandum referenced "several opportunities" for the marketing of insurance to, for instance, Sheraton's 1.2 million credit card holders, Avis's 1.5 million credit card holders, Levitt's home owners, and ITT's more than 200,000 shareholders. Then, six days later and with Lazard's help, ITT bought a 6 percent "toehold" in the Hartford for $64.7 million (1,282,948 shares at $50 per share) from Insurance Securities Inc. (ISI), a San Francisco–based investment fund focused on the insurance industry. At the time, Geneen said publicly that the purchase of the shares, which made ITT the largest shareholder in the Hartford, was "an excellent investment in a leading company in the fire and casualty field." ITT had paid a premium to market of around 20 percent to obtain the big block of the Hartford stock. Geneen also said that the managements of the two companies had spoken about "areas of mutual interest." But the main reason for the purchase of the shares, according to Howard Aibel, ITT's general counsel, was "the long-range possibility that in the future we would be able to merge or make some other affiliation with Hartford Fire."

The "long-range possibility" came precisely forty-four days later, on December 23, 1968, when, with Lazard at its side, ITT made the largest hostile takeover offer in corporate history when it unilaterally announced publicly its $1.452 billion "bear hug" offer to the board of directors of the Hartford Fire Insurance Company. The Hartford, founded in 1810, once had insured both Abraham Lincoln and Robert E. Lee. At the time of ITT's hostile offer, the Hartford was the fifth-largest property and casualty insurer in the country. Bradford Cook, a former SEC chairman, said of the two corporate adversaries: "Hartford—she's a blue-blooded lady, ITT—she's a lady of the night." In typical ITT fashion, the initial offer was about 40 percent more than the Hartford's publicly traded value.

Felix had orchestrated much of ITT's machinations regarding the Hartford: he convinced Geneen of the deal's wisdom, advised him about how to go about stalking the prey, and had been in a position to know that the 6 percent block of stock was available. Lazard was one of ISI's important brokers, and Felix's partner Disque Deane had arranged for the sale of ISI's Hartford shares to ITT, for a fee of more than $500,000.

From a regulatory point of view, ITT's decision to pounce on the Hartford could not have come at a more inopportune time, literally two months after the Celler commission had started looking into the perceived runaway power of corporate conglomerates. More disquieting, though, from ITT's perspective, was that there was also a new sheriff in town in the Justice Department in charge of antitrust matters. His name was Richard W. McLaren, and in contrast to his immediate predecessors, he held the somewhat novel view that conglomerate mergers should be challenged by the federal government based on section 7 of the Clayton Act, enacted by Congress in 1914 to strengthen the Sherman Antitrust Act of 1890. Section 7 prohibits mergers and acquisitions where the effect "may be substantially to lessen competition, or to tend to create a monopoly."

McLaren explained his views to John Mitchell, Nixon's attorney general designate, and to Richard Kleindienst, his deputy, at an interview at New York's Pierre hotel, Nixon's transition headquarters, in December 1968. "I had an understanding with them when they offered me the job," McLaren later explained. "I made three conditions: that we would have a vigorous antitrust program; that we would follow my beliefs with regard to what the Supreme Court cases said on conglomerate mergers, and the restructuring of the industry that I thought was coming about in an almost idiotic way; and, third, that we would decide all matters on the merits, there would be no political decision."

On January 16, 1969, just three weeks after ITT made its hostile offer for the Hartford, the Justice Department sent Harold Williams, the CEO of the Hartford, a letter asking for all the information in his files about the potential deal. The Justice Department had put ITT and the Hartford on notice that the Nixon administration would likely oppose the merger on antitrust grounds.

Remarkably, McLaren was a Republican and was serving in a Republican administration, which most observers assumed would take a pro-business stance on antitrust matters. Soon, though, Mitchell was espousing McLaren's views. The attorney general said in a speech in June 1969 to the Georgia Bar Association that "the future vitality of our free economy may be in danger because of the increasing threat of economic concentration." He noted that mergers involving conglomerates had increased to 91 percent of all mergers in 1968, from 38 percent in the years 1948 to 1951. "These facts require us to move aggressively to counteract this trend," he said. None of this commentary could have pleased Geneen, CEO of the nation's largest pure conglomerate and a significant contributor to Nixon's presidential campaign. Indeed, from 1961 to 1969, ITT had acquired fifty-two domestic and fifty-five foreign corporations—thirty-three of the acquisitions coming in 1969 alone. ITT was in the Justice Department's crosshairs. When McLaren decided to seek a preliminary injunction against ITT's $148 million acquisition of Canteen Corporation, which was set to close on February 18, 1969, Geneen felt he had been provoked. And an unhappy Geneen would soon become a major White House concern.

Today, in an era when cost savings are the sine qua non of most mergers, McLaren's objections to the ITT-Canteen merger on antitrust grounds seem stunningly antiquated. Yet for much of the first Nixon administration, his views ruled and had to be accommodated. Indeed, on April 29, the same day of the Canteen suit, Geneen wrote Felix of his worry—presciently as it turned out—that antitrust storm clouds were gathering in a far more substantial way than even when the Justice Department had blocked ITT's acquisition of ABC, almost a year earlier.

McLaren's increasing aggressiveness aside, ITT pushed ahead with its pursuit of the Hartford in the spring of 1969, even though it fully expected the Justice Department to oppose the merger. In that vein, for $24.4 million, ITT acquired, with Lazard's help, another 458,000 Hartford shares at an average price of $54 per share. Now ITT owned 1,741,348 shares at a total investment of $89.1 million—a considerable sum at the time. To protect its investment, ITT, with Lazard's help, had to make sure the Hartford merger passed muster with both the Justice Department—a mighty big obstacle considering McLaren's ongoing opposition—and the IRS, which still needed to rule that the proposed stock merger would be declared tax free to the Hartford shareholders. Geneen exhorted his team to use its "full panoply" of resources to put "inexorable pressure" on the insurer. And the feisty Brit pursued a parallel path in Washington. "I think that during the ensuing delicate period our posture should be one of extreme alertness and in your own apt phrase from an earlier conversation, one of 'inexorable pressure'—right up to and through the moment the deed is officially consummated," one ITT board member wrote Geneen early in 1969. As it turned out, through a series of extraordinary and unprecedented meetings with McLaren's bosses, Felix was the man who, in large part, orchestrated the application of the required pressure. That "inexorable pressure" would eventually lead to the humiliating resignation of an attorney general—Richard Kleindienst—and would sully Felix's golden reputation for years.

On April 9, the Hartford board capitulated to ITT's takeover tactics, and the two companies signed a merger agreement. Felix had just returned from a two-week vacation in Vail. On his first day back in the office, he attended the firm's operating committee meeting, had lunch with André and Pierre and Michel David-Weill, the three of whom together owned the majority of the Lazard firms in Paris and New York, and headed over at 6:00 p.m. to meet with Geneen.

He was present two days later for the ITT board meeting, on April 9, when the merger agreement with the Hartford was approved. But the specter of McLaren loomed over the deal. On June 23, the Justice Department announced it planned to oppose the Hartford merger—as well as ITT's proposed acquisition of the Grinnell Corporation, yet another Lazard assignment—on antitrust grounds.

The consummation of the Hartford merger, as mentioned, was also contingent on the Internal Revenue Service ruling that the ITT stock being offered to the Hartford shareholders would be tax free. In other words, it was essential that when the Hartford shareholders exchanged their shares for new ITT shares, this exchange be free from capital gains tax at the time of the exchange. This is a fairly standard provision in most stock-for-stock merger agreements—just as it had been essential for Lazard in the ITT-Avis deal—and the IRS usually grants the request since, when a shareholder later sells the new shares, a capital gains tax is levied, so taxes are not avoided, only deferred. But of course, there were any number of important rules that came into play for the IRS to agree to the tax-free request; an extremely important one required ITT *not to own* any Hartford shares at the time the *Hartford* shareholders voted whether to approve the ITT deal. That vote was scheduled for November 1969—and of course, ITT had become Hartford's largest shareholder.

Obtaining the IRS's tax-free ruling involved intense political pressure as well, but first André had to execute an arcane cross-border deal with the help of his old crony Enrico Cuccia, who was, to say the least, André's equal at subtle manipulation. That immensely complex deal, which amounted to illegal stock parking, would add immeasurably to Felix's mounting woes and almost lead to his professional undoing, and, many believed, led to André Meyer's death.

While ITT had its merger agreement with the Hartford, the IRS required that the company, in order to receive its tax-free ruling, dispose of its newly acquired 1.74 million Hartford shares, some 8 percent of the then-outstanding Hartford shares. The ITT management focused immediately on this conundrum. (Geneen did take time out to invite Felix, in writing, to become an honorary member of the International golf club in Bolton, Massachusetts. "The course is scenic and exacting," Geneen wrote. "It has a few water holes and many natural hazards that call for accurate shooting." But alas, Felix didn't play golf.) It was not as easy as just selling the shares in the market. First, selling this large a block of stock, despite the merger agreement, would most certainly depress the Hartford stock price. Second, that price had already fallen well below ITT's average cost of about $51 per share and was trading around $37, giving ITT a paper loss of almost $24.5 million. ITT had no interest in perfecting that large a loss by selling the shares outright in the market.

The Hartford shares had fallen mainly because of the general uncertainty about whether the deal would close. The Justice Department's opposition to the merger—indeed to ITT's entire merger program—merely compounded the problem of unloading the Hartford shares. Geneen decided that Felix was the only man who could help. On June 20, 1969, Howard Aibel, the ITT general counsel, wrote Felix: "Now that it looks like we will have a meeting of the Hartford shareholders, we must get busy on the job of disposing of the Hartford shares which ITT owns."

By the beginning of August, having failed to find a solution on his own, Felix turned to André, who was at his house in Crans-sur-Sierre, to see if he had any clever ideas. That was when André hit upon the idea of having ITT sell the stock to Mediobanca. He knew Cuccia could make a decision quickly, and Felix had also taken Cuccia to meet with Geneen a month earlier in New York. Felix later testified to the SEC that André chose Mediobanca because "he thought they had the size, to my recollection, and that Dr. Cuccia was intelligent and aggressive and wanted to build up a relationship with ITT." Left unsaid by all was the belief—alas, unprovable—of some Lazard partners that André and his friends together owned a controlling chunk of Mediobanca beyond the 10 percent stake owned by Lazard in New York, making Mediobanca's help in this matter inevitable and personally profitable.

Throughout August, Felix sent André a number of telexes, some typographically very difficult to read, that outlined the proposed deal. André suggested that three representatives of ITT meet with Cuccia in the Paris office of Lazard on August 28, 1969. André attended this meeting. His recollections about what happened in Paris in August 1969 came years later, in 1974 and 1975, as a result of any number of lawsuits that ended up being filed against Lazard for its role in the ITT-Hartford merger. By the time of his testimony, he wanted to distance himself from the deal. He said he provided no advice to Cuccia about how to conduct himself with the ITT executives because "Dr. Cuccia is a very cold blooded man and very clear and very realistic."

The day after the Paris meeting, Felix sent a telex (through ITT World Communications) to André in Paris. "Have talked to both Geneen and Howard Aibel and believe that the economic features of transaction are okay but that the lawyers cannot sign until draft agreement has been cleared with Internal Revenue," he conveyed. "Believe it would be unwise and probably impossible to close transaction with Cuccia subject to reversal in November if subsequent problems with Internal Revenue Service but believe we should have IRS ruling as well as clearance of this transaction within framework of IRS ruling by September 15. ITT lawyers are therefore being instructed to get text that is acceptable to Cuccia and which in their best judgment would be consistent with IRS and bring it back here for clearance with IRS. Geneen most grateful for your efforts. Warm regards, Felix." Despite his obvious involvement in the deal, Felix would later seek to distance himself from it as well, giving life to the old Wall Street adage that success has many fathers and failure is an orphan.

Finally, on October 13, 1969, the IRS ruled that the ITT-Hartford merger would be treated as a tax-free combination as long as ITT "unconditionally" disposed of all of its Hartford shares. On October 14, John Seath, ITT's vice president and director of taxes, wrote to the IRS and asked if it would find ITT's selling the shares to Mediobanca a satisfactory fulfillment of its requirement. Seath insisted that the proposed sale would be "unconditional," "as required by your ruling," and further elaborated: "There are no conditions on Mediobanca's ownership of the Hartford shares. It can hold the Hartford shares; it can give them away; it can sell them to ITT's competitors; it can vote as it wishes on any matter on which shareholders vote." Seath's characterization of the arrangement would later be determined to be misleading at best, when the whole transaction came under intense legal scrutiny for duping the IRS into providing the tax-free treatment. Seath also conveniently left unsaid whether Mediobanca intended to take any actual economic risk by purchasing the shares. Felix would later testify that he believed "Mediobanca had the option to make it riskless." Whereas the IRS took six months to issue its first ruling, with the heat ratcheted up and the clock ticking, it ruled one *week* later, on October 21, that the proposed deal with Mediobanca would "constitute an unconditional disposition of stock for purposes" of satisfying its October 13 ruling.

On October 28, 1969, Tom Mullarkey, Lazard's in-house counsel, called the ITT legal department to say that he had just returned from Milan with word that Cuccia had finally signed off on the October 7, 1969, version of the ITT deal—the very version that the IRS had signed off on a week earlier. He also said that Mediobanca was now awaiting payment of a commitment fee equal to .765 cents per Hartford share, or a total of $1,332,131.22. The payment to Mediobanca was approved and money wired the next day to Les Fils Dreyfus, in Basel, to pay such funds to "Lazard Frères & Co. for the account of Mediobanca."

The soon-to-be-infamous October 7 seven-page document memorializing the agreement between ITT and Mediobanca raised circularity and obfuscation to an art form. There was a technical requirement that Mediobanca sell any shares through Lazard after first notifying Lazard in writing of its desire to do so. Lazard had also been authorized, if asked, to provide a minimum price at which Mediobanca could sell the shares to a third party, which was a mechanism designed to prevent Mediobanca from simply dumping the shares on the market to get rid of them at any price. Lazard sought, and received, an indemnification from ITT for the work it was to perform under the ITT-Mediobanca contract.

In his "Memorandum to the File" regarding the closing, Samuel

Simmons, ITT's European general counsel, acknowledged being told by Cuccia that Mediobanca had selected a third-party resale option in the contract; this meant that Mediobanca, with Lazard's help, would hold on to the shares until it found third-party buyers willing to pay more for them than ITT had. Mediobanca never intended to take any risk itself with regard to the shares and would simply pay over to ITT whatever price it got for them, less any fees and sales commission it was entitled to. Per the agreement, any profit or loss on the shares would be remitted to ITT. But this is hardly the same as an actual sale. The contract's convoluted and murky language—and its implications—would subsequently subject ITT, Mediobanca, and Lazard to a massive, decade-long legal battle and the attendant fiasco of negative publicity. Critics charged that ITT, with Lazard's help, was simply placing the stock with Mediobanca—to comply with the IRS requirement—and in the process, while receiving large, no-risk fees for themselves, buying more time for the Hartford stock price to recover sufficiently to avoid a loss on the original purchase, which is exactly what happened.

This was the sum and substance of the IRS's March 1974 conclusion about the matter. As immoral as that scheme may have been, Cuccia's letter to Lazard choosing the third-party sale held one more nugget of impropriety: to wit (in keeping with Lazard's private new arrangement with Mediobanca), "as consideration for all your [Lazard's] services, including the safekeeping of such Shares, you shall, on the completion of the sale of all of such Shares," receive *half* of the profit, if any, as well as half of the up-front fee—the $1,332,131.22—or more than the $660,000 that Mediobanca received for doing the deal in the first place. So Lazard not only received a $1 million fee for advising ITT on the merger and handling the exchange offer for the Hartford shares; it also had cut a separate, undisclosed fee deal with Mediobanca. Lazard also received a $500,000 fee for brokering ITT's original purchase of the 1.7 million Hartford shares. On November 5, 1969, Walter Fried, on behalf of Lazard, signed the Cuccia letter and returned it to him. Lazard did not—at this time anyway—disclose to ITT its fee-splitting deal with Mediobanca. Felix would later say that he had forgotten about this fee-splitting arrangement during his early discussions with Geneen about the potential deal with Mediobanca.

On November 10, in all of twenty-three minutes, in Hartford, the Hartford shareholders approved by a vote of 80.37 percent to 2.78 percent what was, to that moment, the largest merger in corporate history. Felix had a full day of meetings, although none of them apparently concerned ITT. He managed to find time for a meeting with a reporter from

Institutional Investor magazine before heading up to see his client Steve Ross.

But the fight was not over, not by a long shot. On May 27, 1970, the Justice Department renewed its vow to proceed with its efforts to block the merger on antitrust grounds if the two companies were actually combined. The trial in the case was scheduled to start in November.

While in the fall of 1970 Felix and Geneen set out to try to negotiate a settlement with McLaren that would allow ITT to hold on to the Hartford, Mediobanca quietly set about reselling its new ITT "N" shares (which in the interim Mediobanca had exchanged for the Hartford stock when the deal closed) on ITT's behalf. What IRS and SEC investigators would later discover about these sales—but no one knew at the time—was that each one contained a highly convoluted, quid-pro-quo benefit for the purchasers, all of whom had ties to Lazard, Mediobanca, or ITT. In sum, Mediobanca had sold all of its "N" shares for close to $113 million and remitted that sum—less fees for itself and for Lazard—back to ITT, turning an almost certain loss on the sale of the shares into a $24 million gain, the difference between the value of the shares at the closing of the scheme with Mediobanca ($112.7 million) and Mediobanca's provisional cost ($88.8 million).

In Washington, negotiations between ITT, its counsel, and the Justice Department were accelerating furiously in an effort by ITT to retain ownership of the Hartford. Felix would be a leading participant in the negotiations with McLaren and his boss, Richard Kleindienst. Attorney General John Mitchell had supposedly recused himself from the ITT settlement discussions because he had previously, in private practice, provided legal counsel to an ITT subsidiary. This did not stop Mitchell from having an important role in the matter, but for the record, anyway, his recusal put Kleindienst, the deputy attorney general, in charge.

In August 1970, Geneen met with Mitchell in Washington. Supposedly, the two men discussed only "conglomerate policy" generally, although three of the Justice Department's four pending antitrust lawsuits involved ITT. ITT's attorneys did try to negotiate with McLaren a few times during the next year or so, and they conveyed a willingness to divest some of ITT's extensive holdings if it could keep the Hartford.

On April 16, 1971, Lawrence E. Walsh, a partner at Davis Polk & Wardwell, a top New York law firm, wrote an astonishing letter to Kleindienst at the request of his client Harold Geneen, urging Kleindienst *not* to appeal any of the ITT antitrust matters to the Supreme Court. He said he had been asked by Geneen to make a presentation to Kleindienst "urging that the Department of Justice not advocate any position before the Supreme Court which would be tantamount to barring such mergers without a full study of the economic consequences of such a step." Walsh wrote that he was afraid that the Supreme Court's record regarding antitrust matters did not bode well for ITT. "To us this is not a question of the conduct of litigation in a narrow sense," he wrote. "Looking back at the results of government antitrust cases in the Supreme Court, one must realize that if the government urges an expanded interpretation of the vague language of the Clayton Act, there is a high probability that it will succeed. Indeed, the court has at times adopted a position more extreme than that urged by the Department." Here was Walsh, whose firm, Davis Polk, had been ITT's outside counsel for more than fifty years, asking the government's top antitrust official not to bring a case to the Supreme Court involving his client that Walsh thought the government would *win*. Walsh knew what he was talking about, too, having served as deputy attorney general—Kleindienst's job—from 1958 to 1960 and as a U.S. district judge in Manhattan from 1954 to 1957. He joined Davis Polk in 1961.

Geneen's choice of Walsh to send the letter to Kleindienst was a clever one for two other reasons as well, despite Davis Polk having had no previous role in the ITT antitrust cases: First, Walsh had been Nixon's deputy chief negotiator at the Paris peace talks in 1969, and even more important, he was the chairman of the American Bar Association Committee on the Federal Judiciary—and so Nixon's federal judgeship appointees had to be signed off on by Walsh. Since part of Kleindienst's job was to appoint federal judges, the two men had become quite close. "It was, I am afraid a rather elliptical observation that meant regardless of the merits of these cases if you look at the record of the Department of Justice in the Supreme Court in any antitrust case, you have to be concerned with the probability of Government success," Walsh would later say. Indeed, from 1960 to 1972, the government won twenty of twenty-one antitrust cases brought before the Supreme Court. Walsh wrote in his letter that "it is our understanding that the Secretary of the Treasury"—John Connally—"the Secretary of Commerce"—Maurice Stans—and "the Chairman of the President's Council of Economic Advisors"—Pete Peterson—"all have some views with respect to the question under consideration. Ordinarily I would have first seen Dick McLaren, but I understand that you, as Acting Attorney General, have already been consulted with respect to the ITT problem and the Solicitor General also has under consideration the perfection of an appeal from the District Court decision in the ITT-Grinnell case." McLaren had lost the Grinnell antitrust case at the district court level and had appealed the result to the Supreme Court. The letter from Walsh, who later became a special prosecutor in the Iran-contra scandal during the Reagan administration, would soon put Kleindienst in a very difficult position indeed. Walsh was asking for a delay in the government's procedural filing that had to be stamped no later than four days from the time of his letter. Kleindienst, in fact, agreed to delay the procedural filing until May 17, but not without first playing some high-stakes Washington poker.

Meanwhile, a few weeks before Walsh sent his letter and in keeping with Geneen's strategy of swarming the enemy, a top ITT executive in Washington, Jack Ryan, ran into Kleindienst at a neighborhood cocktail party in suburban McLean, Virginia, where they lived five houses from each other. Ryan asked for and received Kleindienst's consent for ITT to plead its case for antitrust relief directly to him. "The door is open," Ryan said Kleindienst told him. Ryan relayed Kleindienst's invitation up the ITT chain of command. And on April 20, 1971, Felix—at Geneen's request, after hearing from Ryan—went over McLaren's head and met privately with Kleindienst for about an hour to lobby the deputy attorney general of the United States on his client's behalf—remember, Felix was also on the ITT board—about the horrors that were certain to befall ITT if forced to divest the Hartford. Ryan had met Felix at the airport and drove him to the Justice Department. "He is a rather quiet individual," Ryan said of Felix. "He did not say much of anything."

Felix had a lot to say, though, to Kleindienst. Since ITT had been claiming it would suffer immense financial hardship if forced to divest the Hartford, Kleindienst had wanted some "recognized financial figure" to appear on behalf of ITT and "make the case." Felix later testified that he went to see Kleindienst that day "at his invitation, to give him what I felt were the economic arguments pursuant to which we couldn't agree to a divestiture of Hartford Fire." He also testified that he told Kleindienst that as long as ITT could keep the Hartford, ITT would be willing to sell Canteen and Grinnell, which together had about $25 million in earnings. "I made the case as best I knew how to make it," he said. In response, Felix testified later, Kleindienst asked him to "make the case" again to McLaren. Oddly, though, Kleindienst did not invite McLaren to the first meeting, nor did he tell his antitrust chief about what Felix said. When asked if Kleindienst seemed "convinced at all" by his presentation, Felix answered, "I thought he might have seemed impressed, but I might have been flattering myself." For his part, Kleindienst later testified that Felix called him up and introduced himself as a director of ITT, said he was not a lawyer, and wanted "to come to my office to discuss some of the economic consequences" of the Justice Department's view of having ITT divest the Hartford. Without hesitation, Kleindienst agreed to see Felix.

On April 20, when, conveniently, he and Felix were alone—"I believe that for the record that any time that I had any meeting with Mr. Rohatyn only he and I were present," Kleindienst testified—Felix made the case, in dramatic fashion, against what Justice wanted: ITT and the Hartford shareholders "would suffer a loss in excess of $1 billion," stemming from a $500 million tax liability that would cause a liquidity crisis at ITT and "interfere" with the company's ability to complete some $200 million to $300 million of foreign contracts that would, in turn, have a negative impact on the country's balance of payments and thus hinder ITT's competitive position internationally.

Also, Felix confided, should ITT be deprived of its competitive position "it might have additional repercussions so far as the general stock market was concerned." Felix asked Kleindienst if he would "direct" McLaren to meet with him to hear the case for ITT's financial hardship. Kleindienst told Felix he would not "direct" his deputy but ask him if he would meet with Felix. No surprise, McLaren agreed to the meeting.

Who knew it was so easy for a perfect stranger—but key advocate for ITT—to have an audience *alone* with the top Justice Department official leading the antitrust prosecution against ITT? Indeed, Walsh later testified that had he been in Kleindienst's shoes, he would never have met with Felix once, let alone four times. "I probably would have had somebody there from the Antitrust Division," he said. "I would do that just to avoid friction with the Antitrust Division, not because I would think it was in any way improper for me to meet with Mr. Rohatyn."

What Felix did not know was that on April 19, the afternoon before his first private meeting with Kleindienst, the deputy attorney general had received two calls, the first from John Ehrlichman, Nixon's chief domestic adviser, and the other from Nixon himself. Both calls concerned Kleindienst's decision to appeal to the Supreme Court the antitrust ruling that the government had recently lost in Connecticut involving ITT's acquisition of Grinnell. "I informed him [Ehrlichman] that we had determined to make the appeal," Kleindienst said, "and that he should so inform the President. Minutes later, the President called me and, without any discussion, ordered me to drop the appeal." A portion of Nixon's recorded conversation with Kleindienst that afternoon follows:

PRESIDENT: Hi, Dick, how are you?
KLEINDIENST: Good, how are you, sir?

President: Fine, fine. I'm going to talk to John [Mitchell] tomorrow about my general attitude on antitrust—

Kleindienst: Yes sir.

President: —and in the meantime, I know that he has left with you, uh, the IT&T thing because apparently he says he had something to do with them once.

Kleindienst: [*Laughs*] Yeah. Yeah.

President: Well, I have, I have nothing to do with them, and I want something clearly understood, and, if it is not understood, McLaren's ass is to be out within one hour. The IT&T thing—stay the hell out of it. Is that clear? That's an order.

Kleindienst: Well, you mean the order is to—

President: The order is to leave the God damned thing alone. Now, I've said this, Dick, a number of times, and you fellows apparently don't get the me——the message over there. I do not want McLaren to run around prosecuting people, raising hell about conglomerates, stirring things up at this point. Now you keep him the hell out of that. Is that clear?

Kleindienst: Well, Mr. President—

President: Or either he resigns. I'd rather have him out anyway. I don't like the son-of-a-bitch.

Kleindienst: The, the question then is—

President: The question is, I know, that the jurisdiction—I know all the legal things, Dick, you don't have to spell out the legal—

Kleindienst: [*Unintelligible*] the appeal filed.

President: That's right.

Kleindienst: That brief has to be filed tomorrow.

President: That's right. Don't file the brief.

Kleindienst: Your order is not to file a brief?

President: Your—my order is to drop the God damn thing. Is that clear?

Clearly upset, Kleindienst later testified, "Immediately thereafter, I sent word to the President that if he persisted in that direction, I would be compelled to submit my resignation. . . . The President changed his mind and the appeal was filed 30 days later in the exact form it would have been filed in one month earlier." Nevertheless, Nixon's message was clear: lay off ITT.

But Kleindienst was nothing if not a shrewd negotiator, and he kept the substance of his conversation with Nixon out of his subsequent discussions with Felix and ITT. On April 29, as suggested, Kleindienst,

McLaren, and the Justice team plus two representatives from the Treasury Department held "a rather large" meeting with thirteen people in McLaren's office to hear Felix's one-hour presentation of how the loss of the Hartford would mortally wound ITT and ill serve the public. The meeting had been scheduled to begin at 10:30 a.m. But Felix kept the group waiting fifty-five minutes because he was upstairs in Mitchell's office working through the DuPont Glore rescue mission.

Felix had told André about his first two meetings with Kleindienst, but at Kleindienst's specific request thereafter he informed no one at Lazard about the sum or substance of the negotiations. In a follow-up four-page letter, on May 3, to McLaren (with a copy to Kleindienst), Felix wrote on his own letterhead from 44 Wall Street—curiously not on Lazard letterhead—that he wanted to "amplify and augment" several points that had been made the previous Thursday "in the hope that its importance will not be overlooked." To wit: should Justice force ITT to divest the Hartford, "ITT would be placed in a very difficult cash position which would severely impact its ability to compete in markets abroad." He further argued that ITT's borrowing capacity would be diminished by the loss of the Hartford earnings, leading to the potential cash drain. Felix argued that the cash drain would hurt the value of ITT's public debt and equity and hinder its ability to raise capital, especially abroad. In closing, he raised the specter that no less than national security was at risk if ITT were forced to divest the Hartford. "Among the adverse consequences to the nation that would inevitably follow from the requisite contraction by ITT of its foreign operations is loss of market shares to major foreign competitors such as Ericsson, Siemens, Philips, Nippon Electric and Hitachi. Loss of market shares abroad can only result in a diminution of the cash, which ITT would have otherwise repatriated to the United States. It would appear contrary to the national interests of this country to take consciously actions which would have such an adverse impact on the balance of payments." Who knew the stakes were so high?

Felix met privately with Kleindienst again on May 10 to reinforce both his May 3 letter and the April 29 presentation, and first suggested the idea that ITT be permitted to keep the non-fire-protection business of Grinnell. Kleindienst later testified he told Felix at the May 10 meeting that McLaren still had not made up his mind. "Rohatyn said it was a serious matter for ITT," Kleindienst recalled, "and wanted to know what was going on with respect to the financial and economic presentation that his company made on April 29. I told him I didn't know and that was up to McLaren and until he came up with a recommendation I wasn't going to bother myself about it."

On May 13, Nixon and H. R. Haldeman met in the Oval Office, and in the context of a discussion about raising money for the president's 1972 reelection, the topic of ITT's pending antitrust settlement came up. "They give us Grinnell and one other merger they don't need and which they've been kind of sorry they got into, apparently," Nixon said on tape. "Now this is very very hush hush and it has to be engineered very delicately and it'll take six months to do properly."

"Does ITT have money?" Haldeman wondered.

"Oh God, yes," Nixon replied. "That's part of this ball game. . . . But it should be later. It should not be right now. . . . Nothing done until the deal is over."

On June 16, Felix received a call directly from Kleindienst's office, asking him to return the call the next morning. It was the rare occasion where Felix, the man whose partners would visibly shudder at the very thought of a call from him, was now put in the position of having to jump as high as Kleindienst said. At precisely 9:30 the next morning, Felix, alone in his Lazard office, called Kleindienst. The deputy attorney general got on the squawk box with McLaren at his side and read the government's new proposal—which he called a "negotiating memorandum"—one that appears to have taken into account Nixon's still-secret directive regarding ITT. Kleindienst told Felix "more or less on a take-it or leave-it basis" that McLaren had recommended that ITT could now *keep* the Hartford if it agreed to divest Avis, Canteen, Grinnell, and Levitt, if it agreed to accept injunctive provisions regarding future acquisitions beyond a certain size, and if it refrained from engaging in reciprocity. In a memo dated the same day as the call with Felix, McLaren had written Kleindienst with his recommendation that he had "come to the reluctant conclusion" that forcing ITT to divest the Hartford would be a mistake. "I say reluctant," he continued, "because ITT's management consummated the Hartford acquisition knowing it violated our antitrust policy; knowing we intended to sue; and, in effect, representing to the court that he needn't issue a preliminary injunction because ITT would hold Hartford separate and thus minimize any divestiture problem if violation were found."

The new proposal, except for the inclusion of the then-struggling Avis, was pretty much exactly what ITT's lawyer Ephraim Jacobs had proposed to McLaren eight months before. Felix concluded the ten-minute call with the Justice Department and called Geneen "within twelve seconds." Both expressed "disappointment and displeasure" with the proposal—with some crocodile tears thrown in for good measure—that now required as many as four divestitures of companies that were never the subject of antitrust suits. But Felix later testified he thought it was a "concrete proposal" that "could be discussed, negotiated and improved upon."

Felix attempted to reach Kleindienst on June 18 to clarify "why all of a sudden we were being faced with four companies" to divest. But he was not able to reach him. On June 29, Felix met again with Kleindienst privately to express disappointment, especially over the demand to divest all of Grinnell, and, according to Kleindienst, "to complain about the rather rigid attitude McLaren was taking with respect to these settlement negotiations, to complain about the rather punitive nature of the settlement negotiations, and the posture of the Government, and that he felt, in his opinion, they were unreasonable." Kleindienst said he told Felix, "I would not inject myself into those settlement negotiations, that that was a problem between the attorneys for ITT and Mr. McLaren and his staff, and that I would do nothing about it." It was another busy day in Washington for Felix. In addition to meeting with Kleindienst, he met with Peter Flanigan, the business liaison at the White House, to talk about matters related to Felix's role in attempting to avert a meltdown among dysfunctional Wall Street firms. But it turned out—according to Flanigan—that Felix also used the meeting to complain some more about the proposed antitrust settlement. "Mr. Rohatyn indicated his belief that the proposal was so tough as to be unacceptable to the company and that the company intended to continue to fight the suits in court," Flanigan said. Flanigan passed Felix's thoughts on to Kleindienst "a couple of days later," and "as I recall his response, it was to the effect that Mr. McLaren had worked out the proposal, and was handling the matter."

On July 2, another federal judge ruled against Justice yet again, and in favor of ITT, allowing it to keep Canteen. A furious series of negotiations between the lawyers for both sides continued for the next twenty-eight days. On Saturday, July 31, the two sides signed a settlement agreement whereby ITT would be able to keep the Hartford as long as it completely divested, within two years, Canteen and the Fire Protection Division of Grinnell and, within three years, Avis and its subsidiaries, Levitt and most of its subsidiaries, and two small life insurance companies. Together, the companies to be divested had revenues in excess of $1 billion; to that time, this was by far the largest agreed-upon, government-ordered divestiture in corporate history. There was also an agreement regarding Justice's concern about reciprocity and an agreement prohibiting

ITT from acquiring any company, for a period of ten years, with $100 million or more of assets without permission of Justice or the Court, or a company in the fire protection business or another insurance company. Geneen called the settlement "in the best long-term interests of our stockholders" and said that ITT would choose to keep the Hartford and to sell Avis, Levitt, and the two small insurance companies. Both Kleindienst and McLaren thought the settlement was a victory for the government, especially given the previous losses on both Grinnell and Canteen.

While those watching the developments closely had no idea that Nixon had personally intervened, questions began to be raised almost immediately about what had *really* transpired to get McLaren and Kleindienst to change course so radically and to agree to a settlement that allowed ITT to keep the Hartford.

Then, on August 23, Justice filed the antitrust settlement documents in court, beginning a mandatory thirty-day public review period. Reuben Robertson, a brilliant young lawyer who had been working with Ralph Nader from the start to block the ITT-Hartford merger, wrote McLaren on September 21 objecting to the antitrust settlement: "We wish to object most strongly to the veil of secrecy that has been drawn over the Antitrust Division since announcement of the decree, which has made full evaluation of the settlement . . . a virtual impossibility." At the end of his cover letter to McLaren, Robertson, seemingly out of the blue, asked whether there was any connection between the settlement and a financial contribution ITT had made to the Republicans to support having the 1972 Republican National Convention in San Diego.

Although Robertson's question seemed a bit odd, in fact it was most perceptive. Some two months before the settlement—around the same time as Nixon and Haldeman's conversation about ITT having plenty of money—Harold Geneen pledged some $400,000 to help hold the Republican National Convention in San Diego. Robertson and Nader had also watched—aghast—as ITT used its cash and its influence to win the approval of William Cotter, the Connecticut insurance commissioner, for the Hartford acquisition: all it took in that instance was for ITT to agree to build two of its Sheraton hotels in downtown Hartford at the very moment the city was struggling—after a failed bond offering—to get its Civic Center project off the ground and Cotter had decided to run for a seat in the U.S. Congress (which he won).

The protests of the media and Nader's Raiders notwithstanding, by the end of September 1971 the U.S. District Court in Hartford had approved the consent decree, as agreed among the parties. Finally, the Hartford deal was a fait accompli.

In early December 1971, Nixon succeeded in getting rid of the "son-of-a-bitch" McLaren by appointing him to be a federal district judge in the Northern District of Illinois, in Chicago. This was a most unusual appointment indeed. Confirmation of federal judges can often take months, following extensive background checks, intense lobbying efforts, support from in-state politicians, and the requisite political wrangling. Not in McLaren's case. This time the confirmation process took four *hours* and had been signed off on by none other than Lawrence Walsh at the ABA. Walsh, of course, was the Davis Polk lawyer and Kleindienst buddy who had written Kleindienst at Geneen's request in the ITT antitrust matters. Not even Adlai Stevenson III, an Illinois senator, was aware of the appointment. The highly regarded investigative journalist I. F. Stone understood what happened perfectly: "McLaren came in like a lion as Assistant Attorney General in charge of the antitrust division and has gone out—a judge."

Robertson also relayed his concern about the potential tie between the ITT contribution to San Diego and the antitrust settlement to someone he thought for sure would care: Larry O'Brien, the chairman of the Democratic National Committee. O'Brien took Robertson's bait and wrote Attorney General John Mitchell on December 13 asking him to explain whether there had been any connection. "Eight days after the selection of San Diego was announced by the Republican National Committee, the Department of Justice and ITT announced agreement of an out-of-court settlement of the three pending ITT merger cases (involving Hartford Fire Insurance Co., the Grinnell Corp., and Canteen Corp.). As national chairman of the Democratic Party, I call on you today in your dual roles of chief law enforcement officer of the United States and chief political adviser to the President"—this a jab, of course—"to make public the full record of your decision to settle with ITT *as well as* ITT's involvement in financing your party's convention next year. . . . At a period in our political history when the American people are seriously questioning the fairness and responsiveness of the political process to *all* the people, I earnestly hope that you, General, will see the urgency of making the record in San Diego–ITT case absolutely clear."

Failing to mention the directive from Nixon, Kleindienst answered the letter for Mitchell, who was still ducking his role in the matter. "The settlement between the Department of Justice and ITT was handled and negotiated exclusively by Assistant Attorney General Richard W. McLaren," Kleindienst wrote O'Brien. This would prove to be a fateful statement by Kleindienst.

While the tempest of the link between the ITT contribution and the antitrust settlement brewed, the biggest bombshell of all came on three successive days beginning on February 29, 1972, when the columnist Jack Anderson, no friend of the Nixon administration, revealed in his column that Nixon and his confidants may *actually* have directed Kleindienst to settle the ITT antitrust suits in exchange for ITT's rather large—at the time—contribution to the Republican National Committee to help San Diego win the 1972 Republican convention, just in fact what O'Brien, Robertson, and Nader had been suggesting. Anderson wrote that he had "evidence that the settlement of the Nixon Administration's biggest antitrust case was privately arranged between Attorney General John Mitchell and the top lobbyist for the company involved. We have this on the word of the lobbyist herself, crusty, capable Dita Beard of the International Telephone and Telegraph Co. She acknowledged the secret deal after we obtained a highly incriminating memo, written by her, from I.T.T.'s files. The memo"—received by Anderson a week before—"which was intended to be destroyed after it was read, not only indicates that the anti-trust case had been fixed but that the fix was a payoff for I.T.T.'s pledge of up to $400,000 for the upcoming Republican convention in San Diego."

Anderson discovered that Kleindienst had lied to O'Brien about his involvement in the settlement of the antitrust cases. Anderson's associate Brit Hume (today a Fox News anchor) confronted Felix by phone—about his private meetings with Kleindienst on the settlement—at Kennedy Airport, when he was about to board a plane for London. "I was supposed to make the case on the economic side of it," Felix told Hume. At least Felix had the good sense not to lie to protect the future attorney general of the United States. "That was again totally stupid [of me]," Felix explained more than thirty years later of his decision to take Hume's call. "Totally stupid. But I was in a hurry. I was waiting to get on the plane and so I took this call. And the guy said to me, 'Do you know about this memo?' And I said, 'Read it to me.' And I said, 'It's complete bullshit.' The notion that this would have been true is, I think, not credible, but that if it were, that Dita Beard would be the intermediary is totally unthinkable."

Anderson wasn't through, though. He then published the Beard memo itself, which was written five weeks *before* ITT settled with Justice. Anderson, of course, did not know of the April 1971 order from Nixon to Kleindienst to leave ITT alone, nor did he mention Nixon's antipathy toward McLaren. The extent of Nixon's involvement would be revealed much later, after the Watergate scandal forced Nixon to release his secret tapes. But Beard's memo implied there was a high correlation between the Justice Department's settlement with ITT and ITT's donation to the Republican National Convention. The memo implicated Nixon, Mitchell (who supposedly had recused himself), Haldeman, and a couple of California politicians. She also implicated her boss, Geneen. Beard claimed to have negotiated the settlement with Mitchell in a private conversation at the Kentucky governor's mansion after the 1971 Kentucky Derby.

With Anderson's columns, the special treatment government afforded rich, powerful corporations and their representatives—long assumed—burst through the dams of secrecy and flooded the media. Felix's one-on-one clandestine, off-the-record meetings with Kleindienst—and the future attorney general's initial denial of them—brought Felix and Lazard to the forefront of the ITT scandal and onto the front pages of the *New York Times* and the *Washington Post*.

The histrionics were a major public relations disaster for all involved, Felix most certainly included. To this point, in truth, Felix's extraordinary prowess as a corporate adviser had been sub rosa, which was just where he, André, and Lazard wanted it to be. Lazard's Avis coup had brought the firm some renown, as had Felix's ongoing involvement with ITT, as ITT's chief investment banker. But these accomplishments were little known beyond Manhattan, if they were even acknowledged there. The Celler commission had proven a revelation, but, as they say, if a tree falls in the forest and no one is there to hear it . . . Even the roles of Felix and his partners in the ITT-Hartford merger—prior to Anderson's cluster bomb—had been understated and barely revealed. ITT's "sale" of the Hartford shares to Mediobanca was discussed only in the barest terms in a paragraph in the public filing related to the Hartford tender offer, with no mention of Lazard's role in unearthing Mediobanca or their mutually beneficial fee arrangement. Buried deep in the public disclosure was the fact that Lazard would receive a fee for its "services" in connection with the Hartford acquisition, with no amount stated. Indeed, the SEC would later question Lazard and ITT about the adequacy of that disclosure.

There was rich irony, too, in that Felix had been an ardent supporter and adviser to the liberal Maine senator Edmund Muskie in the 1972 Democratic primaries, and now Anderson's columns put him in the unlikely position of having to defend big business against Nixon's antitrust department—that alone must have caused the liberal Felix much angst. (To cover Lazard's bases, André gave $90,000 to Nixon's 1972 reelection campaign, making him one of the top ninety-five contributors to Nixon.) Indeed, Kleindienst himself cited Felix's ties to the liberal Muskie as evidence that the Justice Department was a bipartisan "open institution ready to consider any citizen's grievance." The private, elusive, enigmatic Lazard was about to have a historic and most unwelcome coming-out party.

The day after Anderson's first column appeared catching Kleindienst in his lie, Kleindienst asked to reopen his confirmation hearings before the Senate Judiciary Committee. A few weeks earlier, he had been nominated to replace Mitchell as attorney general, after Mitchell announced he was going to run CREEP, Nixon's 1972 reelection campaign. Kleindienst's request was most extraordinary. After all, on February 24, after two days of testimony, the Senate Judiciary Committee had voted 13–0 (with two abstentions) to approve his nomination to be the new attorney general. Kleindienst would have been confirmed by the full Senate in a nanosecond. But he persisted in order to attempt to clear his name, and quite the opposite occurred. The most unnecessary hearings became highly partisan and lasted twenty-two days throughout March and April 1972. And Felix was front and center. Literally.

When the hearing opened, at Kleindienst's side were both McLaren and Felix, "the two persons with whom I had any dealings in connection with these matters," Kleindienst said. Kleindienst "categorically and specifically" denied both influencing the outcome of the ITT settlement and seeking a donation from the company in return for a favorable outcome on the antitrust cases. "I set in motion a series of events by which Mr. McLaren became persuaded that he ought to come off his position" requiring ITT to sell the Hartford, he explained. He said his meetings with Felix were merely a courtesy to help facilitate the discussions that changed McLaren's thinking.

Fatefully, he made no mention of his discussion with Nixon nearly a year before. And when asked by Senator Ted Kennedy, Democrat from Massachusetts, whether the White House had contacted him about the ITT lawsuits and settlement, he perjured himself. "No, sir," he told Kennedy. When Senator Birch Bayh, Democrat of Indiana, asked Kleindienst the same thing, he said he did not "recollect" talking to anybody at the White House about settling the ITT case—a simple lie. For his part, Judge McLaren backed up his boss's account of the events and added: "In conclusion, I want to emphasize that the decision to enter into settlement negotiations with ITT was my own personal decision; I was not pressured to reach this decision. Furthermore, the plan of settlement was devised, and the final terms were negotiated, by me with the advice of other members of the Antitrust Division, and by no one else."

Felix then took the microphone and repeated, now for the senators and the public, his considered view of the dire consequences posed by the potential divestiture of the Hartford, and not only for his number-one client, ITT.

In hindsight, Felix's belief that the divestiture of a large insurance company could potentially bring down the whole economy seems phantasmagoric. He said Geneen deputized him to prepare a presentation to use with the Justice Department. "I was thought qualified in these areas as an economic and financial specialist," he explained. He recounted his meetings with Kleindienst and McLaren, backing up the versions of these two men. "Every meeting was on the record," he said. "No meeting or telephone conversation was held in a covert or surreptitious manner. There was no hint of favor offered or sought."

He failed to grasp, it seems, the perquisites ITT received by virtue of the very access itself, let alone the benefits of the resulting settlement that avoided the much-feared Supreme Court test. Jack Anderson, on the other hand, fully grasped the significance. "The suggestion that discussions with Rohatyn about the case could not possibly count as negotiations, since he was not a lawyer, must have amused investment bankers everywhere," he wrote in his 1973 recollection, *The Anderson Papers*.

> For Rohatyn was the boss of many lawyers, including the ones who were negotiating with McLaren; he had behind him a prodigious career of putting corporations together and taking them apart; Geneen's purpose in dispatching him to Washington obviously was to raise the ITT argument to a more potent level than mere lawyers had been able to do. When Rohatyn was not educating Kleindienst, moreover, he was closeted with Mitchell, helping the Administration to prevent the collapse of Wall Street firms that had used their customers' money and couldn't pay up. So far as impact on the negotiations was concerned, it would have been better for the public weal if Kleindienst had negotiated with one hundred ITT lawyers rather than one Rohatyn.

Felix also volunteered his thoughts about how he had come to be mentioned in Anderson's second column on the unfolding Dita Beard scandal. He said he had been at Kennedy Airport awaiting an outbound flight and "talking with my children on the telephone," who told him that Hume had called from Washington "asking urgently that I speak with him." Even though he did not know Hume, he returned his call from the airport. For those people who know Felix and have tried to get him on the phone and who never get a return call, this must have come as quite a revelation. In any event, he testified that Hume read him the Dita

Beard memo and asked him if the ITT contribution figured into the settlement discussions. "Let me say now that I do not know Mrs. Beard and, in fact, had never heard her name before talking with Mr. Hume," he explained. "Moreover, I never knew of an ITT commitment of the San Diego Convention Bureau until December 1971"—despite being an ITT board member—"when I read about it in the public press. This was six months after the antitrust settlement had been reached. Therefore, it was literally impossible for me to have participated in any conversation regarding the commitment."

Throughout the first day of the hearings, other senators pushed Felix, McLaren, and Kleindienst on the circumstances surrounding ITT's antitrust settlement and the implications of the Dita Beard memo, but the troika held firm in their incredulity about any connection. Still, a clear impression had been left that Felix had asked for and received extraordinary access to the top government officials charged with deciding to pursue, or not, a historic antitrust case against his biggest client. What's more, Felix's intervention worked, even though he told Senator Bayh that he felt "my influence and persuasiveness was obviously wasted" when he went back to see Kleindienst in his office to complain about the harshness of the settlement proposal after the June 17 telephone conversation. Felix moments later recanted his false modesty.

"Is it a fair assessment of your value to ITT to say your influence was wasted when the one divestiture that was going to do the most damage to the company, Hartford, was not successful?" Bayh wondered.

"I would hope I did play a good part, Senator, because I think it was the right thing to do," Felix replied.

"So you cannot say your influence went to waste?" Bayh replied.

"No, sir, I amend that statement," Felix said.

From there, not surprisingly, the senators wanted to hear from Dita Beard, especially after Kleindienst testified that the implications of her memo were "categorically false" and McLaren said about it, "I think those are terribly serious charges and I implore the committee to bring her in here and make her say under oath what she said in there." Kleindienst later testified that the Beard memo was "nothing but a memorandum written by a poor soul, a rather sick woman." Several Democratic senators agreed they would not approve Kleindienst's appointment as attorney general until Beard had testified. But she had disappeared. When she resurfaced a few days into the hearings, the FBI reported that she was in a Denver hospital with a serious heart ailment after none other than G. Gordon Liddy, an ex–FBI agent working for Nixon's reelection campaign who had previously organized the arrest of Timothy Leary in

Millbrook, New York, had whisked her out of town after Anderson's first two columns appeared. (She did eventually testify, from her hospital bed surrounded by senators, without conveying much of substance.) The remainder of the hearings had a theater of the absurd quality, whose folly is far less amusing when one considers that not one but two attorneys general—Mitchell and Kleindienst—perjured themselves in their testimony. Kleindienst was eventually confirmed, but not before the prelude to the Watergate tragedy had been played.

Indeed, at the White House, there was growing concern about the tenor of the Kleindienst hearings. Two of Nixon's closest advisers, Chuck Colson and John Dean, from the outset had questioned the wisdom of Kleindienst's insistence on the hearings. Now there was word that the SEC was beginning its own investigation into possible insider trading charges against some ITT executives, who may have sold ITT stock in and around the announcement of the merger with the Hartford (and later reached settlements with the SEC). As part of that investigation, the SEC had begun to demand of ITT all relevant documents, a subject of much controversy in the wake of the reports of document shredding in Dita Beard's ITT office as she was whisked out of town. The task fell to Colson to investigate the contents of the increasingly worrisome trove of ITT memos that had been produced. Ehrlichman and Fred Fielding, an assistant to John Dean (and later White House counsel to George W. Bush), also reviewed all of the ITT documents, including thirteen "politically sensitive" ones that ITT's lawyers had delivered to Ehrlichman at the White House on March 6. On March 30, Colson authored a confidential memorandum of his own to Haldeman, Nixon's chief of staff, about what he had discovered. The memo is nothing short of astounding; it would have been explosive had it come to light at the time it was written.

Colson warned his boss, "The most serious risk for us is being ignored . . . there is the possibility of serious additional exposure by the continuation of this controversy. Kleindienst is not the target; the President is . . . but the battle over Kleindienst elevates the visibility of the ITT matter and, indeed, guarantees that the case will stay alive. Neither Kleindienst, Mitchell nor [Robert] Mardian [a Justice Department official] know of the potential dangers. I have deliberately not told Kleindienst or Mitchell since both may be recalled as witnesses and Mardian does not understand the problem." Colson proceeded to describe the contents of a handful of, to that point, supersecret memos that directly contradicted the testimony Mitchell, Geneen, and Erwin Griswold, the solicitor general, had given in the previous weeks to the Senate Judiciary

Committee. Kleindienst repeatedly perjured himself in his testimony. Colson revealed to Haldeman his discovery of letters that voided Griswold's testimony that he had made the decision not to appeal the Grinnell case to the Supreme Court. These letters credited John Connally, then Treasury secretary, and Pete Peterson, then commerce secretary, with directly intervening in the decision. (Felix became the trustee of Peterson's blind trust, created when he joined the Nixon administration, on May 25, 1971, in the middle of Felix's and ITT's intense lobbying of the government for a settlement of the antitrust lawsuits; Peterson is, of course, now the über-respected chairman of the Blackstone Group, one of the world's biggest private-equity firms.)

There was also a memo to Spiro Agnew, the vice president, from Ned Gerrity, at ITT, addressed "Dear Ted," that outlined Mitchell's agreement to talk to McLaren after Geneen had his meeting with Mitchell to talk only about antitrust policy, not the ITT cases. Both Mitchell and Geneen testified they only spoke about antitrust policy in their thirty-five-minute meeting in August 1970. "It would carry some weight in that the memo [from Gerrity] was written contemporaneously with the meeting," Colson wrote. "The memo further states that Ehrlichman assured Geneen that the President had 'instructed' the Justice Department with respect to the bigness policy. (It is, of course, appropriate for the President to instruct the Justice Department on policy, but in the context of these hearings, that revelation would lay this case on the President's doorstep.)" Colson revealed another internal ITT memo "which is not in the hands of the SEC" that "suggests that Kleindienst is the man to pressure McLaren, implying that the Vice President would implement this action. We believe that all copies of this have been destroyed."

Colson also reminded Haldeman of a memo from Herb Klein, Nixon's communications director, to Haldeman dated June 30, 1971—one month before Justice reached its settlement with ITT—outlining ITT's $400,000 contribution to the San Diego convention. Mitchell was copied on the memo. "This memo put the AG on constructive notice at least of the ITT commitment at that time and before the settlement, facts which he has denied under oath. We don't know whether we have recovered all the copies. If known, this would be considerably more damaging than the Reinecke statement," where Ed Reinecke, the California lieutenant governor, recanted statements he made that he had spoken to Mitchell about the ITT contribution.

In the Justice Department files, Colson found a number of incriminating documents, among them an April 1969 memo "from Kleindienst and McLaren to Ehrlichman responding to an Ehrlichman request with respect to the rationale for bringing the case against ITT in the first place." A year later, Ehrlichman wrote a memo to McLaren explaining that he had discussed with Mitchell his meeting with Geneen. Mitchell could give McLaren "more specific guidance," Ehrlichman wrote. Five months later, Ehrlichman wrote to Mitchell again complaining about McLaren's pursuit of ITT and reminding Mitchell of an "understanding" with Geneen.

Finally, on May 5, 1971, came the pièce de résistance: another memo from Ehrlichman to Mitchell "alluding to discussions between the President and the AG as to the 'agreed upon ends' of the ITT case and asking the AG whether Ehrlichman should work directly with McLaren or through Mitchell." Colson also wrote about a memo sent to Nixon on the same topic at about the same time. "We know we have control of all copies of this," he said, "but we don't have control of the original Ehrlichman memo to the AG. This memo would once again contradict Mitchell's testimony and, more importantly, directly involve the President."

Colson knew that his discovery of these memos—indeed their very existence—meant trouble, big trouble. He had locked away in a safe most of the dangerous memos, but not all copies of all of them could be located. So, that same day, in the early afternoon, Colson and Haldeman spent an hour with Nixon in the Oval Office. Thanks to Nixon's penchant for recording conversations in his office, even a small portion of the taped transcript of their meeting reveals Colson's extraordinary concern about how explosive it would be for Nixon politically if the hidden memos were discovered and released publicly, the depth of which was quickly conveyed to the president.

COLSON: . . . merely to say to you that, that I've looked at every shred of paper and . . .

PRESIDENT: You've seen it all?

COLSON: I've seen it all.

PRESIDENT: And it isn't good.

COLSON: It scares the living daylights out of me.

Colson then told Nixon he had found the explosive May 5, 1971, memo, where Nixon and Mitchell spoke about the "agreed upon ends" of the ITT antitrust cases.

COLSON: The most dangerous, the most dangerous one we don't know how many copies were made of which is, which is our problem. And we have all of our copies [*noise*] in a safe, uh, but we don't know what happened to it in the Justice Department and we can't find all the copies at Justice. And that's a May 5, 1971 memo from Ehrlichman to the Attorney General in which he talks about the sessions between you and the Attorney General on this case and on . . .

PRESIDENT: That's right.

COLSON: . . . these quite agreed upon ends in the resolution of the ITT litigation. Well that memo, if that came out in that Committee would, would be pretty tough right now, uh, because that would lay it right into here. And we think we've got control of it, but the point Bob makes this morning, and I've discussed some [of] these memos, is very valid that with or without these hearings if these goddamned things leak out now they're gonna be just as big an explosion.

HALDEMAN: Well, if someone's got a copy of that memo, it's gonna be used.

COLSON: Whether there's hearings or not.

HALDEMAN: Whether there's hearings or not, whether Kleindienst stays here or goes . . .

PRESIDENT: Yeah.

HALDEMAN: . . . off to the moon.

Colson's March 30 memorandum to Haldeman, the one-hour conversation between them and Nixon the same day, and more than thirty years of historical perspective combine, in retrospect, to make the final ten days of the Kleindienst hearings more or less irrelevant. Kleindienst and Mitchell lied throughout, to protect the discovery of the fact that Nixon had ordered the Justice Department to go easy on ITT.

For Nicholas von Hoffman, then a *Washington Post* columnist, the absurdity of the hearings—even without the full extent of the conspiracy being then known—was reason to pen a column replete with pointed zingers questioning the morality of all involved. One of these barbs would stick in Felix for years. "Very occasionally," von Hoffman wrote in summarizing the first two weeks of the hearings, "they'll ask a question of Felix Rohatyn, the little stock-jobbing fixer from ITT who went to Kleindienst to get an antitrust break for his wee, tiny multi-billion dollar conglomerate." Von Hoffman continued, "Kleindienst let it out that little Felix the Fixer, Rohatyn, is a Muskie adviser on economic matters. The presidential candidate's headquarters confirmed this, saying Felix had worked with Muskie on an ignoble piece of legislation which allows stockbrokers to gamble with their customers' money." He said the biggest loser of all was McLaren, who "walked into the hearing room less than two weeks ago a highly respected man," but that his "fumbling" answers about why he had reached a settlement with ITT on more favorable terms than he had first proposed were pathetic. "They don't want antitrust, not Felix the Fixer, not the troubled McLaren or Kleindienst, who says he can sleep at night," he concluded. *Felix the Fixer.* That hurt and annoyed Felix for years.

As his final testimony and the hearing itself wound down toward the end of April, Kleindienst chose to emphasize the "important" role Felix played in the settlement. He said he'd come "to regard" Felix "with a very high degree of regard."

At one point, nearing the end, Kleindienst described himself as unmovable in the face of outside pressure and influence. "I am kind of a stubborn, bullheaded guy myself," he said.

"Why did Rohatyn keep coming back if you are so stubborn and bullheaded?" Senator Kennedy wondered.

"He is a persistent little fellow himself," Kleindienst answered, to laughter. "And it did not do him any good, you know. It did not do him any good. He achieved one thing, and Mr. Rohatyn is a very bright, able man, and I think a very fine man, he achieved one thing, he got me to inquire of McLaren whether he would be willing to hear this presentation and I think, as Felix will tell you right now, that that is all he got."

"That is pretty significant the way it turned out," Senator Kennedy said.

"Yes, it was," Kleindienst replied.

"It was not any small achievement," Kennedy continued.

"Yes, I agree," Kleindienst said.

Indeed, the record is crystal clear that the last words uttered in this extremely controversial, convoluted hearing, where perjury and obfuscation abounded, involved the role a diminutive refugee investment banker from New York played in settling, to that time, the largest antitrust case on record.

On April 28, the Judiciary Committee voted, 11–4, to reaffirm its support for Kleindienst's nomination, in effect ratifying its unanimous February 24 recommendation.

Kleindienst, the perjurer, became the country's sixty-eighth attorney general on June 8. Nine days later, on June 17, the Washington police arrested five burglars, organized by E. Howard Hunt and G. Gordon Liddy, as they were installing more bugging devices in the Watergate offices of the Democratic National Committee. On June 30, the Senate Judiciary Committee asked the Justice Department to reexamine the entire seventeen-hundred-page record of the Kleindienst hearings for possible evidence of perjury. So now, incredibly, three weeks after his confirmation as attorney general, Kleindienst's Justice Department was investigating the potential felonious behavior of its leader. On April 30, 1973, Kleindienst resigned as attorney general, after less than a year in office, and eventually pleaded guilty to the misdemeanor of lying at his own confirmation hearing. The controversial plea bargain saved him from jail time and from disbarment. He was the first former Nixon cabinet official to plead guilty to a crime as part of the Watergate scandal. What role ITT's $400,000 pledge and Dita Beard had in all of this was never made clear, although Larry O'Brien said later in his life that he believed the burglary of his Watergate office was done in large part because of the questions he raised in his letter to Mitchell about the connection between the ITT antitrust settlement and ITT's $400,000 pledge to the San Diego Convention Bureau. And of course, we all know where the break-in at the Watergate led. It is not crazy to see the thread that connected ITT's acquisition of the Hartford, and the ensuing fight for antitrust approval, to the Watergate scandal and the resignation of President Richard M. Nixon—and the corresponding loss of confidence in the institutions of American government. The blueprint for Nixon's cover-up of the Watergate scandal can easily be seen in the lies that Mitchell and Kleindienst uttered before the Senate Judiciary Committee—Kleindienst at his own confirmation hearing no less, a hearing he himself demanded and at which he still committed perjury—and in the clandestine, but secretly taped, conversations of Nixon, Haldeman, and Colson to try to figure out what to do if the shit hit the fan. And Felix's role in all of this, although not nefarious by the standards of the Nixon gang, cannot be overstated.

A MAN AS assiduously public as Felix is has had many opportunities over the years to buff the stories that constitute the Felix Rohatyn genome. His years spent explaining his treacherous actions in the ITT-Hartford merger are no exception. In an October 1975 profile of him in the *Wall Street Journal*—while the public ITT controversy had died down but the private investigations still raged on—he chalked up his mistakes to simple naïveté. "One thing I learned from it all is that I should never talk to a government official alone, not even just to have a beer," he said. "Now when I talk to one, I make sure to have eight other people in the room with me." Some thirty years later, his own naïveté remains his explanation, the story by now having acquired the Vermeer-like gloss of many of his tales. "I did something stupid," he explained, "because I think I was very inexperienced in terms of public things. I clearly was used by ITT and by the Nixon administration as part of the scenario that would get McLaren to change his antitrust position."

At the time, though, he did not think he was being "used" by ITT and Nixon. "I thought it was straight up, which is why I say I was naive, to say the least," he said, "because the notion that sort of by the normal course of events I would be invited to meet with the deputy attorney general to make an economic case with nobody else in the room, today I would find that beyond belief. So that's why I say I was really, truly naive. On the other hand, to this day, I am convinced that ITT should've let this thing go to the Supreme Court and that we would've won . . . that we would not have lost the decision and that ITT made a big mistake in settling and that in settling that they gave away much too much, that it was a silly case, that there was no antitrust issue, [and that] the business of 'potential entry' is nonsense." He continued: "The notion here that I would show up and brilliantly convince them that the economic case was overwhelming—I believed it, and I thought, 'Gee, isn't this exciting,' which shows how you can delude yourself in terms of your sense of importance."

As further evidence of his naïveté, Felix cited his decision to appear at Kleindienst's side at the first day of the Senate hearing, *alone*. "I went down to this hearing without a lawyer," he said. "Next to Kleindienst and McLaren. And I walked into this hearing room with this mob in there, and Jack Anderson tried to interview me, and the television cameras—and I thought, 'Shoot, what am I doing here?' So I called André. I said, 'Get me a lawyer. I have to have a lawyer.' By lunchtime, I guess, I think it was Sam Harris or Sy Rifkind, I forget which one was there."

Still unanswered in Felix's mind, all these years later, is whether André may have, for lack of a better description, set up Felix to take the heat publicly for the firm's role in the ITT-Hartford mess. Why else would he not be provided with a lawyer to accompany him to these high-profile hearings? he wondered. "When I thought back on it, [André] was pretty relaxed about my going down to this hearing," Felix reflected. "Nobody asked me if I had a lawyer or who was gonna go with me. And I've never quite resolved . . . whether André knew anything about what was going on or whether Geneen had talked to him or something, but that is still a completely unresolved question."

Of course, Felix believes nothing good came out of the experience. "It was all downside," he said. "Kay Graham called me one day and—after—this was then or a little later, and said, 'Look, you have to get off this ITT board.' And I said, 'Well, you know, if I resign from the board, everybody's gonna think that I believe Geneen is guilty or that I'm guilty, so I can't do it 'cause I don't believe he's guilty.' She said, 'You know, you will never be able to work in a Democratic administration again if you don't.' I said, 'Well, I'm not sure that I'm ever gonna be invited in any case, but so be it.' " He also believed his career had been badly damaged by the negative publicity, which was also taking its toll on his family. He and his wife had recently separated, and his three sons were attending a French school on the East Side of Manhattan. "And they would get insulted, not only by the other kids, but by some of the teachers," he explained, adding that insults were along the line of " 'Your father is this ITT man.' Because they had no clue what this was all about."

CHAPTER 6

THE SAVIOR OF NEW YORK

Needless to say, the relentlessness of the scandal involving ITT and Lazard was not welcome news at 44 Wall Street. Until these hearings, the firm had steadfastly—and successfully—remained out of sight. This had been André's strategy, and it had served him and the firm well. But by the early spring of 1972, Lazard's role in ITT's deal making and Felix's testimony in the Kleindienst hearings had put the firm on the front page. The *New York Times* and the *Washington Post,* almost alone, had been reporting about Felix's and Lazard's role in the ITT-Hartford scandal regularly in early 1972, but the reporter Michael Jensen's lengthy article in the May 28 Sunday *Times* Business and Finance section, titled "The Lazard Frères Style: Secretive and Rich—Its Power Is Felt," shined the spotlight on the firm as a whole. "The world of investment banking is powerful and secretive, but probably none of the handful of wealthy financial houses that dominate the field is quite so powerful, or so secretive, as Lazard Frères & Co.," Jensen wrote. The article proceeded to describe André's role at the center of Lazard and also noted his extreme preference for secrecy. A former partner told the newspaper that actually André was not particularly shy "but simply liked to control what was said about him."

Jensen revealed, in annotated fashion, for the first time the names of the firm's twenty-one general partners as well as seven limited partners, volunteering that they had "no voice in management." Among the partners was a French count, Guy Sauvage de Brantes, the brother-in-law of Valéry Giscard d'Estaing, the future French president; the former ambassador to NATO Robert Ellsworth, who was described as being close to President Nixon; C. R. Smith, the former secretary of commerce in the Johnson administration; and André's twenty-six-year-old grandson, Patrick Gerschel. Felix, then forty-three, was described as potentially being "Mr. Meyer's heir-apparent."

Ellsworth was a particularly interesting and politically motivated hire. He had been a congressman from Illinois before Nixon plucked him to be ambassador to NATO. He had been friendly with Nixon and also with John Mitchell, and it was Mitchell who urged Felix to interview Ellsworth about joining Lazard. Felix agreed, and when André returned from Switzerland, Lazard hired Ellsworth. "André was impressed that I was close to the White House," Ellsworth said. Ellsworth was a Republican in a sea of Democrats at Lazard, at the very moment—given the ITT mess—Lazard needed some friends in Republican Washington. But André didn't really have a job for Ellsworth, and as he had no experience being a banker, there was a daily shadow dance for a substantive role. André suggested that Ellsworth, who because of a chronic back ailment stood behind a tall desk in his corner office, lead something called Lazard International, which was one of those periodic efforts to forge a working relationship between the London, Paris, and New York houses. "André didn't know what it really did, and I didn't know, either," he told Cary Reich in *Financier.* "I mean, it was actually ridiculous—the concept of having something called Lazard International. What would it do? Lazard *was* international."

Next, André asked Ellsworth to report to him the doings at the annual meeting of the International Monetary Fund and also arranged for him to serve on the boards of both General Dynamics and Fiat. Then they would worry together some more about what Ellsworth should do. "I'd go over to his apartment on Sunday afternoon, and we'd talk about that," Ellsworth explained. "Then he'd say, 'Now we're going to get organized. Next Sunday we'll have Felix over.' So Felix would come over and enter into the conversation, but nothing ever happened." Ellsworth quickly concluded that he was to be nothing but a high-paid promulgator of "trivial political gossip" who might help the firm influence the Nixon administration. After around three years of this nonsense, he left Lazard to go back into government as President Ford's deputy secretary of defense.

At more or less the same time that the Senate Judiciary follies were at full throttle and Jensen's article appeared, the Securities and Exchange Commission was conducting its own investigation about the legality of ITT's stock sale to Mediobanca. Both Felix and Tom Mullarkey, Lazard's general counsel and one of the chief negotiators of the Mediobanca transaction, testified.

Mullarkey was up first. He coyly described his position at Lazard as being "in charge of the back office." The SEC investigators, naturally, were quite focused on Mullarkey's role in the Mediobanca transaction. He claimed to be but an insignificant associate carrying out the orders of his boss, Walter Fried. He explained how he had been sent to Milan at the end of September 1969 to meet with Cuccia, the head of Mediobanca, and testified that they met for "four or five hours" but only discussed the side agreement between Mediobanca and Lazard. He said he had no role in the overall agreement between ITT and Mediobanca. He explained that while he took note of the $1.3 million fee that had been negotiated between ITT and Mediobanca—of which Lazard would receive half—he was not in a position to negotiate it or to inquire about it. He was really nothing more than a clerk.

Five days later, just as the Kleindienst hearings were winding down, Felix testified for close to six hours in hearing room 488 at the SEC's offices on North Capitol Street. Felix said he assumed André sent Mullarkey to Milan, and that he "had nothing to do with it." Here Lazard was entrusting a crucial aspect of the largest deal in corporate history with by far its best client to an errand boy, which seemed hard to imagine. Felix did concede that he reviewed several interim drafts of the final agreement between ITT and Mediobanca and found the deal to be "an unusual transaction, sure." When asked if it occurred to him that the entire transaction might be a "sham," Felix replied, "Well, I have learned not to, you know, not be my own lawyer," referring to his all-too-fresh experience at the Kleindienst hearings.

The SEC lawyers pressed Felix hard about whether or not he knew Lazard would get half of the $1.3 million commitment fee Mediobanca received at the time of the closing of the stock transfer. "I can't answer that question," Felix replied. "I am not sufficiently acquainted with the actual details of how the contract worked and how this applied to the profit." But he did recall telling Geneen before the end of October 1969 that "Lazard would get half of whatever Mediobanca got." Felix also testified he never knew about the November 3, 1969, understanding between Mediobanca and Lazard that effectively confirmed that Lazard would get half of the profits from the sale of the ITT stock plus half of the commitment fee. He said he found out about its existence only *ninety days* before his April 1972 testimony. And he reiterated his testimony that he had no idea how the $1.3 million fee came about.

Today, Felix's take on these events is that he and André had a clear bifurcation of responsibility on the ITT-Hartford deal, which, while unusual, was not one Felix had any intention of violating. André was his boss, after all. "I just distanced myself from it because it was André's stuff, and I wasn't about to get in between André and Mediobanca or Gianni Agnelli," he explained. "André was on the board of Fiat and Mediobanca. He was head of Lazard Paris. I don't remember another deal where there was almost a division of labor between André and myself on the same deal, not on Avis, and then after that fairly rapidly I was doing more and more things totally on my own." His explanation seemed hard to believe given how important the Hartford deal was to his best client, ITT, and that he was an important member of the ITT board of directors. He continued, about André: "Agnelli was his client. Cuccia was his client. Geneen was his friend, and I also was very, very careful not to get in between Geneen and André because when Geneen invited me on his board, it was against André's wishes, essentially, because André wanted to put either himself or Stanley Osborne on the board because André didn't think a young Jewish Polish refugee should go on the board of this big, prestigious, white-shoe American company, that that was sort of an overreach. So there were these things in the background."

On June 16, 1972, the SEC charged ITT, Mediobanca, and Lazard with violating sections 5(a) and 5(c) of the Securities Act of 1933, essentially for knowingly failing to register with the SEC the by now infamous 1.7 million shares of the Hartford that ITT owned and "sold" to Mediobanca with Lazard's help. In retrospect, these were narrow violations—the failure to provide adequate disclosure to potential buyers of the ITT stock—especially given how exhaustively the series of transactions related to the ITT-Hartford merger had been investigated by the insurance commissioner of Connecticut, the Justice Department, the Senate Judiciary Committee, and now the SEC. But the violations as charged by the SEC were no small matter, for the Securities Act of 1933 and its required disclosures form the bedrock of our capitalist system by insisting on adequate and thoroughly vetted disclosure to investors by corporations seeking to sell securities. Violations of such simple and basic requirements were tantamount to sticking a finger in the eye of the system. For Lazard, and by implication for Felix (who was in charge of the ITT-Hartford deal), to be accused of violating such basic disclosure as part of its cloak-and-dagger operation with Mediobanca was as appalling as it was astounding. The SEC sought a "final judgment of permanent injunction restraining and enjoining" ITT, Mediobanca, and Lazard and their officers, directors, partners, and employees from in effect selling shares of ITT until a "registration statement" had been filed with the SEC as to such securities.

At about this exact moment, Senator Kennedy called William Casey, the SEC commissioner, to inform him that André Meyer was a family friend and a trustee of the Kennedy family's charitable foundation (presumably Kennedy didn't need to remind Casey of his friendship with Felix). Indeed, André kept a "simple gold Tiffany clock" on his office desk inscribed: "To André—with deep appreciation and affection—Rose,

Eunice, Jean, Pat and Ted." Kennedy told Casey that André was a "man of high reputation" who "had been very helpful" to the Kennedy family. He also said that André was "concerned that the firm would be named and perhaps besmirch his reputation." Casey later testified that he thanked Kennedy for the information about André and assured the senator "the case would be considered on its merits." Still, Casey thought it "improper" for a regulator to receive such a call from a senator. Improper or not, Casey did intervene to Lazard's immense benefit by overturning the SEC staff's recommendation that would have added a charge of *fraud* to the list of accusations against ITT and Lazard and could, once again, have put Lazard out of business. The other SEC commissioners accepted Casey's decision not to include a fraud charge.

In any event, the defendants took the SEC suit sufficiently seriously that exactly four days later, on June 20, 1972, all parties reached an out-of-court settlement. Lazard agreed to the precise relief the SEC sought and in particular agreed to be enjoined "from offering to sell the securities of International Telephone and Telegraph Corp., unless a registration statement has been filed with the Commission, and from selling or delivering after sale the securities of International Telephone and Telegraph Corp., unless a registration statement is in effect with the Commission as to such securities."

Stanley Sporkin, the SEC's enforcement chief and later, for fourteen years, a federal judge in Washington, D.C., said the SEC's action at the time against ITT, Mediobanca, and Lazard, while appearing to hinge on a technicality, was virtually unprecedented. "That was big, big stuff in those days," he explained. "It was never done before. It can't be compared with today's standards. Any lawsuit by the government in those days against major corporations like ITT, Mediobanca, and Lazard was big stuff. In those days, if you sued a big company, that was a big thing. Nobody wanted to be sued by the SEC, particularly Geneen, who wanted to be cleaner than Caesar's wife." Sporkin credited his colleague at the SEC Irwin Borowski with developing the legal theory under which the three defendants were prosecuted and agreed to settle the charges. "He was an extraordinary intellect," Sporkin said of Borowski. "He was a Talmudic scholar and he developed a theory for suing ITT that was a very esoteric—almost Talmudic—allegation and it worked and he was right." He said the speed of the settlement was a tribute to the wisdom of Borowski's legal theory and the practical astuteness of the defendants' high-priced attorneys. "They realized, correctly, that the best thing to do was to settle these claims and not let them fester." Most important, though, the settlement between the SEC and Lazard was accomplished "without trial or argument of any issue of fact or law" and did not "constitute any evidence or admission by" Lazard or its partners or other employees "of any wrongdoing or liability for any purpose." In other words, the horrifying public humiliations that Felix and Lazard had suffered for four straight years since the start of the Celler commission hearings in 1968 would, theoretically, be put to an end. Lazard issued a rare public statement, which it hoped would finalize the matter:

> Since the SEC's complaint was filed late last Friday, we have had an opportunity to review it. The substance of the allegation is that Lazard Frères rendered some professional services in connection with the sale by Mediobanca of shares of ITT Series N Preferred, and in some instances, as broker, executed orders for the sale of such shares, and that additional registration was required and was not had. Whether registration was required is a highly technical question. Our eminent counsel have expressed their opinion to the Commission that such registration was not required. However, we have no desire to engage in protracted litigation over so technical a question, and in order to avoid such time-consuming litigation, we have consented to the entry of an order which enjoins Lazard Frères in the future from selling unregistered securities of ITT. Our policy has always been meticulously to observe the securities laws and to act only in reliance on advice of counsel whenever any questions were presented. We have no intention of departing from that policy in the future.

But Lazard's settlement with the SEC did not finalize the matter, as Lazard had hoped. The ITT-Hartford merger was simply a bad penny, and unfortunately for Felix and Lazard there was no predicting where it would turn up next. Two weeks after the settlement, the first of several shareholder lawsuits were filed against ITT and its board of directors, including Felix. Hilde Herbst, a housewife from Jamaica, Queens, had purchased one hundred shares of Hartford Fire for $39.75 per share on April 29, 1970, and exchanged them for the ITT "N"-preferred in the tender offer in May. She sold the "N" shares on August 4, 1970, for a profit of about $700. Herbst, who emigrated from Germany to Queens in 1937—like Felix, a refugee—was educated in Germany "as long as Mr. Hitler let me." She never graduated from high school. In her complaint, she and her lawyers alleged that ITT's representations made in the exchange offer for Hartford Fire "with respect to the federal tax consequences of the acceptance of the Exchange Offer were false and misleading." In other words, Herbst was suing because she feared—and her lawyers clearly agreed—that ITT had erroneously received a favorable tax ruling from the IRS related to the acquisition of the Hartford and that should that tax ruling be changed—something the IRS was looking into at that very moment—there would be adverse tax consequences for her and her fellow Hartford shareholders.

THERE WAS NO disputing the magnitude of the shock wave that Jack Anderson unleashed with his reporting about ITT and its aggressive tactics for gaining the government's approval of its merger program. But ITT's aggressive corporate behavior wasn't restricted to improperly seeking to influence top Nixon administration officials about M&A deals; ITT was also not beyond trying to overthrow foreign governments. And once again, Anderson and his colleague Brit Hume were at the center of the storm. Among the documents ITT released during the Dita Beard circus was a pile of twenty-five memorandums that disclosed ITT's efforts to prevent the 1970 election of Salvador Allende, a Marxist, as the president of Chile. Since ITT owned several businesses in Chile, including the national phone company, Geneen had been worried that the election of a Marxist might result in the nationalization of the ITT companies. His meddling in Chile, with the CIA's aid and approval, was meant to somehow prevent the Allende election. Geneen had pledged $1 million of ITT money to the overthrow effort. "Secret documents which escaped shredding by ITT show that the company maneuvered at the highest levels to stop the 1970 election of leftist Chilean President Salvador Allende," Anderson wrote in his first column about ITT's effort in Chile. "The papers reveal that ITT dealt regularly with the Central Intelligence Agency and, at one point, considered triggering a military coup to head off Allende's election. These documents portray ITT as a virtual corporate nation in itself with vast international holdings, access to Washington's highest officials, its own intelligence apparatus and even its own classification system. They show that ITT officials were in close touch with William V. Broe, who was then director of the Latin American Division of the CIA's Clandestine Services. They were plotting together to create economic chaos in Chile, hoping this would cause the Chilean Army to pull a coup that would block Allende from coming to power." A second column revealed ITT's offer, through Felix's fellow board member John A. McCone—who also just happened to be a former CIA director—to Henry Kissinger, then Nixon's national security adviser, to "assist financially in sums up to seven figures" in any effort the U.S. government may have been planning to prevent Allende from taking office.

Not surprisingly, these revelations added a new, even more nefarious element to the ITT stew of gluttonous misbehavior. Just after the Kleindienst hearings wrapped up but before the Senate had voted on his appointment as attorney general, Senator Frank Church, Democrat of Idaho, decided to convene a hearing of a subcommittee of the Senate Foreign Relations Committee to investigate the allegations that ITT had attempted to meddle in the internal affairs of Chile. Unlike with the Kleindienst hearings, though, the subcommittee agreed that "to insure a fair and balanced investigation," the hearings—sure to be controversial—should be postponed until after the 1972 presidential election. The Church hearings, which commenced on March 20, 1973, also sought to ascertain the broader influence of multinational corporations in U.S. foreign and economic policies.

Felix, as an ITT board member, appeared before the Church Committee on April 2, 1973. After he was sworn in but before his questioning began, the public was treated once again to a passing glimpse of the increasingly close ties between the power of government and the power of Wall Street. In this instance, the curtain was pulled back on the long personal relationship that Felix had with Charles Percy, then the senator from Illinois and previously the chairman and CEO of Bell & Howell, a Lazard client. Felix met Pete Peterson through Bell & Howell as well, after Peterson himself served as chairman and CEO of the company from 1963 to 1971, following Percy. And then, of course, Felix had served as the trustee of Peterson's blind trust. "In accordance with the practice that I have followed in the past, when witnesses have been before us that I personally know, I would like to indicate that Felix Rohatyn, a partner of Lazard Frères, was very active with me in business," Senator Percy conveyed to the audience. "Lazard Frères were bankers for Bell & Howell Co. I am sure that Mr. Rohatyn knows that my friendship with him and business acquaintanceship with him and relationship with him would not in any way interfere with my constitutional responsibilities in helping to conduct this investigation"—thank goodness for that!—"but I welcome him to this forum." Under questioning, Felix testified that the topic of Chile and whether ITT's assets there would be nationalized was a constant one at ITT board meetings in the spring of 1970, including whether ITT's insurance would cover any potential problem. But he insisted that the ITT management never informed the board of either Geneen's meetings with Broe or ITT's million-dollar offer, just as he had insisted that he was unaware, as an ITT board member, of the $400,000 San Diego contribution.

"Do you feel as a director you should have been informed?" wondered Jack Blum, the committee's associate counsel.

"I think that is a very difficult question, Mr. Blum," Felix responded. At which point Senator Church interjected, "What makes it difficult?"

"Well, Senator, what makes it difficult was the fact that the offer was not accepted," Felix answered. "I believe that a management committing a company, prior to committing the company has to go to its directors."

"But the offer," Senator Church countered, "if Mr. Broe's testimony is accurate, the offer was not made upon condition that the board of directors would subsequently approve it or ratify it. It was made outright. ITT was prepared to offer a substantial fund if the CIA would be a conduit, and the purpose of the fund was to help finance the election of Mr. Alessandri [a rival to Allende] as President of Chile. I think that is a very significant offer of a large amount of money that would plunge the company deeply into the internal politics of a foreign country. You say it is a difficult question when you are asked whether such an offer ought not to be communicated to the directors of the company. What makes it difficult?"

"Well, Senator," Felix tried again, "I said the question that I was raising was indeed whether Mr. Geneen did make an unconditional offer. If he did make an unconditional offer then it should be passed by the board before the offer was made. If Mr. Geneen was engaging in an exploratory discussion subject to coming back to the directors with a proposal, did he have one, then that would be another thing."

"So if Mr. Broe's testimony is accurate, in your judgment, it would have been the kind of offer that ought to have been first communicated to the board of directors before being made to an agent of the CIA?" Senator Church wondered.

"If it were an unconditional offer, yes, sir," Felix allowed, completely ignoring the propriety of a major U.S. corporation enlisting the help of the CIA to interfere in the politics of a sovereign country.

This very question—of propriety—was very much on the mind, though, of the committee's chief counsel, Jerome Levinson, as well as of Senator Church. "Mr. Levinson is asking, if I understand it, if there isn't another consideration here, and that has to do with the propriety of making any kind of offer at all for such a purpose, whether it is conditional or unconditional. I think that is a very legitimate question," Senator Church said, adding that other CEOs with business in Chile at the same time had testified that ITT's offer was "highly improper" and unacceptable. "You are a member of the board of ITT," Senator Church continued. "Do you take a different view?"

Now squarely on the hot seat, with the real issue joined, Felix responded, "No, Senator. I am sorry if I didn't make myself clear. I didn't say that had Mr. Geneen made such an offer for the purposes as you stated them and had he come to the directors and asked us to approve it I am not at all sure that I would have. In fact, I think I would probably have objected to it. I am dividing the question into what does a management have the authority to do without asking the board from the question had they come to the board would we have approved it." But for whatever reason Felix still had not made his thinking clear to the committee, prompting Senator Church to once again wonder, "But do you want to leave the record in such form as to support that ITT's management has the authority to dabble in the politics of foreign countries without prior approval of the board?"

"No, I certainly wouldn't," Felix answered. "I couldn't leave the impression that the board or at least I, as a director, am insensitive to the propriety of a management interfering in the internal political activities of a foreign country. However, as I said before, the management of the company assured me and assured the other directors that they had not done so." Felix admitted that the board itself had never undertaken an investigation of Geneen's activities with the CIA in Chile although two law firms were engaged to study whether ITT would be able to obtain the insurance payments. Felix ended his testimony by making it clear that under no circumstances would he have considered a payment to the CIA by ITT to be an expense "in the ordinary course of business" that could be made without the board's approval.

AS THE WASHINGTON wrangling continued unabated, back in New York—as if in some parallel universe—Felix set about rehabilitating his teetering reputation. *BusinessWeek* obligingly served his cause, with a March 1973 cover story, "The Remarkable Felix G. Rohatyn," a paean to Felix's M&A prowess (and his facility with some members of the press). The lengthy profile, just weeks before his Chile testimony, featured a youthful and earnest picture of the forty-four-year-old Felix, calling him a "model of the new breed" of investment banker, and, thanks to the information released by the Celler commission, listed ten years of Lazard's M&A deals and corresponding fees. The magazine mentioned in passing that Felix was "reluctantly exposed to the public eye" by the congressional "flap" over ITT and the Hartford, preferring instead to concentrate on his fascinating background and his role advising the leaders of corporate America.

The piece added to Felix's growing mythical status a jewel of a story about how one of his partners, the avuncular Albert Hettinger, had recommended that Felix meet with Hettinger's acquaintance Paul Williams, the president of O. M. Scott & Sons Co., the rural Ohio manufacturer of lawn-care products. Williams had wanted to find a way to buffer the perceived cyclicality of Scott's business by merging the company into a larger, more stable conglomerate. Felix flew to Marysville to the rescue. "You would not believe what a wonderful place it was," he said in the *BusinessWeek* article. "They even offered me apple pie. I decided then and there this company had no business merging with anyone." Felix succeeded in dissuading Williams from making the deal with a small chemicals company. But when Williams called Felix again a year later, in 1971, to say that a large company was preparing a bid for Scott, the concern in Williams's voice gave Felix the idea that ITT should buy the company instead. He called Geneen. "I told him that it was a business I found attractive because much of their product is sold in hardware stores, and I'm a great believer in hardware stores as outlets," Felix told the magazine. "We would have to accept a certain amount of dilution [to earnings], but in a company of ITT's size you wouldn't even notice it." Within four days, Geneen had met with Williams and a deal had been hammered out, agreed to by the boards of both companies, and announced publicly. ITT paid Lazard $400,000 for its week of work.

Such a charming story added immeasurably to Felix's status. Here was an investment banker making clear he was above doing a deal for a fee; here, apparently, was an investment banker who stood for something far more valuable than a fee—the ability to provide impartial, non-self-interested advice to a CEO who was not even his client. So what if Felix was the only source of this self-serving gem. Scott was a precious piece of Americana—"They even offered me apple pie"—that required the right home, which, it turns out, just happened to be ITT, Felix's best client.

The *BusinessWeek* article once again raised the specter of succession at Lazard. And again André lavished praise on Felix, his protégé. Felix "can negotiate anything," André said, an extraordinary blessing indeed from the master negotiator himself. André also allowed that Felix had been one of the few Lazard partners to generate business. "In my lifetime I have given opportunities to many people," he said, "and only some of them have been able to grasp that chance. Felix did so in such a way that I don't believe personally that I would have been able to do so well." But as ever, Felix seemed preoccupied with doing deals, and his unwillingness to take the reins in New York from André left the older man with considerable agita, or so he claimed. "I am sorry that Felix is so highly motivated in what he is doing," André said. "I have said that I consider him my son, and I would not say that if I did not mean it. I had hoped that he would take over this firm, but he has turned me down." For his part, Felix said, "I do not think I could do what Mr. Meyer is doing but I know I can do what I am doing, and do it well. I think what I am doing is important to the firm, and I want to keep it that way."

Naturally, this being Lazard, there was more to this matter of Felix and succession than met the eye. There was also André's reaction to Felix being on the cover of *BusinessWeek*. "André didn't like it one bit," Felix explained years later. Indeed, according to Felix, André was sufficiently jealous of this press coup that he insisted that Felix arrange for *BusinessWeek* to put them both on the cover. "I had the worst time with André about that article," Felix explained. "I mean, I didn't quite know how to—because I knew they were doing an article. I didn't know it was going to go on the cover. And when they said to me that I was going to be on the cover, I said, 'But I've got to talk to Mr. Meyer, I mean, he's going to go ballistic.' " When Felix spoke to André about it, André told him, without a trace of irony, " 'This will be terrible for you. It'll be terrible for you. You know, all this publicity, it'll come back to haunt you. But I want to help you, [so] tell them that I'd be willing to go on the cover with you.' And I said, 'Well, thank you very much.' " But the *BusinessWeek* editor Lou Young, who was a friend of Felix's, wouldn't hear of it, according to Felix. As a compromise the magazine agreed to include a separate boxed spread, in the article, on André alone. As to why he never wanted to succeed André, despite the attendant prestige and power of such a promotion, Felix confessed a truism about Lazard that defies the conventional wisdom about ambition on Wall Street. "André first talked to me about running the firm sometime in the late sixties," Felix confided. "And I knew that wasn't serious. This was André venting. It was our little theater. He would ask, knowing that I would say no. But I also knew, because I had seen it happen with other people, that the moment you said yes, you were dead, especially if you were in the firm to begin with. . . . I was always convinced that André, who was a very lethal person if you didn't handle him right . . . that the first time I tried to exercise any kind of control would be my last." The extraordinary insight that a partner as important as Felix would be eviscerated the moment he tried to assume or to exercise a leadership role at the firm is essential to understanding the post–World War II Lazard history.

Despite not wanting to "run" anything at the firm, Felix was the head of the corporate finance group, which was essentially the M&A group. One week after his Church Committee testimony, Felix penned a rare and now infamous—inside Lazard anyway—memorandum to the thirteen bankers who worked for him in the M&A group. "I am still far from satisfied with the operation of this Department," he wrote. "Let me remind you of our objectives: 1) Coverage of existing corporate clients to protect existing positions and generate business. Performance: Poor. 2) Execution of transactions created by others within the firm. Performance: Satisfactory. 3) Creation and generation of new business ideas. Performance: Poor. Great scattering of effort. No intellectual discipline. No follow through. If it doesn't work the first time, forget it. Conversation is no substitute for business."

But Felix was just getting warmed up. "Every member of this Department, but especially the *Senior* members, *must* realize they have a direct P & L responsibility to the Firm," his memo continued.

> This is even more acute in the kind of times our business is entering into. We can no longer afford the luxuries we have indulged in for the past 20 years of carrying unproductive senior personnel. It is unfair to the productive ones and demoralizing to the junior members. I am perfectly aware of the fact that performance requires both luck and perseverance. Nobody can force luck. Perseverance, however, requires a level of intellectual discipline that I find woefully lacking in the Department and that *has* to change. There will be clearer assignments, that is *my* responsibility. There will be better follow through, that is *your* responsibility. There will be less time wasted with unrealities. There will be *more profit* or there will be *less costs.* Our business is about to enter the *Dark Ages.* Because of the policies that Mr. Meyer has imposed on this Firm we have a chance of surviving and emerging stronger than ever when the bloodletting is over and many of our competitors fall by the wayside. We can only do it if we have no fat and if we perform. I leave you to reflect on this.

ON MARCH 6, 1974, just as depositions in the Herbst shareholder lawsuit were in full swing, the IRS decided to revoke, retroactively, its original two rulings that the ITT-Hartford merger was tax free to the Hartford shareholders—one month before the statute of limitations on the original ruling would have expired. The revocation was an unprecedented and highly embarrassing development for ITT, the IRS itself, and of course Lazard, since once again the shady nature of the deal was reiterated.

The IRS's 110-page ruling explained why the service had changed its mind. According to the IRS, though, the document has been destroyed, in keeping with its policy to shred all rulings that are more than three years old; all other copies seem to have disappeared. Therefore, the only insight into the ruling's content comes from some brief press reports at the time. "We believe," the IRS report stated, "the subsequently developed evidence establishes that the ITT-Mediobanca transaction was not consummated in accordance with the representations made to the Service in ITT's ruling application. Rather, ITT was aware that Mediobanca did not want to assume any risk and intended to sell the stock transferred to it. ITT then styled the transaction to take on the appearance of a sale to satisfy us, when in reality, Mediobanca was an agent, broker, or best efforts underwriter for the sale of the shares on behalf of ITT and did not acquire any interest in the shares."

In the wake of the IRS reversal, ITT moved quickly to try to assuage growing shareholder unrest related to the tax consequences of the Hartford merger. By letters dated March 11 and April 4, 1974, ITT agreed to reimburse the former Hartford shareholders: "In the unlikely event that the exchange is ultimately adjudicated to be taxable, ITT will reimburse any Hartford shareholder whose net overall tax liability with interest (taking into account any other years involved) is increased as a result of the imposition of tax liability on the exchange of his shares." Needless to say, the IRS's change of heart and ITT's immediate concession to the former Hartford shareholders began to make Hilde Herbst, the housewife from Queens, look like a very smart lady indeed. A couple of months before the IRS issued its new ruling, on January 16, 1974, Herbst added Lazard as a defendant to her shareholder suit. Following the revocation of the 1969 tax ruling, the IRS made tax claims against a number of the former Hartford shareholders. Consequently, these shareholders filed some 950 petitions against the IRS in U.S. Tax Court, seeking to fight these new tax bills.

As a result of ITT and the ITT board of directors being named a defendant in Herbst's original lawsuit, and then since Lazard had been added as a named defendant, Felix, André, and Tom Mullarkey all testified in the case. As Yogi Berra would say, it was déjà vu all over again. Felix testified twice in the Herbst matter. On November 16, 1973—before the IRS's new ruling—he testified about the circumstances related to ITT's "sale" of the 1.7 million shares of the Hartford stock to Mediobanca. And once again, he stuck to his story of having no role whatsoever in the transaction between ITT and Mediobanca and that only André and Tom Mullarkey were even the slightest bit involved, and then only tangentially.

When Felix testified again in the Herbst matter, for two and a half hours on April 24, 1974, it was six weeks after the IRS had reversed its ruling. Felix's story did not change. "My recollection is of minimal involvement," he said.

Mullarkey also testified twice in the Herbst matter, immediately following Felix's testimony. This time around, he shed a little more light on how he had come to work in the back office—"this was receipts and deliveries of securities, payments, sales, all the trivia that makes a banking firm operate internally." It turns out that André had reassigned Mullarkey, then an associate, to work in the back office for the partner Walter Fried in late 1969. Fried had become ill in December 1969 and taken a leave of absence from the firm (before passing away in October 1972). He originally suffered from circulatory problems, and then had a nervous breakdown. Mullarkey described him as "a very sick man" and said that André had moved Mullarkey into the back office because of Fried's deteriorating health.

For the first time, Mullarkey acknowledged his own role, along with Cuccia's, in the creation of the November 3, 1969, side agreement between Lazard and Mediobanca with regard to ITT's "sale" of the Hartford shares. "Fried instructed me shortly before I went over there"—to Milan to meet with Cuccia on a Saturday in late September 1969—"to see what Cuccia wanted us to do because we had responsibilities under the basic ITT contract. We would be a courier, a custodian and we made some market valuations and it was really to find out how Cuccia wanted this handled, so I really went over with nothing but to talk to Cuccia about what he had in mind." He came back to New York with Cuccia's handwritten notes of the agreement, showed them to Fried—but, he testified, no one else at Lazard—and continued to work with Cuccia on drafting the document. He knew his place. "Because I was an associate in the firm at that time and I had no direct access to Mr. Meyer," he testified.

For the first time in the whole blessed ITT-Hartford matter, André Meyer was obliged to testify. He did so on four separate occasions in March and April 1974, in the Lazard offices at One Rockefeller Plaza. The transcripts showed him to be quite firm in his recollections, and often quite loquacious. He characterized his role as extremely minimal and restricted solely to his initial contacts with Harold Williams, the CEO of the Hartford, in the fall of 1968, and with Cuccia, the CEO of Mediobanca, in the summer of 1969.

Like Felix and Mullarkey, André put the responsibility for Lazard's role in the ITT-Mediobanca stock arrangement at the feet of Walter Fried, the dead man, an Austrian immigrant whom André described as a "self-made man," a very simple man, a very modest man who came to Lazard as an accountant. "Mr. Fried was in this firm 15 years before or 17 years before I came to this country, and I had before not the slightest idea about rules or regulations or tax or overall fiscal and administrative policy as it existed in the United States and I was relying and always relied and everybody in this firm was relying entirely on Mr. Walter Fried," he testified. "It was a great loss when he died. He was a tower of strength and had the full confidence of all the partners. He was the kind of young grandfather of everybody in this firm and everybody can tell you that."

At various times in the almost eight hours of testimony, André became quite irritated with Leon Silverman, Herbst's attorney. "Mr. Silverman, I am an old man and I have taken three pills this morning to be able to be with you, to be able to do the job of trying to answer properly but I am not going to speak of things that I don't know in which I have not been involved in." When Silverman asked André if he understood the inner workings of the Lazard mailroom, André could take it no more. "This firm has always been very carefully run. Its existence is 130 years and we never had any problem of any kind." He was then asked how the mail was routed around the firm, and he replied:

> I have no idea. Really, I don't know. I have told you and I am prepared to repeat that my role in the firm has always been very clear. I would like to say something which may not please my counsel because I am doing more than answering the questions but I feel that I should tell you. I was a Frenchman and I flew from France in 1940, a few hours before the Gestapo came to my apartment to pick me up. I was not persona grata, and the best evidence is that I was denationalized by the Pétain regime, and that same day as General de Gaulle was denationalized, I was on the first list. In the first week of August 1940, I arrived in this country with my wife and my two then young children and I was a refugee, in fact, I did not speak a word of English. I don't speak too well still, but I have never taken one lesson of English. For two years I was sick. The doctors said that there was a cancer of the pancreas; it was not so, and in 1943 I came to the firm with the minimum of knowledge and I learned but I relied on the people who were in this firm and with good people in whom I had confidence. I did not interfere with what they were doing because this firm never had any trouble and had a very clean balance sheet and was considered as a firm of high standing. Step by step I took responsibility of the firm and I am proud with what I did with it but I did not disrupt a lot of things. Among the things that I did not disrupt because I was very ignorant about it and I knew my limitations

with such things was what we call the inside machinery and about Walter Fried, a man who was, I believe here since 1930, even before and who has been successful and a young employee and who has shown a lot of quality and who became the head of the accounting department and then his activities were broadened. I had to learn from him many things in many respects and I tried step by step to make of this firm, as I said, one of the most respected and one of the largest firms in this town in every respect but it has been a full time job. I was lucky enough to have competent and serious people who were following the machinery and I relied upon them. I thought that it might have been useful for me to give you that little bit of background. My role consisted of many things in this firm in respect to its policy, in connection with the kind of business that we are doing and more especially the one that we should not do but my principle also was, after a decision is made after the policy has been established, not to have interfered in the implementation of the things which were done. I have had in these 35 years enough to do in respect to that battle in that jungle of Wall Street, in doing a certain number of constructive things and in maintaining a tradition and this has been really my job, and I am even too old to pursue that job in my judgment, but when you ask me who was opening the mail, I will be ashamed to tell you I don't really know.

Finally, though, in the remaining moments of André's testimony, Silverman asked him about the critical unanswered mystery. How could Felix, the head of Lazard's mergers business, essentially eschew responsibility for one of the most crucial aspects of his most important client's most important deal at the most important time? "What department did the ITT-Hartford merger fall into or under?" Silverman asked.

"Rohatyn," André answered.

"That would be new business?" the lawyer wondered.

"Yes," André replied.

"What department did the ITT disposition of the Hartford stock fall under?" Silverman asked.

"I don't believe that we have created a special department for that," André answered.

"Would that be new business?" Silverman asked.

"Mr. Rohatyn was the director of ITT and he was the liaison in the matter of that kind between the Lazard firm and the ITT firm, and as I told you, this firm is a very compact firm, including the partners and messenger boys and which has between 200 and 240 people," André explained. "Things are not that compartmentalized as they would be in Merrill Lynch."

"But Mr. Rohatyn would have been in charge of the ITT-Hartford merger as it affected Lazard?" Silverman asked again.

"Yes, but he was also helping or helped by a certain number of people who were dealing more in the machinery or with the legal work," André offered.

"Are you telling me that in the matter of the ITT-Hartford that would fall under new business, Mr. Rohatyn would not perform every single function that had to be performed in connection with it?" Silverman asked incredulously.

"Yes," André replied.

"Are you also telling me that in such a situation Mr. Rohatyn would be the partner who would be the supervisory person of all of the little functions?" Silverman asked.

"No, not the supervisory necessarily for all," André answered. "The machinery agreement and so on, I would say no, but if it comes to discussing with the chief executive of the company, it is certainly not Mr. Mullarkey or Mr. Fried who would do it."

That is as close as André got to trying to discern the logic of how Felix abdicated his advisory role for ITT at such an important moment. In any event, soon after the IRS ruled that the ITT-Hartford merger was now taxable to the Hartford shareholders, ITT made its offer to cover the taxes payable for any of the still eligible Hartford shareholders. In keeping with our litigious society, following this announcement by ITT four new derivative shareholder lawsuits were started against ITT. The Herbst case was settled in and around the first week of April 1977, with ITT agreeing to pay each original Hartford shareholder $1.25 in ITT stock for each of the twenty-two million Hartford shares, or about $27.5 million in ITT stock, and also agreed to indemnify any Hartford shareholders for any future tax liabilities that might arise from the IRS decision. Lazard and Felix were released from all the claims of the shareholder lawsuits.

DESPITE THE DEPOSITIONS, the never-ending lawsuits, and the harsh glare of negative publicity, Felix remained convinced he had done nothing wrong in his advocacy of ITT's goals, and so set about once again doing what he knew best how to do: advising on landmark M&A deals. And of course, he continued to rehabilitate his tarnished image. Both of these goals were happily advanced in one particularly timely pairing of June 1974 articles, one in *Time* and the other in the *New York Times*. Written once again by the reporter Michael Jensen, who had written about Felix and Lazard often in the past years, the *Times* article described Felix as a "merger mastermind" for his deft architecture of a cleverly conceived and structured rescue of the struggling Lockheed Aircraft Corporation by Textron. Felix's idea, as Lockheed's adviser, was to have Textron invest $100 million in the ailing Lockheed in exchange for a 46.8 percent interest in the company. The Textron investment would have also, crucially, relieved the federal government of some $250 million in controversial loan guarantees made to Lockheed's banks. These guarantees, approved by Congress by a single vote, saved Lockheed from bankruptcy in 1971. The Textron equity investment also convinced Lockheed's banks to convert $275 million of debt to preferred stock, reducing Lockheed's interest expense by $100 million in the first two years after the restructuring. "It's far and away the most intellectually satisfying thing I've been involved in," Felix told the paper. The generally laudatory article did contain the requisite cheap shot from an unnamed competitor, no doubt jealous of Felix's continued acclaim. "Nobody's better than he is," this person told the *Times.* "His ability is that he turns people on. With the backing of Lazard, he's able to get good people. I don't think all that highly of Felix, but that doesn't mean he isn't as good an investment banker as there is on Wall Street. The problem is that no one is a saint." The article correctly linked Felix's "rise" to two "powerful forces," André Meyer and Harold Geneen at ITT, the same two mentors Felix still credits. But it also offered the thought about Felix, presumably Jensen's own, that "some of his successes, generally heavily publicized, are considered on Wall Street to be as much a triumph of public relations as a display of financial acumen."

The *Time* article turned the epithet "Felix the Fixer" on its head, making it a laudatory reflection of his skill in putting together the Textron-Lockheed deal rather than a von Hoffman–esque reference to his unfettered access to political power. "If he pulls it off, it will be the investment banking deal of the decade," one corporate executive told the magazine. Felix described the deal to *Time* as "very satisfying from an aesthetic point of view."

Felix's efforts to resurrect his reputation had been boosted enormously by both the Jensen and the *Time* articles. He was once again heralded as the boy wonder of Wall Street. Rarely complacent, though, he used the opportunity afforded by the blast of favorable publicity—and the quieting of the negative—to, for the very first time, put a toe in the water of public policy debate. Obviously for years, on behalf of his clients, he had been cleverly pulling the levers of power in Washington, but this was something entirely different; this was Felix using his considerable intellect to take a stance politically. (More than thirty years later, he is still at it.) In a two-thousand-word essay on the Sunday *Times* editorial page, in December 1974, Felix boldly endorsed the idea, then being floated by several congressional Democrats, to resurrect the Depression-era Reconstruction Finance Corporation. The original RFC, commissioned by Congress in January 1932 with the former Lazard partner Eugene Meyer as its chairman, eventually disbursed some $10 billion in capital, both debt and equity, to struggling American corporations. Forty percent of the RFC's capital went to financial institutions. The original RFC effectively pumped badly needed capital into corporate America when the public markets were still having trouble providing that service. The economic struggles of the early 1970s had revived the idea in Felix's mind. He wanted the U.S. Treasury to capitalize the new RFC with a $5 billion equity pool, plus the authority to offer an additional $10 billion in federal guarantees, all of which could be used to again inject fresh capital into struggling American corporations, not unlike how Textron's offer to inject $100 million into Lockheed proved pivotal. "The RFC, therefore, should become a revolving fund—hopefully a profitable one—which steps in where no alternatives are available and which steps out when the public interest has been served and normal market forces can again operate." Felix suggested that the private sector would finance the Treasury's contribution to the RFC by having those companies earning more than $1 million donate 1 percent of pretax profits annually to the Treasury. In five years, the government would be repaid, he believed.

The financial establishment warmed to Felix's proposal. "I agree emphatically," said Gus Levy, Felix's friend and the managing partner of Goldman Sachs. "It is essential we move in this direction," William McChesney Martin, the former chairman of the Federal Reserve, wrote the *Times*. But politically, where Felix often had a tin ear, the proposal was virtually dead on arrival. "If Lockheed is the kind of example Rohatyn is thinking of, he's dead before he starts," one senior congressional staffer told *Forbes*, in a typical comment. "Remember the vote on the Lockheed debt guarantees? It passed by one vote in the House and two votes in the Senate. Today the leadership wouldn't even bring it up!" Wisconsin's Democratic senator William Proxmire dismissed the idea as "a formula for protecting buggy whip manufacturers."

If by late 1974 Felix had begun the process of public rehabilitation, it was equally true that there was hardly a government entity that had not investigated, or itself been the subject of an investigation into, Felix's and Lazard's role in ITT's acquisition of the Hartford. The insurance commissioner of Connecticut had ruled twice. The federal courts in Connecticut had ruled repeatedly on the matter of ITT and antitrust. The state courts in Connecticut had ruled on Ralph Nader's lawsuits. The House of Representatives had conducted hearings into boxes of purloined ITT documents. The Senate Judiciary Committee had dredged up the whole sordid affair as part of the Kleindienst confirmation hearings. The Justice Department had settled antitrust claims against ITT after intervention from Nixon, Kleindienst, and Felix. Justice was also looking into charges of perjury against the witnesses at the Kleindienst hearing, including both Kleindienst and Mitchell, the current and former attorneys general. The SEC had settled securities fraud violations against ITT and Lazard before shipping the documentary evidence to the Justice Department. Nixon's White House was up to its eyeballs in trying to influence the outcome of the antitrust matters, thanks to ITT's intense lobbying efforts and its substantial donation to the Republican National Convention. The IRS had reversed its original rulings about the tax-free nature of the deal, and the original Hartford shareholders affected by the new IRS ruling had sued for damages. Shareholder litigation abounded. One could reasonably expect that by 1975 enough would be enough in the matter of Lazard, Mediobanca, ITT, and the Hartford.

And once again, one would be wrong. After reviewing all of the documents in the case ad nauseam, the SEC decided once more at the end of 1974 to open up a new investigation into whether ITT had violated certain provisions of federal securities laws in conjunction with its acquisition of the Hartford. Once again, the Lazard leadership found itself facing intense scrutiny. Felix would testify twice more, as would an increasingly ailing André Meyer.

The major focus of the SEC's *second* examination into the ITT-Hartford matter was Mediobanca's subsequent profitable resales of the ITT "N" stock, in 1970 and 1971, to what turned out to be an internecine web of companies one way or another affiliated with Mediobanca, Lazard, or both of them. Then, in two instances, the affiliated entities that bought the stock, at a profit as well, turned around and *sold* businesses they were investors in to ITT—all at the exact same time. The coincidences were too delicious for the SEC to ignore but proved exceedingly difficult to pin down precisely. Felix, of course, told the SEC that he knew very little, if anything, about the ITT-Mediobanca deal and very little, if anything, about these derivative sales. If any of these questions were irritating to Felix, it was not apparent. He seemed especially gracious . SEC lawyers—several of whom he had befriended over the years- they with him.

FIVE MONTHS LATER, in May 1975, a serendipitous phone call while he was once again working the corridors of power in Washington, D.C., would do far more for the resurrection of Felix's reputation than would his first op-ed piece in the *New York Times* or a feature about him in *Time* magazine. That fateful call from Hugh Carey, the New York governor, seeking Felix's help in solving New York City's looming fiscal crisis—a debacle Felix to that point had no inkling about—would transform Felix from a controversial man, reviled by editorial writers, into one of the most famous and highly respected men in the country. He would become the savior of New York City. Felix's adulation among common New Yorkers was such in the mid-1970s that cabdrivers would not let him pay for his fares and cops would volunteer to ferry him in their cruisers to his appointments. He started hanging out at Elaine's, the very social East Side pub, with the likes of Clay Felker and Jimmy Breslin.

According to Felix, one day in May 1975 he had been at a meeting at the SEC unrelated to its new ITT-Hartford investigation—he was now part of an advisory commission on the National Market System—and afterward paid a social visit to Senator Henry M. "Scoop" Jackson, Felix's ally in his effort to reestablish the Reconstruction Finance Corporation. "I got a call from David Burke, who was the chief of staff to Hugh Carey and who used to be Ted Kennedy's chief of staff," he explained. "He said the governor would like to see you urgently. I said, 'I'm about to take the shuttle back to New York, I'll stop in your office.' I go in there, and Carey is there with Burke, and Burke I had known a little bit. Burke used to also work for Howard Stein at Dreyfus, and is a remarkable, remarkable man. Carey goes over this thing with me, or Burke does, about the financial situation of the city." Carey and Abe Beame, then mayor of New York, had been to see President Ford with an urgent request for the federal government to provide $1 billion—"$1 billion being wildly less than we needed," Felix explained years later—to New York City in order to prevent a bankruptcy in the next thirty days. Ford told the mayor and the governor he would not help. Remember the infamous blaring *Daily News* headline "Ford to City: Drop Dead"?

Governor Carey then turned to Robert Strauss, the ultimate Washington insider, to see if he could twist Ford's arm. Felix explained: "Strauss says, 'No, I can't do anything, but I know somebody who's very smart

Rohatyn. Why don't you ask to see him.' I know hat's when Carey put in the urgent call to Felix and ckson's office. After Burke explained the dire sit- lix, " 'What would you think would happen if the aid, 'Well, I think it would be a terrible thing if mean, I think you have to try to avoid that at n't believe that that can happen.' 'Well,' he said, 'would willing to help us and take on the job of spearheading that?' I said, 'No, I can't do that. I don't know anything about city finances, but, you know, if you were to form a small group, a bipartisan group, including Republicans and Democrats, you know, four people, I'd be certainly willing to participate, but I have to clear it with my senior partner. And if you do that, I would urge you to have one of the people that you appoint be Judge Rifkind' "—Lazard's lawyer throughout the various pieces of ITT litigation. "Carey says yes, call Rifkind. I call André. I say I really have to see you tomorrow, or whenever it was, and I'd like Judge Rifkind to be there. And I thought, 'André will never let me do this' "—prompting the question of why Felix thought André would not allow him to step into the city's financial breach. "I had spent almost two years on the New York Stock Exchange, and then, oh, what else, on ITT, and André would just say no," Felix explained. "In 1975 André was pretty tired by then, and he said, 'How long do you think this will take?' I said, 'I have no idea, but I think we want to try to gear it to create something that would enable the city to finance, and at least to get back to the capital markets, and once that happens, I'm gone. You know, and that should be it. A month, two months, three months, max.' " And that is how Governor Carey created the so-called Crisis Panel, the precursor to the Municipal Assistance Corporation, or MAC, just as Felix had suggested.

The three other men on the panel were Simon Rifkind, Felix's lawyer and friend; Richard Shinn, the CEO of Metropolitan Life Insurance; and Donald Smiley, the CEO of R. H. Macy & Co. With the thirty-day drumbeat pounding, the four men began a round-the-clock effort to fashion a solution to the impending crisis. "For the last two weeks, life for the four men has been a succession of crises involving bill-drafting sessions until long after midnight, city-hopping trips starting as early as 7:30 a.m. on a helicopter from La Guardia Airport, and hurried conference phone calls to Governor Carey, Mayor Beame and other key officials," the *Times* reported, breathlessly, in June 1975. There were lots of helicopter trips between Albany and Manhattan, shuttling between meetings with legislative leaders and Mayor Beame at Gracie Mansion. "They may be new to the problem," one state official told the *Times*. "But they've quickly become comfortable with it. And most important of all, they have no evident political bias and no fear of speaking frankly. Why one of them simply told the legislative leaders: 'You're facing a financial Dunkirk. And you have to deal with it accordingly.' "

Felix said his involvement with MAC, which is generally credited with constructing a financing mechanism that allowed New York City to avoid bankruptcy, was his single proudest professional achievement. His image was that of the crisis's honest broker, prescribing the tough-love cure to all who would listen. "I didn't tell the Republicans one thing and the Democrats another," he said. "I just told them the unvarnished facts, as brutally as I knew how, but without being brutally rude. I just said, 'Look, the patient has cancer. It isn't my fault. You have the choice of letting him die or taking the cure. The cure will be painful, and it may not work. But the risk of not taking the cure is far greater.' "

The MAC platform also provided the much-needed salve to begin to repair the wounds that Felix had suffered for more than six years as a result of his work with Geneen on the Hartford acquisition. He was now happily lionized on the streets of New York. And his courtship of the press accelerated, as he intentionally became the MAC official willing to take the time to explain the complicated financial machinations to the often clueless political reporters. After he had devised and sold a $2.3 billion financing plan, in September 1975, that saved New York from default, Felix's friend Mike Burke, then president of Madison Square Garden, sent him a note: "Congratulations, Sisyphus should have learned to roll with Rohatyn. He would have made it."

Now that Felix was becoming a public figure of international renown, details of his private life began creeping into the press. For the first time came word of his marital problems. Felix had married Jeannette Streit in 1956, and together they had three sons. She worked, at least for a time in the 1950s, at the United Nations in New York, translating long Spanish and French speeches into English virtually simultaneously with the spoken words. During periods of crises, as in the Middle East in November 1956, the hours were long and demanding. "Plays hob with my domestic life," she told the *Washington Post.* That Streit ended up working at the UN was probably no accident. Her father, Clarence Streit—a writer—joined the *New York Times* as a reporter in 1925 and, in 1929, was sent to Geneva as a foreign correspondent to cover the League of Nations. He stayed for ten years, and while there he developed his own plan for a union of fifteen democratic nations, including the United States, that would closely resemble today's European Union. He wrote a book on the eve of World War II, in 1938, *Union*

Now, that detailed his thinking about how the union of nations would work. It "electrified the nation," became a best seller, and was hugely influential on college campuses.

In the late 1960s—when he was still married to Streit—Felix began a long affair with Helene Gaillet de Barcza, now Helene Gaillet de Neergaard. He had grown apart from his wife even before his public profile soared. "Jeannette was very intelligent, genteel and decent," a friend recalled, "but she was also very introverted." Added Felix: "She was an extraordinarily bright, intelligent, very high-quality person." (Streit declined to be interviewed.) Felix met Gaillet, by then separated from a Hungarian count, at a dinner party he and Jeannette had been invited to in 1967 in Greenwich Village. Gaillet was seated between the host and Felix, without giving him much thought. Toward the end of the evening, as music was played, Felix asked her to dance. He was quite taken with her from the start. At the time, she was said to closely resemble the beautiful French actress Anouk Aimée. Gaillet had emigrated from France to the United States in 1946; supposedly her family of eight was the first to fly commercially as a family across the Atlantic.

A week later, Felix called Gaillet and asked her out for a drink. She declined. He called the following week, and again Gaillet declined; just over a difficult marriage and with two young children to raise on her own, she had no interest in dating a married man. Felix proceeded to call her every week for the next six weeks until she agreed to go out with him. "At some point six or eight weeks after I originally met him, I said yes," she explained. "Now, don't ask me why I said yes. I suppose his persistence and his charm. He was not a physically very attractive man, but he was extremely charming and, of course, brilliant. But at the time I didn't know he was brilliant. I just knew that, I suppose, his persistence broke down my wish to not go out with a married man. And I went out for a drink with him." After the drink, Felix asked her to dinner. They tended to stay in the Yorkville section of Manhattan, where there were lots of bars and ethnic restaurants. Even though Felix was not particularly well known at this time, he wanted to be discreet, so they would frequent the same three local restaurants of Polish, Hungarian, and German extraction. In each restaurant, they had the same meal every time. After these dinners, Felix would ask to go back to her apartment. But Gaillet said no, until finally her resistance broke down once again and she agreed. They became intimate. "We would meet, and then he would leave right after for the country"—he and his family had a house in Mount Kisco. "But at that time, I did wonder to myself why am I doing this, knowing that he was very, very much married and knowing that it was never going to lead to anything for me. And I wasn't in love with him. He was not in love with me. It was not even a great affair. You know what I'm saying? It was just something that was happening. But in a sense, I enjoyed having an affair with him, because we always had dinner, and that was always the interesting part, the conversation."

Several months into the affair, Felix decided they should rent a pied-à-terre where they could meet regularly. He paid in advance, in cash, for a year's rental on the small apartment in a brownstone on East Sixty-second Street, between Park and Lexington avenues. They stopped having dinner and would just meet at the pied-à-terre for an hour or two, and then go their separate ways. Gaillet did not have a key to the apartment and, over time, began to notice she was not the only woman to be there with Felix. On occasion, she would see someone else's earrings or lipstick lying around.

According to Gaillet, one of the other women he was seeing at the same time—a married woman—tried to blackmail Felix, demanding that he buy her a fur coat in exchange for her not telling his wife about their affair. But Gaillet said she didn't much care about these other women. "I didn't have any kind of reason to be possessive about him or him of me," she said. "And we liked what that situation was like." One late afternoon, about a year into the affair, Gaillet and Felix had agreed to meet at the apartment. But Gaillet was uncharacteristically delayed by the fact that her apartment at Madison and Ninety-sixth had been all but destroyed by a fire. Fortunately, neither she nor her children were in the apartment at the time. In all the commotion, she remembered she had agreed to meet Felix (Gaillet pronounces his name with a slight French accent, *Fay-leex*). She scurried down to East Sixty-second Street and found Felix, who, while sympathetic, was not particularly happy that his evening had been ruined. He offered to help her financially. She accepted from him, right then and there, a check for several thousand dollars, made out to cash, to see her through this very rough patch. "Which I thought was incredibly generous," she said. But at that very moment, he also stopped calling her. The affair was over until, six months later, Felix called her "out of the blue" and asked her to meet him at the pied-à-terre. They resumed the affair "as if we had seen each other the week before."

Four weeks later, he announced to her: "I am madly in love with you. I have to live with you. I'm going to separate from my wife, and we're going to live together." Gaillet was surprised by this declaration, for she was not particularly in love with Felix since their relationship had become fairly one-dimensional. "I actually fell madly in love with him once we started living together," she said. He told her to find an apartment to rent, and he would move in with her and get a separation from his wife. Gaillet quickly found and rented a sixteen-hundred-square-foot penthouse apartment, with a wraparound terrace and a fireplace, at the Hotel Alrae, at 37 East Sixty-fourth Street (now the luxurious Plaza Athénée). There were round-the-clock doormen and room service available from the Henry IV restaurant.

At the time Felix and Helene were living at the hotel, newspaper and magazine articles about Felix made no mention of his affair. Rather, he was described as living the life of the somewhat disheveled bachelor in a rundown "residential" hotel. The articles clearly conveyed a sense that Felix did not care about money or particularly how he lived. His accommodations at the Alrae were often described as "less than sumptuous" and "small," and no mention was ever made of his infidelities. He was portrayed as living a modest and cerebral bachelor life, with time spent reading mysteries and histories and chatting with his friends in art, publishing, and political circles—an image that served his purpose in the middle of the excruciatingly difficult negotiations with the New York City unions during the fiscal crisis. His "humble" abode at the Alrae was, according to a 1976 profile of him in the *Times*,

> stuffed with books, magazines, camping and sports equipment belonging to him and his three sons, and bikes. The wines in the front closet are humble Côtes du Rhône. His car is a four-year-old BMW station wagon, also stuffed with camping gear. Rohatyn's suits are anything but modish. To the disgust of Lazard's senior partner, André Meyer, Rohatyn appeared at the Governor's side during a weekend of particularly momentous meetings on the city's fate last fall, wearing a black turtleneck sweater. His trench coat with button-in lining is the only overcoat he owns and his safari hat from Hunting World is the result of a sudden revelation, walking past that 53rd Street store in the rain, that "my head was getting both cold and bald." He travels with a small vinyl flight bag, the kind the airlines give away free or for next to nothing.

But the *Times* article was one big head fake. Yes, Felix lived at the Alrae, but not alone. He lived there with Gaillet, and it was plenty luxurious, she said, although these facts were never reported. He certainly was not living the life of a bachelor, because she was with him there from the beginning of the affair until its end. Although not as opulent as the Plaza Athénée today, she said, their penthouse apartment was actually quite elegant. The hotel was filled with an international money crowd. "It was a very, very, very subtle, private hotel in the middle of New York,"

Gaillet explained. They entertained often there the likes of Harold Geneen and other rich and powerful people. (Her children were away at boarding school during this time.) And of course, Felix was becoming fabulously rich at Lazard.

They also rented an apartment next door and broke down the wall for Helene to have a photography studio. They paid $6,000 a month for the space, a tidy sum in those days. Felix covered all their costs and encouraged her to stop working at her day job so that she could be free to travel with him wherever he went. She did as he wished. "And I therefore started my photography career, and as I evolved and became more and more of a successful photographer, he, in his own way, became more and more a public figure, because he was then working with the City of New York, with the finances," she said. "He also got Lazard Frères to move from Wall Street to Rockefeller Center, because he was sick and tired of commuting to Wall Street. He used to drive his BMW down to Wall Street every day, and he got sick and tired of that. And so when we moved into the Alrae, the first thing he did was to get André Meyer to move the firm to Rockefeller Center so he could walk to work."

They lived at the Alrae together for around five years, beginning in 1970. Streit and their three sons lived a mile farther uptown on Park Avenue. In 1972, Felix's wife asked for a separation, and Felix acceded to her wishes. He said publicly at the time that the papers he signed gave her much of his modest fortune. (But he did not divorce Streit until 1979, just before he married his second wife, Elizabeth Vagliano.) Needless to say, his separation from his first wife would take its toll on the previously close relationship he had with his three sons, Pierre (a glass artist living in the south of France), Nick (a financier and New York socialite, like his father), and Michael (a composer and screenwriter in Manhattan). For years, the family had enjoyed weekends together at their country home on six hilly acres in Mount Kisco, in Westchester County. The house abutted a lake that would freeze in the winter, and Felix and his sons would play hockey on it. "These things happen without being anybody's fault," Felix explained about his separation. He and Gaillet rented a house one summer in Ridgefield, Connecticut, to be near Felix's children in Mount Kisco. But Felix grew bored with Fairfield County, and he and Gaillet decided thereafter to rent a "summer shack on the beach" in the Hamptons, where they hung with his artsy friends and enjoyed intimate dinners, where the ideas of Felix's favorite writers, among them Thomas More and Montaigne ("civilized skeptics, not ideologues"), were discussed.

Gaillet said she and Felix were incredibly happy, living a carefree life and enjoying each other's company without any strings attached. They would go on ski vacations together in Alta, Utah, and Felix's three sons and Gaillet's two daughters would be there as well. (Much later, one of Gaillet's daughters dated Pierre Rohatyn for about a year.) Gaillet lived with Felix at the Alrae throughout the ITT-Hartford fiasco, through his testimony in front of the Senate Judiciary Committee, through his daily vilification in the press, and through the numerous investigations by the IRS, the SEC, and the lawyers pursuing shareholder lawsuits. "I was very much on the sideline of all this all the time," she said, "because I went to dinner with him every night. Every night we had drinks with somebody. He didn't drink. He would never drink more than a glass of wine in one evening, always a glass of red wine. He would never drink a second glass of wine. We first would meet people for a drink someplace, and then we would go to dinner with someone else, and then we would go possibly have an after-dinner drink with someone else. He would drink water, soda, or a juice." She never saw him betray any concern whatsoever about being at the center of the ITT controversy. "This man never showed his emotions on his sleeve," she said. "This is a man who kept everything in his brain, and he kept it all churning all the time. You would never have known that he was under so much pressure. It was more like, 'I have to go to Washington. Do you want to go with me?' And he was at the hearings. And then he would come back at night, and we would have dinner. He would never complain about something or share about the pressure."

Felix was becoming more and more famous. He was on the precipice of superstardom, thanks to his work with MAC and New York City. Helene, too, had developed a fine reputation as a photographer. "What happened was, as my career as a photographer progressed, his career as a well-known financier-politician developed at a fast clip," she explained. "Both our careers developed at a fast clip. And what happened during the last year to two years of our living together, we started seeing each other less and less, because I had more and more bookings, more and more travels for my photography. He had more and more demands on his time. And he was getting to be a very famous person. He was always in the papers. He no longer was as interested in me as he had been to start with. And I have to tell you, when you look at the psychology and the development of our affair, our getting together and then breaking up, it is exactly the stepping-stone situation of a man who is in a marriage, which is extremely dull, who finds an exciting woman, who lives with her for a while, and who then finds another woman who's going to get him completely out of his first marriage, then affair, and then into it. And that's what happened when he met Elizabeth Vagliano, who he's married to still today." On their regular skiing trip to Alta, in January 1975, they met Vagliano, who was there with her children. Gaillet thought nothing of the chance encounter, even though she does recall Felix commenting on her. "I was the stepping-stone that allowed him to end his marriage, to walk out of it, to leave his children, and to develop this whole side of his life, which was so exciting and different from being just a banker at Lazard," Gaillet continued. "And then he met Elizabeth, who pulled him out from living with an artist. What do you want with this artist? What do you want with this photographer? She'll never get you to where I can get you. And Elizabeth got him there, which was the society, the big boards, the big thing. You know, the entire spectrum of life that they started living, which I would never have gotten there, because it's a kind of life I'm totally not interested in."

In December 1975, there was a major show of Gaillet's photographs in Paris. She had photographed famous people the world over, from Louise Nevelson to Mick Jagger to Aristotle Onassis, with whom she had had a brief affair on his Greek island, Skorpios, four months before his death in March 1975. (Gaillet had first met Onassis with Felix and André over dinner in New York. And Onassis gave Gaillet an open invitation to visit Skorpios, either with or without Felix. One day, some months later, Gaillet was in Paris on her way to Kinshasa to photograph the 1974 Muhammad Ali–George Foreman fight. She was speaking to Felix on the phone when he told her that the fight was postponed for some five weeks. She asked him if she should instead go to the Greek islands. Why not? Felix replied. Felix called Onassis on Skorpios, and with Onassis's approval gave Gaillet his number. Onassis encouraged her to come to his island, and the rest is the stuff of history.) Gaillet had also taken a series of erotic photographs. "Clay Felker said it was the best hung show in New York," she said with a laugh. She went over to Paris several weeks before the big opening to help out at the gallery. She ended up being in Paris for around five weeks.

Although their careers started to affect their relationship, Gaillet said, she and Felix had worked things out and had even agreed to get married at a church on the top of Alta Mountain around Christmastime 1975, soon after she returned from Paris. The photography show was a huge hit. Felix came to Paris for it. And both Michel David-Weill and André were there with their wives. Some four hundred people showed up. The show began at six at night, and the party did not end until midnight. "We had closed down the entire street around this gallery," she said. "It was a huge success. Felix came for the opening. And we had decided after the show that we were going to regroup. We had decided. In my mind, I thought he had agreed. Because we were going to get married. . . . He was so excited that I was becoming more of an international scope of person. At the time I did not know that he was then already going out with Elizabeth."

When she returned to the Alrae from Paris, Gaillet discovered that Felix had moved out. She thought she was coming back to America at the height of her artistic success to get married to Felix Rohatyn. And instead, he left her. She was devastated. "I came back to a totally empty apartment," she said. "There was only my clothes left, and the furniture of the hotel. And he had moved out. And I had no forwarding address. So I called up his secretary, Sally, who said to me, 'I'm sorry, but I cannot tell you where Mr. Rohatyn is—he's on a trip,' or some excuse. The emotional impact of coming to this empty apartment, you have no idea. In fact, I never picked up a camera again. I have never done photography again since then."

The following Monday, Felix's secretary asked Gaillet to join Felix for dinner, at 8:00 p.m., at the "21" Club, on West Fifty-second Street. "And so I get all dressed up," she said. "I am completely devastated. I was tongue-tied during the entire dinner. I could not talk. And he said to me, 'I have to move on with my life. I need more space. I love you, but I have to do something else.' Of course, then I was not aware of the fact that he was already getting quite involved with Elizabeth. And so that was the end of the affair. That was it. And I never saw him again. That was it, that night. You have no idea. It took me five years to get over this . . . it was the worst thing. It was worse than the fire; it was worse than anything else. I mean, it was just absolutely terrible. Terrible, terrible, terrible. It took me five years to get over the breakup with him. And I still have dreams about him. It's so unbelievable. The impact of this life I had with him is so enormous that I still dream of him in my life." Felix paid for her to stay at the Alrae for another year or so, but then she had to move out and start all over again.

She bears no ill will whatsoever toward Felix, in part because that is not her nature and in part because she acknowledges that Liz Rohatyn took Felix to a place and a stature in New York society that she could never have done. But she knows Felix was deceitful throughout their eight years together, carrying on with other women on a regular basis. Even though she no longer knows, she doubts he has settled down. "No, no, no, no," she said. "You don't understand this kind of mentality. This is a person who has to go for the kill every time. I mean, for the win. It's not a matter of having affairs. It's a matter of sexually getting somebody and then, you know, screwing them two or three times and then that's it. That's done. And then no more. And then getting another one and getting another one. I mean, everybody's written about this kind of mentality or character or personality. That's what he's like. He needs to be the conqueror, you know? He needs to conquer women."

Gaillet said that after they broke up, and while Felix was dating Elizabeth, he also had an affair with Jackie Kennedy Onassis, following the death of Aristotle Onassis. "It was all over the papers," she said. "Their picture was in the paper everywhere." Felix and Gaillet, André and Bella, and Jackie would often dine together at André's apartment at the Carlyle. Felix had been the one who had introduced Gaillet to Onassis, and he knew about their brief affair. Felix's affair with Jackie ended, Gaillet suspected, because even for Felix the glare of publicity around Jackie was too intense, and put less of the limelight on him. "I wasn't there," she said, "but I imagine that it was too much publicity for him to handle at the time. He just wasn't that kind of person. He really preferred to be sort of in the background." She said Felix even dated Marie-Josée Drouin, who is now married to the financier Henry Kravis. Felix's only comment about his time with Helene was: "Look, I was living with a woman for a number of years. And that broke up. And a year or so later I was with another woman, who became my wife, whom I've been married to for twenty-seven years."

FELIX'S SUCCESS AS an investment banker had now been conjoined with his increasingly fawning press notices—whether they were for helping solve the Wall Street back-office crisis or for leading the efforts to solve New York City's fiscal mess—making him "one of the most influential and interesting bachelors around." He was a frequent guest at many of the toniest social gatherings in New York, all the while giving the general public the impression that he was living alone at the supposedly downmarket Alrae. "In those days," said a woman who knew him well, "Felix tried to be very counter-Establishment, very tough, smart and independent. He used to say, 'I own only two suits, the one I'm wearing and the one that's at the cleaner's.' The first night we went out, we drove through Central Park in his beat-up car. It was spring, and the apple blossoms were in bloom. 'Do you see those flowers?' he asked me. 'Take a good look, because I'll never send you flowers. I don't believe in things like that.' " He was said to have dated both Barbara Walters and Shirley MacLaine.

Somehow, Felix kept churning out important deals. For instance, in July 1975—in the midst of the intensity of New York's crisis—he recommended that United Technologies, the Hartford-based manufacturer of jet engines, look seriously at buying Otis Elevator Company. United Technologies wanted to diversify its revenue and profitability away from its dependence on fickle government contracts. Harry Gray, UT's CEO, took Felix's advice. United Technologies pounced on Otis by launching, on October 15, a hostile tender offer for 55 percent of Otis's shares, for $42 each. Otis resisted and called in Morgan Stanley to help it find a "friendly" suitor—to no avail, as UT raised its offer to $44, in cash, and Felix and Lazard would add another pelt, and client, to their belt. For not the last time, Felix was favorably compared to Henry Kissinger—at the very moment Kissinger was at his most powerful. "He is the Henry Kissinger of the financial world," Donna Shalala, Clinton's future secretary of health and human services and now the president of the University of Miami, told *Newsweek* at this time. "He's as brilliant as Henry, as European as Henry, makes as many deals as Henry. But he's nicer than Henry."

But Felix's deification in Manhattan meant little in Washington. Not only had President Ford turned a cold shoulder to New York City's fiscal crisis, but Felix could not avoid the SEC's ongoing investigation of the Hartford deal, even of its most obscure details. In his final deposition in the second SEC investigation, on February 3, 1976, Felix started modestly by explaining to the SEC's lawyers that since his previous testimony, Governor Carey had asked him to get involved with the New York City financial crisis. There was a brief nod of recognition but little interest. The SEC lawyers were now all business.

For the first time, they were very focused on even the most minute details of the transaction, having by now dissected the whole series of events for more than four years. Of all things, the SEC now wanted to know what Felix knew of a small Italian auto parts company, Way-Assauto, which ITT bought rather unexpectedly in 1971. Seventy percent of Way-Assauto was owned by the Griffa family and 30 percent by an investment company controlled by the powerful Agnelli family, the principal owners of Fiat and close associates of both Cuccia and André. The sequence of events is complicated, but somehow ITT ended up buying the company for $22 million at the end of May 1971 (actually $20 million in cash from ITT and $2 million in cash Way-Assauto had on its books that ITT allowed the sellers to withdraw at closing) in a deal brokered by Lazard. Why Felix, André, or Lazard would have any involvement in a deal of this size in Italy is, of course, a good question. "It was just a relatively small acquisition that I had really little to do with," Felix said. "Nor did the firm really." How, then, does one explain Lazard's $300,000 fee? The simple answer no doubt is that the tiny deal involved not only the Mediobanca stock deal but also two of the firm's biggest and most important clients, ITT and the Agnellis—more than sufficient justification for Felix's and André's involvement. The SEC pressed Felix on whether he made any connection between Mediobanca's sale of 400,000 ITT series "N" shares at $55 per share, or $22 million, to IIA, an entity controlled by the Agnellis, and ITT's agreement to purchase, also for $22 million, Way-Assauto, a parts supplier to Fiat, all at exactly the same time in the first part of 1971. Felix demurred, but conceded there did seem to be a clear, indisputable relationship between the two deals.

The SEC lawyers were also quite curious about how another in-the-money option from Mediobanca to buy thirty thousand ITT series "N" shares ended up in the estate of the longtime Lazard client Charles Engelhard at the same time that Engelhard sold an investment company he owned a big stake in, named Eurofund, to ITT. Engelhard's equity partner in Eurofund? None other than Lazard Frères in New York. It turned out that Engelhard and Lazard controlled 28 percent of Eurofund through their limited partnership, Far Hills Securities. Perhaps the most curious testimony from any of the bankers at Lazard was that of Mel Heineman. At the time of Heineman's testimony before the SEC in September 1975, he was thirty-five years old and had ten months earlier been promoted to partner at Lazard, after six years as an associate. Although he graduated from both Harvard and Harvard Law School, it is doubtful his extraordinary education could have prepared him for his experience at Lazard. He had been part of the ITT team working on the Hartford exchange offer, literally counting the shares tendered. He recalled for the SEC having been sent to Mediobanca in Milan twice: first in November 1970 and then from January 12 to 17, 1971, to do something or other with regard to Mediobanca's resales of the ITT series "N" stock or perhaps something having to do with Way-Assauto; in any event he was not at all certain what he was doing in Italy in January 1971.

His testimony provides a rare—and often humorous—glimpse into the life of an associate at Lazard at that time. Heineman's description of his responsibilities as a young investment banker contrasted deliciously with the highfalutin role typically portrayed. But Heineman was quite serious about one thing: no matter what, he told many of his colleagues at the time, he had no intention of going to jail to protect Felix. "There was no reason for me to do anything for Felix," he said thirty years later, "because, Lord knows, Felix hasn't done anything for anyone else."

For the SEC, he recalled attending a meeting at Mediobanca's offices where eight or ten Mediobanca bankers, including Cuccia, were gathered. "The only recollection I have of that meeting," Heineman explained in his deposition, "is that it involved certain tax problems that had something to do with the Way-Assauto transaction. The meeting was populated by Italians, except for me. My recollection is that approximately 95 percent of the conversation was in Italian with an occasional lapsing into English for my benefit." He did recall reporting what he could about the meeting—which was very little indeed—to his client Stanley Luke at ITT. "The reason that I recall with such precision is that it interrupted a very nice dinner that I was having with my wife," he testified. "I remember that very concretely." He also remembered *not* reporting anything about his five days in Italy to Felix, who was his boss, although he said he had no idea if Felix was working on the Way-Assauto transaction. "The only recollection that I have, in terms of reporting after that meeting, is and you will understand, being an employee of Lazard, being very anxious to get home, having been in Italy for five or six days, I remember placing a call to Mr. Rohatyn, basically to tell him that there had been such a meeting and the extent to which I might have known what happened, and to ask him permission to come back. My recollection was that Mr. Rohatyn was not interested in any details of that meeting whatsoever, and merely suggested that the proper course for me would be to pass them on to Stanley Luke. Mr. Rohatyn said that after I reached Luke, I should come home."

When the SEC lawyers asked André, at the end of October 1975, if he had sent Heineman to meet with Cuccia, he said, simply, "No," before adding, "Mr. Heineman is a nice man but [I had] not very much to do with him."

When asked if he knew what the Way-Assauto transaction was all about, Heineman said he did not, nor had he heard about it before being sent to Italy. "What was your understanding before you went to Italy about what you would be doing there?" he was asked.

"To the best that I can recall, I went to Italy to be of assistance to Dr. Cuccia who was, I gather, perhaps a client of Lazard, or there was some relationship and I was sent there to be of assistance to him. That is all that I frankly remember about it." During his testimony, Heineman must have realized how strange it sounded for him not to know why he was being sent to Italy for five days or what the people were talking about when he got there, so he volunteered the following: "At the time I went to Italy, I was at Lazard for under two years. I was an associate in the mergers and acquisitions area, as I previously testified. As I conceive of it now, and definitely as I conceived of it at the time, my function with respect to the trip was a clerical function. There would be no reason, in my judgment, for anyone to necessarily explain details of the transaction to me, other than what I was supposed to do. Certainly, I would have nothing to do with the kind of policy questions that you think you are asking me, which I said I did not know."

The opposing SEC attorney found this a bit hard to believe. "I still don't understand, even generally, what you were supposed to do over there," he said. "Could you be more specific about it? I am sure you received instructions more general and more specific than just 'Go to Italy, and help Dr. Cuccia.' "

"To the best of my recollection, I was sent to Italy to be of assistance to Dr. Cuccia," he replied. "I may have taken some language with me on paper, and I have no recollection whether I did or didn't, but I am quite clear on the fact that, as far as I can recall it, there were no specific instructions given to me, nor did I consider that to be in any way extraordinary."

Now, even though Felix deemed the early 1970s to be the Dark Ages of investment banking, for a graduate of Harvard and Harvard Law to be sent to Italy for five days, with his wife—including two days spent skiing in Saint Moritz before taking a bus to Milan—and to have absolutely no idea what he was sent there to do, or why, is quite peculiar, even by the rigidly hierarchical standards of behavior that ruled at Lazard at that time. What is even more ironic is that Mel Heineman would, after the incapacitation of Tom Mullarkey—whose testimony he seemed to be aping—become Lazard's general counsel and the keeper of most, if not all, of Lazard's most precious secrets. Eventually, he would become the consigliere to both Felix and Michel David-Weill and serve on the firm's executive committee. Perhaps his ability to accept an amorphous assignment overseas for a clandestine series of transactions was a crucial litmus test of his suitability for the job he would hold for most of his thirty years at the firm. Some of their former partners said that Mullarkey and Heineman—both bankers turned Lazard general counsels—agreed to take the legal reins of the firm in return for substantial compensation in order to keep them quiet about the ITT matters. (Heineman very graciously declined repeated requests to be interviewed extensively for this book.)

Mullarkey, too, once again testified twice before the SEC, on January 31, 1975, and then on March 5, 1976. In the course of his testimony, which included the usual inability to recollect most things, he said it now seemed to him after much study that the sale of Way-Assauto to ITT and the purchase by the Way-Assauto sellers of 400,000 ITT "N" shares "were linked."

Mullarkey was also asked about a somewhat mysterious payment of

$520,000 made by the Agnellis to Lazard—but actually paid by Les Fils Dreyfus in Switzerland—in June 1971 that represented four years of advisory services to Fiat and the Agnellis. In his June 1975 written testimony to the SEC—prepared with Mullarkey's help in Switzerland—André explained that since 1964 Lazard had "rendered advisory services" to the Agnellis and their affiliates, including "general advice with respect to markets in relation to securities in the United States," "discussions of trends in foreign exchange and commodities," "opinions about the American economy and investments in North American companies," studies of attempts to sell various Agnelli businesses, studies of the Italian aircraft industry, and "studies of possible Fiat participation in Chrysler's European operations and in the Citroën automobile enterprise." These were the services rendered that resulted in the $520,000 fee paid in 1971 as well as an additional $200,000 fee paid in December 1973. After 1974, Lazard firmed up its fee arrangement with the Agnellis, receiving $600,000 per year, to provide an annual valuation of the family's various investments. One SEC attorney, Gary Sundick, asked Mullarkey if he was satisfied with André's written explanation of the services he provided to Fiat and the Agnellis to earn the fee.

"Mr. Sundick, are you, in effect, asking whether I'm going to impeach the integrity of my senior partner?" he replied, incredulous. "Is that your question?"

"I'm asking what your belief is and whether you have—", Sundick tried to answer, before being cut off.

"Mr. Sundick, my senior partner is a man of great integrity," Mullarkey stated. "If he told me this, I have no reason to dispute him."

When asked by Sundick if anyone had ever told him there was a link between IIA's purchase of 400,000 "N" shares and the sale of Way-Assauto to ITT and Les Fils Dreyfus's purchase of 100,000 "N" shares, the sale of 30,000 of those shares to Charles Engelhard, and the purchase by ITT of Engelhard's Eurofund, Mullarkey answered that, of all people, Simon Rifkind, the Paul, Weiss lawyer who had ferociously defended Lazard over the years, had told him the transactions *were linked*—a rather remarkable admission, not only because the conversation was covered by attorney-client privilege but also because for years no one had been a more reliably resolute defender—albeit well paid—of Lazard's mischievous behavior than Rifkind.

"Anyone else?" Sundick inquired.

"It's my present impression that anybody, even of the meanest intellect understands these transactions were linked," Mullarkey answered. His March 5, 1976, deposition was the last one taken in the matter.

One of Mullarkey's longtime partners said years later that Mullarkey told him he would often wake up in the morning and be sick to his stomach—literally throw up—before the many days when he had to deal with the ITT litigation.

Years later, Felix reflected upon the entire incident and the countless investigations. "André found some people who could buy the stock," he said. "And did he have any arrangements with them that were silent? I don't think so, but maybe he did. I don't know." As the investigations persisted, Felix said he found himself increasingly being blamed by André for the fiasco (along with Walter Fried, of course). "André was already fading," Felix continued, "and André really disappeared more and more and forgot more and more and remembered less and less as time went on. And I found André more and more saying, 'This is Felix's deal.' Did I feel very comfortable about that? No. But what was I gonna do about it?"

The SEC finished taking depositions in the spring of 1976 and encouraged Lazard's legal teams at Paul, Weiss and Fried Frank to make whatever arguments they cared to on their clients' behalf. On May 14, 1976, Rifkind wrote a cover letter to Irwin Borowski, the SEC attorney, seeking a negotiated settlement. Rifkind's letter made clear the seriousness with which Lazard was taking the SEC's latest enforcement action—and, as the SEC's Stanley Sporkin explained, with good reason.

Both Rifkind and André's attorney Samuel Harris had made eloquent, if not completely factual, arguments for their clients' innocence and unimpeachable integrity. Unfortunately, though, their lengthy treatments seemed simply to disappear into the SEC's black hole as the months passed and the investigation continued. Over the summer of 1976, while on a visit to London, Harris wrote a moving letter to Borowski on Claridge's hotel letterhead. "Dear Irwin," he wrote, "I am deeply grateful to you for letting me know that I need not worry about anything recurring with respect to the Lazard matter during my brief business visit here . . . to me, the most important matter on my business agenda is the Lazard investigation because it involves the reputations and careers of these fine human beings. I can't begin to emphasize how strongly I feel about the possibility of André Meyer ending an extraordinary career, which has involved conferring tremendous benefits on men and women in many nations—particularly in the U.S., France and Israel—with a suit in which he is named by the Commission as a party defendant."

Finally, on October 13, after many years of depositions, the examination of boxes of ITT documents, and the relentless effort to stitch together precisely what Lazard, Mediobanca, and ITT had pulled off, the

SEC ruled, deeming "it appropriate . . . that proceedings be instituted with respect to" ITT and Lazard regarding potential violations of the Securities Exchange Act of 1934 having to do with ITT's disposition of the Hartford shares to Mediobanca and Mediobanca's sale of those converted shares to two buyers that simultaneously sold their companies to ITT. Somewhat surprisingly, however, after all the years of effort, the SEC also agreed to a settlement proposal, as being "in the public interest."

The settlement proposal, proffered by ITT and Lazard, permitted them to consent to the SEC's findings and its penalties "on the basis that nothing contained herein is an adjudication with respect to any matter referred to herein." Lazard agreed, within forty-five days, to "adopt procedures that will insure that it properly ascertains and records all fees received by it and the basis for such fees." Lazard also agreed to provide companies on whose board a Lazard banker sits with "full and complete" information, in writing, about all of the fees Lazard receives, in whatever form, from that corporation. Finally, Lazard agreed, upon request, to provide any former shareholder of Eurofund with a copy of the SEC order. For its part, ITT had the burden of amending its annual reports for the years 1969 through 1976, within ten days, to include the SEC's order. Within forty-five days, ITT agreed to set up a committee of independent directors of its board to review the SEC's order, and the related findings of fact, to determine what could be done to prevent a recurrence of such activities.

Sporkin's current views notwithstanding, by any measure these reprimands were light indeed. The *New York Times* reporter Judith Miller wrote a 408-word story about the settlement that the editors deftly tucked inside on page 78. She conceded the twenty-six-page settlement document shed "new light on one of the most complex and controversial mergers in corporate history," but her story never bothered to share with the paper's readers what that beacon was revealing, probably because she had not previously covered the story and was not in a good position to know. She quoted Rifkind's view that "Lazard firmly believes that its conduct throughout these transactions was in compliance with all legal requirements and in accord with high professional standards and that all appropriate disclosures were duly made."

To be sure, the SEC's single-spaced compendium displayed, in sumptuous detail, Lazard's role in the unprecedented transatlantic journey taken by the now-infamous 1,741,348 shares of the Hartford. The SEC's accounting explained that once ITT bought the Hartford shares, with Lazard's help, the shares became "a serious problem" because obtaining a favorable IRS ruling required that ITT divest the shares before the Hartford shareholders were to vote on the merger with ITT. But the market for the thinly traded Hartford shares had fallen far below the $51 per share that ITT had paid for them, making Geneen reluctant, to say the least, to sell them at the current price. ITT turned to Felix to find a solution. He tried, without luck, to find a buyer in the United States. He then appealed to the vacationing André, whose suggestion of Mediobanca set in motion a series of events that led eventually to the resales of the by-then-converted ITT "N" shares to two buyers, Charles Engelhard and a fund controlled by the Agnellis, that in turn each sold a company, Eurofund and Way-Assauto, respectively, where they held large stakes, to ITT. The SEC's basic conclusion—utterly correct—was that ITT bought these two companies, in effect, with their own "N" shares while allowing the owners of the companies to profit not only by receiving a premium for their companies but also by converting the proceeds of those sales into the in-the-money options on the ITT "N" shares that Mediobanca had in effect granted to the sellers of the companies.

The SEC also noted the abundance of fees that Lazard pulled out of the entire series of deals, starting with the ITT-Hartford merger itself. It was the gift that kept on giving. First, Lazard received $500,000 for brokering the sale of the 1.7 million Hartford shares to ITT. Then the firm received $1 million for its advice to ITT in the acquisition of the Hartford. (Another, tiny investment bank, Middendorf Colgate, also received $1 million.) Lazard also received half of Mediobanca's commitment fee from ITT for agreeing to "buy" the 1.7 million Hartford shares. That came to about $684,000, which Felix may or may not have remembered to tell his client Geneen about. Lazard also initially received half of another $359,000, or about $180,000, in selling fees Mediobanca received for the disposal of the "N" shares, but after the IRS reversed its 1969 ruling, in 1974, Lazard returned these fees because after the IRS raised questions, Mediobanca decided the money had been sent to Lazard erroneously. Lazard also received the $520,000 "settlement of fee—Agnelli" by way of Les Fils Dreyfus for, as André described, years and years of Lazard's to-then-free advice to the Agnellis on any number of topics. Lazard took no fee from Eurofund for negotiating the sale of ITT because it was also a principal, for which it received a profit of more than $1.2 million on its $450,000 investment. Lazard received another $250,000 fee from ITT for its advice with regard to the liquidation of the securities in Eurofund and for the reinvestment of the cash. Finally, Lazard received brokerage commissions on the sale of the 441,348 "N" shares that Mediobanca had sold through Lazard, 400,000 of them to Salomon Brothers and 41,348 of them in the market. In sum, Lazard had received well over $4 million in fees stemming from this one transaction, at a time when large cooperative apartments in tony buildings on Park Avenue were selling for around $50,000.

Whether all this added up to *criminal* activity on the part of Felix and André became the next crisis these two bankers, somewhat unexpectedly, had to face. It seems that Sporkin, at the SEC, had urged the U.S. attorney in the Southern District of New York, Paul Curran, to convene a criminal grand jury to investigate and to decide whether to *indict* Felix and André in the ITT matter. The convening of the grand jury was said to have occurred during the seemingly endless delays in the second SEC investigation. (The SEC investigations and the shareholder lawsuits were directed at Lazard, the firm, not the individual partners, although if the punishment were severe enough, the cost to the partners could have been substantial.) Now, though, a criminal grand jury investigation raised the possibility, for the first time, that Felix or André could go to *prison*. Here, André's deteriorating health played a significant role in persuading the U.S. attorney not to call for his appearance. But Felix was young and vibrant and had been very much involved, as we have seen, in the events that resulted in the ITT-Hartford scandals.

Felix would have to appear before the grand jury. And he was scared shitless. The task of preparing him for his appearance, which he had to do alone, without counsel, fell to his partner Bob Price. Price had joined Lazard four years earlier, in December 1972, as a forty-year-old vice president working for Felix in the corporate finance group. He had exactly zero formal training in M&A but was well known to both André and Felix as the man who masterminded the Republican John Lindsay's improbable victory in the 1965 New York City mayoral election.

After engineering Lindsay's victory, Price became one of his two deputy mayors, a position he held for about a year, with some controversy. After leaving the Lindsay administration, at the end of 1966, Price joined the Dreyfus Corporation, which controlled the Dreyfus Fund, one of the largest mutual funds at the time. After two years at Dreyfus, he set out on his own and created Price Capital Corporation, an early version of today's hedge funds. Price Capital did not achieve what its founder hoped, though, and so when André and Felix asked him to join Lazard at the end of 1972, he readily agreed. On February 7, 1974, Price became a Lazard partner. In 1968, he had also given Lazard and Felix a gift, in the form of a fully negotiated deal between Lorillard, the tobacco company, and Loews, the insurance conglomerate run by the Tisch family. Since the Dreyfus Fund owned a significant amount of Lorillard stock,

Price could not get the fee he felt he had earned for putting together the deal. Instead, he gave the fully negotiated deal to his friends Felix and André, the finishing touches of which were made at the now-defunct Christ Cella steakhouse on East Forty-sixth Street. The Loews deal gave Lazard its second million-dollar M&A fee. That's not all Price gave Felix. He also introduced Felix to Elizabeth Vagliano, now Elizabeth Rohatyn, Felix's second wife. Vagliano had been a secretary in Price's law office.

The grand jury investigation, though, forced Price to earn his keep at Lazard. In 1959, he had been an assistant U.S. attorney in downtown Manhattan. In the mid-1970s, in the midst of the second SEC investigation, Felix and André desperately needed Price's legal expertise. Price relentlessly coached Felix on his grand jury appearance, even going so far as to sneak him into the hearing room after hours to conduct mock question-and-answer sessions. "I came into the firm a year or two after Sporkin had started the investigation," Price explained thirty years later. "So I was totally free. I wasn't part of the ITT-Hartford transaction. André liked me and asked me to give him advice about how to handle things, and the thing was that Sporkin had decided to have a major grand jury investigation until Felix and Sam Harris, from Fried Frank, calmed Sporkin down and made him see this wasn't the way he was going to succeed in life. And then I gave them [Felix and André] the advice that they should offer to appear before the grand jury for questioning. What they would say was secondary. Getting them to accept the concept of appearing before the grand jury, though, was earthshaking." Price said his "job was really to coach them on answers and get them ready for the grand jury and to give them truthful answers that skipped the truth." He said that Paul Curran, an old friend, had given him the key to the grand jury room so that the night before Felix was to appear they could both go in together. "Felix sat in the chair, and I bombarded him with questions so he wouldn't go into the pit cold," said Price.

In the end, Felix dodged the bullet. Whether because the evidence was inconclusive or because political strings were pulled or because, as Price suggested, Sporkin—who later became a federal judge—decided it would be a poor career move to mess with the powerful Felix, the prosecutors and hence the grand jury lost interest in the case, not unlike how the former SEC investigator Gary Aguirre claimed the SEC lost interest in his 2005 investigation of insider trading by the well-connected Arthur Samberg, CEO of Pequot Capital, and John Mack, CEO of Morgan Stanley. But there was a lot of arm-twisting along the way. "Sporkin was all over Lazard like a blanket," Price said. But then Felix started to romance the SEC investigator, and, according to Price, by the end of the process "Sporkin was in Felix's pocket." Price explained that Felix had many meals with Sporkin down in Washington to try to convince him to let the matter drop and had his powerful Washington friends, such as Ted Kennedy and Jacob Javits, also weigh in on his behalf. "But who do you know who goes before a grand jury and doesn't try to do that?" Price asked years later, rhetorically. Paul Curran's son James got a job at Lazard at around the same time—1976—and worked at the firm until the early 1980s. In the end, the matter got "stale" and the "file was lost," Price explained. The SEC and Sporkin decided to reach a settlement agreement with Lazard instead. Sporkin's boss at the SEC was Felix's old friend Bill Casey. After Casey became director of the CIA, Sporkin followed him to the agency and was his general counsel. When Casey died in office, Sporkin won his appointment to the federal judiciary. He is now a partner in the Washington office of the Wall Street law firm Weil, Gotshal. Had the "broad investigation" in front of the grand jury "proceeded," Price said, "Sporkin wouldn't have become a judge but would have had a helluva story."

Felix adamantly and repeatedly denied having any recollection that he was the target of a criminal grand jury investigation into the ITT matter. "I'm not denying that it happened," Felix said. "I'm just telling you that I have absolutely no recollection." But the very idea that someone had even suggested such a thing was anathema to him. He repeatedly made it clear he did not want the thought even mentioned. "The notion that I could appear as a defendant in front of a grand jury without it getting into some newspaper or some column or something is just not credible," he explained. "It just couldn't have happened." There are no records that can be checked about withered grand jury investigations; by law, grand jury records must be sealed or destroyed, if they were ever kept in the first place. All that can be relied on is the recollections of people involved at the time, some thirty years ago. Felix has one supporter for his view, who was there at the time and would know: Stanley Sporkin. Sporkin, who has nothing but good things to say about Felix, said he never asked the U.S. attorney's office to convene a grand jury investigation into Felix's role in the ITT matter. But one former Lazard partner, Disque Deane, said he recalled that around this same time, André offered Sporkin a job at Lazard; Sporkin denied this was true. Paul Curran, the U.S. attorney, would not say whether or not he convened such an investigation. Along with other Lazard partners at the time, Bob Price was equally adamant that the grand jury investigation did happen. "I swear on the Torah it is true," said Price, who is Jewish. Deane, a close friend of Price's, said he, too, believed that Felix and André were the targets of a grand jury investigation and that Felix had appeared before the grand jury. "Yes," Deane said. "I will confirm that, yes." He said Price is telling the truth. "The soul of the earth and very honest," he said of his former partner. "He'll tell it the way it is."

Deane said that while the partners at Lazard did not talk about the investigations, they were extremely scared about the potential outcomes. "Because the firm could have been put out of business," he said. "So it was a very scary time at the firm." Deane, whom Felix referred to as his "blood enemy," described how, in his opinion, Felix avoided indictment. "Well, because Felix knew nothing about the inner workings of André Meyer and all his friends in Europe," he said, "Felix just appeared as an implementer, not as the brains. The brains of the whole transaction was André Meyer. . . . You see there's a thread to this whole thing. Felix is a very intelligent person. And Felix is smart enough to keep out of the way of these, what I would call criminal activities. The parking activities and all. These were criminal activities. And he did. And when someone asked Felix what he knew about the parking, he said, 'I knew nothing about it.' And that was so." He said André and Felix used their connections in Washington to make the whole matter go away, with but a slap on the wrist from the SEC. "But," he said, "we thought that any minute they might come down with some type of an order that would basically put Lazard out of business. . . . Felix Rohatyn is the greatest escape artist of all time." Patrick Gerschel, André's grandson and a partner at Lazard at the time, was no friend of Felix, Deane, or Price. But he, too, remembered clearly that both his grandfather and Felix were targets of the grand jury investigation. Why would Felix deny the matter ever occurred? "Felix would deny that he was walking across the street if he thought he could do it," Gerschel said.

In any event, with the federal grand jury and the SEC both safely tucked away, the only remaining open issue in the matter was how much ITT would have to pay the IRS to settle the tax indemnity it had provided to the Hartford shareholders. In typical ITT style, it was not going to concede an inch without a substantial legal fight. Within weeks of the IRS's change of heart, in March 1974, ITT filed a suit against the IRS and its commissioner, Donald Alexander, seeking a judgment declaring Alexander's revocation invalid. In June 1975, the U.S. District Court in Delaware dismissed the complaint. But in early 1979, both a federal court in Delaware and the U.S. Tax Court thwarted the IRS and reinstated the acquisition's original tax-free status. On behalf of the IRS, the Justice Department appealed these new rulings, and finally, in May 1981,

ITT agreed to pay $17.8 million to the IRS in exchange for the IRS agreeing not to pursue tax claims against the former Hartford shareholders. "We are very pleased to have this litigation behind us," Rand Araskog, ITT's new CEO, told the *Times*. "While we have felt that our position that the exchange was not taxable was correct, the legal issues involved are extremely complex and the final outcome in the courts was uncertain." In any event, the settlement was well below the $100 million ITT originally thought the tax indemnity would cost.

Now the final open question was at hand: What effect would the years of litigation, and its attendant publicity, have on Lazard's reputation in general and on Felix's in particular? Felix's highly prized reputation for secrecy, elitism, and unimpeachable advice had been broadly challenged by his role in arranging for and then defending ITT's high-profile acquisition of the Hartford. Despite the deal being his most important client's most important deal, he sought to portray himself as detached from it and uninvolved, especially when the seas started to swell. This is simply implausible, especially for a banker so facile with numbers and insights who prided himself on the depth of his understanding for his clients and their aspirations. Now, of course, it would have been terribly inconvenient for Felix to admit the extent of his involvement. Far better, he and André must have decided, to pin the tail on the nervous and thankfully deceased Walter Fried, their administrative partner who, according to Cary Reich's description of him in *Financier,* "was unable to push a paper clip across a desk without clearing it first with Meyer." Mullarkey, who replaced Fried as Lazard's administrative partner after Fried's nervous breakdown, told the SEC that even someone of the "meanest intellect" could see that all the transactions were linked, which is about as close as anyone at Lazard ever came to admitting to the authorities that the deals had a mastermind. "It was brilliantly conceived, just brilliant," Mullarkey would later confide to Reich. "There were a lot of minions involved—myself, Felix and some other people. But the conception of it was André's." Mullarkey's recollection of the Hartford deal sounded much like Deane's recollection. Concluded Reich: "It was, unquestionably, one of André Meyer's greatest deals."

André was quite ill by this time, so if there was to be fallout from the years of negative publicity, the brunt of it would chiefly be felt by Felix, and perhaps to a much lesser degree by Michel David-Weill, who had moved to New York in 1977 to take over the day-to-day operations of the firm in the wake of André's incapacity. Michel said much later he was glad not to have been in New York during the ITT tempest and claimed to know nothing about the grand jury investigation. But he also said he was certain that the ITT conflagration was ultimately what killed André.

ON SUNDAY, September 9, 1979, André—the man his partners referred to without irony as Zeus—died at a hospital in Lausanne, Switzerland, near his beloved mountain home in Crans-sur-Sierre. The *Times* reported he died after contracting pneumonia, but he had been ill with cancer since the death of Pierre David-Weill in January 1975. The *Times* also reported he left behind a fortune, estimated at between $250 million and $500 million, although when the final assessment was made some years later, André had left a calculable estate of $89.5 million. Disque Deane explained that he believed André had moved out of his estate into trust funds several hundred million dollars before he died. André had also asked him on at least one occasion to take what he assumed were priceless paintings—they were wrapped in brown paper—with him on a jet to Paris in order to remove them from his estate and the purview of the Internal Revenue Service.

After his death, forty-one of André's paintings, by such masters as Bonnard, Cézanne, Corot, Degas (his 1884 portrait of Mary Cassatt), Pissarro, Picasso (his 1905 *Boy with a White Collar*), van Gogh (his 1888 *The Bridge at Trinquetaille*), Rembrandt (his 1635 portrait of Petronella Buys), Renoir, and Toulouse-Lautrec, were auctioned off at Sotheby's on October 22, 1980. Unlike those of his partners George Blumenthal and the David-Weills, André's collection was not judged by experts to be exceptional.

"It was not so much a sale as a social event," Cary Reich wrote in his biography of André. When all the hysteria had concluded, André's collection was valued at $16.4 million, some $2 million more than the auction house had anticipated. Not included in the auction was Picasso's *Homme à la Guitare*—itself valued at $1.9 million—which he had bought with his friends David Rockefeller and David Sarnoff and which had been promised to the MOMA. "It was a typical rich man's collection," one art expert sniffed at the time. "He had the names, but he didn't have the best examples of those names. People were stunned that such second-rate pictures brought that kind of money." Concluded Reich: "The prized André Meyer collection, in short, had been a glorious triumph of mystique over substance."

Even the so-called André Meyer Galleries of European paintings, which opened at the Metropolitan Museum of Art in March 1980 on the second floor of the new Michael C. Rockefeller Wing, were a mirage.

While André had served on the Met's board (taking Bobbie Lehman's seat) from 1968 until his death and had given $2.6 million to the museum to pay for the cost of the construction of the new wing—with twenty-four thousand square feet of exhibition space—that was to house the museum's huge collection of European art from the nineteenth century and that would bear his name, none of the work exhibited there was from André's collection. At the time of André's death, Douglas Dillon, the chairman of the Met's board of trustees and a former secretary of the Treasury, said the new André Meyer Galleries would "stand as an enduring memorial to an extraordinary patron of the arts and an extraordinary man." The Met's timeless homage to André lasted fewer than a dozen years. In 1992, the museum undertook a gut renovation of the André Meyer Galleries, and in 1993 the redesigned exhibition space reopened, without the slightest mention of the former Lazard partner. "The Meyer Galleries were as crisp and as modern as the Rockefeller building itself," wrote Paul Goldberger, then the architecture critic at the *Times,* "and they were something of a disaster: with paintings hung on movable partitions set on the diagonal on a wide open floor, they looked more like an art show at the Javits Center than the centerpiece of the greatest museum in North America. Designed to last forever, they looked temporary. Everything in those galleries, from the art on the walls to the visitors trying to find their way through the aisles, seemed forlorn, confused, lost."

A few weeks after André's death, his *Times* obituary was entered into the *Congressional Record,* along with numerous paeans to his illustrious career. "Timeliness, style and charm—as well as wisdom and astuteness—were a part of all that he did," the New York senator Jacob Javits said at the time, "and powerful leaders of our country and other free world countries were beneficiaries of these attributes as well as of his sage advice. André Meyer was a very dear friend and adviser and the many hours I spent with him over the years were among the most fruitful in my life. His passing is a singular and irreplaceable loss to those who like me were personally close to him and to his wife, Bella"—who died five months later in Paris—"and also to American and international institutions of business, education, culture, and health and to the worlds of international finance and private philanthropy." At André's memorial service, held at Temple Emanu-El on Fifth Avenue in New York, Felix delivered one of the most emotional eulogies. "Rohatyn's voice cracked as he recounted how he still instinctively reached for the phone to call his mentor," Reich wrote, and then quoted Felix: "Sometimes I imagine what the conversations would be like, what he would say, but I can't be sure—it's left a terrible void. . . . Behind that stern, forbidding, and sometimes theatrical façade lay a man who was really yearning for affection. In my youth, he was an Olympian figure: Zeus hurling thunderbolts. Then he was my teacher. He taught me not only to achieve perfection, but to do it in style."

Somehow, the Teflon investment banker was able to achieve just what his mentor had taught him.

CHAPTER 7

The Sun King

"Poor Michel." It is hard to fathom these two words together. After all, Michel David-Weill, now seventy-four, unerringly courteous, gracious, and polite, described once as "the living legend of French capitalism," is one of the world's wealthiest men. Thanks in large part to the equity he inherited as a direct descendant of the founders of the Lazard banking empire, the elfin, cigar-chomping Michel had a net worth in 2000 estimated by *Forbes* to be about $2.2 billion and supposedly, through his "mysterious labyrinth of interlocking investments," controlled assets "worth five times as much." At that time, even without the multiplier effect, he was listed as the eleventh-wealthiest person in France and owned one of the world's one hundred best private art collections, with a specialty in French paintings from between the seventeenth and the nineteenth centuries. Indeed, as an expression of his love of art, at the end of 2003 he pledged $10 million for the creation of an English painting gallery at the Louvre. He also has one of the world's finest collections of mortgage-free and seductively exclusive high-end real estate—where he displays his priceless art—including a Fifth Avenue apartment facing Central Park, a Parisian mansion just off the Boulevard Saint-Germain-des-Prés, and massive country homes in Glen Cove, Long Island, and Cap d'Antibes, along the French Riviera. He also used to have a home in Jamaica but sold it. A more recent update of Michel's wealth is difficult to obtain as, somehow, he has succeeded in persuading *Forbes* to leave his name—and fortune—off the latest annual lists of the world's wealthiest. But suffice it to say, the value of his impressive set of assets, all told, is well north of $1 billion. Still, despite his extraordinary wealth, there is about Michel a certain loneliness, even wistfulness, that can evoke among his acolytes the occasional feeling of sympathy for the burden carried by the last male heir in the David-Weill family tree. But for his partners, these feelings of empathy, experienced generally over cigars and lengthy, *intime* conversations on the couches in his large Rockefeller Center office, were fleeting.

During his twenty-five years at the helm of Lazard, Michel used his Gallic wiles to massage his partners' considerable egos. He loved to refer to Lazard as the *"haute banque d'affaires vis-à-vis the world."* He once described what he meant by this: "To me it is a state of mind, not an activity. It is a firm which puts itself at a level parallel with the level at which decisions are made in enterprises. It means that you remain at the decision-making level, that you give advice at that level, that you *think* at that level and that you remain exclusively at that level." This is a rather remarkable insight into why Lazard—for all the implied arrogance—was the envy of other bankers, as no other head of a Wall Street firm described his strategy this way.

But Michel also reveled in old-fashioned autocracy. He could be unabashedly Machiavellian. He alone set the all-cash compensation levels of his partners through an annual, almost medieval, bloodletting that involved his partners' post–Labor Day pilgrimage to his corner office to plead, on bended knee, for an appropriately robust amount of succor. Michel's return to his 820 Fifth Avenue co-op—purchased from the estate of the CBS mogul Bill Paley—each September from his villa in Cap d'Antibes signaled the beginning of what at Lazard became known as the "silly season," when grown men and women prostrated themselves to kiss his ring in exchange for a few—million—pieces of gold. From October 1 to around December 20 of each year, he would see the New York partners one by one in his office to discuss their compensation and tell them what their new percentage of the profits would be for the coming year. Each partner's name would be written down on his yellow pad and his longtime assistant, Annik Percival (who had also worked for André), would arrange for the visits by calling up the partners and chiming in her *séduisant* French lilt, "He is ready for you now." Michel was always prepared for the meetings, where the individual partners would plead their case for their own performance. He always seemed to know who *really* did what each year.

What's more, Michel would engage in a sporting bit of negotiation if that was appropriate. A partner unhappy with his compensation could usually get Michel to cough up some more dough out of his own pocket—"perhaps," he would say, "a little bit more for you"—but usually not convince him to alter the given percentage, for that information was widely disseminated among the partners and therefore could be noted and debated. There was no discussing secret arrangements, obviously. On balance, though, the partners recognized that under Michel's patronage, in some years they got paid more than they probably deserved and in some years less.

Some partners, noticeably Bob Lovejoy, Lou Perlmutter, and Jon O'Herron, were the "early runners" and could usually be seen making a beeline to Michel's office soon after the yellow pad appeared around October 1. Others held back cagily, waiting for Michel to come to them. "I guess the thinking of the 'early runners,'" one partner said, "was that they thought if they got to Michel early they might get more for themselves, since the pie was finite." Naturally, in such a closed system, the role of politics and favoritism was colossal, and "side deals" between Michel and selected partners were known to be commonplace. But no one, except Michel, knew the exact specifics of the side deals. Rumors abounded, however, especially when it came to the side deal cut by Damon Mezzacappa, the partner in charge of Lazard's capital markets business. The rumor was that Michel had granted Damon a percentage of the pretax profits generated by his business, to be distributed at his own discretion. When the truth about Damon's deal became known—around 1998—his partners were flabbergasted.

Michel was generally happy to reward his partners well, often better than they could possibly be paid at other firms. He was long-term greedy and knew that if the pie kept getting bigger, he stood to make more and more money himself, as he had the largest profit percentage by far. Mostly, though, Michel was interested in his partners' ability to generate fees—as he himself had little ability or desire to do so. "Frank Zarb once told me that when he walked into Michel's office, he felt like he was being looked at as a bag of gold and was being weighed as a bag of gold," a longtime partner remembered. "It was like we were bringing bags of gold to Michel, and he would allow us to take a little bit off the bottom, and then he would put the rest in his pocket." Jean-Claude Haas, a debonair senior Lazard partner in Paris, once said, succinctly, "Objectively, Michel is the landowner and everyone else is a tenant farmer. They get rich but they're still tenant farmers." Frank Pizzitola, another longtime partner, described Michel's unique system of remuneration in this way: "This is not a partnership. It's a sole proprietorship with fancy profit sharing."

✻

Michel David-Weill, son of Pierre, grandson of David, and great-grandson of Alexander, joined Lazard Frères in 1956, at age twenty-four, after graduating from the Lycée Français in New York and the Institut des Études Politiques in Paris. Michel and Felix became Lazard partners on the same day in 1961. From that point on, like fraternal twins, they maintained an odd sort of symbiotic relationship. Their offices were right next to each other at One Rockefeller Center, although Michel's was easily twice the size of Felix's. And they spoke only French to each other. But they would never *tutoyer,* or use the familiar form of the language. They lived less than a block away from each other on Fifth Avenue, but they never socialized. Felix brought in significant amounts of business; Michel would only occasionally meet with clients. One former Lazard partner, who knows them both well, once said, "You would need many advanced degrees in psychology to figure out their relationship." Between 1965 and 1977 Michel spent very little if any time in New York, given Felix's increasingly exalted status and André's iron grip on the New York partnership.

He was not an unknown in New York, though. At the request of both his father and André, Michel had spent several years in the mid-1950s serving an apprenticeship at both Lehman Brothers and Brown Brothers Harriman, the über-WASP, two-hundred-year-old private bank still located near Wall Street. He worked in New York until 1965, when he returned to Paris to work with his father. He remembered his early years in New York with some fondness. He "did things as a helper—very ordinary things," he said once, and recalled receiving "an extreme degree of attention" from André. Only later, when Michel arrived in New York to take over, did he, too, feel André's wrath. Before that, though, when Michel was somebody André found it important to cultivate, he worked with André on one of the first hostile takeovers ever, the 1964 unsolicited tender offer for Franco Wyoming Oil, a Paris-based company with diverse interests in ranch land in the western United States, oil and gas reserves, and a valuable portfolio of oil company stocks. Michel found him charming.

André had asked the young Michel to analyze Franco Wyoming's assets. The analytical exercise wasn't for Lazard acting as agent for a client; the task was to decide whether the partners of Lazard, acting as *principals,* should buy Franco Wyoming. "If you don't see us getting back two hundred percent of what we put in, then forget it," André told Michel, according to an account of the deal in Reich's *Financier* (an earlier *Fortune* article put André's supposed hurdle rate at 150 percent). Michel's analysis determined Lazard would make 197 percent on its money, and "I had to persuade him the other three percent," he recalled. At the time, many Wall Street analysts thought Franco Wyoming was vulnerable to a takeover because its oil and gas assets alone were worth more than the current share price, with the $40 million stock portfolio as additional gravy. Management of the company was thought to be opposed to any takeover, but André determined, correctly, that their opposition would be little impediment to victory since the company's stock was owned largely by Europeans and was held in French banks. But no one ever thought the partners of a Wall Street firm would launch a hostile offer against a public company. (Even today the idea is anathema to financial buyers, such as private-equity firms and hedge funds, let alone an established Wall Street firm.) But André decided to do that very thing, enlisting in his effort—in a rare example of three-house unity—Lazard partners in Paris as well as the Pearsons, who controlled Lazard in London. On April 8, 1964, large ads appeared in the financial press announcing the tender offer. The Lazard group wanted two-thirds of the company's stock and offered $55 a share for it, or a total of $45.1 million. At the time, the shares were trading at $48.50, up from $40 a few weeks before the offer. Predictably, the Franco management, based in Delaware, fought the Lazard bid by filing a suit to block it and by sending a letter to shareholders urging them not to tender. A month later, though, Lazard had emerged with an easy victory. A group from Lazard walked into Franco Wyoming's annual meeting in Wilmington, Delaware, and voted its newly acquired shares. "The president stepped down," Michel recalled. "And one of us walked up to the podium. It was the only *physical* takeover I've ever seen." In the end, Lazard decided to liquidate the company, and the partners pocketed a fortune, estimated at $25 million, "close to three times what we put in," Michel said. But as Cary Reich pointed out in *Financier,* "The real significance of the Franco Wyoming deal wasn't the huge capital gain Lazard reaped. It was that an eminent group of investors, led by one of the world's most prestigious investment banks, had mounted a tender offer against the target company's wishes, had weathered the storm and had won. The hostile takeover had, in a sense, finally come out of the closet."

❧

By the mid-1970s, the ongoing ITT-Hartford scandals, combined with André's health problems and Felix's refusal to manage the firm, created a serious leadership vacuum at Lazard. The firm was starting to drift and lose focus. The day after Christmas 1974, André began to seriously address the issue for the first time. In a "Memorandum to Partners," he wrote, "After 35 years of management of Lazard Frères & Co., New York, and because of the irregular condition of my health, I have decided, effective the first of the year, to reduce substantially my activities and my responsibilities for the day to day operations of the firm. I will continue as a general partner, having the same role as in the present Partnership Articles."

With this memo, Meyer set off a succession battle at Lazard that raged for the next thirty years. Never again, despite many high-profile attempts, would authority and control at Lazard be vested so clearly in one man as it had been during Meyer's long reign at the *haute banque d'affaires.* He had been both chief deal maker and chief administrator. It is a failure of imagination that still haunts Lazard. No doubt, though, André thought he had a workable solution when he appointed a new management committee, with Felix and Howard Kniffin as its co-chairmen. Kniffin joined Lazard in 1946 and became a partner in 1952, nine years before Felix and Michel. There were six other partners at that time. Per André's edict, the nine-member management committee, "composed of men in whom I have the greatest confidence"—including Disque Deane, Patrick Gerschel, Tom Mullarkey, and Frank Pizzitola—was to be "responsible for the co-ordination of all firm activities and for daily conduct of its business" and was to meet every day at 8:45 a.m.

Meyer also spelled out, briefly, an ownership arrangement for Lazard, a yoke that existed until 2005. "My family and I, together with the David-Weill family have arranged for establishing and maintaining the stability of a fixed capital of $17,500,000, of which our two families will own roughly 75%," he wrote. "We will all be signing new Partnership Articles before January 1 which will implement the Management Committee and establish the fixed capital." As of that date, André had $3.187 million of capital in the firm. Pierre David-Weill had $3.215 million. Felix and Kniffin each had $700,000.

As the all-powerful "partners under section 4.1" of the partnership agreement, André and Pierre David-Weill set the all-important partnership percentages. Before he cut his stake back, André had 13.236 percent of the net profit in 1974, which translated into almost $1.1 million in compensation for him that year, given that New York made $8.1 million in net income before taxes. Pierre David-Weill took just over $750,000 that same year from the New York partnership. Felix, who had the second-largest percentage as of 1974, at 10.796 percent, took home $875,000.

Indeed, given the contents of section 4.1, it is understandable that Pierre David-Weill was the *only* man André referred to as *his* partner. On the occasions when Pierre came to New York from Paris, André would relinquish his desk to him and sit in a seat on the side. "So as to show who was in charge," one former partner recalled. This partner also remembered that Pierre was known around the firm—but never to his face—as "Pinky" because of his red hair and "flushed complexion." (In his younger days, Michel, too, had red hair.) In the 1920s, while still a young man, Pierre collected the finest examples of Art Deco—the "modern art" of the day—and filled his Paris apartment on Avenue Émile-Accolas with avant-garde works by La Fresnaye, Matisse, Picasso, and Balthus. According to one observer, Pierre's apartment had "become a veritable private museum" of Art Deco. He commissioned the painter André Masson to come to his apartment to paint him two huge surrealistic murals, which were displayed in his dining room. He also hung in the apartment two absolutely remarkable surrealistic tapestries by Jean Lurçat. Pierre also commissioned the sculptor Alberto Giacometti to create radiator covers for his apartment.

Robert Ellsworth once said that Patrick Gerschel, André's grandson, told him, "Pierre was so smart that he was smart enough to hire André Meyer and trust him." Michel believes his father never received enough credit for reviving both the Paris partnership and his own fortune after World War II. "My father had, in my opinion, an exceptionally hard life, but he was exceptionally courageous," Michel explained.

> But because if you think about it, there is a fellow who at the age of thirty-two has no money left, and has to fight. And has to fight to get the firm back on track. At age forty, the firm is taken from him, and the Germans come in, and he has to fight to liquidate the firm decently so that nobody gets hurt. At age forty-two, he arrives back in the U.S., which he had never lived in but had visited plenty of times, and has to fight with Washington because of the Trading with the Enemy Act because of the way the liquidation involved money coming from elsewhere. Then he has to deal with André Meyer, which was not that easy. Then in 1945, he has to rebuild from scratch Lazard Frères Paris. From scratch. There was nothing. There was not an office. There was not an employee. Not an easy life.

The partnership economics made clear, though, that after André reduced his stake to 7.236 percent, as promised, this was now Felix's firm—at least from a day-to-day perspective—indicating definitively that the entire ITT-Hartford fiasco had little effect, if any, on the trajectory of his career. Felix retained his partnership share of 10.796 percent, so he would take home $1.1 million in 1975 (the firm made $10.2 million that year). Pierre David-Weill took the next-largest share at 9.431 percent, while André, who had the largest share in 1974, reduced his share, per his memorandum, in 1975 to 7.236 percent.

Within two weeks of André's memo, fate intervened, and Pierre David-Weill died unexpectedly. At Pierre's funeral, Disque Deane, by then a very wealthy man, was said to have made change in the collection plate. (Deane denied this.) "He was an immortal," Patrick Gerschel said, with some sarcasm, about Pierre. "So everyone at the funeral, which was in a big church in Paris, was in their finest uniform. But his mistress wasn't allowed to come. She had to send a wreath." Pierre David-Weill was buried in the Montparnasse Cemetery, in Paris, in the same catacomb as his father, grandfather, and brother François, who died tragically in 1934, at age twenty-seven, after the plane he was piloting crashed on landing at Orly Airport in Paris. After his father's death, Michel took over the running of the Paris partnership, but he remained some distance removed from New York, as André's intimidating influence was still strong, despite his Christmas memo. When the partnership agreement was amended next, six months later, to account for the hiring of two new partners and the retirement of one other, Felix had his percentage lowered slightly to 10.671 percent, and Pierre David-Weill's stake had been shifted, per the partnership agreement, into the David-Weill family account under "Lazard Groupement," which now received 18.735 percent of the firm's profits.

But this new arrangement lasted barely a year, as Felix continued to have little interest in managing the firm. Around Thanksgiving 1975, with Felix increasingly consumed with solving New York's fiscal crisis and André debilitated by the pancreatic cancer that had been diagnosed in January—indeed, after an immediate operation, doctors gave André forty-eight hours to live, which he characteristically defied, but he had slowly been reduced to wearing a bathrobe and slippers around the Carlyle while awaiting his daily toast and tea—Lazard Frères in New York turned to an outsider, Donald Cook, then sixty-seven, to be the firm's "managing partner," effective March 1, 1976. Cook had been a close friend of André's, as well as chairman of the SEC under President Harry S Truman and the CEO of American Electric Power for fourteen years in the 1960s and 1970s. In the quaint argot of a simpler era on Wall Street, a *Times* article explained that André had been looking for "an industrial man." Cook was given a 4 percent profit share; Felix's share was *increased* to 11.5 percent (in 1976, Felix was paid $1.43 million; he took no compensation as head of MAC); and André's was decreased again, to 6.56275 percent. "I have a certain degree of influence but I am not the boss," André told the *New York Times*. "The new boss is Mr. Cook. The managing partner of the firm is Don Cook."

In the same article, which mentioned the ITT-Hartford fiasco only in passing, André lavished praise on Felix yet again. "Mr. Rohatyn is a very important man," he said. "He is absolutely unique. He could have been boss years ago if he had wanted it, but he wasn't keen for the responsibility." Indeed, the article touted Felix as a potential New York City mayoral candidate or for an important position in the Carter administration. Felix denied an interest in politics and said he didn't want to move his family to Washington "at this stage in my life."

In an article five months earlier that attempted to predict who might end up in a Carter cabinet, even though it was still some two months before the election, Felix was of course mentioned as a potential for the Treasury post. He had been part of a gathering at the "21" Club in Carter's honor hosted by a group of New York businessmen in angling mode. He said, though, going to the nation's capital was "not something I yearn for." In another *Times* article, in March 1976, this one a fawning profile in the Sunday magazine titled "The Wizard of Lazard," he also denied interest in going to Washington. But it was more in the nature of—in keeping with the Nixonian shadow still looming in national politics—a nondenial denial. "Suppose I was appointed Secretary of the Treasury," he mused. "Can you see me driving up to the gates in my old BMW?" The *Times,* though, made clear Felix's associates "say" that the Treasury position would be "welcomed."

The *Times* profile thought it curious that André would have selected Cook over Felix to run Lazard, but as usual, Felix proclaimed no interest whatsoever in running the firm. "I run my side of the business—corporate finance—with enormous freedom and that's all I want to do. That's enough." He confirmed Meyer's assertion that he could have run Lazard at any time had he wanted to. "What I do for this firm," he said, "I do it in my head. I can do it from here. I can do it from Morgan Stanley, or from my apartment at the Alrae. So if I didn't like this decision, I could leave. But it was something Mr. Meyer and I agreed to between ourselves."

Unfazed by the internal politics or Lazard's idiosyncratic history, Cook set about, at his own peril, actually trying to *manage* the firm. On July 2, 1976, he reiterated the existence of the three-person management committee with himself as chairman and Felix and Kniffin as the other two members. Mullarkey was an ex officio member. Cook promised a further "reorganization" of the firm's "structure" in "due course," with "priority consideration" to be given to a "New Business Department." On August 19, six weeks later, Cook made good on his promised reorganization by announcing, in a seven-page, double-spaced memo, that the "New Business Department" would be reorganized and expanded to form the "Corporate Finance Department." Cook explained the title "New

Business Department" was actually a "misnomer" since new business development occurred not just in M&A but across various of the firm's products. "Felix Rohatyn will, of course, continue as Partner in Charge and Frank Pizzitola will serve as Deputy Partner in Charge of the reorganized and expanded Department," Cook wrote.

But Cook also recognized the reality that Felix had "substantial public service demands" on his time and would be out of the office frequently, requiring "Cook [to] spend a large part of his time in the overall coordination of the activities of the Corporate Finance Department." Cook discerned that certain Lazard partners were "business getters," chief among them Felix, while others were "business processors," such as Mel Heineman. The failure to formally recognize these distinctions between the Lazard bankers, Cook suggested, resulted in a number of "readily apparent" disadvantages, including "an inadequate flow of new business into the firm," "an uneconomic utilization of the talents of the partners," and "difficulty in organizing a suitable program for the development of new business opportunities." So Cook's reorganization formalized these distinctions between the banking partners and grouped them into "business getters" and "business processors." In his conclusion Cook wrote, "It is believed that the above described reorganization and expansion of the 'New Business Department' to create the 'Corporate Finance Department' should result in making it possible to achieve a significant increase in the net income of the firm. This reason alone suggests that the fullest measure of cooperation should be given by each and every member of the Department to achieve the desired result. Of course there are other reasons as well for expecting that cooperation. That cooperation is earnestly requested." His huge, sprawling signature ended the memorandum.

Predictably, Cook was a disaster, principally because the unruly bunch of "jungle warriors" had no interest in being managed *at all*. And of course, because André still breathed. Cook attempted to run Lazard "like a business," one former partner explained years later. He organized meetings that nobody attended and asked partners to tell him what they did all day long. They ignored him. "And it went from bad to worse," Patrick Gerschel said. "And it got more and more peculiar. He had these decoration ideas. And so the whole place started getting decorated in pinks and mauves, with his wife. And I thought, 'Okay . . .' " Then one day a sign appeared on Cook's office door—"Trespassers will be shot, by order of Donald Cook." In the end, "some of the other partners simply cut his balls off," said someone who worked with Cook. "He fizzled from day one." Said another, Cook "thoroughly alienated people." As Felix suspected, chances were good that any effort at all by anybody to manage

Lazard would have alienated people. Cook just happened to be the guy who tried.

Seven months after Cook's hiring, in September 1976, André and Michel tried to calm the growing unrest in the firm with a poignant, confidential, five-page typewritten memorandum sent to, simply, "The Partners" and signed by both men in their own hand. The memo began:

> At the suggestion of Donald Cook, this memorandum was prepared during his visit to Switzerland to deal with some aspects of the organizational structure and the distribution of responsibility and authority among the partners of the firm. . . . We have been fortunate in adding Don Cook to the team, as a partner in the firm and he has been with us for almost four months. During this time, he has had an opportunity to become acquainted with the partners, the firm's business, and the means by which the firm's business is handled. In addition, he finally took a much needed vacation and has now returned, both rested and largely free from his nagging problem of laryngitis. His full availability is of considerable help to us in completing our overall plans for the management of the firm for the foreseeable future.

André and Michel then laid out the second stab at a management committee to run the firm's "day to day operations," which consisted of Cook, Felix—when he was around—Howard Kniffin, who by now was ill with emphysema and on doctor's orders to slow down, and Mullarkey, the firm's general counsel, as an ex officio member. Patrick Gerschel was appointed the secretary of the management committee. The committee was to meet at 8:45 a.m. each business day, just like the first one. Cook was named chairman and was "known as the Managing Partner." But in a foreshadowing of the future, André and Michel made clear in the memo they remained in charge.

They concluded the September directive with their belief that their partners would do as they instructed. Pointedly missing from Cook's authority was the ability to set partner percentages. The memo was both the beginning of the end of Cook and the first evidence of the inevitable coronation of Michel as the Lazard patriarch. Four days after this memorandum landed on partners' desks, Cook invited all partners to an afternoon meeting in the large conference room on the thirty-second floor of One Rockefeller Plaza. "The meeting is important and we would appreciate it if you would make an effort to be there." Almost no one showed up.

Lazard was obviously suffering one of its periodic generational crises, which, in a firm so utterly dependent on the machinations and idiosyncrasies of its Great Men, are to be expected. Through the sheer force of his personality, will, and searing intelligence, André had resurrected Lazard from irrelevance and made it one of the most important firms on Wall Street. This was not a firm, like Goldman Sachs, Morgan Stanley, or Merrill Lynch, that worshipped at the altars of a unifying, all-powerful corporate culture, where professional management deployed well-schooled armies and abundant capital to solve clients' problems. Lazard had nothing to sell but the power of its exceptional people and their ideas. With André quite ill and the "flamboyant" Felix largely focused on the problems of New York City, Lazard was facing a Job-like test.

A January 1977 *Times* article, "End of an Era at Lazard," exposed the festering sore by focusing the spotlight squarely on the nagging question of who, if anyone, could succeed André. His debilitating illness (the details about which he coyly tried to sidestep, calling it "strictly confidential, very painful and not something you brag about") had kept him away from the office he had once ruled with an iron fist for going on two years. Felix wouldn't consider it. Kniffin was ill. Although André had recruited Cook to run the firm, the *Times* article served to undermine his authority, as had the September memo from André and Michel. The story also confirmed that Michel was the only potential leader of Lazard with the legitimacy that ownership and bloodlines bestow. Cook had no legitimacy because he had no ownership and no power of the purse, the true Wall Street currency. André "didn't do what an institution builder has to do, which was to put in place a plan for pulling out," one Lazard observer said. "He didn't do it but kept talking about doing it, which was even *worse.*" Much the same thing would be said over time about Michel.

The reasons Cook's efforts flopped were made evident by his comments to the *Times*. Cook explained that the old Lazard management style—and here he drew a picture of a hub and spokes for the reporter—was a wheel with Meyer at the center. "He was obviously the dominant figure but the wheel-and-hub organization no longer will produce the best results for the firm." In the Cook regime—and here he drew another diagram—Lazard would be run in a pyramid structure, with a board of directors at the top, a CEO beneath the board, and executives reporting to the CEO, a "more classic" corporate structure, he explained: "I'm the resident bureaucrat; what I can do for this firm is be the architect of the transitional period."

Clearly Cook had failed—really failed—to understand the Lazard ethos. Felix told the *Times* that he agreed the firm was in a transitional period, but he knew better than to concur that Cook's management approach would work for Lazard. "When you no longer have a Mr. Meyer," he said, "you have to change your method of operation—and we have. Mr. Cook is the managing partner and he runs the firm but no one of us will make a policy decision without conferring with the other. . . . We act as partners, not as servants." Cook's influence waned steadily from the moment the article appeared. His economic stake, though, remained at 4 percent, while Felix's fell to 11 percent. "There was a sense of drifting here," one Lazard partner observed at the time. "It was a discouraging period."

Competitors began to notice. "We saw them drifting downward and becoming uncompetitive," the unnamed head of another investment banking firm told *Institutional Investor* at the time. "They were losing clients and not leaving a good impression on the clients they had. André was elderly, sick, but still not willing to turn over the reins completely." Michel would later say of that rudderless time, "The risk was not of losing business. It was of losing people. That we were losing clients was unimportant, curiously enough. We were losing people. That was serious. . . . But the people were getting discouraged. Morale was bad. The eternal question was 'What is the future in this place? Should I stay? Should I not stay?' People are extraordinarily easily disquieted, and extraordinarily easily quieted."

Behind the scenes that year, somewhere between the dimly lit corridors of Lazard's Paris office on the Boulevard Haussmann and André's Swiss chalet, a fierce debate was once again raging about the future of the New York partnership. Unlike the Rothschilds, Lazard had no rule against a non–family member running the firm. André's fifty-one-year tenure, including thirty-four years at the helm, after having been among the most respected foreign currency traders in France, was clear evidence that the David-Weills didn't have the same concerns as the Rothschilds about looking outside the family for leaders. But it was obvious to André and to Michel—and to all the other partners at the firm, too—that Cook was not the answer. It was equally obvious that André could no longer be expected to run New York—not to suggest he wasn't still very much active in the firm from his outposts at the Carlyle and in Crans-sur-Sierre.

Felix should run the firm, they decided. He was an obvious choice. He was the preeminent investment banker of his generation. He knew how "to bring business." He was exceedingly well known. He spoke fluent French, German, and English. He understood both the American and the European cultures. In short, a Great Man. Just what the firm needed.

But Felix was heavily involved with solving the New York City financial crisis. "He was politicking," according to Patrick Gerschel. And there was the persistent, nagging matter of Felix being steadfast in his refusal to accept the job. Publicly, he had always hidden behind events of the day. He couldn't run the firm, because he was solving the Wall Street back-office crisis, or was too busy being tarred by the ITT scandals, or was swamped by his commitment to MAC. Or he was doing deals. He once again told André to forget it. "I told him it wouldn't be good for him and it wouldn't be good for me," Felix told *Newsweek* in 1981. "It was a very subtle psychological situation."

There is no doubt Lazard would be a different firm today had Felix agreed to run it. He strongly believed in André's dictum that small is beautiful. He was frugal, he was discreet, and he could be ruthless. Felix was far more risk averse than André and shunned the principal investments that André, for a time, reveled in. Felix is said to favor government bonds for his personal investments and pointed out that he lives far less ostentatiously than his peers, which is probably true as a relative matter, despite his Fifth Avenue apartment, his Southampton spread, and his Wyoming ranch. Such fiscal conservatism paid off for Lazard at least once, in the early 1970s, when other firms were struggling financially—which Felix saw firsthand as head of the Crisis Committee of the New York Stock Exchange. "We were riding through the early Seventies on a mountain of treasury bills," Mullarkey once said.

Many of Felix's former partners could never figure out, though, why he never accepted his mandate to run the firm. Some understood his reluctance, since the task was a thankless one and he was so gifted at making them rich by bringing in so much business. Others, less charitably, pinned his refusal on selfishness. "Felix only cares about Felix" is the sum and substance of this argument. It wasn't selfishness, Felix countered, but realpolitik. "The Lazard I knew, you couldn't run it and do business at the same time," he explained. "And I would rather do business. And so it was that simple. Also, I knew that as long as André was really halfway healthy, the moment I accepted to run the business, I would become his number one enemy. And so there was, from that point, it was not a winner."

WITH FELIX REFUSING to take the job, there was only one person who could—Michel. "The firm was very lucky I existed," Michel would jokingly say several years later. Maybe, in truth, he was the only person with all of the required legitimacy, authority, and DNA. And André insisted upon it. "André was just really in very bad shape," Felix said. "I didn't want to do it. And Michel clearly was the only candidate, and actually was the right candidate." Perhaps that was Felix's greatest insight. He recognized the inherent danger for him in attempting to run a firm where the majority owners—Michel and André—were intensely hands-on and opinionated. Perhaps he had been cognizant of what happened to the dignified Frank Altschul, who like Felix had no ownership in the firm. Felix had the legitimacy and the authority for the post but not the bloodline. With Michel running Paris and so clearly focused on his birthright—"I was born to great opportunity and perhaps a little too much responsibility," he once said—Felix simply capitulated to the inevitable, however inconvenient it proved to be for Michel, who would now have to be a bona fide globe-trotter. Thanks to the Concorde, the plan was for Michel to spend three weeks each month in New York and one week (and two weekends) in Paris. Indeed, he was such an inveterate frequent flyer of the Concorde that he always had reserved for him both seats in the first row of the cramped jet, one seat for him and the other for his slim Louis Vuitton briefcase. To accommodate his new schedule, Michel bought an apartment at 810 Fifth Avenue, where Nelson Rockefeller had lived. (A few years later he moved next door, to 820 Fifth.)

The partnership agreement was rewritten to account for Michel's important new role in New York. Michel's capital account showed him to have just over $3.5 million in the firm, an amount previously shown under the Lazard Groupement account representing the stake in New York held by the French families. Most important, of course, Michel joined André, as of September 1, 1977, as one of the "partners under section 4.1," which, in effect, gave him absolute authority over the firm. Michel's arrival in New York as a general partner signaled the end of Cook's role as the interim leader. He hung on until the early 1980s, but his partnership shares slipped continuously, from 3.5 percent in January 1978 to 2.5 percent in September 1978 to 1 percent in 1979 and thereafter. Cook was another failed experiment. Meanwhile, Felix's stake was reduced—at his suggestion—to 8 percent from 11 percent, in January 1978, and again, to 6 percent, in September 1978, where it stayed for some time. Upon his arrival in New York, Michel picked up the bulk of his father's stake in the New York firm, at 9.36031 percent, just below the 9.431 percent his father had. Michel and André, "acting jointly," were the partners under section 4.1 and therefore set partner compensation.

Michel assumed control of the New York office in September 1977 without much fanfare. "I had the feeling, and Mr. André Meyer had the feeling, that the time had come," Michel said. He was forty-four years old.

On his first day, André told him, "Too bad, you have come too late. And I said, Why? He said, Because the great age of investment banking is over."

The world received the news of Michel's ascendancy from *Fortune* magazine, in a carefully scripted article, "Passing the Baton at Lazard Frères," in the November 1977 issue. Michel was careful to make clear that he intended to run the firm just as André had: low overhead, M&A-focused, stay small.

Lazard still had about 250 employees, just as it did ten years earlier, with about thirty-two partners. At the same time, other firms, such as Goldman Sachs and Morgan Stanley, were beginning to grow their workforces; Morgan Stanley, which had been Lazard's size, was now more than a thousand people. But Lazard's small size kept the firm obscenely profitable, which redounded to the partners' benefit. In 1971, for instance, New York made $13.1 million of net income before taxes, a little bit more than London and four times as much as Paris. By 1977, Lazard in New York made $15.4 million. "It's the biggest racket on Wall Street," Disque Deane told *Fortune*.

In the *Fortune* piece, Felix made clear he remained dedicated to helping New York City. "I do believe I've made a difference in New York," he said. "And to me the greatest sin one can commit is not to participate where one can help." But another partner confessed to the magazine that "André can't control Felix" anymore. Indeed André had asked Felix to reduce his time at MAC and return his focus to Lazard. "Because I love him, and think he is terribly smart, I've tried to explain," Felix said of André. "I've told him that everyone has some indulgence. Some people indulge in beautiful women. . . . MAC is my indulgence, my *péché mignon*." André's reported response: "Get it out of your system."

Naturally, there was intense speculation inside the firm about how Michel would run it. Some believed that, compared to André anyway, Michel was "lovely," "nice," and "courteous," and hoped that the manic intensity of the firm would be curtailed. Speculated Disque Deane: "The partners' blood pressure will go down, there will be fewer ulcers and maybe some people will take a day or two of vacation." The latter thought, of course, was a reference to the fact that André rarely took vacations—even when he was in Switzerland, he was always working—and didn't like his partners to take them, either. Mullarkey used to tell his wife to tell André, when he called Mullarkey on Sunday mornings, that her husband had gone to church, simply to avoid the senior partner's regular calls. That was but one of many legendary stories about the lengths André would go to in order to thwart his partners' vacation plans. But the

Fortune article also tipped the partners to the fact that wholesale cuts in the partnership ranks were coming, an exceedingly rare occurrence for Lazard, where most partners considered their position a tenured one.

Michel, however, made clear that he viewed the "optimum number" of partners to be twelve, since "it's possible to get that number around a conference table"—not that the Lazard partners had ever met to decide anything of substance about running the firm before (or very often since). The article suggested that the new, smaller group of partners would form the basis of an "inner circle" of leaders who would begin to resurrect the firm. Michel also indicated a willingness to allow Lazard partners to once again make private-equity investments, a throwback to Lazard's pioneering days of the 1950s and 1960s. André had pulled back from this activity in the 1970s because corporate merger activity made the cost of such deals for financial buyers prohibitively expensive and because principal investing required a time horizon that André's illness began to rob him of. Michel believed the private-equity angle would help Lazard attract new bankers. His mantra was simply that a few Great Men could transform the franchise. According to *Fortune*: "The appealing atmosphere of a small organization coupled with the chance to build wealth, he reasons, could bring Lazard the brains that might otherwise be attracted to its larger, more visible competitors."

THERE WAS ONLY one subject where the *Fortune* article went off the rails: Was there to be a meaningful role for Patrick Gerschel, André's grandson? Although Michel had literally just taken over, there remained speculation about who would succeed *him*. As Michel had four daughters, none of whom was interested in working at Lazard, the inevitable focus fell on Gerschel. The perspicacious and pugnacious Gerschel became, in 1971, at all of twenty-five years old, one of the youngest partners in the history of the firm. By 1977, Gerschel had become one of only three New York partners who was also a partner in Paris. The other two were André and Michel (although Michel kicked Gerschel out of the Paris partnership soon after he took over after Pierre's death in 1975). His grandfather was referred to as Zeus, making Gerschel "Son of God" and creating much resentment of him among the other partners.

In the late 1960s, Gerschel had graduated from Cornell and had moved to Paris to become an assistant bureau manager for NBC News. He knew nothing about television journalism, but his grandfather was, of course, intimate friends with David Sarnoff, the man who controlled RCA, NBC's parent company at the time. After a couple of years in Paris, André asked his newly married grandson to join Lazard in New York, in October 1969—just as the ITT-Hartford deal was about to close. Gerschel had grown up in the corridors of Lazard at 44 Wall Street, under his grandfather's tutelage, since the age of five. He worked summers at Lazard all through college. Unlike André's son Philippe, who declined his father's persistent efforts to have him join Lazard and instead became a scientist, Gerschel had Lazard in his DNA. André hired him to work full-time in the research department writing due diligence reports on companies in the underwriting queue. Although he considered it a "rather menial" job usually "done by a lady in the syndicate department," Patrick loved it. He was paid $22,000 a year, then the lowest level of compensation for a Lazard professional. He felt like he was thrown into the pool to see if he would sink or swim. He received no special attention from his grandfather and indeed felt like he was starting at the very bottom. "You know a clerk is a clerk," he said.

Soon, he was told to move over to the corporate finance department—really M&A—to work in Felix's group. His pay was increased to $35,000 per year. "It was a very curious kind of place," he said. "You would be told to write a report, which you wrote, and you never knew whether it meant anything or not. In fact, there were times I would write reports over a week and spend all night, every night for a week, getting a report done, hand it in to Felix, and he'd throw it in the trash." Felix would ask him to write a memo about, say, Gulf & Western, then an important conglomerate, and then change his mind about the need for it. "People who write memos drive Chevrolets," Felix told him. But somehow, Gerschel found a way to feel okay about Felix's mercurial behavior. "At least you got your day," he said. "The worst thing would be if he hadn't asked you."

To André's grandson, Lazard at that time was somewhere between Kafka's *The Trial* and the Fellini movie *Amarcord,* with George C. Scott's performance in *The Hospital* thrown in for good measure. "This was cuckoo land with very, very, very smart, able people who knew something," he said. "There are no people like that on Wall Street today, maybe Bob Rubin." Gerschel rose quickly through the ranks of the firm, with André's blessing, having one of the highest percentages—at 4.455 percent—of the firm's profits and one of the largest capital accounts, at $1.4 million, almost three times that of Felix. "I owed and he knew I owed," Gerschel said of his relationship with André. François Voss, the longtime French partner and Gerschel's relative, believed that Gerschel simply did not have the requisite personality to one day be the senior partner of Lazard. "To be number one at Lazard, you have to—how can I say?—show to the world that you deserve it by the way you are presenting yourself," he said. "It's a very important job."

Many at Lazard believed that Gerschel's presence was André's not-so-subtle effort to keep control of Lazard in the Meyer family. The first inkling of trouble, in this regard, was young Patrick's elevation to a full partner, nearly immediately upon joining the firm. "It was a shocking breach of investment-banking etiquette," Meyer's biographer wrote in *Financier.* Gerschel was said to be brusque, arrogant, and condescending toward the other partners. "At first, Patrick was just a nuisance," recalled one former Lazard banker, "but then he became a pain in the neck. André kept pushing him into the middle of conversations with business people about their problems, and Patrick wasn't capable of handling it. The clients rejected the premise that Patrick was a proper lead man for their business. He lost us at least two clients that I'm familiar with." Disque Deane, no friend of Gerschel's, said André's grandson badly overstepped his perceived authority. "Patrick was trying to become the senior partner of the firm, and Felix did not want to work for Patrick," he said, adding diplomatically: "Patrick is a different type of person." As the secretary to the management committee, Gerschel found that job required him to report to Cook what various partners were working on, including Felix, "since he never talked to Cook in his life. So guess what kind of position that put me in? And I wasn't smart enough to know it. I should have made a beeline for the door right then."

In the 1977 *Fortune* article, Gerschel compounded his problems with Felix by being quoted saying he hoped Lazard would attract more "avaricious" people, people more like D. K. Ludwig, the secretive billionaire industrialist known as the "father of the supertanker," and less like Felix, who "seems to put fame above fortune." "Most Lazard partners would rather be like Felix Rohatyn than D. K. Ludwig," he lamented. With uncharacteristic understatement, Gerschel confided that his relationship with Felix "wasn't very good" after the article came out. Felix said of the Ludwig comparison, "I thought that was an asinine remark and I still do. If I'm setting an example, I think I'm egotistical enough to believe I'm not that bad an example. And I think people who spend some of their time not just grubbing around doing business are better people. And ultimately they become better businessmen than rich young kids who think the world is nothing but money." But Gerschel also believed that the "end" for him "came long before that. The end came the day I entered." As proof, he pointed to the contrast between his own treatment at Lazard and Michel's. "André Meyer's view of life is that he would put my foot in the stirrup, but I had to climb on the horse," he said. "David and Pierre believed that Michel should be put on the horse." He continued: "There are two things that work in an investment bank, ability and legitimacy, all right? Felix believes and believed that I was incompetent. That destroyed ability. And when André Meyer refused to put me in the saddle, that destroyed legitimacy. Game over. *'Bien vaincre,'* as they say in French."

Soon after Michel arrived in New York, Felix demoted Gerschel to a limited partner, with André's blessing. But André remained hopeful, Gerschel said later, that somehow his grandson would be restored to his full partnership over time. "He loved that firm more than he loved many things, including his family," Gerschel said. "But he wanted his family taken care of." He said he had a "very unique altercation" with Felix beyond what was said in the *Fortune* article but would not elaborate because "it truly doesn't help me very much." For his part, Felix said that Gerschel harbored the "total" fantasy that he could run Lazard. "He was just a young man who thought his family positions entitled him to authority in the firm," Felix said. "And he got into difficulties with some of the people, and finally I think André had to let him go." So it was André, not Felix. In any event, Gerschel received a letter from DeForest Billyou, the former ITT lawyer then at Paul, Weiss, informing him what it meant to be a limited partner at Lazard.

He was no longer permitted to step foot on the partners' floor. He was no longer permitted to attend partners' meetings. He was no longer able to use Lazard stationery. "I was a special case," Gerschel said. "To get rid of the Meyer influence that had beaten the shit out of all these characters for years. I was between a rock and a hard place. And, man, I should have been smart enough, tough enough and smart enough." He moved down to an office on the thirty-first floor of One Rock and put up some green curtains. Then Felix had the idea that Gerschel should open a Lazard office in Texas. Then André had the idea he could open an office in San Francisco. "I said, 'Don't be so silly,' " Gerschel recalled. "Ain't going to San Francisco. I ain't going to Texas. I may go somewhere else to get a job . . . because I knew it was over." He talked to Wertheim, a small investment bank, about going there. He thought about selling used equipment from Alaska to the Philippines and Iran. He then learned how to work on the floor of the American Stock Exchange, with a defrocked priest. "That was sorta fun," he said. He did a quick deal with the Bass brothers in Texas and made some money. Finally, he landed on the idea of working with Jerry Speyer to recapitalize the Tishman Company into something called Tishman Speyer, now one of the largest real estate developers in New York and the owner of Rockefeller Center. He turned to André to help accomplish the deal, and quickly Michel was brought in with a few other Lazard partners as well. They all made money.

Gerschel became a limited partner on January 1, 1978. He still received his partnership points, which remained fairly steady at a sizable 4.45 percent, and he still had his capital account. A little more than four years later, Michel fired him from even that tiny role. In a one-paragraph letter, signed by Michel but not on Lazard letterhead, Michel invoked his power under section 3.2 of the Lazard Frères & Co. partnership agreement, which clearly stated: "If in the sole and unreviewable determination of the Partner under section 4.1"—Michel—"it shall be in the best interest of the Partnership and of the remaining partners desiring to continue the firm for any general or limited partner, other than André Meyer, to retire, he may be required to retire upon the request of the Partner under section 4.1 as of any future date which he may determine." Gerschel keeps a framed copy of the letter on his desk at Gerschel & Co., his private investment firm on Madison Avenue. He had to sue Lazard to get his capital out, since Michel didn't want to give it to him.

THE IMPLEMENTATION OF Michel's vision for Lazard began in January 1978 with the rewritten partnership agreement. Michel's new percentage share rocketed to 19.05387 percent, and he alone became the all-important partner under section 4.1 of the firm's new partnership agreement. Michel agreed, though, that "decisions" made pursuant to the agreement "shall be made after consultation with André Meyer," but with Meyer ailing steadily, Michel now controlled the purse strings, alone. Furthermore, the new agreement announced that André, Patrick Gerschel, Disque Deane, and Howard Kniffin were "retiring" as "general partners" to become "limited partners." Joining them as limited partners were Ned Herzog, Stanley Osborne, and Fred Wilson. Also shoved off to sea as limited partners were Patrick Gerschel's siblings, Laurent and Marianne Gerschel. Patrick's brother and sister had never been involved in the business but had each received some 2.7255 percent of the firm's profits in 1976. The new partnership agreement spelled out for the first time that all of André's family interests taken together had to equal 67.301 percent of Michel's family interests taken together. So, in 1977, all of the Meyer family stake totaled some 17.3352 percent of the profits, making the David-Weill stake equal to some 25.7552 percent of the profits. In other words, together the two families were taking out more than 43 percent of the profits in New York—a fact that over time would be a serious drain on the firm, especially since, with André gone, none of these beneficiaries, including Michel, were bringing in much business, if any, to the firm.

Many of the partner profit percentages were shifted about as well, without any discernible pattern. The ailing Kniffin's stake was reduced to 1 percent from 4.5 percent and Felix's take was reduced to 8 percent from 11 percent. Donald Petrie, one of the key figures in the success of Avis, returned to the firm as a partner, with a 2.5 percent stake.

Michel had taken the first steps in reducing the size of the firm in keeping with his statements to *Fortune*. And his concern was justified by the deteriorating financial performance of the New York partnership. Yes, Lazard in New York had made $13.1 million in 1971, 44 percent of the three houses' net income of almost $30 million. But that number had fallen steadily, reaching a mere $8.1 million in 1974—the "Dark Ages" on Wall Street, according to Felix—before increasing again in the mid-1970s, to $15.4 million in 1977. In 1978, though, net income fell again, dramatically, to $11.9 million in New York, well below the profitability of London, which was $16.8 million. Even the much smaller Paris house was no longer far behind New York, earning $6.7 million in 1978.

Michel determined he had to fix New York—and fix it he did. "In New York, if you had asked people around Wall Street if I could have been successful, I think the answer would have been no," he said in 1981. "They would have told you three years ago that the idea of sending a young Frenchman, nice, wealthy, relatively well educated, into a jungle like Wall Street, and especially into a jungle like Lazard Frères that was full of talented but very difficult personalities, was ludicrous." In 1988, Michel said of his first days in New York: "At that time and even seen retrospectively, the odds seemed to be against me. But I never had doubts. Difficulties, yes. Doubts, no."

Still, by July 1978, Michel was feeling sufficiently well about his growing importance at the firm that he decided to have a coming-out party of sorts for the French business community in the pages of *Le Nouvel Économiste,* a respected business journal. There, for all his wealthy friends to see—and for one of the first and last times—was, on the cover, a half-smiling forty-five-year-old Michel, resplendent in an expensive gray three-piece suit, vest buttoned tightly, save for the requisite one at the bottom. His jet-black hair (where had his red hair disappeared to?), unparted, was slicked back well off his prominent brow. Inside, another picture, slightly out of focus, showed Michel seated in a sparse conference room in Paris below four black-framed pictures of his forebears, with a caption citing him as "the heir of a celebrated line of bankers."

The article added to the growing mythology of Lazard as an incredibly secretive, incredibly powerful collection of important men doing important business around the globe. Many of the old chestnuts were trotted out: an ability to control billions of dollars at a moment's notice with only the tiniest drop of capital—$17.5 million in New York and 17 million francs in Paris; the spartan, almost unforgivable working conditions, where every two partners shared one secretary, in shabby leased offices; the importance of being long-term greedy by offering unparalleled advice to CEOs as opposed to simply loaning money.

There was hardly anything secretive about such a prominent and fawning article. But there were some subtle (and not-so-subtle) messages being conveyed by Michel to his partners, including the public reinforcement of the importance of partnership at the firm and the refutation of Cook's failed management philosophy. "It is a Lazard rule: No pyramid structures," Michel explained. Sorry, Mr. Cook. The article concluded by affirming that Lazard had "stayed true" to established principles of private European investment banks of the nineteenth century—"a sanctuary where all the different threads of a tightly knit network come together and where decisions are made whose authorship is given to others"—and left readers with a little morsel from Stendhal, where the arriviste protagonist of *Lucien Leuwen* wonders why his father, the banker, is keeping four foreign exchange traders waiting for him in the lobby of his office. His answer: "Their job is to wait for me. My job is to read the paper."

THE MID-1970S were a period of profound change across Wall Street. The back-office crisis of the early part of the decade, which Felix had helped to solve, resulted in any number of old-line brokerages being merged out of existence and others being liquidated. Then, on May 1, 1975, the SEC ordered the end of fixed commissions on stock transactions. "After 183 years of doing business under fixed commissions, Wall Street will have to respond to the challenges of free enterprises," Donald T. Regan, then the chairman and CEO of Merrill Lynch, told the *New York Times*. Added Billy Salomon, the head of Salomon Brothers, "There was a time when a client handled by X firm stayed with that firm. Today it's a dog-eat-dog world." That decision began to break the clubby covalent bonds that had existed between many Wall Street firms and their corporate and institutional clients. This benefited firms outside of the club (many of which happened to be predominantly Jewish), such as Lazard, which had lower overhead and could gain access to new clients as a result of the rapid breakdown of the conventional order. The decline in brokerage-fee revenues further exacerbated the need for the large brokers to consolidate, so, among others, Bache Halsey Stuart, itself formed by the merger of Bache & Company and Halsey, Stuart & Company, bought Shields Model Roland. Then Paine Webber bought Mitchell Hutchins. If this weren't enough commotion, a number of the old-line investment banking partnerships were facing succession issues. Not only was Lazard struggling with succession, but so were Allen & Company, where Charles Allen Jr., then seventy-four, was slowly disengaging from the highly secretive media boutique; and Dillon, Read & Company, where Clarence Dillon, then ninety-four, no longer came in to the office. Sidney Weinberg, Gus Levy, and Bobbie Lehman—giants among men—had died. Pete Peterson, Felix's old friend from Bell & Howell and the Nixon administration, had left Washington in 1973 to help rescue the financially troubled Lehman Brothers, after turning down an offer from André to come to Lazard. Then there were both Loeb, Rhoades & Company, run by John Loeb, then seventy-four, and Kuhn, Loeb & Company, run by John Schiff, then seventy-three. Both of these firms were pondering their future, given the aging of their leaders. The two even considered merging their complementary businesses as a way to compete more effectively. In the end, both Loeb, Rhoades and Kuhn, Loeb ended up being bought, at separate times, by Lehman Brothers.

Michel, ever protective of his birthright, determined early on not to let Lazard fall prey to the merger forces running rampant on Wall Street. He needed to make Lazard more profitable and the Lazard partnership more meaningful. His decision to demote seven partners (including Mel Heineman) and then force another seven (including André, at his request) to become limited partners sent a powerful message. "It was a Napoleonic first act, if you will," one partner remembered. "I am sure it was all calculated to instill fear and trembling in the troops." Many said Michel took a page from Voltaire, in *Candide,* where the great French writer explained how the British executed one of their own admirals who lost an important battle *"pour encourager les autres"* (to encourage the others). Michel also declared that for the next four years, he had no intention of promoting any internal candidates to the partnership ranks, a decision that added to the frustrations of the firm's long-suffering younger bankers. One of the demoted partners, Peter Lewis, remembered being "disappointed" by Michel's decision but also understood his logic for it, given that Lewis's main focus at Lazard to that point had been on Blackwell Land, the huge agricultural enterprise in California owned by the original family heirs, including Michel, individually and not by the firm. Lewis eventually became a partner again after he "reinvented himself as an M&A banker." Peter Smith, who also was demoted, reclaimed his partnership two years later. Mel Heineman thought his demotion related directly to his SEC testimony and his clear-eyed sentiment that he would not go to jail to protect Felix. Not surprisingly, Felix took a different view of the cuts. "We cut back quite a bit," he said. "It was a brilliant piece of work." He noted that as a result of the cuts, a Lazard partnership was now more "meaningful," as in, the remaining partners all made more money. "It was a difficult, thankless task," he added.

Michel elaborated: "Particularly during the years when Mr. André Meyer was sick, there was a natural tendency to satisfy the ambition of young individuals by naming them partners relatively quickly. But to me being a partner is not an honor; it is either a fact or not a fact. It is much better to be a highly paid senior vice president when you are in fact doing the job of a senior vice president than to be a partner, which attracts other partners' attention to the fact that you're not completely right to be one." Or, put another, more metaphorical way, Michel explained, "It was like looking in the mirror. You don't realize you're gaining weight, until one morning you look at yourself and realize you're getting fat. Then you do something about it." In another act laden with symbolism, Michel moved into André's old office but was careful to keep André's desk exactly as it had always been, untouched. He moved his own desk into the opposing corner, near where his father had a desk during his infrequent visits to New York. He kept the Lazard offices as drab as ever and echoed André's old saw: "Luxury helps at home, not in the office." Partners noticed that while Michel may have occupied André's office, he was not André. "Mr. Meyer wanted to know every time a pebble turned over," the partner David Supino told Cary Reich approvingly. "Not Michel." Michel also, for the first time, invited Lazard Brothers, the U.K. affiliate still owned 80 percent by S. Pearson & Son, to invest $1.5 million in the fixed capital of Lazard in New York and to receive a 1.5 percent stake in the firm's profits. "It is a little different if you are a partner of the owner than if you are just a cousin of his" is how Michel put it at the time. This was a critical first step toward Michel realizing his vision to reunite the ownership of the three houses of Lazard. "The relationships are getting closer and closer all the time," Michel explained. "I have a sense of being at home when I am at Lazard Brothers. To me it's very much a part of the family."

But perhaps his most important initial decision was to recruit four highly productive partners from Lehman Brothers to Lazard in New York. The defection of the Lehman partners—known as "the Gang of Four"—in the wake of the Kuhn, Loeb merger, was organized and led by James

W. Glanville, an oil and gas banker with one of the largest ownership stakes in the Lehman partnership, and included Ian MacGregor, the former chairman of AMAX, a U.K.-based minerals and coal giant, Alan McFarland Jr., and Ward Woods, two younger partners who had worked with Glanville. "Last month, four Lehman partners chose the more measured music of Lazard, with its golden notes and emphasis on solo turns, over the orchestrated innovations of the much larger Lehman firm," *Fortune* reported in September 1978.

Notwithstanding the sweet music being composed in the pages of *Fortune,* this was a *highly* controversial decision inside both firms, the reverberations from which are felt by many of the individuals involved to this day. Glanville hated that Pete Peterson was pushing Lehman to become a full-service firm and opposed him openly on the executive committee. Beyond that, he just hated Peterson. The feeling was mutual. "Before coming to Lehman Brothers," Peterson told Ken Auletta in *Greed and Glory on Wall Street,* "I was told the firm itself was seriously divided and Jim Glanville was at once very productive in the energy area and perhaps the most divisive and even vindictive of the partners. I found both statements to be accurate." One month before his first discussion with Michel about decamping, Glanville asked Lehman to write a $5,000 bonus check out to William Loomis, an associate who worked for Glanville. Peterson and the executive committee rebuffed Glanville since determining bonuses was not the purview of an individual partner but rather the responsibility of the firm. "So it is to be war," Glanville wrote Peterson after the rebuff, in July 1977.

Soon Glanville "whispered" his displeasure with Peterson and Lehman to the Lazard partner Frank Pizzitola, who knew Glanville from energy deals. Thanks to Pizzitola, Glanville met with Michel in August 1977—just before he took control—to see "what Lazard might be like under its new managing partner." In December 1977, Lehman completed the acquisition of Kuhn, Loeb, but the tension between Glanville and Peterson continued. Michel and Glanville met again in the spring of 1978, and afterward Michel urged Glanville to meet with Felix. Felix met with Glanville several times and even volunteered to reduce his percentage of the firm's profits to help recruit the Lehman team. (Felix voluntarily cut his points by 25 percent, to 6 percent, from 8 percent, in September 1978, which cost him $240,000 that year; Michel, too, reduced his points to 13.2 percent, from 19.1 percent, but his stake went back up to 18 percent the next year while Felix's take stayed fixed at 6 percent.)

On the morning train from Connecticut, Glanville confided to his old client—now a partner at Lehman—MacGregor that he was thinking of moving to Lazard and that he "trusted small firms," a phrase that became a bit of a mantra for the Lehman crowd at Lazard. "Count me in, Jimmy," MacGregor said. Woods and McFarland joined the others. With word beginning to leak out, though, Glanville needed to move quickly. Michel interrupted his August vacation and took the Concorde back to New York to negotiate with each man individually—Glanville won a 3.75 percent stake; MacGregor 2.5 percent; Woods 2 percent, and McFarland 1.45 percent. The Gang of Four also flew to Switzerland to meet with André. "I was very well impressed by their perfect manners," André said at the time. On August 8, the four submitted their resignations to Peterson, and the next day he announced the departures in the midst of a strike of New York newspapers. Peterson hoped the news would go unnoticed. But he was also extremely upset at the time about the unprecedented raid. "Peterson was not happy for a minute after we hired those people," Michel said, with some understatement. "But my personal relationship with him has remained quite good." There were rumors of "angry shouting, sealed desks, chauffeurs dismissed, lawyers hired," according to *Fortune*. To which Auletta added: "Door locks were changed, credit cards were canceled."

Michel let it be known he had trekked down to One William Street to tell Peterson what he had done. "With his big cigar, like he was on some sort of French diplomatic mission," Peterson recalled. And according to Auletta, at some point Peterson went to see Michel to warn him that Glanville was "poison." Glanville hired the ubiquitous Simon Rifkind to fight Lehman, after, according to Glanville, Peterson "cancelled the bonus of my secretary and of the other secretaries who were leaving." Other charges were leveled at Glanville as well by his Lehman partners. First, according to *Greed and Glory on Wall Street,* members of the Lehman executive committee accused the Gang of Four of attempting to buy a real estate asset from one of their oil and gas clients, without telling the firm the client had made the offer to them, a charge Glanville vehemently denied. Peterson said he called a meeting of Lehman's top partners to discuss what Glanville had done. He invited the tax partner to show the other partners the papers related to the Glanville deal. "Everybody was pretty appalled," Peterson recalled, and the committee voted unanimously, 8–0, to tell Glanville that he had to leave the firm. The following Tuesday, Michel made his pilgrimage down to One William Street to see Peterson and tell him that the Gang of Four were coming to Lazard. "And I just sat there and kind of smiled," Peterson said. "Obviously Glanville had told [Michel] nothing about this whole situation. But

Glanville had undying enmity for the firm and for me and so forth. And that was my last year of contact with André and Michel. I virtually never talked to them again."

The second charge against Glanville, equally serious, was that he was anti-Semitic. The short, stocky Glanville was a Texan, born and bred. His father was a history professor at Southern Methodist University. Glanville graduated from Rice with a degree in chemical engineering, and then went to graduate school at the California Institute of Technology. All he wanted to do was work in the oil business, and he started his professional career as a petroleum engineer for what is now Exxon-Mobil. Lehman recruited him to be an oil and gas banker in 1959, and according to Auletta, he became a Lehman partner in 1961 (*Fortune* said 1963). In an interview with Auletta, Glanville answered the charges of anti-Semitism: "It is the sort of typecasting you give to someone when you can't figure out what to say about them." Glanville's Lehman partner Lew Glucksman, a Jew and occasional ally of Glanville's, said of him: "People have said Jim Glanville is anti-semitic. That's bullshit! He was a guy with lots of strong opinions on every subject in the world."

Twenty-eight years later, the rift caused by Michel's recruitment of the Gang of Four is still palpable. Actually, the Gang of Four was really the Gang of Six because two Lehman associates—Bill Loomis and, two months later, Dod Fraser—were part of the block trade. (Ultimately, Loomis would have more impact on the future of Lazard than anyone else Michel had recruited that September day.) Sitting in his office at Bessemer Securities in Rockefeller Center, Woods reluctantly confided: "Pete is a friend of mine now, and I have great admiration for him. He wasn't then. It was a very difficult separation, so I'd rather not talk about it. It was very bitter. Let's put it this way. I came back from visiting clients. And I got a call in Tulsa. I was on my way back. I got a call in Tulsa from my secretary, in tears, because she'd been kicked out of the office and it was locked. And then we had a settlement, which I negotiated with Pete, and it was over. But there was a little scratching around. They tried to make it difficult. They were very angry. We had a significant percentage of the clients in the firm, and we were lucky enough that most of them went with us."

For his part, Felix never liked Glanville as a person but respected his effectiveness as a banker. He sided with his friend Pete Peterson on the subject of Glanville's anti-Semitism. "I mean, Glanville was a really difficult, very difficult, very rather sinister person," Felix said. "I mean he was very, very racist, very anti-Semitic." Indeed, Glanville gave his critics all the ammunition they needed about his anti-Semitism in a 1980 letter he wrote to his former Lehman partner George Ball, who had once been an undersecretary of state and was a close friend of Peterson's. (When Ball joined Lehman in 1966, Frank Altschul wrote a letter of "congratulations" to Bobbie Lehman.) Ball had authored a piece in the *Washington Post* critical of Israeli policy. Glanville wrote him: "My view on U.S. relations with Israel completely in line with yours (as they should be, as I learned from you) but I doubt if they receive much sympathy from the members of your Executive Committee. The members of that Committee are overwhelmingly of one ethnic persuasion with the exception of one gentleman who found it necessary to change his name in order to disguise his heritage"—a reference to Pete Peterson, who is Greek. "This is the same Committee that exhibited such glee over the opportunity to delete four Presbyterians from their list of partners." After Glanville's letter became public, many Lehman partners demanded that Peterson initiate a libel suit against him. "Glanville wrote one of the most blatantly anti-Semitic letters I've ever read, about how my partners' first loyalty was to Israel and not to the United States," Peterson said. "And the chairman has hidden his ethnic persuasion, which was ridiculous. Everybody knew I was Greek. So what? And it was just vile. And my partners are now absolutely furious. And they wanted to sue him for libel and so forth. I said, 'Look, in this business of an eye for an eye and a tooth for a tooth, everybody gets disfigured ultimately, and let's just forget it. And I'll call and tell Michel and I'll see if I can get a commitment from him that he totally clamps down on Glanville.' "

Peterson called Michel and asked to see him, but not in his office at Lazard. They agreed to meet at Michel's Fifth Avenue apartment "with his big cigar and so forth." They sat down together to discuss Glanville's letter. "And I recall saying," Peterson said,

> "Michel, I have been in this business now for a while. I know it's a very tough business. But I assume there are levels below which we don't stoop. And somehow the questioning of the patriotism of some of the firm's partners strikes me as well below the levels that are appropriate and acceptable behavior." So I said, "I'm going to show you this letter. And then all I ask from you is a commitment that you're going to get Glanville and set him down in your office and tell him he can never, ever again do such a thing." And then he lit up that big cigar. He said, "Well, everybody knows that Glanville's a bigot, but he produces a lot of business." I said, "I thought I was having a discussion with you on another level. I know he produces a lot of business. I know he is one of the

biggest producers. But I'm approaching you on a level of civil behavior." And Michel then said, "Well, he has a lot of clients." So I got up and walked out, and I don't think I ever spoke to him again."

For his part, Michel said he has always maintained a cordial relationship with Peterson.

Controversies aside, Michel had sold the Gang of Four on the wonders of Lazard. Woods recalled what he had said to them:

> There was a place in the world for people, serious people with global connections who can do things on a more sophisticated, less bureaucratic, individual basis, where there will be three, or four, or five partners who you can trust to go out and represent—or maybe ten partners, if you get really lucky—who can really go out and sign up any company and have the sophistication, the knowledge of the business to actually be able to do what the client has asked you to do, in a way that the client is happy and comes back. It's that simple. Michel said to me, "We don't need money. Swiss Bank Corp. wants to put in $500 million and have Lazard be a global investment bank like Goldman Sachs, or like Morgan Stanley. I don't want to do it. We don't need to do it. We have this wonderful franchise that no one else has, and we'll nurture it. We've got partners in Paris, partners in London. They're there and they are part of Lazard. They do share business. And we've gotta fix New York. But we're going to fix it."

Woods also spoke to Michel about Felix and his role. And Michel told Woods that Felix had offered to cut his percentage so the Lehman partners could join the firm with a proper economic incentive. "And frankly, we talked about Felix," Woods said. "Felix was a wonderful partner. He never was political. He didn't give a shit. He was very pleased to have me do business. He never tried to interfere or anything. He has his guys, and those guys knew where their bread was buttered. But I wasn't one of those guys. And he was great. We had a good time."

But the new partners had to make some adjustments before the good times started. First, One Rockefeller Plaza was no One William Street. Whereas the Lehman bankers were happy to display their immense wealth both in their opulently appointed offices *and* at their homes, Lazard's offices remained shabby. "We live in cramped quarters—it's like something out of Victor Hugo's *Les Misérables*," Pizzitola told *Fortune.* Then there was the famous lack of infrastructure. Bill Loomis wrote an amusing memo to Sid Wolf, the resident Dickensian overseer, about the woeful state of the firm's photocopiers. (Many partners thought there was something poetic about a man named Wolf being responsible for keeping costs at the firm low.) "As is often the case," Loomis wrote, "I find myself on Monday morning sending out a series of tables to clients that appear to have been photocopied in Moscow in the 1920s. It is particularly aggravating after working hard to have the final product so unprofessional in appearance. A second frustration with our machines is that frequently they don't work at all. One recent week the machine on 32 broke literally every day. While I appreciate maintenance is always a problem with these machines, this one is clearly a piece of junk. It is very depressing at night to go floor to floor trying to find a machine in reasonable working order." He recommended Wolf replace the machine on the thirty-second floor with "a very sophisticated and expensive" one that could produce work that "is professional in appearance." Another Lazard banker called Wolf and asked him for a new bookcase after something fell on the old one and it shattered. "And he says to me, 'André wouldn't like it.' And I said, 'Sid, he's been dead for four years, buy me a new one.' "

For his part, Glanville told Cary Reich, with amazement, "The secretaries have to go outside to buy typewriter ribbons. We don't stock them here." But he drew the line of his frustration at the infamous Lazard weekend list, which André had instituted with a certain amount of logic. The idea was that each partner had to give André the number to reach him. "You don't have to say with whom," Michel once explained—with, according to Reich, "a Gallic twinkle in his eye"—"but you have to say where." André would distribute the list only to his *real* partner, Pierre, not to the other titular partners. Michel at least had the decency—at Loomis's urging—to distribute the weekend list around to all the partners, as a way of inculcating in them his inviolate philosophy, learned from André, of always being available to clients and to colleagues. "We are in a service business," he reminded everyone.

Glanville would have none of the weekend list. "Do you want to know what I do with it?" he once asked a visitor. "I put it right in there," pointing to his trash can. Glanville also did not take kindly to the micromanagement of his expenses. Wolf used to produce printouts of partners' telephone calls, and then attempt to figure out which calls were business related and which were personal. The personal calls were charged to the partner's internal expense account. One day, Wolf had examined Glanville's calls and found that he made a call or two to Darien, Connecticut, where he lived. Wolf sent Glanville a bill for $1.25. The immensely wealthy Glanville never paid the bill, so Tom Mullarkey, Wolf's boss, showed up in Glanville's office to demand payment. The two had quite a row, needless to say, and never spoke again.

Woods also was surprised to find his partners a bit demoralized. "I found a group of very smart, very experienced, and generally beat-up partners, who had survived under André Meyer, in what must have been the most brutal environment, but enormously intelligent and capable," he said. Loomis recalled that Lazard had a reputation as a "dark place" and that "André Meyer was someone you would not want to work for." He explained that one of the Gang of Four told him after they arrived at Lazard, "Don't kid yourself, if André were running the place, we wouldn't be here." He himself "was horrified by how backward it was." He was one of only six associates, and there were no analysts (the most junior professionals, generally right out of college, who are expected to crunch all the numbers and do whatever they are told to do by the associates). "We were treated like serfs," Loomis said. "There was no communication between the partners. There were no [deal] books. Analysis was a letter."

But the Gang of Four, led by Glanville, did do a fair amount of business at Lazard. "My clients are my friends," Glanville was fond of saying. Indeed, Damon Mezzacappa, formerly Lazard's longtime head of capital markets, believes that in terms of clout with his clients, Glanville nearly rivaled Felix. "He had a powerful grip on his clients," Damon said. Roger Briggs Jr., a longtime investment banker, remembered when he was at Salomon Brothers working on a deal where Lazard and Glanville were Salomon's co-advisers. "We went to this meeting, and the first thing Glanville does is turn to us and ask, 'Do you guys have the books?' " he said, referring to the presentation bankers often prepare for their clients. Briggs said he couldn't get over the fact that the Lazard bankers had produced nothing in writing but Glanville had figured, correctly, that the Salomon bankers would. "That's how great his relationships were with his clients," Briggs continued. The second thing he remembered about Glanville was how after asking about the books, he turned to the associate and said, "Could you go downstairs and get me a couple of cigars." He said he felt he had just witnessed the essence of Lazard.

Not a single one of the crew Michel recruited from Lehman is still at Lazard, and not a single one—aside from perhaps Loomis—was able to crack the Lazard code. One observer close to Lazard believed the Lehman group, particularly Woods, McFarland, and MacGregor, were unsuccessful at Lazard because of their own inability to adapt to the firm's quirky nature. MacGregor was the first member of the Gang to exit

Lazard. Two years after he arrived, the British prime minister, Margaret Thatcher, recruited MacGregor to run the failing government-owned British Steel Corporation. Incredibly, the Thatcher government agreed to compensate Lazard for losing MacGregor's services. Naturally, this was extremely controversial, especially when it was revealed that the British government had agreed to pay Lazard up to $4.1 million depending on whether MacGregor achieved certain milestones (a total of $2.2 million was actually paid to Lazard). Several members of Parliament described the payment as "monstrous" and "farcical."

Michel conceded the MacGregor episode "created somewhat of a problem" as the Scot had just arrived at Lazard. Michel said MacGregor believed the British Steel job to be "the crowning challenge of a long career." But he said the payment "was presented in a light which did not please me very, very greatly." MacGregor became a Lazard limited partner in July 1980. He proceeded to "restructure" British Steel by ruthlessly cutting a hundred thousand jobs, many of them in Scotland. The many who despised him afterward dubbed him "Mac the Knife." Ward Woods, who was immensely successful at Lazard, left in 1989 to become CEO of Bessemer Securities, a private investment fund affiliated with the Phipps fortune. Over the past few years, he and his wife have donated $40 million to Stanford University, Woods's alma mater. Alan McFarland also left Lazard in 1989, to start his own investment banking boutique, McFarland Dewey & Co.

While the Lehman group struggled to adjust to its new surroundings, where the ghost of André loomed large, Michel was having his own problems escaping the influence of the former senior partner. He may no longer have stepped foot into the Lazard offices, but whether in Crans-sur-Sierre or at the Carlyle, André was giving Michel fits. Long gone were the days, in the early 1960s, when André romanced Michel, his only partner's son. Now Michel was the boss, and André was having difficulty coming to grips with that. Felix said André made life "miserable" for Michel. "I remember Michel coming to see me after some great scene with André where André just—André could lash people pretty badly," Felix explained. "Also, he could second-guess people, which was always an uneasy thing. It made life very difficult for Michel. I was kind of surprised that he was able to take it and carry on. But it was obviously the right decision." André's treatment of the young Michel bordered on the humiliating. "André Meyer treated Michel extremely badly," one partner remembered hearing. "There were times when he would take him up to the Carlyle and literally undress him, tell him, 'You're not up to running this bank. You were born with a silver spoon. How dare you think you can take my role?' You know, really tough. He almost reduced him to nothing. To tears, in fact, is what a lot of us were told." Frank Pizzitola remembered a lunch at the Carlyle with André, Felix, and Michel, where André spoke of Michel in the third person, as if he weren't there. "He is a boy," Pizzitola recalled hearing André say. "And Michel just began filling up. It was a real punch to the gut."

Michel remembered well what it was like for him in New York the second time around while André was still alive. "When he did ask me to come back, it was extremely difficult," he said. "He was not terribly well. He was not often in the office. He was very, very—I could say physically jealous that I was leading the firm. I knew that it would be difficult because the normal way for that gentleman was to take every decision." Even on his deathbed, André would summon Michel up to the Carlyle and demand that he respond to one question after another for him, causing Michel to go back and forth to the office to search for an answer. Michel added, in another interview, that at the beginning of his tenure running New York "I was not sure I could, and I was very *iffy* for a while in my relationship with André Meyer. But my relationship vis-à-vis the place changed overnight. This place was in good shape because of André Meyer. It had extremely low overheads. Comparatively, we have high overheads today. I have been a spendthrift by comparison. It was making money in bad times and in good. Consequently, the partners were not wondering whether they would eat the next day—which in New York is truer than you think. Wall Street is a dangerous place. You are on top of the world one day and out of a job the next."

Michel recalled the essence of the psychological warfare in which André would engage, the André method. André had the ability to make powerful men fear him, among them such shrinking violets as David Rockefeller, Bill Paley, David Sarnoff, and Bobbie Lehman. "Bobbie Lehman I can testify to it because I was present during one conversation and he was obviously petrified by André," Michel explained. "He had the art of making people feel guilty. Finally, I discovered that, and it didn't work with me anymore. It dawned on me that it was maybe not on purpose, but a trick. All of us can be made to feel guilty. It's very easy. I think I even know how to do it, but I've always consciously refrained from doing it because of my experience with André Meyer. He used that too much."

Compounding Michel's expected problem with André was yet another problem, this one unexpected—an inkling of wanderlust on Felix's part. Having just turned fifty, Lazard's most important business generator and by far its most famous partner was casting about. "There are just so many deals you can make before it takes on a certain sameness," a banker who knew Felix told *Newsweek* in 1981. Ever since his friend Harry Oppenheimer's Anglo American Corporation had taken a meaningful stake in Charles Engelhard's company, Felix had gone on the board as Oppenheimer's representative. Eventually, he went on the board of Anglo American, too. One day, around the time that Michel took over New York, Oppenheimer approached Felix about heading up Oppenheimer's growing business outside of South Africa. The job, which Felix opted not to pursue, would have been based in London. Felix also indicated to Governor Carey that after three years as the chairman of MAC, he intended to step down. The July 1978 *Times* article announcing this news indicated Felix was "about to leave the spotlight and is wrestling with the problem of what to do for an encore." According to the *Times*, he sat for a "long, reflective" interview in his "small, spare" Lazard office and confided: "I will always invent deals. But simply doing deals does not fulfill my life. I certainly don't expect that doing deals will be 100 percent of my professional life. But it may be 90 percent for the next two or three years. I need two or three years to think through and analyze the jumble of sensations and flashes that I have."

The article, as usual, turned out to be quite a kiss to Felix. "Unlike most governmental officials, Mr. Rohatyn is accessible, informative and frank," wrote the *Times* reporter. "He not only enjoys power, he courts it and he is indefatigable in pursuit of the solution to whatever problem he is working on." Something must have been in the air that day thirty-two floors above the street in Rockefeller Center because it is clear that Felix, while not exactly humble, displayed a rare semblance of self-awareness bordering on humility, a trait not typically associated with an investment banker, let alone one of Felix's stature and accomplishments. "My being able to command press, to command space, is one of my weapons for dealing with politicians," Felix said. "Politicians equate words written about one with power, and now I will be written off as a power. This is an interesting test of character for me. Giving up power is like giving up smoking." (Felix had been a big smoker—as many as two packs a day—in college and in the army, until his first wife convinced him to give it up.) Felix also reflected upon how he felt when Geneen invited him onto the ITT board. "That was really something," he said. "I have always been a maverick, an outsider. I didn't have the right background or go to the right schools. I am not a big club-man. I am not a big school-reunion man." The *Wall Street Journal* also profiled Felix, with his tenure at MAC supposedly coming to an end. "He is the Big Apple's Henry Kissinger, an institutionalized compromiser," the paper wrote. "He's the darling of the city's powerful news media. He's a skillful financial mechanic. He is, of course, Felix G. Rohatyn. While other public officials have fallen, Mr. Rohatyn has flourished during the fiscal crisis that littered New York City's sidewalks with broken careers." As to what he would do after MAC, he told the *Journal* he just wanted "some breathing room right now" but admitted he was "going to miss the exposure." (The speculation turned out to be moot since Felix stayed as chairman of MAC for another six months, and then came back *again.)*

A few months later, Felix gave a luncheon speech at the Pierre hotel, before the French-American Chamber of Commerce, that not only continued to show his palpable melancholy but also was a damning assessment of President Carter's first two years in office. "Our economy is out of control, our currency is in danger, our institutions of government is *[sic]* unresponsive or inept. . . . We are at war today. With inflation, with unemployment, with lack of education, with racial discrimination. We are, furthermore, not winning. If we lose, our system of government may not survive." Felix then added an unfavorable comparison between New York's now-solved fiscal problem and the burgeoning one in Washington: "If the President loses this fight, if, collectively, we cannot create the climate to help him to win, the result will not be noteholders with a moratorium imposed on them or a wage freeze on the unions, but it could be the end of a form of government which, since the days of the French Revolution, had done more for people than any other system ever invented. There will be no winners or losers then, simply the history of another nation that was unable to count its blessings and lost sight of its values." Felix made these comments almost six months to the day *before* Carter's infamous "malaise" speech to the American people.

Felix gave another interview, also in his "modest, somewhat cluttered office" in Rockefeller Center, in February 1979 to *W,* the fashion bible, just as his MAC responsibilities appeared to be ending. His reflections about his public tenure were a mixture of pride, melancholy, and pure ego. "Being in the public eye really grabs you," he said. "It's very heady stuff, a businessman all of a sudden becoming a star. Suddenly I find myself on the front page of the *New York Times,* and I read what I say and I begin to think I'm a pretty smart fellow. I'm not sure that's all to the good." With his time freed up from MAC, Felix said, "I'm going to try to patch together my private life, which I have neglected. I plan to spend a little more time with my children"—then twenty, eighteen, and fifteen years old. "I'll do some writing, listen to some more Bach and Mozart, read some books and go to the theater. I'll be a private citizen but not uninvolved." Interestingly, he made no mention of Lazard or of his impending nuptials to Elizabeth Vagliano.

CHAPTER 8

FELIX FOR PRESIDENT

In the end, of course, Felix stayed at Lazard and redoubled his commitment to the firm and to doing deals. His timing was impeccable, as the stock market was about to embark on an unprecedented bull run. As a corollary, the size of M&A deals—and the fees paid to investment bankers, who often receive a fixed percentage of the total consideration—exploded as well. "From my point of view, my position at Lazard was quite ideal. . . . I spent a huge proportion of my time, certainly in the seventies and even into the eighties, on the stock exchange crisis in the seventies and on the city all the way through, and I can't imagine any other place giving me that luxury," he said. "Now, I made up for it by making a lot of money for them."

Michel and Felix worked out what Michel described as a "bicameral" approach to running the firm. They had a symbiotic relationship. Michel took care of the day-to-day management that Felix abhorred. Felix used his unparalleled access and M&A skills to keep Lazard at the top of the deal league tables. They made each other even richer. They shared, at least in the early years of their partnership, a similar devotion to low overhead, business lines (like M&A) requiring little capital, and a desire to remain unique. They thought about resurrecting Lazard's risk arbitrage and private-equity businesses. And Michel wanted to increase the firm's municipal bond trading business. Mostly, though, they focused on giving the respected bankers who worked there the room to run, increasingly free from André's micromanaging. "In the last couple of years we have probably had four, five or six different partners working start to finish on large transactions, partners other than me and André Meyer," Felix told *Institutional Investor.* "They are capable of taking on a piece of business and putting it through without the need for me or the equivalent of André Meyer getting involved. That's a new thing around here, people going off on their own. It gives a dimension to the place and a spirit it didn't have. We've had a flowering of people who had been in our shadows." In the old days, he continued, "We had André Meyer as a superstar and me as a junior superstar. People were encouraged to bring in business but they weren't left alone, partly because André had great difficulty trusting anybody other than a very, very small number of people. He would go along with me doing my own thing but not many other people. It takes a while for people to come out of that. If you asked me whether there has been any real change in what we are trying to do, I would say, no there hasn't. But in terms of how we do it, of course there has. You don't go from Julius Caesar to the Third Republic without having a change in how you do business." Observed one partner, fresh from a two-week, uninterrupted vacation in Mexico that was far from civilization, *"That's* the new Lazard."

Felix also made another attempt to instill a little discipline in the M&A team. He demanded, in a January 1979 memo, that associates in the group monitor the "broad tape," the old-fashioned paper version of the "crawl" that now appears at the bottom of the CNBC television screen, and immediately inform the "senior members" of the group of any M&A deals "within minutes of the announcement in order that we inform our clients in a timely manner." He instructed the associates, on a rotating basis, to write a one-page synopsis of the relevant deals. Felix's memo was an early and modest effort at marketing Lazard's services. He wanted the associates to answer the question "Should we call either of the companies involved to determine if our services may be useful and, if so, is there evidence to suggest, such as by means of a review of the directorate of both companies, who in this firm should make such a call?" But within a month, the system Felix had tried to set up had already malfunctioned. In a memo to all the partners, including Michel and Felix, Frank Pizzitola observed, "The procedure outlined in Felix Rohatyn's memorandum of January 24th, a copy of which is attached, appears to have broken down. We are going to make another concerted effort to see if this system will work to the benefit of us all."

Regardless of the system failure, in quick succession, the firm—principally Felix—represented United Technologies in its acquisition of Carrier, the air conditioner manufacturer; ABC in its acquisition of Chilton Books; and Unilever in its acquisition of National Starch. Indeed, the money once again started rolling in. After the shaky transition year of 1978, the firm earned $54.5 million in 1979, with fully 46 percent of that amount, or $25.3 million, coming from New York. Lazard as a whole had never earned more than $40 million in a given year and now had cracked the $50 million level. Felix earned more than $1.5 million in 1979; Michel made more than $4.5 million, just from New York *alone.*

The partner Frank Zarb, for one, remembered this period as golden. "One year, we paid our entire expenses by the end of February," he said. "Invariably, we did the same thing. We'd look at the pipeline in December. Felix would panic. We'd put together a new business committee, have a new business committee meeting, talk about lists and bullshit. And by February, we were all so busy we couldn't go to meetings anymore. Year after year after year."

In the spring of 1979, two lengthy magazine articles—one about André in *Institutional Investor*, the other about Felix in *The New Yorker*—added immeasurably to the firm's growing luster. The Cary Reich article in *Institutional Investor* about André, coming some five months before his death, was both an homage to his legacy and an early obituary. One observation, by the partner David Supino, captured André's mysteriousness. "He has a European penchant for elegant inconspicuousness," Supino said. "Even if everybody knows who he is, nobody knows all the facts." In short, it was the portrait of a man in full, complex and brilliant, relentless and flawed.

The New Yorker article coincided with Felix's brief departure from MAC and with a pair of testimonial dinners designed to honor the key participants in the more than three-year drama to save the city. One dinner was to honor Victor Gotbaum, then the executive director of the city's biggest municipal employees union. The ordeal of saving New York from bankruptcy had forged—for a time—a formidable friendship between Gotbaum and Felix and their wives. At the first testimonial dinner, more than thirty years ago, Felix described Gotbaum as "today probably my closest personal friend."

The closeness of their friendship would often find its way into print. Gotbaum was the best man at Felix's 1979 wedding to Elizabeth Vagliano, one month after *The New Yorker* article appeared. Indeed, it was Victor Gotbaum who convinced Felix, while walking on a beach in Southampton, that he had better propose to Elizabeth or risk losing her. "Liz was getting very frustrated with it and was very negative about the whole thing, the way Felix was behaving," Gotbaum explained. "We took this famous walk on the beach, Felix and I, and I said, 'You know, what the fuck's holding you up?' He made all kinds of excuses about money, how you'd lose this and you'd lose that, and so I gave him my customary stuff. I said, 'Felix, you're full of shit, you know, you're just full of shit. You're insecure about it, okay, but you're not going with anybody else. You seem to care for her a great deal.' I said, basically—in much better language than this—'Shit or get off the pot.' "

The four were regular dinner companions, and the Gotbaums rarely failed to appear at the Rohatyns' annual Easter egg hunt in the Hamptons. And thanks to Felix, Gotbaum's son Josh was a partner at Lazard for thirteen years, beginning in 1981. "Felix wanted him," Gotbaum said of how his son ended up at Lazard. "We used to congratulate each other that we had two sons that were smarter than we were. Josh in my case and Nicky in his case." It was an unexpected friendship, this one between the refugee multimillionaire investment banker and the labor leader prone to Khrushchevian acts of violence. Felix used to refer to them as the "municipal 'Cage aux Folles' " and talked repeatedly about their close personal friendship. In his speech at the Gotbaum dinner, Felix described their first meeting, in July 1975. "We had an extraordinarily enlightening night, which ended at five in the morning with Victor pounding his shoe and being very vocal and intimidating." Felix's retort to Gotbaum after that episode: "Look, you're not Khrushchev and this is not the U.N. So stop pounding." Gotbaum said that his display was simply part of the early theater of the principals' staking out their positions.

But something happened to this beautiful friendship. Inexplicably, Felix no longer speaks with Gotbaum, one of the saddest developments in the former labor leader's life. Some mark the day Gotbaum retired—in 1987—as the city's most powerful labor leader as the day Felix lost interest in him. But the break became complete when Felix returned to New York in 2001, after serving as ambassador to France. "It didn't unwind," Gotbaum said. "It didn't unwind. I think a better word is it somehow dissipated. And somehow began to disappear. And I think a lot of it had to do—it wasn't just Felix, it had to do with me also. He became very rich indeed. I think the best way of saying it is we grew apart."

For a moment or two in the 1980s, Gotbaum toyed with the idea of running for mayor of New York City. As he was thinking about this decision, he shared his private ruminations with his dear friend Felix, who supposedly told Gotbaum that he was sorry, but he just would not be able to publicly—or privately, for that matter—endorse him for mayor. Now, lacking the endorsement of his high-profile partner in solving the city's financial crisis put Gotbaum in a most difficult position. When he left Felix's apartment after this conversation and got into his waiting car, he did two things. First, he decided to terminate his nascent efforts to become mayor; and second, he cried. Although Gotbaum said years later that he never seriously considered running for mayor and didn't recall crying in his car (what man would?), he did remember talking to Felix about the possibility and being very disappointed about how nervous Felix seemed to be about the prospect of his running for mayor. "Felix was very nervous about it in terms of his growing constituency," he said.

"That bothered me. That bothered me because I wasn't going to run for office, you know. I figured, fuck it. Why the hell he was nervous, I don't know. And you know, it just reached a point where I almost told him, like, 'Felix, fuck off. I'm not running for office and that's it. And, you know, let's cut the shit.' But he was very nervous about it. The truth is that if he said he wouldn't support me, I'd have gone anyhow, and, guess what, he'd have looked like shit if he didn't support me. So I just really didn't care in that sense. One, I wasn't going to run, and two, if I ever decided to run, I had him by the balls, because there's almost no way he could get out of supporting me."

The New Yorkerr piece made another point. While Felix's involvement with the city's financial crisis consumed much of his time for three-plus years beginning in 1975, neither he nor Lazard charged the city a penny. Nor did Lazard charge the city for the services of the other partners who, on occasion, worked with Felix on MAC. This was not as crazy as it sounds. The three houses of Lazard took precisely this tack during the franc crisis of 1924, when together they eschewed their fees in favor of copious amounts of favorable publicity. True, Lazard was by no means a charitable organization, as Felix had told the Celler commission in 1969, but the amount of glowing press coverage that Felix, and by extension Lazard, received was immeasurable and invaluable. Felix's increasingly high profile, according to the *New York Times*, "propelled him to national prominence and showered more incidental publicity on the firm than it desired." The *Times* got half of it right: Felix had become a national figure, but nobody inside Lazard was complaining anymore about the firm's increasing renown. The days of André's false modesty were decidedly over.

Soon enough, Lazard would be asked for its professional advice to solve the financial problems of other cities in crisis, such as Detroit, Cleveland, and Washington, D.C. "I like big cities," Felix told *Newsweek*. "Civilization grows there. Religion develops in the open air, I suspect. But civilization—that is in the cities." Lazard was also asked by the state of Illinois to help with a crisis in public education finances and by the U.S. Treasury to help it evaluate the proposed $1.2 billion—later $1.5 billion—federal bailout of the Chrysler Corporation. (Lazard had been an adviser to Chrysler but had resigned over "policy differences.") Felix's role in the Chrysler bailout caused him once again to champion a new version of the Reconstruction Finance Corporation on the editorial page of the *New York Times*. "Somebody told me we were getting to be the Red Adair of municipal finance," he said at the time.

Felix estimated that *had* Lazard charged MAC for its services, the bill would have been in the range of $2.5 million. And Lazard was the only adviser to MAC to serve pro bono; Paul, Weiss, Simon Rifkind's law firm, albeit at a reduced rate, billed MAC—and received—$500,000 for the legal work necessary to set up the corporation. But when he resolved to leave his position at MAC, in January 1979, Felix "felt that it was unfair to expect his partners to continue on the old basis," Andy Logan wrote in *The New Yorker.* The Lazard partners met to discuss the situation and decided to continue the firm's advisory work with MAC, since the firm possessed an immense institutional knowledge about the city's financial picture. The firm also decided, though, to ask for a monthly retainer, at a reduced rate, which also specified that Felix would not receive his percentage share of the pretax income the MAC fees generated. The new chairman of MAC, George Gould, recommended hiring Lazard at a modest annual retainer of $250,000 (assuming this was all profit, Felix's sacrifice for not taking his 6 percent share was to have been $15,000). Representatives of Ed Koch, the new New York City mayor, were present at the MAC board meeting two weeks later when the board unanimously approved the Lazard arrangement.

It turned out, though, that after Felix had independently made some negative comments about Koch's proposed city budget, Koch decided to take his anger out on Lazard and its proposed financial arrangement with MAC. Before going to the dinner to honor Felix, Koch gave an impromptu interview to the *New York Post* where he derided Lazard's hiring, without a competitive bidding procedure, as "certainly a moral conflict of interest." When asked by a reporter if he was going to confront Felix with this issue at the tribute, Koch demurred. "This is Felix's Bar Mitzvah, and you don't say mean things to the Bar Mitzvah boy," he said. A predictable firestorm ensued. Two days after the *Post* story appeared, Lazard resigned its MAC assignment. "The privilege of public service does not carry with it the obligation to be subjected to needless abuse," the Lazard partner Jack Tamagni wrote MAC in the firm's letter of resignation. Governor Carey, the board of MAC, and Simon Rifkind all defended MAC's hiring of Lazard and urged the firm to reconsider.

A barrage of positive publicity for Lazard ensued, including a lengthy assessment of the matter in London's *Economist,* which hailed Felix's long record of "notable public service" and blasted Koch for remarks the magazine found to be "both ill-timed and needlessly offensive, apparently calculatingly so." More favorable press came when the *Daily News* reported that the city had actually asked Lazard to serve as *its* financial adviser, for a $500,000 annual fee, but that the firm turned down the opportunity out of concern about a possible conflict of interest with what Felix had been doing with MAC. (Dillon Read took the assignment, and the fee.) The *News* described the whole matter as "a pretty shabby episode" and said that "Ed Koch would be a lot better mayor if he would learn to use his brain before shooting off his big mouth." Koch made a feeble attempt to apologize to Felix. Those "who want to run the city should stand for election," he went around town saying. To which Felix replied, "I don't accept that notion. Nothing precludes me from criticism. I pay taxes. If you pay to see Isaac Stern and he gives a bad performance, then you reserve the right to criticize that performance. And the critic doesn't have to have had violin lessons."

A month after the testimonial dinners, Governor Carey asked Felix to *return* to MAC as its chairman. George Gould had resigned after only five months. Some Lazard partners believed Felix engineered Gould's resignation so that he could get back the powerful position he missed. "If Guidry can pitch relief for the Yankees, I guess I can pitch relief for the governor," Felix said, doing his best common man imitation. Lazard also returned to advising MAC, once again without pay. The next day Felix and Koch supposedly patched up their differences, although the tension would linger for years. The recollection of Koch accusing Felix and Lazard of having a "moral conflict of interest" still rankles. "I thought it was outrageous," Felix said in 2005. "I still do." But the two men were able to let bygones be bygones. "Well, he didn't hurt me," Felix allowed. "I mean, if he said that and if it had been true, that would have been a different thing. But no, he popped off in terrible taste and I reacted. After a while, we both grew older and we were both out of power. And he's an amusing guy, and every once in a while we have lunch together." Felix's return to MAC and the ongoing kerfuffle with Koch seemed to reinvigorate both Lazard and Felix (after he got back from his honeymoon), and now, led by the "bicameral" team of Michel and Felix, the firm began a lengthy renaissance, but not one without more than a few bumps in the road.

ON SEPTEMBER 9, André died at the Nestlé Hospital in Lausanne, Switzerland. He had turned eighty-one six days before. André's death, of course, occasioned yet another rewriting of New York's partnership agreement. Michel now had the absolute authority, under section 4.1, to unilaterally make all decisions for the partnership. He no longer had to check with anyone at all. Publicly, Lazard liked to keep the fiction alive that New York had merely $17.5 million of capital, when in fact the partners' capital totaled close to $31 million, still unbelievably modest for a Wall Street firm—not that Michel or Felix found there to be a particular need for more money.

In the French tradition, a photograph of André was placed above his Lazard desk with a ribbon of black crinoline draped across one corner. One year to the day exactly, Michel removed the desk and the photograph. Outwardly, Michel had great respect for André, but according to one partner, "the fact was that he did not like André's ghost lingering around." Indeed, in the early days of Michel's stewardship, one of the quickest ways to become, in the words of one partner, "persona non grata" would be to invoke the memory of how "Mr. Meyer" would have done this or that. Michel slowly but surely began to put his own imprint on the firm. In addition to the high-profile Lehman Brothers raid, he made a few hires in the municipal finance area, authorized the new partner Frank Zarb to set up the "International Group" to advise sovereign governments, and promoted Stanley Nabi, who had been president of the New York Society of Security Analysts, to head and increase the assets of Lazard Asset Management, or LAM, after the death of Engelbert Grommers.

Mostly, though, Michel kept the firm focused on M&A work, and in 1979 alone Lazard advised RCA on its $1.3 billion acquisition of CIT Financial (Lazard's former partner in André's hugely successful SOVAC deal); Reliance Electric on its $1.2 billion acquisition by Exxon; United Technologies on its more than $1 billion acquisition of Carrier; and International Paper on its $805 million acquisition of Bodcaw. "They are making a fortune right now," a partner at a competitor told the *New York Times*. "They are a merger house, and mergers have hit it big." Indeed, Lazard would have its best year to that time, in 1979. In New York, profits had risen almost twofold from the year before. In 1980, the firm made even more money—$84.1 million, $39.2 million from New York and $29 million from London. In the two years since Michel had taken over the New York office, pretax income had risen from $12 million to $39 million. His five-year stewardship of Paris had increased pretax income from $6.8 million in 1975 to $15.6 million in 1980—thanks to Paris's involvement in a wildly profitable partnership that produced precious-metal coins for the 1980 Moscow Olympics. Felix made almost $2.4 million in 1980, and Michel, from the New York profits alone, took home more than $7 million.

The firm was on an unprecedented roll, and Michel's leadership was winning some fast converts. "In any walk of life I have been in, you have six months to fail and two years to succeed," Michel told *Euromoney* in March 1981. "The first six months here [in New York] were crucial. The arrival of the people from Lehman was more than an accolade. It was manifest proof that important people outside, who had their professional life at stake, were willing to agree with me and the partners here that this was a place which had a great future. For the outside world, it was probably the most important event. But to me the most important and the most difficult task was to take hold of a nebulous something and that was not made very easy by the presence of André Meyer."

One important convert, Damon Mezzacappa, then forty-five years old, came from Morgan Stanley, one of Lazard's main competitors, in March 1981 to establish at the firm a capital markets business. Capital markets—the underwriting and trading of stock and bond issues—had long been dormant at Lazard. Occasionally, it is true, Lazard would underwrite an offering for a favored client—such as the IPO of the Washington Post Company for the former partner Eugene Meyer, or of Avis for Geneen at ITT, or of Pearson, in the U.K., for the Lords Cowdray and their heirs—but after André Meyer's arrival in New York these underwritings were few and far between. From André's and Felix's perspective, the reasoning was simple. Underwriting required an ever-escalating amount of capital and a sales force of fancy brokers to sell the underwritten issues. With scale, it could be very lucrative and provide wonderful access to clients at the important moment of seeking capital. Accordingly, underwriting remains very competitive, with ongoing pressure on the prices firms can charge for the service. With the M&A business so ebullient and so profitable, requiring no capital, the logic was impeccable for Lazard to stay away from capital markets, where the competition was fierce. Michel, though, was willing to risk a bit more of the firm's slowly growing capital on the selective underwriting of stocks and bonds for the firm's growing stable of clients.

For this task, he recruited the Harvard-educated Mezzacappa, "the Peacock," as he was known around the firm in later years because of his ramrod-straight posture, his impeccable dress, and his penchant for preening. Immensely charming when he wanted to be and tough as shoe leather when he had to be, Mezzacappa and his wife, Liz, who ran a travel agency, were fixtures on the New York social scene, looking lithe and resplendent in the pages of *W* and the *Times*'s Style section cavorting with the jet set at their homes on Fifth Avenue, in Southampton, and in Palm Beach.

At first, Michel offered Mezzacappa a 2 percent partnership stake, but then reduced it to 1.75 percent because, Michel told him, "It would be a mistake to bring you in at 2 percent because there are these guys, like Tamagni here and others, who are at 1.75 percent or whatever and I don't want to offend them." (Tamagni was actually at 2.25 percent, along with a slew of others such as Ward Woods, Frank Zarb, Jon O'Herron,

Don Petrie, Lou Perlmutter, and Peter Jaquith. In 1981, 2.25 percent in New York was worth $1.125 million.) Mezzacappa experienced immediate culture shock. But, he said, "for me it was all about the future. I was either going to succeed or not. I was really quite sure I would succeed, and I saw it as a great opportunity, which it was because Lazard Frères needed me. Goldman Sachs didn't need me. Salomon Brothers didn't need me. There was definite evidence that Lazard had a banking franchise, either real or potential. They certainly had corporate relationships." But "they didn't know how to sell anything," he continued. "They had half a dozen guys down there, and they had weak leadership and very little authority and basically just syndicated this stuff and sold it into the Street and sold it, less reallowance, to bond brokers. I mean, if they were underwriting a deal for ITT, the rest of the Street would be out of bonds and they wouldn't know how to sell them, so they would sell them to a broker who would then sell them to another dealer." Here he laughed from the belly. "And so I met with a lot of animosity when I arrived."

Lazard's fledgling capital markets department was then housed on the thirty-first floor of One Rock, one floor below where the high-powered partners, like Felix and Michel, sat. These operations could not have been more different from what Michael Lewis satirized in *Liar's Poker* about the trading powerhouse Salomon Brothers. There was no football field expanse of humming computer screens and ribald traders. Rather, there was a modest, decidedly low-tech, L-shaped configuration of consoles with strange buttons and attached phone headsets. Equity guys were to one side, debt guys to another. The municipal team was around, too.

Mezzacappa first encountered resistance from the irascible Tom Mullarkey, who believed he ruled the roost on the thirty-first floor. "That was Tom's job, just to be difficult and not give anyone anything," Mezzacappa recalled. "He was trying to maintain his control of that floor, the trading floor." He then encountered Walter Eberstadt, a relative of one of André's favorite investing partners, Ferd Eberstadt. Mezzacappa became "quite fond" of Eberstadt over time, but at the beginning "he couldn't figure me out or what I was all about." Mezzacappa said he found that Stanley Nabi was running LAM "quite badly," with assets under management falling to $1 billion, from $1.4 billion when Nabi took over. And then there was Charlie McDaniel, who was running the trading operation. "A nice man but he wasn't building anything," Mezzacappa recalled. His first day at Lazard, Charlie asked Damon to lunch. "Charlie had a couple of martinis, and he sort of told me the way things ought to work, and I just kind of listened and took it all in," he said. Mezzacappa fired McDaniel five months later. "It was going to be my way, not his way," Damon said. His "way" meant recruiting about eight of his "guys" from Morgan Stanley, among them Mike Solomon, Phil Young, Harlan Batrus, Harry Rosenberg, John Connors, and Rick Levin. "We built a pretty good operation and made a lot of money for the firm," he said.

And Mezzacappa made a ton of money for himself as well. Eventually, he worked his profit percentage up to 4 percent, which in the late 1990s was worth more than $8 million in cash per year, excluding the infamous side deal that he cut with Michel. That deal, on top of his $900,000 salary (at least in 1999) and his percentage stake in the overall New York partnership—which "became a bit of a sore point to the other partners," Damon acknowledged—equaled another 5 percent of the pretax profits of the capital markets business, with a cap of $3 million. One of his former partners said many of the bankers were "absolutely shocked" by how much Mezzacappa was making with his side deal and described him as a "*ganef*" (Yiddish for thief or scoundrel). "So for a while, I was making my salary, my 4 percent, and another $3 million," he said with a faint smile, a total of around $12 million a year by the late 1990s.

❋

Another increasingly crucial aspect of the effort to resurrect the Lazard franchise during Michel's first years in New York was the acute need to hire and train a new breed of junior bankers, known on Wall Street as associates, for the rapidly changing, increasingly analytical world of M&A transactions. At Lazard, being an associate meant nothing more than being an apprentice. André used to boast of only needing "a yellow piece of paper and a pencil" to do deals, a siren song that future partners like Jon O'Herron would still sing well into the 1990s. Felix used a slide rule to check numbers and still has not mastered the use of a computer. Michel, too, has no computer skills. When Loomis told Michel in the early 1980s that Lazard actually had *a* computer, he said, "Really? Where is this computer? I must go and see it." The need for associates with more relevant skills was therefore of only passing concern to them, for Michel rarely, if ever, worked on deals and Felix, being Felix, used other partners as his associates and they, in turn, used the hook of a high-profile "Felix deal" to get the best talent to work for them. But as Felix observed, condescendingly, other partners at the firm were now capable of executing M&A deals from beginning to end without his help. And these partners, chief among them the new Lehman recruits, needed able associates.

Loomis recalled how the ground shook when Lou Perlmutter, the new partner from Merrill Lynch, put together the first client presentation book for Colgate, the consumer products company. "It was very controversial," he said. But Michel slowly began to get with the program and authorized the upgrading of the associate pool. In the winter of 1979, Sherwood "Woody" Small came from Lehman, and Philip Keevil came from Morgan Stanley, via Oxford, Unilever, and Harvard Business School. "Then for the first time, we considered people from business school," Loomis recalled, with great moment. Other firms had been recruiting from business schools for years. But not Lazard. Lazard's recruiting of young bankers—who, in truth, were thought of more as clerks than as young bankers, let alone as potential future partners—was limited to a highly restricted pool of family friends of the existing partners, sons of the rich and famous or of clients, and frustrated associates at elite law firms or at other investment banks. The decision to recruit from a business school led to the arrival in 1980 of two Harvard Business School classmates, Luis Rinaldini and Mina Gerowin, the first woman professional ever hired by Lazard and the last for another four years. Lazard would never be the same.

Gerowin, who grew up in New Rochelle, where her father had a business importing fabric, had been a lawyer for Nestlé in Switzerland and for the law firm Brown & Wood, and decided she wanted to be an investment banker. A family relative introduced her to Philippe Herzog, a longtime partner at Lazard in Paris and the brother of André's wife. She remembered interviewing with Herzog and a few other longtime Lazard partners at the dilapidated offices on Rue Pillet-Will in Paris. She noticed during her interviews that each of the Lazard bankers had a pronounced nervous tic. This made her nervous, too. "I mean, what are these guys up to?" she remembered wondering. "But I realized later that nobody has put a dime in for years and what they're doing is just brushing the peeling paint off their heads, and when I came out, there was peeling paint all over my head." She got an offer, and André decided she should start working in New York, even though she had interviewed in Paris. Gerowin was André's last hire. Mullarkey had promised her she would make just as much at Lazard as she had as a lawyer for Nestlé. But the offer turned out to be $4,000 a year less. "And I didn't want to be their prisoner," she recalled. So she went to Harvard Business School instead. "Well, they kept saying, 'Where are you?' I said, 'You promised me more money, and if I don't get it, I'm not coming.' " After graduating from business school in August 1980, she joined Lazard in New York. "First of all, it was so dilapidated in New York," she said. "You're talking threadbare tan carpet. You would walk in, and a little old black man would be asleep on the front desk on the thirty-second floor. Fast asleep.

There'd be a leather couch with its seams split open and a threadbare tan carpet and a dead palm tree that stayed there for at least five or six years. Charming."

Soon enough she received the requisite advice from one of the old-time partners—in her case, Fred Wilson—about how to survive at Lazard: "Fred comes in and he lectures me, 'You know you have to understand life here, Mina, you're in the Byzantine empire and they were all in training. They're all baby barracudas. Felix is the biggest barracuda, but everybody's a baby barracuda. You gotta learn to swim. Then just remember, in the hallways you can survive anything but a direct hit. Learn to dodge.' " And her reaction to this advice? "Oh, shit," she thought, "what have I gotten myself into? And there was rule number one through ten, at the end of the day: Just never let them see you cry. Never."

After Princeton and four years before attending Harvard Business School, Luis Rinaldini had worked in the office of the renowned architect Philip Johnson. He worked on the Sears Tower in Chicago and Avery Fisher Hall in New York. A friend recommended that he try to get a job at Lazard. "I didn't have a clue, because I was an architect," he said. He called Alan McFarland, one of the new Lehman partners, and McFarland told him: "You don't really sound like you have the right qualifications, so I don't know." McFarland, "probably to brush me off," suggested Rinaldini call Mullarkey. "Mullarkey's only job was to say no," Rinaldini remembered. "I must have called him ten or fifteen times"—Mullarkey would never take the call.

> Finally I called him on a Friday afternoon, and he was very funny, and he said, "Goddamn it, my secretary's gone, you got me! You are so bloody persistent you might as well come in here and see me." He sat me down and asked me a bunch of tough questions, and he said, "Look, I like you and this might work, but I don't actually have any influence on this process. The guy you have to see is Pizzitola. But don't think it means you are going to get a job here. All it means is that you get to see Pizzitola."
>
> So I went to see Pizzitola, and he asked me questions up and down: Who's your grandfather? Who's your father? Who's your mother? What's your uncle do? I couldn't figure out what the hell he was asking, and I finally realized he was just checking to make sure I wasn't related to anyone important or anybody that Michel knew or some friend of Felix's so when he booted me out the door he wasn't going to hear from somebody who would say, "How could you throw Luis Rockefeller out the door?" Once he established he *could* throw me out the door, he then started

> asking me why I thought I could do the job. I said, "Look, I think I am relatively smart, and more importantly I work harder than anybody I know. If someone is willing to stay up until ten, I'll stay up until eleven. If someone is willing to stay up until eleven, I'll stay up until twelve and get it done." It was sort of the right answer for a tough, grizzly old guy.

Rinaldini was hired, and as he liked to say, "I was the first, the first Lazard associate hired out of business school because they always used to hire laterally."

He shared an office with Arnold Spangler, "who was five years older and still being treated as an associate." What Rinaldini found was a "bunch of old guys, like my age now, who had been in business for a bunch of years . . . very serious senior guys, with three or four younger guys around to crunch their numbers for them, so it really wasn't an investment banking firm in the way we know it today, it was a collection of industry and finance specialists, and then they decided to hire a couple of people out of business school."

Rinaldini, who went on to work extensively for Felix on deals for the next ten years, was well aware of his mentor's import when he arrived at the firm. "Felix had a reputation at the time that was both a little bit notorious and a little bit noteworthy," he said. "I was aware of a visible effort to manage it intelligently. He felt maligned by what had gone on in the ITT case and didn't feel that it was fair. . . . I think the biggest issue on that was just that it was in the press and it was very visible in the press and it was just one of those things that was very unpleasant for him personally after all the work that he had done and all the effort that he had made to be prudent, conservative, and sound. I think he was concerned that after all that, people would only remember him for something that had the opposite connotation. But he certainly outlived that issue and came out the other end."

THE LEHMAN BANKERS were behind these first tentative steps to hire the few younger professionals with business school training, rather than with legal training. On the one hand, their desire for the new MBAs paralleled their own success, which was palpable, doing deals at Lazard. They needed bodies to help them process the deals. But another phenomenon was at work as well, whether or not anyone at Lazard was cognizant of it. The early 1980s was the dawning of the age of widely available—and utilized—spreadsheet software. In late 1981, two software entrepreneurs, Mitchell Kapor and Jonathan Sachs, formed Lotus Development Corporation, outside of Boston, and began designing what became Lotus 1-2-3, the first commercially accepted spreadsheet software. It hit the market in January 1983. Lotus 1-2-3 was an immediate sensation, selling $53 million the first year, $157 million the second year, $200 million in 1985, and $250 million in 1986.

Lotus 1-2-3 without doubt materially contributed to the quantum increase in M&A activity from the early 1980s to today. Of course, the spreadsheet software was simply a catalyst for a greater confluence of factors. To be sure, if the economic conditions were not ripe for change or if the CEOs of corporations didn't view mergers and acquisitions as a means of achieving their perceived goals or if they had been unable to execute on the promise of the deals they consummated (and in many cases, they did not), then the deal boom would never have occurred. "I think it really became the means by which previously disconnected parties were able to communicate with each other in a format and in a language that was common; it was a numercial language at some level that people used within their organizations and between themselves and their clients or their customers or whatever," said Jim Manzi, who became CEO of Lotus in 1984. "And as a result it became a very powerful lingua franca for what was going on in that age. I don't know that it was seminal, but it was a spark. I think that's probably overstating it, but I think it's absolutely a big piece of the zeitgeist at the time, you know it was the technical part of the zeitgeist." So just as the elimination of fixed commissions in 1975 forever altered the Wall Street landscape, so, too, did the viral utilization of spreadsheet software—first Lotus 1-2-3, which over time was overwhelmed by Microsoft's Excel—among bankers and their corporate clients shake up the established hierarchy. But whereas the ending of fixed commissions was a brokers' problem, the spreadsheet revolution utterly demystified the role of the M&A bankers. Manzi called it the "democratization of Wall Street."

For the first time, the mystery of the numbers was eliminated. The deal alchemy that seemed to be the secret reserve of a select group of highly intelligent, experienced, plugged-in investment bankers was now available to all. Eventually, competition among financial institutions intensified to provide high-margin, prestigious M&A advice, as new entrants, such as commercial bankers, were able to do the same analysis as the investment bankers. Financial models could be shared among bankers and among their clients. Assumptions could be tweaked simply by altering a number in a cell. Multiple scenarios could be run quickly. How much one company could afford to pay for the shares of another could be determined easily. Internal rates of return could be calculated instantly, as could earnings dilution. A certain numerical precision overtook the world of deals—so-dubbed analysis paralysis.

Now, inevitably, some of this precision proved to be false, and expensively so. And a backlash against the commoditization of advice followed, too. Manzi himself was one of many CEOs who came to recognize, over time, that the value of a banker's judgment was more important than his or her ability to perform a financial analysis. "There are some incredibly smart people who have worked in investment banking before, during, and since [the spreadsheet revolution] who understand that it isn't really only about the numbers but it's really about the judgment being applied and whether there is sort of core economic logic here and whether the resulting team is going to be able to execute on what they're contemplating as opposed to this sort of stupid half-inch-deep thinking about the numbers squaring in the spreadsheet," he said. "And you know there are only a handful of people who are great at that." And that is one of the reasons why some ten years later, in 1995, Manzi selected Felix and Jerry Rosenfeld, then both at Lazard, to help advise Lotus against IBM's unwelcome, hostile $3.5 billion cash offer.

*

Nineteen eighty-one dawned with Lazard as the number-one adviser worldwide in M&A deals, having participated in some forty-five deals worth $12 billion. The firm also had a record year financially, earning $84.1 million in pretax income from its three houses. Michel was firmly ensconced, having—with the help of the Lazard partner Bruno Roger in Paris—convinced the new Socialist French president, François Mitterrand, not to nationalize the Lazard partnership in Paris as part of Mitterrand's plan to nationalize *all* the French banks. Even Lazard's rival Rothschild could not avoid nationalization. Although it was touch and go until the ultimate moment—when having less than 1 billion francs in deposits became the criterion used to decide the matter—Lazard was the only French bank anyone had ever heard of that avoided nationalization. This carefully orchestrated and heavily lobbied-for piece of good fortune put Lazard on a path, for much of the 1980s and 1990s, to ratcheting up its market share—and profits—in France to the stratosphere. There was simply nowhere else to turn in France for independent M&A advice in those days. "We explained to Jacques Attali and Michel Rocard [two key advisers to Mitterrand] that we were not a bank," Michel said, with perfect logic as always, "but rather we were a service company." This was a major victory for Lazard's longtime strategy of cozying up to politicians—by hiring them into the firm, by contributing financially to them, or merely by socializing with them, whatever it took—wherever it did business. In 1988, for instance, thanks to that fateful decision in 1981, Lazard's pretax profits in Paris reached their all-time peak of $109 million, up from $10 million in 1984. "They understood before anyone else that it was at the intersection of politics and business that the opportunities to make the most money were the greatest," Bernard Esambert, a longtime Rothschild partner and adviser to the French president Georges Pompidou, said of Lazard.

For his part, in 1981, Felix was back focused nearly exclusively on deals, although he remained chairman of MAC. The new partners were making meaningful contributions. Damon Mezzacappa had begun to build a small but profitable capital markets business. Overheads remained low. Lazard was poised for what proved to be a remarkable run of increasing profitability, just as the M&A market exploded in a rare confluence of large strategic mergers and the emergence of well-financed corporate raiders and buyout shops. Nineteen eighty-one was also the year that Felix and Lazard were able to—finally and quietly—put the ITT scandal behind them. ITT reached its $17.8 million tax settlement with the federal government in May, effectively ending a seven-year legal battle. (In 1981, Felix also turned over his ITT board seat to Michel.)

Ironically, just as the ITT matter was quietly wrapping up, Felix was perfecting his status as a national figure. There was no one catalyst for this, of course, as his reputation as a deal maker had been acknowledged for years. And his role as chairman of MAC allowed him to claim, with justification, a good measure of the credit for helping New York solve its fiscal problems and establish an institutional mechanism for preventing a recurrence.

The tipping point for Felix, though, was the election of Ronald Reagan, an unabashed conservative ideologue whose policies and rhetoric reintroduced the politics of polarization to the national debate, a schism that exists to this day. From the inauguration of 1981 on, and for the next eight years, Felix became something of an unguided political missile, a prominent card-carrying member of the political opposition—albeit without portfolio. His pronouncements as a quasi economist and political commentator were dark and foreboding and foretold of gloom and doom—the Dark Ages memo writ large—in almost stunningly perfect contrast to the Reagan rhetoric of optimism, hope, and "the shining city on the hill." The media loved Felix for it and rewarded him with prominence in the debate. In April 1981, the *New York Times* put Felix on the front page of the Metro section, in another one of its periodic kisses to him. There seemed to be no apparent news peg, other than a general desire to criticize Reagan economic policies that were not yet even three months old. He was interviewed, over breakfast—dry toast, orange juice, and coffee—both at his 770 Park Avenue duplex and in his Lazard office. "I believe in the free market," he said, "but I do not believe in laissez-faire. I do not believe that, at the end of the 20th century, in complicated, advanced industrial societies, an absolute free-market system exists or is desirable. If it does not exist, I do not think we should pretend we can cure the problems that we have with simply free-market solutions." His remarks were meant to be criticisms of how the Reagan administration was, in Felix's judgment, already mismanaging the economy. He referred to Reagan's "supply-side economics" as "an oversimplification" and "Keynes in drag."

According to William Serrin, the *Times*'s labor reporter, Felix was "demanding a fundamental change in the relationships between capital, labor and government. A new social contract must be established, he believes, between these three institutions if the American economic system is to know the productivity and abundance that has characterized it in most periods since the Civil War." Once again, Felix called for the reestablishment of the Reconstruction Finance Corporation as a way to facilitate the bargaining among competing interests that he felt must occur to "bring new vigor to the American economy." And then, with the venue switched to his Lazard office, he unleashed his parade of horribles, a veritable catalog of the social ills that have plagued American society for decades and of which we still have no resolution: "We have an educational system where a high school education means nothing. A society where families don't provide ethics; an illiterate Army that is being provided the most sophisticated weapons at enormous costs—weapons they don't know how to use. We produce tens of thousands of lawyers, tens of thousands of business school graduates who are utterly of no use to society, instead of producing more chemists and people who know how to run factories. We cry about productivity, and the children of plant foremen want to be computer programmers. The contradictions—Karl Marx's contradictions—seem to have arrived." Wow. Felix's own contradictions and complexities were such that one was torn between thinking him prescient and astute and thinking him more akin to a broken clock, which is still accurate twice a day. For much of the Reagan era, Felix predicted the decline and fall of American society at the very moment American economic and political power was reaching its zenith worldwide.

Many of his prognostications appeared in the pages of the *New York Review of Books*. Robert Silvers and Elizabeth Hardwick, the co-editors of the *Review,* became his friends. But he often also voiced his concerns in the op-ed pages of the nation's foremost newspapers. He gave numerous speeches. In March 1982, in the thick of the Reagan recession, he blasted Reaganomics in a speech before the Conference Board, a New York–based business think tank, as placing the U.S. economy on the edge of "economic disaster." He urged Reagan to convene a "summit meeting" of administration and congressional leaders plus Paul Volcker (the chairman of the Federal Reserve) to "grapple with the national economic problems." His dire warning about the "growing misery and despair among millions who cannot find work and untold others who have given up trying" was that "violence is the handmaiden of despair. It does not take a soothsayer or an alarmist to predict that, if this process continues into the summer, it may be a very hot summer indeed." Felix impressed one Democratic U.S. senator—Thomas Eagleton, of Missouri—so thoroughly that he introduced legislation in 1982 for a constitutional amendment—the Rohatyn Amendment—that would have permitted naturalized, foreign-born citizens such as Felix to run for president or vice president. Eagleton had been moved by his "unbounded admiration for the intellect and skills of Felix Rohatyn."

In a tongue-in-cheek letter to Felix in November 1982, Eagleton wrote, "I am getting calls from all over the country about Felix Rohatyn for President. However, some of my callers raise some delicate points. 1. Your first name, i.e. Felix. Some callers think you are a 'cat.' Therefore 'Felix' has to go. 2. 'Rohatyn' is hard to spell and pronounce. It looks like shit on a bumper sticker. Therefore, based on 1 and 2, we are changing your name to: Sterling Patriot Jefferson." The letter continued in this vein. "In short, Felix," the senator concluded, "you are on the way to the White House if we can totally re-make you in almost every respect." Said Felix: "Eagleton liked me."

One of those old-fashioned, massively voluminous *The New Yorker* profiles about Felix appeared in January 1983, giving him another platform for his ongoing criticism of Reaganomics. As the economy began to recover throughout 1983, Felix remained skeptical. "It's a normal recovery after a recession," he told Charlotte Curtis, then the society columnist for the *New York Times* and later its opinion page editor. "But it looks like the validation of a program"—Reaganomics—"that's deeply flawed." Curtis reported about a speech Felix gave to Fordham University's graduating class the week before. "The war we are going to fight is not with the Soviets," he told the students. "It is here at home. It is a war with lack of education, racial discrimination, crumbling cities and dying industries, enormous disparities of wealth and privilege. This is a war we can lose. If we [do], the result could be a dangerous willingness to experiment with political extremism of the right or the left. Political extremism of any type is the enemy of freedom. It is a bridge to nowhere."

ATTEMPTING TO ARTICULATE and grapple with these massive problems would, one would assume, be an all-consuming task. But for Felix, in truth, it had the quality of an extracurricular activity. He remained very much in the thick of the fresh and growing wave of mergers and takeovers, many of them originating in an unfriendly way, then sweeping across the country. The media exacerbated the excitement level by covering these battles as if they were high dramas. And the middlemen—bankers and lawyers—were portrayed as rock stars, albeit with an intellectual bent. "For the handful of men who orchestrate such takeovers, the work is heady, frantic and exhilarating—a crucible in which careers are made or broken," the *Times* allowed in 1982. "The group is comprised mostly of confirmed workaholics, who see the corporate battles in personal terms. Indeed part of the game is to see who outsmarts whom and takes home the prize." The article quoted Felix: " 'There are some fairly gigantic egos involved in all this.' " And the deals were big, too. There was DuPont's $7.5 billion acquisition of Conoco, after Conoco successfully eluded the hostile entreaties of Seagram (represented by Felix) and Mobil. Then Mobil and U.S. Steel battled for Marathon Oil, which U.S. Steel won for $6.2 billion. Then Mesa Petroleum attempted to take over Cities Services (known as Citgo). This prompted Citgo to turn the tables and attempt a takeover of Mesa. Ultimately, Gulf Oil emerged as a white knight and scooped up Citgo for $5.1 billion. This was just the tip of the merger iceberg. While there were more mergers in 1969 (6,107) than in 1981 (2,395), the dollar value of the mergers in the early 1980s had skyrocketed to $82.6 billion in 1981, from $23.7 billion in 1969.

Since the investment bankers advising these companies on these deals got paid on the absurd formula based on a percentage of the deal value, fees for bankers and lawyers exploded, too. On the DuPont-Conoco deal alone, the professional advisers walked off with more than $40 million in fees. First Boston, representing DuPont, and Morgan Stanley, representing Conoco, were paid $14 million each for their advice. First Boston received $18 million for representing Marathon in its sale to U.S. Steel. Not only did 1969 seem long ago in terms of the dollar value of M&A deals, but also with M&A fees it seemed an eon before. How quaint did Lazard's million-dollar fee for the McDonnell-Douglas merger—the first million-dollar fee—seem now?

Naturally, the increasingly large fees paid to M&A bankers caught the attention of critics. And just as naturally, bankers defended their excessive compensation, as they always do. A typical defense came from Stephen Friedman, then a leading M&A adviser at Goldman Sachs, who later led the prestigious firm with Robert Rubin before each entered national politics: "These fees don't come from widows and orphans. They come from people who are more than capable of strenuously negotiating over the amount of the fee. Fees are the purest form of competition. The companies have full knowledge of what other banks are getting for similar deals and the service provided, and they are not shy."

Felix, though, having perfected the art of cognitive dissonance, alone among his peers criticized the growing fees. "The level of fees is so different depending on what happens—and that's the unhealthy element," he told the *Times*. An apex of sorts was clearly reached during one of the most infamous takeover battles of all time—the 1982 fight for Bendix between Martin Marietta, Allied, and United Technologies. Bendix, led by its charismatic CEO, William Agee, took the offensive by launching a hostile offer for Martin Marietta, another aerospace company. Martin Marietta, now partnered with United Technologies (represented by Felix), countered with its own bid for Bendix. Ultimately, though, Allied won Bendix, but not before Bendix had acquired 70 percent of the public equity of Marietta and Marietta had acquired 50 percent of the public equity of Bendix. Allied ended up with Bendix and 38 percent of Martin Marietta. The two-month battle during the summer of 1982 played into the media's fascination with takeovers. There were the high-profile bankers of course, including an increasingly prominent M&A banker at First Boston named Bruce Wasserstein, but this mess had four huge corporations fighting a public war on multiple battlefields. There were more fronts than World War II. There was even the additional spice of the revealed affair between Agee and Mary Cunningham, one of his executives. Felix was outspoken in his criticism of his fellow bankers in this episode, too. "There's a general perception that investment banks' fees are too high, and that they don't earn them," he said. "That opinion is so widespread that the investment banking community had better pay attention to it, or someone will pay attention for us."

His fellow bankers, though, waved off Felix's criticisms. "Sour grapes," they replied, especially since Lazard increasingly seemed to be on the losing side of many of the deals or else was just missing them completely—and therefore missed out on many of these big fees. One unnamed banker suggested Lazard had "lost some standing on Wall Street" as a result of the growing success of competitors such as Wasserstein at First Boston and Marty Siegel at Kidder, Peabody, an old-line firm that had, under Siegel, developed a "takeover defense service" for companies fearful of getting taken over. Felix dismissed the competitors' observations. "Anyone can win as long as they're willing to pay anything," he said. "I think we gave correct advice" to United Technologies in the Bendix deal—to not pay up to win. To the increasingly voluble charges from the competition that Lazard was becoming less and less relevant, Felix said simply: "Time will tell whether we're an anachronism. But if our choice was changing to conform to what I take to be a general degradation of quality in investment banking, I'd rather go out of business."

It was left to no less a social critic than Michael Kinsley, then a top editor of the *New Republic,* to call Felix on the carpet for his bewildering trail of contradictions. The occasion was Kinsley's lengthy March 1984 review, in his own magazine, of Felix's *The Twenty-Year Century: Essays on Economics and Public Finance,* Random House's 175-page collection of his various ruminations on the state of the world. The title of the review, "The Double Felix," was a clever pun and foretold Kinsley's apt criticisms. "Rohatyn's progress from Felix the Fixer to Felix the Philosopher is one of the great public relations ascents of our time," he wrote, with an insight seemingly overlooked by everyone else. "The transformation has been so complete that even *The Washington Post* forgot along the way that he first hove into view (and got his nickname) as a minor figure in the Watergate scandal." Kinsley recounted the many twists and turns of Felix's involvement in the ITT-Hartford scandal and, with a fair amount of awe, professed jaw-dropping astonishment at Felix's ability to extract himself from the mess. "Chuck Colson put Watergate behind him by finding religion," Kinsley wrote, no doubt with a wry smile. "Felix Rohatyn has gone further: he has become a secular saint. He is simultaneously a leading member of the business community and the official investment banker of the New York left-wing intelligentsia." Kinsley pointed out that Felix's central thesis, whether perceived from the political left or the political right, was the maintenance of the status quo. "The terribly conservative essence of Rohatyn's philosophy is fear of change," he wrote. "He would invest the leaders of today's elites with extraordinary power and money in order to preserve the industrial, geographic, and financial status quo."

As Felix continued to lead Lazard's M&A practice and was, by design, its most prominent figure, Michel quietly set about accomplishing the few goals he had set out for himself and the firm when he took over from

André. Mezzacappa's capital markets group slowly began to grow. Municipal finance did, too, after Michel recruited a few bankers and traders from other firms. Michel also turned his attention to improving the asset management department, a backwater at the firm that he thought, through annual fee income, might help balance out the cyclicality of the high-margin M&A business. To do that, on Mezzacappa's recommendation, he hired from the outside Herb Gullquist and Norman Eig, the two heads of Oppenheimer's successful asset management business.

But the hiring of Gullquist and Eig created an ethical dilemma for Lazard from the outset, although Felix was not bothered by it. It turns out that Oppenheimer had *hired* Felix to sell Oppenheimer's mutual fund business, giving Lazard the unique opportunity to discover who, according to Leon Levy, the legendary founder of Oppenheimer, were the "best and brightest" fund managers and to woo them. "To me, this was an outrageous breach of ethics," Levy wrote in his 2002 memoir, *The Mind of Wall Street*. When, at a meeting at Lazard to discuss the matter, Levy complained to him about the hiring of Gullquist and Eig, Felix responded: "Look, this conversation is going nowhere. All of us have been through a divorce, right? Well, this is like any divorce where you have different sides." Unmoved, Steve Robert, then president of Oppenheimer, barked to Felix, "You're right. It's like a divorce but it's like a divorce in which your lawyer is sleeping with your wife."

Once they were on board, Michel pretty much left Eig and Gullquist alone to run their separate fiefdom, and they rewarded him by delivering steadily increasing and consistent financial performance. Along the way, of course, there were the occasional bumps. Inconvenient partners were jettisoned unemotionally. Before the arrival of the two men from Oppenheimer, Lazard Asset Management, then a tiny operation managing money for a few clients, was run by Stanley Nabi. But a year after their arrival, Eig and Gullquist called Nabi into a conference room. "We don't like you," Nabi said the "blunt and combative" Eig told him. "We don't want to work with you." Nabi said nothing. He left the firm shortly thereafter.

As the firm started to grow and new business lines such as capital markets and asset management expanded, Michel's laissez-faire management style began to show its flaws. True, André's iron grip had produced the ITT-Hartford fiasco, but that could *almost* be excused as his failure to grasp how the regulatory rules were changing around him while he continued to take full advantage of the old clandestine and clubby mores of Europe's postwar reconstruction. Felix, who obviously knew better, said he was only peripherally involved and, in any event, also claimed to be smart enough not to challenge André's will. While Felix's frequent attempts to wash his hands of the ITT scandals strain credibility, it is also abundantly clear the scandal had no effect whatsoever on Lazard's business. But Lazard would begin paying a price for Michel's management philosophy and for his decision to grow the size of the firm.

CHAPTER 9

"The Cancer Is Greed"

The first cracks in Lazard's carefully constructed facade came at the beginning of January 1984. Just after the new year, James V. Pondiccio Jr., thirty-seven, the firm's former assistant head trader, pleaded guilty in federal court to the charge of violating insider trading regulations. Felix and Lazard had been hired by Joseph E. Seagram & Sons, the liquor giant, to advise and to structure a $2 billion hostile tender offer for St. Joe Minerals Corporation, the nation's largest lead producer. Seagram's hostile tender offer for St. Joe was launched on March 11, 1981. Shortly beforehand, Pondiccio caught wind of it and bought call options on St. Joe's stock through family members' accounts at another brokerage. According to the U.S. attorney's office, Pondiccio made $40,000 after the St. Joe stock rose with the tender offer. Seagram later dropped its bid after Fluor Corporation made an even higher bid for St. Joe and Seagram decided not to compete. Pondiccio faced a maximum penalty of five years in prison and/or a $1,000 fine.

While insider trading had long been an unfortunate fact of life on Wall Street, the SEC chairman John S. R. Shad made the prosecution of insider trading a top priority after taking over the commission in May 1981. During the year ended October 31, 1979, the SEC filed only seven insider trading cases. In the year ended October 31, 1983, under Shad, twenty-four insider trading cases were filed, and another seventeen were filed between November 1 and January 1, 1984. Of course, the late 1980s would bring a plethora of high-profile and embarrassing insider trading scandals to Wall Street—the Pondiccio case was simply one of the first involving a Wall Street trader. But it was not the last, and not even the last that year at Lazard.

On December 10, 1984, Danny Davis, then thirty and considered one of the top salesmen in Lazard's equity department, "calmly handed a co-worker the phone numbers of his next of kin," opened one of the windows on the thirty-first floor of One Rockefeller Plaza, and jumped out, plunging to his death. He left a wife and one young child and a new $300,000 Tudor home in Scarsdale they were renovating. The SEC probed the circumstances surrounding his suicide because of suspicious trading activity in several stocks favored by Davis, particularly Value Line, a publisher of investment information, the IPO of which Lazard had recently underwritten. The regulators requested Lazard's trading records in Value Line from December 5, 1984, to December 13, 1984, during which time the stock declined to $23.25 per share, from $31.50, after a poor earnings announcement. (The SEC now says it has no records of the Davis investigation.) The firm also investigated the Davis suicide, Michel said later, to see if any impropriety had occurred, and found nothing amiss.

The Davis suicide followed by a few weeks the embarrassing leak to the *Wall Street Journal* of a detailed confidential Lazard study of a potential $4 billion takeover of Allied by United Technologies, one of Felix's best clients. Lazard had done the work at the request of Harry Gray, UT's chairman and CEO, a year after United Technologies, with Felix advising, lost Bendix to Allied. Bankers do these kinds of analyses all the time, of course, but rarely, if ever before, had the press obtained one and reported on it. Much to Lazard's embarrassment, the leak naturally scuttled any potential deal. This is not the way you want your trusted M&A adviser to behave. Felix launched an internal probe into the source of the unwanted disclosure. "I think there were three people in this firm who had access to that report," he said later. "We satisfied ourselves, as much as you can ever satisfy yourself, that it didn't come out of here. We turned the place upside down."

WITHIN WEEKS OF the United Technologies leak and Davis's suicide, another, more outrageous scandal began to unfold, involving John A. Grambling Jr., a former Lazard associate, and his supposedly unwitting accomplice, Robert M. Wilkis, then a Lazard vice president. Grambling came to Lazard, after a stint at Citibank, in the early 1980s through the auspices of Jim Glanville, his fellow Texan. Grambling's father had been the CEO of a Texas utility, and the Gramblings were one of the wealthiest families in El Paso, where he grew up—in other words, a typical Lazard hire. But Grambling didn't last long at Lazard. He left under mysterious circumstances a year or so after he arrived. The suspicion was that, among other reasons, he was quietly dismissed after he made unwelcome sexual advances toward Mina Gerowin in an elevator at One Rockefeller Plaza. After Lazard, Grambling went briefly to Dean Witter Reynolds. In 1983, he set up Grambling & Company, with offices in Greenwich and on Park Avenue.

Soon thereafter, he became aware that Husky Oil Ltd., a Canadian company, had put its American subsidiary, RMT Properties, up for sale. RMT owned and operated oil wells and refineries in several western states and also distributed its products through eight hundred gas stations. RMT's revenues were in the hundreds of millions of dollars, and it employed thousands. Grambling won the bidding for RMT with an offer of $30 million. He also realized RMT required another $70 million of working capital to run the business. So, in total, he needed, he believed, an even $100 million to buy the business and run it. Despite being from a wealthy family, Grambling had nothing close to the money required. But as the mid-1980s were the early days of the leveraged buyout, or LBO, craze, Grambling figured he could borrow the money, all the money, from others. And that is what he set out to do. First he turned to the finance subsidiary of General Electric—then called General Electric Credit Corporation—to get the bulk of his $100 million. But in September 1984, GECC pulled the plug after it decided Grambling was paying too much for RMT.

Fearful the sale would fall through after GECC pulled out, Husky introduced Grambling to one of its main banks, the Bank of Montreal, to see if it would finance the deal. Husky also offered to guarantee any loan the Bank of Montreal agreed to make, effectively eliminating the bank's risk. The Canadian bankers quickly analyzed the deal and came to the conclusion the RMT opportunity made sense, especially with the Husky guarantee. The sellers had given Grambling a January 1 deadline to close the deal, making the time short for the Bank of Montreal and its Manhattan law firm, Shearman & Sterling, to complete the loan documentation.

In the midst of that process, on December 7, Grambling came up with the nifty idea that he would also ask the Bank of Montreal for a separate, personal loan of $7.5 million. As would be typical in an LBO, he told the Bank of Montreal, he had incurred numerous expenses—for lawyers, accountants, and consultants—as the deal came together, and his personal cash to pay the cost of these professionals was virtually nonexistent. So not only would the entire purchase price of $100 million be borrowed; Grambling intended to borrow an additional $7.5 million.

In truth, he needed the other $7.5 million to pay off a host of increasingly irritated creditors nationwide, from whom he had borrowed money previously and had no way to repay. In evaluating the creditworthiness of the proposed $7.5 million loan, the bankers asked Grambling for a copy of his personal balance sheet. Grambling provided the document, which showed, among other things, that he owned 375,136 shares of Dr Pepper. In November 1983, Forstmann Little & Co., a large New York private-equity firm, had agreed to buy all of Dr Pepper's publicly traded shares for $22 each, a total of $512.5 million. The deal, *according to Grambling,* was to close no later than January 22, 1985, and Grambling's shares were about to be bought by Forstmann Little for a total of almost $8.3 million. In fact, though, Forstmann Little closed the Dr Pepper deal on February 28, 1984, not January 22, 1985—an easily verifiable fact that should have been (but wasn't) the first tip to everyone that something was terribly amok. Understandably, the Bank of Montreal demanded Grambling's Dr Pepper shares as collateral for the $7.5 million personal loan. Those shares, soon to be turned into cash, the bankers reasoned, would be the best security should Grambling fail to repay the personal loan.

Dr Pepper had hired Felix and Lazard to sell the company beginning in July 1983. Felix conducted an auction and found Forstmann Little, which agreed to pay $22 a share, in cash, for a company that had been trading at around $13 per share. For the impressive feat of getting shareholders an almost 70 percent bump in value, Lazard earned a $2.5 million fee. The Dr Pepper sale to Forstmann Little was one of the largest LBOs to that time, and so the deal—even though Felix was one of the more outspoken critics of the LBO frenzy and the so-called junk bonds used to finance it—was big news around the firm. Although for some reason the Canadian bankers missed the fact that the Dr Pepper sale had *already closed,* they asked Grambling how the bank could get its hands on the Dr Pepper stock as collateral. Grambling directed them to Wilkis, the Lazard vice president with whom he had shared an office, a secretary, and a brief career at Citibank.

The Bank of Montreal banker called Wilkis, who walked him through the public documentation of the Dr Pepper buyout—he did not work on the deal—and, mysteriously, confirmed the erroneous January 22, 1985, closing date, three weeks after Grambling's RMT deal was to have closed. In a follow-up call, Grambling again directed the Canadian banker Ivor Hopkyns to Wilkis. "Ivor, call Bob Wilkis again," he told him. "The stock is in my Lazard Frères account, and Bob can give you the necessary details." When Hopkyns called Wilkis again to get the Dr Pepper stock information, Wilkis responded, "I can't give you that information. I'm not John's account officer. For the details on John's stock, you have to ask someone in the back office." Increasingly frustrated with figuring out how to get the collateral he needed, Hopkyns asked Wilkis if he was authorized to sign the document transferring Grambling's Dr Pepper stock to the bank. "No," Wilkis replied. "I am an associate, not a member of the firm. Only a partner can sign such a transfer. You're going to have to get a firm member to sign any kind of transfer document." Hopkyns then called Grambling to complain that the personal loan could not be closed "until we have the ownership facts for the assignment" of the Dr Pepper shares. Grambling responded to this problem by saying, "Everything has been straightened out at Lazard, Ivor. Bob just needed to get the numbers. He has them now waiting for you. Just give him a call."

Hopkyns called Wilkis again, and the Dr Pepper stock information was now available. Wilkis told him: "I just received a call from the record keeper at Continental Illinois Bank"—the paying agent for the Dr Pepper stock. "This is how John holds his stock. There's 181,000 shares of stock in his own name, certificate number DX67144. He owns another 194,036 shares in the name of E. F. Hutton and Company, certificate number DX24618." Continental Illinois Bank's contractual obligation was to disburse cash to Dr Pepper shareholders in exchange for their legitimate shares. The company Forstmann Little formed to buy Dr Pepper signed a nonpublic contract with Continental Illinois Bank on February 22, 1984—six days before the closing—requiring the bank to perform this function until six months after the closing date, which would have been at the latest August 28, 1984. Forstmann Little placed an ad in the *Wall Street Journal* announcing the closing of its acquisition of Dr Pepper on March 7, 1984.

Clearly unaware of the specifics of the closing and having been deceived by Wilkis, Hopkyns made note of the certificate numbers and forwarded the information to his Shearman & Sterling lawyer, who was preparing the crucial consent and agreement document that was to have assigned the Dr Pepper stock as collateral for the $7.5 million personal loan. The Shearman & Sterling attorney, James Busuttil, reconfirmed the information himself with Wilkis, by telephone, and asked him who from Lazard would be signing the consent form. "I can't sign and I don't know who John is going to get to sign the consent," Wilkis explained to Busuttil. On December 24, 1984, Busuttil had the consent form hand-delivered to Wilkis at Lazard's Rockefeller Center offices. The signature lines were left blank.

Four days later, Grambling showed up at Shearman & Sterling's offices in the sleek new Hugh Stubbins–designed Citicorp Center at 599 Lexington Avenue in midtown Manhattan. He was there to close on the $7.5 million personal loan and carried with him the all-important, and now signed, consent and agreement form. There had been two signature lines on the document, and both were filled in. The first line was signed "Lazard Frères & Co.," and in the same hand just below was what purported to be the signature of Peter Corcoran, a longtime Lazard partner in New York who had come to the firm in the early 1970s, also from Citibank. Underneath Corcoran's signature was another signature, that of "Robert W. Wilkis, Vice President." The quaint Lazard signature documents showing which partners could contractually bind the firm had been around for decades. The Grambling closing was a clear instance where the importance of the accuracy of that authority became essential. The documentation for the personal loan to Grambling was complete, and together Busuttil and Grambling called Hopkyns in Canada so that Busuttil could inform his client that a Lazard partner—Corcoran—had indeed signed the crucial form. Hopkyns told Grambling he wanted to speak with Corcoran to confirm he could legally bind Lazard, a point that Hopkyns had become sensitive to after his earlier calls with Wilkis.

"Reaching Corcoran might be a problem," Grambling replied. "I think Corcoran may already have left for vacation." Hopkyns called Lazard and confirmed that Corcoran had left for the New Year's holiday. Grambling offered to get a phone number where Corcoran could be reached. He then called Hopkyns. "I've gotten the number, Ivor," Grambling told him. "Corcoran's already in Miami. He's at 305-940-7536." Hopkyns made the call, and a man answered. "Peter Corcoran?" he asked. "Yes, this is he," the man said. After Hopkyns identified himself as the Bank of Montreal banker, Corcoran supposedly replied, "You're calling about the consent form I signed for John. I am a general partner at Lazard Frères and have been for years." This Corcoran—who was really Grambling's accomplice Robert Libman—told Hopkyns that he had known Grambling at Lazard, and despite Grambling's departure from the firm, "I anticipate that Lazard Frères will be doing a great deal of business with John's companies in the coming year." This Corcoran confirmed to Hopkyns he had signed the consent form and that he was authorized to do so. After hearing Corcoran's confirmation, Hopkyns authorized the closing of Grambling's $7.5 million loan. Acting quickly, Grambling approved the transfer of the funds out of the Bank of Montreal's Park Avenue New York office to his highly agitated creditors—banks in Kansas, Texas, Arizona, Connecticut, and Tennessee.

Meanwhile, the real Peter Corcoran *was* on vacation. But not in Miami. He was in Vermont with his family for a ski holiday. About two weeks later, on January 15, another Bank of Montreal banker, Scott Hean, who was busy trying to put the finishing touches on the $100 million loan needed for Grambling's purchase of RMT, recalled that the bank had not yet received the cash from the sale of Grambling's Dr Pepper shares, which was the security for the personal loan. Hopkyns called

Wilkis. When will the Bank of Montreal get its cash pursuant to the consent and agreement that Corcoran and Wilkis had signed? Hopkyns wondered.

"I don't know what you are talking about," Wilkis said.

"I'm talking about the agreement you signed, the consent I have a copy of, here right in front of me," Hopkyns said. "It bears your signature, Robert W. Wilkis, and—"

"You have a problem," Wilkis said. "My middle name is Mark." Wilkis hung up the phone.

Hopkyns called the Lazard main number. He asked for Corcoran. "Corcoran here," Corcoran said.

Hopkyns knew instantly upon hearing the *real* Peter Corcoran's voice that the Bank of Montreal, as Wilkis had said, had a problem, a big problem. Busuttil called Tom Mullarkey, the Lazard general counsel and chief firefighter, to find out what was going on. "No," Mullarkey responded, "Corcoran and Wilkis did not sign that document that you have in front of you." He asked Busuttil to messenger over a copy of the document.

On January 17, Lazard, through Mullarkey, provided Shearman & Sterling with its official response to the Grambling matter. "Dear Mr. Busuttil," Mullarkey wrote, "I have your letter dated January 16 enclosing a copy of a Consent and Agreement purportedly signed by Lazard Frères & Co. Before you sent the letter to me with its enclosure, I informed you that the Consent and Agreement was spurious. Manifestly, we have no intention of complying with its terms. Thomas F. X. Mullarkey." The Shearman attorneys and others would make much of Mullarkey's use of the word "spurious" instead of a more precise word, such as "a forgery" or "fraudulent," but clearly Mullarkey and Lazard had denied the authenticity of the consent form and would not comply with its terms.

Hopkyns called Grambling for an explanation. "I don't know what's happening at Lazard," Grambling asserted. "But it sounds like a technical error regarding whose signatures can technically bind the firm. Wilkis and Corcoran must have fouled up. Remember, Ivor, I worked there, so I know how they make these mistakes. Someone's trying to cover his ass. I'll make some calls and get to the bottom of this." Later that night, Grambling gave Hopkyns his explanation: "I just got off the phone with my wife. She read me the mail delivered to our home in Connecticut. E. F. Hutton remitted my Dr Pepper proceeds to my account at Coronado Bank in El Paso, Texas. The transmittal voucher was in today's mail. The stock had been cashed on the fifteenth, just like we expected, but it was sent to the wrong place."

According to a *Wall Street Journal* article from March 1987 summarizing the whole Grambling affair: "The truth was that Mr. Grambling didn't own a single share of Dr Pepper. The documents were forged; so were the signatures of Messrs. Corcoran and Wilkis. The Libman balance sheet was made out of whole cloth. The Peter Corcoran that Ivor Hopkyns had phoned in Florida was, in reality, Robert H. Libman doing an impersonation." Grambling and his Florida accomplice, Libman, had systematically set up a nationwide Ponzi scheme designed to defraud banks all across the country. The idea was to keep one step ahead of the old creditors by borrowing money from new ones and using the proceeds to repay the old. In the end, of course, that can go on for only so long. They tried to steal a total of $36.5 million and made off with $13.5 million "without pointing a gun at anybody," as the *Journal* put it.

Brian Rosner, then the Manhattan assistant district attorney, who successfully prosecuted Grambling and Libman, explained to the *Journal*: "It's called robbing Peter to pay Paul, and as long as it works, as long as the money comes in, no one knows he's being victimized. . . . No one is more complacent than a banker who has been repaid." In May 1987, after a lengthy investigation into Grambling's activities, which revealed that he had been stealing at least since college, the acting state Supreme Court justice Herman Cahn sentenced Grambling to between seven and two-thirds and twenty years in a state prison after he pleaded guilty to thirty-two counts of fraud. He had separately received a four-year sentence from a federal judge in San Diego for attempting to defraud a bank there as part of the overall scheme. The state prison time for Grambling began after the federal prison time was completed. Grambling's prison sentence, at the time, was one of the harshest ever for a white-collar criminal. (Libman received a six-month sentence after pleading guilty more rapidly than Grambling, who attempted to commit even more of these crimes while awaiting sentencing.)

What has remained less clear in the whole Grambling affair is the role of Wilkis. Shouldn't he have been aware of the implausibility of Grambling having more than $8 million worth of Dr Pepper stock when Forstmann Little had bought and paid for the company nearly a year before? Nobody, no matter how wealthy, leaves $8 million worth of stock lying around for eleven months when it could be turned into badly needed cash. Wilkis also admitted knowing that Grambling had asked their mutual secretary, Sheila, to send him a bunch of Lazard stationery, even though he no longer worked at Lazard. Wouldn't that have been a tip of odd behavior? At one point, as the fraud was being sorted out, Jon Greenblatt, a Shearman & Sterling litigator assigned to the case, told Rosner he thought Wilkis "was Grambling's accomplice" and that would be made clear after Rosner interviewed Greenblatt's clients at the Bank of Montreal. "But it sure looks like Grambling had Wilkis working for him," Greenblatt told Rosner. Lazard hired Martin Flumenbaum, a litigator at Paul, Weiss, to represent it and Wilkis—indicating that Lazard felt Grambling had taken advantage of Wilkis and Lazard did not need separate counsel. In his first discussion with Rosner about the matter, Flumenbaum told him, "Wilkis was duped by Grambling. He can fill in a lot of what you need to know to make your case." According to *Swindle,* Rosner's 1990 book on the Grambling case, by mid-February 1985, Flumenbaum had successfully negotiated with Rosner "full transactional immunity" for Wilkis. "That means you can't be prosecuted for any crimes derived from what you tell me," Rosner told Wilkis, unless he were to later lie in front of the grand jury, should he be asked to appear.

With full immunity in hand, Wilkis laid out his version of what had happened between him and Grambling. "In early December, I gave him a call," he began. "Lazard had just finished a big deal that I was involved in, and I wanted to let people know what I had done. I sat down at my desk with my Rolodex, and started calling everyone on my cards—classmates, associates, acquaintances—just to let them know. Grambling was one of the dozens of people I called." When Rosner expressed surprise at this boastful behavior, Wilkis said, "I was just tooting my own horn. That's the way the Street works. Wall Street, I mean. You have to let people know what you've done, and that you're around, so they think of you in their next deal."

Grambling then called Wilkis on December 19 and told him about the pending RMT deal and how he needed some help with the Canadian bankers. Wilkis explained to Rosner he thought maybe Grambling would be a new client and was worth helping. "And he tells me how he has this problem with bankers," Wilkis told Rosner. "They're Canadians, real slow, dim-witted, he says. And he has to explain to them how, because of a leveraged buyout, his Dr Pepper shares are worth so much in cash. Now, Lazard had done the Dr Pepper deal, so I knew about it. And, we're talking, and I ask, 'How many shares,' and he goes '360,000 or so.' And I think, 'Jesus, when he was here everybody knew he was filthy rich, a Texas oil brat, but here's this guy, he has 360,000 shares of Dr Pepper hanging around'—and I do some quick calculations in my head, that's $8 million we're talking about—'and he hasn't even converted the stock yet.' You see, the stock had been convertible for months, with mid-January 1985 being the cutoff date. And this guy, I'm thinking, he has so much fucking money he doesn't even notice that his stock can be converted to $8 million of cold cash immediately.

"So, he asks me if I can talk to these dim-witted Canadians. 'You know,' he says, 'they don't understand LBOs and high finance, and if you could just explain to them how the deal worked, and how the money comes out at the end.' And I agree. Why not? If I can help the guy out in such a little manner on such a big deal, why not? So I say 'yes,' and Hopkyns, the Canadian banker, calls that day. I explain the LBO to him, and the cash conversion process."

"Did you tell Hopkyns that Grambling owned 360,000 shares of Dr Pepper?" Rosner asked.

"I told him I wasn't Grambling's account officer, and couldn't give details about Grambling's stock," Wilkis replied.

"Did you disagree with Hopkyns when he referred to Grambling owning 360,000 shares?" the assistant DA said.

"No," Wilkis responded. "I thought Grambling was a multimillionaire. The rumors, from when he was at Lazard, were that he was worth $50 million. So $8 million of Dr Pepper stock was just, yeah, it seemed right." Astonishingly, Rosner had granted Wilkis immunity without having checked something as simple as when the Dr Pepper deal had actually closed. The information about Continental Illinois Bank's role was not publicly available, and so Wilkis could not have seen it, and even if he had, the bank's job would have ended, contractually, five months *before* Wilkis and Grambling claimed. Rosner had been duped by Wilkis.

Wilkis then recounted for Rosner the calls about signing the consent form and his unwillingness to do it because he had no authorization. He said he didn't think too much more about the whole thing until January 15, when Hopkyns called looking for the Dr Pepper money. He then relayed the "You have a problem" conversation. Wilkis said it didn't take long for the Lazard bankers and lawyers to figure out what Grambling had done. "Christ, I could have killed that shit," Wilkis told Rosner. "All of a sudden my job is on the line. The first reaction of everyone is that I helped him do this."

Rosner wrote that Wilkis threw his hands in the air at this point. "Of course, I did help him," Wilkis said. "But even saying that makes me feel like a jerk. Credibility is important on the Street. All of a sudden, after so many good deals, my credibility's down the drain. Now Wilkis is the sap who got done in by Grambling." Wilkis explained he called Grambling and "cursed him out" and then Grambling turned on him, saying, "How dare I accuse him of forgery." Wilkis recounted a few more relevant details for Rosner, who then asked him if there was anything else. "No, but, that son-of-a-bitch hurt me," Wilkis said. "Here's a guy born with a silver spoon in his mouth, and I'm just a poor schmuck just trying to make my money the old-fashioned way, and this is what the guy does to me."

Apparently, though, Wilkis had long before run out of patience trying to make money the old-fashioned way. Since at least November 1979—more than *five years* before his conversation with Rosner—he had been systematically uncovering inside information about Lazard's merger advisory assignments and revealing it to a ring of bankers led by the now infamous Dennis Levine, as chronicled in James Stewart's *Den of Thieves.* This revelation makes it even more implausible to the layman that Wilkis could have simply been Grambling's innocent dupe.

Wilkis met Levine in 1977 at a cocktail party given by the Citicorp chairman, Walter Wriston, for new Citicorp employees. Unlike Levine, who was a gruff, uncultured kid from Bayside, Queens, Wilkis had far more of a classic Lazard background for someone not related to a CEO or French nobility. He grew up in Baltimore, a product of Orthodox Hebrew schooling. He was a graduate of Harvard University and Stanford Business School. Raised an Orthodox Jew, he had taught handicapped children in the Boston public school system after college but also worked at the World Bank and had spent a summer at the Treasury Department, where he researched economic issues. He thought of himself as politically quite liberal. He had married a Cuban-born woman and spoke five other languages fluently: French, German, Italian, Arabic, and Hebrew. By the time he had graduated from business school, which he detested, his wife, Elsa, was pregnant, and his mother was getting divorced. Wilkis needed money. The job offer from Citicorp provided him with a steady income. But he hated Citicorp, too, seeing it as stuffed full of Waspy "corporate types." Only Levine showed an interest in him and would tell him, "You know, we're just nice Jewish boys in a hostile, WASP environment," while trying to get Wilkis to skip out of the office for an afternoon diversion. One evening, while the two were socializing, Levine told Wilkis: "I knew after I was bar mitzvahed that there was an inside track and information was the key." He would often add that his "dream of dreams" was "the euphoria, the omnipotence of reading on September 12 the *Wall Street Journal* of September 13."

When the two friends came up for promotion the following year, the focused, hardworking Wilkis was promoted, but Levine was not. Levine left Citicorp soon thereafter for a job at Smith Barney, then an independent brokerage and now, ironically, part of Citigroup. During his first week at Smith Barney, he called Wilkis and told him to buy a stock. "Just buy it," Levine told him. "Don't ask any questions." Wilkis bought several hundred shares, and the stock price subsequently rose dramatically. "See, Bob," his friend said, "I am going to take care of you." Smith Barney shortly thereafter moved Levine to its Paris office, which he did not like because it was far outside the information flow. At around the same time, Smith Barney had hired J. Tomilson Hill III, from First Boston, to set up an M&A business at the firm, in a belated effort to cash in on the growing merger boom. Levine desperately wanted to get into Smith Barney's M&A group and regularly asked Hill if he could join. Eventually, Hill, who now is a wealthy vice chairman at the Blackstone Group and runs its hedge fund business, relented, and Levine moved back to New York and joined the M&A group. Levine and Wilkis celebrated Levine's move at a fancy Manhattan restaurant where they swilled bottles of Château Talbot '71. Levine also told Wilkis he had opened a Swiss bank account, at Pictet & Cie, in Geneva, one of the secret accounts he would use to make insider trades.

Over time, Levine's ruminations about the possibility of profiting from insider trading began to make more and more sense to Wilkis. Soon after Levine left Citicorp for Smith Barney, Wilkis left for Blyth Eastman Dillon, where he worked briefly, before moving again, to Lazard, to work for Frank Zarb in the international department. Levine had been urging Wilkis to get to a place, like Lazard, that was heavily involved in mergers, since that's where the excitement was and the potential greater for insider trading. Wilkis later said he just wanted to be able to put his language skills to work and to find a way to help people in a banking capacity. Levine's idea had been for Wilkis—and other members of the circle—to listen for information about pending mergers Lazard was working on while Levine would do the same at Smith Barney, where he worked before moving to Lehman Brothers and then to Drexel. Other co-conspirators at Lehman Brothers and the law firms Wachtell, Lipton and Skadden, Arps soon joined the circle. "You gotta do it," Levine told Wilkis. "Everybody else is. Insider trading is part of the business. It's no different from working in a department store. You get a discount on clothes you buy. You work at a deli. You take home pastrami every night for free. It's the same thing as information on Wall Street."

"I'm scared," Wilkis replied.

"Look," Levine continued. "It's foolproof. And I'd love to give you tips. But you gotta get set up like the big guys. You gotta open a foreign bank account so that it will all be confidential."

When Wilkis still expressed discomfort, Levine pounced. "I know you want to help your mother and provide for your family. This is the way to do it. Don't be a schmuck. Nobody gets hurt."

In November 1979, years before the Grambling swindle about which he claimed innocence, Wilkis took the hint. He convinced his wife to take a family vacation to Nassau, in the Bahamas. While there, Wilkis took all of his $40,000 in savings and, following advice carefully given to him by Levine, opened a "Swiss bank account" at Credit Suisse. He was "Mr. Green" and his dummy Bahamian corporation had the name "Rupearl." Since he was isolated from M&A deals in Zarb's group, Wilkis now sought to befriend the Lazard bankers in M&A to find out what they were working on. He passed this information on to Levine, using code names.

Since Lazard was much more involved in the flow of M&A deals than Smith Barney, Levine naturally wanted to work there to fuel his scheme. He interviewed several times at Lazard, but there was no interest in him, given his gruff manner and his common upbringing. The rebuffs, though, fueled Levine's desire to get back at the firm.

Swiss bank account in hand, Wilkis finally gave in to Levine's ongoing exhortations for more and better inside information about Lazard's merger activity. One Friday evening in May 1980, around 8:00 p.m., Wilkis allowed Levine into Lazard's offices, and once there he began rifling through the desks, papers, and Rolodexes of the Lazard partners. According to *Den of Thieves,* Levine even admired Lou Perlmutter's "cache of Cuban cigars." Michel said later he discovered Levine had searched his office as well. Levine found documents—and copied them—about the French oil company Elf Aquitaine's pending acquisition of Kerr-McGee, another oil company. (The deal did not happen after the French government nixed it.) He also took a chart showing where all the Lazard partners sat so that in the future, when he discovered which partners were working on which deals, he would know the offices to search. Wilkis told Levine about United Technologies' entry into the Bendix fray, making Levine $100,000 after he bought stock before the announcement. Much inside information passed between the two men. In 1984, Wilkis told Levine about Lazard's advice to the Limited in the company's efforts to buy Carter Hawley Hale Stores, a department store chain. The deal did not go through, but Levine still made $200,000.

Wilkis had also recruited a Lazard junior analyst, Randall Cecola, to help him in his quest. They used to walk home to the Upper West Side together after work. One evening in 1983, after Wilkis had moved into Lazard's M&A group, he and Cecola had dinner together at La Cantina, a now defunct Mexican restaurant on Columbus Avenue. He confided to Cecola the whole scheme; Cecola was an enthusiastic participant. Cecola immediately told Wilkis about a deal he was working on—an improbable hostile bid by Chicago Pacific Corporation for Textron, the Providence-based conglomerate. Wilkis called Levine and told him the news. Levine bought 51,500 Textron shares, and Wilkis bought 30,000. Two weeks later, Chicago Pacific announced its tender offer for Textron, which also ultimately failed. But Levine and Wilkis each made money, $200,000 and $100,000, respectively, during the run-up after the announcement.

However, the size and timing of their trades were such that they attracted the attention of the SEC, and an investigation commenced. They were each subpoenaed to testify about the Textron deal before the SEC, and Levine appeared on November 14, 1984—one month before Wilkis said he was first asked by Grambling to help him out. The SEC investigation led to the downfall of Levine and Wilkis, among others, and exposed the largest insider trading ring in American history.

Den of Thieves, although it was published in 1991, never made the connection between Wilkis and Grambling. Nor did the prosecutor Rosner make the connection between Wilkis and Levine before giving Wilkis immunity in the Grambling matter. Indeed, that Wilkis got immunity was itself amazing. To this day, Rosner said he never thought Wilkis was anything more than a duped bystander in the Grambling matter, an observation that—while Rosner no doubt believed it and getting Wilkis to finger Grambling was essential to his conviction—could not possibly have been accurate. In February 1987, in the midst of the still-pending Grambling mess, Wilkis was sentenced to two concurrent 366-day prison terms, in the Danbury prison camp, for his role in the insider trading scheme. For his part, Cecola pleaded guilty to one count of tax evasion and to failing to report his insider trading profits. He was suspended from the Harvard Business School, where he had enrolled after leaving Lazard. Wilkis made about $4 million from the illegal trades, including $2.7 million in 1985 alone, while still at Lazard, when he stole information about twelve pending deals and traded in their securities. Wilkis pleaded guilty to four felonies and settled insider trading charges with the SEC by disgorging what was left of his illegal profits—some $3.3 million—and a new Park Avenue apartment. He was left with only $60,000 in cash, a Buick, and his 321 West Seventy-eighth Street apartment. With considerable understatement, Grambling said in an interview that he was "perhaps not the best person to talk about Lazard." He lives in upstate New York, near Catskill State Park, with his second wife, whom he met while incarcerated.

All of these criminal indiscretions stuck a dagger into the Lazard corpus, missing by mere inches the heart of the firm but badly damaging its sacred reputation for honesty and integrity. True, the firm tacked awfully close to the wind during the ITT scandals a decade earlier, but until Pondiccio, Wilkis, Cecola, and Grambling, no Lazard employee or former employee had been convicted of wrongdoing, let alone—according to the public record anyway—illegally profited from insider information or from forgeries.

Despite supposedly having been the target of a criminal grand jury investigation during the previous decade, Felix was not pleased. In March 1987, one month after Wilkis's sentencing, Felix wrote "The Blight on Wall Street" in the *New York Review of Books,* in which he denounced the increasing lack of morality in the investment banking profession. He warned, "As the revelations of illegality and excesses in the financial community begin to be exposed, those of us who are part of this community have to face a hard truth: a cancer has been spreading in our industry, and how far it will go will only become clear as the Securities and Exchange Commission and federal prosecutors pursue the various investigations currently under way. The cancer is greed." He pointed out to his readers that he had been an investment banker for more than thirty years. "It has been an honorable profession," he wrote. "I want it to stay that way." But lately, he added, "too much money is coming together with too many young people who have little or no institutional memory, or sense of tradition, and who are under enormous pressure to perform in the glare of Hollywood-like publicity. The combination makes for speculative excesses at best, illegality at worst. Insider trading is only one result. No firm, even my own, is immune from it, no matter how carefully it handles sensitive information. We have to rely on the ethics and the character of our people; no system yet invented will provide complete assurance that all of them will behave ethically." That was as close as Felix got then to any mention of his Lazard colleagues Pondiccio, Davis, Wilkis, Cecola, and Grambling.

More than twenty years later, Felix said he was "thunderstruck" when he realized one morning at breakfast, while reading the *Wall Street Journal,* that Lazard had been involved in many of the deals in which Levine had confessed to engaging in illegal trading. He said he immediately summoned Mullarkey to his office to figure out what had happened. Mullarkey quickly uncovered Wilkis's phone records indicating ongoing conversations with Levine. These records were turned over to the SEC. Felix also called the lawyer Marty Lipton, at Wachtell, Lipton, for advice, the firm's new go-to crisis adviser after the deaths of Sy

Rifkind and Sam Harris. "And I just couldn't get over it," Felix said. "I mean, it was the worst thing that could happen, especially in a small firm."

With criminal behavior rampant right under his nose, Michel's focus could not have been farther away. He had been busy, across the Atlantic Ocean in London, putting the final touches on one of the most important—and little appreciated—moves in the firm's history, that of wresting back control of Lazard Brothers in London from S. Pearson & Son and creating a unifying ownership umbrella for the three houses for the first time since 1919. The creation of Lazard Partners, the name given to the new entity created in May 1984, was the essential first step in Michel's personal mission to unify the firm. As Kate Bohner, a former Lazard junior banker turned journalist, so eloquently put it in *Forbes,* Lazard, like Caesar's Gaul, had always been divided into three parts: Lazard Frères, the largest, most high-profile, and generally most profitable, in New York; Lazard Brothers, the most insular, in London; and Lazard Frères & Cie, the smallest and most enigmatic, in Paris. Right from the start, the three houses had always been independently run to take full advantage of the indigenous quality that each firm possessed in its own country. Until 1919, some combination of the Lazard and Weill families had always owned the three firms, although the precise calculus of their equity splits is no longer known. In 1919, of course, the founding families brought in the industrialist Weetman Pearson to recapitalize Lazard Brothers in order to prevent its possible liquidation and to satisfy the Bank of England that the firm was no longer majority owned by Frenchmen. In the early 1930s, Pearson's ownership of Lazard Brothers had rocketed up to 100 percent in the wake of the trading scandal perpetrated out of the Brussels office. After the David-Weills paid off their accumulated debt to Pearson, the Pearson stake in Lazard Brothers returned to 80 percent.

The catalyst for the creation of Lazard Partners turned out to be Rupert Murdoch, the Australian press baron and powerful chairman and CEO of News Corporation, who had started buying shares of Pearson with the hope, no doubt, of obtaining the publishing assets. To combat the potential risk that Murdoch might get control of Pearson and that somehow, as a result, Lazard Brothers would fall into unfriendly hands, Michel told the Pearsons he would buy—with his own money—a sufficiently large stake in Pearson to thwart Murdoch's advances. In return, he wanted to be able to purchase enough of Pearson's stake in Lazard Brothers to ensure the firm's independence should Murdoch get control of Pearson. The resulting agreement, Lazard Partners, was Michel's exceedingly complex first step in regaining family control of Lazard Brothers from Pearson, with the hope of eventually uniting all three houses. The deal also successfully thwarted Murdoch. The new holding company was to own 100 percent of the stock of Lazard Brothers, 24 percent of the capital of Lazard in New York, and 12 percent of the capital of Lazard in Paris. (Lazard Partners would also receive 12 percent of the annual profits in both New York and Paris.) The basic idea of the plan, which required the approval of the Pearson public shareholders, was for Pearson to exchange its—by then—79.4 percent direct ownership stake in Lazard Brothers for equity positions in *each* of the three houses. Pearson's revamped ownership package constituted a 50 percent stake in Lazard Partners plus a direct 3.7 percent stake in the capital of Lazard New York and a direct 4 percent stake in the capital of Lazard Paris. When the direct and indirect stakes were collapsed together, Pearson ended up exchanging its 79.4 percent stake in Lazard Brothers for 50 percent of Lazard Brothers, 17.4 percent of Lazard in New York, and 10 percent of Lazard in Paris, plus a right to 10 percent of the annual profits of the New York and Paris partnerships. Not only did the Pearson shareholders have to approve the deal, which they did in June, but all the various valuations of the three houses, relative ownership stakes, and equalizing payments had to be blessed for "fairness" given the numerous conflicts of interest among the various shareholders (chiefly Michel)—a task that fell to the small and prestigious merchant bank Cazenove & Co., which signed off quickly.

Not surprisingly, of course, this deal was not only about Pearson. It was also about Michel getting greater control of the three houses. He and his immediate family ended up with a 17.9 percent stake in Lazard Partners, in exchange for their 15 percent stake in Lazard Brothers and for a portion of their ownership of New York and Paris. In addition, Michel continued to own "substantial" stakes in New York and Paris. But that is not all. He also arranged for Eurafrance, a French private-equity firm controlled by him and his French partners, to invest $46.3 million for a 20.8 percent stake in Lazard Partners. A few of the partners in New York ended up owning 6 percent of Lazard Partners; an even smaller number of partners in Paris owned 5.3 percent of Lazard Partners. In the end, though, Michel and Pearson each controlled half the votes of Lazard Partners.

In addition to the economic arrangements, the deal sought to "establish procedures for encouraging co-operation between the Three Houses," a chronic unsolved problem in the firm's long history. There was little likelihood that Lazard Partners would quickly lead to international cooperation, but it did occasion the creation of a new, seven-member partnership committee, of which Michel installed himself as chairman.

The May 1984 Pearson prospectus provided another one of those rare glimpses into the profitability of the three Lazard firms. As on the other occasions, what was confirmed was how fabulously profitable the firms were—and had been for years. For instance, in 1983, New York earned £55 million ($80 million) before distributions to partners and taxes, while Paris earned £7 million (FF 83 million) before such distributions. London, which was not a partnership, earned £13.4 million after paying its managing directors but before paying taxes.

Left unsaid in the Pearson public pronouncements about the deal was that Michel would now have, for the first time, effective control of the three separate houses of Lazard. The financial press, though, picked up on the import of the announcement. *BusinessWeek* viewed the deal as Michel "finally exorcising Meyer's ghost." What's more, the consensus seemed to be that Michel had accomplished something—the reunification with London—that André simply could not have or would have had no interest in trying given his general disdain for Lazard Brothers, despite his ownership stake and his board seat. Indeed he had been to London only once after World War II, convinced that the British had somehow been responsible for the collapse of France in 1940. "It was Michel's doing," Felix said at the time. "I don't think André could have done it." Added Michel: "Already I feel a fantastic current of interchange between the firms. It's rather amazing. There's much more openness and less secrecy."

But in a potential harbinger of trouble, Thomas Manners, then a vice chairman of Lazard Brothers, told *BusinessWeek* he had his doubts about how easy it would be for his colleagues in London to adapt to the fact that their firm was no longer a wholly owned subsidiary of a respected British institution but was instead under the control of a Frenchman, who also happened to be the last remaining scion of the founding families. "I wouldn't be telling the truth if I didn't [say I] have some concerns," he confided. "The American system involves a harder sell than I would like to adopt. Sometimes American attitudes work well in this country. Sometimes they don't."

Human beings instinctively resist change. And for M&A bankers, who are so heavily invested in maintaining the status quo, that instinct is calibrated at a level far higher than the norm. But there was no denying, by the mid-1980s, that Michel's leadership was transforming Lazard. André's stifling, autocratic style, which had led the firm to drift aimlessly during the final years of his long illness, had given way to Michel's reign of charmed and enlightened imperialism. "You kiss Michel's ring in this firm" is how one Lazard "insider" explained it to the *Wall Street Journal.* "He's as much an absolute ruler as the old man was, just in a different way. Michel has better manners. He's an iron fist in a velvet glove. Meyer was just an iron first." Michel had shown an eagerness to pursue new business lines—for instance, Mezzacappa's extremely profitable capital markets effort, Zarb's international advisory group, and municipal finance underwriting—and to revitalize older ones, such as asset management or two of André's favorite areas, investing in real estate and private equity. Waves of people were hired to run and staff these new efforts and to expand the older ones. This was all in addition to the bankers hired to help Felix grow the M&A advisory group, still Lazard's most important, most prestigious, and most profitable business. By 1984, the combined firm had some 1,350 employees—600 in London, 400 in New York, and 350 in Paris—a near doubling from when Michel took over in 1978.

As the firm grew and became more profitable, it was inevitable that from time to time, the press would shine a spotlight on some of the newer partners—to their ongoing peril, of course, as Felix's body language about anybody but him courting the press remained quite articulate. In July 1985, *M,* an affiliate of *W,* did a feature story with many photographs on Ward Woods, the former Lehman partner, who was becoming increasingly successful at Lazard. The article referred to Woods as "the sporty banker" and featured the preppy Andover grad hunting quail on a Texas prairie, helicopter skiing in Snowbird, Utah, and fly-fishing for silver salmon "150 miles from nowhere" in Alaska. And Michel himself began to speak of Mezzacappa in glowing terms. "I think very highly of him," he told the *Wall Street Journal* in a rare 1984 front-page profile of the firm. "When you speak of influence in the place, the greatest one is me, the next is Felix, but after that it's Mezzacappa." The fact that the same article quoted an unnamed Lazard "veteran" complaining about Mezzacappa's behavior—how he was "not above dressing down someone in public. He's a ranter, a screamer, a volatile, emotional guy"—seemed irrelevant because, this same person said, "Michel goes anywhere the dollar goes and Mezzacappa's operations have been extremely successful."

The *Journal* piece even went so far as to state, without qualification, that Felix was no longer "as influential at Lazard as he once was." This observation had started to appear with some regularity in the media during the early 1980s. True, as competition among investment banks for M&A business had intensified, Lazard missed some deals that in the past the firm would rarely have missed. So competitors felt freer to take the occasional potshot at Felix, albeit always anonymously. And certainly, some partners inside the firm would not have been unhappy to see Felix take a nick here and there, despite how fabulously wealthy he was making them all. In truth, though, Felix had lost none of his power and influence at Lazard. He was still by far the firm's dominant rainmaker. Furthermore, his decision to fix his stake of the profits at 6 percent, far less than he was entitled to, meant that his partners all got paid more than they deserved. And this fact alone made his behind-the-scenes manipulation of people and events at Lazard as effective as ever.

Indeed, if there was even the slightest doubt about the length of Felix's shadow at the firm, and beyond, in the second half of 1984 two slavishly fawning cover stories in national magazines about him—and him alone—definitively put the lie to all the wishful, envious thinking among his competitors and partners. But all the attention on Felix probably made them all the more envious and wishful. In the first article, Felix allowed the best-selling financial writer David McClintick to follow him for ten days as he jetted around the United States, France, and the Middle East. The resulting piece in the *New York Times Magazine* was titled "Life at the Top: The Power and Pleasures of Financier Felix Rohatyn." Even though McClintick confessed that Felix "was very reluctant to allow this reporter to travel with him, and agreed only after two days of fitful ruminating," what followed was a breathless account, in diary form, of the world according to Felix.

Here, in living color, was the Jewish refugee Felix cavorting "in a tan wool jacket, a navy crew-neck sweater, a white shirt with open collar and light beige corduroy slacks" at the Rohatyns' annual Easter egg hunt at his Southampton spread with the Gotbaums, Kissingers, Paleys, and Oscar de la Rentas. Every so often, the host would excuse himself to take a call from Leslie Wexner, then as now the founder, chairman, and CEO of Limited Brands, the large retailer. When McClintick started following him around, Felix was in the midst of advising the Limited on its hostile $1.1 billion bid to acquire Carter Hawley Hale Stores.

The Limited deal became the leitmotif of the piece. There was Felix flying to Los Angeles to testify in some Limited-related legal proceeding. When that didn't happen, he turned around and flew back to New York, where he collected Liz, and together they took the Concorde to Paris. In the Concorde lounge, they chatted up Philip Beekman, the president of Seagram, about some unexplained trading in the shares of Colgate Palmolive and wondered if Seagram was about to make a bid. Both Seagram and Colgate were Lazard clients. The Rohatyns declined the pre-takeoff champagne cocktails but went for the fresh caviar and a glass each of iced vodka. Felix was going to Paris to speak with the French president, François Mitterrand, a close friend. Once there, he shared with him some informal and unofficial advice about what was going on in the United States. Then Liz joined them for lunch. Afterward, they visited a Pierre Bonnard art exhibit. A stroll around the city was canceled so Felix could return to the Hotel Lancaster, off the Champs-Élysées, to participate in a conference call about the Limited deal. There was a visit, the next day, to have coffee with his mother and stepfather at their spacious apartment, just off the Place du Trocadéro.

Afterward, the Rohatyns were tracked as they flew to Jerusalem for a withering procession of meetings to help raise money for the Israeli Museum, where the Dead Sea Scrolls are kept. There were visits with Teddy Kollek, the mayor of Jerusalem, and a banquet at the Knesset. At each event, the Rohatyns were treated like royalty. (Liz, after all, had once appeared alongside the future First Lady Jacqueline Bouvier in an East Hampton, New York, fashion show.) Various sightseeing tours were canceled for the ubiquitous calls back to New York for the Limited. But there was time for a visit to Yenon, a settlement of about six hundred Jews from Yemen, about an hour southwest of Jerusalem. The Rohatyns were introduced to the village elders with much enthusiasm. And then the dancing began, with Felix and his bride quickly joining in with the hora, a traditional Israeli wedding dance. No doubt exhausted himself, McClintick observed: "A week and a day after his frequently interrupted Easter egg hunt, five days after a quick trip to Los Angeles and back, barely two days after arriving in Israel from France and 24 hours before he must board an all-night flight from Tel Aviv to New York, the world's most eminent investment banker is dancing like a teen-ager." As they say in the biz, you can't buy that kind of publicity.

The Limited would eventually fail in its effort to win Carter Hawley Hale. But given his continuing concern about his fellow bankers' behavior in this and other hostile deals, he used the *Times Magazine* platform to rail, once again, against his chosen profession. "I guess I'm getting to be like a friend of mine, a very successful defense contractor, who says to me, 'It's more and more difficult for me to run my business because I don't believe in the defense budget.' Sometimes it's getting more and more difficult for me to do the things we do, because in the last analysis, I don't think that's what I want on my tombstone."

What he did want on his tombstone, of course—former U.S. secretary of the Treasury—was also a topic of discussion between Felix and his muse. "This is my time," he told McClintick when asked about his interest in a cabinet position. "There's going to be an enormous amount of financial engineering required to redo the national and international financial systems that have grown out of control and are going to have to be put back together. It won't necessarily be me, and I truly don't yearn for it, but it'll be people like me"—and then he made his pitch. "There are going to have to be people involved in public policy who understand financial structures, and who understand the relationship between financial structures and the real world. There are lots of people who understand financial structures but who don't understand the real world, and vice versa. At least I've had experience with both." The *Times Magazine* article followed on the heels of the publication of his collected essays and speeches, which itself spurred a wave of media focus on Felix from *CBS Morning News, The MacNeil/Lehrer NewsHour,* and, according to McClintick, the possibility of *Time* putting him on the cover. (It never happened.)

Then, as if all that were not enough, four months later, in December 1984, Felix appeared on the cover of *Institutional Investor,* the industry trade magazine, doing his best imitation of Fred Astaire. Felix appeared in white tie and tails, top hat and dancing stick. "Felix: The Making of a Celebrity" the cover screamed. Finally, in one neat package, was the Felix phenomenon captured in all of its deconstructed complexity: the consummate deal maker, the media manipulator, the social doyen, and the frustrated wannabe high-level political appointee. Clients and rivals weighed in on his supremacy as a corporate adviser. "I am satisfied with the counsel Felix gave us," commented Leslie Wexner, despite the Limited's failure to win its prize, "and I would use Lazard again for other acquisitions"—something Wexner did repeatedly from then on. "You can't underestimate the longevity factor," said a competitor from Lehman Brothers. "Felix has been doing deals since I was in second grade." And there was the requisite homage from one of his partners. "His mere presence at the firm helps me wherever I go in the world," purred Lou Perlmutter. "I may bring in a new client, but the fact that he's one of my partners is very important."

The competitive daggers were out in full force, though, when it came to commenting on the surfeit of Felix's fawning press coverage. One competitor chirped: "When he sneezes, the *New York Times* gets a cold." The iconoclastic *Washington Monthly* was quoted wondering just how Felix does it: "What is it about Felix Rohatyn? Is it an elixir that wafts from his pores? He has become the 1980s version of Henry Kissinger, the powerful figure whose mere presence stupefies usually capable journalists." The answer is simply, like Kissinger, Felix worked—and works—

hard at carefully managing his persona, working far harder at it than he leads anyone to think he does. And hard and time-consuming work it is, too. He benefited immeasurably, of course, from his understanding with Michel that he *alone* would be the public face of Lazard. He wooed reporters with pithy quotations and unalloyed access. Among the all-time favorites was his description of what would happen to New York City if the city's officials didn't get serious about the looming fiscal crisis: "Bankruptcy is like stepping into a tepid bath and slashing your wrists. You might not *feel* you're dying, but that's what would happen." He also socialized with leading reporters, columnists, and editors, inviting them for meals at the Four Seasons, the Regency Hotel, Elaine's, "21," or his Fifth Avenue apartment, where he and Liz had moved from 770 Park, to discuss the weighty issues of the day.

He also made good copy, since he seemed willing to take contrarian and controversial positions, on the record, whether about public policy or the investment banking profession. But he also kept after reporters, working them relentlessly with a combination of charm and exactitude to convey his views until the moment of publication made his further effort irrelevant. Felix's mastery of the media was a potent and effective cocktail that pushed his profile higher and higher. With tongue firmly planted in cheek, the *Institutional Investor* editors put together "The Felix Index," which tracked Felix's press notices and assigned them points depending on whether they were mere mentions—1 point—or a major cover story or profile: 20 points. The chart rises from a score below 10 in 1970, when ITT's hostile deal for Hartford started, to something like 150 in 1984, with the rash of cover stories and the publication of his book. Felix took it all in stride. "Certainly over the past ten years I have had an extraordinarily supportive press," he said. "I've gotten beaten up on occasion, but that has been the exception."

Perhaps no banker ever, not even J. P. Morgan in his day, had lavished on him the amount of favorable ink that Felix now garnered. The irony, of course, was that all of this publicity and political positioning came at the outset of Reagan's second presidential term—and there was never even the slightest chance Felix would be part of a Republican administration, let alone one as conservative as Reagan's. And as had been cataloged endlessly, Felix was increasingly bored with doing deals and, apparently, had little ambition to make more money than he already had. The reaction inside the firm to the Felix publicity parade was predictably schizophrenic: on the one hand, having Felix and Lazard featured so prominently was great for business, which meant that all partners would benefit financially; but on the other hand, there was increasing resentment, as the firm grew, over the fact that no one seemed to recognize that Lazard was becoming far more than just Felix. There was also a general sense that perhaps enough was enough. "I have compared him to a great fish," Mayor Ed Koch said at the time. "A great fish that leaps from the ocean into the brilliant sunshine so that everybody can see his beautiful golden scales. And that's all right, that's reasonable. *But every day?*"

BUT EVEN AS Felix continued to preen, there was no challenging Michel. The creation of Lazard Partners not only solidified his control but also gave him an added patina of authority for having pulled off the unexpected. A few months after the ink was dry on the Lazard Partners deal, Michel maneuvered Ian Fraser out as chairman of Lazard Brothers. He looked Fraser "straight in the eye" and told him, as if he weren't even there, "Ian Fraser is a brilliant deal maker but he is a lousy administrator," and then threw in for good measure that "next time we must have a good manager." John Nott, the defense minister in Margaret Thatcher's government and during the Falklands War, succeeded Fraser. Michel also seemed content, for the moment, to allow Felix to get the public glory while he added to his already enormous wealth.

And there was no arguing with the firm's performance under Michel's leadership. Lazard was making lots of money, and so were its partners. The *Wall Street Journal* reported Michel made $50 million in 1983, and that his net worth was north of $500 million. This fact, along with section 4.1 of the partnership agreement, made Michel's power absolute. But Lazard was still not functioning, from a management point of view, the way other, more professional, less idiosyncratic Wall Street firms were. Hiring was haphazard. Mentoring and training were nearly nonexistent. Internal financial controls were archaic at best. Every important decision—compensation, partnership percentages, promotions, senior-level hiring—required Michel's sole approval and sign-off. For all practical purposes, Michel had pretty much retained André's "sole proprietorship" approach to running the firm, even if there was now a velvet glove on the iron fist.

CHAPTER 10

The Vicar

But slowly, at least one person inside the firm began to feel the need to fill the organizational vacuum, with the hope of bringing the woefully byzantine firm into the latter half of the twentieth century. While the task had a Sisyphean feel to it, William Loomis—known to everyone at the firm as Bill—decided the time had come to attempt the impossible: modernize Lazard. Not that he had any special qualifications for the job, other than the desire to do it. Tall and handsome, he looked like a slightly less angular version of the late writer George Plimpton, which gave him a somewhat ministerial air. Some of the partners referred to him as the Vicar, while the younger bankers called him Lurch. According to the *Financial Times,* Loomis "spent part of his youth hanging out with Muslim rebels in the Sulu Sea, off the Philippines, and wandering through Asia on a grant to write fiction in the style of Somerset Maugham." Loomis once elaborated on this phase of his life in a letter he wrote to a young Lazard associate after he resigned. "At the risk of intruding on your personal life, I'd like to offer a couple of observations," he wrote in 1988. "Some of your frustration I may have avoided by flying to Afghanistan on graduation from college, with an Olivetti portable typewriter and a change of Khaki pants, only to emerge by freighter from Borneo a year later. Having spent time previously in India, I already knew that the Peace Corps was the U.S. Army of altruism. I never considered graduate school, architecture or otherwise, as a substitute for dusty Jeep rides, shooting with a Pathan tribesman or small boats in the Sulu Sea. In short, I forgot about my resume and decided I would figure out a career later."

Like the firm he loved, Loomis's often enigmatic and inscrutable behavior masked his ambition. Loomis worked in New York until around 1980, became "the world's best associate," and was outspoken about the need to improve the pay and the training of the younger Lazard bankers, all of whom he thought were underpaid, compared with Lehman, and had no idea what was expected of them to become a partner. In need of a "new experience," though, and frustrated by Michel's decision not to make any new partners for the time being, Loomis asked Michel if he could go to Hong Kong with Steve Oliver to start an advisory business there. "I was concerned that I was ever more expert at analysis and at observing partners but not having the opportunity to develop the client skills which would be needed when I was a partner later," Loomis explained. East Asia Partners, as it was called—Michel wouldn't allow them to use the Lazard name—was 20 percent owned by each of the Lazard houses, with the balance being owned by the C. V. Starr affiliate of AIG, the big insurer, and by Loomis and Oliver themselves. After two years, Lazard bought AIG's stake in the business. All parties did "okay," Loomis said, but the business wasn't "important" or much supported by Lazard.

Meanwhile, in New York, Lazard's M&A business was booming. Loomis wanted back into the action. He returned to New York, and as of January 1, 1984, became a partner. Almost immediately, he began discussing with Michel and Felix ways to improve "organizational discipline." Loomis was partial to writing detailed, often passionate memos to Michel and Felix about his ideas for the firm. In an early missive, he made the heretofore-unheard-of argument that Michel needed to appoint one partner to coordinate the assignments for and evaluations of the junior professionals, including the making of all hiring and firing decisions for these bankers. This task, Loomis supposed, would take about half of the chosen partner's time. He volunteered for the job. As he saw it, his mandate would be to coordinate all staffing of associates on M&A deals, requiring partners to go through him—Felix's recommendation—as new assignments came up, as opposed to going directly to their favorite associates, as had been the custom. He also described the need to quickly "weed out" a handful of poorly performing associates and to hire replacements, of higher quality, "aggressively."

Loomis, correctly, foresaw looming danger for him as he set about breaking the thick glass of inertia at the firm. The memo to Michel was liberally sprinkled with caution flags. "Anyone who does this job will be subject to a lot of pressure and criticism," he wrote, adding parenthetically, "Whenever a partner is unable to have four people in Kansas City on a Tuesday, the person co-ordinating assignments will be the focus of direct and indirect criticism." With regard to assigning associates to deals, he asked for "the authority I need to intercede forcefully in the interest of priorities, balancing work etc. All of this involves consulting partners and senior associates, but at the end of the day, the system won't work if going around me is an easy alternative for people. (This is more of an issue at the outset when people will try it.)" And as for hiring people, Loomis wrote, "As long as I do this job, I don't want anybody hired informally by others without consulting me before a job offer is made. It is counterproductive to have inefficient people leave only to be replaced by other weak people."

In the wake of the numerous breaches of ethics and judgment that Lazard had just suffered as a result of Michel's laissez-faire management style, it was hard for Michel—or anyone else at the firm for that matter—to argue that the disciplines and controls were not necessary. In fact, they were needed, desperately. The firm had grown, but the internal systems had not kept pace. Michel moved Loomis's office to be near his on the thirty-second floor of One Rockefeller Plaza so they could speak regularly. But this being Lazard, the boldness of Loomis's approach caused some to begin to lay traps for him. Felix, for one, didn't want to run the firm, of course, but was none too happy when someone else stepped into the vacuum to try to run it, either. And neither Felix nor Mezzacappa was particularly pleased that Loomis had increasingly unfettered access to Michel.

While Loomis tilted at these internal windmills, Felix kept his focus on his high profile and on his high-profile deals. One of the more notorious deals at the time was Ron Perelman's 1985 bold and successful hostile bid to take over Revlon, the cosmetics company. Felix represented Revlon, thanks to his enduring friendship with its CEO, Michel Bergerac, a Frenchman whom Felix had met when Bergerac was one of Geneen's top lieutenants at ITT. While far from the biggest deal, at a mere $1.83 billion, the Perelman-Revlon fight seemed to have it all: an upstart corporate raider, using money borrowed with the help of Michael Milken, trying to buy one of the world's best-known consumer brands, versus a proud corporate pillar, run by a sophisticated Frenchman, desperately hoping to avoid his clutches. The process dragged on for months, with Bergerac and Felix bringing in Forstmann Little, the buyout firm, to put together a competing bid. At each turn, Perelman and Milken raised their price until finally the Delaware Supreme Court ruled that Revlon had put itself up for sale and had to sell itself to the highest bidder—the precedent forever more known as being in Revlon Mode—which turned out to be Perelman. "This damn thing turned into World War III," commented one of Perelman's lawyers at the time. The fight had cost Perelman $500 million more than he originally offered for the Revlon shares. (He still owns Revlon, but it has been one of his poorer investments.) And of course, the deal was an investment banking fee bonanza. Lazard was paid $11 million for its advice to Revlon, one of its largest fees ever to that point. But this was chump change compared with the $60 million Milken's firm, Drexel Burnham, pulled out for financing Perelman's deal and the $30 million Morgan Stanley received for advising Perelman and selling off some of Revlon's assets. "It's the deal of the century," one banker said at the time.

If that were the case, it was not for long. A little more than a month after Perelman won Revlon, GE announced that it was buying RCA, a longtime Lazard client, for $6.3 billion in cash, plus the assumption of debt. The GE-RCA deal was, to that moment, the largest non-oil deal in corporate history and reunited RCA with the company that started it some fifty-five years earlier. The combination was a corporate bombshell and has turned out to be one of the most successful mergers of all time, as NBC remains one of GE's most important assets. And it was Felix who got the ball rolling on the deal. He was "a regular breakfast companion" of Jack Welch, the GE chairman and CEO, although Lazard was not GE's banker. And of course, since André first wooed David Sarnoff with a $100,000 check to the UJA, Lazard had always been close to RCA and had a board seat for many years. Welch asked Felix at a breakfast in October 1985 to arrange a meeting for him with Thornton Bradshaw, the chairman of RCA. Felix happily complied (for this is an investment banker's dream, no matter how jaded). Cocktails were arranged between Welch and Bradshaw at Felix's apartment for the afternoon of November 6.

The landmark deal was announced a mere thirty-six days later after the usual furtive negotiations over price and legal terms. At one point, on a Saturday late in the negotiations, Felix took the Concorde to Paris to visit his ailing mother. He returned the next day to resume his position. There was lavish front-page coverage of the deal in both the *Times* and the *Wall Street Journal,* highlighting Felix's role in bringing the two sides together. A week later, *Time* weighed in with a rare business cover story, "Merger Tango," about this deal and others. Felix sat down with the magazine's editors and, in typical fashion, again criticized his profession for potentially endangering the country's financial system. "Today things are getting badly out of hand," he said. Although soon enough he would be wooing Perelman, he railed against Perelman-style takeovers, financed by junk bonds and "excessive risk taking." He called on the government to help. "The integrity of our securities markets and the soundness of our financial system are vital national assets that are being eroded today," he testified before the Senate in December 1985. "Actions are required to help them." And he offered any number of solutions to help ward off the impending disaster. "The way we are going will destroy all of us in this business," he told the *Time* editors. "Someday there is going to be a major recession, major scandals. All of us may be sitting in front of congressional committees trying to explain what we were doing."

Felix, as usual, was partly correct. There would be a major market correction, in 1987, and a plethora of corporate scandals. Ironically—and unbeknownst to Felix—another Lazard banker, Marcel Katz, engaged in illegal activity related to the GE-RCA merger. Katz, then a twenty-two-year-old recent Brown University graduate, was a financial analyst on the deal. He passed along inside information about it to his father, Harvey Katz, a wealthy Houston businessman. Harvey Katz and his father-in-law, Elie Mordo, made more than $2 million in illegal profits by trading in the stock and options of RCA before the GE-RCA deal became public. When confronted by Tom Mullarkey, the Lazard general counsel, about how it came about that his father had traded so extensively in the RCA securities before the GE deal was announced, Marcel denied passing along the information to his father. Marcel resigned from Lazard in February 1986, four months after he started and two months after the announcement of the GE-RCA deal. In August 1986, the SEC and the Katzes reached a settlement whereby Harvey Katz agreed to pay a fine of $2.1 million and repay more than $1 million in illegally obtained profits. Mordo agreed to give up $1.1 million in illegally obtained profits. As for Marcel, the SEC charged that he "knowingly disclosed to Harvey Katz material, non-public information" that he had gleaned from working on the deal at Lazard. As part of a consent decree with the SEC, Marcel agreed to be permanently barred from working in the securities industry.

But there seemed to be no stopping the Wall Street deal machine and the riches bestowed upon the people who put the deals together. Despite Felix's claim to modesty, his lifestyle improved steadily throughout the 1980s. Whereas he had once lived at the supposedly shabby Hotel Alrae and drove a beat-up BMW station wagon, with the help of his partner Alan McFarland (who was president of the co-op board) and Liz's social connections—and his own growing wealth and fame—he moved to a duplex at 770 Park Avenue, at the southwest corner of East Seventy-third Street, considered one of the best buildings on Park. Today, Felix has all the obvious trappings of considerable wealth but is careful not to go overboard in the vein of Steve Schwarzman, Saul Steinberg, or Dennis Kozlowski. He and Liz now share a full-floor co-op apartment, facing Central Park, at tony 810 Fifth Avenue (at Sixty-second Street), decorated in simple elegance by the Boston designer William Hodgins with Impressionist paintings and eighteenth-century pastels and drawings. In the early mornings Felix could be spotted strolling down the fourteen blocks of Fifth Avenue on his way to Rockefeller Center, as he had always wanted to do when he convinced André to move the Lazard office uptown. Eight hundred ten Fifth is much like Felix—refined, unobtrusive, elegant, and exclusive.

And they have the requisite shingle-style mansion less than a mile from the beach on South Main Street in Southampton, where he invited McClintick to witness his annual, boldfaced-name Easter egg hunt. Another house they own in Southampton, which used to be where Liz summered, occasionally gets rented out to the likes of Barbara Walters. The Rohatyns also own a beautiful, intricate—and huge—log cabin home, designed by Liz's nephew, some seventy-two hundred feet above sea level, outside Pinedale, Wyoming, where they spend most of August and enjoy fishing and bird-watching. "Modest" is not the word that best describes these various real estate holdings but neither is "ostentatious." For his part, Felix has a number of fine paintings in his Fifth Avenue apartment. Jane Engelhard, the socialite wife of his former client Charles Engelhard, gave him a lovely Vuillard portrait of a woman. André Meyer gave him a wedding gift of an extraordinary Monet landscape painting of a small town in Provence nestled in and around a hillside, all seen from a distance. He also gave Felix a Bonnard painting of a seated woman who appears to be preparing to wash some clothes. Felix also has a few Canalettos here and there. But one has the sense that art is not his passion.

THE ROHATYNS' FACILE command of the New York social scene in 2006 makes it easy to forget that in 1985, Felix and Liz were at the epicenter of a self-inflicted if well-intentioned social faux pas. In a November 1985 speech at the City Club of New York about mass-transit financing, Felix made some comments about New York socialites, partially in response to a recent speech by Senator Pat Moynihan about the growing disparity between rich and poor in New York City. Felix chastised the city's upper crust by claiming that "while dazzling benefit dinners are attended by our richest and most elegant New Yorkers, and millions of dollars are raised for our golden institutions, it is increasingly difficult to find money for less glamorous needs. If our wealthiest institutions were to exercise more restraint over the proportion of charitable funds they try to absorb; if our most energetic, glamorous, and wealthy citizens were to become involved with community houses, the 'Y,' shelters for the homeless and programs for unwed mothers, then New York would be a much better place for her citizens." Sitting in the audience at the City Club that day was

Kathleen Teltsch, the *New York Times* reporter who covered charities. She dutifully reported Felix's concerns. In separate remarks to Liz Smith of the *Daily News,* Elizabeth Rohatyn echoed her husband.

The Rohatyns' comments fell with a thud on their intended recipients. But they weren't done roiling the waters. In January 1986, Felix told the *New York Times*, "There is so much concentration on the gala and on catching a glimpse of the gala-goers, we are losing sight of the purpose of the exercise. The opulence of some of these affairs becomes an embarrassment when one remembers the misery the charity is trying to alleviate." Then followed Ron Rosenbaum's definitive take on the matter in a *Manhattan Inc.* cover story, which, though a bit of a send-up, explored not only the reaction from New York society but also some of the Rohatyns' proposed solutions. Rosenbaum interviewed the Rohatyns at 770 Park, surrounded by "porcelain and damask," and during his interview they all enjoyed "sherry and biscuits." He asked them about the firestorm of reaction from their socialite friends.

"They said they were pleased that two people have stood up and said much of what they were thinking about," Liz replied.

"But sweetheart," Felix interjected, "I think in fairness that what was equally important is how many people in our circle of friends who are involved in these things didn't really speak to you. It's a very eloquent silence."

"It's a pregnant silence," Liz said.

When told by Rosenbaum that his article would be published in the magazine about six weeks after the interview, Liz said to Felix: "We'll just have to plan to be out of town then, dear."

The coup de grâce was a nasty, unsigned May 1986 article in the fashion industry bible, *W,* ominously titled "Felix the Cat and Snow White vs. the Social Sisters," which recounted the Rohatyns' battle with the then-all-powerful social doyennes Brooke Astor, Annette Reed, and Pat Buckley. The article suggested Felix had raised the issue to curry favor with New York's governor, Mario Cuomo—with whom he shared an interest in Sir Thomas More, the sixteenth-century statesman and martyr—in hopes of becoming Cuomo's secretary of the Treasury should Cuomo be elected president, or decide even to run. (Felix's later response: "Ludicrous.") The *W* article included this tasty morsel from one "Socialite B": "How dare they? The Rohatyns have a right to spend their money—if they spend any—with any charity they like. And so do I, and so do you. It amazes me that someone who works at Lazard Frères, which is not a place that you put your money if you're in a charitable mood, thinks he has the right to dictate how Annette or Pat or any of the others spend their time and effort. These women have gotten into the trenches for the Met and the Library and AIDS and everything else. So some of the parties were fancy. Some of RCA and GE's profits are fancy too. Does Felix criticize them? You bet your life he doesn't."

In the face of this controversy, a quite normal urge would be to lie low for a while and keep out of the press, especially if the new matter doesn't juxtapose particularly well with all that had just transpired. Felix, though, chose not to follow this path. Instead, he remained true to his unarticulated philosophy that there is no such thing as bad publicity. A week after a *Newsweek* article rehashed the charity ball debate, he was quoted in the *New York Times* talking about the quality of the *wines* in the Lazard wine cellar and engaging in some polite banter with Robert Pirie, the CEO of Rothschild in North America, whose office was three floors below Felix's in Rockefeller Center. "What we serve," Felix said, "is not the crown jewel of our escutcheon." To which Pirie observed, "I've drunk Felix's wine, and he's right." Pirie, of course, could boast of the finest corporate wine collection and select simply from among the "homemade reds," including the Rothschilds' Château Duhart-Milon and Moulin des Carruades. "He gave me a Lafite-Rothschild," Felix told the *Times,* referring to one of the world's most expensive wines, "and I almost went to work for him as a result."

Felix was also being urged to challenge the U.S. senator Alfonse D'Amato, Republican of New York, in the 1986 election. He declined. "It's just not something I could do well or be comfortable doing," he said at the time. "Besides which I promised the Mets I will play shortstop for them next season." Upon hearing this, Frank Cashen, then general manager of the Mets, wrote Felix a letter. "Having followed your career with great interest, I was pleased to learn that you are now committed to playing shortstop for the Mets during the pending season," Cashen wrote. "To this end, I have enclosed your official 1986 Uniform Player's Contract and trust the terms are satisfactory." Felix declined Cashen's offer, too. "I was thrilled to get your letter with the contract for next season," he wrote back.

> Imagine my dismay when, upon closer reflection, it now appears that I will not be able to play for you in 1986 for the following reasons: (1) My arrangements with Lazard Frères include noncompetitive clauses. It seems to me there is not much difference between a hostile corporate takeover raid and a high inside fastball thrown at somebody's ear. We are both in show business and I am afraid that our lawyers would feel that I should stick to our kind of show biz. (2) I am sure that Rafael Santana

is a serious hard-working young man with a great future with your club. I shudder to think what would happen to his morale if, all of a sudden, he found a 58-year-old, left-handed shortstop on your roster. I don't want to risk creating such unrest. (3) Last, but not least, I must come to the issue of money. Your proposed contract at $75,000 per year seems to me somewhat on the skimpy side even though I recognize that my fielding has been erratic and that in my last full season (fraternity college in 1949), I hit only .089. In addition, I should point out that your proposal is way below the minimum wage scale set by the Investment Bankers' Benevolent Association and that $75,000 is what one of my very junior partners earns in one weekend, working on a deal that doesn't even go through. Nonetheless, I do appreciate that, under the circumstances, your proposal undoubtedly appears generous to you.

In response to Felix's letter, Cashen said, "I really didn't feel I wanted to give him the minimum, because of who he is"—major-league rookies in 1986 received a minimum of $60,000. "But his experience seemed a little thin." Felix's decision may have saved him from a salary cut of 99 percent, but it also cost him a World Series championship ring.

Felix's growing fame, though, could not insulate him and his family from the randomness of big-city life. Three times over the years, Liz Rohatyn was mugged on the streets of the Upper East Side. First, a bicyclist ripped a gold chain off her neck on Madison Avenue, then her wallet was stolen on Fifth Avenue, and, finally, her Hermès handbag was grabbed after she and Felix left a friend's Passover seder on East Sixty-second Street and were almost home. Felix said a waiter at Arcadia, a nearby restaurant, remarked, "God, how can they do this to you? You saved the city."

Around the time Felix was joking around with the Mets, Michel, previously quite press shy, chose to announce his arrival on the international social scene. In the summer of 1986, while on his annual flight from Lazard, he permitted both the fashion reporter Christa Worthington and a photographer from *W* to visit him and his family at Sous-le-Vent, his aerie in the French Mediterranean town of Cap d'Antibes, near the Italian border. The resulting three-page color spread on the oversized pages of the mid-August issue of the magazine featured large pictures of many of the rooms and charming gardens of his "summer retreat," described as a "pink stucco wedding cake of a mansion with cool marble stairways, grand Moorish archways, potted lemon trees on its myriad of terraces and so many servants that one rarely sees the same domestic face twice in the course of an afternoon." There were revealing pictures of "Monsieur," clad only in his bathing suit, "conducting business" on the phone at the beach, thanks to a telephone cord that snaked throughout the vast property (it was before the days of commercial use of cellular phones). Right on the first page, *W* got in an ironic dig at Felix, which of course was the point of Michel agreeing to the article in the first place. After explaining that Michel made $50 million in 1985 as the "world's best-paid banker" (and supposedly $125 million in 1986), Worthington wrote: "But when it comes to personal publicity, the kind that one of David-Weill's employees, Felix Rohatyn, routinely attracts, this wheeler-dealer couldn't, frankly, give a damn. 'I don't know who you are. I don't know what you do, but I know you are famous,' is the punchline of the New York anecdote that makes him guffaw."

The reaction inside the firm to the *W* article about Michel was one of stunned amazement. "This was just a terrible article in *W,* a terrible article," remembered Damon Mezzacappa, himself no stranger to the society pages. "It was kind of silly. It showed Michel sitting in his bathing suit with a big cigar"—actually it was one of the few times Michel was pictured without his cigar—"and it was pretty unflattering, pretty unflattering." In retrospect, Mezzacappa viewed the *W* article as the distinct point in time when Lazard began to change, and not necessarily for the better. Michel had decided he now wanted some of the recognition that for years had been Felix's exclusively. "Michel really started to love the press attention," Mezzacappa said. "And Felix got pretty angry about it because the roles had changed, and a tension developed between the two of them." Michel's comings and goings began to show up in the society pages, and his picture graced, among others, the pages of *Forbes, BusinessWeek,* the *New York Times,* and the *Wall Street Journal.*

WHILE FELIX FOUND himself momentarily subsumed by his charity crusade and Michel by his own extraordinary foray onto the pages of *W,* Bill Loomis was embarking on a lonely crusade of his own: nothing less than a total revamping of the infrastructure and the quality standards for Lazard professionals, partners included. In September 1986, he wrote Michel a lengthy confidential treatise about what he thought needed to be done to maintain and increase the worth of a Lazard partnership, absent which he feared the position would be devalued. The memo at once highlighted Loomis's substantial intellect and writing skills, the depth of his appreciation for the firm's uniqueness, and, of course, the quintessential irony that now that *he* was a partner he wanted to raise the bar higher for other candidates. There was also a masterful display of sycophancy and advocacy. Loomis began: "In *Euromoney* six years ago, you said about becoming a partner, '. . . if you are serious with yourself, you will know it at the same time as I shall know it.' This is a wonderful statement. It motivated me, encouraged me to develop substantively, and at the same time, provided reason for patience. The values appeared to be leadership in terms of transactions and relationships, independent judgment and already acknowledged stature within the firm. Partnership was also valuable because there were so few."

The problem, as Loomis saw it from his perch, at all of thirty-seven years old, was that the standards for a Lazard partnership had been increasingly lowered—partnerships had become a "reward" for "hard work and excellence"—from the amorphous and subjective standards articulated by Michel in *Euromoney.* A "two tier" partnership structure had evolved: the real, rainmaker partners were getting paid a profit percentage of 1 percent or above, and as the standards fell, partners who were focused only on executing deals were getting paid far less. "Such a change at Lazard is analogous to going off the gold standard at a time when other firms are more rapidly devaluing the currency of partnership," he continued. "The standard for partnership is a critical part of our franchise which is in danger of being eroded, almost imperceptively, in a series of individual decisions. As other firms become institutions where partnership is merely a title, Lazard should be moving in the opposite direction, as the stature of partners is critical to differentiating the firm commercially." Without a midcourse correction, Loomis feared, Lazard would by the early 1990s have sixty to seventy partners (which is exactly what *did* happen). "In terms of motivating young people, we will be in a box with a wrenching purge as the only alternative to mediocrity," he wrote presciently. He urged Michel to reduce the partnership ranks by "four or five" and to tighten the selection process. "The ability to be generous with the economics of partnership should not extend to generosity with the position itself, or it will lose value. The issue is criteria and absolute numbers, now and in the future. This is not a subject where consensus and exclusivity are contradictory concepts. Lazard would benefit from a return to partnership as your personal, and closely held, prerogative."

There had surely been nothing like this Loomis memo in the 138-year history of the firm. In the early days, partnerships were passed within the Lazard or David-Weill families, or among their close friends, and from father to son. Then André had divined, in his own judgment, who from outside the founding families was worthy of a Lazard partnership. True, unlike many other early Wall Street partnerships, Lazard had always been open to inviting non–family members into the firm—a point that Michel made frequently.

By 1986, the explosion of M&A deals and the introduction of spreadsheet software had exponentially increased the need for junior bankers with greater technical skills. For the first time, Lazard now had ambitious associates, many of whom were recruited from MBA programs or other firms. They were not content to just have a *job* at Lazard; they demanded a *career* at Lazard that included a clear shot at becoming a partner.

ONE PART OF this initiative was to find a new partner to work in London for Lazard New York. Now, the mere thought of this was plenty controversial inside Lazard, regardless of who was hired for the post. Since the creation of Lazard Partners in 1984, Michel had taken some preliminary steps to have New York and Paris work more closely with London. Given the historic idiosyncrasies of the three firms, cooperation was not natural, especially with London. Not only had André and Felix basically ignored Lazard Brothers, but also Pearson's fifty-three-year control of the firm made it a far different culture from that in New York or Paris, despite being in many of the same business lines. London was not a partnership, and since the near liquidation in 1931 senior bankers there had no share of the profits. Lazard Brothers—often referred to as the "House of Lords" because of the preponderance of British aristocrats working there—was by and large a far more insular, genteel, and haughty place than its scrappier and meaner cousins in Paris and New York. "They were Pearson men," one former partner recalled. "They were—you know what they were? It was almost a priesthood. As far as they were concerned, they were in an independent bank with a shareholder, and they would not be intimidated or altered in their course."

Then there was also the matter, discussed rarely and only sotto voce, that some of the leading lights at Lazard Brothers may have harbored more than a passing feeling of anti-Semitism, which, given the very Jewish nature of both New York and Paris, could not have facilitated cooperation. (Michel denied feeling any sense of anti-Semitism directed toward him but conceded that at Lazard Brothers such sentiments were possible. "I don't think these people thought for a minute to be anti-Semitic, but they didn't think for a minute of recruiting any Jewish people, either," he said.)

In any event, with Lazard Partners more than two years old and Michel feeling the tug of his DNA, he decided the time had come to attempt to forge a greater sense of business cooperation among the three houses. To that end, he decided Lazard Frères, the New York partnership, should have its own representative in London, working out of the Lazard Brothers offices. The idea was not only to promote cooperation among the three houses and to participate in cross-border M&A transactions but also to begin to transfer the cutting-edge M&A techniques—the firm's intellectual capital—to London from New York. While all of this sounded rational, many of the leaders of Lazard Brothers suspected that what Michel really wanted in London was a spy who would allow the Sun King to get increasing control of London, too.

In November 1986, Loomis recommended for the job a thirty-three-year-old American, Robert Agostinelli, who was then head of Goldman Sachs's M&A business in London. After a four-hour interview the prior evening, Loomis wrote Michel, "In my judgment, we should hire him, and I believe that there is now an opportunity to hire him."

Agostinelli, born to immigrant Italian parents outside Rochester, New York—where he was known as Bobby—graduated from St. John Fisher College, a Jesuit school in Rochester, and from Columbia Business School. Agostinelli had wanted to work for Lazard after graduating from Columbia. He had even managed to work his way into the office of the Lazard partner Disque Deane, whereupon Deane offered him a job and asked him how much he expected to be paid. The going rate for associates on Wall Street at the time was $35,000 a year. However, Agostinelli recalled telling Deane, " 'Given the opportunity and the ability to work with you, I'll take a discount. I'll take $25,000.' Because I thought that was the right way to deal with this guy." Deane was appalled. "Let me understand this," Deane said to Agostinelli. "You want me to pay you $25,000 a year for me to make you a multimillionaire? Son, don't you realize that this is a guild? That Lazard is one of the great Florentine guilds? That I'm one of the richest men on Wall Street today, and it's all because of learning at the right hand of André Meyer, and we're giving you—we don't hire people."

Deane urged Agostinelli to go work on Wall Street for a "wire house" for three or four years before considering a return to Lazard, which is pretty much what Agostinelli did. Spurned by Lazard, Agostinelli first went to work for Jacob Rothschild and then Goldman Sachs. Reinvented as Robert, a suave, sophisticated, energetic international financier with extravagant tastes and slicked-back jet-black hair, who pretended to speak Italian but could not, he worked briefly in New York at Goldman before being dispatched to London to build the firm's fledgling M&A effort there. "I thought my career was over," he said about the move overseas and away from the Goldman power center at 85 Broad Street in New York.

But in fact, he caught the wave. American know-how was beginning to have a major impact on London's financial markets at the very moment the M&A boom had spread to Europe. Goldman, led by Agostinelli, started to dominate the M&A league tables in London. Agostinelli started to get noticed, including by Michel, at the very moment he began to feel the intellectual pull, yet again, of Lazard.

"Bob is not normal," Loomis's memo to Michel about Agostinelli continued. "He has been successful at Goldman, in part, precisely because he is not typical of Goldman." But there were words of caution, too. "Bob clearly has a large ego," he wrote, "and can be abrasive. . . . Quite apart from where he might actually be from, imagine him as a tough, confident Italian kid from Brooklyn who is in a hurry and is not willing to let anyone get in his way. He could be an enormous asset." Loomis strongly urged Michel to meet Agostinelli and consider him for the posting at Lazard Brothers. Soon enough, the requisite Michel meeting had been arranged, this time for breakfast at Michel's apartment at 810 Fifth Avenue. After a long chat, Michel told Agostinelli, "You are Lazard, and you should be a partner of Lazard. Certain things exist, and other things don't exist—this exists. You are a partner. You belong in Lazard, and you need to come here." Agostinelli joined the firm as a partner in early 1987.

Having successfully orchestrated Agostinelli's arrival in London, Loomis turned his attention again to recruiting junior bankers. On January 20, 1987, he wrote Michel another confidential memo about his assessment of the Lazard associates and the need to actively recruit more of them. While noting that six associates had left the firm in the past year (including Mina Gerowin, the first female associate), he was complimentary of the ones who remained. But the combination of the associate departures and the pickup in M&A business made the need for new associates acute. "There are, for example, more partners than associates in M&A and Corporate Finance in aggregate," he wrote. He recommended to Michel an active recruiting campaign and even outlined the names and assessments of seven candidates then under "serious consideration" for jobs at the firm. Today, of the seven, three are partners at private-equity firms, one is a member of Parliament, one owns his own information services firm, and one, Michael Price, rose up the ranks at Lazard to become a partner. In the late winter of 1987, as the market was reaching dizzying heights, Loomis met with MBA candidates at Wharton and extolled the virtues of Lazard and how the firm prided itself on being different. It was an extremely seductive elixir. "Even senior people at other firms know remarkably little about Lazard," he told them. "We see no advantage to publicity. Indeed, there is a private quality integral to our franchise." He dismissed many of Lazard's competitors as "processors of capital" and celebrated the firm's differences. "We will not be all things to all people," he said. "The world is large and our firm is small. We will, however, continue to find companies that do not want to go through the checkout line of a financial supermarket." Furthermore, Loomis took up the fight for the junior professionals at Lazard who were expected to slavishly put together materials for a client meeting, only to be excluded from it at the last moment. Life at Lazard for the younger bankers was always a hard one, caught as they were between extreme overwork and the desire to emulate what they perceived as the idealized version of the suave Lazard partner who never unbuttoned his suit jacket in the office, all the while swilling Évian and smoking Montecristos. They often worked in sweatbox-like conditions, literally. In the summer, the air-conditioning in One Rockefeller Plaza was turned off at 11:00 p.m. One year, in the early 1990s, as the late evening hours bled into the early morning, and it became hotter and hotter inside the Lazard offices, the young male bankers still there took to sitting at their desks in their T-shirts and boxers. Finally, after a few days of this, a group of them worked up the courage to ask the administrative partner, Nancy Cooper, if she would ask the building management to keep the air-conditioning on until 2:00 a.m. "You people are the most ungrateful group we've ever had at this firm," she told them, completely seriously.

LOOMIS ALSO FOCUSED on the concerns he had long harbored about his partners' lack of interest in a coordinated, dedicated, and professional new business development effort. He was greatly bothered both about the tendency of many Lazard partners "to wait for the phone to ring" to get new assignments and about preparing for the day when Felix retired from the firm or was no longer generating his perennial huge M&A fees. "There is a need to increase our ability to *generate* business in a tougher environment in order to balance our established ability to *execute* business," he wrote Michel. "We still have to spread the ethic of business development beyond Felix Rohatyn. In the absence of addressing these issues, we are likely to earn $50–$75 million less." The problem, as Loomis perceived it, was that Luis Rinaldini, "an extraordinary investment banker," who previously had been asked to lead the new business development effort, didn't have "a 'strategy' to increase our business." Indeed to Loomis, Rinaldini was "a particularly ironic volunteer as there is no demonstrated (versus expressed) inclination toward new business on his part, no consistent record of working effectively with peers and subordinates, scant inclination to organization, and a lexicon (e.g. 'control,' 'idiots,' 'screwed up,' 'inefficient') which hardly inspires confidence in his ability to *encourage,* as opposed to *discourage,* entrepreneurial activity by others who have equally large egos and ambitions." His perfectly logical solution was to have those partners skilled at developing new business teach those who were not and then to establish a set of loose and modest new business "goals." Loomis was right about the importance of these initiatives, of course, but like a battleship in the open sea, Lazard would not be turned around quickly or easily.

Six months later—just after the Black Monday stock market crash, when the Dow Jones average lost 22.6 percent of its value, or some $500 billion, in one October 1987 day, and when nerves were still a little raw from the market's fall—Loomis wrote a firm, three-page typed response to Michel's simple question to him of what is "wrong" with the associates. Loomis explained that while the quality of the associates had improved throughout the mid-1980s, the quality of their professional lives had deteriorated. He recounted for Michel what his partner Jon Kagan had recently told him. "When I was an associate, I learned a lot from Jon O'Herron, but now I sense that young people are missing that experience. Now O'Herron talks to Golub, Golub talks to Mohr, and Mohr talks to them." He also railed against many of his partners' tendencies to ask associates to create overly lengthy presentations to be used in client meetings. Loomis called this phenomenon the "blue book syndrome" since Lazard's corporate logo was often displayed in dark blue, or on a dark blue background, and the covers of these presentations were dark blue as well. Loomis took his partner Lou Perlmutter to task in the memo on the matter of "personal respect" for his fellow professionals. "One example says it all," Loomis wrote. "Lou Perlmutter did not want Jamie Kempner to do the McGraw-Hill 'blue book' analysis. When a conflict on McGraw-Hill became apparent, he did not bother to tell Jamie to stop work on the book. Three days later, he returned Jamie's two-day-old phone message, and Jamie asked Lou the status. The response? 'Oh yes, I thought Loomis would have told you that it's dead because of a conflict.' "

On Halloween 1987, two weeks after the crash, Loomis wrote Michel another emboldened memo, this one, essentially, about how to make Lazard a great firm. This goal was "of paramount concern" to him now that his fortieth birthday was on the horizon. His comments were made against the backdrop of the crash and the fact that, in New York, Lazard was on its way to making $133 million pretax, down some 26 percent from the $168 million the firm made the year before. "Associates understand very well that investment banks are under pressure and that Lazard may be under pressure in the future," he wrote. "We do not need references to André Meyer in 1974. Associates have already been offended by Felix gloating in the newspapers, as he did two weeks ago, about the Wall Street associates who would no longer earn $650,000 a year."

He then tackled the even more divisive issue of relative partnership pay and offered Michel, unsolicited, ways to redress the inequities he perceived. "The current partnership distributions are analogous to transfer payments and social security in the national budget," he wrote. "On the whole, there is a tendency to be more generous with the last generation than with the next generation. The partners in the middle and upper end, like myself, should accept the necessary dilution in current income, if the result is a bolder plan for a stronger partnership." He recommended that Michel cut the profit percentage of Bob Lovejoy, a former partner at Davis Polk who had joined Lazard the year before as a partner. Michel was considering paying Lovejoy a healthy 1.75 percent (worth about $2.3 million) of the pretax profits, up from 1.189 percent (worth about $2 million) in 1986. Loomis thought Lovejoy should be kept at his 1986 percentage or even decreased to 1 percent (which would have been worth about $1.3 million, a significant pay cut). He proposed taking from Lovejoy and giving to partners such as Luis Rinaldini (an increase to 1.25 percent, from 1 percent) and giving four younger partners a twenty-five basis-point increase as well. "The current plan," he told Michel, "risks keeping Bob Lovejoy and losing Luis Rinaldini, instead of just risking the loss of Bob Lovejoy." Needless to say, Lovejoy and Loomis were never close.

Loomis also urged Michel, "at the risk of seeming incorrigible," to institute partners' meetings. "I believe this firm has to evolve toward *real* partners, and thus, *real* partners' meetings," he wrote. "The two are inseparable." In closing, Loomis made certain Michel understood how respectful he was trying to be. "You have created this firm as it now exists with all of its stature and potential," he said. "The firm of André Meyer and his employees did not, could not, have such opportunities. You talk about firms of national character. You have a great firm that is fundamentally French in character, and another which is British in character. What you are still lacking is an American partnership. You can create a broadly based and self-perpetuating firm in New York—a great firm—only with partners."

Michel said he appreciated these insights.

FIVE MONTHS LATER, in March 1988, Loomis broached the matter of "blue book" banking again, this time in a memo to both Michel and Felix. Very little of substance had changed since he first expressed his opinions to Michel. And then in April, all of Loomis's boundless ruminations congealed in a four-and-a-half-page, single-spaced manifesto to Michel following a breakfast the two had together. "Fundamentally, the issues of concern are competitive strategy and competitive appetite for success," he wrote. "We have two philosophical alternatives. *We can place, or we can win. A firm cannot win by seeking to place.* Your comments about patience, about the ability to sustain the loss of 75% of the partners, about keeping the doors open and not forcing business and about Felix's simple cure of getting two or three major deals in the newspaper—left me deeply disillusioned. If the objective is only to place, then these statements are consistent."

Loomis then criticized what he perceived had been years of drift at the firm. "This is the time to be commercially aggressive," he wrote. "And we have, after all, missed important opportunities. We came to junk bonds too late, valuation expertise too late, business development too late, industrial focus too complacently, business organization not yet, the concept of investment of resources in business segments not yet. The business has changed and we do not own a self-perpetuating franchise. It is not enough to be a larger Lazard of the 1970's in the 1980's. We must be the Lazard of the 1990's, now. It is deeply troubling to me that Wasserstein, Wilson and Volker [*sic*]"—Bruce Wasserstein, Ken Wilson, and Paul Volcker—"albeit for different reasons, all explored Lazard and then went elsewhere. We can rationalize individual decisions but collective judgment is indicative. And Wasserstein, in particular, having seen us, chose to compete with us." Loomis then recounted, with names, the "deep-seated constructive frustration about our lack of competitive strategy and drive" that he had been hearing from a diverse group of bankers he described as the "best under the age of 50 plus Damon" Mezzacappa. "People are crying out for direction, an organization, a desire to be the best in a changed and changing competitive environment."

Loomis continued by praising Michel as "extremely wise" but fretted that the firm could not "win" with the "dilution inherent" in having Michel running Lazard in New York and Paris and worrying about the problems of Lazard in London. He then lit into Felix in a most ungenerous way. "And Felix is both able and 60 in a world that is able and 45," he wrote.

> Contrary to his stature internally at Lazard, there is a widespread consensus of takeover specialists outside the firm that Felix is too conservative and is simply no longer a leading factor in the industry. Meanwhile, he "sits" on our best resources when our best resources should be encouraged to blossom. This is a lesser but still important aspect of our future business strategy. Felix's interests do not necessarily coincide with those of the firm. In a laissez-faire administration, he would, consciously or unconsciously, leave the status-quo for the next 3–5 years, not upsetting his apple-cart, thereby leaving a sudden and substantial void upon his departure or retirement. Felix can be an asset or a liability—depending on your decisions now. Since he can be a constructive genius or a destructive force, much more deliberate thought needs to be given to his role from the perspective of others here. People like me are being encouraged by his conduct to view him as an adversary to progress. This is sad as I admire him and respect him. We need to find a better way to allow Felix to flourish and others to benefit (rather than rebel) from his presence in the future. As opposed to concentrating Lazard's efforts around Felix, we need to focus our attention on the rest of the firm. Let's build up something else of value which he can adapt to gracefully—eventually.

Finally, after all the critical words, Loomis offered his solution. He believed Michel should lead and delegate, by appointing—and overseeing—a new management committee comprising Mezzacappa, from capital markets, Norm Eig, from asset management, and . . . Bill Loomis, with a "disproportionate responsibility for banking." He wrote that this was only one alternative but urged Michel to give it a try. "If in 2–3 years, this does not work, so be it," he continued.

> The risk of the firm taking a bold step now is less than the risk of the firm not taking it. I am young and ahead of my time. (But I am also ahead, after all, of David Verey.) There would be more pressure to increase the percentage of Ward Woods (producers like Felix, Ward, and later, Luis, should receive resources, respect, fame and cash but not the right to terrorize organizations and harass young people at the firm), and you need to hear the opposition of Lou Perlmutter. Beyond that, there would be the natural but strong resistance to change and direction

> where there has been a lack of commercial discipline. I am prepared for that as long as I have your support and a close relationship with you. I am less prepared for more large committee meetings which mimic the more serious focus of the 25 professionals at Wasserstein, Perella. And I am not anxious to be Lazard's Oliver North who takes the next 25 hills without authorization and is anointed or disowned according to the ultimate result.

He urged Michel not to let the good men of Lazard go stale.

As if this were not aggressive enough, a month later Loomis urged Michel to take on London next. He said London "is a long-lasting boil which should be lanced, once and for all, and then healed by respect for national tradition within certain parameters of commercial conduct and respect for you. Any other approach is, at best, confusing and has nothing to do with the tradition of Lazard. *You are that tradition.* My fear is that you, like the British, draw back because one is British and one is French, and it all fits into an inherited history of political sensitivities. You are above such defensiveness by your authority, which we, the Americans—the youngest and thus the most brash of the lot—have recognized out of personal and commercial respect for you as Lazard." For Loomis to be flying this aggressively close to the Sun King could result in only one of two outcomes: either his own feathers would shimmer in the reflection, or he would end up like Icarus, tumbling to his death.

For a while, remarkably, he soared. The former "world's best associate," whose father was a respected career naval officer, was about to get a battlefield promotion. Somehow he had turned all of this frank talk into career advancement. Just eleven days after his "lance the boil" memo, in a May 20, 1988, memo to the "Banking Group"—most of the New York partnership—that could have been written by Loomis himself (and probably was), Michel and Felix sounded the trumpets, albeit in a low-key way. "The excellence of our partners and associates, as well as our business philosophy, have allowed us in the past few years to outperform other firms," the memo said. "At the same time, our banking business is larger, more complex and faces tougher competition in the future." Felix and Michel wrote that Lazard had a finite "window of opportunity" to exploit the unresolved internal problems of larger firms and the still evolving role to be played by several emerging advisory boutiques. "We need to address successfully difficult issues of organization, priorities, allocation of scarce resources, new undertakings, momentum and accountability for performance," they continued. "Without fundamentally changing the nature of the Firm, a more formal process and some centralization of authority are required to achieve our banking objectives."

With that, Loomis became the firm's first official head of investment banking. To be fair, through the André years, of course, others such as Felix, Frank Pizzitola, and George Ames had loosely held the reins of the firm's advisory business. But they all understood the pointlessness of the role in a small firm so totally dominated by the presence of André Meyer (in Felix's case) and Felix (in Pizzitola's and Ames's cases). Loomis became the first person under Michel's leadership to successfully maneuver himself into a position of relative authority just as it was beginning to mean (a little) something more than just being a clerk for André or Felix. Loomis was to "work closely" with Mezzacappa to ensure an "effective relationship" between banking and capital markets, and, of course, he was to "seek guidance" from Felix and Michel, "as appropriate."

The memo was eerily reminiscent in its conclusion of those few written some fifteen years earlier when André pretended to cede some of his absolute authority to Donald Cook. "We also intend to continue to use small meetings with a few partners to discuss issues of business direction or potential engagements with policy implications for the Firm," they concluded. Loomis's promotion was an "evolution not a creation" that sprang from his initial and ongoing concerns about the proper treatment of the junior professionals. This had led him to be given incremental responsibility first for recruiting, then for assignments, then for a general review of the promotion process, then to head of banking. In a firm famous for the independence of its idiosyncratic bankers and where Michel *alone* still made all the important decisions regarding partner pay, promotion, hiring, and firing, for Loomis to be named head of banking appeared to be, at best, an oddly Pyrrhic victory. But there was no denying his role, pretty much out of nowhere, as a member of the loosely taken management committee and the important symbolism of moving his office, at Michel's request, to between Michel and Felix.

But Lazard being Lazard, May 1988 would mark for Loomis the beginning of a thirteen-year period that left him resembling Saint Sebastian, where his "authority was always informal" and his frustration was always immense, caught between the Sun King and an ever-changing committee of senior partners ready, willing, and able to launch arrows at him. Whereas Felix had an intuitive sense that a management role of any kind at Lazard "was not a winner," Loomis, whether through ambition or naïveté, possessed no such instinct. He would have to learn the hard way.

The first indignity came within ten days of his appointment. *BusinessWeek* ran its first-ever cover story about the firm (as opposed to just about Felix)—and Loomis was not even mentioned. The article, titled "The Last Emperor," featured on the cover an imperious-looking Michel, hair slicked back, holding one of his ubiquitous Cuban cigars. He acknowledged that as a man with four daughters, none of whom had an interest in finance, he was likely to be the last David-Weill to lead Lazard. But at a mere fifty-five years old, he was quick to point out this was not about to happen anytime soon. "It's more than probable that the firm will move outside my family when I die or retire," the emperor acknowledged. "I'm getting used to the idea—slowly." One of the reasons he was in no hurry was simply how well the firm was doing and how fabulously wealthy he was becoming as a result. "Compact, steady Lazard Frères, meanwhile, is thriving as never before," the article stated. For the first time since the creation of Lazard Partners forced the firm to reveal five years of its historical financial performance, Michel shared the firm's financial performance: In 1987, New York made $134 million before taxes (but down from $168 million in 1986); Paris made $70 million pretax (up from $36 million in 1986, reflective of the firm's luck and skill in avoiding nationalization); and London made $58 million (although this number is after payments to partners, whereas the New York and Paris numbers are before those payments).

Michel received in 1987 about 20 percent of the profits from New York alone, or some $25 million, and likely another $20 million or so from the other two houses. Not a bad haul, making him one of the wealthiest bankers on Wall Street with a net worth around $1 billion. (Michel, though, was a distant runner-up to Mike Milken, of Drexel Burnham infamy, who made $550 million in 1987.) Felix's 6 percent take put his 1987 pay at around $8 million.

The *BusinessWeek* story also trotted out the usual Lazard myths—some of them patently untrue—and embellished upon them. Back was one of Michel's favorite descriptions of the firm as a *"haute banque d'affaires,"* an elite private bank. "To me, private banking is a state of mind vis-à-vis the world," he explained yet again. "It means not being in the way, being one who helps instead of being a power unto oneself. I see our role as very, very modest." He shared this same mantra with the new young hires, when he met with them once each year. There was also mention of Lazard's renowned frugality with regard to office space, with a new twist: When workers found a "magnificent slab" of marble in the Lazard lobby on the thirty-second floor of One Rock that André had considered "ostentatious" and ordered covered up with drab wallpaper, "there was serious discussion around here about putting the wallpaper back," one partner said. Michel made the decision to reveal the marble. "That's the new Lazard," the same partner said, joking. "Damn the overhead." There was the de rigueur discussion of Felix's prowess as a deal maker, his devotion to public service, and the need for Lazard to prepare for the day when he was gone. "It is beginning what might be called its post-Felix era," *BusinessWeek* confided, "which is greatly complicated, to be sure, by the fact that Rohatyn is still very much a force at the firm." But there was also the acknowledgment that the firm had grown and Felix, alone, could no longer generate sufficient business to cover everyone's high-level compensation expectations. "Lazard is not exactly kicking down the door any more in terms of major new business coming to Felix Rohatyn," Eric Gleacher, then head of M&A at Morgan Stanley, told the magazine hopefully. But Michel dismissed this speculation. "The intimacy between Felix and I," he said, "has been the cornerstone of the firm's success—not *a* cornerstone, *the* cornerstone." Take that, Loomis.

Part of Lazard's problem was the "cruelly ironic" fact that—as the economist Joseph Schumpeter said about capitalism itself—the seeds of its own destruction were being sown by its own unparalleled success. As Felix aged—he was sixty at the time of the *BusinessWeek* piece—he was steadily selling off the firm's historic clients, among them RCA, Revlon, and Owens-Illinois. Loomis had recognized this as a problem but had had no success in solving it. This dilemma, while hugely lucrative in the short term as large fees rolled into the firm, presented Michel with the long-term conundrum of somehow attracting new clients.

Lazard had always resisted prostrating itself for business. "The best way to get business is over the transom" is how the onetime partner Bob Lovejoy put it, much to Loomis's ongoing consternation. Unlike the other, far better capitalized Wall Street firms, Lazard had few ways, other than sound advice, to get its hooks into new clients. The firm didn't make corporate loans and rarely underwrote corporate bonds, high-yield bonds, or corporate equity. Once the leader in principal investing—the buying and selling of companies for its own account—Lazard had long ago abandoned the business, leaving behind the possibility of healthy profits and a steady stream of captive clients.

The article revealed that while there would be no changes to the basic business model, created by André, of offering blue-chip clients world-class advice, Michel was now prepared to make tweaks on the margins. First, following Loomis's recommendation, the firm would make a stab—perish the thought—at actually calling on clients with thoughtful M&A ideas. Partners made a list of likely prospects and organized themselves into four separate teams of about twenty professionals each, including six partners per team. Each team was responsible for particular industries. Loomis was to assist coordination among the groups as well as be part of the group focused on the retailing and financial services industries. This *surely* had never been done before at Lazard. "Everything is being done to fan out clients and encourage quite a number of people to go out and get business," Felix said.

Another new development was the introduction of a $1.5 billion white knight fund—so called because the firm used the capital to help corporations under attack from raiders by putting a slug of stock into friendly hands—to be called Crossroad Partners and headed by Lester Pollack, the former general counsel of Loews Corporation (a Felix client) and a former partner of Odyssey Partners, an early private-equity fund. Ali Wambold, another Lazard partner, by way of Lehman Brothers, was to work with Pollack on investing the fund.

The fund, to be an entity separate from Lazard, had a five-member board made up entirely of Lazard partners, including Michel. The Lazard partners invested $60 million of their own money in the fund. And of course, Pollack and Wambold would remain partners of Lazard. (Lazard changed the name Crossroad Partners to Corporate Partners after lawyers told them they had to, and the fund ended up being $1.55 billion, less than the hoped-for $2 billion.) The idea for the fund was for Lazard to buy between 10 and 40 percent of the stock of a company under attack from an unwanted suitor. By putting a chunk of stock into friendly hands, the raiders would, theoretically, go away. "The gist is Corporate Partners represents a pool of capital to invest in the company to allow the company to do something constructive and have the time to do it," Pollack said.

This was a different strategy by far from the one André used to buy Avis and Matador Ranch, but that didn't stop Pollack from spinning Lazard's historical success in principal investing to his advantage in promoting the new fund. "Lazard in Paris has been operating as a principal, acting as a friendly shareholder, for a long time and has been very successful," he said. "Lazard in New York has also acted as a principal from time to time and has done very well at it. Because we do act as principals, as proprietors, we have longstanding relationships with corporations. We're on a lot of boards not only of clients but other companies where we provide an active director role. Other investment-banking firms are finding ways to buy market share through use of their own capital. That's the phenomenon of bridge financing and the like. We're not in that business."

Wambold, who had conceptualized the fund, tried to slice the Lazard difference even thinner. "I think if you asked Michel whether he is an investment banker investing in companies, he would tell you the answer is no," Wambold said at the time. "He would say he is a senior partner of an investment-banking entity. He is also an investor. We are very suspicious of mixing the two mentalities because there is always the danger of using capital on the investment side to generate fees on the current income side. You're making $20 million on the income side, while putting $300 million at risk on the investment side." Before long, Lazard and Corporate Partners would find there were big risks investing this fund, risks that reflected very poorly on Lazard. But with the new Corporate Partners fund at least Lazard could say it was back in the often lucrative business of private equity, with its own differentiated twist.

THE ARTICLE ALSO announced that Lazard had hired J. Ira Harris, then fifty, as a senior partner in M&A, from Salomon Brothers, where he had built up the firm's Chicago office into a big moneymaker. Harris, a walrus of a man who was born in the Bronx and played stickball growing up—he could hit the ball three sewer lengths—had known Felix for years and had worked on the opposite side of many deals with him. Harris remained in Chicago—although he often shuttled back and forth to his palatial home in Palm Beach and to New York—where he built up a Lazard office by hiring a number of new partners, including William Gottschalk and Jeffrey Golman. Lazard, oddly, took to marketing the "Felix and Ira" show—"two mature bankers with decades of experience behind them, men whom a corporate executive can trust" is how the overture went. Of course, Felix and Ira couldn't have been more different—the massive, gregarious, and outgoing Harris loved spending time with clients playing golf or attending Chicago Bears football games, whereas the aloof and cerebral Felix rarely socialized with clients; it has been suggested that Felix's idea of a good time in Chicago was to "speak to the Economic Club." Ira, meanwhile, organized an annual golf tournament in Chicago that attracted around a hundred of the nation's top executives. There is even an Ira Harris sandwich at a local Chicago deli.

But the tag team proved effective—for a while—with Ira playing a prominent role at Lazard in a number of legendary deals: representing the special committee of the board of directors of RJR Nabisco during the infamous saga that resulted in the largest leveraged buyout of a company until late 2006 (and a $14 million fee); the sale of Kraft to Philip Morris; the merger of Primerica with Commercial Credit; the sale of Associates Financial from Gulf & Western to Ford; and Bridgestone's acquisition of Firestone. Felix and Ira worked together on these deals, with one pinch-hitting for the other in meetings if needed. "It's not bad having Babe Ruth as a substitute" is how Harris described his partnership with Felix to the *New York Times*.

Despite his success at Lazard, which would have put him in the top of the partnership percentage ranks, the financially conservative Harris maintained a special arrangement with Michel whereby—unlike every other Lazard partner—he was paid a large fixed salary that worked out to around a synthetic 3 percent stake of the firm's profits with a significant upside potential based on his own performance *only*, without having any actual percentage of the firm's overall profits, which of course depended on how all the partners together performed. On the one hand, this spared Ira from having to make the annual fall pilgrimage to Michel's office in New York to determine his profit percentage, and also absolved him from liability in the event something went wrong and partners' capital accounts were docked. His thinking was that since he had spent twenty-five years making his money at other Wall Street firms before coming to Lazard, he had no intention of losing it there if someone did something stupid—another bit of prescience on his part. When other partners became aware of Harris's deal with Michel, some of them became so paranoid that they scurried around trying to figure out what he was getting that they weren't. One of them was so concerned that he marched into Tom Mullarkey's office to demand to know what was going on with Ira's deal. "None of your goddamn business," Mullarkey told the startled partner on his way out.

The May 1988 *BusinessWeek* cover story also revealed that Michel had—for the first time, but not for the last—assiduously courted Bruce Wasserstein in 1987, just as Bruce was deciding whether to leave First Boston, the Wall Street firm he had helped build into an M&A powerhouse. As Loomis alluded to in his manifesto, in the end Wasserstein and his partner Joseph Perella, and a handful of other First Boston bankers, including Chuck Ward, started Wasserstein Perella & Co., an M&A boutique that competed against other Wall Street firms and went on to have many successes during its twelve-year life. "The Fortune 500 is our target clients," Wasserstein told the *Wall Street Journal* in February 1988 on the day he left First Boston. "We think the custom-tailored merchant bank is the wave of the future. We want to be the Lazard of the 90s." At the *real* Lazard, meanwhile, there was great relief that

Michel and Bruce couldn't agree on the terms under which he would come to the firm. "The Wasserstein thing was viewed with horror because it looked like Michel might be going back to importing top partners instead of promoting from within" was how one relieved Lazard M&A banker put it. Loomis obviously had a different view, that somehow Lazard was so impaired that more money could be made competing against it than working for it.

LATE IN THE summer of 1988, Loomis tried again to convince Michel that the banking group needed more structure to become more productive. He noted for Michel that despite having better and more bankers, banking's revenues were trending down in 1988 both absolutely and compared with those of other firms. He also pinpointed one of the firm's key problems: the failure of the partnership to function as one. He then bemoaned as a "major problem for us"—correctly as usual—the firm's complete lack of accountability. "Accountability for partners at Lazard is not a clear concept, or, at least, does not closely track our goals," he continued. "Accountability tends to be perceived as individual in nature and either a negative incentive (fear of failure) or an endorsement of raw personal ambition (to become a hero)."

Lazard also had no formal training program for new hires or even anyone who gave much thought to what happened to new employees when they arrived. In this sense, and in many others, the firm was totally Darwinian, a fact Loomis lamented, metaphorically. "Interestingly, the 'freedom' of being left to sink or swim in a pool of 100 individuals increasingly raises the question at all levels, 'What are we doing and what am I part of?' " He further explained to Michel that some partners recommended to him shrinking Lazard back to a few partners and associates. "Simple is best," goes this argument, "and all the problems disappear—just fire people." Loomis preferred, though, to find a way to work more effectively with the existing talent. To that end, he told Michel, "We have to be willing to make real changes in our daily pattern of doing business."

He then proposed the previously discussed radical solution—radical for Lazard anyway—of dividing banking into four industry-focused groups. "The partners would be evaluated, in large part, by the ability to work effectively together," he wrote. The beauty of this structure, Loomis believed, would be a more productive and accountable banking effort where junior bankers could be more efficiently employed, mentored, and evaluated and where the productive senior partners could lead by example for those less productive. "Instead of simply being busy as individuals, we need to focus attention on how we become more successful as a firm," he concluded.

Loomis's proposal was thoughtful and well conceived—and utterly ignored by Michel and Felix. Loomis was right that above all Michel and Felix favored the status quo. Loomis was wrong in that the firm was doing fine—in 1988, New York made $141 million, up from $134 million—and the two leaders were each making tremendous amounts of money. His recommendations all but ignored, Loomis entered one of his periodic phases of introspection and frustration. On November 30, Michel announced that his first head of banking would be giving up the post after a mere six months. "Bill Loomis has decided to turn his attention full time to client relationships and transactions," Michel informed the firm. In his place, Michel had asked the partners Tom Haack and Nat Gregory "to assist the Banking Group in various roles previously undertaken by Bill." An odder duo of leaders could not have been conceived. Haack was the son of the former president of the New York Stock Exchange whom Felix worked with on the back-office crisis of the early 1970s, and Gregory, a North Carolina native, had been an academic at the University of Chicago and worked at Bechtel before coming to Lazard in 1983 with no previous investment banking experience.

Although their tenure was brief—Loomis returned to head banking six months later—Gregory was the embodiment of the sink-or-swim mentality then pervading the firm. On one of his first days at Lazard, at the last minute, Lou Perlmutter dragged Gregory into a meeting with the top management of Beatrice Foods. The Beatrice executives—led by the company's CEO, Jim Dutt—had flown to New York from Chicago because they were concerned that someone was buying up their stock and wanted advice on how to react to the potential threat. But after greeting the executives, Perlmutter left Gregory alone in the meeting and disappeared for thirty minutes. One of the Beatrice executives asked Gregory, who was in his mid-thirties, how long he had been at Lazard. "It was one of those moments where you had to decide how you were going to play the fish," Gregory remembered. He chose candor. Here he was faced with a group of nervous executives looking to their investment banker for advice and succor and the partner was nowhere to be found, leaving a neophyte to deal with the situation.

Soon after the Beatrice fiasco, Gregory found himself on another high-powered deal for which he was ill prepared. The raider Victor Posner had assembled a large minority stake in one of Lazard's Chicago clients, and Gregory was sent to the company along with the partner Arnold Spangler. But neither of them was particularly proficient in the emerging art of takeover defense. When they returned to New York a few days later and Gregory was informing Ward Woods about the developments, Felix popped his head into Gregory's office. He didn't like what he heard Gregory saying, and he ordered Woods to fire Gregory on the spot. Woods ignored Felix, and Gregory stayed. He became a partner in 1986. By late 1988, he was running banking. "Running banking at Lazard was like being dean of a business school," Gregory said. "It was not an easy thing to do because, as you know, it was Michel's firm."

INTO THIS RELATIVE anarchy, intense quirkiness, and immense prosperity strolled Steven Rattner, the one Wall Street investment banker who was every bit as scarily talented, media savvy, and professionally and politically ambitious as Felix and who, much to Felix's surprise and eventual dismay, refused to be cowed by the Great Man's prowess or play by his long-established rules. The impish Rattner, a former *New York Times* reporter in Washington and London, joined Lazard as a partner from Morgan Stanley, where he had run media investment banking and had made it one of the top groups on Wall Street. He was all of thirty-six years old, but his slight build and elfin appearance made him look even younger. He turned out to be a huge business generator for Lazard, but he often came across as cool, aloof, and indifferent. Surviving depressions and wars was one thing, but the conflict that would soon erupt between Felix and Steve, whose father-son relationship for a time mirrored in many ways that between André and Felix, would test Michel, and Lazard, as never before.

CHAPTER 11

THE BOY WONDER

Steve Rattner, pride of Great Neck, New York, a wealthy Jewish enclave some twenty miles outside of Manhattan along Long Island's North Shore, joined Lazard in the early spring of 1989 with surprisingly little fanfare, especially for someone as well connected in media circles as he. Ironically, as the discussions with Steve originally unfolded, at his own insistence, he was willing to consider leaving Morgan Stanley only if Lazard would allow him to do something *other* than media banking. And the firm, with Loomis as chief negotiator, was more than willing to try to accommodate Steve's wishes. After an often tortured five-month negotiation, where, much to Michel's chagrin, he initially said he would come to the firm before equivocating, he was hired at Lazard as the partner in charge of a new group providing advice and capital in "special situations," an oblique reference to his desire to work with smaller, "emerging growth" companies as either a principal or an agent and to help build Lazard's nonexistent high-yield finance business. Hiring Steve for this role not only satisfied him but was all of a piece with the firm's desire to reinvigorate its long-dormant private-equity business, as evidenced by the creation of Corporate Partners and the much smaller Centre Partners, another Lazard-affiliated fund that invested about $150 million of the partners' money in LBOs.

A brief *Times* article about Rattner's hiring explained he would head a new group "providing advice and financing in special situations, including restructurings, recapitalizations and leveraged acquisitions"—none of which sounded the slightest bit like advising media and telecom tycoons on their M&A deals. Rattner elaborated on his new assignment in the article and about why he moved from Morgan Stanley. "Lazard has been in the junk bond business for about a year," he said. "My mandate is to take that embryonic effort and turn it into a very successful group. Morgan Stanley is probably the best firm on the Street at what it does. But I just found the attraction of a small private firm, and particularly the job that was created, to be irresistible." To his new team, Steve quickly recruited from within the firm two experienced vice presidents, Tim Collins, one of the few people to ever leave Lazard and return, and Ken Jacobs, who had recently joined Lazard from Goldman Sachs.

But it was a classic bait-and-switch moment, whether intentional or not. One day early on, Felix, Michel, and Damon Mezzacappa decided that Steve had gotten control of too many of the firm's limited resources, and in any event they didn't really want to pursue the business that Steve described. Felix had always been an outspoken critic of Mike Milken and the use of high-yield bonds to finance takeovers, so for Steve publicly to commit the firm to that line of business, while innocent enough, rankled him. Quietly but definitively, Steve's "special situations" group was dissolved even before it began. Steve felt the firm had snookered him but quietly accepted his fate. "In two days the whole thing was gone, and I became just another partner doing my business," he said. "I kind of shrugged and went on. . . . I don't remember enough about it to know whether Bill was just trying to pat me on the head. I honestly don't remember. I also don't know whether Bill knew it was never going to happen and just wanted to get me there, which you know is the way of the world and I have no problem with, or whether he honestly thought it was going to happen and he got his legs cut out from under him by Michel or Felix."

It was his baptism to the ways of Lazard. Rather than stew or bolt, though, he got over the incident and quickly returned to calling on his old media clients, much to the consternation of his new partners Luis Rinaldini and Ali Wambold, who had been running Lazard's loosely focused media effort and had actually suggested recruiting Rattner to the firm as Wambold had known him well at Lehman Brothers. They felt the sharp edge of Steve's elbows. "What I didn't really understand is that Steve from a business point of view was a loner," Rinaldini said. "He didn't want to have a shared team in this area. I had done a lot of media business. I had actually done Comcast, and he had done it from the Morgan Stanley side, and initially I said to him, 'Why don't we sit down and figure out how we can work together and who does what.' And he kind of looked at me with a blank stare and said, 'Why would I want to do that?' "

Steve soon became the partner in charge of the firm's media and telecommunications banking practice. Or as one of his many freely available biographies puts it, "Mr. Rattner founded the firm's Media and Communications Group and was involved in many of the largest and most important transactions in the industry." Charitably, Rinaldini said he didn't feel Steve had pushed him out of media. "It's tough competition," he said, "which is different than being cut out. I wasn't going to be the media star, because we already had one of those—Steve—so you say, 'Okay, can't do that. Okay, I'm not going to be the star of the basketball team, I'll try football.' "

Steve's ability to overcome the initial confusion derived, in large part, from both his quiet confidence and his mighty ego, which is often a prerequisite for success in the competitive sea of investment banking. He had the confidence of a man who believed that the world would provide what he needed when he needed it. Steve had—and has—an unrequited ambition and an ability to manipulate and court the press that rivaled—and rivals—Felix's. His genuine friendship with Arthur Sulzberger Jr., the publisher of the *New York Times,* whom Steve has known since they were both young reporters together at the *Times* in Washington, has been much documented and is replete with multiple instances of public support of one for the other, often in Sulzberger's paper. In short, Steve had his own Great Man credentials and was determined to use them for his own advancement both at Lazard and beyond.

Before Rattner's arrival at Lazard, the firm had quite purposefully not made group-head designations by industry despite Loomis's urging. Michel had the long-held view that specialist groups would balkanize the firm. True, there was a small, world-class effort advising companies in, or near, bankruptcy, led by the brilliant longtime partner David Supino, but that effort obviously cut across all industries. Lazard bankers had always prided themselves on being generalists, with no specific industry expertise and with world-class M&A execution skills. Furthermore, if a client wanted to raise debt or equity capital rather than, say, make an acquisition, the client's Lazard banker would execute that transaction regardless. It was also a given that Felix would lead the charge on the firm's big deals (because more likely than not he would have received the client's call in the first place) and then rope in acolytes as needed. It was also gospel that by his own choice, Felix would have no administrative responsibilities in running the firm's banking operation: He would only do deals. Period. Of course, Felix didn't want anyone else running the firm, either, a doctrine that made Lazard somewhat out of control operationally, as Loomis had the scars to prove.

Steve's hiring exacerbated the long-overdue metamorphosis inside the firm toward industry specialization—a change other firms had long ago adopted—a process that would hasten his blowup with Felix as the two clashed repeatedly over roles and responsibilities on the firm's high-profile media deals. So, in addition to Supino's restructuring group (which the firm disbanded in 1992 despite its being arguably the best on

Wall Street), at the urging of Ira Harris the firm hired on its second try, in January 1990, Ken Wilson, a onetime Salomon Brothers partner, to start, run, and build up the so-called FIG group (coverage of financial institutions, such as banks and insurance companies). Michael Price was hired a little before Steve, also from Morgan Stanley, to focus on technology and telecommunications. Previously, of course, Michel had poached the Lehman Brothers gang, led by Jim Glanville, in 1978, to focus mostly—but not exclusively—on oil and gas clients. And there had always been "industrial men," such as Frank Pizzitola and Donald Cook, at Lazard. These hires were all in addition to the seemingly random, so-called Felix hires, generally a group of his former clients or high-level political acquaintances with little banking experience whom Felix convinced Michel to hire. None of these men remains at Lazard, a testament to, among other things, Felix's transient loyalty and their own shortcomings, in many cases, as bankers.

The creation of these new industry groups necessitated, of course, the hiring of additional bankers to be part of them; on Wall Street, it was simply inconceivable to be a group head without a group. Lazard was starting to grow its historically modest head count. As with nearly everything else at the firm, though, the hiring process at that time was antiquated and convoluted. In early 1990, Michel had urged his partners to hire people based on their "human qualities" rather than just their professional qualifications. "Intelligence . . . spark . . . humor . . . wit . . . and a paradoxical mind . . . boring people are bored here . . . unhappy people remain unhappy however diligent or skilled they may be technically," he said. There was also the acknowledgment at the time that Lazard had never been very good at nurturing. "The firm has been relatively unsuccessful with those who want a lot of guidance, structure and rationality," the partners observed. Nevertheless, despite Loomis's efforts, there was no "hiring on campus" as with other investment banks, meaning that no Lazard professionals appeared at the top business schools to interview slates of eager MBAs. Nor did Lazard retain executive search firms to fill positions. Rather, the way to be hired at Lazard as a neophyte was through enlightened nepotism or luck—or both. If you knew someone who worked there, you had a shot, although not a very good one. (Not so long ago, the lucky few who managed to somehow wrangle an interview often heard nothing back from the firm afterward.) This explained, in part, the presence at the firm of people such as Thomas Pompidou (whom peers took to calling "Thomas Pompidant"), grandson of Georges, the former French president; Lou Gerstner III, son of the former CEO of IBM; Gregory Salinger, son of Pierre, John F. Kennedy's press secretary; Anne Bevis, granddaughter of Dwayne O. Andreas, the founder of ADM; Mike Dingman Jr., son of the CEO of Wheelabrator-Frye; and Lyle Wilpon, nephew of Fred, the owner of the New York Mets.

Steve had moved with Eric Gleacher, a former marine and later the founder of the M&A boutique Gleacher & Co., to Morgan Stanley from Lehman in the spring of 1984, primarily because Morgan Stanley was then, and today still is, considered the bluest of the blue-blood investment banking firms, with the best and most loyal clients. In 1984, Gleacher was hired from Lehman to run Morgan Stanley's new M&A department. Steve went with him. For Steve, the Morgan Stanley business card would certainly prove that the Jewish kid from Great Neck and former reporter had begun his ascent of the investment banking summit.

In short order and true to form, Steve attracted attention at Morgan Stanley. He recalled later for *Vanity Fair* how "soon after I got to Morgan Stanley, I wrote a memo saying that one of our major objectives had to be to handle a significant sale of a major television station. This was the sine qua non." He was a vice president, head of the firm's media and communications group, and worked on a number of increasingly high-profile media deals, including those defending CBS from the hostile entreaty of Ted Turner and helping the Pulitzer family evade A. Alfred Taubman's unfriendly advances toward the *St. Louis Post-Dispatch*. He also—per the script—advised Henry Kravis and the investment bankers who owned KTLA, an independent TV station in Los Angeles, on its sale to the Tribune Company for $510 million, then the largest amount ever paid for a single television station. The station's owners doubled their money, at a profit of $255 million, three years after buying it from the movie star Gene Autry. The *New York Times* included Steve in a story about Wall Street's "upstarts," and *Channels* magazine featured him in a story. He spoke of the "big money" to be made from companies "ripe" for deals and of the "frightening" similarities between M&A advisory work and reporting. "I used to develop sources, now I develop clients," he said.

He was also the subject, in 1986, of a revealing and lengthy profile in Charles Peters's iconoclastic *Washington Monthly,* "Hello Sweetheart, Get Me Mergers and Acquisitions: The Rise of Steven Rattner." Steve said he was worried about the appearance of the article—"nothing good was going to come of this," he explained—but decided to cooperate after a few months of stonewalling the reporter. "If something is going to get written, you're generally better off cooperating than not cooperating," he said in acknowledgment of his journalistic roots. Although less fawning than the profiles of Felix in *The New Yorker* or the *New York Times*

Magazine, the *Washington Monthly* piece was a watershed nonetheless, for it tried to capture the gestalt of what was luring the best and brightest minds of a generation into the then-obscure profession of investment banking. Here for public consumption was the story of Steve Rattner, the well-off oldest son of successful New York businesspeople, who was willing to chuck away his career at the top echelons of journalism for Wall Street. Of course, Steve had chosen to cooperate with the magazine; he had agreed to allow himself to become this iconic figure. Word was, though, among some Morgan Stanley associates working with Rattner at the time, that Steve bought up all the copies of the magazine in the vicinity of the Morgan Stanley building on Sixth Avenue (whether out of embarrassment or pride is not clear). In any event, this was not your usual investment banker. The buzz was he was making about $1 million annually, a staggering sum at the time for a young banker.

Aside from his legendary drive, the Rattner résumé is fairly straightforward, without any of the Sturm und Drang Felix experienced. Yet there is a certain inevitability about him, in a John P. Marquand *Point of No Return* kind of way. He is the eldest of three siblings, with a sister who is a gynecologist and a brother, Donald, who is an architect. His parents owned and operated Paragon Paint, a Long Island City paint manufacturer, before its liquidation in the late 1990s. His father ran the business successfully for forty years. When his parents divorced, his father left Paragon Paint, and his mother took over its day-to-day operations. (The business had been in her family originally.) In short order, she ran it into the ground after trying to bust the company's small labor union and after being cited repeatedly by the National Labor Relations Board for malfeasance.

But the Rattners prided themselves on their intellectual bent as well. Selma, Steve's mother, had a graduate degree in architecture. In the 1980s, she was an adjunct professor at the School of Architecture and Planning at Columbia University and taught at the New York School of Interior Design. She was very knowledgeable about the work of James Renwick, the architect of Grace Church, at the edge of Greenwich Village, and of Saint Patrick's Cathedral, on Fifth Avenue. Steve's father wrote nine "serious plays," including one, *The Last Sortie*, that was staged as part of T. Schreiber Studio's 2000–2001 theater season on West Twenty-sixth Street alongside a production of Wendy Wasserstein's *The Heidi Chronicles*.

"It's tough to be a first child brought up in a place like Great Neck and not be a little hard-driving," Steve once said. Peter Applebome, a reporter and editor at the *New York Times,* also grew up in Great Neck and described the town, in part, as a "kind of 'Goodbye, Columbus' suburban experience—privileged, insulated, largely Jewish but essentially secular—so familiar as to occasion an almost reflexive rolling of the eyes." After graduating from Great Neck North High School in 1970, Steve moved on to Brown University, from which he graduated in 1974 with honors in economics and received the Harvey A. Baker Fellowship, awarded annually for graduate study abroad to members of the graduating class who have "high scholastic standings; have participated in college activities; and have shown qualities of leadership."

While in college, he devoted himself to the *Brown Daily Herald*, furthering an interest in journalism that had started in high school. When he was a senior at Brown, he served as the editor; he was the chief writer of editorials and the overall leader of the paper. In keeping with the times and the function of the editor of a college newspaper, he was an aggressive and outspoken critic of the university's administration and especially of Donald F. Hornig, Brown's president. Rattner believed Hornig to be isolated and detached from the students and kept a running tally of the number of days since Hornig last met with students in a public forum (674 and counting, as of October 1973). Steve facetiously hoped Hornig wouldn't "surpass Babe Ruth's mark."

Steve's final editorial urged his fellow students not to let "those folks in University Hall and the office building and in all the departmental offices get away with things that they shouldn't get away with. And that's one of the main things we tried to prevent this past year. We blew it occasionally, but we think we came up with more heads than tails . . . for God's sake let the *Herald* know when your blood boils. You're all we've got, folks." Next to these strident words was a picture of a long-haired, baby-faced Steve Rattner and four of his colleagues, unsmiling and buck naked, strategically holding posters of themselves naked (yes, it's complicated) with the request that students "get involved" by joining the staff of the paper. Steve is sitting, with his poster facedown in front of him, revealing his bare chest. He has long since made his peace with Brown; he has given at least $500,000 to the university's endowment and is now the chairman of the Budget and Finance Committee of the university's Board of Fellows.

From Providence, Steve shot straight to the top of the journalism profession, serving as clerk for the legendary *New York Times* man Scotty Reston—an assignment that has been described as "the most honored job for a young man in journalism, something like beginning a legal career as a Supreme Court clerk." Steve had been planning to use his Harvey A. Baker Fellowship to attend the London School of Economics in

September 1974 and then move on to law school. But fate intervened when he applied for a summer job in 1974 at the *Vineyard Gazette,* on Martha's Vineyard, and met on-island with the paper's owners, Mr. and Mrs. James Reston. He got dinged for "not being folksy enough" for the Vineyard, and so lined up a summer job at *Forbes* instead. But in June, Scotty called him up out of the blue and asked whether he wanted to come to Washington to be his clerk at the *New York Times.*

One of the great attractions of the apprenticeship with Reston, of course, was the expectation that at its conclusion, the *Times* would proffer a full-time position to the tireless clerk. Steve was a natural at the *Times,* reveling, at all of twenty-three, in his stature as a full reporter on the metro desk of the world's most important newspaper. He hung out with Paul Goldberger, then twenty-five and on his way to being the *Times*'s influential architecture critic and a Pulitzer Prize winner. Some of their former *Times* colleagues believe Rattner, for a time, modeled himself after the über-sophisticated Goldberger, soaking up the latter's savvy knowledge of contemporary art, fancy clothes, and New York culture. "Steve and I were both involved with plenty of women, but somehow we still found lots of time to hang out with each other," Goldberger told *Vanity Fair.* "We used to shop for art together and we spent Saturday wandering down Madison Avenue going to art galleries. He started collecting contemporary prints and at times he bought the same things I had on my walls. People said I gave him a sensibility. Maybe. He gave me a lot of good companionship and a loyal friendship that lasted 20 years."

Steve moved quickly from the metro desk to a coveted role covering energy policy during the oil crisis of the late 1970s, when his reporting from the Middle East impressed his bosses. "I don't know how people get to be so smart, so savvy," the *Times*'s former business editor John Lee recalled about Rattner. "He walked in the door and knew what to do." In April 1977, at twenty-four, he won the plum assignment of covering Carter's energy policies in the *Times*'s Washington bureau. "Something no one of my age or experience had any right to," Steve recalled. Eventually, he covered economic policy. "He was very bright," said Bill Kovach, the former bureau chief and the founding director and chairman of the Committee of Concerned Journalists. "His ideas were faster than his ability to talk." It was in Washington, not surprisingly, that Steve befriended Arthur Sulzberger Jr., the current chairman of the New York Times Company and its controlling shareholder. The Rattner-Sulzberger clique also included the other twenty-something reporters Jeff Gerth, Phil Taubman, and Judith Miller, whom Rattner dated for much of the time he was in Washington.

Together, Rattner, Miller, and Sulzberger and his wife, Gail, rented a house, the Blue Goose, on Maryland's Eastern Shore, sealing their lifelong friendship. "There is no one outside my family to whom I'm closer than Steve Rattner," Sulzberger has said. When Rattner was a *Times* reporter, he referred so regularly to Arthur's father, Arthur Ochs Sulzberger, by his nickname, Punch, that Joe Laitin, a spokesman for the Carter Treasury Department, asked Rattner if he was indeed a member of the family. Rattner's response: "No, but you're not the first person to ask me that." Sulzberger junior, nicknamed "Pinch," is regularly quoted about Rattner and is one of his firmest public champions. "What I like about Steve is his mind," he said once. "It is always a challenge to keep up with him." They take vacations together, "something tough and invigorating," such as scuba diving in the Cayman Islands or hiking the Appalachian Trail. Almost every New Year's Eve, the Sulzbergers and Rattners celebrate together. The two are so close, in fact, that Sulzberger, for a time, regularly faces questions about whether Rattner would one day join the New York Times Company in some partnership role. So far, both parties deny the likelihood of this happening.

Steve also developed close ties with many of the younger Carter administration officials, as often happens between reporters and their sources. This kind of relationship is a sensitive one, comprising daily calibrations of where lines should be drawn and how thickly. These decisions are immensely personal, reflecting the values, morality, and character of each party as much as anything. There are no written rules or laws, only constant judgments. Some reporters choose to be aloof, drawing the line at social interaction. Others choose a more intimate path, believing a complete understanding of the personal and the professional will provide rare insight and access. There is no right answer.

But a reporter's power to influence is substantial, as can be the consequences of choices made, or not. For an ambitious young man in his mid-twenties, this can be extremely heady—but complicated—stuff. Steve clearly understood the power he possessed and the choices that had to be made. He wrote about it for the Brown alumni magazine in 1980. "For my part, I have tried to walk something of a middle line, although frequently wondering whether my friendship with people working in government on issues similar to those I report on compromises me," he wrote. "I have particularly avoided friendships with officials with a leadership role on issues I cover." But he certainly cut it close. He shared a house on Martha's Vineyard with Ralph Schlosstein, who was then working for Stuart Eizenstat, Carter's chief domestic policy adviser. He was also friendly with Walter Shapiro, a Carter speechwriter, and with Josh Gotbaum, who held many positions in Democratic administrations and who later, for a time, was Rattner's partner at Lazard. He was friendly with Jeffrey Garten, who worked for Secretary of State Cyrus Vance.

Steve quickly grasped the power his position gave him to influence policy and to influence careers. He walked a tightrope here as well, but generally in favor of his distinguishing characteristic of cozying up to important people. He wrote approvingly of Robert Strauss, the ultimate Washington insider and dear friend of Felix's, that he "has always been careful, as he collects friends, not to collect them indiscriminately." His 1980 *New York Times Magazine* cover story on G. William Miller, Carter's Treasury secretary, described "Bill Miller" as "businesslike as his dark suit, white shirt and striped tie. Poise and self-confidence are key components of that executive image, as is a strong measure of personal control." For his part, Felix attributed to Miller a good measure of the blame for the failure of his Textron-Lockheed rescue deal when Miller was CEO of Textron. A profile of George Shultz, Nixon's Treasury secretary and Reagan's secretary of state, included the softball "The lack of force in Mr. Shultz's manner belies an abundance of force in Mr. Schultz's ideas." Just as he had aspired to be the overzealous college newspaper editor, Steve naturally sought to be influential as a Washington reporter for the *New York Times*. "The thing I loved about reporting was the actual impact on events," he once said. "Helping inform intelligent opinion, affect administrators' judgment of things." Which, when he did, "made me feel it's all worthwhile."

In a move of questionable judgment, though, Steve risked throwing away his growing influence at the *Times* when he flirted dangerously with the all-important line between reporters and their sources. The Council of Economic Advisers was central to Rattner's economics beat, as was its chairman Charles Schultze. Over time, Steve developed a high regard for Schultze, a very high regard. In 1979, he applied for the position as special assistant to Schultze. The job was not dissimilar to that of being Scotty Reston's clerk. It entailed working on economic reports, handling the press, and managing the staff of the council. It's "the world's best job in economic policy if you're not a big enough shot to be a principal," according to Susan Irving, who got the job instead of Rattner.

The *Times* never knew that Steve had attempted to cross the line from reporter to source, and so there were no repercussions for him or for the paper. The incident behind him, Rattner kept reporting on the Carter administration's economic policy and continued to write glowingly of Schultze. He described a series of lectures Schultze gave at Harvard as "a modern classic, the *Das Kapital* of the regulatory reform movement."

In the spring of 1981, Steve got promoted to be a foreign correspondent, as the rookie in the three-man *Times* London bureau. The Schultze matter proved, among other things, though, that Rattner was getting antsy at the *Times*. In truth, Steve had been considering the switch to investment banking for some time but held off in favor of moving to London, reasoning that he could always be a banker but the chance to report for the *Times* from London was once in a lifetime.

Helping him to make this decision was his friend Arthur junior, who had been a foreign correspondent for the Associated Press for two years, in London, in the 1970s. Pinch also shared with Steve some names of people to look up while in London, one of whom was Maureen White—his future wife—who was working for a Japanese TV agency. (They didn't hit it off at first; Sulzberger had to reintroduce them when they all had returned to New York City. They were married in June 1986 at the Lotos Club on East Sixty-sixth Street.) Of his time in London, the consensus seemed to be that Rattner's reporting from there was less inspired than it had been in Washington, in direct proportion to his distance from the nerve center of American power. He worked with another *Times* legend, R. W. "Johnny" Apple Jr., the bureau chief, covering the Falklands War and reveling in the older man's insatiable appetites. "Steve and I talked about architecture," recalled Apple. "He did up his flat in London in a modern style very successfully. London is not a late town, and we were working late hours, because of the timing in Argentina, and we'd end up at 12 at night, and to unwind we'd go to Joe Allen's in Covent Garden to eat and drink double margaritas on the rocks, which Rattner christened 'Depth Charges.' "

One of Steve's best *Times* articles, in which he compared the productivity of a Ford plant in Germany with one in England, ended up in the Business section, an ocean away from the *Times*'s front page, to which Rattner had grown accustomed. But he also has conceded, in a rare moment of self-doubt, that his skills as a writer were limited. "I once watched Apple write a cover story for the *Times Magazine* in four to five hours with a glass of vodka next to his computer," he told *Vanity Fair*. "Johnny was so talented. I was only the palest imitation. The story in London was more of a writing story than a reporting story. It was my belief that the great correspondents were great writers, and I always thought I was, at best, an ordinary writer." There was also the matter of making money and accommodating his soaring ambitions. Some believe Rattner's move to banking was a prescient acknowledgment that the world was changing quickly; others believe he was motivated by a desire to get rich. Steve said his decision was simply a matter of calculating his best option. "I wasn't going to go into the clergy," he said.

Maureen White told the *Washington Monthly* in 1986 why her husband had moved from journalism to investment banking: "It begins to get on you after a while that you are writing about people who have more power than you, more influence and more money and are not any more capable. Why in God's name are you trailing them around the world and writing about them when you are smart enough to make the money and have influence commensurate with theirs?"

Amen.

But how was Rattner to make the jump from reporter to investment banker? The tried-and-true way at that time, in 1982, especially for someone changing careers, would have been to go to business school, suffer through a two-year MBA program, and come out the other side as an associate at a Wall Street firm after successfully navigating the randomness of the on-campus interview process. To accomplish his move to investment banking, though, Rattner chose the much faster, higher-percentage approach of soliciting the former Carter administration officials he had carefully cultivated, many of whom were now on Wall Street.

Steve spent a "week or two" in New York, seeking the counsel of the top bankers at the best firms about what he should do next, as if no one had anything better to do than help further Steve Rattner's career. With the help of Bob Strauss, the doors were opened to him across Wall Street. First stop for Steve was his good friend Roger Altman, Carter's former assistant secretary of the Treasury, then at Lehman Brothers. They had dinner in downtown Manhattan to discuss Steve's future. Come to Lehman, Altman urged, convinced Rattner possessed the secret DNA of investment banking—the ability to gain the confidence and trust of important people and the intelligence to synthesize complex financial information. "He could understand the interplay of legal, tax regulatory, and finance questions, very complex stuff, to look at things like a three-dimensional chess game," Altman has said. He also spoke with Bill Miller, the former Treasury secretary whom he had profiled. Miller thought Rattner a "brilliant guy" and wanted him to join him at G. William Miller & Co., a merchant bank he started in Washington in 1983. Rattner met with Ken Lipper, then at Salomon Brothers, and Ace Greenberg, the longtime head of Bear Stearns & Co. He met with Bob Rubin at Goldman Sachs. After a cocktail of some Macbeth-like soul-searching as to whether investment banking would be fulfilling or meaningful enough and an evening of extreme drunkenness with Sulzberger in London, Rattner bolted the *Times* and joined Lehman. Sulzberger, while disappointed, understood his friend's decision.

Steve had no idea what bankers did or how they did it. Nevertheless, "it was like a match to dry wood," Jeffrey Garten, then also at Lehman, has said. "I have never seen anything like it. He was effective from day one. He had a gift of expression. He was a great briefer. He capitalized on the similar requirements of journalism and investment banking—to encapsulate a complicated subject and make it appear you know more than you do."

BY THE TIME Steve left Morgan Stanley for Lazard, he had perfected many of the nuances required to be a successful banker, and his career appeared headed on a higher trajectory. Despite his relative youth, he brought with him to Lazard a highly coveted asset—a stable of devoted, M&A-savvy clients, among them the cable and wireless tycoons Craig McCaw, Amos Hostetter, John Kluge, and the young Brian Roberts, now the acquisitive CEO of Comcast. Hostetter, whose cable company Rattner sold, actually offered to pay Lazard a fee higher than Rattner felt appropriate, so "Steve insisted that I reduce what I was proposing," Hostetter recalled. These ironclad relationships would prove invaluable to Rattner.

Of course, if you are an M&A banker, extraordinary client relationships aren't all that useful without deals to do. Consider the timing of Rattner's arrival at Lazard: April 1989 was but seventeen months after the October 1987 market crash, when the Dow Jones Industrial Average fell a stunning 22.6 percent in two trading sessions alone, effectively ending five years of wild speculation and merger mania. The severity and magnitude of the collapse, rivaled at that time only by 1929, initially paralyzed the country's deal-making machinery: CEOs and investors were petrified, having lost billions of dollars, and bankers and lawyers found themselves in one of those periods of uncertainty when deals come unhinged.

Only, this time, something unusual happened: in one sector of the deal-making world, activity actually *increased*—for so-called leveraged buyouts, where private-equity firms, run by such men as Henry Kravis and Ted Forstmann, use lots of debt to buy and "take private" companies that previously had traded in the public markets. There were two principal reasons the LBO market stayed hot after the crash of 1987. First, the price of public equities looked cheap, as stock had just fallen by more than 22 percent, and in many cases by far more. For instance, GE dropped to $43 per share on October 22, 1987, from $60 per share on October 7, 1987, a nearly 29 percent fall in two weeks. Second, and this is a bit of a mystery, financial institutions, such as banks and insurance companies, along with public investors, continued to finance these kinds of deals. The lines of fear and greed had not yet crossed. Since Lazard had no deal-financing capability to speak of and Felix had spent years publicly denouncing the use of so-called junk bonds to finance leveraged buyouts, Lazard missed many of these often very lucrative transactions. Compared with every other firm on Wall Street, Lazard may as well have not even been in the high-yield finance business. Rattner, though, had hoped Lazard would underwrite many more such high-yield financings, despite Felix's public objections to the product.

And so by the start of 1988, this unusual confluence produced all sorts of LBOs, culminating in the epic (and well-chronicled in *Barbarians at the Gate)* battle to take private RJR Nabisco, which Kohlberg Kravis Roberts won for $25 billion in cash, topping bids by Forstmann Little & Co. and Shearson Lehman. Hundreds of millions of dollars in fees were paid to bankers to advise on and to finance the RJR deal, somewhat mitigating the toll the crash was taking, at least on Wall Street. Lazard, led by Felix and Luis Rinaldini, his then golden boy, had the lucrative assignment advising the special committee of the RJR board of directors in its consideration of the bids; the firm earned $14 million for its trouble.

The true fallout from the crash of 1987, though, did not hit Wall Street until almost two years later, during the summer of 1989, when the financial markets buckled amid the effort to finance the LBO of United Airlines, a $6 billion deal and one of the largest of the so-called employee-owned buyouts. Lazard was advising United, thanks to the management relationships of Eugene Keilin, whom Felix had recruited to the firm from MAC. At the eleventh hour, Citibank pulled its financing commitment for the buyout after failing to syndicate the huge loan package. Syndicating a loan—the time-honored practice of dividing it among other financial institutions—is an essential part of corporate finance, as no one bank would ever want to have on its own balance sheet the full exposure of a particular credit. Failure to syndicate a loan is the death knell of a deal and means that the market has voted no on its efficacy. Don Edwards, a Lazard associate and brilliant recent graduate of the University of Illinois, had been working on the United deal with Keilin and Ron Bloom, a vice president, running spreadsheet scenario after spreadsheet scenario on his computer. Edwards nearly physically collapsed along with the deal. "This is the junk-bond market's October 19," Rattner told the *Wall Street Journal* at the time, comparing the collapse of the United deal to the day the stock market crashed in 1987. "This looks like a cataclysmic event." The aftershocks of the United deal's end spread virally. So finally, two years after the crash, the M&A and financial markets imploded, causing scores of highly indebted companies to file for bankruptcy and bankers to lose their jobs. It is hard to overestimate the effect the combination of the crash and the closing of the financial markets had on deal makers. Felix had proved prescient about the dangers of junk bonds and too much corporate debt. Fear and loathing had returned to Wall Street.

AT THE SAME moment that the global financial markets went into a deep freeze, Lazard announced a historic development. For the first time, a single person—Michel—took executive control of the three Lazard houses. The "retirement" of Sir John Nott, who since the creation of Lazard Partners in 1984 had been the chairman and chief executive of Lazard Brothers, gave Michel this unprecedented opportunity. Nothing had changed in the ownership structure of the three firms—Michel and Pearson were still the largest shareholders—but the typically low-key announcement was momentous. "Our clients want to have the advantage of speaking to two and sometimes the three firms combined," Michel said. "Having a [single] chairman will make that easier. The three firms have some difficult sorting-out to do, all the time. If it is done for a time with one single voice, the sorting-out will be very easy."

Michel told the press that Nott, the British defense secretary during the Falklands War, accomplished in his five years at the helm of Lazard Brothers "what he set out to do and now he wants to do something else." Nott did not comment publicly about his departure, although his memoir, *Here Today, Gone Tomorrow,* recounts any number of his frustrations working for Michel. Several of his colleagues, though, confirmed he was furious at Michel, especially for his increased meddling in the business of Lazard Brothers since the formation of Lazard Partners. Michel's insistence from the start that David Verey, then thirty-three, be named as Nott's deputy caused Nott some anguish, especially since Verey leapfrogged a bunch of older, more seasoned partners to get the job.

And of course, the appearance of Agostinelli in London further infuriated the independent Nott. "Michel was starting to exert control," the former Lazard partner Jeremy Sillem explained. "And Robert was the instrument through which the New York partnership expressed their disdain for London. And their contempt for it. Because he would go and see companies in the U.K. and not tell anybody in London about it. I'm sure he was encouraged to do that by Michel. But Nott didn't really get along with Michel, and in particular, Michel used Robert Agostinelli—being

American—and must have encouraged him to stir it up to make all kinds of trouble in London. And in the end, it undermined John Nott's authority. And he basically told Michel it was either Agostinelli or him. And it was Agostinelli. Agostinelli stayed and Nott left." (In his memoir, Nott claimed to have fired Agostinelli before deciding to leave himself after another six months.) Two years later, at the end of 1991, Michel relinquished his chairman title at Lazard Brothers to Verey. "David has been doing the job anyway," he told the *Wall Street Journal*, which pointed out that the "change won't significantly diminish Mr. David-Weill's power at the firm . . . but it does make room for a younger generation of executives."

THIS WAS THE backdrop for Rattner's rather subdued arrival at the firm. He quickly established that he would be *the* media banker, relegating Wambold to work with Lester Pollack on the Corporate Partners fund and Rinaldini to return to the generalist ranks. Among Steve's first actions was to serve as the placement agent for a novel $300 million private-equity fund focused solely on investing in media and communications companies. Lazard invested $7 million in the new fund, to be called Providence Media Partners, along with Jonathan Nelson and Greg Barber, two partners of Narragansett Capital, who together invested $10 million. Steve also negotiated for himself and for Lazard one of the sweetest fee arrangements in capital-raising history. Since some of the Providence fund had been committed at the outset, Lazard was to raise only $175 million. For that work, the firm was to be paid a 1 percent placement fee, or $1.75 million, plus—and highly unusually—one-third of the General Partner's carried interest, or profits. Since the fund was enormously successful—returning to investors four times the amount of money invested—Steve figured the General Partner made $100 million, of which Lazard took around $33 million. But Steve had a side arrangement with Michel that gave him 8.25 percent of the firm's take, amounting to some $2.72 million for Steve alone, leaving the Lazard New York partners with around $30 million. Talk about unprecedented!

Despite the continuing pall cast on the financial markets by the collapse of the United Airlines buyout, Steve wasted little time in revving up his deal machine, which quickly erased any lingering concern on his part about what he had been hired to do at the firm. By the end of his first year at Lazard, aside from the Providence Media mandate, Rattner had advised the cable mogul Jack Kent Cooke on the $1.6 billion sale of his cable properties to a consortium of TCI and Intermedia. He sold KKR's Storer Communications cable business to TCI and Comcast (for a $10 million fee), and he represented his friend Craig McCaw on McCaw Cellular's $6.1 billion hostile acquisition of the TV broadcaster LIN Broadcasting (for a $14 million fee). These were major deals, and major accomplishments for any banker, especially given the rocky markets.

Felix, too, of course, had managed to maintain his usual whir of activity. He and his partner Jon O'Herron found themselves deeply immersed in the controversial and landmark $15 billion merger between Warner Communications and Time Inc., creating Time Warner Inc. The deal, which started out as more or less a merger of equals between Time and Warner, quickly dissolved into one of the most contentious and litigious deals of all time after Paramount Communications, another Lazard client, made a last-minute hostile offer for Time. In response, Time, advised by Bruce Wasserstein at his new firm, Wasserstein Perella, changed the structure of the deal with Warner by agreeing to acquire it in a highly leveraged transaction that would burden the combined company for years. The merger, which Rattner also helped out with as needed, marked the culmination of Felix's longtime association with the Warner CEO, Steve Ross. Felix claimed never to really like Ross because he felt his greedy behavior caused him to do some unsavory things. He remembered receiving a call at his house in Southampton years later from Ross, when he was near death, claiming to be in Dallas, picking out a horse for his daughter Nicole. Skeptical that Ross was well enough to travel, Felix called his friend Paul Marks, the president of Memorial Sloan-Kettering. "Paul, I just got a phone call from Steve Ross from Dallas," Felix reported. "I did not know he was able to travel. Paul said, 'He can't. He's at Sloan-Kettering right now.' Steve Ross stage-managed his life until the end."

By this time Felix had also met the Hollywood legends Lew Wasserman and Sid Sheinberg, the two men who ran MCA, the owner of Universal Studios, the powerful film and television studio. MCA had attempted a hostile offer for SeaWorld, a theme park operator, that Felix eventually sold to Anheuser-Busch for $1.1 billion. After the SeaWorld deal was over, Wasserman asked to come by and meet with Felix at his Lazard office. "Which was typical of Lew," Felix said. He expected to be lambasted for the outcome of SeaWorld. Instead, Wasserman asked him to join the MCA board. "If we can't beat you, we want you to join us," Wasserman told him. Flattered, Felix explained his long-standing relationship with Ross at Warner, a major MCA competitor. With Ross's consent, though, Felix joined MCA's board, which included his old friend Bob Strauss, the Washington lawyer.

The years after the 1987 crash were funny ones on Wall Street. LBO firms were having a bonanza taking private public companies whose share prices had fallen precipitously. CEOs of American companies were running scared, out of fear that if they didn't take steps to improve the productivity of their businesses the sharp-elbowed LBO financiers would target them for a takeover. The steep drop in share prices in the United States also attracted the attention of foreign buyers, especially the Japanese. The high-profile deal that started the Japanese buying spree here was the successful $2.6 billion acquisition of Firestone, the iconic American tire maker, by Bridgestone, the leading Japanese tire manufacturer. Lazard and Felix, representing Bridgestone, put the two companies together after the Italian tire maker Pirelli, backed by the French tire maker Michelin—a onetime Lazard client—made an unfriendly $2 billion offer for Firestone. The Lazard bankers were so angered by the fact that the Michelin-Pirelli team had made such an audacious move without Lazard that the firm quickly sought out Bridgestone to make a superior—and successful—bid. Bridgestone's acquisition of Firestone was the largest Japanese purchase of an American company at the time, but obviously was not the last such large purchase.

Felix was not a stranger to the Japanese. He had represented Sumitomo Bank when it had acquired 12.5 percent of Goldman Sachs, in 1986, for $500 million (which turned out to be a fabulous investment). But the Bridgestone-Firestone deal was far more iconic. Not only did corporate America seem particularly vulnerable post-crash, but there was likely no more quintessentially American company than the ninety-year-old Firestone Tire and Rubber Company of Akron, Ohio. There were a number of years, before the Japanese economy crashed, when American politicians became frightfully concerned that the Japanese were "buying up our country." This fear reached a symbolic peak, of sorts, in 1989, when the real estate subsidiary of Mitsubishi took control of Rockefeller Center. Around the same time, Sony purchased Columbia Pictures from Coca-Cola for $3.4 billion. Soon, Congress was holding hearings to assess the potential fallout from these acquisitions.

Felix testified at the hearings despite having played a meaningful role in bringing about the worry—however silly and nonsensical it was—in the first place. He focused on the coming economic dangers for the U.S. economy in the 1990s if the federal budget was not balanced and long-term interest rates reduced. He also criticized the many Lazard competitors that were using their own capital to make risky bridge loans to help their clients complete leveraged acquisitions. "Market conditions may occur under which a bridge loan cannot be refinanced," he correctly predicted. As to the concern about foreign acquisitions, Felix simply acknowledged that it "is becoming an area of increasing economic and political importance," and then sought clarification on the rules of engagement. Afterward, more than one of his partners remarked on the level of cognitive dissonance that Felix must be able to withstand after, on the one hand, actively participating in the acquisition of American companies by Japanese companies and, on the other hand, being able to testify before senators trying to come to terms with the phenomenon—and not even acknowledge before them his own role.

Maybe it was because he was not yet finished playing that role. In the fall of 1990, Felix's friend and literary agent, Mort Janklow, asked him to lunch at the Four Seasons restaurant to meet Michael Ovitz, the über–Hollywood talent agent, who was then the head of the Creative Artists Agency. Ovitz had just represented Sony in its acquisition of Columbia Pictures, and Felix had never met him before. He was plenty controversial, even in those pre-Disney years, for it was rare for someone who was not an investment banker to play a central role in a high-profile corporate marriage. But such was Ovitz's standing at that time that he was uniquely able to pull it off, much to the envy of traditional bankers. Perhaps, Felix thought, Ovitz was cooking up some new corporate assignation, and that was why Janklow wanted Felix to meet him. "Lunch at the Four Seasons, and breakfast at the Regency, are at the heart of New York finance, the arts, publishing and high-level gossip," Felix once observed. "You do not go there if you want privacy. You go there if you are not averse to publicity." After Felix and Ovitz chatted a bit about their mutual experiences working with Japanese companies, Janklow left the two men alone.

Ovitz then told Felix he had been working for more than a year with a Japanese company, Matsushita, that was interested in buying MCA. Ovitz said Matsushita believed MCA's mix of business—movies, theme parks, and music (after Felix had just sold them Geffen Records)—would mesh well, in a Sony–Columbia Pictures way, with its consumer electronics business. Ovitz insisted on confidentiality and told Felix the Japanese would walk away if there was a leak. He asked Felix to speak to Lew Wasserman about the possibility of a deal. "By asking me to arrange a meeting with Wasserman to broach the possibility of an acquisition of MCA, he was making me an interested party to a possible transaction and at the same time, as an outside director, putting me at somewhat of a fiduciary obligation to try to give his transaction a fair hearing," Felix recalled.

Thus began the usual two months of intense deal making between the unlikely protagonists—the Jewish Hollywood royalty, on the one hand, and the conservative, secretive Japanese businessmen, on the other. Felix remembered one Sunday night dinner, in November 1990, between the two sides held at the Hôtel Plaza Athénée, ironically the very site of Felix's lengthy affair a few years earlier with Helene Gaillet. It was "one of the oddest dinners I have ever attended," filled with awkward silences between the top brass of both companies, punctuated by equally awkward non sequiturs, duly translated. The first course was melon and prosciutto. "I hear you have very good melons in Japan," Sid Sheinberg observed. To which Masahiko Hirita, a Matsushita vice president, responded: "Yes, we have wonderful melons because we have very well electronically heated hothouses." This went on for three hours. "I thought I was in a Kafka novel where the central character never knows whether he is crazy or everyone around him is crazy," Felix commented later. But the deal progressed, despite concerns about the cultural fit—and the potential political fallout. To try to grapple with the latter, Matsushita agreed to spin off to MCA shareholders WOR-TV, MCA's independent television station, and to transfer MCA's concession in Yellowstone Park to a new, American operator. Wasserman and Sheinberg were to be left alone by the Japanese to continue to run MCA.

When the deal was announced just before Thanksgiving 1990, it was, at $6.6 billion, the largest nonindustrial deal to that time. "This deal might be another feather in my cap and in Lazard's cap," Felix remembered, "but I still had a bad feeling about the whole thing." His instinct was correct. The deal was a total bust. Less than seven years later, and without a word to Wasserman or Sheinberg, Ovitz advised Matsushita in the sale of MCA, for almost $6 billion, to Seagram. (That deal proved to be a disaster, too, and Seagram eventually unloaded Universal to what became Vivendi Universal, an overly ambitious former French utility then run by the former Lazard partner, Jean-Marie Messier. Once again, Universal proved poisonous. To avoid a possible bankruptcy, Vivendi ended up selling Universal to GE, which combined it with NBC.)

All of these deals—whether by Felix or Steve or many others—were large, high profile, and industry transforming, the completion of which meant big fees for Lazard. The MCA deal was particularly sweet not only because of the ongoing dearth of M&A deals but also because the financial advisers—Ovitz and Allen & Co. for the Japanese and Lazard for the Californians—were small boutiques, not the big Wall Street behemoths, a further validation of the Lazard business model. Generating these fees, of course, year in, year out, was essential to Lazard because it has always been, basically, a one-product firm: providing financial advice on M&A transactions. So while the larger, multiproduct Wall Street firms, such as Goldman Sachs, Merrill Lynch, Morgan Stanley, and Citigroup, have many ways to derive fees from their clients, especially from raising debt and equity capital for corporations, Lazard had, by design, precious little of that capability. The word around Lazard, repeated like a mantra every January, was, "Now we have to start again from scratch." Somehow, just as Frank Zarb had described, year in, year out, Lazard was able to do just that.

In the post-credit-crunch environment of the early 1990s, Steve's ability to generate high-margin M&A fees was, not surprisingly, getting him noticed in the corner offices of Lazard's thirty-second floor, where Felix and Michel held court. Not only did Steve generate large M&A fees; he did so with clients that were not traditional Lazard clients. This gave him increasing authority and power. He was, of course, being well paid—to the tune of millions of dollars per year—and before long he was also being recognized and rewarded with leadership positions. At the end of 1990, the introspective and cerebral Loomis, then forty-two, had managed to regain his balance as the firm's loosely acknowledged head of banking, as Lazard referred to its leader of investment banking. Loomis was to provide some leadership and direction—a task he did minimally, at best, given his natural reserve and the constraints placed on him by Felix and Michel—and, most important, once a year, conduct performance reviews and pay the nonpartners. Michel still set partner pay at that time, an increasingly deeply flawed system that led to acute paranoia among partners but kept everyone on edge and completely loyal to Michel. But Loomis still had time for his thoughtful, if somewhat inscrutable, observations about the state of the partnership.

He delivered one such tome in March 1991 to his banking partners. "After one year of some involvement on my part in the coordination of our banking business, it might be worthwhile to share observations," he wrote, with some modesty. One of his main points was to confirm that Lazard was doing quite well, especially when compared with the disarray being experienced by the bigger Wall Street firms after the credit crunch. That said, though, he enumerated eleven "observations, more or less obvious," that he believed had the ongoing potential to hinder the firm in the future. These ranged from the usual laments about proper use of scarce professional resources to how to continue to compete effectively against the firm's two largest perceived competitive threats. "Wall Street remains in disarray," he wrote. "Having said this, Morgan Stanley and Goldman Sachs are effective competition, not only because of their excellence but also because they have in common an enormous sense of drive currently and an almost imperial sense of an international approach."

Loomis's paper also acknowledged that Lazard was "not a place where anyone is going to direct activity and bestow efficiency on the rest of us. Some of the inefficiency is inseparable from the strength of the place and some is a lack of effort on our part as partners day to day in a host of little ways. It is our problem and thus the solution is a shared response." The treatise continued in much this vein before concluding existentially:

> Success and happiness at Lazard flow from similar characteristics. By and large, the partners who are most successful here on a sustained basis combine individual talent with a natural or acquired tendency to present Lazard to major corporations rather than using our franchise to rise or fall as individuals. Success as an individual is only an indirect and cumulative result. We can't do this without seeking out those who have something different to say or who can contribute a judgment before the die is cast. Similarly, there is a correlation here, among partners and associates, between the causes of success and happiness, as those seem most at ease who are most inclined to consult with others frequently and casually. A more solitary approach has an increasingly unattractive risk/reward ratio internally . . . and externally. And it diminishes the personal privilege of being part of a partnership.

Once again, Loomis had produced a document the likes of which had never before been seen around the firm's threadbare hallways. In his professorial tone he had created a gumbo, with one dollop of positive reinforcement and a whole lot of opaque scolding. How this went down with his partners is tough to know for certain, but it would be hard to think it too dissimilar to castor oil. The document never made it to the nonpartners. Furthermore, there was not even the slightest perceptible change in the way the partners acted, approached new business, or worked with the junior professionals. Lazard remained as quirky, as dysfunctional, and as successful as ever.

Much of this absurdity was celebrated in a little-read October 1991 profile of Michel—"It's Good to Be the Emperor"—in *M, Inc.*, Felix's friend Clay Felker's short-lived successor to *Manhattan Inc.* The heavily edited piece, written by Suzanna Andrews, celebrated both Michel and the firm and pointedly did not look under any rocks. "Today, Lazard is arguably the most profitable and powerful mergers house in the United States," the article purred. "In Europe, where it owns huge stakes in major continental corporations, Lazard is the most feared bank. And now, on the eve of the European economic integration next year, Lazard

Frères is the investment banking firm in position to garner even more riches and more power. As Lazard's power has grown, so has the mystery surrounding David-Weill, its all-powerful éminence grise." The article portrayed the dapper Michel standing in his Paris office in front of the priceless portrait of his grandfather by Édouard Vuillard, the family friend.

Felker gave Michel plenty of ink to convey his oddly charming quirkiness and aphorisms. "Every firm over the years basically developed their identity," Michel said of investment banks. "At least it's a great belief of mine that the walls speak to the people that are inside the walls, and that you can change everybody but they still speak the same language as in the past." Michel was celebrated for appearing to give his partners freedom to do their jobs, without the bureaucracy of Lazard's larger competitors. Much was made of his desire to collect bankers unlike others on Wall Street. Felix the immigrant. Steve the former *New York Times* reporter. Bill Loomis, who wanted to write in the style of Somerset Maugham. Luis Rinaldini, the former architect for Philip Johnson. "We have an emphasis on being individualists," Felix said. And supposedly everyone got along just fine. "It's like a family," Rinaldini said. "You know this brother is a drunk, this one works hard. You know that this sister is artistic and this one isn't."

But the reality, touched on only briefly in the piece, was far darker. Michel had collected around him a unique group of people at once brilliant and insecure, hugely ambitious yet deeply risk averse, all of whom were willing to trade obeisance to Michel for nearly risk-free wealth. Michel tended exceedingly well to the proper care and feeding of his high-strung thoroughbreds. Felix, of course, was Exhibit A of this phenomenon. Lazard was "my home," he said. But as Andrews discovered, he proved highly sensitive to questions about this fact. She asked him about his supposed ten-year rolling employment contract with Michel. "The question touches a nerve," Andrews wrote, "because Rohatyn refuses to answer me and ends the interview." But, a fine reporter, she asked Michel about the contract. "Felix has always had an immigrant's mentality," he said. "He's always very concerned about security. So we have conversations or arrangements so that he feels that he is definitely at home." But others saw this odd dynamic between Felix and Michel as symptomatic of the firm's manic nature. "The place is totally overwrought," one competitor observed. "I'm sure you see this kind of thing at the entertainment companies, but by the standards of finance, it's off the scale."

And Michel was behind it all. "I am the resident psychiatrist," he said. "You know that I am a great believer that the faults of people are very often more determining than their qualities. I look very carefully when I have somebody. I say, what is his fault? Where is the break in his personality which will motivate him?" What was his own weakness? Andrews wondered. "I don't mind at all that anybody is as good as me," he responded. "But I don't like when people are better." In truth, Michel was highly motivated by his ability to say no to other people, both socially and professionally. "I am equidistant from people," he once famously told Anne Sabouret, a French journalist who in 1987 wrote a book about Lazard. Michel told Sabouret he looked for ways to limit his "perimeter of suffering." Surrounding himself with expensive art and other tangible signs of his wealth was one way to rejuvenate after his days at his Lazard office. "I really need this confrontation with beautiful things to maintain my balance," he said. "It gives me back my sense of joy of living." To Andrews, he confided that another way he limited his perimeter of suffering was to be mostly alone. "It's not bad to be isolated," he said. "I think a lot is taken out of you by the urge to conform, and I never had that. I had no urge to conform. I was not with other kids. I was not part of a group."

This sense of being apart informed the way Michel and Felix directed the firm professionally, too. Felix, of course, was a leading critic of the Wall Street fads of junk bonds, bridge loans, and advising corporate raiders, a source of huge but unsustainable profits at places like First Boston and Drexel Burnham in the 1980s. Michel defended Felix and the firm's decision to keep away from most of the faddish behavior, a variation of the ability to just say no. "We pride ourselves that we don't have to do anything," Michel said often. "It's an illusion that you have to rush into anything."

When Michel did emerge from his cocoon, it was usually in the company of women. "My friends are mostly ladies," he told Andrews. "I do not like men socially that much. At work they are interesting. But in life women are more interesting." Atypically on Wall Street, Michel often spoke to his partners about the need to bring to deals the tactical skills of a woman. "Michel always says that you need a certain degree of femininity to be a good investment banker," explained Robert Agostinelli. "You have to be intuitive and sensitive. You know, men don't often get a lot of things." Added Michel: "Men very often lose all sense of proportion." Andrews described Hélène Lehideux, Michel's wife and the daughter of a once-prominent French banking family, as "a beautiful woman who in many ways is as socially reserved as her husband. But when she summons, *le tout Paris* responds." A "Parisian socialite" told *Women's Wear Daily,* "She has a way of getting everyone to show up." In keeping with Felker's purpose of lusciously laminating Michel's image, no mention was made of his longtime affair with Margo Walker, a woman well known in the exclusive world of Locust Valley, Long Island, where Michel owned a weekend estate. Andrews would reveal the affair between Michel and Walker to the general public in her next, explosive article about Lazard just over four years later.

CHAPTER 12

THE FRANCHISE

On Java, the most populous island in Indonesia, there is a fable about a beautiful but deadly tree—known as the upas (the word means "poisonous" in Javanese)—that emits such noxious odors that nothing around it can grow. A Dutch physician who visited the island in 1783 and claimed to have seen the tree firsthand wrote of it: "Not a tree nor blade of grass is to be found in the valley or surrounding mountains. Not a beast or bird or living thing, lives in the vicinity." No less an authority than Erasmus Darwin, grandfather of Charles, repeated the tale eight years later.

The effect of the upas is a useful metaphor to describe the fate of many, if not all, of the partners who toiled away in anonymity for Felix while he became an investment banking legend. His modus operandi was to have at least one, more junior, partner work for him on all of his important deals and be responsible for coordinating the larger team that did the actual deal execution—due diligence, crunching the numbers, putting presentations together, staying up all night, and so on—while he wisely focused his energy on coaxing along the principals and wowing the board of directors. But the landscape is littered with frustrated bankers who worked for Felix—no doubt thinking it was a ticket to stardom, only to be disappointed to find there appeared to be no limit to Felix's own ambitions. "[Felix] has been cutting people off at the knees for years," one man told *New York* magazine in 1996. "Anyone who has gotten close to him has gotten fucked."

One of the best-known examples of this phenomenon is the well-documented story of the former Lazard partner Peter Jaquith. A graduate of Andover and Dartmouth, Jaquith joined Lazard in 1970 after having been an associate at Shearman & Sterling, the Wall Street law firm. He worked for Felix on many deals, including those for Seagram. "He was my chief lieutenant," Felix told the *New York Times* in a lengthy profile of Jaquith. "When transactions needed financial and legal structuring, he worked on that." Jaquith was one of Lazard's best-paid partners and accumulated a fortune, with all the requisite toys, of some $20 million at one time. But according to the *Times* article, which chiefly described his sad descent into drug addiction and destitution, Jaquith began to resent his "secondary role" at Lazard. He remembered a closing dinner in 1981 for a Seagram deal, held at the "21" Club, where Edgar Bronfman, the Seagram CEO, singled him out for public congratulations. Bronfman's father had been the man who, more than twenty years earlier, had advised Felix to get out of foreign exchange and work on mergers at Lazard with André.

Felix, sitting nearby, was not happy. "I think Felix was jealous," Jaquith explained later. "Right after that, he took me off the account." What's more, after the Seagram dinner, Jaquith claimed, Felix increasingly shut him out of other deals. Fed up, he left Lazard in 1985. Felix rejected Jaquith's assessment. "I was happy with his work and sorry to see him go," he told the *Times*. After Lazard, Jaquith had successive jobs at Forstmann Little, at Bear Stearns, and even at his own investment firm, Tilal, an acronym for "There Is Life After Lazard." His own arrogance and addictive behavior contributed mightily to his professional and personal demise. Finally, after years of struggle, at the end of 1997 he broke his addiction to alcohol and crack cocaine. He tried to return to Lazard. He made an appointment with Michel and went to see him at his new office in 30 Rockefeller Center. "We met at his office, and I told him I knew some of his executives had left and he might need someone," Jaquith explained. But of course, it was not to be. Michel wrote him a letter, saying, "As you may know, we have always had a policy of not rehiring people who have left"—which wasn't exactly true. In editorializing about this scene, the *New York Observer* wrote, "Mr. David-Weill apparently lacked the empathy to reach out even a little—not necessarily by hiring Mr. Jaquith, but certainly he could have done something that would give his former colleague some support. Mr. David-Weill may have inherited a fortune, but he seems to have squandered a more valuable asset: his character." Jaquith now lives alone in a small apartment in Pasadena.

There are other, far less dramatic examples of the frustrations felt by partners who worked for Felix. David Supino, like Jaquith a former associate at Shearman & Sterling, also worked briefly for Felix. He recalled a deal early in his career at Lazard when Felix's client Charles Revson wanted to buy a small private company in Boston. Felix asked him to go to Massachusetts and perform the due diligence. Once there, Supino understood that the CEO wanted a higher price for his stock than he wanted the other stockholders to receive. With his legal background,

Supino quickly realized "this was illegal." He reported the discussion to Felix. "Felix took in what I was saying, and the next day I was taken off the case," he remembered, explaining that the deal never happened.

Supino, who speaks fluent French, also worked with Felix on a number of early Franco-American, cross-border deals. He recalled that Felix made it very clear that Felix alone would speak to the CEO and Supino would not. Once when the CEO called Supino and Felix was not around, word got back to Felix about the conversation. "That's the way Felix liked to run things, and if in fact you departed from that stratification of duties, then he got very upset," he said. "I remember one time he called me up and he said he had heard I had talked to [the CEO] and he said, 'How could you do this? It is terrible.' He was yelling at me." Supino concluded that working for Felix was "very difficult because it was unrewarding. He never wanted you to get any credit with the client or for that matter within the firm. What I observed working for Felix was that Felix had a track record of having young partners or senior associates work for him and for one reason or another they fell out with him. He dismissed them from working for him, and thereafter their careers were stalled." While Supino found the assignments "interesting" and "exciting," he decided that working for Felix was "a dangerous position for me to be in at the firm" because it was "at best a dead end and at worst a death sentence."

He decided that to survive at Lazard, he had "to engineer a way to get out from under Felix's thumb." In 1980, he got a call from Art Newman, then a partner at Ernst & Young, asking him to get involved with the financial restructuring of the White Motor Company, one of the largest American truck manufacturers. White, based in Cleveland, had recently filed for bankruptcy. Supino saw restructuring-advisory assignments as his ticket to getting away from Felix. He grabbed the opportunity and created one of the best restructuring practices on Wall Street. He forged a successful career at Lazard, away from Felix. Felix's initial response to Supino's decision? "David, I don't understand why you are working in the cancer ward." Supino described Felix as "a very insecure person" who "is the ultimate user. Once he has no use for you, he tosses you aside like yesterday's stinking fish."

Luis Rinaldini also knew this to be true about Felix, although since he is still a working banker he is more diplomatic about it than Supino, who has retired from Lazard. Upon joining Lazard as an associate in 1980, Rinaldini quickly perceived that Felix was always looking for bright, hardworking, ambitious associates to work for him. "He wasn't interested in explaining things to people," he said. "He wasn't interested in training anybody, he wasn't interested in mentoring people. He just wanted someone who could read his mind. So when he said, 'Have you thought about that?'—like Radar on *M*A*S*H*—I said, 'Yeah, here it is. Weren't you going to ask me about this analysis?' We just clicked and we got along and I ended up working on most of his things."

It wasn't quite that simple, though. Rinaldini recalled that Felix would often ask three or four people to do the same task. "I never really knew if this was on purpose or because he was not sure of where to go and was just starting four people going to see what they would come up with or because he had forgotten he'd given it to three guys and gave it to the fourth guy or because he was just actually starting four hares running just to see which one would run the fastest. But it was very sort of capitalistic in that sense. There was a bid and an ask, and if the bid and the ask were right, he'd buy." He seriously doubted that Felix did this in a haphazard way, if only because he was so brilliant and so hands-on. "He could tell you the numbers," Rinaldini recalled. "He could memorize. He had a great memory. He'd look at it once and memorize it. You'd go into his office with one analysis, and then come back with another, and he'd find a mistake. The EPS was $1.15 in the last presentation, and now it's $1.17 in this presentation, and he'd say, 'I thought this was $1.15, how could that happen?' " This being the days before computers were prevalent—not that Felix used a computer anyway even when they were—Felix "would literally take out his slide rule and check your numbers" and find the mistakes.

Mostly, though, Rinaldini credits Felix with teaching him that, like the rich, "CEOs are different" from you and me. Felix's partners found him to be the most astute CEO "psychiatrist" they had ever seen. "What he really did is he managed the amount of information and the way it was communicated to the people he talked with," Rinaldini said.

> The only other person I saw who had the same kind of natural talent for doing that was Steve Rattner in the sense that you could see the change when he got on the phone. Because so-and-so was on the phone, Felix kept it concise. He edited well. He didn't bring in all this extraneous shit. What I call this is synthesis. You take 170 different inputs and you don't discard 167 of them and say what matters are these three, you say, taking it all together, these are the things that matter—this matters, this matters, and this matters, we've taken everything into account. . . . It's kind of like Felix being Radar for them. And they say, "Fabulous, that's what I need. I need a guy who can cut through all these financial equations . . . and tell me what matters for the decision I am trying to make."

In the wake of Jaquith's falling-out with Felix, Rinaldini became Felix's new wingman. "He was Felix's butt boy," was the way the partner Ken Wilson described him. "He kind of treated him like dog meat." The Time-Warner merger, the GE-RCA deal, MCA's purchase of Geffen Records, the sale of SeaWorld to Anheuser-Busch, the sale of MCA to Matsushita, the infamous RJR Nabisco sale to KKR—all these, and more, fell to Rinaldini to execute. He was completely under Felix's spell, a phenomenon Wilson found absurd coming from a firm such as Salomon Brothers. "I was really shocked, a senior guy like Luis doesn't seem the guy who'd be running around, you know, at Felix's beck and call," he said.

But like those before him, after some ten years at Felix's side, not surprisingly Rinaldini began to chafe and feel increasingly frustrated. "The only issue I had with Felix ever is that Felix was not able or willing to transfer his clients on to the younger people," he explained. "So I would talk to him about that and say we ought to have a lunch with Jack Welch, or on this Warner stuff, let's pick two or three areas where I can take charge. Otherwise, you don't advance." Like other homegrown Lazard bankers, he found that when he became a partner and was expected to bring in business, he was at a loss about how to do so, having worked for Felix all those years. What Supino knew intuitively, Rinaldini learned the hard way. "Clearly when I was made a partner, I wasn't ready for the commercial side," he recalled. "I could certainly act like a partner, talk to any CEO in the world, go to any board meeting. I knew I wasn't ever going to embarrass myself. . . . I'd learned how to behave in grown-up company, but pitching new business and getting out, getting hired on my own without the Felix crutch, was very hard work." It dawned on Rinaldini that "even though I was having a fabulous time" working for Felix on all of these landmark deals, "I kind of had to find a way to break off and do things on my own. And that was actually difficult because I was so involved with all of the things that he did that I probably didn't do it very elegantly and I was clumsy about sort of breaking away from things."

His frustrations with Felix came to a head at a dinner Michel held for a small number of partners in 1991 at his apartment at 820 Fifth Avenue. The idea for the dinner had been to clear the air of the frustrations felt by some of the younger partners toward the older partners, the thought being that the older partners, such as Felix, needed to begin relinquishing control of some coveted accounts so that the junior partners could develop commercially. Rinaldini, who grew up in New Rochelle, cultivated an image as a "fiery Argentine" after his father, a doctor, moved the family to Argentina when Luis was in college. Rinaldini is a fierce and well-regarded "gentlemen's" polo player and once commissioned a six-foot-by-four-foot oil portrait of himself—costing upwards of $30,000—wearing his polo uniform and holding his mallet and helmet. At Lazard, Rinaldini was known to be emotional and capable of losing his considerable temper. There are stories of associates nearly being hit by one of his absurdly wide Gucci loafers after he chucked it in a fit of pique.

The dinner started out innocently enough with a discussion about how to help younger partners develop better commercial instincts, a subject Rinaldini had some strong opinions about. But he wasn't the only one who had these feelings. Others did, too. As the Château Latour flowed at the dinner table, Damon Mezzacappa voiced his concern that the discussion hadn't yet been frank enough. The group moved to the living room, and the debate sharpened. "I think Luis had one drink too many," Mezzacappa remembered. "And he went off on a tirade. He attacked Felix a little bit and used a bunch of four-letter words, something we never did in the presence of Michel, frankly out of respect. Felix was sitting there. And well, that was the end of Luis."

Rinaldini unloaded on Felix all of his pent-up frustrations during the past ten years. According to those who were there, it was a painful moment to endure. "It was difficult for me to get out from under Felix because every time I tried to go out and do things on my own, I'd get five things handed to me that I had to do," Rinaldini recalled. "And they were important. So I was kind of living under the gun and pressure from Felix that you've got to do this, this, and this. The firm wasn't doing anything to help on this front, and you can't complain when you get to play for the Lakers, but you've got to understand there were pressures involved, too. It's not all fun and games. I mean, there was zero career development, to put it in the simplest terms. I kept saying, 'So, what am I going to do? Go to battle with Felix?' I mean, fuck it. First of all, it would be horrendously stupid, and second, I would lose. So why do I have to make that choice?"

In retrospect, Rinaldini thinks he was being too forceful an advocate for change before Michel and Felix were ready to change, if ever. "I think for both Michel and Felix that was kind of too cosmic," he said. "It was like, 'What are you talking about? Go back to fucking work!' " For his part, Felix said he had no recollection of the evening or the incident whatsoever. Immediately after the dinner, though, he took Rinaldini off all of his deals. Rinaldini spent another ten years at the firm doing what deals he could on his own before leaving to join First Boston in London.

Jeffrey Leeds, a former vice president at Lazard who worked for both Felix and Steve on many deals during his six years at the firm, has an entirely different take on his time working for Felix. It was a more charitable view of what it was like working for one of the legends of investment banking, and it is a view shared by many of the younger nonpartner bankers who felt under less pressure from Michel to originate deals and fees. "Felix's view," Leeds explained, "would be, 'Excuse me, what do you mean by loyal? You're right I don't have this sense of politics within the office. I'm just trying to do great work here, work that's interesting. And if I ask you to work on this project with me, it doesn't fucking mean that we just got married. I'm sorry but nobody told me that was the deal.' He had no interest in mentoring. When I worked for him, as I said to him recently, 'You weren't nice, you weren't charming, but I fucking learned a lot.' . . . But I didn't really feel like I was owed anything. Some of these other people may have felt they were owed something."

Younger bankers at the firm referred to Felix as "the Franchise" and would exclaim—perfectly seriously—"What a Franchise!" after Felix's role on an important deal became known. Leeds elaborated: "I think it was clear to those of us who worked there that there was a hierarchy of talent and productivity. And other people on Team Lazard would score touchdowns, but that was only after Felix had carried the ball to the one-yard line or they would fake it to Felix and someone else would have an open field to carry the ball and they would spike it as if it were them. But you take Felix off the team, you suddenly find that you're going nowhere and all there is is a cloud of dust."

❦

Steve Rattner, who was at the emotional partners' dinner at Michel's apartment, didn't speak up. Rinaldini's concerns were not his concerns. He had his own clients. And they were hiring him and Lazard to do deals, lots of deals. Bankers at all levels were increasingly cognizant of Rattner's growing importance inside the firm. He had no intention of haphazardly stumbling into Felix's orbit; if he and Felix were to work together, it was going to be on Steve's terms and as close to equals as could be managed. Steve was able to pull it off because his deal-making prowess stood in bold relief to that of almost anyone else, and particularly when compared with Loomis's less than robust contributions. Felix had assigned Loomis to, among others, ITT, International Paper, and Leslie Wexner and the Limited, but increasingly, the often difficult Wexner was taking his business elsewhere. Ironically, in earlier years, Loomis had ridden his singular success with the Limited to a Lazard partnership. In truth, only Felix and perhaps Ira Harris were bringing in as much business as Steve.

And the more junior bankers were clamoring to work for him, a sure sign in the Darwinian canyons of Wall Street that Steve was gathering some serious momentum. One of those, Peter Ezersky, had come to

Lazard as a vice president from First Boston in 1990 as an M&A generalist. He arrived at Lazard exceedingly well informed about what it took to succeed there. "Kiss up, crush down" was how the junior bankers described his approach. By the first quarter of 1992 he was quietly discussing with both Rattner and Loomis his desire to join Steve's media group. In March the matter was coming to a head. Loomis decided to put his thoughts on paper. It is not clear how helpful he was to Ezersky as he wrestled with the prospective move. "As a generalist who is both exceptional and just below the level of partnership, you find assignments complicated by your role vis-à-vis some of our partners in relationships which are complicated by their nature. Specifically, the partners only partially involve you in decision-making while leaving you fully to deal with the result. . . . As a positive incentive, you correctly observe that Steve Rattner combines remarkable ability, good communication and advice, a willingness to delegate, when appropriate, and important business." Loomis conveyed his bias toward having Ezersky stay a generalist. Still, he said he would support Ezersky in his switch "provided that you think about it for a couple of weeks and have one more conversation" with Michel since "you are close enough to the point of consideration [for becoming a partner] that it would be foolish from your personal perspective to change your role without his support. And from the firm's perspective, you also have an obligation, in such case, to explain the sources of your frustration in a candid and explicit manner with specific examples for illustration. You should not silently leave us with the unpleasant while you escape to the pleasant. . . . And you are Lazard, so you share responsibility with the rest of us." Wow. What a heavy trip to lay on a young banker simply endeavoring to pursue a new area of interest. In short order, Ezersky had his conversation with Michel and moved to join Rattner in the media group. The buzz around Lazard was that the inhabitants of the two corner offices on the thirty-second floor had begun to take serious notice of Steve's commercial success and the tilt of the firm toward him.

Loomis was clever enough to perceive the shifting sands around his feet but not fleet enough to move them. He needed much of the summer of 1992 to come to grips with what was happening. The opening salvo came in April 1992, when he once again returned to one of his favorite themes of the late 1980s: to wit, Lazard's banking effort remained too irrationally organized to be maximally productive. Lazard's corporate coverage effort was chaotic and lacked a central authoritarian to direct traffic flow. "The dilution of effort is greater when one takes into account differences in partners' relative abilities to lead major business effectively," he wrote Michel, Felix, Damon, and Steve. "It would be more commercially productive to agree on the universe of companies, the lead partners, and then have anything else subject to prior review and consent (with a negative bias)."

Once again, Loomis was not wrong. At Lazard, there was no central authority when it came to deciding how partners should spend their time. Any many partners liked it that way. So what if other firms were centrally organized and professionals were held accountable? Lazard was different. Bureaucracy was minimal, and despite Loomis's repeated efforts—and best intentions—the resistance to his entreaties remained intense. There was a meeting a week later between Michel, Felix, Steve, Damon, and Loomis, who for a while formed a sort of informal executive committee. It was clear by this time that 1992 was going to be a tough year for M&A deals in general, and that meant that a tough year loomed for Lazard despite its increasing market share in M&A deals. This group of partners met to try to figure out what the firm should do, if anything, to address the situation.

Loomis returned to his favorite theme, that the firm needed to get more organized. "But Felix was part of the problem," one partner recalled, "because he didn't want to get more organized. He liked it unorganized." After the meeting, Michel asked Loomis to summarize in writing what had transpired for use at a subsequent meeting. Agreeing may have been Loomis's first mistake. Loomis quickly compounded his ongoing problems with Felix by trying to carve out a bigger role for himself at the firm, with more responsibility. He confessed his belief that "I have contributed to some of the progress of the firm internally" and then added, bizarrely, "As I believe other partners would say, I have been most successful when the contribution is a lot of little steps which are separately not very visible and not designed to credit me." He recognized, though, what others had been whispering about him: for whatever reason, he wasn't doing a lot of business. "There is a tension with how I can be effective with clients," he wrote. "It is easier for me to help with a sales pitch, participate in some Nestlé discussions and join a partner for a board meeting, than it is for me to become the primary partner on six or more relationships and to be effective (and here) internally." But as this was what partners at Lazard were *supposed* to do, he made himself vulnerable to attack from the ones, such as Felix and Steve, who were doing just that.

Nevertheless, he threw down the gauntlet. He said he doubted he could do "much more" running banking unless: "(i) There is consensus on what I term an 'operating approach' instead of changing theories and strategies; (ii) Felix is supportive instead of oscillating between support at one time and undercutting at another; this is less a matter of my feelings than of an impediment to my effectiveness; and (iii) Within Banking, and excepting those (including myself) on our committee, Michel has to be willing to have me set Banking partner percentages with him, and this needs to be known informally but broadly."

He had touched the third rail of investment banking at Lazard. Although he worked well with Felix in his early years at Lazard on deals for the Limited and for Revlon, among others, when it came to matters of firm management, the two clashed repeatedly. Now Loomis had openly criticized Felix. Worse, he had attached to the memo a copy of Felix's "Dark Ages" memo from nineteen years earlier, a crass document that reflected poorly on Felix and that one could easily have assumed would never see daylight again since many of those partners who had originally received it had long since left the firm. Predictably, Felix was incensed. No doubt Felix's ongoing refusal to run banking himself and his not wanting anyone else to run it, either, contributed greatly to Loomis's frustrations.

But Loomis had also, equally momentously, demanded the right to help Michel set compensation for the bankers in the firm, excepting the most senior. As this had always been solely Michel's responsibility (and before him, André's) and the major source of his ongoing relevance and power, this could only have been viewed as an attempted suicide on Loomis's part. He must have sensed it, too. The memo concluded, archly: "Alternatively to all the thoughts in this memorandum, I am happy just to work on companies. I enjoy it; it is easier for me; and, in the ensuing disarray, I will have no difficulty attracting the best people to my projects. What I am unwilling to do is either lend my credibility to more futile organizational exercises or to try to do the difficult without your substantive support on a sustained basis. I am happy to have you meet privately on this subject."

Since Michel spent the better part of every summer at his spectacular seaside villa, Sous-le-Vent, the matter seemed to go dormant for a few months while he was away. It was obvious, though, that Michel was not going to allow Loomis to have any role in setting compensation. Still, Loomis's logic for asking to have this authority was impeccable. There was no other way, really, to get a banker's attention and cooperation than to determine his pay. For Loomis to be effective as head of banking, this was a necessary authority and one held by other heads of investment banking on Wall Street. The opposite is also true. Without this authority, Loomis's fate was sealed because he would have difficulty being effective. If Loomis had not been such a student of the firm's history, his demand could be derided as foolish and naïve. Instead, it was the opening salvo in the increasingly impossible task of getting Michel not only to confront the larger question of his own future succession but also to address the smaller question of managing the firm more efficiently as it grew. "He never would give an inch," Loomis said later of Michel. "And I'd say, 'You know, how can I influence behavior in these people if they know not only that you solely decide their percentage but secondly that you solely talk to them at year end about what they're doing?' " But this being Lazard, Loomis's frustrations were not only with Michel's viselike grip on authority but also with Felix's incessant undermining. His feud with Felix had now bubbled up into the open, just as Steve and Felix were starting to get along well. "Bill wrote it down and Michel gave it to Felix and that was the end of Bill," a partner recalled. Loomis kept pushing, though. "I would always say that I had responsibility without authority," he said by way of explanation.

He now decided to take on Damon Mezzacappa, the head of Lazard's small but highly profitable capital markets business, who had often been described as the third most important partner at the firm after Michel and Felix. In two separate and lengthy memos—over time some partners gave up caring what Loomis did, or did not do, just as long as he agreed to stop copying them on these long diatribes—during the first two weeks of August 1992, Loomis, under the guise of passing on an increasingly emotional set of other people's views, in effect ratted out Damon to Michel (while he was in the south of France) by enumerating a fulsome list of problems that seemed to be engulfing the capital markets group: political infighting derived from Damon's cocksure behavior, unjustified requests (in Loomis's view) for additional resources, incompetence in pitching Lazard's financing capabilities to clients, and a total lack of a "cohesive plan or organization to the overall effort." He conveyed to Michel that he keeps being told by bankers asked to work more closely with the capital markets effort that "it's a mess down there. Nobody who is already there really knows who they are working for or whether the partners agree on anything."

But it was in "Capital Markets (II)," his second memorandum on the subject in as many weeks, that Loomis took off the gloves. He named names. In but one example of four, he explained to Michel that Felix had asked him to speak to Steve Niemczyk, then a senior vice president working for Ken Wilson in the FIG group, about the firm's still uncertain role in a proposed IPO of Van Kampen Merritt, the former wholly owned money management subsidiary of Xerox. "After some fearful hesitation,

Steve explained to me that a meeting to 'pitch' the business at Xerox should have been a formality, confirming the assumed lead role," Loomis wrote. But "the oral presentation was a complete disaster. This was reportedly because of the inability to limit the number of participants (nobody can make a decision) and the lack of any prior discussion within Lazard of the oral portion. The subject matter was passed from one to another randomly. Thus, Xerox heard a rambling prologue from Luis followed by Jeremy, I believe, stating that we don't risk capital, and so on, through the *six* Lazard participants." Lazard eventually won a lead role on the underwriting, but Xerox decided to sell the company instead for $360 million to Clayton Dubilier & Rice, a buyout firm.

Then Loomis relayed a story about Joe Maybank, at that time a vice president in banking, who had been asked to join Lazard's fledgling high-yield finance effort. Maybank had been concerned about infighting in the capital markets division. Loomis reported to Michel that Mezzacappa's response to Maybank on this score was, "Look, it's not important that these people don't get along with each other because they all report to me, and that's a problem I take care of." Loomis followed this example with yet another about how Ken Jacobs, a young banking partner, had agreed at Loomis's suggestion to spend some of his time talking to his clients about using Lazard for high-yield financing. But when Jacobs talked to Al Garner, then the head of high-yield finance at Lazard, Garner was dismissive of the potential assignment. According to Loomis, Garner told Jacobs, "How can we be sure we get paid for thinking about this? Can you assure me that they won't take our ideas and shop them? Is this a real assignment? Why should we devote time to this instead of other stuff?"

Having furnished these examples to Michel, Loomis then turned to what he categorized as the "underlying causes" of the problems, which he felt needed to be "addressed openly and with some friction." Among these was his observation that "Damon is quite good at creating business units and talent . . . up to a certain point. He then falls back on three flaws," which he was more than happy to describe. First, "he senses that you are fearful of capital exposure or losses and preys upon his perception of you and passes it on to the others under him as a fundamental premise." Second, he resisted "shared responsibility and accountability" between bankers and his capital markets teams. Third, "it suits his own importance to have conflict, once business units or partners exist, for him to mediate as the sole mediator." The other partners in capital markets, with a single exception, were described as "not that strong individually and feel beholden to Damon. . . . These are not brave men, but they are capable men if effectively led and woven into the fabric of the firm's overall perspective on business."

No surprise, Loomis described his relationship with Damon as poor. "I am viewed by Damon as a threat, active or in remission depending on the week or month, and only as an ally on a specific issue when he senses that I, at least partially, already agree with his own plans or conclusions," he wrote. "(Having said this, I think that you could put Daffy Duck in my role, and Damon would be defensive, as I am sure I could get a dozen Morgan Stanley partners to agree.)" Loomis, who, after he wrote this memo, occasionally referred to himself internally as "Daffy Duck," offered Michel two options for capital markets: do nothing or undertake a substantive revamp, the details of which were then undetermined.

To further illustrate his concerns, Loomis shared with Michel a copy of a memo he had asked the partner Kim Fennebresque to write about his recent experience on a financing project. Loomis had recruited the flamboyant Fennebresque to Lazard the previous year after First Boston had let him go "in the wake of difficulties the firm suffered in connection with a problematic bridge loan," according to the *New York Times*. Fennebresque's wife, Debby, and Loomis's wife, Kirstin, were good friends, and the wives played an important role in bringing the husbands together. Not surprisingly, Fennebresque's memo bolstered Loomis's view that the capital markets effort at Lazard was badly broken. "Those responsible for the capital raising process at Lazard appear to view the protection of the firm's capital as their principal function," Fennebresque observed, in a concise summary of Lazard's longtime strategy that Loomis seemed eager to change. "Having been at a firm which did not view that as its function at all"—First Boston—"I can readily appreciate that notion. However, as we appear to be in an era where capital raising is going to be an important long-term aspect of providing client service, perhaps, a more balanced view should be considered. Risking capital is a pejorative term here, and it should not be."

For his part, Mezzacappa had no idea Loomis had written these critical memos to Michel about him and his department. The two men did not get along. Mezzacappa described Loomis as "an empty suit," "a fraud" who was "full of shit," and "in way over his head." He added: "Loomis learned to talk in riddles. He learned to talk a language that only Michel could understand. And people thought there was deep meaning there, but it was all just bullshit."

The tortured Loomis, whose political instincts were, if nothing else, finely tuned, must have known Sisyphus's boulder was about to smother him. Apparently without having been prompted, he sent Michel a handwritten letter—*the day before* he sent the "Capital Markets (II)" memo—voluntarily reducing his prospective partnership percentage for 1993 to 1.8 percent, from 2.5 percent in 1992. He had been pondering the decision for two months. Aside from Felix, no other Lazard partner had ever *voluntarily* reduced his percentage, and Felix had done so to be assured of his freedom from internal politics while still feeling free to contribute to them. Loomis, on the contrary, seemed to be acutely frustrated and just plain angry. Reducing his percentage was a quasi protest vote—although he was not doing anything as rash as resigning and would still be making $3.3 million a year. "The purpose in telling you now is so that you can take it into account in your overall percentage calculations," he explained to Michel.

In taking this unusual step, Loomis became preoccupied with how it would be perceived by the other partners, as the list of partner percentages circulated each January was proof positive of whose star was rising and whose was falling. "As importantly, I want you to know before you review your list further with other partners," he continued. "This should not appear in September as an apparent outcome of any particular conversation. My decision is, in fact, independent of conversations and events this fall." In truth, Loomis's decision was hardly voluntary; he was shoved aside by the firm's more powerful partners, whom he had systematically alienated. "There was a cabal that came after him," one partner remembered. "I think Rattner was a part of that. Mezzacappa was definitely part of it. And Felix was part of it. . . . They thought he was a do-nothing partner who took a lot of money out of the place."

Not the slightest inkling of this Sturm und Drang filtered down to the rank and file in the firm. Which is probably as it should be. Certainly, the associates knew the firm was basically dysfunctional, not as a commercial enterprise to be sure, but rather as a social community. Internal calls to peers would often go unreturned. There was little cooperation among the three houses. Partners always seemed to be angry at one another or rarely spoke. Partner meetings were infrequent and accomplished little. There was a widespread feeling among the bankers that Loomis played favorites, promoting his acolytes at the expense of those less attentive. "There absolutely was a cult of Bill," Kim Fennebresque said, in a typical rendering of the "FOB" phenomenon. "I had drunk the Bill Loomis Kool-Aid big-time from the day I got there, and I thought everybody did, but it turned out that Bill had engendered some enmity, which surprised me." Mezzacappa thought Loomis's habit of playing favorites drove some good people to leave the firm. "I think Bill does have qualities of leadership," he said. "But he punished people who didn't support him, which was an extraordinarily mean thing to do if you are a leader. I remember when Bill took over banking there were certain guys who were in and certain guys who were out. Just extraordinary. You can't do that."

Habitually, like a swallow to San Juan Capistrano, Michel returned to Manhattan from Sous-le-Vent after Labor Day. His return signaled the start of the annual groveling about compensation. That was to be expected. What was unusual in 1992, though, was the terse, Kremlinesque memorandum Michel distributed to the banking group on September 22. "Steve Rattner and Kim Fennebresque have accepted, after consultation with Felix Rohatyn, to take on responsibility for coordinating the Banking Group," the memo began. "Obviously this will be done in concert with Felix Rohatyn and Bill Loomis as well as myself. Bill Loomis has agreed to take on additional responsibilities regarding the coordination of the 3 Houses and international business, which is increasingly important to us. Bill will also devote more time to developing business. Because both Steve and Kim will continue to work with clients, it will be important for everyone to give them their fullest cooperation. I hope and expect that we will thus all meet the challenges of a relatively difficult period."

Although plenty amorphous, this news shot through the firm like a bolt of lightning. In the imperious Lazard partnership, the always inscrutable and enigmatic Loomis was one of the few relatively accessible authority figures. Not only had he had a hand in hiring most, if not all, of the junior bankers then at the firm, but he also seemed to be one of the few partners who at least gave an impression of caring for them. But even this was a mirage. Whether it was Rattner, Fennebresque, or Loomis running banking didn't much matter: pay for midlevel nonpartners continued to be relatively low compared with other Wall Street firms, and the grunts that passed for performance reviews were equally disappointing. Indeed, in 1991 more than one associate received no performance review at all from Loomis and was able to calculate the amount of his annual bonus only by grossing up for taxes his bank account balance after it was spit out of a Rockefeller Center ATM machine one late December day. "What the fuck was that all about?" Fennebresque remembered wondering at the time.

Indeed, there was always a Kafkaesque quality to the annual performance reviews, which merely added to the firm's iconoclasm. Unlike other investment banks, Lazard never asked junior bankers (let alone partners) for a written self-assessment of performance in any given year, nor was it ever clear to the junior bankers whether the partners had ever been asked to put performance assessments in writing. Certainly, no such evaluations were ever shared. Rather, year after year the heads of banking always told at least one associate the same thing: You are doing an excellent job, but unfortunately you are working for the "wrong" partners—a message taken to mean that there were Great Men at Lazard, and not so great men, and that the poor soul had better figure out a way pretty darn quick to start working for the Great Men if he was ever to have a chance of becoming a partner. Of course, he had very little control over whom he worked for or on what assignments, and so was left with a bit of a political Catch-22, Kafka-style.

For his part, Steve took the news in stride. He recalled that after Felix "decided he was going to decapitate Bill," there was a "big leadership vacuum," and since "I had done a couple of big deals, they asked me to head banking. I said I wasn't going to do it alone. Kim was very close to Bill and Bill wasn't happy. I figured having someone with another set of relationships within the firm doing it with me would be a good thing." He had not known Fennebresque very well at all up to that point, although now they are the best of friends. "While I wasn't sure whether we would work well together, I felt that having a partner in this venture was more likely to lead to success than not. I think I was right about that but not right enough to make it work."

Fennebresque was positively stunned by—and considerably wary of—the news that his good friend Loomis had been demoted and that he had been asked to take his place. "Someone told me Loomis was going to be out as head of banking, and I was so not plugged in I said, 'Pffft. Not a chance,' " he said. "I said it totally unencumbered by the facts, but I said it with some conviction because it was unimaginable to me that Bill would be out. But at one point, Michel called me into his office and said, 'We're going to make a change. Bill is going to go back to being just a banking partner, and I've asked Steve Rattner to run banking, and he has told me he won't do it unless you do it with him.' " Fennebresque asked Michel if he could think about his answer; Michel gave him the rest of the day. He said he wanted to think about the new assignment because "I didn't want to do it. I didn't want to do it. I had been in management before."

He knew Steve a little bit by this time. He had first met him when Steve was thinking about leaving Lehman and Fennebresque interviewed him at First Boston. And Maureen, Steve's wife, had known of Kim from her days working at First Boston "because I was a colorful and funny guy," he said. But for Fennebresque there was also the problem of his friendship with the now-deposed Loomis. "I used to go by and see him every day, literally," Fennebresque said. "Just to smoke cigars and bullshit together. For all the acolytes and sycophants around Bill, I was his best friend in short order." And there were concerns that Felix didn't particularly like Fennebresque and resented the way Loomis had engineered his arrival at the firm. "I mean, what the fuck?" Fennebresque said. "I went to see Bill, and he said, 'Kim, I told Michel I didn't want to do this anymore. I told him this a month and a half ago.' And of course, I didn't know all the intrigue that led to that, but he said, 'I don't want you to give this a second thought. This is a good opportunity for you, and you should do it. I want you to do it. You have my blessing.' "

Fennebresque said he quickly left the building without speaking with Steve for fear that Michel would call him back and insist that he take the job then and there. He met his wife and another couple for dinner.

> I was unbelievably morose at dinner, and no one could figure out why, and my friend said, "What's wrong? What's the matter with you?" I was just stunned. I was stunned by being there just eighteen months. I was shocked by Bill. The whole thing shocked me. It made no sense to me. So I told my friend what happened, and he said, "That's great!" I said, "No, this is the beginning of the end of my time at Lazard." He said, "Why?" I said, "Because it's not the kind of firm, especially in banking, where management takes you anywhere. The guy who runs the firm has his name on the door. I'm not getting his job. I'm going to have this job, and then I'm going to get thrown out or thrown back into the population or leave because I'm miserable or something. But this dog is not going to hunt, and I don't want to do it."

Despite his better judgment and instincts, what choice did Fennebresque have? Michel wanted Steve to take the job, and Steve wouldn't take it without Kim, so Michel basically insisted that Kim take the job. Not only had he been at the firm a brief time; he had not really produced much business, either. "Steve Rattner was a luminary and I wasn't," he said. He knew there would be a rash of undefined envy, especially from the Loomis loyalists. ("Kim used that position to aggrandize himself to an extent" was the typical refrain of one partner close to Loomis.) There was also the difficulty of the job itself. "I thought managing the Lazard partners was like herding cats," he said. "I described it once to someone as when you are the managing partner of the banking group at Lazard, your job is to throw chum in the shark tank and try to stay in the boat." And then there was the matter that although the press release read that Steve and Kim were co-equals, such was not even close to being true. "I had zero illusions about that," Fennebresque said. "It was Batman and Robin. But Steve Rattner, to his credit, for which I will be undyingly grateful, always played it like we were equals."

Since no one expected banking to change much regardless of who ran it, the two aspects of this unexpected news (unless you had been privy to the confidential memos) that really got people talking were, first, the acknowledgment of Rattner's continued meteoric rise and, second, just who the heck was this guy Fennebresque, anyway? Rattner's rise into this thankless role was not surprising given how much business he was bringing in; he exuded confidence and connectedness, and there was that inevitability to him. Steve had learned at Morgan Stanley the kinds of things the best firms did to get that way, and he was prepared to try to implement some of those at Lazard. "Virtually every reporter thinks he'd be a great editor and wants to be an editor because he thinks it's more interesting," Steve said. "And virtually every banker thinks he should be running something. I was not any different in that respect. I didn't have huge ambitions, but I had been a banker for ten years at that point, and there was clearly a vacuum of leadership at the firm."

Fennebresque was a different story. He seemed nothing more than a (most un-Lazard-like) stereotypical 1980s "Master of the Universe" banker: the tall, lithe, articulate Fennebresque, with a wicked sense of humor and permanently slicked-back hair, had spent fourteen years at First Boston, where, he said, "Bruce was king the whole time," referring to Bruce Wasserstein, the firm's M&A rainmaker. But behind that facade was not only a remarkably decent person but also one whose confidence had been badly shaken during the market meltdown. He had been named one of First Boston's fifteen "franchise partners." But in November 1990, First Boston fired him. "I got fired partially because I had a big mouth and partially because the place was hemorrhaging and coming apart and they wanted some blood and I was senior blood so they took me out," he explained. He was forty years old, married, with kids—and terrified. When First Boston went private in 1988, he had been strongly urged to buy stock in the firm using a seven-figure loan from the company. The value of the stock quickly decreased, but the loan was still payable. He was in financial distress. "Everyone was dying," he explained. "Every morning you'd pick up the paper and read that Merrill Lynch was laying off five thousand more people. It was awful. A terrible time to find a job." He had been looking around for something new for only a short time but was increasingly depressed about his future.

Thanks to some behind-the-scenes communication between his

wife and Loomis's, though, Loomis called him that November and invited him to lunch at the China Grill on West Fifty-third Street. They discussed Fennebresque's plight. When he got home that night, he found a long handwritten letter from Loomis waiting for him. "The letter was unbelievably touching," he recalled. But he still thought there was little chance of his being hired at Lazard; after all, Lazard was an M&A shop, and Kim had focused on financing LBOs at First Boston—plus, he was unemployed. Two weeks later, Loomis called and told Fennebresque he had been speaking to Michel about him. "I wonder if you would like to come by and see him and spend half an hour?" Loomis asked. "I told him you were someone he should know and he's someone you should know." He told Loomis of course he would come by and see Michel but thought, "I need a courtesy interview like a hole in the head. I'm looking for a job and this is a bad time to find one and I can't waste my time. But Bill Loomis has been unbelievably kind and I'm going." As he walked across Fifth Avenue in front of Saint Patrick's Cathedral from First Boston's office on East Fifty-second Street, he ran into George Shinn, then chairman of First Boston. He greatly admired Shinn—"The only hero I've had in business," he said—but hadn't seen him in a few years. They had a conversation about Fennebresque's new forlorn status during which Shinn told him everything would be fine, even though things at that moment looked particularly bleak. "I was raised Catholic," Fennebresque explained. "I am no longer a Catholic, but as my wife says, 'Once you are a Catholic, you are always superstitious.' " He walked into Michel's office at the appointed hour "and I sit on his couch and he's sitting in his chair and there's a big, not elegant—especially for a man who is the personification of elegance—hardware store kind of clock on the wall. And I sit down at 4:30 and the clock starts going around and around and the next thing I know it's 7:05 and I say to myself, 'Here I am, an out-of-work stiff, spending two and a half hours with Michel Fucking David-Weill. What's this all about?' "

After he told Michel up front he had been fired by First Boston (to which Michel responded, "Yes, I know"), they spent the rest of the time "talking about everything under the sun." By the time he got home, Loomis had already called to tell him that Michel wanted him to become a partner at Lazard but first he had to meet with Felix and Damon. He did that the next day. "I went in and spent fifteen or twenty minutes with Felix, and Felix, as he always is, was unbelievably gracious, which I always find nice, and I met with Damon, and he said, 'Don't worry, I've been fired a bunch of times, too,' and it was a very pleasant conversation.

Next thing you know it was January 1 and time to report for work. The single happiest day of my life, I believe."

The night before he started at the firm, he thought he should read the partnership agreement, a copy of which Loomis had sent him. Like so many others before him, he quickly discovered that the slim document gave all power to Michel, through section 4.1. "And it says such and such and such and such can happen only with the agreement of the partner in paragraph 4.1," he said. "Paragraph 4.1 this and paragraph 4.1 that—I nicknamed Michel that: '4.1.' And I remember the next day I walked into Bill's office, and you know me, I'm a bit of a wiseass and people don't know exactly how to read that, and so I walked into Bill's office and said, 'Who do I give my comments to on the partnership agreement?' And you could see the blood drain from his face: *What the fuck have I done bringing this asshole in here?*"

Fennebresque said it took him all of "thirty seconds" to figure out the Lazard culture. "If it takes longer than that, you're really, really stupid. . . . It comes at you like a fire hose—it's cold and powerful and it didn't bother me at all. I think the human condition is that people like to be led." What he had figured out instantly, of course, was that Michel made all the decisions, it was his firm, and "we were all staff." The only possible exception was Felix, an insight he got when he went to a meeting with both of them shortly after his arrival and they started talking in French to each other. "He wasn't in the family," Fennebresque said of Felix, "but he gets to eat with the family."

FENNEBRESQUE TOOK THE co-head of banking job, despite his misgivings. When Annik, Michel's secretary, called him the next day and asked him to come see "my boss," he joked with her: "Aah, it's not a good time for me." As he feared, Michel insisted he accept the job. "There was nothing about it I wanted," he said, looking back. "There was no glory to it. Nothing." With it, he moved his office right next to Steve's on the thirty-second floor of One Rock, and he received a raise. When he arrived at Lazard in 1991, his partnership percentage was 0.65 percent (worth about $860,000 that year), fairly modest as a comparative matter. (Steve's was closer to 4 percent, or some $5.3 million.) "Jeez," Loomis told him, "that's kind of low." Fennebresque concurred. At the end of his first year, Michel raised him up to 0.966643 percent. Now that he had been asked to become co-head of banking, he insisted on getting another raise. "Can you take it to 1 percent?" he demanded, with a smile. Michel gave him 1.1 percent, worth about $1.4 million in 1992.

The first thing the dynamic duo had to absorb was the deaths of two of the more important senior partners in the New York firm: the sudden one of Jim Glanville, sixty-nine, as a result of injuries suffered during an automobile accident in Houston, and the not unexpected one of Tom Mullarkey, fifty-nine, the longtime consigliere, who had had a stroke in 1987. Although Mullarkey had returned to work after a few months, the effects of the stroke were obvious. He roamed the barren halls of the firm like a character out of a Dickens novel. He died of brain cancer at his home in Locust Valley. He had devoted the last years of his life to philanthropy, a not unnatural extension of his responsibilities at Lazard, where for years he had saved the partners from one near-death experience after another—from the numerous ITT-Hartford-related investigations right up through the sentencing of Robert Wilkis for his role in the Dennis Levine insider trading scandal. That task now fell to Mel Heineman, the former lawyer and associate on the ITT-Hartford deal, who had been Mullarkey's apprentice for years. He would have his hands full.

For his part, Glanville was the last member still at Lazard of the original Gang of Four Lehman partners Michel had recruited in 1978. Glanville had been fairly productive at Lazard but could never adapt to the parsimonious culture. And his anti-Semitic bent rightly made him an enemy of Felix, never a good thing for anyone working at the firm. His most enduring legacy, it turned out, was the indefatigable Loomis, despite the recent turn of events. Loomis delivered the eulogy at Glanville's funeral. He said that Glanville had taught him that investment banking was about judgment and understanding people with "a little arithmetic tossed in." He acknowledged that Glanville did not fit well with the Wall Street community. "Fiercely blunt, Jim was a great intellect mixed with equally great emotions and encrusted with character." To illustrate, Loomis repeated one of Glanville's favorite stories: "There was a fella with a dry hole and some limited partners who weren't too happy. One of the limited partners said to him, 'You have to understand that for $10,000 I can get a New York lawyer to tie you in knots for five years.' And the Texas fella said, 'No, you have to understand that for $25 I can get a Mexican to blow your head off . . . right now.' " Glanville, Loomis said, understood the dry-hole business.

Meanwhile, Corporate Partners, Lazard's white knight fund, was itself learning rapidly about the dry-hole business, an education that would shortly prove further detrimental to the firm's reputation. The fund got off to a rough start. It was originally slated to be $2 billion when the fund-raising began before the 1987 market crash, but Lazard decided to stop the fund in August 1988 at $1.55 billion, when money for such efforts all but dried up. Then Lester Pollack, the fund's chief executive, tested his investors' patience by not making the fund's first investment until Christmas 1988, more than a year after the money had been raised. Around that time, Corporate Partners announced a $200 million convertible preferred stock investment in Transco Energy, as part of Transco's acquisition of a gas transmission subsidiary of CSX. It turned out that Lazard had advised Transco, a Glanville client, on the acquisition and received a fee for its advice. This was the exact opposite of the kind of deal Corporate Partners said it was in business to do—first, the Transco deal with CSX was friendly, so no thwarting of an unwanted interloper was necessary, and second, Lazard had received an advisory fee. Pollack, though, denied any conflict of interest or deviation from the fund's strategy. "They asked us to consider this, not the other way around," he said. (Corporate Partners' actual investment in Transco ended up being $120 million; the fund made a $65 million profit on the deal.)

The fund's next investment came six weeks later—$300 million of preferred stock, convertible into a 7.7 percent stake of Polaroid. This was more like it. Polaroid had been under attack from Shamrock Partners, Roy E. Disney's investment fund, which was trying to get control of the instant-film company. The combination of the investment by Corporate Partners, the sale of another chunk of stock to an employee fund, a stock buyback program, and a favorable court ruling led to Polaroid's successful rebuff of Shamrock. But it was a Pyrrhic victory, for Polaroid shareholders would have been better off with the Shamrock cash: Polaroid filed for bankruptcy in 2001 after the advent of digital photography made its business untenable. Corporate Partners did well, though, realizing a $215 million profit on its Polaroid investment.

More than another year passed before Corporate Partners made its third investment, in June 1991—$200 million for a 17 percent stake in Phar-Mor, a private Ohio-based deep-discount retailer (the fund ended up investing $216 million). The fast-growing Phar-Mor then operated 255 stores in twenty-eight states and had revenue of more than $2 billion. This investment, too, was outside the fund's stated mandate. Phar-Mor was private and claimed to need the new capital to grow, not to rebuff an unwanted suitor. From the outset, though, there was speculation that Phar-Mor actually needed the Lazard money to pay its vendors, who had been complaining about late payments from the company. Corporate Partners rejected the thought that Phar-Mor was financially distressed. "You should view our investment as a vindication of the company," David Golub, a vice president at Corporate Partners, said at the time. The Lazard partner Jonathan Kagan agreed to go on the board of

Phar-Mor and quickly deflected questions about when Phar-Mor would go public—something other investment bankers had been urging the company to do—by saying that Phar-Mor "clearly chose to work with us because it's not eager to go public at this time." A year later disaster struck. On August 4, 1992, the company abruptly fired its founder, Michael Monus, and its CFO and announced that the FBI and the U.S. attorney had started a criminal investigation. Two weeks later the company filed for bankruptcy protection and announced that Monus and three other executives had systematically defrauded the company of more than $400 million "in a fraud-and-embezzlement scheme dating back to 1989." Corporate Partners sued, among others, Coopers & Lybrand, Phar-Mor's auditors, claiming that the accounting firm had participated in the fraud by certifying inaccurate audits. The head of Coopers at the time said Corporate Partners was "trying to shift the blame for their inadequate due diligence and judgment." Regardless of who was to blame, the fact remained that Corporate Partners had made a terrible investment, and all but $77 million of the $216 million was lost. The next investment, $83 million in Albert Fisher Group, a U.K. food distributor, also proved troublesome. The fund lost all but $37 million of the original investment.

Then, fortunately, Corporate Partners' performance began to improve. The fund invested $146.5 million in First Bank System, which in 1997 bought U.S. Bancorp and took its name. The fund made almost $700 million on that investment. Good fortune struck again when, through Steve Rattner's relationship, Corporate Partners invested $300 million in Continental Cablevision. When the US West Media Group bought Continental in 1997, the fund made nearly a $600 million profit. In total, over its initial twelve-year existence, Corporate Partners invested $1.35 billion in nine companies and received in return $2.99 billion, for a profit before fees and carried interest of $1.64 billion. Private-equity funds are judged on how well their investments perform over time, a calculation known as the internal rate of return, or IRR. Corporate Partners' IRR during its existence was 15 percent, net of fees and carried interest; investors received an annualized return of 15 percent per year. That placed its performance in the top quartile of such funds.

❧

Bill Clinton's victory in the 1992 presidential election handed Lazard another unexpected problem: a glum and cranky Felix Rohatyn. After twelve years of Republican Party rule, Felix rejoiced in the election of a Democrat to the White House. But Clinton's election soon became bittersweet for him, when he came to the realization that he was not going to be named Treasury secretary, the one government post he had long coveted.

During the Reagan and Bush years, he had become a national figure, saved New York City, and, through his ubiquitous writings, led the lonely crusade against any number of Republican fiscal and monetary policies he deemed misguided. But he also made a few political mistakes that seem obvious in retrospect but were in keeping with his worldview. First, he supported Ross Perot, his former client at EDS. This was done partly out of loyalty and partly because Felix believed in much of what Perot had to say. To this day, though, Felix disputes the extent of his support for Perot and believes the press and the Perot campaign overstated it. In any event, he was not as early and as loyal a supporter of Clinton's (although he certainly came around) as were the expert fund-raisers Roger Altman and Bob Rubin—who together had, for instance, raised 20 percent of the money raised privately for the Mondale campaign in 1984—and this hurt him politically when the short lists were shortened even further. Felix's real political Achilles' heel, though, was his complete disinterest in political fund-raising. He was happy to give money to the Democrats—and lots of it—but could not be bothered to raise the mother's milk. What others were willing to do, he was not. No fund-raisers at his Fifth Avenue apartment or Southampton home. No dialing for dollars or putting the squeeze on his wealthy friends for a politician.

His thinking was admirable enough, but the disconnect was also painfully obvious: in a political age when plum cabinet positions are often the reward for the hard work of a campaign, to try to play by different rules was not a winning strategy. For one of the world's best strategists not to comprehend that simple reality was stunning. Rattner remembered Felix coming into his small office, where he had moved so that he and Fennebresque could be nearer each other. "Felix liked to walk the halls, which was one of his good qualities," Steve said. "He came in my office one day after the election of 1992 and he said, 'You know, I used to think that being a policy guru and saving New York was enough to become Treasury secretary, but I found out that you really have to be in the mix and you really have to raise money. It's not going to happen for me.' I felt sorry for him." If Steve learned anything from Felix's misfortune, it was the old saw about money and politics; he and his wife, Maureen, have since become among the most effective fund-raisers in the Democratic Party. He also took up his pen again. Soon after Clinton's election, Steve wrote his first *New York Times* op-ed piece, "Short-Term Stimulus? Long-Term Error." He admitted he was a Democrat (although he gave $500 to Dole for President in October 1987) and urged the new president to focus on crafting long-term economic solutions, such as encouraging investment and increasing productivity.

AS IF THE foibles of the Phar-Mor investment and Felix Rohatyn weren't difficult enough for the firm to digest, two investigative reporters for the *Wall Street Journal* chose the same moment to focus an unwanted spotlight on Lazard's tiny—but suddenly quite potent—municipal bond underwriting department. Ever since Felix had helped solve New York City's fiscal crisis, Lazard had been asked to help other cities with financial difficulties. For these advisory assignments, the firm received monthly fees.

Naturally, Felix himself didn't have the time or the inclination to personally work on all of these assignments on a day-to-day basis, so at Michel's urging, Lazard hired a cadre of people into the banking group for this purpose, the most prominent being Eugene Keilin, the former executive director of MAC, and Franklin Raines, who would later become Lazard's first black partner and the CEO of Fannie Mae (where his reputation would be badly tarnished by scandal). An offshoot of the business of providing advice to municipalities was the business of underwriting their bond issues, which raised money from the market to build hospitals, schools, and roads or was used for a municipality's "general obligations." From the outset of Michel's management of the firm, he sought to build up the municipal finance department—both by hiring traders who bought and sold municipal securities and by hiring bankers whose job it was to win underwriting mandates from state and local governments (although in those days if Lazard was hired as a financial adviser to a municipality, the firm was precluded from acting also as an underwriter). The effort remained small but profitable, in the typical Lazard mold.

That began to change in 1985, when Felix decided to hire Michael Del Guidice, the chief of staff to New York's governor, Mario Cuomo, to run the municipal finance business. Felix obviously knew Del Guidice well from his work with MAC and his numerous interactions over the years with Governor Cuomo. And certainly Del Guidice knew his way around the corridors of political power on the state level and knew how municipal underwriting assignments were awarded. Of course, he had never before worked on Wall Street or managed a group of bankers, but that was a minor detail; Lazard was well known (as were many other Wall Street firms) for providing a warm bath to former government officials with no prior Wall Street experience. "Del Guidice was really more of a political operative than he was a banker, and if anything, he took some pride in the fact that he wasn't a numbers guy, that he was more a relationship guy, a connections guy," observed one Lazard partner. Del Guidice, whom Mezzacappa, his boss, described as "a nice guy who was in way over his head," set out quickly to hire some new bankers with close ties to state government officials, figuring correctly that this was the way to win underwriting mandates. He was, after all, one of those guys himself. Among his hires were Richard Poirier Jr., a cigar-smoking six-footer from Prudential Securities, and Mark Ferber, then thirty-four, a supposed superstar municipal finance banker in Boston who had previously worked for First Boston and Kidder, Peabody.

Soon enough, the marketing skills of these two men became apparent to their colleagues in the department. "Ferber and Poirier were two of the most productive bankers in the country," recalled one partner, "doing some of the biggest deals ever done. They were very aggressive guys in seeking business. Poirier was more 'I'm gonna go through that brick wall and get that business, and if you're standing in front of that brick wall, I'm going through you, too.' Ferber was much smoother. Ferber was more 'How can I get the most leverage I can out of the system?' " Both of them knew the municipal finance business far better than Del Guidice did and by the early 1990s had started operating independently of their titular boss. "Del Guidice had two guys that were bigger guys than he was," one Lazard partner remembered.

Just how much bigger became clear in a surprising, twenty-eight-hundred-word front-page *Wall Street Journal* article in May 1993 that focused on how Poirier, who joined Lazard the same month as Rattner, was able to make Lazard the top underwriter of municipal securities in New Jersey in 1992, when as recently as two years before Lazard had not underwritten a single bond for the state. The article credited Poirier's stunning success in New Jersey to his political connections, particularly with Joseph Salema, the chief of staff to Governor Jim Florio, and with Florio himself.

Florio appointed Salema's brother-in-law, Sam Crane, to be state treasurer at just the same moment that Lazard was chosen to lead a $1.8 billion "general obligation" bond issue that the previous state treasurer had opposed both issuing and choosing Lazard to manage. Lazard made $10 million for its role in the underwriting. The article also described Poirier's ability to win a slew of state hospital underwritings, despite little experience in that discipline and despite the recommendations from hospital officials that other firms be hired instead. "We had selected Prudential," one hospital executive told the paper, "but then all of a sudden we got a call. It was obviously controlled by the governor's office." Poirier also won for Lazard the coveted role of advising the state's turnpike authority on the sale of $2.9 billion of bonds in 1991 and 1992. New Jersey paid Lazard a $2.3 million fee for that advice.

The article revealed, though, that the SEC and the U.S. attorney's office in Manhattan were investigating Poirier's actions in relation to the sale of the turnpike bonds. Poirier's success in New Jersey notwithstanding, the *Journal* reporters also pointed out that his previous interactions with officials in Florida and Kentucky had gotten both him and Lazard into hot water. Lazard's lead underwriting of an $861 million bond offering for the Florida State Board of Education quickly turned sour amid charges that it had mispriced the deal. The outcry led to an inquiry about how Lazard had been chosen in the first place, and the answer—Poirier's political connections—led Governor Lawton Chiles to ban Wall Street firms that make political contributions to state officials from underwriting state bonds. In Kentucky, Poirier's handling of a $250 million turnpike bond caused state officials to write a "blistering" ten-page memo accusing him of "lying, making unauthorized trades on the state's behalf and overcharging the state by more than $1 million." Poirier's "attitude was antagonistic," and the deal "recalled many of the boilerroom tactics of an era we hoped was behind us." Poirier refused to be interviewed for the article. At least one of his former partners at Lazard believed that the highly damaging *Journal* article appeared because a number of competitors and colleagues, including Ferber, were just "getting even with Poirier" because he was so aggressive.

When the *Journal* next appeared the following Monday, there was a letter to the editor from "Lazard Frères & Co." complaining about the article's portrayal of both Poirier and the firm. "We are dismayed by the article that appeared on page one Friday about the work of a partner in our Municipal Finance Department, and we take issue with its tenor as well as its specifics," the firm wrote. "Our review of the matters discussed in your article has not brought to our attention any evidence of illegality. Our code of conduct, subscribed to by everyone from our more senior partners to our most junior employees, states clearly our policy that all business affairs be conducted on the highest ethical level. Nothing falling short of this will be tolerated." The letter pointed out that the firm had met with the *Journal* reporters as they were preparing the article but that Lazard's input did not make it into the paper. "The day-to-day efforts of individuals in our firm to formulate innovative responses to the extremely complex financial issues that confront our state and local authorities were disregarded in exchange for the drama of unproven insinuations of improper influence," the letter concluded. Before long, the firm would rue the day these words were written.

The same day the firm's letter appeared in the *Journal*, Rattner wrote Michel a memo suggesting that he was already tiring of the job as co-head of banking—a mere eight months after his appointment. He had run the weekly partners' meetings, given reviews to some of the junior bankers, and tried to give input to Michel on the partnership percentages, a process he called "tinkering with tenths," a reference to his minor role in trying to influence Michel's thinking. "If you go back in time (and it was before my time), no one was running banking," Steve explained. "Bill was the first one to try to run banking. He was quite good at it in a certain way, but—and Bill would be the first one to admit it—it still had a long way to go to really be effective. Kim and I were trying to take it to the next level. We met with enormous resistance from all the old guard, although Felix was relaxed about it," since what Steve and Kim were attempting rarely affected Felix. And of course, Felix was then still fond of Steve and his successes. Steve's frustrations, and even some of his thoughts, were curiously reminiscent of many of Loomis's feelings about being head of banking. "You asked that I try to articulate the key elements of my coordination responsibilities and what might be done to arrange them in a way that satisfies everyone's needs," Steve wrote. "Let me reiterate at the outset that my first choice is to be relieved of all of those responsibilities for the reasons that we have discussed. While I understand why this might not make sense for the Firm, I'm not concerned from my own standpoint about any reverberations." He recommended nothing less than dismantling much of the internal banking infrastructure that he and Loomis had so carefully constructed in the past decade. He was immensely frustrated and thought the time had come to "eliminate my efforts to influence decisions as to the direction of the Firm. The many conversations that I have had with you, Felix, Damon, Mel and others and the several significant analyses that have been prepared regarding size, profitability, productivity, etc. have taken an extraordinary amount of time. At this point, I've expressed everything that's on my mind so it would be relatively easy to relieve myself of this activity."

Despite this diatribe, which few knew about, once again not much changed outwardly. Summer was right around the corner anyway, and that meant Michel's departure for Sous-le-Vent and the general disappearance of most other partners to their fancy homes in the Hamptons, the Vineyard, the Hudson Valley, Litchfield County, or Wyoming, among other places. After Steve had written the memo, Fennebresque remembered one "summer evening" when he and Michel were "bullshitting" in Michel's office and the topic of managing the banking group came up. Michel had been doodling on a piece of paper, and then he said to Kim, "The problem is, you know, that you and Steve want to manage the banking group and the banking group is really the heart of the firm, and it's really my firm." To which the startled Fennebresque responded, " 'I've got that message, pal. I get it. My foot's coming off the accelerator.' So, um, that was quite a telling moment." From that evening on, Fennebresque said, he was far more low-key about his already subdued efforts to run banking. "I didn't see any reason to increase the enemies list or make the enemies list," he said. He resolved to let Steve be even more out front managing the banking partners than before. Together, they continued to interview some big-name M&A bankers, such as Geoff Boisi, Roger Altman, Joe Perella, and Tom Hill, about coming to Lazard (all of whom declined), but mostly they focused on doing deals.

Like the few before him, Steve had quickly discovered the frustrations and the thanklessness of the task Michel had given him. He was frustrated with his inability to get things done with Michel's incessant micromanaging and undermining. He felt he was wasting his time and energy on trying to reform a system that would not be changed, at least not as long as Michel retained the power of the purse and Felix was free to meddle. He decided he was spending his time unwisely on internal matters when he could spend it far more profitably with clients.

In coming to the decision to abdicate his position as head of banking, Steve had an obvious role model at Lazard: Felix. Through all the changes taking place on Wall Street generally and at the firm specifically, Felix remained the embodiment of the Lazard culture and ethos, and he had never chosen to manage anyone or anything. Aside from Michel, he was the highest-paid partner at the firm. He just did his deals and anything else he wanted. True, Felix tended to thwart the careers of the young partners who worked for him, but Steve didn't care about that. He would be different: he had his own clients, and he had shown a willingness to bring *Felix* into major deals (for instance, AT&T's acquisition of McCaw Cellular, which generated a $20 million fee) as often as Felix had brought him into deals. Felix actually seemed to *like* and *respect* Steve, and he even started to acknowledge around the firm and in New York social circles that Steve appeared to have the potential to match, one day, Felix's business-getting acumen. And since Michel valued what Felix did more highly than what anyone else at the firm did, it wasn't difficult for Steve to figure out what he should do, not only at the firm but also beyond it.

Fennebresque put Felix's continuing importance to the firm in perspective. He remembered being called by a reporter in 2004 who was writing a story about Bob Greenhill on the eve of the incredibly successful IPO of Greenhill's eponymous investment bank. "And this guy didn't know what he was talking about," he recalled. "And he referred to Greenhill as the best investment banker of his time. And I said, 'You could have the opinion that he was in the top echelon, but you can't say anyone was the best banker of his time if they lived when Felix Rohatyn lived. You just can't say it. You can say he's in the top echelon. You can say he's in the pantheon, but you can't say he's the best.' "

What makes Felix's singular success as a banker so remarkable is that he has sustained his relevance to corporate executives for so long and across so many industries. It seems not to matter to Felix or to his clients whether he understands their business. This fact is so profoundly counter to how every other major Wall Street firm designs its investment banking business—which is to have far younger deal makers specialize by industry and by product—that Felix had become an anachronism, the exception that proves the rule. Lesser bankers at inferior firms have attempted to imitate Felix's style and generalist approach with predictably disastrous results. His edge is his extraordinary level of deal experience and his consummate judgment—plus a killer Rolodex. It is nearly impossible to ignore a phone call from Felix Rohatyn—regardless of whether you are a CEO, a politician, or even one of his former partners. Indeed, simply seeing "Rohatyn, Felix" on the caller-ID screen caused the men (and a very few women) of Lazard in their forties, fifties, sixties—themselves earning millions of dollars per year, thanks, in large part, to Felix—to shudder visibly, interrupt a phone conversation with a client, and scurry down the threadbare, tan-carpeted hallways to Felix's lair. It was not unlike how a misbehaving middle school student reacts upon being summoned to the principal's office—with a predictably similar outcome.

Befitting his status, lesser partners sought him out as a sounding board on deal ideas—and, of course, to see if they possessed the right stuff to be a Great Man, too. In one particularly humorous example of this testing, Michael Price called Felix and suggested that the Agnellis, the Italian industrialists who controlled Fiat, might want to think about acquiring the then-struggling Chrysler. Price then contritely choked into the phone, "Dumb idea? Okay," and hung up. Adapted from the cynical French moralist François La Rochefoucauld, the Lazard credo—"It is not enough for you to succeed; others must fail"—had Felix's fingerprints all over it. He charmed his partners—to say nothing of his clients—and rewarded them with a meaningful percentage of the profits when he needed them to execute his prodigious deal flow. At the slightest whiff of resentment, disloyalty, or burnout, Felix would dispatch them to irrelevance and excommunication, in some out-of-the-way hovel, before shining his beacon and affections on the next rising Lazard star. He was immensely feared around the halls of Lazard—just as his mentor, André Meyer, had been—but could not even for a moment be ignored, so long as he continued to produce 80 percent of the deal flow and profits. No one at Lazard had anything like Felix's client list, CEO access, or annual revenue production. Felix spent his time where it could be used most profitably. Being such an effective banker and of such enormous importance to Lazard's profitability meant that he was fabulously well paid. By 1995, the rumor mill pegged Felix's compensation at more than $15 million, all cash—which even for the top bankers in the frothy 1980s and 1990s was an attention grabber. But in truth, he could easily have demanded even higher compensation—and gotten it—because he was that good and that important to the firm, a fact that Felix belatedly came to realize but never did anything about.

Felix relished his Great Man status as much as he relished having nothing to do with the day-to-day running of the firm. The poorly lit, unadorned, dingy corridors became his stage. When he would stroll with intent past Deirdre Hall and Catherine Cronin, his double-barreled secretarial guard, he was all Great Man, in his off-the-rack suits, blue and white Brooks Brothers oxford cloth, buttoned-down shirts, and Hermès ties. He was always completely in character, as if he were a larger-than-life Mickey Mouse making his entrance into Disney World. Generally speaking, it was no fun being the end point of one of his journeys. So, while he was impossible to avoid when he wanted you, he became expert at evading your gaze in the narrow One Rock hallways, pretending not to have heard a "Hello, Felix" from a lesser partner or junior professional, preferring instead to stare ahead icily—unless of course you happened to be one of the few attractive young women rarely in Lazard's employ. Then Felix could be exceptionally fine-tuned to your presence. Rumors abounded of his occasional indiscretions with the younger female professionals. But they were mostly unfounded. He was just a notorious flirt, and his conversation could be jam-packed with innuendo.

CHAPTER 13

"Felix Loses It"

No doubt Steve's evolving mimicry of Felix received a significant boost on November 10, 1993, when the *Wall Street Journal* published a story—written, the paper said, without the help of Steve, Felix, or Michel—on the front of its third section with the headline "Rattner's Star Rises as a Deal Maker at Lazard Frères." In exploring the question of what happens when Felix, then sixty-five, "slows down," the *Journal* concluded, "The clouds are parting just a bit with the emergence of Steven Rattner, a 41-year-old specialist in the type of media mergers driving the current acquisition boom." There was the view, espoused by an unnamed "observer," that Steve was now "sharing Felix's aura." Steve was said to have generated for the firm the second-largest pot of fees after Felix—and twice as many as his nearest rival—while also continuing to serve as co-head of banking and to chair the Monday partners' meetings when Michel was away (all while seeking to abdicate the role). His pay was said to top $5 million a year, enough to easily afford, the *Journal* revealed, his Dakota co-op overlooking Central Park, where the walls "are studded with prints by Andy Warhol and Roy Lichtenstein"; his "country house" in Kent, Connecticut; and his eight-seat Cessna that he flies to his "beach house" on Martha's Vineyard. The paper reiterated Steve's "media savvy" and described his close friendship with Arthur Sulzberger Jr., including their now legendary workouts at the gym and a scuba-diving vacation on Little Cayman Island in the middle of the recently commenced battle for the hand of Paramount Communications—with Felix and Steve advising—between Viacom and QVC Network. Steve's "my best friend," Sulzberger repeated. The *Journal* reported that Steve punctuated his obvious wealth with "regular-guy touches," such as taking his twin boys to school at Temple Emanu-El on the "crosstown bus" and attending parents' night there while at the same time "juggling calls" on his cell phone from Marty Davis, the CEO of Paramount, at a crucial moment in the deal.

In the unwritten—but well-known—rules of Lazard, the *Journal* article about Steve was just the kind of self-aggrandizing publicity that only Felix, and occasionally Michel (since not even Felix could squash that), were allowed. The risks for other bankers who dared swim in these waters were great indeed. Steve, though, "did not obviously completely appreciate the extent to which Felix had no interest in anyone competing for his oxygen," one former partner explained. But he was prepared to try to swim in the riptide anyway. At least, in this instance, Steve could claim not to have spoken to the *Journal*'s reporter, although some of the personal details in the article would seem hard to know unless Steve had confided them. The article also conveyed the risks to Steve "of having a high profile" at Lazard and not being Felix or Michel. "Most other senior Lazard bankers labor in obscurity, by their own choice and the firm's," the article said. Accordingly, Damon Mezzacappa told the paper, Steve's rise had engendered a "predictable amount" of "jealousy and resentment" around the firm. A hint of Felix's reaction to the *Journal* story appeared in *The New Yorker* a few days later. Under the title "Felix Rohatyn in Autumn," a swan song to the man who a few weeks before had stepped down—once and for all—as head of MAC after eighteen years, Felix acknowledged there was the lingering question of what would happen at Lazard when its "biggest rainmaker" decided to slow down. Over breakfast of dry toast in his Fifth Avenue apartment, Central Park spread before him, Felix confided to the reporter that "while he has left MAC and no longer suffers well all the details of investment banking, he has no intention of fading from the scene."

As it turned out, the *Journal* article was only the opening salvo in Rattner's sophisticated media assault. At the same time that the troika of Michel, Felix, and Steve were supposedly *not* speaking with the *Journal*, they were fully engaged in helping the writer Ed Klein, the former editor of the *New York Times Magazine*, put together a profile of Steve that would appear in the January 1994 issue of *Vanity Fair*. Apparently, the idea for the article came about when Klein happened to run into Felix after the announcement of the AT&T-McCaw deal and, after Klein congratulated him for it, Felix charitably and accurately gave full credit for the origination of the transaction to Steve. Before cooperating with Klein, though, Steve knew he should get Felix's approval. Steve discussed with Felix what Klein had in mind. "He said, 'You've worked very hard. You deserve some attention, and you should do it,' " Steve remembered. "And what I didn't understand is that he didn't mean it, and even if he thought he meant it, he didn't mean it."

The front-page machinations of the then-raging battle for Paramount Communications provided the perfect amber to examine the vicissitudes of the—until that moment—symbiotic father-son relationship between Felix and Steve. Atypically, Felix was incredibly gracious—up to a point—in his comments to Klein about Steve, being more laudatory about his younger partner than he had ever been in public about any of his Lazard partners. The resulting article, titled "Paramount Player," was the first time the firm or any of its partners had been featured in the gossipy *Vanity Fair.*

Needless to say, though, the Klein piece caused a sensation and set in motion a series of events that would forever change Lazard. Right from the opening blurb, the article foreshadowed trouble. Next to a full-page picture of Steve, arms folded, eyes piercing, in his Lazard office, the theme of the article was revealed: "Among the financial wizards involved in the Paramount takeover is a New Age breed of Wall Streeter: 41-year-old Steven Rattner, the former *New York Times* reporter who, as a partner at Lazard Frères, is fast becoming the most prominent investment banker of his generation. Bosom buddy of Arthur Sulzberger Jr. and whispered successor to the legendary Felix Rohatyn, Rattner regularly commands multimillion-dollar fees and bonuses, but, he tells Edward Klein, he isn't in it for the money." As the curtain rises, Klein rapidly brings together the globe-trotting Paramount protagonists for a hastily scheduled Saturday morning strategy session in the Columbus Circle office of Marty Davis. Viacom had just revised upward its original offer for Paramount. Felix was there, as was Dick Beattie, the head of the prestigious New York law firm Simpson Thacher. But the focus of the vignette was Steve. The scene included the requisite description of the opulent Paramount offices, of Felix huddled with Davis awaiting Steve's and Beattie's arrival, and of Steve giving some advice to the Paramount executives about a technical aspect of Viacom's revised offer and whether it would stand up to scrutiny in the face of rival bidding from Barry Diller at QVC. There was also some novel reportage from inside the Paramount board of directors meeting of presentations Felix and Steve were making just as Viacom decided to raise the cash portion of its offer. The article noted that the Paramount board swiftly endorsed the new Viacom deal.

Missing from this mise-en-scène was Ira Harris, the Chicago-based Lazard partner who had known Marty Davis from the Bronx and who had worked with Felix—and Davis—in 1989 on the $3.4 billion sale of the Associates from Gulf+Western (thereafter renamed Paramount) to Ford Motor Company. Inside Lazard, bankers noted with interest Felix's decision to exclude Harris from the Paramount deal and replace him with Steve. "Paramount was Ira's relationship," Mezzacappa said. "But before you knew it, Felix and Steve were carving it up, and I think Ira felt that it happened to him on two or three occasions and he was pretty angry about it. When he came in, I think he thought it was going to be the Felix and Ira show and it wasn't." For his part, Harris told his partners: "Everybody in the firm knows who brought in the Paramount relationship. But life goes on."

Much of the *Vanity Fair* piece was given over to revealing aspects of Steve's personal life and to attempting to answer the central question of whether he was the man to succeed Felix at the firm. Klein, a longtime colleague of Steve's from the *Times,* seemed to be advancing Rattner's cause. "Today, when C.E.O.'s want to do major media deals, they no longer pick up the phone and ask for the Gleachers, Hills, and Wassersteins—all stars in the 1980s and all still active to one degree or another in the 90s," he wrote. "Often, the person they think first of calling is Steve Rattner." There was the requisite homage from Steve's mogul friend Arthur Sulzberger Jr. And then Felix added his rarely bestowed imprimatur. "André Meyer used to say that you can explain things to people, but you can't understand for them," he told Klein. "Which means that if you're going to be an adviser to important people, you not only have to have the intellect to decide the right advice but also the authority to have that advice be listened to. The other person has to recognize you as a peer. Steve clearly has all that."

Steve's reaping so far, the article revealed, had already yielded him a rich harvest. His annual compensation for 1993 had increased to "about $8 million" (some 60 percent more than the *Journal* estimated a month earlier) from the $60,000 he received in 1982 as a *Times* reporter. The Rattner's foundation by then had assets of $2 million (now more than $3 million, public records show). Also reiterated in the article were Steve's perks: the Dakota apartment, noticeably underdecorated, did hold his burgeoning collection of modern prints, among them those by Ruscha and Motherwell, in addition to those of Lichtenstein and Warhol. And then, of course, there was the ubiquitous twin-engine Cessna 421—since upgraded—on which Klein accompanied Steve for a trip up to Providence for a Brown trustees meeting. Then there was the house on Martha's Vineyard, although no mention was made of the one in Kent, Connecticut. Somehow, though, Steve and Maureen, with Klein's help, turned all of this conspicuous consumption into an example of the "upright, self-depriving attitudes of the Bill and Hillary Clinton era," a soon-to-be-plenty-ironic observation. Maureen explained that she had no interest in going back to Wall Street "because we don't need to add to our income level" and because "we already live well below our means, and I don't want any more money." She said when her children get older she would look for something "more socially useful [to do] with my life."

Steve elaborated extensively on this theme of modesty. "At times," he said, "it crosses my mind: What am I doing this for? But I think, I wouldn't quit and do nothing, because it would set a terrible example for my children. . . . We live comfortably but have deliberately changed our lifestyle little since our children were born, largely to prevent their values from being adversely affected"—and here he referred again to a detail *someone* supposedly told the *Journal*. "When I take the boys to school, it is on the M72 bus, even though a car and driver is certainly within our means. Maureen buys their clothes from discount catalogues, not trendy Madison Avenue boutiques. . . . I often take the subway to and from work, in part, because I don't see how one can have a view about the problems of the city without experiencing the city on at least some level as typical people do." This lovefest did contain a few shots across Steve's bow, though, some surreptitious, some direct. One of his "best friends" described him as the "Michael J. Fox of investment banking." For his part, as he puffed away on his cigar, Michel listed Steve as merely *one* of the firm's important partners, preferring instead to tell Klein how well positioned the firm was in its three financial capitals. He brushed aside talk of successors and the future. But "a friend of both" Felix and Michel told Klein: "Felix has always been a problem for Michel. Felix has always been a very big producer for Michel, but if you're the guy who owns the business, you say to yourself, 'This guy Felix controls too much of the business, and what happens if he gets hit by a bus?' So Michel has tried to get away from the star system and diversify the business by bringing in new blood and integrating his three firms to make a network."

Steve's remarkable financial performance in such a short time appeared to provide Michel with the outlines of a much-needed insurance policy for the inevitable day when Felix decided to leave the firm. And Felix was aware of this. Along with his unqualified praise of Steve, he served up what could only be taken as a warning. "Talking about an heir is a meaningless thing in a firm like ours," he said. "I came to this firm in 1948, when André Meyer was the senior partner. Since 1948 we've had two men running this firm—André and Michel. Michel and I became senior partners on the same day in 1961, and we go back to the days of André. We have an extraordinarily close relationship. We have similar European backgrounds. I'm 65 and he's 60. We'll be around for a while. I can't transfer my background and my relationship with Michel to someone else." He then continued, more explicitly: "We're all worried for Steve about this story that you are writing. I've been through stories like this at Steve's stage in life. The firm was a lot smaller then, but still these kinds of articles inevitably create internal tensions. The mergers-and-acquisitions side has become very personalized and show-biz. In M&A, you have marquee players. Obviously, being a marquee name is nice, as long as everything is wonderful. But it makes you a target. People are unforgiving if you falter. . . . It's heady stuff, a little scary, because for every marquee name that stays up on the marquee, there are 10 shattered names on the sidewalk."

AN ADVANCE COPY of the *Vanity Fair* article, sent by the editor Graydon Carter, landed with a thud on Felix's desk. He obviously knew the extent of the praise he had lavished on Steve, but when he read the article in toto, he was beyond incensed. The combination of the boardroom leaks, the top billing given to Steve, and his fey stabs at humility sent Felix into the stratosphere. "Felix went berserk. Berserk," according to one Lazard partner at the time. Another said, "*Of course* Felix was pissed." Still another: "Felix ran that deal, not Steve." Steve's nearly five-year honeymoon with Felix evaporated like rain in the Sahara. "He goes hot and cold on people," one partner said of Felix, echoing the earlier observation about Felix's successive loyalties. "Steve was his favorite son for a while. He was going around telling people, 'Steve's my guy, and when I can't do this anymore, Steve's the guy.' And then the *Vanity Fair* piece came along." And that was the end of their relationship at Lazard. The *Vanity Fair* article was "a real oh-shit moment," Felix said subsequently. "Michel and I were appalled."

It wasn't just Steve's shameless self-promotion that so upset Felix. The Paramount deal was one of Felix's most important and complex assignments of the decade. Not only did the spotlight's glow on Steve necessarily detract from the light on Felix, or so Felix thought; there was also the revelation of those confidential details from inside the boardroom. After he read the galley, Felix insisted that Marty Davis be called immediately and informed about the article's contents. Steve was in Arizona at a conference when he got Davis's call. "Marty went berserk," Steve recalled. "And he had every right to. We were in the middle of a deal. He called and screamed at me, which he did all the time, so there wasn't anything unusual in that." Steve denied to Davis he had been the source of the boardroom leaks. Felix, though, blamed Steve. "Steve," Felix said publicly, "made it seem like he was talking right out of the boardroom." Questioning another partner's loyalty and judgment, in public no less, was the worst sort of professional affront. Steve once again denied he was the source of the leaked information. "That's bullshit," Felix insisted.

(Steve continues to insist he was not the leaker and that a careful rereading of the article will reveal Deep Throat; a subsequent *Vanity Fair* article about Marty Davis showed *him* to be the "loose-lipped cannon.")

As the *Vanity Fair* article came out in the middle of the Paramount deal—a deal experience he now believes was a "horror" and "one of the most awful deals that I've ever worked on"—Felix felt obliged to take action against his younger partner. "Steve was almost fired over that," Felix said. "I demoted him on the deal and put Bob Lovejoy on it. The only reason I didn't take him off the deal completely was because it would have created press stories." The consensus among the senior partners was that the *Vanity Fair* article was a mistake for Steve and for the firm. "I have the utmost respect for Rattner," Damon Mezzacappa said. "I think he is a brilliant guy, very open, at least with me. And direct. And honest. I'm a big fan of Steve's, a big fan. But I raised hell with Steve when they did that article in *Vanity Fair,* and I told him I thought it was a stupid thing to do and I was really pissed off at him. He was surprised. He thought it would be helpful to the firm. Well, it was helpful to *him."* For the more junior bankers at Lazard, so steeped in deference and the importance of hierarchy, the *Vanity Fair* story was a serious wake-up call about Steve's ambitions. In particular, the quotation that set tongues wagging incredulously from the Hudson River to the East River was Steve's entirely serious description of taking his kids to school on the crosstown bus, "even though a car and driver is certainly within our means." In any event, this high-profile saber rattling was beginning to remake the secretive, mysterious Lazard into a noisy public battlefield.

The fallout was immediate. The first person to become radioactive was Kim Fennebresque, though he had nothing to do with the article, nor was he even mentioned. Fennebresque decided he no longer had the stomach for the battles raging inside the firm. Whether it was Felix being increasingly irked by Steve's favorable publicity or Loomis's brooding in exile, the fun had vanished. When the Loomis loyalists wanted a scalp, they came after Fennebresque's. His higher profile and marginal productivity made him a sitting duck. Plus, he always knew the job as co-head of banking "was a death sentence." And then he had a falling-out with Loomis himself, who a few months after he took the job began to think Kim "was disloyal to him" because he stopped coming around as often to seek his counsel on how to run banking. "But I really wasn't doing much," he said by way of explanation. "I was there to help Steve. I was not there to be a hero." Loomis and Fennebresque stopped talking. When he got a call from a headhunter at the start of 1994 about a senior position in investment banking at the Union Bank of Switzerland in New York, complete with a multiyear, multimillion-dollar contract, Fennebresque pursued—and then took—the job "purely for the money" and the financial security. The memory of the seven-figure debt to First Boston remained fresh. He left Lazard without saying good-bye to Loomis, a recollection that still makes him a little melancholy. "I was unbelievably happy for the first eighteen months at Lazard," he said. "I was proud to be a partner there. The name was incredibly lustrous. I loved using the words 'my partner.' I just loved the whole thing. And then that one night when Michel said, 'Will you do this?' I never recovered. I became unhappy, and I knew it was a ticking bomb. I knew the day I got it, it was a ticking bomb and it would go off and blow up."

Michel made no effort to change Fennebresque's mind—not that he expected that to happen. "My guess is that in the end he didn't care," Fennebresque said. He called Steve and told him of his decision to leave. Steve said he "sensed that this was coming." Maureen called Kim in tears. Fennebresque's wife was pregnant with their fourth child, and Maureen told him, "You know, you and Debby will now have the time and money to really enjoy this," he said. "It was really a bittersweet moment for the Rattners and the Fennebresques."

Steve was now all alone running banking, although he had successfully dished off many of the more ministerial duties to Steve Langman, a vice president, as he had wanted to do. This gave him more time to focus on deals and his outside interests. He more or less gave up trying to make reforms. "When I ran banking the first time, our mistake was to think we could accomplish as much as we set out to accomplish," he said. "Bill was good at it in part because he understood the limitations of what could be done in the context of the firm and 150 years of history. London. Paris. New York. Michel. Felix. The feudal lords, all this stuff. I was more naïve." But there was still the small matter of Felix's continuing rage. Unlike Kim, Steve had an ability to generate huge fees that made him nearly untouchable in the mercenary Lazard firmament, but he soon realized that he could no longer effectively run banking without Felix's support.

And it was obvious around the firm that his heart was not in it. He was aloof, cool, and distant within the firm's corridors, although he could turn on the charm with clients and in social settings. Some of the other, long-tenured partners were beginning to be put off by his diffidence. His year-end obligation to the nonpartners became even more perfunctory than it had been the year before; the highlight of the five-minute sessions was being able to see, up close, the original Warhol lithographs alongside the black-and-white etchings of old New York on the walls of his office.

It was nearly impossible to carry on a conversation with him, as he rarely made eye contact with subordinates and preferred monosyllabic responses. He executed this duty with a detached efficiency. Steve said he did not think he was particularly good at running banking at that time. "I didn't and I still don't particularly like conversations where people are trying to figure out what's in it for them," he said. "But I do enjoy the process of trying to move the firm forward, getting good people to come, thinking through the business and strategy, and going to get clients."

Steve walked away from the job as head of banking after the 1994 bonus and review period; Michel selected Ken Wilson to replace him. "When Steve arrived at the firm, Felix embraced him," Mezzacappa remembered. "He was young enough to be Felix's son. He was extremely talented and bright. My guess is that he was the most intelligent. It was all fine until Steve started getting some press—because the rule was you don't do that, only Felix can get the press—and Felix was unhappy about that. That's when the strain developed. Steve didn't back off, because he had his own clients. He wasn't in a position like everyone else—dependent on Felix's castoffs. He didn't back off, and of course Michel tacitly encouraged it because Michel liked to see division among the partners because it gave Michel the opportunity to come in and say, 'See, they can't operate without me.' "

❦

WITH THE EFFECTS of the *Vanity Fair* article still reverberating around the firm, the lymphatic cancer in Lazard's municipal finance department continued to spread. The *Journal*'s 1993 unflattering portrait of Richard Poirier's unsavory behavior in New Jersey coincided with the news, reported aggressively by the *Boston Globe,* that Poirier's partner Mark Ferber had quit Lazard in Boston, along with all eight members of the office, to join the regional brokerage First Albany Corporation as vice chairman and co–chief executive officer. "The guy's a good guy," one Lazard colleague told the paper. "He's not irrelevant. But it's not Felix Rohatyn. He was a very junior partner."

Thanks in part to well-crafted tips from many of Ferber's enemies, including Poirier, the *Globe* had a sixth sense that there was more to the story of Ferber's departure from Lazard than was readily apparent. Such was Ferber's stature that in the past, when he left Kidder, Peabody for First Boston and then First Boston for Lazard, a meaningful portion of the state's financing business followed him to his new firms. This is no small accomplishment for a banker. In explaining his success, Ferber had always maintained it came as a result of his knowledge of the intricacies of state government and his relationships with state leaders, rather than from any hidden arrangements. As expected, within days of Ferber's departure from Lazard, First Albany started to be included in the syndicate of firms underwriting Massachusetts's bonds. Then came the news that the Massachusetts Water Resources Authority, charged with cleaning up Boston harbor, had voted to move its $2.375 million, four-year advisory contract from Lazard to First Albany. First Albany, a tiny firm that did not even rank among the top hundred brokerages, would be paid nearly $600,000 a year for its financial advice. "In our view and in the view of the financial services industry generally, the transfer of the former Lazard team to First Albany positions First Albany as one of the most qualified financial advisers in the country," the head of the MWRA, Douglas MacDonald, wrote to explain his group's decision after the Massachusetts inspector general, Robert Cerasoli, raised questions about it. Cerasoli remained concerned, though, about potential conflicts of interest between the people and firms awarding and benefiting from the state contracts and demanded that all advisers to state agencies disclose all potentially conflicting arrangements. He also didn't believe First Albany was qualified for the assignment or deserved the same compensation for it that Lazard had received.

To comply with the inspector general's request, on May 27, 1993, Ferber—now at First Albany—wrote a one-paragraph letter to the MWRA, his client, revealing the existence of a contract between Lazard and Merrill Lynch, the MWRA's lead underwriter, under which they split more than $6 million in fees and commissions in exchange for Ferber and Lazard recommending that state agencies in Massachusetts use Merrill for financing and interest-rate swaps, a way for municipalities to reduce their interest costs. Merrill also paid Lazard $2.8 million in "consulting fees," and in return Ferber "was expected to help introduce Merrill Lynch to his contacts in government agencies" with the expectation that these agencies would choose Merrill Lynch as an underwriter of bonds and other financial transactions.

At the same time, of course, Ferber and Lazard were supposed to be giving the firm's municipal clients in Massachusetts unbiased, independent advice. The Lazard-Merrill arrangement, eerily reminiscent of Lazard's undisclosed deal with Mediobanca in the 1960s, ran from December 1989 to December 1992 and had never before been disclosed to the water authority. When the *Globe* broke this story on June 21, the paper reported that during the time period covered by the contract, Lazard helped "select Merrill Lynch as the agency's bond underwriter and has been involved in overseeing its work." The nub of the problem, the *Globe* wrote, was that "while by no means illegal, the fee-splitting arrangement between Lazard Frères and Merrill Lynch is a symptom of an underregulated municipal finance industry, where political connections can often bring more dividends than the substance of an underwriter's proposal and where hidden conflicts often abound."

When asked at the time to comment about the arrangement with Merrill that he engineered, Ferber told the *Globe*: "I'm not telling you it's pretty but there is absolutely no violation of my fiduciary responsibilities." When Douglas MacDonald heard about the existence of the Lazard-Merrill contract, he was not happy. Still, he told the paper he felt that the water authority's "interests were protected" by Ferber's earlier oral disclosure to the authority's director of finance, Philip Shapiro, of the existence of Lazard's contract with Merrill. Cerasoli, though, first heard about the Lazard-Merrill contract in the *Globe* story. In a letter to MacDonald two days later, he wrote he found it "especially alarming" that MacDonald had told the paper about Ferber's "unwritten disclosure" of the contract to Shapiro when more than three months earlier Shapiro failed to disclose any knowledge of the contract to the inspector general's office during an interview about the matter. Now, clearly exercised, Cerasoli started a full-scale investigation of Ferber's behavior. Even MacDonald began to realize he had been duped.

A month later, with the controversy still percolating following the MWRA's decision to bar all of Lazard, Merrill, and First Albany from working with or for the agency, First Albany's board of directors voted "to terminate the employment" of Ferber. The *Globe* had also revealed that while Lazard and Merrill had their contract and First Albany had been an underwriter of Massachusetts bonds, First Albany had also paid Lazard and Ferber $170,000 for general corporate financial advice. A September 1993 *BusinessWeek* cover story featured the controversy and described Ferber as "the investment banker who played by his own rules." Richard Roberts, an SEC commissioner, told the magazine that Ferber's side deals "violate everything that a financial adviser is supposed to be about: impartiality, objectivity, third-party advice." Ferber disagreed. "The contract, as reviewed at the time by Lazard's general counsel and as drafted by a major New York law firm, did not violate any laws, regulations, ethical standards or fiduciary duties owed by this or any other financial adviser," he said. A Lazard spokesman sought to pare responsibility for the matter away from the firm. He said that the "contract clearly envisioned disclosure to Mr. Ferber's clients" and that Ferber had "assured us that he did so." Merrill described the contract as "proper, ethical and legal." The inspector general, meanwhile, continued his probe throughout the summer and fall of 1993.

Inside Lazard, the senior partners were working with Wall Street's best lawyers to formulate a legal strategy to deal with the growing scandal. Loomis wrote a September 9 memo to Mel Heineman, with a copy to Michel, recommending that the law firm Cravath, Swaine & Moore be hired to work with Wachtell, Lipton, Lazard's usual outside counsel. "I believe that our best assets are our franchise, or reputation, and our leadership, Michel. Both of these may erode as defenses if we engage in a protracted process of attrition which leaves us small but not unique—an ideal target," he said. He recommended closing the municipal finance department immediately and establishing a blue-ribbon panel to review Lazard's activities in municipal finance as well as the industry as a whole across Wall Street. "The problems of business practice would be those common to other firms and constitute industry reform by the first example of how to avoid problems, having forthrightly addressed them on our own," he wrote. His recommendations were ignored—until it was almost too late.

On December 16, Cerasoli released his report, and in a cover letter to Massachusetts's governor, William Weld, he wrote that what he had uncovered was "so extraordinary and compelling" that he felt the need to make a public disclosure and "accentuate the need for a dramatic switch away from business as usual in negotiated bond sales, toward a policy which favors open and competitive bidding. The issues are national in scope and not solely those of the Massachusetts Water Resources Authority." The inspector general's December report revealed that Merrill and Lazard had misrepresented their relationship in disclosure statements made to the MWRA. The report also disclosed that Ferber had been coaching Merrill's bankers about how to win business from the state and revealed helpful information about what other underwriters had proposed in their efforts to win business. Even worse, "the evidence suggests that despite Merrill Lynch's disclaimer, [Ferber's] advocacy of Merrill Lynch as a member of the Massachusetts Water Resources Authority's underwriting team was a *quid pro quo* for the firm's delivering lucrative business to him in other deals, including out of state deals." Documents showed that Ferber told his counterpart at Merrill that Ferber "works to make a positive spin for Merrill Lynch's performance at every turn" but that he wanted business in return, from Merrill, with "his name on it." The documents show further that Ferber had given the Merrill banker a "warning that without a return on his investment, he will hurt us. I will discuss this in more detail when I have a chance to reflect on it—right now, my mind is mush." Not only did Merrill then direct non-Massachusetts business to Ferber and Lazard—they worked together in Washington, D.C., Indianapolis, Arkansas, Florida, Michigan, and for the U.S. Postal Service—but this led to the advisory contract between the two firms, initially for an annual retainer of $800,000 for 1990, and subsequently increased to $1 million annually for 1991 and 1992. Cerasoli also documented other instances where Ferber had tried to pressure other investment banks to throw some business his way in exchange for favorable treatment from the agencies he represented: the report stated that Goldman Sachs accommodated Ferber's requests and received underwriting business, while Lehman Brothers ignored him and was cut out of the underwriting syndicate. Merrill was an enthusiastic player in Ferber's scheme. Wrote the Merrill banker Jeff Carey to his bosses: "We need to find a way to 'reach' Ferber since everyone acknowledges that he will not only shape the [MWRA's] evaluative process but also critically influence the finance committee and Board actions" in selecting bond underwriters.

The inspector general's report went on in this vein to detail other breaches between the two firms and the fiduciary duties they owed to the citizens of Massachusetts. "In summary," Cerasoli wrote,

> I have provided this information to you because it contradicts the disclosure made to MWRA by Merrill Lynch that its contractual relationship with Lazard Frères & Co. "was not in connection with its provision of, or expectation to provide services to the MWRA. . . ." On the contrary, one of the most disturbing implications of these communications is that Merrill Lynch did not tell the MWRA the truth in its disclosure statement (i.e., that it expected [Ferber] to encourage the Authority to give the firm business). Just as important is the fact that Lazard Frères, which owed its loyalty as a fiduciary to the MWRA, mistreated the Authority and put it at risk. The MWRA contracted with Lazard Frères, on the assumption that it would be its advocate, and paid the firm a premium, approximately $600,000 per year for its financial advisory services, despite the misgivings of some Board members about the amount of the contract. Any expectation that paying a high fee would translate into quality was not met. Instead, Lazard Frères treated the MWRA as collateral to increase its own profit by seeking and obtaining other business with the Authority's underwriters.

It is difficult to conceive of a more damning indictment of Lazard and Ferber's behavior—a mere six months after *Institutional Investor* had lionized the firm and Michel, in a May 1993 cover story, as seeking to be the paragons of ethical behavior on Wall Street. Without its carefully cultivated reputation for independent and unbiased financial advice, the firm might as well not exist. But there was no firm-wide statement from Michel or from Mel Heineman, the general counsel, about Cerasoli's report. There was no discussion at all, in fact, about these allegations, at least among the rank and file at Lazard.

As the paper that broke the story, the *Globe* had a field day with Cerasoli's report. On December 17, the paper faithfully described the report's scathing contents on the front page and also revealed that the "dealings" between Merrill Lynch and Lazard had "become the focus of federal and state investigations" in which "thousands" of pages of subpoenaed documents were being reviewed to "determine if Ferber violated his fiduciary responsibilities as financial adviser to the MWRA and other agencies through his ties to Merrill Lynch." Ferber's lawyers called the inspector general's report "outrageously erroneous, incomplete and out of context." But MacDonald, the MWRA executive director, said the report "is really unbelievable. If what is alleged in these documents is true, we're talking about a very serious statewide problem, not one confined to the MWRA."

The press coverage of Cerasoli's report led to another bit of bad luck for Lazard and its municipal finance department. Michael Lissack, a senior investment banker in the public finance department of Smith Barney, read an article about the report while on vacation in Florida and realized the Massachusetts state investigators were missing another important—and quite complicated—part of the emerging illegal activity that had been occurring in municipal finance departments across Wall Street, including at Lazard. From the beach, he walked to a pay phone and placed what started as an anonymous call to the U.S. attorney's office in Atlanta "to let the government in on Wall Street's dirty—but very profitable—little secret." For several years, he told them—in an act of betrayal that would not win him many friends on Wall Street but would get him "whistle-blower" millions—investment banks had engaged in systematic, industry-wide overpricing of securities sold in connection with certain municipal bond transactions. Hundreds of millions of dollars in illegal profits had been pocketed by Wall Street. Lissack stressed that these overpricing practices—known as yield burning—were the true scandal on Wall Street, for they infected thousands of transactions across the country and touched nearly every public issuer of municipal debt. Yield burning was hurting the Treasury, the bond markets, and taxpayers far more than any market-splitting arrangement.

Thanks to Lissack's call, Lazard would soon be embroiled in yet another scandal—the so-called yield-burning scandal—to go along with investigations into the questionable behavior of both Poirier and Ferber. There was now a nagging sense that Lazard, despite its immense prestige and profitability, was dangerously out of control and a pattern of criminal malfeasance had emerged. Not surprisingly, the federal authorities were by now in regular communication with the Lazard senior partners and the firm's lawyers about the goings-on in the municipal finance department. There was the possibility that the firm would be prosecuted under the Racketeer Influenced and Corrupt Organizations Act, known as RICO, which would likely put the firm out of business. One partner recalled, sadly, "Lazard was told by the feds, 'Hey, look, guys. You got two bad actors. Ferber and Poirier. Kidder went down. Drexel went down. We're really trying to be sensitive to the fact that we can put companies out of business, because we see we can do that, just by suggesting something. You know, the RICO word. So we're just letting you know.' And we cooperated like sons of bitches. So then all of a sudden, along comes yield burning. It's like, 'Holy shit. We are teed up like nobody else is teed up.' And our pitch to clients does not have a broad appeal: it's trust and close relationships, and all that. And we ain't got much capital. And we were teed up."

To this point, the New York papers had no coverage of the matter. But in May 1994, the *New York Times* weighed in with a devastating thirty-four-hundred-word article about Ferber and Lazard. There wasn't anything particularly new in the article, but since it was the *Times,* Lazard felt the need to react to it. Two days after the article appeared, a memo was sent to the firm's partners and vice presidents, under Michel's name (but clearly written by lawyers), seeking to definitively refute its implications. "Many of you undoubtedly read with great frustration" the Ferber story, Michel wrote. "While the article covers old ground, yet again, it is important to note a few key points which the article mischaracterizes or fails to reflect, despite our best efforts to educate the reporter."

The firm's view, as articulated by Michel's memo, was: "The New York partners who approved the 1990 contract between Lazard and Merrill Lynch believed it to be entirely proper and it was reviewed by counsel. It provided that Mark Ferber would provide consulting advice aimed at improving Merrill Lynch's marketing of municipal swap transactions (in return for an annual retainer), and that Lazard and Merrill Lynch would jointly pitch swap transactions to Lazard municipal underwriting clients (in return for a split of the fees paid by the municipal client). We were of the view that Ferber had negotiated the contract at arm's length and that it involved a fair exchange of legitimate consulting services for appropriate compensation." Michel denied the contract was kept "secret" and stated that Lazard had insisted that disclosure clauses be added to the contract to ensure that Ferber explained to clients that "Lazard had a swaps-based relationship in those situations where Merrill Lynch was pitching swaps to Lazard's financial advisory clients." Michel wrote that Ferber had informed the New York partners "both in writing and orally" that he made proper disclosure of the relationship "wherever Merrill Lynch was proposing swaps to Lazard advisory clients." As to the Massachusetts inspector general's allegations against Ferber, whom the firm by this time no longer had access to, Michel wrote that Lazard had "stressed" to the *Times* reporter that "we were profoundly disturbed" by them and that if Ferber had indeed breached his fiduciary duties to the firm's clients, as alleged, this behavior was "abhorrent," adding, "We could not have been stronger on this issue, and it disappoints us that the story as printed fails to reflect this." In closing, Michel wrote that the firm would await the outcome of the two investigations into the matter. "In the interim, we intend to continue to assist them to the best of our ability," he stated.

Michel's Cartesian logic was, as usual, impeccable. But the fact remained that despite the precise explanation, Lazard had entered into a most unusual arrangement with one of its competitors to the apparent detriment of its clients—a cardinal sin if your reputation is premised on offering unbiased, independent advice. "Seldom do you see two national firms coming together to co-pitch business," a managing director at another firm told the *New York Times*. "You might see a regional and a national, but rarely two nationals." In October 1994, the SEC informed Lazard, Merrill, and Ferber that it intended to file charges against them all "for maintaining a secret contract to split millions of dollars in bond fees." In January 1995, in order to avoid a lawsuit from their dealings with the District of Columbia, Lazard and Merrill each agreed to pay $1.8 million. And by the middle of 1995, Richard Poirier decided to quit Lazard amid the ongoing SEC and U.S. attorney investigations into how he and Ferber won business for the firm.

❦

Despite the increasingly public nature of the feud between Steve and Felix because of the *Vanity Fair* article—now compounded by rising concerns about the mushrooming municipal finance scandals—Steve's deal-making prowess continued unabated. And what was fascinating about his oeuvre was how it sprang mostly from a well of his personal relationships—not all that dissimilar from the way André worked. First, in late 1993, came the blockbuster $13.9 billion sale of McCaw Cellular to AT&T (for a $20 million fee) that forever transformed the wireless industry in this country from an entrepreneurial endeavor to a high-stakes, well-capitalized, essential service. Steve, of course, represented his friend Craig McCaw. Then, in July 1994, he represented his friend Brian Roberts in the first of several of Comcast's audacious and transformative deals, the successful hostile acquisition, with its partner Liberty Media, of the home shopping network QVC, a deal that thwarted the merger between QVC and CBS. The QVC deal proved to be incredibly lucrative for Comcast; in December 2004, Liberty bought Comcast's 57.5 percent in QVC for almost $8 billion, a stake Comcast had bought, with Rattner's help, for $1.9 billion. Just as the AT&T–McCaw Cellular deal was closing, in September 1994, the Ziff family (and in particular Steve's friend Dirk Ziff), of New York, hired Steve and Lazard to sell, discreetly, the Ziff Davis Publishing Company, the nation's leading publisher of computer magazines. Before long, Steve had contacted Forstmann Little, and the firm quickly made a preemptive bid, buying 95 percent of the company for $1.4 billion. Forstmann's offer of speed and certainty to the seller had prevented other buyers from having a chance to get the business. But others were still interested. Ten months after Forstmann closed the Ziff Davis deal, the SoftBank Corp. of Japan formalized its interest and bought the company for $2.1 billion, a profit of $700 million for Forstmann—one of the more stunning and lucrative buyout deals of the 1990s. Steve advised Forstmann on the sale. Then, if all this wasn't enough, Steve represented another buddy, Amos Hostetter, in the sale of his cable company, Continental Cablevision, for $10.8 billion to the telephone company US West.

Felix was busy doing deals, too, including the landmark sale of the software pioneer Lotus Development Corporation, the maker of Lotus 1-2-3 and Lotus Notes, to IBM for $3.5 billion in cash, at that time the largest software deal ever. The deal was also notable because IBM, the bluest blue-chip company in corporate America, had launched a surprise all-cash $60-a-share hostile bid for Lotus on June 5, 1995, a premium of nearly 100 percent to where Lotus was trading before the offer. Everyone considered Lotus dead in the water given IBM's offer. Felix, who had no idea how to use a computer, worked on the Lotus deal with his partner Jerry Rosenfeld, who had joined Lazard in 1992 after a stint at Bankers Trust. Rosenfeld knew the Lotus CEO, Jim Manzi, well from their days together at McKinsey & Company, and Rosenfeld had, typically, introduced Felix to Manzi in an effort to seal the relationship between Lotus and Lazard.

When IBM launched its hostile bid, Manzi called Rosenfeld and Felix. After initially rejecting IBM's all-cash offer, Lazard and Lotus negotiated to increase the IBM offer from $60 a share to $64 a share. Lazard received a $9 million fee for its work. Ironically, six months before IBM launched its bid for Lotus, Manzi had feared this very thing and had confided his concern to Felix. "I'm a bit worried that IBM might try to do something hostile with us," Manzi said he told Felix. "This was six months beforehand. And Felix said, 'Don't be stupid, they would never, ever do anything like that, that's not the way they operate,' or words to that effect." They still joke about the turn of events today.

Lazard, thanks to the dynamic duo of Felix and Steve, had become *the* premier media and communications advisory firm on Wall Street. But all was not well in paradise. The two men were like prizefighters circling each other warily in a title bout, and the challenger's incessant rope-a-dope had just opened a bloody gash under the eye of the aging champ. There was a moment early in 1995 when Felix considered leaving Lazard altogether. He had been skiing in the picturesque village of Zürs, Austria, with his wife when he got a call from Roger Altman, the Clinton confidant and friend of Steve's who several months before had resigned his position as deputy Treasury secretary. Altman was still close to Clinton, of course, and Clinton had authorized him to talk to Felix about becoming the next president of the World Bank, replacing Lewis Preston, who had just told Clinton that he was ill with the cancer that would soon kill him. The Rohatyns were very friendly with the Prestons, and Felix knew of Preston's illness and that he had told Clinton he would be stepping down. Altman told Felix: " 'You know, Clinton really likes you. He thinks you'd make a great World Bank president. [Treasury Secretary Robert] Rubin doesn't like [James] Wolfensohn, who was the leading candidate. And if you told us you'd be interested, you would get appointed. But also remember that you really should—if you do, you should be able to make a moral commitment for two terms, which would be twelve years.' "

Felix asked Altman for a few days to think about the offer. He was very intrigued for any number of reasons—among them, his growing frustration with the dynamic inside Lazard. But he had never *run* anything before, let alone something as massively bureaucratic as the World Bank. "Running a big bureaucracy was never my cup of tea," he said. And Elizabeth was dead set against it. Aside from the requisite move to Washington, there would have been extensive travel worldwide to attend ponderous meetings. And there was also the twelve-year commitment, which would have put Felix close to seventy-eight years old by the time he left the job. Felix called Altman and told him he would pass. Wolfensohn got the job and served for ten years. There was only the barest mention in the press that Felix had been considered for the post. But that mention revealed to the outside world a character flaw. "I didn't want the World Bank," he reportedly said. "But I almost took it so Jim Wolfensohn wouldn't get it."

But that was sufficient to suggest that Felix was getting antsy at Lazard, leading to a palpable and discernible shift within the firm: after years of anticipation, the end of the Felix era was at hand. And Lazard bankers were no longer able to ignore just how formidable Steve had become. He sensed it, too, no doubt, and gave up his head of banking position in 1994 in favor of being a senior "deal guy" without any administrative duties. He even replaced his longtime assistant, Cathy Mignone, with Sally Wrennall-Montes, the taller and more attractive assistant of Christina Mohr, one of his less powerful partners. Ken Wilson took over from Rattner as the fifth head of banking at Lazard in six years, which suggested to the professional rank and file that the feuding was perhaps making Lazard unmanageable. When Felix decided not to take the World Bank job, he virtually ensured that, as painful as it was for all involved, his white-hot resentment of Steve would intensify throughout the year.

For his part, whether intentional or not, Steve knew just what to do to make Felix crazy. He continued to elevate his intellectual profile by writing "thought" pieces for the *New York Times.* And then Steve and Maureen started to raise their social and political profiles as well. As a first step, the Rattners and their four towheaded children—Rebecca, the twins Daniel and David, and Izzy—moved across Central Park from the funky and elegant Dakota on Central Park West to the ninth floor of the highly exclusive 998 Fifth Avenue. For this privilege, they paid close to $10 million—what looks like a steal nowadays. The McKim, Mead & White–designed building, built in 1912 as the first luxury apartment house on Fifth Avenue above Fifty-ninth Street, is exceedingly exclusive even by Upper East Side standards. The building once was home to the Astors, the Guggenheims, and the Nobel Prize–winning statesman and lawyer Elihu Root, who was the first fancy to move from downtown to 998 Fifth, paying rent of $25,000 per year. The full-floor apartments are huge, at about five thousand square feet. Michael Wolff, Steve's former colleague at the *Times,* unable to contain his jealousy after a visit there, wrote of the Rattners' apartment: "The elevator opened into a massive foyer that in turn opened into an even larger anteroom (all of these rooms were the size of other people's two-bedroom apartments) that opened into the main gallery running in front of Central Park and the Metropolitan Museum of Art. The room was a careful, muted, just-so green affair, with much elaborate and detailed plasterwork." He failed to mention the apartment's marble.

Among their new neighbors was Joseph Perella, an accountant's son who, like Steve, had risen to the very top of the investment banking profession, first at First Boston, then at Wasserstein Perella. When Perella split with Bruce Wasserstein in 1993, Lazard heavily recruited him to come to the firm. But in the end, Perella chose Morgan Stanley. When the Rattners applied to get into the building, a Lazard partner's wife wrote an unsolicited letter trashing Steve and Maureen. Nonetheless, the Rattners were approved. (In addition to their home on Martha's Vineyard, they own a horse farm in North Salem, New York, in the upper reaches of Westchester County, that they bought after selling their home in nearby Bedford, for $7.8 million, to a partner at the Blackstone Group, where they had moved after selling their home in Mount Kisco.)

Steve was a large donor to his alma mater, Brown University, and had joined the Brown board of trustees. He also was on the board of trustees of Channel 13, New York's public television station (and later became the chairman of the board after Henry Kravis stepped down). Since he had amassed an impressive collection of contemporary prints and the Met was across the street, he joined Michel on that board, too. His friend Arthur Sulzberger Jr. invited Steve to join the board of Outward Bound, which he did for a time. He became a member of the prestigious and highly selective Council on Foreign Relations. The council has been the most powerful private organization in U.S. foreign policy since it began in 1921, with the help of the former Lazard partner Frank Altschul. Felix is also a member. Steve is on the board of directors of the New America Foundation, a Washington-based public policy institute that has as its mission "to bring exceptionally promising new voices and new ideas to the fore of our nation's discourse." He has served on a number of public commissions and committees, including the International Monetary Fund Advisory Committee, the President's Commission to Study Capital Budgeting, and the International Competition Policy Advisory Committee.

And true to her word, Maureen sought to devote her time and energy to public service as well. Until 2006, she was the national finance chair of the Democratic National Committee and, according to *her* biography, is an "active national and international human rights advocate." She serves as a U.S. government representative to UNICEF and as the chair of the Leadership Council on Children Affected by Armed Conflict. The couple, among the very top Democratic Party fund-raisers, became very close to the Clintons, especially during the second term. They once stayed in the infamous Lincoln Bedroom at the White House. They were frequent guests of the Clintons at Camp David. They have given hundreds of thousands of dollars to Democratic candidates around the country and to the party itself, according to public records—other reports put their giving for the Democrats in the millions. The Rattners caused a momentary fillip in the fall of 2005 when they publicly announced their support for the reelection of New York City's mayor, Michael Bloomberg, a Republican, whom Steve believes is the best mayor since La Guardia.

Steve also continued to attract—or to court, depending on your point of view—publicity. In September 1995, *Broadcasting & Cable* magazine featured him in a two-part interview on the state of media and telecom mergers. "The subject is so provocative, and his treatment of it so comprehensive and valuable, that the editors are publishing the Rattner interview in two parts, this issue and next," the magazine purred. The magazine's cover photograph showed a confident and inscrutable Steve, collar unbuttoned on his Paul Stuart shirt, Hermès tie knotted handsomely. The interview conveyed that Steve could be at once *extremely* chatty and remarkably astute—as one might expect—about the doings in the media and telecom industries. He made a number of bold—and correct—predictions: that intense competition among telecom service providers would lead to a financial bloodbath, that cable and radio broadcasting would see further consolidation, and that video on demand would be a powerful force. "Why would you go to a video store if you could call up, five minutes before you wanted to watch it, and get any number of movies to start when you wanted, to play, pause, fast forward, rewind?" he mused. Remember, this was 1995. The interview, which mentioned Lazard not at all, further incensed Felix, although, except for professional jealousy, it is difficult to discern why. He called Michel at home one weekend morning to complain after the appearance of the *Broadcasting & Cable* interview. "Oh, Felix, go back to bed," Michel reportedly responded.

But the publicity coup de grâce came in October 1995 when *Vanity Fair,* again, featured Steve in an article about the top fifty members of "the New Establishment," without putting on the list anyone else at Lazard, including Felix. Sandwiched between Esther Dyson (information newsletter guru) and Gordon Crawford (famed media and entertainment investor), at number 43 on the list, was Steve, pictured half smiling with his arms crossed confidently. (He has since fallen to number 99 out of a list of 100.) "There are lots of young, hotshot investment bankers on

Wall Street, but in the telecommunications-and-media business Steven Rattner is the hottest shot," the magazine gushed. But in a mere 250 words there was much to feast on for Rattner's growing number of enemies inside Lazard. Among the most incendiary were these: "He keeps secrets like a priest and has a way of putting older men at ease" (neither was true if Felix was to be believed). "He has a Rolodex to kill for, and the guest lists at his Martha's Vineyard parties boggle his clients' minds, helping him win business and press. He flies his own plane, is investing in a disco on Martha's Vineyard with his pals Strauss Zelnick, Dirk Ziff and Carly Simon, and has an expensive art collection, but says money doesn't drive him." And the pièce de résistance: "Sniping colleagues say Rattner doesn't like to share his deals with Rohatyn, even though Rohatyn brings Rattner in on his." Even though this wasn't completely true—Rattner brought Felix into the McCaw Cellular deals, for instance—the two men stopped speaking completely. "That last article," Felix said later, without the slightest sense of irony, "was bad for the younger people here"—not that he had ever shown one whit of evidence that he cared about Lazard's younger bankers. "It hurt morale. People who yearn for publicity and exposure don't realize how dangerous it is in terms of business. Clients do not want us to go public on their deals."

Some of the qualities that made people perceive Steve as having a cool side—aloofness, elitism, lack of a common touch—seemed all to be operative in some of the interactions he has had with his neighbors on Martha's Vineyard, one of the two very pricey, hard-to-get-to, and breathtakingly beautiful islands off the southern coast of Massachusetts. Just after Steve started at Lazard, in April 1989, he and Maureen bought a 1930 shingle-style home with five bedrooms on close to thirty-two waterfront acres on Obed Daggett Road in West Tisbury. The purchase price was $1.99 million, which "sounds like a Wal-Mart price, and by today's standards it definitely is," one longtime Vineyard resident said. In December 1990, Steve subdivided the property into two parcels, the one with the house on 10.88 acres, and the other, 21.09 acres of undeveloped land. (In 2001, he transferred the two parcels into Maureen's given name—Patricia M. White—and today they are appraised for real estate tax purposes at $23.2 million.)

By the summer of 1994, Steve found himself tussling with his neighbors over two projects, one of his own making and one not, but both engendered a fair amount of local controversy. In June 1994, he proposed building a 110-foot wooden seasonal pier off Lambert's Cove Beach on his property. The pier, to have been the first along the northern coast of the island in modern times, would lead to a floating dock, where his boats could be tied up. The problem he was trying to solve with the pier was that "our beach has become quite rocky, and particularly when there is any surf, bringing our boats into shore to load or unload our four small children can be a tricky and potentially dangerous exercise." The conservation-minded Vineyarders were quite opposed to Steve's dock. As the proposal was awaiting final approval and as protests from neighbors were mounting, Steve agreed to drop the proposal on the condition that his dozen or so neighbors sign a covenant forbidding the construction of piers along the northern coastline. Although the agreement was never signed, he decided to shelve his plan for the pier.

Meanwhile, a few months after the pier controversy, Steve faced another problem. His immediate neighbors to the east, Margaret Smith-Burke and Cary Hart, wanted to develop their eighty-one-acre parcel on Vineyard Sound. The idea, approved by the West Tisbury Planning Board in 1995, was to subdivide the eighty-one acres into four lots, three of which could have one house on them and one of which could have two houses. Steve had opposed the development, such as it was, every step of the way.

But after the planning board ruled against him, he took the additional step of filing a civil lawsuit, on October 4, 1995, in Dukes County Superior Court against the planning board, Smith-Burke, and Hart. The gist of Steve's lawsuit was that the owners of the new homes in the subdivision would be using the same dirt road that he used to get to his house. He complained that the dirt road was not suited to the extra traffic. The case went through the system for four years until Steve fashioned on a brilliant and unique solution: no doubt at Steve's suggestion, Brian Roberts, his longtime friend and client at Comcast, bought the whole property and put an end to the dispute. In July 1999, two Philadelphia attorneys, on Roberts's behalf, bought the eighty-one acres from Smith-Burke for $12 million, and then Roberts had constructed on the property a sixteen-thousand-square-foot home designed by the architect Robert A. M. Stern.

That matter solved to his liking, in March 2000 Steve rekindled his effort to build his controversial pier, this time at 130 feet in length and 320 feet farther east. Not surprisingly, the new pier project once again engendered much vocal opposition. "Being tone-deaf comes with the territory," one of Steve's Martha's Vineyard neighbors said about him. By the time a public hearing was set for October 2000, Steve had decided to change the proposal from a 130-foot pier to a much smaller, 24-foot pier that would connect with a seasonal floating metal dock that he already used. The new pier would, he said, allow his family to get to the floating dock "without having to wade through three feet of water" at high tide. Steve was the only person to speak at the hearing in support of the pier. Those opposed were outspoken and presented a petition with two hundred signatures against the building of a pier. Even his neighbor Brian Roberts was said to oppose the project. In the end, in December 2000, the Martha's Vineyard Commission voted 9–1 against even the slimmed-down pier.

Once again, though, Steve took refuge in the legal system. In early January 2001, his attorney filed a five-page complaint in Dukes County Superior Court asking that the commission's decision be reversed and the pier project approved. The commission voted again to reject the pier in June 2001. While Steve continued to press his case, he unwittingly galvanized an unprecedented coalition against any future piers or docks jutting into the water on the north shore of Martha's Vineyard. The conservation commissions from the four towns that border the north shore voted to preserve the shoreline and keep it free from piers and docks. The Martha's Vineyard Commission then voted unanimously to recommend the designation. Slowly but surely, voters from each of the four towns approved the designation, with Steve's hometown of West Tisbury approving the measure 59–7 in March 2002, effectively killing Steve's effort to build the pier.

Finally, during the summer of 2004, Steve threw down one more challenge to his neighbors: a rough proposal for a large new home on his property to be designed by his brother, Donald. To meet the Vineyard's strict guidelines for homes that tower above the tree line, the builder had proposed that "much of the property would be removed and carted away" by hauling out an estimated five hundred truckloads of dirt and thus lowering the siting of the new house so it would not extend above the tree line. Since there are no limits on the size of single-family homes on Martha's Vineyard as long as the onerous restrictions on building heights and setbacks, among other things, are met, the West Tisbury Planning Board could not stop the project although it tried to thwart it by referring the matter to the Martha's Vineyard Commission. The planning board asked Steve "to exercise restraint on his property." In September 2006, the Martha's Vineyard Commission voted 10–3 not to block the Rattners' plan to move their existing home to an adjacent lot and then to construct a new "trophy home" consisting of 15,575 gross square feet on the original home site overlooking Vineyard Sound.

❋

Within days of the second *Vanity Fair* article in as many years that featured Steve, the shoes began to drop in the firm's municipal finance scandals. On October 26, 1995, a federal grand jury indicted Ferber on sixty-three counts of fraud, attempted extortion, and acceptance of gratuities as part of his scheme to pressure Wall Street firms to give Lazard business in exchange for recommending them as underwriters of municipal bonds. A three-month trial in federal court ended in August 1996 with Ferber's conviction on fifty-eight of the counts. He was sentenced to thirty-three months in McKean federal prison in Bradford, Pennsylvania. He also was fined $1 million.

The same day Ferber was indicted, Lazard and Merrill each agreed to settle charges with the SEC that they willfully violated Rule G-17 of the Municipal Securities Rulemaking Board requiring securities firms to "deal fairly with all persons and . . . not engage in any deceptive, dishonest, or unfair practice." The SEC faulted Lazard for failing to have "a procedure" in place to accurately determine whether or not Ferber had told his New York partners that he had disclosed to his clients the existence of the Lazard-Merrill contract. But, the agreement said, Lazard's partners knew about the Lazard-Merrill contract and knew that it "created at least a potential conflict of interest for Lazard" and "Lazard did not take adequate steps to ensure that Mark Ferber met his obligations to disclose the true nature and extent of the contract." The SEC censured the firm, which, together with Merrill, agreed to pay a $24 million fine—$12 million each—to settle the charges. At the time, the fine was the largest in the municipal finance industry. Lazard issued a statement confirming the settlement agreement and pointed out that the investigation "uncovered no evidence that any of Lazard's other partners had knowledge of, participated in, or approved of any such misconduct" and that "Ferber actively misled his Lazard partners concerning disclosure of the contractual arrangement" with Merrill. The firm said it was "saddened by Mr. Ferber's apparent violation of the Firm's ethical standards." Much of the reporting about the municipal finance scandals couldn't help but mention Felix, since it was so ironic that Lazard—the firm synonymous with the man who saved New York—was caught up in a major scandal involving cities and states all across the country. "He was upset that his name was appearing in press stories about this," said one partner. On November 30, 1995, years after Loomis had recommended it, Lazard disbanded its municipal finance department and quit the business.

OBVIOUSLY FRUSTRATED WITH a dynamic inside Lazard that resulted in costly scandal in the municipal finance department, to say nothing of the titanic struggle over supremacy between himself and Steve, Felix made a bid, in February 1996, to become vice chairman of the Federal Reserve

Board. The ill-advised effort, which all agreed was for a position well beneath his stature and accomplishments, ended swiftly in about a week when Felix withdrew his name from consideration in the face of seemingly endless protests from Senate Republicans—and without a hint of public support from Clinton during the ordeal.

Felix's mysterious desire for the Fed position had its origins in his own ample ambition, his frustration at not being selected Clinton's Treasury secretary, and, of course, his overwhelming—and now painfully obvious—desire to leave Lazard, but only for a position in government that was worthy of him.

During the mid-1990s, Felix had been closely monitoring the U.S. economy as it emerged from the Gulf War recession and before it exploded during the late 1990s. He felt that the economy could sustain a real growth rate of greater than the 2.5 percent per year White House economists were modeling and, accordingly, that Alan Greenspan's effort to slow the economy by doubling interest rates in 1994 and 1995 to 6 percent was simply bad monetary policy. In hindsight, doubling interest rates in twelve months without so much as a hint to the market *was* poor monetary policy, as the bond market plunged, which proved fatal, or nearly fatal, for, among others, Kidder, Peabody, the venerable investment bank founded in 1865; Orange County, California; and the Mexican economy. (Nowadays, the Fed telegraphs monetary policy months in advance.)

Alan Blinder, the Fed vice chairman, had long been frustrated with Greenspan on any number of topics, from interest rates to his own lack of career advancement, and so when his two-year term expired in early 1996, he chose not to seek reappointment and returned to Princeton. Felix had his opening. When Laura D'Andrea Tyson, head of the National Economic Council, canvassed Felix's views as to possible successors to Blinder, he surprised her by volunteering himself for the position. She tried to talk him out of it, explaining Blinder's frustrations with Greenspan, the position's inherent flaws, its subordinate role, and that it required attendance at boring meetings—in sum, not at all a role for a Great Man of Felix's experience, reputation, and proclivities. Felix liked to suck the air out of every room he entered; the conflict with Greenspan would be inevitable, and not pretty to watch. "We're friends," he explained to Tyson about Greenspan. "We've known each other for a long time. It would be different because we're friends. I would be able to have more influence."

Clinton loved the idea. He was eager for resolution on this whole question of real growth rates—and of course, a crumbling bond market would not be welcome news at election time. "We'll have a really interesting debate, a national debate about this issue between the Fed chair and the vice chair," he said privately. Clinton loved the politics of the Rohatyn appointment, too. The president could reappoint Greenspan, not inevitable at that precise moment as his term was to expire in a few months, and know that his man Felix would keep a close eye on the uncontrollable Fed chairman, a Republican no less. Tyson tried to persuade Clinton, to no avail, that economic warfare at the Fed served no purpose. In the end, though, she informed Felix of the president's enthusiasm. Thinking he had Clinton's support, Felix began calling in his chits from his corporate chieftain friends, and they responded by lobbying their contacts in Washington on Felix's behalf. Felix failed, though, to inform Michel that he wanted to go to the Fed. "That didn't make Michel happy," one observer said.

Then Blinder called. "Why are you doing it?" he asked Felix. "I'm leaving because I can't stand it." He conveyed to Felix the same message that Tyson had: everything at the Fed revolves around Greenspan; the staff is the next all-powerful force, implementing the chairman's bidding and "squelch[ing] dissident thoughts or alternative thinking unless Greenspan agreed," according to Bob Woodward's *Maestro*. Felix's wife, Liz, was in violent agreement with Blinder. "You're crazy," she told her husband. "You're lucky they don't lock you in a closet. Nobody will ever see you again. How would you have felt, when you were chairman of MAC, if Hugh Carey had put in Alan Greenspan as vice chairman of MAC? Would you have liked that?" Felix told Liz, "No, probably not." What Tyson, Blinder, and Liz had underestimated was Felix's twin desires to escape the Lazard insanity and to have, finally, a Jean Monnet–like chance, however modest, to influence the national political debate. For his part, Felix again badly misjudged the politics of the situation.

On January 19, 1996, the *Wall Street Journal* reported that Clinton was likely to name Felix to the vice chair post at the Fed, with all the usual plaudits about Felix's investment banking prowess, including the nugget "Unlike some previous Fed vice chairmen, Mr. Rohatyn probably would be seen as Mr. Greenspan's likely successor—if the Fed chairman were to leave office while a Democrat was president." Opposition from the Republicans on the Senate Banking Committee to Felix's nomination was swift—and devastating. The Republican senator Connie Mack, from Florida, blasted Felix immediately and publicly as a dangerous, big-government, liberal interventionist. Senator Al D'Amato, then the chairman of the Senate Banking Committee and a Republican from New York, didn't need to say much of anything; after first contemplating a run against D'Amato, Felix had opposed his reelection in 1992. Republican congressional staffers sent Senator Mack a memo complaining; "Put simply: R-O-H-A-T-Y-N spells stagflation," a reference to the low-growth, high-inflation 1970s. Felix was caught in a political vortex the likes of which this experienced man of the world could hardly imagine. On the one hand, the Republicans controlled the Senate, making iffy the ratification of any Democratic nominee of a Democratic president in the highly partisan Clinton Washington. Therefore, the boisterous opposition from the Republicans was to be expected and could easily serve as cover for the more subtle machinations going on behind closed doors. This, in fact, is what occurred, Woodward argued. He claimed both Rubin and Greenspan were sufficiently lukewarm about the Rohatyn appointment that they effectively killed it. Greenspan, the Republican, subtly communicated his indifference to the Republican senators. And Rubin served as the messenger.

"What will happen if we send you Greenspan as chairman and Rohatyn as vice chairman?" Rubin asked Senator Robert Bennett, Republican of Utah, on the committee.

"We will confirm Greenspan in a heartbeat," Bennett answered, "and Rohatyn will not get out of committee."

"Yeah, but they go together," Rubin responded. "We'll send them up together."

"It will take a nanosecond to separate them," the senator responded, "and Greenspan will be confirmed . . . and Rohatyn will be filibustered until Connie Mack doesn't have a breath left in his body."

Rubin had got what he came for.

Next came the requisite well-orchestrated media assault challenging the wisdom of Felix's economic views about growth rates. On January 29, the *Washington Post* ran a front-page story reporting that many economists, including Greenspan, doubted the higher-growth-rate scenario. Paul Krugman, then a Stanford economist and now a columnist for the *New York Times,* wrote in the *New York Times Magazine* that higher-growth-rate proponents like "financier-pundit Felix Rohatyn" were living a "delightful fairy tale." He continued, "In fact, the so-called revolutions in management, information technology and globalization are vastly overrated by their acolytes."

And that was pretty much it. On February 12, Felix sent his withdrawal letter to Clinton and spoke with Rubin and Greenspan.

A few days later, after it was over, Felix received a call from the White House telling him Clinton would be at a $1,000-a-plate fundraising dinner February 15 at the Sheraton Hotel in New York and wanted to publicly thank him. When Felix arrived at the Sheraton, he ran into Vice President Al Gore and told him he could not stay for the dinner because he had something else to do. Although the president had never publicly stood up for Felix as his nomination was going down in flames, at the Sheraton, Clinton lambasted the Republicans for playing politics with the Rohatyn nomination. "An example of what should not be done that most people in this room are familiar with was the outrageous political treatment of my intention to nominate Felix Rohatyn to be the vice chairman of the Federal Reserve." He then asked Felix to stand and take a bow, but Felix had already left the event. Somebody stood up, and people started to applaud anyway.

Felix basked in the momentary glow of the president's adulation, as reported in the press, but the whole Fed incident was an ugly one for Felix and for Lazard—on many levels. To that point, much of the internal squabbling among the senior partners had been kept quiet, even to others working at Lazard. But the Federal Reserve debacle made clear to all that Felix wanted out of the firm and that his younger partners were expecting him to leave. How else to explain his desire to aggressively seek a subordinate position that seemed well beneath his aspirations and capabilities? "Michel has been buttressing himself" for the day Felix would leave, one partner observed. "And the Fed thing shows how right he was to do it. It's out in the open now that Felix has basically said, *I want to get out.*" Although it was not a job that made a whole lot of sense for Felix, he was not happy the Fed appointment did not happen. He was cranky and displeased. Word started to get around town that he was badmouthing Steve wherever and whenever he could. "Felix is angry and bitter," Steve told a friend as these stories reached his ears. "He's not aging well."

Finally, the volcano erupted. In the second week of March 1996, the reporter Suzanna Andrews struck again, with a cover story for *New York,* whose title, "Felix Loses It," was emblazoned in thick black seventy-two-point type underneath a less than flattering close-up of a piqued Felix. The *New York* piece laid bare just how horrible and irreconcilable the differences between Felix and Steve had become. There, for the first time in living color, was Felix's anger about the *Vanity Fair* articles, the Paramount leaks, the mischaracterization of Steve as his "protégé," the jealousy over Steve's relentless social and political climbing. Andrews wrote that Lazard was a "mean" place, and it was true.

The story came about serendipitously. Andrews had been interviewing Felix in his new, most un-Lazard-like, luxurious office in 30 Rockefeller Plaza (where Michel was said to have chosen the carpets) for a story she was writing for the March 1996 *Institutional Investor* about Gershon Kekst, the dean of Wall Street public relations and a longtime Felix friend. Kekst had been heavily involved in the Paramount-Viacom deal, and Andrews wanted to talk to Felix about Kekst's role for the profile.

Given how upset Felix continued to be with Steve for the *Vanity Fair* piece and for his role in the Paramount deal, unbeknownst to her, Andrews was merely touching a match to *very* dry wood. "I don't believe Felix ever intended that this would be an on-the-record attack," Andrews explained some ten years later. "I think if Felix had had his way, I was to be yet another reporter going out, getting the dirt on Steve, and writing a story about how Steve Rattner was under fire at Lazard and should lose his job because he had really messed up the Paramount deal. And Felix's fingerprints would not have shown up on the story at all. That's how I believe he expected it would go, which is why he never bothered to put the interview on background, or off the record. I think he was playing a game the way he'd played it with reporters for so long, he'd forgotten the original rules."

During the on-the-record interview about Kekst, Felix spewed venom, unsolicited, about Steve. "Steve is so monomaniacal," Felix blurted out in a fit of Freudian rage. "He wants a job in the Clinton Administration. Eventually he wants to be Treasury secretary, and he's trying to get it by getting media attention and by social climbing, without doing any public service. He should do public service, but he doesn't care about anything, not music, not art, not politics. He just wants to get ahead." Felix also told Andrews that "Steve's position at the firm is by no means secure." Andrews took it all down. When Steve coincidentally had sushi lunch at Hatsuhana with Andrews a day or so later just after she had heard Felix's diatribe, she told him about the incident. "I hope you throw away your notebook," Steve told her. She did not, of course, and ended up writing the single most inflammatory, unscripted, and revealing article in the firm's history.

Investment banking is a confidence game, and no single firm in the post–World War II years had been better than Lazard at continuously using and controlling the press—whether by serendipity or by design—to weave a magical spell about its uniqueness and moral and intellectual superiority. This proved to be very good for business—a form of catnip for clients. Much of the carefully cultivated mythology about the firm carried with it significant elements of truth: Lazard *was* different from other Wall Street firms. For a long time, Lazard was able to attract the most successful, most intelligent, most differentiated bankers. Year after year, it was able to pay its partners, in cash, far more money than they could have made at other Wall Street firms, all from the tiniest base of capital. There was indeed alchemy in the firm's ability—with very little at risk but its reputation—to turn its partners' relationships and advice into vast wealth. Long before other firms, the Lazard brothers recognized the importance of international finance, and its interconnectedness, and established indigenous and respected firms in the three global money centers—Paris, London, and New York. And only Lazard had André Meyer and Felix Rohatyn, two of the most powerful and successful investment bankers of the last fifty years.

But the fairy tale was taking a dark turn. Under Michel's leadership, Lazard's historically tiny head count had grown significantly, along with its revenues and its profitability. Michel, though, was far less of a hands-on manager than André had been, and things started getting out of control: a rash of problems befell the firm, from scandals involving insider trading and municipal finance to internal battles among the partners for Michel's favor. Then there was the inevitable generational question of succession. Michel had four daughters with interests outside of finance, and besides, Lazard was no place for a woman. Felix had no interest in running the firm but continuously thwarted those people who tried. Inevitably, as both Felix and Michel got well into their sixties, the younger partners began to chafe and push for more responsibility and a clarification of the firm's—and their own—future. Most of these unorganized and inchoate efforts by the younger partners went nowhere, effectively quashed by their own lack of coordination or the power of Michel and Felix to derail them or a combination of the two. Lazard was not a happy place; Andrews was right, it was *mean.* Only Steve, for the first time since Michel took the mantle from André, had the power—through his growing revenues and public profile—to challenge Felix. The truism that Wall Street runs on personal alliances and enmities was laid bare, by Andrews, in the pages of *New York* magazine.

After stating that Felix's surprise bid to be vice chairman of the Fed seemed nothing more than an inelegant effort to leave the firm, Andrews observed that "in the past few years, Lazard has begun to change in ways that have loosened Rohatyn's grip—changes not just in the mix of business at the firm but in the growing influence of a generation of younger partners." She quoted an unnamed "younger partner" who confided his view that "there is a perception that Felix is part of the problem" and then repeated a joke making the rounds inside the firm: "What's the difference between God and Felix Rohatyn? God doesn't think he's Felix Rohatyn." The article described how Steve was "a yuppie version" of Felix, with his deal success, his media attention, his enormous Rolodex. Then there were the descriptions of the "widely coveted" invitations to the Rattners' apartment on Fifth Avenue, where the likes of Mickey Kantor, Vartan Gregorian, and Henry Louis Gates would be celebrated, or to their annual August cocktail bash on Martha's Vineyard, where the First Family were regulars, along with friends Harvey Weinstein and Brian Roberts. The Rattners' stay in the Lincoln Bedroom in July 1995 "is known by all who need to know," Andrews wrote, noting that the visit included "private time for bonding" with the Clintons.

The idea that Steve had become Felix's protégé—an idea that both men for a time actively encouraged—was conveniently debunked. Felix "never wanted" a protégé, offered an unnamed friend of Felix's. "You have to understand," this person continued, "Felix is *alone*," and despised the idea of a chosen successor. Felix believed Steve was way out ahead of his skis. "Felix has worked so hard," said another Felix stalwart. "He suffered in the war and under André. He did MAC. I think it is emotionally and intellectually insulting to him that Steve Rattner would be considered his heir apparent." The Freudian aspect of the feud was difficult to ignore. "I don't understand why a man like Felix, who has done so much good and who is recognized for it, cannot be at peace," a source told Andrews. "Steve is a good banker. He has very limited experience in terms of the kinds of businesses he has handled. He has not achieved much on the public service front yet. Why does Felix feel the need to crush him?" Another friend of Steve's told Andrews: "Maybe Steve wants to be president of Brown or the Metropolitan Museum, maybe he would take a deputy-secretary job in Washington, but I don't think he's kidding himself about being Secretary of the Treasury in fifteen years."

Nowhere, of course, in the *New York* article was there any admission from Felix that perhaps Steve, so very much like Felix himself, had actually outmaneuvered and outperformed the older man in this extremely high-profile, high-stakes game. Maybe such an admission would have required from Felix the kind of self-awareness he does not possess. But even an amateur psychologist could quickly conclude that Felix's actions during the mid-1990s—the lashing out publicly, the accusations of professional indiscretion, the contemplation of the World Bank job, the bid for the Fed—were also obvious signs of jealousy and frustration. Said another man, who claimed to know both Steve and Felix well: "The son is getting too successful, so what does the father do but go after him for things he suspects are in himself?" Said another "mutual friend": "I know both Steve and Felix well enough to say they are the same man."

Right on cue, Arthur Sulzberger Jr. rose to Steve's defense in the *New York* article. He was one of two people quoted on the record on Steve's behalf; the other was Steve's friend and former *Times* colleague Paul Goldberger. "It is almost a crime that a story in *Vanity Fair* should help or hurt anyone," Sulzberger said, and then referred to Felix's accusation that Steve had been the source of the leaks from the Paramount boardroom. "It's like asking if a story in *Midnight Magazine* can affect you. It's so fucking vacuous. Hurting Lazard is antithetical to everything Steve believes in. Whether or not it was another source, I don't believe adults would deal with it this way." He explained Steve's media savvy as a natural outgrowth of having been a reporter for so many years, unlike Felix, who had to work hard to cultivate and seduce journalists. "Steve doesn't collect people," the publisher of the *Times* continued. "He attracts them. I have seen Felix at more events than I have seen Steve. You can't accuse Steve of being a media climber without saying that he and the publisher of the *New York Times* had desks next to each other for two and a half years. Steve is good with the media because he was a talented member for many years. It's not true of Felix or lots of other people who have had to learn it for their own particular purposes."

Reflecting back some ten years later about the generational struggle between Felix and Steve at Lazard, Sulzberger remarked:

> Culture change is hard. Culture change is hard in any organization. What Steve was trying to do at Lazard was to bring that culture into line with where people had gone already. The culture of large companies in the 1950s, 1960s, and 1970s was driven by the deals that people made who had the experience of the 1930s and 1940s. What were the experiences of the 1930s and 1940s? Great Depression and World War II. And so you had a generation of people coming in to work in the 1950s and 1960s and really achieving authority in the 1970s, 1980s, early 1990s. And the deal was this: "I saw the Great Depression. You don't fire me, and I won't ask about being fulfilled . . ." But now you've got a whole new generation whose life experience is the 1960s. And they're saying, "Wait a second, my whole life is about more freedom, more flexibility. And by the way I grew up in the fat times. I could go across the street and get another job, and then if I don't like that, I can go across the street and get another job. So I want to be happy. I want to be fulfilled. I want my voice heard." So you've got those two cultures coming into

> friction as you have a shift in leadership taking place. And this is not a Lazard problem. It's not a New York Times problem. It is the cultural shift that had to take place in this country.

In truth, along with the generational and cultural clash that it exposed, the *New York* article itself was also a masterpiece of Steve's ability to manipulate the press for his own benefit. After Steve heard from Andrews at Hatsuhana that an assault on him was coming, it is clear from the published article that any number of sources were mobilized on his behalf to mitigate the damage. There were the obvious sources, of course, such as his über–*Times* friends, Sulzberger and Goldberger, but there were, naturally, any number of unnamed sources that steered Andrews toward a far more favorable appraisal of Steve than the one Felix had presented to her. Indeed, the very title of the piece, "Felix Loses It," suggests that the editors of *New York* thought that *Felix* was the one whose judgment deserved questioning, not vice versa. There were deft touches such as blaming the boardroom leaks found in "Paramount Player" on Marty Davis, thereby deflating a large part of Felix's proclaimed source of anger with Steve for the *Vanity Fair* article. And there were unattributed quotations from current and former partners that damned Felix for his treatment of them over the years. "The success and the dysfunction of Lazard," said one, "has a lot to do with Felix's role. He isn't interested in managing, or teaching, or leading. When someone gets out of line, he crushes them and walks away."

Then there were other masterful pieces of obfuscation and irrelevance, such as a purely gossipy item about Michel that had never before appeared in print: to wit, that when in New York he had been carrying on a longtime, discreet extramarital affair with the "socialite" Margo Walker, who lived (and lives) around the corner from him in Locust Valley, Long Island, on an estate—previously owned by J. P. Morgan Jr.'s son, Junius—that Michel helped her to buy in 1994. The not-so-subtle message, of course, was that the fish rots from the head.

CHAPTER 14

"It's a White Man's World"

There is a much-discussed story in the Lazard annals about a private-jet trip that the CEO of an important client took with Michel, Lou Perlmutter, and their wives down to a gathering at Caneel Bay in the U.S. Virgin Islands. "And here they are at twenty-five thousand feet," explained a Lazard partner.

> Three odd couples. The CEO is a good guy, Midwestern, good-looking, white button-down shirt. Just what you would expect. And somehow the discussion got to be about the difficulties of getting into college in the U.S. And the CEO starts telling the story about his seventeen-year-old son, eighteen-year-old son, who was going to be taking the SAT test and how they hired a tutor for the English and the math. Once or twice a week you have these prep sessions. Anyway, they hired a teacher from the school, he was at a private school, and they hired a teacher. So the CEO and his wife are out one night and the wife gets sick and asks to come home early. And they come back after forty-five minutes or so or something like that, and they find the kid in the sack with the SAT prep teacher. Lou Perlmutter can't believe this story. The CEO is sort of baring his soul a little bit. Well, Lou didn't know what to say. The first person to speak was Michel, who offered his very French way of consoling, of expressing his sympathies for the CEO. His comment was, "Well, I think an experience like that can be very valuable to a young man." Lou said that one incident just summarized Michel's view of sexual harassment: It's open season. It's part of life. And everybody's behavior in the firm, you know, followed down from that. And that led to the whole lack of discipline and lack of accountability.

Sadly, this is an accurate assessment of the plight of women at Lazard. Equally discomfiting, there is no question that the firm's treatment of its women over the years has derived from, shall we say, the *Eu-*

ropean sensibilities of the firm's most senior partners. André had many affairs, as did Pierre David-Weill. Michel said his father was "a natural" with women because he was quietly confident and very charming. "I have never seen it to that extent," he explained. "He just found it so normal and evident that if a lady was beautiful and he found her attractive why didn't they go to bed together? Why not? I think women were pretty convinced but disarmed in a way. All their defenses were useless. So he was very gifted that way." Michel's stepmother was not happy with the arrangement but accepted it, more or less. "I mean it's a fact of life," he said. As for his client's son, Michel said—years later—"He was a lucky young man."

Less than a mile away as the crow flies from Viking's Cove, Michel's Locust Valley home, sits Morgan's Island, a 140-acre boot jutting into Long Island Sound, due north of Glen Cove and adjacent to the 110-acre tidal lake known as Dosoris Pond. Morgan's Island, also known locally as East Island, is connected to Long Island by a stone bridge J. P. Morgan Jr.—Jack—had constructed using stones taken from the demolished Harlem Bridge in Manhattan. In 1929, just to show that the partners of the house of Morgan still had plenty of cash at their disposal after the market crash, Morgan's son, Junius Spencer Morgan, built Salutations, a forty-room stone mansion on what has become known as West Island, or Dana's Island, an eighty-eight-acre heart-shaped promontory adjacent to his father's island. Son and grandson Morgan lived like the barons they were on these two adjacent islands off the Gold Coast of Long Island; many scholars believe that F. Scott Fitzgerald memorialized the two islands in *The Great Gatsby* as West Egg and East Egg. In April 1960, Junius Spencer Morgan celebrated at Salutations, along with eight hundred invited guests, the first anniversary of the historic merger of Guaranty Trust and J. P. Morgan & Co. He died six months later, at age sixty-eight, from ulcers suffered on a hunting trip in Ontario. After Junius's wife, Louise, died in 1993, her estate put the mansion up for auction.

The buyer, who paid "several million dollars" turned out to be Margaret "Margo" Walker, Michel's longtime mistress. With Michel's help, she had already purchased three of the five houses on West Island. At Salutations, there is an indoor swimming pool and an outdoor swimming pool; an indoor tennis court and an outdoor tennis court. There are beautiful gardens and a stunning view across Long Island Sound. In 2000, Walker bought the fifth house on the island and now owns the island and all the houses on it. She rents them out to a well-heeled crowd, once they have passed muster with her. Among the renters have been Stephen

Volk, since July 2004 a vice chairman of Citigroup, and Richard Plepler, an executive at Time Warner's HBO. Jeff Sechrest, a current Lazard partner covering the media industry, also rents a house from Walker. In years past, three former Lazard partners, Robert Agostinelli, Steve Langman, and Luis Rinaldini, now head of Groton Partners, his own advisory firm, have also rented from Walker. So far, she has refused the repeated requests of her A-list renters to buy the homes.

After driving over the short stone bridge, all the renters arrive at a closed iron gate. To gain access, they punch a secret code into an electronic monitoring system, which opens the gate. Two roads wind through the spit of land, Salutation Road and Pond Road, but access to them is restricted unless you have the code that opens the gate. Walker has been described less than favorably, when she has been described at all. "She has this house with birds that fly around inside," a "friend" told *Vanity Fair* in 1997. A "New York fashion editor" also told the magazine, "She's a total eccentric. She'll walk you around her properties in spiky heels. Margo must be—what?—in her 50s? But she's still the complete sweater girl, always perfectly groomed." She has two children with her former husband, David Walker.

Neighbors, of course, wonder where Margo, a local real estate broker (whom, although he disputes it, Michel once tried to get his partner Disque Deane to hire; Deane declined), got the money to buy the properties, which are now said to be collectively worth around $100 million. All roads—correctly—lead to Michel. "Fees for services rendered," sniffed one former Lazard partner. Having a wife and a mistress has occasionally led to some curious, schizophrenic behavior. A Lazard partner tells the story of how he was outside Michel's office one day—waiting to go in to see him—when he overheard Annik having to juggle phone calls from the two women simultaneously. On one phone line was Margo, for whom Annik was arranging a private jet to take her to Moscow, at a cost of $100,000. On the other line was Hélène, reminding Annik to return rented videos to the video store in order not to be charged a two-dollar late fee. During one of our many interviews—this one at his magnificent Paris home—I asked Michel about his relationship with Margo. Moments before, he had introduced me to Hélène, his thin and somewhat dour wife of fifty years, as she walked through the grand living room where we were meeting. Although *New York* disclosed the relationship in 1996, Michel seemed to shudder visibly at the question and asked me, for the only time in all of our many meetings, to turn off the tape recorder. He then proceeded to explain that while it may be difficult for an American to understand, he had been able to create for himself loving relationships with both of these women. He said he loved both Hélène, the mother of his four daughters, and Margo, whom he has been with for some twenty-five years. They both understand the arrangement, although he conceded that Hélène might be less sympathetic to it than Margo. Margo knows, he said, that he would never leave his wife but believes "half of Michel is better than the whole of someone else." How very French.

His sensitivity on the subject, while perfectly understandable, derives not from any personal shame but rather from, he said, the love he has for his wife. Hélène, he said, had suffered from the affair's disclosure and from the chattering of her friends in New York. (In Paris, her friends are more accepting, he explained.) His concern is for "my wife, who is not terribly sensitive, but is fairly sensitive to the subject," he said. "And I love her dearly." Michel said that he lamented his wife's pain in this regard but that Margo continues to be an equally important part of his life: they still travel together to exotic locations around the globe and see each other in the "country" on Long Island. Whereas in the past Michel would occasionally go out with Margo in New York City, now they are far more discreet socially. Yes, he explained, he did help Margo with the "financing" of the purchase of the houses on West Island, but the Junius Morgan house was an "opportunity" because it was being sold in distress by Mrs. Morgan's estate. And about that he was certainly correct. One person who understands well Michel's approach to women explained: "He adored his girls, but he's French, so he's, you know, women are there to be dressed and fed and fucked."

Another, possibly apocryphal, story about indiscretions with women involves Felix. In the 1970s, before he remarried, he had quite a reputation as a ladies' man. In one particular tale, André Meyer came looking for Felix one day in his office, only to find the door locked. This was unusual at the time. So André, a man without much patience, knocked briskly on the door and called Felix's name. No answer. André knocked again. Still no answer. Finally he yelled, loud enough to be heard around the floor, "Felix, why don't you go to a hotel room like the rest of my partners!"—a perfectly logical request given that many of his partners *did* in fact have hotel rooms. Word was that Felix was behind locked doors with the actress Shirley MacLaine. Others remembered the incident well but said Felix was there with a secretary, who shortly thereafter enrolled—at no cost to her—in business school and later worked on Wall Street.

In an interview, Felix said he had heard this story about him before many times. And he was not happy to be asked about it. "No, it didn't happen," he stated firmly. "I didn't need the office to get laid." He said he never dated Shirley MacLaine and may have been on a date with Barbara Walters—despite their liaisons being much rumored—"once," along with Howard Stein and his wife at a Chinese restaurant. In 1977, about a year before he remarried, Felix moved from the Alrae, where he had supposedly lived the bachelor life, into a duplex on the twelfth and thirteenth floors at 770 Park Avenue. His partner Alan McFarland was the president of the co-op board, and he helped Felix get into the building. "Getting into our building was a real pain in the ass," McFarland said. "I had to do a favor for a friend who was the executor of the estate, selling it to Felix." After Felix got into 770 Park, McFarland watched as he "moved from bachelor around town to marry Liz and set up shop in this huge apartment in the back of my building." But apparently, Felix had not settled down completely. As the story goes, according to a former partner, two hookers showed up at the same time one night in the lobby of 770 Park, and each of them asked for Felix. Both Felix and McFarland ended up in the lobby to settle the dispute. Still, Felix had a reputation around both New York and Lazard of being an inveterate flirt. "When I was there he had a terrible reputation, I mean for having affairs and for hitting on women," said a young woman who was at the firm around 1990. "I mean, he was like notorious."

Needless to say, this misogynist, profligate behavior, such as it was, trickled down throughout Lazard. There was one horrible story about a particularly attractive secretary in the bond department, who had coincidentally dated Robert Agostinelli when Robert was still an undergraduate at Columbia. "Like all these beautiful young girls, she wanted to build herself a career," one Lazard partner recalled. "She was going to school, and she got a job working at Lazard. And she was very good-looking. I'm sure she got the job—she's smart, too—but she got it because she was really beautiful." Anyway, one night, she called Agostinelli in London, where he was working for Jacob Rothschild, years before he came to Lazard.

Previously, when they would occasionally speak, Agostinelli would try to warn her to be careful about Wall Street bankers. "And sure enough, she got taken to one of these parties by this preppy crowd—one guy from Lazard Brothers and one guy from Lazard New York—and they allegedly date-raped her," a Lazard banker said. "They fed her a Mickey and viciously raped her in this guy's Park Avenue apartment." But the two Lazard bankers were not prosecuted. "Lazard being the way it is, they were both eased out," someone familiar with the incident explained. Bill Loomis chalked up the firm's shameful treatment of its women to a number of factors. First, he said, "I think the firm was small and had no tradition—as Wall Street generally didn't—of treating women with equality of opportunity." There was simply no infrastructure at the firm, or any policies, to deal with issues such as sexual harassment, diversity, recruiting, or mentoring. The bigger, more institutional firms, such as Goldman Sachs and Morgan Stanley, were able to focus on improving these problems far more quickly than Lazard. Lazard's DNA continuously rejected any kind of bureaucracy to handle such things. Stuff happens. Move on. "We were kind of putting bricks together," Loomis said, "not pulling levers."

Very slowly, Loomis said, this began to change, but not always very successfully. There were no women professionals at Lazard—other than the secretaries—until around August 1980, when Mina Gerowin was hired, fresh out of Harvard Business School. Before Gerowin, the Lazard old-timers have a vague recollection of another woman professional being hired. "She'd been there for a couple of months," remembered one. "But she'd been killed off is my understanding, brutally." Given that the law of the land with regard to employers' discriminating against women had been in place since the Civil Rights Act of 1964, Lazard was not exactly acting in an enlightened way. But with Gerowin, the firm made a *tiny* bit more of an effort. Related by marriage to André Meyer, she was a lawyer and a Baker scholar at Harvard Business School. She had worked for Nestlé in Switzerland and spoke fluent French. She was one of the first women to attend classes at Amherst College before graduating from Smith. When she arrived in the late summer of 1980, the firm had her share an office with Peter Mattingly on the thirty-second floor—the partners' floor—at One Rockefeller Plaza. She would be sure to be seen by one and all. "It was a very small firm," Gerowin recalled. "I doubt if there were three hundred people, counting the coffee ladies. And you got a desk, and you punched all these numbers by hand. You had little HP calculators and that's it. No computers, no nothing. Lots of paper. Lots of models by hand." She also got plenty of unsolicited advice from various partners about how to survive at Lazard. But none of this advice prepared her for the education she received within weeks of joining the firm. She had been assigned to work with clients in the industrial heartland, which didn't necessarily play to her international experience. In any event, one day early on, she found herself riding the elevator with another associate, John Grambling Jr. (the same man who later spent years in prison for masterminding any number of schemes to steal millions of dollars from North American banks). Grambling had been working with Felix on a deal with Renault, the French carmaker. Once in the elevator with Gerowin, Grambling started to grope her and push himself on her.

She was appalled. "I told him to fuck off," she said. She knew from then on that she, too, needed to become more barracuda-like. She decided to get even, in her way. "I'm so frosted at this," she said. "This sleaze, his wife had a baby the week before. That's when I said, 'Screw this, get yourself on the French deal, he ain't going to last long anyway, the way the kid's behaving.' I didn't know about the other stuff at the time. I just knew this guy did not understand reality." Soon after the incident, when she saw Felix talking to one of the senior Renault executives in the thirty-second-floor hallway, she went up to them and, in perfect French, offered to help out on the deal. Grambling spoke no French. Next thing she knew she was on the deal and Grambling was gone.

She worked for several years on various assignments for Renault as it slowly acquired Mack Trucks—first Renault took a 10 percent stake, then 20 percent, then 40 percent, until eventually Mack became a wholly owned subsidiary of Renault. It was very touch-and-go and very hard work. She had no life outside the firm. She worked directly with Felix and with David Supino. After Renault increased its stake in Mack to 40 percent, in 1983, Lazard received a huge fee, something like $8 million, one of the largest fees in its history to that point. But Felix never thanked Gerowin for her hard work.

Of course, there was more insult. Once, Allan Chapin, then a partner at Sullivan & Cromwell, the law firm (years later Chapin was briefly a partner at Lazard), organized a closing dinner for a Renault-Mack deal at one of the private clubs on the East Side. But the club did not allow women as members, nor did it, incredibly, allow women to enter the dining room. When Gerowin tried to join the dinner, she was not permitted into the dining room. The matter greatly offended the CFO of Renault, for whom the dinner had been arranged. "He heard what was happening," Gerowin recalled, "and says, 'Renault is owned by the government of France, we are a fair and equal opportunity employer. We cannot have a to-do. So I will go and have dinner with Mina.' " So the guest of honor left the event and had dinner with Gerowin. "His answer to Chapin was, '*Il y a mille restaurants au New York.*' There are a thousand restaurants in New York. You schmuck. You had to put it in this one? So he and I went and had dinner and the rest of them went to Allan Chapin's dinner and the next morning I explained to George Ames what had happened at the dinner. I didn't realize that this guy also told Michel."

Michel decided that Lazard's honor had been impugned, and for a brief time Sullivan & Cromwell was in the penalty box with Lazard. But only for a brief time. "So did these things happen?" Gerowin asked rhetorically. "You bet they did. I told you, 'You just never let them see you cry.' Actually, things reached a point where I didn't even cry. I would just be seething, absolutely seething." She often felt she would be assigned work the male bankers didn't want to do. And there was also the problem that some of the partners did not want to work with a woman. "You'd walk into their office, and they'd go into a cold sweat," she said. The best it got for her, she explained, was when after she had done some work for Ward Woods, he managed to give her a backhanded compliment at the year-end review meeting. Gerowin was told that Woods said: "I don't know why she's here. I don't think we should have women here. . . . But you know what? If we've got to have them here, I gotta say she did a hell of a good job." Recalled Gerowin: "I can deal with a guy like that."

After Gerowin had been at Lazard for a few years, the firm decided to hire a second woman banker, Linda Pohs. Pohs had been working at First Boston. There was a partners' meeting where the subject of hiring her came up. Jim Glanville spoke up at the meeting. "Why are we firing Mina?" he said. "She's getting the hang of it. The work seems okay. I don't understand why you're firing her for some unknown." Another partner corrected Glanville's misimpression of what was going on. "So someone finally said, 'We're not firing Mina,'" Gerowin recalled being told after the meeting. "This would be a second woman. And Glanville's answer was, 'I thought the EEO meant we only had to have one.' This should set the tone for you."

In August 1985, Gerowin's brother was killed in an airplane crash. Naturally, this caused her to rethink her goals and how she wanted to spend her life. She had given her all to the firm for the previous five years and received little but grief in return. "It was so brutal," she said. "I mean, my brother's death made me realize, you know what? I need a life. I'd given these guys a life." The tipping point came a couple months later when Bill Loomis asked her to lunch. "You're not being very productive lately," he told her. "I say, 'My brother died two months ago. We're still trying to find the airplane and lift it.' This was off of Block Island, and this guy looks at me and says, 'That was two months ago.' And it was like a snap awakening." She left Lazard about a year later, after being transferred to another department, to head up the restructuring advisory effort at Dean Witter, the brokerage firm that would later merge with Morgan Stanley. One longtime partner recalled that Gerowin did have a difficult time at the firm, partially for reasons unique to her and partially for reasons related to the slow changing attitudes toward women on Wall Street. "From the beginning, she had an unhappy experience," he said. "She didn't get along with partners. Frankly, I think it was very difficult then to be a woman. But I actually don't think it was about her being a woman; it was more just her working relationships and the work. At the time, though, the firm was extremely chauvinistic, as was Wall Street."

Gerowin may have paved the way for other women bankers at Lazard, but their task was no less imposing. Linda Pohs left the firm before the decade was out and soon thereafter married David Supino. Michael Carmody—a woman—joined Lazard after Pohs but left before her, supposedly a victim of unkept promises and harassment from the likes of Jim Glanville, Luis Rinaldini, and Felix. When she was pregnant, a Lazard partner said to her: "Why don't you just go home and do what you do best and have your baby?" After she was fired by the firm and threatened to sue, Wachtell, Lipton was brought in. She was said to have received a $1 million settlement from the firm and has moved to South Africa.

Sandy Lamb came from Mutual of New York. Christina Mohr came from Lehman Brothers. Kathy Kelly came from First Boston and Rothschild. Jenny Sullivan, Mary Conwell, and Susan McArthur all joined. These women were part of the general hiring wave on Wall Street in the 1980s that even Lazard could not avoid, per Loomis's recommendations. "And while we were one of a group of people, they built that firm on our backs," Kathy Kelly said. "And it would have been nice to have shared in the rewards. And I don't believe that by and large we did." The business was rapidly changing from being one where white men met and solved the social issues of mergers to one where white men met to solve the financial and social issues. The new crop of hires was proficient in the use of the computer programs that did the analytical work of relative valuation and dilution. These analyses became a new and integral part of the deal business. "And it was the beginning of seven of the most wonderful years of my life," Kelly said. "I have even tears welling in my eyes. Absolute, sheer unadulterated hell. But waking up every day was a pleasure because every day was an intellectual dialectic. Every day was a challenge. And you were working with people who weren't just smart. You could feel the tangible difference between yourself and their IQ. I mean, it was phenomenal." The new hires—men and women—were simply "utils," as one of them explained, "cogs in the machine." The problem for Lazard became what to do with the "utils" as they progressed and showed genuine promise as bankers. "Obviously that's where it becomes an issue," explained one of the women professionals at that time. "Because at the point at which you're no longer a util, there's a question of whether you become additive or a threat. Or just expense. You know what I mean? So it was a bit of a struggle without a lot of thought process around what you did with people in that gap between the time they were utils and the time they became gray-haired themselves. Let's just say there was a pretty long gap where you had to kind of fend for yourself."

To succeed at Lazard, the women bankers, even more so than the men, had to figure out a way to bring in business, the coin of the realm. Whereas some of the male bankers were paid well and were promoted for working on Felix's deals and "carrying his bags"—a role that had its own costs—and others seemed to get the deals that came in over the transom, neither of these more traditional avenues to success seemed to be available to the few women bankers at Lazard. Felix never chose one of the women as his understudy, although many of them said he was pleased to flirt with them and to work with them occasionally. Most of the women at Lazard could not figure out how to play this game or lost interest in trying. "It's a white man's world," one of them said. Kathy Kelly, for one, eschewed her social life for some seven years in favor of her Lazard career, and then on the day she thought she would finally be promoted to partner, she was fired.

"I believe that Bill Loomis, acting in my best interest, was absolutely right in letting me go," she said. "However, I don't believe if I had been one of the guys that I would have been let go." Christina Mohr gave it her all. She transformed herself into a tough, no-nonsense street fighter who refused to kowtow to the men at Lazard. She fit the stereotypical profile of the successful tough-as-nails female Wall Street banker. She occasionally smoked cigars. Within two *days* of giving birth to her children, she was back at the office. Nobody, at any level, worked harder than she did. She was not much fun to work for. She carved out for herself a niche of the clients that nobody else at Lazard wanted—in retail and in consumer products, ironically the traditional route of the outsiders and the immigrants. She started bringing in clients and winning business. She also sought to mentor the few younger women at the firm and act as a role model for them. She became the first female M&A partner at Lazard, in 1990. "I remember Michel saying to me at one point, you'll become a partner the year after it is evident to everyone that you are one," Mohr recalled. Added Loomis: "I think that Christina Mohr is a classic example. To be successful at Lazard as a woman partner, you had to be *better* than your peers."

Then there was the unique case of Marilyn LaMarche, who worked for many years in the backwater that was Lazard's equity syndication department. She was a bit of an anomaly, though. There was a time—almost laughable now—in the late 1970s and early 1980s when Lazard was considered a bulge-bracket equity underwriter. Lazard rarely led a deal (even though it was the lead underwriter for the IPO of the Henley

Group in 1986, one of the largest IPOs of all time), but the firm would be included in almost every equity underwriting syndicate because that's the way it was done at the time—when client relationships and capital were less important than the fact there was this set group of firms that did equity underwriting. LaMarche had Lazard's relationships with the institutional investors that bought the equity, and the firm made a fair amount of money as a result. Finally, in 1987, she was named a partner at age fifty-two. One of her partners explained why, in his opinion, LaMarche received this special treatment. "Basically she came back to her desk one day," he said, "and I understand there was a *turd* in a Baggie in her desk."

Another woman, Sandy Lamb, worked with David Supino on restructuring deals, and she became the second female Lazard partner in banking in 1992, when Supino's restructuring group was having a big financial impact on the firm in the wake of the slowdown in the traditional M&A business. The firm seemed to be slowly making some progress by the early 1990s with regard to its treatment of women. Lazard hired a woman named Nancy Cooper to create and run some sort of HR department, the firm's first such effort (and a miserable failure). Cooper was even a partner for a short time.

But that progress quickly came to a complete halt in the aftermath of the hiring of a beautiful young woman, an undergraduate at the highly regarded Wharton School at the University of Pennsylvania. Her name was Kate Bohner. She was athletic, tall, and striking, with long blond hair and long, muscular legs. When Bohner was in her junior year at Penn, she happened to be at a dinner party in New York on Valentine's Day 1987. She was seated next to Kim Taipale, an up-and-coming vice president at Lazard living in the East Village. They got to talking, and Taipale asked Bohner what she was thinking about doing for the summer between her junior and her senior years. Bohner said something about working at Goldman Sachs, and Taipale urged her to come to Lazard instead. Michel had just decided to shake things up at Lazard Brothers by installing a team of Lazard New York bankers there with the hope of having some of the American M&A techniques rub off on the British (who, of course, were disdainful of the whole exercise). Michel had asked Robert Agostinelli, Steve Langman, and Taipale to move to London to set up the Lazard Frères outpost inside Lazard Brothers. "Michel sent us over there to wind them up," one of them said. Taipale said the group needed a summer analyst. Would Bohner be interested in the job?

Bohner spent the summer in London working with the three New Yorkers, in a bull-pen-like setting, at Lazard Brothers. Their desks were catty-corner to one another. Bohner, then barely twenty, had a front-row seat on the deal business, Robert Agostinelli–style. "And there were no walls, so I could hear them negotiating, and I learned so much through osmosis," she said. This was a wonderful experience for Bohner. She had never before been exposed to international finance. She grew up in Wilmington, Delaware. Her father was chairman of the English department at the University of Delaware, and her mother was a poetry professor in the same department. When Bohner was a high school freshman in Wilmington, she was on the varsity lacrosse team. When she was fifteen, her mother left her father for her lacrosse coach. The coach happened to be a woman. "Remarkably, it wasn't as jarring as people assume," Bohner later wrote. "The experience taught me about a new type of permissive pluralism that I had not encountered before."

What she may not have fully realized, though, was the effect she had on men. After graduating from Wharton in 1988, she joined Lazard full-time, in August, in New York, as part of the two-year analyst-training program. But the uncontrolled, unhealthy Darwinian Lazard environment may have been a seriously wrong choice for her. She was like catnip. "I was very naive," she explained. "I was very young, extraordinarily naive. I had no idea what I was getting into. I mean, remember I didn't grow up in New York and both my parents were professors." She said that various partners—Agostinelli and Loomis, among them—tried to "protect" her from the lecherous behavior. They "still wouldn't have been able to protect me, because you can't," she said. "There wasn't a culture there, in terms of the abuse, to prevent the abuse. And the obvious sort of sexual harassment."

Shortly before Thanksgiving 1988, she received a call from her former London colleagues telling her to be on a plane to London that night to work on a deal with Agostinelli, Langman, and Taipale. What was supposed to be a few days turned into a six-month assignment, living in a swank London hotel, ordering room service and expensive champagne—and charging it all to the client. "Back then, if I was a client and I had seen the amount of expenses that we had, I would've been, like, horrified, totally," she said. Her roommates in New York would bring her clothes to Lazard at Rockefeller Center, and her secretary would FedEx them over to London. "I lived at Claridge's for six months," she said. "And my bill was like £87,000. They said I'd be home for Thanksgiving. I didn't get home for Christmas or Easter. So I just lived in a hotel and I worked from, like, eight in the morning until ten at night because room service closed at ten-thirty at Claridge's. I just did that every day." There is an old saw on Wall Street told to young new recruits: "You won't know your children. But you'll get to know your grandchildren really well." Bohner was quickly discovering the meaning of that remark. Her professional and social life revolved around her colleagues in the London office. Before long, she started dating Steve Langman, then a vice president and later a partner. Langman was married. They dated for the balance of Bohner's time at Lazard. Langman decided to leave his wife, even though she was around eight months pregnant. Bohner was also said to have dated the flamboyant Agostinelli, who had taken to having a gourmet chef prepare his meals for his overseas first-class flights and having Frette sheets FedExed to his hotel rooms in advance of his arrival.

When she returned to New York, she was put in the oil and gas group, working with the senior partners Jim Glanville and Ward Woods. This proved to be quite treacherous for her. She started working on the IPO of Sterling Chemicals, a private company based in Houston owned by the iconoclastic investor Gordon Cain. One late afternoon, she and Glanville were in Glanville's car on the way to the airport to catch the last plane to Houston to work on the offering. By this time, Glanville was well into his sixties, overweight, and craggy. According to Bohner, he had his driver purposely get lost in Queens, and then, when it was obvious that the last flight to Houston had been missed, he suggested that they take the first flight out in the morning. "I didn't understand that he was hitting on me," she said. "I was that naive. I was that weird. . . . And then he sent me flowers the next day, and the flowers, I didn't have a doorman, so the flowers came to the office, and I opened up the card [when she got back from Houston] and I was like, 'Oh my God!' So I just ripped up the card and threw it out and said they were from my brother."

J. Virgil Waggoner, the CEO of Sterling Chemicals, also gave Bohner an earful when she showed up for the meeting in Houston. He said to her: "I don't understand why a girl like you is doing this. You're a beautiful girl. Why don't you just get married?" Bohner described sitting at the conference room table with Waggoner—known to all as "Virge"—after he finished making his comments. "I took it seriously, 'Oh, I actually really enjoy my work,' like I actually answered the question. I mean, can you imagine?" Later, when she was at the printer putting together the prospectus for the Sterling IPO, the CFO of Sterling saw her and asked her to get him a cup of coffee, with cream and sugar. The man later apologized for thinking she was a secretary and not part of the deal team. "It was sort of just like constant," she said. The oil and gas group was clearly the wrong place for Bohner, and Ward Woods, of all people, recognized that fact. Woods recommended to Loomis that Bohner be transferred to another group. "She's getting killed," he told Loomis.

But the shenanigans did not stop. Michael Price, then a young Lazard partner, got a firm reprimand from Bill Loomis for joking with Jamie Kempner about whether or not he had had sex with Bohner yet. Bohner was working with Kempner on the Sterling IPO, and he was her mentor. Price's comment was inappropriate and outrageous—as Kempner was, and is, happily married—and Loomis let Price have it in the form of a warning that such behavior would not be tolerated. Christina Mohr introduced Bohner to a young banker from Salomon Brothers who was working with Mohr on a deal. The idea was that Bohner should meet some people her own age. They dated a few times and, the rumor goes, had sex in the small library at Lazard. Then there were the unfounded rumors going around the office that she had sex with the bisexual fellow in charge of the night word-processing department. And with Mark Pincus, a fellow analyst. And Luis Rinaldini. And there was the rumor that she had oral sex with Felix, also in the library. Felix used to stop by Bohner's office regularly to chat with her when her office was, briefly, on the thirty-second floor of One Rock. The rank and file couldn't help but chuckle at the fact that Felix barely knew the names of people who had been there for years but made a point of spending time with Kate, a twenty-two-year-old financial analyst. But these rumors persisted, even though some clearly were not true.

Kate recalled, "When somebody confronted me with the rumor about her and Felix, I said, 'You can't get fired for that. You can only get promoted for it.' So that's why it circled the firm, because I was just so pissed at this point. I was so tired of all the chitchat I couldn't take it anymore." Rumors about Bohner and all sorts of Lazard bankers had become a staple around the firm. "The tally of people Kate slept with around the firm got up to around fifteen," one former partner said.

Many of the stories about Felix pursuing the younger women at the firm were more rumor and innuendo than anything else. "I think that it is a remarkable sense of delusion for someone such as myself or perhaps even Linda [Pohs] or Michael [Carmody] to think that they were going to compete with Shirley MacLaine or Barbara Walters for Felix," Kathy Kelly said. "Did Felix ever put his hand on your shoulder and come close to you? Yes, that's Felix's way. He's a warm guy. But that's not sexual harassment. He's a flirt. And that's part of the goddamn job. And you know why it was part of the goddamn job? Because that's exactly what you do with your clients. You flirt." For his part, Felix claimed to be "blissfully unaware" of all the sexually aggressive behavior that had been so much a part of Lazard over the years and said he could no longer even recall names such as Gerowin, Pohs, Carmody, Kelly, Mohr, McArthur, and

Bohner. "Without going into personalities," one woman banker explained, "I think that was the time at which there were some dark forces around Lazard. And I do think that there was at least one individual who was not fair. And who did not treat me well. And since at Lazard you were kind of waiting to turn fifty-five, I kind of looked at how old I was, looked at when I would turn fifty-five, and looked at these people and said, 'Maybe there's a better place for me to wait out the next ten years than getting picked on by these characters.' "

But there was more. A senior vice president of Lazard, well on his way to making partner, was a regular visitor to Bohner's office after she moved down to the thirtieth floor. The senior vice president would come by and chat, no doubt as he had seen Felix do with Bohner any number of times. Loomis became a little concerned by his increasingly random visits to see Bohner. Loomis's office was right next to Bohner's, part of the plan to try to protect Kate by letting people know that Loomis would be watching. After all, the senior vice president was married with children. And Loomis was becoming all too aware of the effect Bohner was having on the Lazard men.

Word had gotten around the firm about the various incidents. Loomis took Bohner out for lunch—a burger downstairs in Rockefeller Center—and just let her know that he was aware of and concerned about the senior vice president's increasing visits. Some two weeks later, Mary Conwell, a banker in Lazard's Chicago office, had come to New York for Christina Mohr's wedding and was staying at Bohner's apartment. Conwell was at the apartment the night that the senior vice president knocked on the door looking for Bohner. He was in an inebriated condition supposedly exacerbated by sleeping pills. At first Conwell told him to leave, that Bohner was not home. He apparently did leave, went for another drink or two, and then returned to the apartment. This time Bohner was home, and the senior vice president was let in. He proceeded to "throw me into a brick wall" in the apartment, Bohner said. He became ill. He supposedly announced to Bohner that he was in love with her and wanted to leave his wife and children.

As appalled as Bohner was, she would never have said anything about the incident, she said, because she had a sense that somehow the victim has a way of getting blamed for these types of things. "If I had gone to Bill Loomis and said a senior vice president came stumbling over to my apartment and threw me into a brick wall, nothing good can happen to my career for saying that," Bohner explained. "There's going to be fifty people in the firm that say it was somehow my fault." Conwell felt differently. She reported the incident to Ken Jacobs and also to Loomis.

"The incident—what I observed of it—was the biggest injustice from a moral standpoint," Conwell explained. Loomis confronted the man. And the firm fired him instantly. Loomis had simply seen and heard enough after decades of the women at Lazard being sexually harassed. The senior vice president became the fall guy for his own lapse in judgment—and that of all the Lazard bankers before him. Bohner said she forgives the man. She even congratulated him years later on his accomplishments since leaving the firm. The incident has done nothing to damage the friendship between Loomis and the senior vice president, either. Loomis has had business dealings with him and they see each other regularly, both socially and professionally.

But after the firing, Bohner had had enough of Lazard—and vice versa. She was simply too disruptive a force at the firm. "I was embarrassed by the whole situation, quite frankly," she said. "I could tell that people were treating me differently inside the firm afterward. And I just felt depressed, and I felt like I'd been ripped off. There were certain people that were really on my side, and then I think there were just certain people that were like, oh God, what a troublemaker, but I don't know, because no one ever really said anything to me. I just sort of dropped into the background after that." She left the firm a few months later after fulfilling her two-year commitment. "They couldn't wait to get rid of me," she said. On that day, the former Lazard partner Ward Woods, who had become CEO of Bessemer Securities, called her and invited her to lunch at Le Bernardin, one of the best restaurants in New York City. While Woods's wife spent her time at their home in Sun Valley, Idaho, Woods and Bohner began a four-year affair. Woods, handsome and charming, had a long track record himself of sexual misadventures, according to his former partners. He also used to carry on his trysts in the corporate hotel suite of one of his Lazard oil and gas clients. Now Woods and Bohner became a public item. They went to parties and restaurants together. They lived together in Woods's Fifth Avenue apartment, where she became familiar to his doormen and his driver. They had lunch every Friday at Le Bernardin. She became well known to the pilots of his private jet.

To Loomis, the firm's record in treating its women employees is nothing to be proud of. "There were a series of very difficult situations involving women ranging from equity to appropriate conduct which were very unpleasant for me, for Michel, and for other people, too," he recalled. But he maintained Lazard did improve in this regard over time. (Could it have been much worse?) "I'd say, in 1980, I think if the place had had a policy, it would have had a policy that there wouldn't be women partners," Loomis said. "And in 1990, if the place had a policy, it would say, 'You know, we need to have more women partners.' "

But to another of Loomis's partners, the firm's troubled experience with women was nothing less than an embarrassing, and long-hidden, fiasco, with the bad behavior condoned by the senior partners. "Kate came into my office one day and was in tears," this partner said. "She said, 'I don't know what to do, blah, blah, blah. I don't know whether to sue Lazard or not.' I said, 'Well, Kate, why don't you think it over?' " He also went to see Michel to talk about the deteriorating situation. "So I went to Michel, and I said, 'Michel, this could really be an ugly scene.' At that point, the Goldman litigation—remember when they got sued for $150 million? Sued by a secretary, there was a big litigation. I went to Michel and said this could be a really expensive thing. And Michel's comment to me was, 'I don't understand the way American parents raise their daughters.' My jaw dropped. I didn't know what he meant by that. As if his predatory partners were not at fault. But he was sort of blaming the women."

The Goldman litigation, though, hit a nerve with Michel. "Then all of a sudden he said we have to stop this," this partner explained. "He didn't send a memo around, but it was understood that you weren't supposed to do this anymore. It still went on, and there were a number of women who left this firm, really wonderful people who left this firm, after being sexually harassed." Lazard assiduously cultivated its image of having the highest ethical standards, of being an independent adviser beyond reproach. "And of being a class act," this partner said, "and it never was."

The fallout from Lazard's experiment in the 1980s—culminating in the myriad incidents involving Kate Bohner—rained down on the firm for many years thereafter. In the mid-1990s, a New York City police detective came to the thirty-second floor at One Rockefeller Center looking to arrest Robert Agostinelli for violating a temporary restraining order his wife had had issued against him. Apparently, this domestic dispute had its origins in the affair Agostinelli had been carrying on with a woman who lived on his block on East Seventy-second Street. He also had an affair with a woman in Chicago, who was said to be a stripper. His American Express bills were said to be on the order of $200,000 a month. (Agostinelli divorced his first wife, Pascale, and later married a European countess and changed his name to *Roberto* Agostinelli.) In the mid-1990s, Christina Mohr left Lazard to become a managing director at Salomon Brothers, what is now Citigroup. Sandy Lamb stayed at Lazard until 2002, although in the late 1990s she was demoted from partner back to vice president. She then founded Lamb Advisors, her own advisory firm, which works with nonprofit organizations.

Meanwhile, as for Kate Bohner, after leaving Lazard, she enrolled at the Columbia University Graduate School of Journalism, on a prestigious *Reader's Digest* scholarship. After graduating in 1993, she became a reporter at *Forbes.* In 1994, she married Michael Lewis, the author of *Liar's Poker,* the classic Wall Street narrative about Lewis's brief tenure at Salomon Brothers. At *Forbes,* thanks to a tip from Ward Woods and help from her new husband, she penned one of the few articles ever written in the English language—before his death—about Édouard Stern, Michel's notorious son-in-law. Even though the article was heavily edited and taken off the cover of *Forbes,* it caused a sensation around Lazard and on Wall Street. Although Lewis once wrote an article about Bohner's perfect derriere, the marriage lasted a mere eighteen months. After leaving *Forbes* in 1997, Bohner co-wrote *Trump: The Art of the Comeback* with Donald Trump. The book hit the best-seller lists in November 1997. As the Internet bubble inflated, she became an on-air correspondent at CNBC, reporting on business celebrities. But in 1998, her contract with CNBC was not renewed. So she then went off to London as president of an Internet venture, Startupcapital.com, backed by the British venture capitalist Stephen Morris. They started dating. When they stopped, in June 1999, her gig in London ended, too. She then became managing editor of JAGfn, a short-lived Internet business news Web site. From there, as the bubble was reaching its dizzying heights, she jumped to E*Trade Financial Corporation as the managing editor of Digital Financial Media as part of E*Trade's short-lived, over-the-top effort to imitate CNBC. In an expensive, glass-walled studio on Madison Avenue in midtown Manhattan, Bohner hosted an hourlong business broadcast over E*Trade's Web site. The *Times* profiled her, as did the *New York Observer.* In the market bust, she lost most of her savings—some $70,000. Eventually, Bohner became the executive vice president of marketing and content for a venture-capital-backed health care device company based in New York and New Jersey. But she is no longer with the company. In the fall of 2006, she started Kate Bohner Productions, a media consulting firm in Boca Raton. And she never remarried.

CHAPTER 15

THE HEIR APPARENT

t is clear that the Suzanna Andrews *New York* article did far more damage to Felix and to Lazard than it did to Steve, thanks to Steve's media savvy and a passel of friends willing to help redirect Andrews's thinking.

Not surprisingly, the article prompted a swift—but low-key—reminder from Michel about the dangers of airing dirty laundry in public. The *New York* article was *bad* press. In a "Memorandum to All Managing Directors and Vice Presidents," Michel wrote:

> We are at our very core a private firm in an environment in which it is increasingly difficult to be so. All of us have seen and read too often in the press the intimate details of issues and conflicts with our competitors. We ourselves have had some instances where comments have been made and misrepresented, taken out of context or isolated from other comments that were made which would have provided balance and have therefore created erroneous impressions. By the very fact of being in the business we are in, we have undertaken obligations of confidentiality and privacy as to our daily affairs. From time to time we may fall short, in the end, though, we can prevent our own undoing. We should avoid any discussion of the inner workings of the Firm or of its people in the press.

The last line, while perhaps not directed at Felix alone, would certainly have been an admonishment of him, a highly unusual zinger for one of the world's most masterful manipulators of the press and his own image.

Three days later, at Michel's insistence, Felix penned his own rather extraordinary near apologia, addressing the *New York* article head-on:

> The article in *New York Magazine* this week was extremely unfortunate. I recognize that it need not have occurred. Although I was interviewed by Suzanna Andrews in a different context than this week's article, I

> nonetheless made many comments to her that were ill advised. Statements about Steve Rattner were inappropriate and inaccurate. It is a fact that Steve is a serious professional of significant talent and achievement whose work is appreciated by me and by everyone else in our firm. In particular, I know that Michel David-Weill has always had and continues to have the highest regard for Steve and looks forward to a long and mutually satisfying association between him and Lazard Frères. I hope this will close an unfortunate chapter that was completely unnecessary and inflicted needless pain.

Ten years after its publication, the article still touches a raw nerve with Felix. But he could not be any clearer about his utter lapse in judgment or any more eager to proclaim his error. "There's absolutely no excuse for it," he said. "You don't criticize a younger partner. You don't do it publicly. You don't speak to a reporter about this." The article was "not one of my crown jewels," he continued, and said it helped to convince him that "I had stayed too long. When you begin to make mistakes like that, you should do something else. And that was a very bad thing. I had never done that before, and I lost my temper." He brought the subject up again another time, in case somehow his mea culpa had not been heard. "Look," he said, "what happened, happened. I'm not proud of it. It should never have happened. And it was extremely painful, I'm sure, for him, but very much for me. And probably for the firm as a whole."

For his part, Steve said of Felix and the incident: "He's a complicated guy. I know him as well as anybody but not well enough to know what really goes on in his head. He blew a circuit breaker and it all poured out, and he would be the first one to say that. As soon as he did it, he knew he made a horrible mistake, but there's no taking it back, and the rest is history."

Armchair psychiatry and near apologies aside, Michel and Lazard now had a huge problem: with no way to rebut it, the worst kind of publicity about the firm and its two most prominent bankers had just been unleashed, giving competitors all the ammunition needed to sow significant doubts with CEOs about the quality of the advice coming from Lazard. And the market for M&A deals was heating up once again.

NOW, OF COURSE, it was time for Felix to leave Lazard. When he would leave and what he would do when he left were details to be worked out. Even though Felix added immeasurably to Lazard's chronic dysfunction, nobody really wanted him to leave. Everybody knew that his prodigious ability to bring business was not going to be easily replaced, even if Steve was getting close. Obviously, the Fed embarrassment and the *New York* article were painful and unfamiliar setbacks. And for sure Steve wasn't going anywhere, given his steep career trajectory and impressive fee-generating ability. "We were both viewed in the firm as important sources of revenue," he said. "I don't think anybody, including me, wanted Felix to leave. I think that Felix basically reached the judgment to leave on his own." In the past, when Michel had been asked about how the firm would manage without the prolific Felix, he would quote Georges Clemenceau, the French World War I leader: "The cemeteries are full of indispensable men."

By serendipity, several months after the *New York* article, Felix and Liz were dining in Paris with Pamela Harriman, then U.S. ambassador to France. "She was a hard woman," Felix said. "One of the toughest women I have ever met." The First Amendment notwithstanding, one of the first things Harriman did at the dinner was complain bitterly to Liz about the fact that the New York Public Library had allowed Sally Bedell Smith, the respected author of *Reflected Glory,* a frank and unflattering portrait of Harriman, to read publicly from her book at a library-sponsored event. Liz, the recently appointed chair of the public library, quickly deflected the inappropriate assault. Felix saw the need to change the topic. He put the spotlight back on Harriman by reminding her about the expulsion from France of five CIA agents, including the station chief, after they were accused of political and economic espionage during her tenure as ambassador.

Then they got down to the substance of the dinner. Harriman told the Rohatyns that night that she had told Clinton she "wanted to go home" and did not want to serve another term as ambassador. "Which wasn't quite true," Felix said. "Because she did want to be renewed but they decided not to." Then, out of the blue, Harriman suggested that Felix think about taking the job. As a replacement for her, Felix recalled that she said, "They ought to have somebody with a European background, like you, as ambassador to France. And there's only you and one other person" being considered for the post—Frank Wisner, a career diplomat then serving as U.S. ambassador to India. "Would that interest you?" "And I said, 'Well, you know, I've never thought of being an ambassador,' which was true. 'But probably France is the only country that I would consider being ambassador because I think I could really do something. But I don't know, let me think about this and I'll talk to Elizabeth and we'll see what we want to do.' "

Felix recalled later talking to his wife about Harriman's proposal. "And I said to Elizabeth, 'What do you think?' And she said, 'Well, you think you'd really like that?' I said, 'I'm not sure, but I do think we ought to get out of Lazard,' because after the Steve business and the Fed, I mean I was gone" mentally from the firm. "And," he continued, "Elizabeth had been urging me to leave already for some time. But she says, 'You don't have to be ambassador to France to have a future.' I said, 'No, but I think we ought to try it.' And she is really terrific. She hated the idea. She had been recently made chairman of the New York Public Library, which is a big deal, and she'd worked hard at it. And to just pull up stakes—she's just had a grandchild and to go to be the wife of the ambassador to France, she thought that was just awful. But she thought it was good for me to get out. . . . So I tell Pamela, 'Yes, I'd be interested, but only if you make the recommendation to the president, you know.' She says, 'Fine, absolutely, we'll do it.' "

As with the Fed appointment, Felix may have thought that his replacing Harriman in Paris was a done deal. After all, he spoke fluent French, had done business in France for decades, and worked for a firm founded by a French family. He also had donated $362,500 in soft money to the Democratic Party in 1995 and 1996 alone. But it was not. The first sign of trouble came within weeks of his return from Paris. He got a call from Janet Howard, who had been Harriman's assistant for some twenty years. The two women had had a falling-out, and Harriman had fired Howard. Howard was furious with her former boss. In their conversation, Felix recalled, Howard told him, "You know, Mr. Rohatyn, I have to tell you that behind your back terrible things are happening and Pamela really doesn't want you to replace her. She wants Frank Wisner."

Felix then called his friends and longtime Clinton confidants Vernon Jordan and Erskine Bowles, who offered to find out what was going on. Jordan reported that Harriman had double-crossed Felix and decided to rally her friends in the State Department to argue vociferously that a career diplomat, such as Wisner, was the right person for the Paris job. Jordan also told Felix that Harriman had suggested that Felix's friendship with Édouard Balladur, the French prime minister and political foe of Jacques Chirac, the French president, would unnecessarily complicate relations between the two countries. Felix was not happy when he heard Jordan's report, especially because, Felix said, he didn't really know Balladur—he had only met him twice—and he got to know him some months before only because *Harriman* had asked him to set up a meeting for Balladur with American CEOs on a visit the French prime minister had in New York. He even had a copy of a "glowing" letter of thanks from Harriman to him for arranging the Balladur meeting. He sent Jordan a copy of the letter. "So I gave that to Vernon, and I said, 'You know, this is a little strange.' "

Months passed and Felix sat in limbo, awaiting a decision from Washington that was not forthcoming. And then fate intervened. On February 5, 1997, Harriman died unexpectedly of a massive stroke just as she was getting out of the rooftop swimming pool at the Hôtel Ritz in Paris. She was seventy-six years old. Her funeral was a state occasion. Just after it was over, Felix and Liz went to London for a long weekend. Felix had decided that if he wasn't offered the job in Paris soon, he would withdraw his name from consideration.

At ten-thirty on the night before the Rohatyns were to leave, he got a call from Bowles in the White House. Bowles told him: "There is still no decision on Paris, but the president wants you to go to Tokyo." Felix was dumbfounded. "After more than six months of hesitating whether to send me to Paris, the president wanted me to go to Tokyo?" he said. He spoke with Vernon Jordan. "Vernon suggested I speak with Bowles," Felix said.

> Bowles was direct. "Felix," he said, "the president thinks you could make an enormous contribution by representing us in Tokyo. Japan is in terrible financial condition. They need help. They know you and they would listen to you. If you tell me that you are willing to go, I am authorized to tell you that the president will offer you the nomination to Tokyo tomorrow." I was speechless. "Erskine," I said, "I have spent a fifty-year career in finance, and of those fifty years I have not spent more than two weeks in Japan. Of two to three hundred mergers or so that I have negotiated, five at the most have involved Japanese companies. I do not speak a word of Japanese; I have practically no relationships there; I know practically no Japanese history. I am utterly unqualified, and I would embarrass myself as well as the president at a confirmation hearing." Bowles was unshaken. "The president thinks you can do the job." "What about Paris?" I asked. "Paris is very complicated; it is still a possibility, but it is a long shot. Tokyo is yours for the asking."

Before he spoke with Bowles next, Felix heard confidentially that Wisner intended to retire. And when he did speak to Bowles, he declined the Japan posting but said he was still interested in Paris. He said nothing about Wisner. The waiting continued. Finally, in April 1997, Sandy Berger called to offer him the Paris job. He could say nothing until after he was confirmed. As soon as he accepted the position, though, he had "really, really terrible" second thoughts about taking it. "What is this? What does one do as an ambassador?" he wondered, suddenly recalling his earlier supposition that ambassadors were simply glorified butlers.

On September 11, 1997, by the unanimous vote of 97–0, the U.S. Senate confirmed him as America's thirtieth ambassador to France. What the Senate also confirmed that late summer day, along with its vote, was what many keen Lazard observers suspected for years: that for all the incredible riches and prestige that Felix, the Great Man, brought to himself and to his partners during his long tenure as Lazard's chief rainmaker, because of his intransigence, his insecurities, and his imperiousness he, unwittingly or not, helped to preside over the slow demise and near destruction of this once-great pillar of the financial world.

By Michel's design, the matter of succession at Lazard—meaning who would lead the firm after Felix and Michel were gone—was always convoluted and fraught with peril. Through the early 1990s, as Felix became increasingly less engaged, there was the perennial question of who could possibly succeed him as the senior deal maker at the firm. The discussion, such as it was, usually focused on finding a new rainmaker in New York, as the United States had historically been the biggest M&A market and the New York partnership was by far the largest of the three Lazard houses. But replacing a banker of Felix's caliber is not easy. Like Halley's comet, a banker with Felix's awesome level of production, year in and year out, comes along rarely—maybe even less than once every seventy-six years, especially in the recent Wall Street environment where the firm, writ large, is what matters, not the individual banker. Of course, in the few years before the *Vanity Fair* article about Steve appeared, Steve had often been mentioned as Felix's protégé and likely successor. In the years after the article, though, such talk died down considerably. In its place was left some vague notion that a group of people—Steve, Ken Wilson, Jerry Rosenfeld, Ira Harris among them—could together serve to replace Felix. This concept appealed to some Lazard insiders—and even to Michel—because it considerably lessened the firm's dependence on the productivity of any one man. For Michel, Felix became like a drug addiction. Michel needed to find a way to wean himself from him.

The Lazard ethos had always been predicated on a Great Man coming along to sustain the firm or reinvent it. So while Michel could rest more easily knowing that the crop of younger bankers he had recruited in the late 1980s and early 1990s were now becoming increasingly productive, he had not yet found someone of Felix's stature to replace him. While Michel may have been searching for the null set, he did continue his quest. There had been the somewhat halfhearted attempt to recruit Pete Peterson when he was leaving the Nixon administration in the early 1970s. Peterson went to Lehman instead and later started the Blackstone Group. There was the short dalliance with both Bruce Wasserstein and Joe Perella when they were thinking about quitting First Boston in 1988. Instead, they formed Wasserstein Perella & Co. In 1993, Michel tried again to recruit Perella when he was leaving Wasserstein Perella. But the chemistry between Michel and Perella was never great, and so it was no surprise when Perella ended up at Morgan Stanley. (Perella denied that he ever considered going to Lazard in 1988 or in 1993.) In the spring of 1995, Michel tried to land John Thornton, one of the top M&A bankers at Goldman Sachs, but Thornton quickly lost interest after Felix disabused him of the notion that he would be running the firm anytime soon. He went on to become a co-president of Goldman.

But this romancing of Great Men had been for the purpose of finding a potential successor to *Felix*. There was still the very important matter, rarely discussed or even speculated about, of who would succeed *Michel*. Michel and his family were the ones who primarily *owned* the firm—ownership also resided with Pearson PLC, the heirs of André Meyer, a French holding company, a couple of the French partners, such as Antoine Bernheim and Jean Guyot, and a handful of the older partners in New York, but without question it was Michel, and pretty much Michel alone, who *controlled* the firm. The working partners were extremely well paid each year, but their percentages referred only to what slice of the pretax profits Michel would agree to give them each year and from what house—New York, Paris, or London—rather than representing an ownership stake. After all, as the longtime partner Frank Pizzitola was fond of reminding everyone, "Lazard is not a partnership. It's a sole proprietorship with fancy profit sharing." Most partners, including Felix, owned nothing. So there was always the question of who would *own* the firm after Michel died, just as he took over ownership after the death of Pierre David-Weill, who owned the firm after the death of David David-Weill, who owned the firm after the death of Alexander Weill. Michel did not have a natural heir to fit into this historical construct, which had served everyone so well for almost 150 years.

Which is why when Michel's thirty-eight-year-old son-in-law, Édouard Stern, at once brilliant and ruthless, joined the firm as a partner on May 1, 1992, speculation intensified in the threadbare corridors that Michel had brought the dashing Édouard in to be *his* designated successor. Not as the successor to Felix, deal man extraordinaire, but to succeed the Sun King himself as owner-operator. Regardless of what

Michel may have been thinking by inviting the highly combustible Édouard into the firm, the decision made many of the already insecure Lazard partners very nervous indeed—even by the cutthroat, Darwinian standards of Lazard, Stern's reputation for being both brilliant and abrasive caught people's attention—and set the firm on a ten-year odyssey to solve the succession curse. David Braunschvig, a Lazard partner until recently, grew up with Stern in Paris and was one of his closest friends. Apparently, the two shared a love of racing motorcycles, playing golf, and chasing girls. Even then Braunschvig could tell there was something special about his friend. "He had immense charm," Braunschvig explained. "It was almost irresistible. When he went into a room and started talking, it commanded people's attention. Not because of the seriousness of his intent, but just, you know, there are people who have a compelling presence. Charisma. He had that from the earliest years."

There were at least three facets of the Stern biography that bedazzled his new partners. First, there was the somewhat mythical story about how at the age of twenty-two he had kneecapped his own father as head of Banque Stern, the family's merchant bank, founded in 1823 to cater to "the needs of the French aristocracy." The Sterns were said to be from the same Jewish ghetto—Francfort-sur-la-Main—as the Rothschilds. For a while, the Stern family had similar aspirations. They lived in a sumptuous mansion near the Eiffel Tower. But Antoine Stern, Édouard's father and the lackluster steward of the bank, was said to be a dilettante who pranced around Paris. He hosted an annual partridge, pheasant, and duck shoot in the Paris environs. But he failed to run the firm as a proper financial enterprise, preferring to use it as a source of his own social aggrandizement. By 1977, the firm was near bankruptcy.

To Antoine, the solution was simple: sell the bank to the Rothschilds, for all of $600,000. Not so fast, Édouard said. Fresh from ESSEC, one of Europe's premier business schools, a black belt in karate, and a chess champion, Édouard—with André Meyer's help—convinced his two uncles Philippe and Gerard and their mother, Alice, that he could run the bank better than his unmotivated father. His uncles and grandmother decided to throw their support behind Édouard, and the sale to the Rothschilds was wisely abandoned. Édouard recruited François Cariès, then the CEO of Banque Rothschild, to become chairman of Banque Stern, and Édouard became vice chairman. "I knew this was the way to learn exactly the business," he said later. But he was branded an enfant terrible by the French press for supposedly kicking out his father, for whom he reportedly had much disdain. "To read the papers, he was just this monster," a family friend said. When asked about what happened at the bank, Édouard, who generally shunned the press, told *Forbes* in 1995, "True, it was the family bank begun by my ancestors in 1823. True, too, it was nearly bankrupt. So what had to be done was done."

The truth, according to Édouard's longtime attorney Kristen van Riel, may be somewhat less sinister. "Everyone said Édouard stole the bank from his father, but he couldn't have," he explained to the writer Bryan Burrough in 2005, "because he didn't own a single share of stock. It was the grandmother and the two brothers who did it! They threw him out! His father was already on the way out when Édouard was brought in to save the bank! Which is what he did." Still, he didn't speak to his father for the next fifteen years; the two reconciled only when his father was dying.

Together with Cariès, Stern turned the bank around, in dramatic fashion. By 1982, revenue had increased to about $110 million from around $6 million. When Cariès left that same year, Édouard recruited, to replace him, Claude Pierre-Brossolette, an old family friend and former special assistant to the French president Valéry Giscard d'Estaing. Other leading French businessmen and financiers were recruited as well. In 1984, he sold the bank to a Lebanese investor for the equivalent of around $60 million today. He retained for himself the right to continue to use the Banque Stern name. That same year Édouard, then twenty-nine, married Beatrice David-Weill, then twenty-seven, the oldest of Michel's four daughters. She was an art historian at the Louvre and said to be stunning. She had apparently been madly in love with Édouard from the time she was fifteen. When she divorced her first husband, it was possible for the two of them to marry. Édouard was "the person she had loved all her life," Michel explained. "She always loved him."

With his personal life squared away for the moment, he quickly set about building a new bank under the Banque Stern moniker. In this new entity, he sought to offer M&A and investment advice, not unlike his new father-in-law's more famous firm—but in a far more aggressive and ruthless way. One of his associates at the time recalled: "Édouard was like a tornado when he came into the office every morning, wondering, 'Who's blood can we spill today?' " In one infamous maneuver, he attempted a hostile takeover of Groupe Rivaud, a sleepy conglomerate owned by two French aristocrats. He failed to get control, but still pocketed $30 million in profit. By 1987, the new Banque Stern was sufficiently vital that Édouard decided it was time to sell. "I thought we were on our way to becoming a big investment bank," said his associate Jean Peyrelevade, who headed the bank from 1986 until its sale. "But it wasn't Édouard's temperament. He was in a hurry." Stern quickly arranged for

Swiss Bank Corporation, now part of UBS, to buy the *new* family firm for a reported $337 million, of which the then-staggering sum of $170 million came to him personally. He moved to Geneva to avoid French taxes. From August 1988 through July 1989, Stern met with a number of Lazard partners, including Bill Loomis and Robert Agostinelli, about the possibility of joining Lazard as a partner. He also talked with Swiss Bank about becoming an M&A adviser there.

But instead of joining Lazard or Swiss Bank, Édouard chose to see how quickly he could turn the $170 million into $500 million. His ability to do just that, within four years, added yet another dimension to his growing legend. In this regard, he was taking after Sir James Goldsmith, the famed British corporate raider, who was Stern's distant cousin. In partnership with Goldsmith, Stern bought a number of hotel properties in Vietnam. Accounts vary as to just how immensely successful the private partnership was, but the two men were said to have split $250 million on a $75 million investment. Stern also bought into Elysée Investissements, a French holding company, where his friend Kristen van Riel was on the board. He was said to have tripled his investment on Elysée, receiving at one point a $150 million dividend from the company. Without question, at a very young age, Édouard had proven his mettle as an extremely savvy investor. He had also become a very rich man in his own right—at one point the thirty-eighth of the four hundred richest French families—and was that rare being, an independently wealthy relative of a billionaire. For Michel, this added to Stern's luster. "Michel found himself in Édouard," observed one David-Weill family friend. On the one hand, Michel had always claimed to be unimpressed by self-made men. His father often told him with regard to André, for instance, "Beware of self-made men because they always think it is their fault." "And I thought it was a wonderful saying," he continued, "because it's so true. Because at least I don't think it's my fault." But on the other hand, he felt comfortable around people with immense wealth. He was also impressed by Édouard's investing prowess.

Édouard also had immense appetites: among them for food, for sex, for risk, and for mercurial behavior. He especially enjoyed dining at Nobu, the notoriously expensive and delectable New York sushi restaurant. "The single most distinctive and unusual characteristic of Édouard's was how much sushi he ate," explained Jeffrey Keil, one of Stern's financial partners. "He could eat fifty or seventy pieces of sushi at one sitting. I'm not kidding. We took turns paying the bill. Usually $300 or $400." There is an apocryphal story about how Édouard was hosting a dinner in a private room at a Paris restaurant in the early 1990s, and all the guests were so busy chatting they had left their bowls of soup untouched—and now cold—in front of them. They decided they would all pour their soup back into the tureen, in the middle of the table, and would have it reheated. When the waiter came around to clear away the uneaten soup, Édouard stopped him and rose from his seat. He then found a little silver knife and made a small incision at the end of his left index finger. Then he placed his hand above the soup tureen, and a single drop of blood from his cut finger fell into the soup. He looked at each of his guests and supposedly said, "Those of you who trust me will help themselves later." He was also said to relish demanding in front of others that his wife fellate him, much to her embarrassment. Jon Wood, a proprietary trader then at UBS in London, recalled flying on a British Airways flight from Miami to Paris and finding that Édouard was the only other person in first class. Stern happened to be returning from his grandmother's funeral in the Bahamas. "Édouard sauntered onto the plane," Wood recalled, "and he immediately started snapping his fingers—'I want to watch this film, eat this meal, and put on my pajamas.' He was hopping mad. He threw the videos on the ground. He didn't put on his seat belt. He demanded to speak to the captain. He said he wanted to get off the plane. I thought to myself, 'What a wanker! Who is this guy?' "

Wood's observation was consistent with Édouard's penchant for irreverence and flaunting the rules. "He was too solitary and too independent to be part of a formal structure," Peyrelevade recalled. Braunschvig saw this as early as age fifteen. "He always wanted to challenge the existing order of things," he recalled. "There were no taboos. This might seem a bit ordinary from an American perspective, but in France a high school education is more strict than it is here, the discipline, the long hours. Many kids, as a result, develop a shy or introverted demeanor. Édouard was always outspoken and irreverent. That's because at an early age he had this sense of self—he was not going to be threatened by any existing order. He wrote his own rules."

This risk-taking extended to his approach to investments. One of these landed him front and center in an insider trading investigation by the British Department of Trade and Industry, or DTI, the equivalent of the SEC. In February 1989, Stern purchased a total of 320,000 shares, worth about £4.7 million, of Consolidated Gold Fields, a British gold company, in the middle of a takeover battle between Consolidated Gold and Minorco, which was the Luxembourg subsidiary of a South African gold conglomerate owned by the wealthy and powerful Oppenheimer family. The Oppenheimers had long been associated with Lazard, first through André and then through Felix. At the time of its bid for

Consolidated Gold, Minorco still owned 30 percent of Engelhard Corporation, a stake that came about as a result of a number of deals Lazard arranged in the 1970s. In 1986, Felix was on the board of Minorco for a year; then Jim Glanville took over his seat. By 1987, Bill Loomis was the Lazard representative on the Minorco board. The Lazard partners Loomis and Agostinelli represented Minorco on its hostile £2.9 billion offer for the 71 percent of Consolidated Gold it did not already own. During a November 1988 meeting, Agostinelli spoke to Stern about Lazard's role in advising Minorco, but supposedly only as a "topical" indicator of the kinds of deals the firm was involved in.

When DTI became aware of the familial relationship between Michel and Stern, the investigators "were concerned to ascertain whether the connection influenced, in any way," Stern's purchase of the shares. Under questioning, Édouard said he had never discussed Lazard's role as adviser to Minorco with Michel, Loomis, or Agostinelli. The investigators were not pleased that Édouard had not told them of his relationship with Michel at the outset, and so sought some answers from Michel himself. Through his lawyer, Michel responded that he had never discussed the Minorco bids with Édouard, nor would he have, and he had no awareness that Édouard had bought the Consolidated Gold shares. Aside from finding that Édouard "deliberately failed to ensure" that the information about his Consolidated Gold purchases was reported properly and that "we are surprised that it did not occur to him that the prudent course of action would have been to give careful consideration to the implications" before buying the shares, given his relationships with both Lazard and Swiss Bank, the DTI investigators concluded, in their *public* finding, "There is no evidence to suggest that either Minorco, Lazard Frères (New York or London), Mr. David-Weill or Swiss Bank Corporation had any knowledge of the transactions in ConsGold undertaken by M. Stern . . . and we have no criticism of them." In any event, Stern lost money on the investment after Minorco's offer for Consolidated Gold did not succeed. Another British conglomerate, Hanson, bought Consolidated Gold in August 1989.

The findings of the DTI investigation notwithstanding, Michel made the decision, as he said, to "try" Édouard in the firm. Michel said he had read the DTI report and was "okay" with it. "I see it as a learning experience," he said. "Édouard is impetuous. He is someone who had success early. There are allowances for that. I have made allowances." But there was opposition to his hiring on both sides of the Atlantic. "In Paris there were people who didn't like him because they didn't like the way he had treated his father," Michel said. "In New York, there were people who didn't like him because they were questioning whether he was rigorous in his behavior." And the partners in London simply thought it wholly inappropriate for someone who seemed like a crook to be at Lazard. Bill Loomis, for one, was not happy about Édouard's arrival in New York. He had formed a negative view of him from the Minorco–Consolidated Gold incident. "I think it had a huge impact on Bill personally because he didn't like Stern from the moment he met him," one partner explained. Others were wary of his mercurial temperament. "He can be absolutely the most charming person, absolutely *séduisant,*" said a banker who had been friendly with Édouard since childhood. "He's witty, very well read, and a great storyteller. And he can be so brutal that men twenty years older than he have left his office crying." Of Édouard, a former Lazard partner in London said, "There was only one person I ever met who made the hair on the back of my neck stand up, and that was Édouard." Added Peyrelevade: "When things didn't go exactly as he wished, he was capable of extraordinary verbal violence."

But Michel plunged ahead anyway. And his logic for doing so, as always, was impeccable. "If you had to choose, in France, a natural leader for the firm, there are very few which would fit the theoretical bill as well as Édouard," he explained.

> There is a fellow who is obviously very enterprising, very, very smart, hardworking, and who is very at ease in the United States, who speaks absolutely perfect English, much better than I do, who has no relationship problems with Americans. They understand him right away. They don't feel he is a total foreigner. He is very wealthy on his own—which for a banker is useful and gives a degree of independence—and is the heir to a banking tradition. His grandfather—I love this one story of his grandfather—was on the board of Banque Paribas, and he was very deaf. They were reviewing credits, and they said, "We are lending 100 million francs to the Ottoman Empire," and he said, "What? What?" "Mr. Stern, we are lending 100 million francs to the Ottoman Empire." And he turned around and said, "A hundred million francs? I would not lend that to myself!" I cite it very often when I speak about banking because bankers forget that there are sums which you shouldn't be lending, even to the credit you adore the most, which is your own. You should just say, "This is ridiculous." So, now the fact that he had married my daughter, curiously nobody believed it, but it really did not enter the equation.

Michel was correct that nobody around Lazard believed that Édouard was at the firm for any reason other than the familial relationship. "Maybe I would have felt different if he was my son because maybe I would have related differently to him, but he was to me one fellow," Michel continued. "Not more, not less than my other partners. It was not because he was sleeping with my daughter that it made any difference. It didn't. Really. Nobody really believed it, they always, they all felt, well, it's more than it seems. No. It was simply an evaluation that—now, I knew that the fellow was not trained to be in an investment bank. He had been more of an entrepreneur, and basically he said so. He had two mothers in life: he had Jimmy Goldsmith and me. He didn't know which way he wanted to go, the Jimmy Goldsmith way or the Michel way." Stern spent much of the first two years at Lazard in New York but shuttled frequently between there and Paris. His New York office was on the thirty-first floor of One Rockefeller Plaza, near Mezzacappa's capital markets operation and one floor below his father-in-law and most of the other banking partners. He had a safe installed in his office, bolted to the floor. This was considered extremely odd even by Lazard standards. Every night, he put his papers in the safe. He was also said to keep a change of underwear in there as well.

Stern was busy right from the start, mostly focused on private-equity investing as opposed to M&A advisory. On the heels of Corporate Partners' Phar-Mor disaster, Stern organized a new, $350 million private-equity fund, Jupiter Partners, focused on management buyouts. He put an end to efforts to raise a second Corporate Partners fund at a time when "there were a lot of questions about Lester's and Ali's judgments," one partner said, speaking of the two men responsible for Corporate Partners. Édouard sent packing Lester Pollack, the head of Corporate Partners. Much of the money for Jupiter came from Lazard partners. He recruited to run Jupiter a management team from outside Lazard, led by John Sprague, who had been one of the early partners at Forstmann Little. But Jupiter made some poor investments during the Internet bubble and, although still in existence, never lived up to expectations. "Jupiter turned out to be a total disaster for the firm," a partner said. "A total disaster." Some partners questioned the wisdom of Stern's decision to end the fund-raising for Corporate Partners II, which could have been a $2 billion fund despite its perceived troubles, in favor of the much smaller Jupiter fund.

Stern also devised a strategy that proved disastrous for Lazard in Asia. He recommended, and Michel agreed, that Lazard open an office in Singapore and in Beijing, both headed up by protégés of Édouard. "This sent a clear message," one Lazard partner said. "Stern was the man. Michel trusts him." Stern also set up a joint venture, called CALFP, with

Crédit Agricole, the large French bank, to structure complex derivatives for clients. Crédit Agricole invested $50 million of the $75 million in capital the venture required; Lazard put up the $25 million balance. Édouard became the chairman of CALFP and received equity in the deal as part of his management arrangement. He could not serve as CEO of the venture, because the Bank of England would not permit it after the accusations that permeated the Minorco–Consolidated Gold deal. So Stern recruited Philippe Magistretti from AIG to head CALFP. He also recruited Bernard Saint-Donat to run CALFP in New York. The venture did very little business, and Saint-Donat and Magistretti squabbled from the outset. Saint-Donat thought CALFP "was a disaster" where the stated purposes of helping Lazard's clients access Crédit Agricole's massive balance sheet masked the "hidden" purpose to create a hedge fund to "make a lot of money" for Lazard. When Saint-Donat complained to Stern that the joint venture was not working well, Magistretti got upset and fired him. Stern then arranged for Saint-Donat to get a new job working at Lazard in New York.

CALFP ended up doing one deal of significance, for Televisa, Mexico's largest media company, and made around $50 million. After that deal, Édouard wanted to sell his equity in the joint venture. Miraculously, Michel and his sister, Éliane, agreed to buy Édouard's stake in CALFP for *$50 million.* Édouard had been given the stake for free. Shortly thereafter, CALFP was closed. Michel and his sister lost their full investment. "I was not sure absolutely that I would lose it," Michel said of that money. "Although it was more probable in my eyes that I would lose it than make it."

Another blunder occurred when Michel asked Édouard to head up the effort to consolidate, into London, Lazard's capital markets business in all of Europe. Édouard offered the job as head of capital markets in Europe to two different people, Anthony Northrop, a longtime managing director in Lazard's London office, and Bernard Poignant, an outside recruit. Poignant got the job, and when Northrop resigned, the Lazard Brothers team was extremely peeved. "I had to clean up Stern's mess," Mezzacappa said. "It's clear that Stern had misled them both slightly." He was also said to have made unauthorized bonus promises on the sly to his cronies. Another time, after Lazard's distressed trading debt desk in New York had accumulated a very large position in the bonds of Eurotunnel, the oft-bankrupt builder and owner of the Chunnel between London and Paris, Stern decided to cause mischief by seeking to use his connection to the Eurotunnel CEO to get the firm hired as Eurotunnel's financial adviser in bankruptcy—an obvious conflict. Stern then called the distressed-debt trader and offered to abandon his effort to get the firm hired if he personally could, as a principal, get a cut of the firm's action in the Eurotunnel distressed debt (the idea is to buy the debt at enough of a discount to par value and hope that it trades up over time). Deeply offended by Stern's request—which had the odor of bribery—the trader promptly called Michel and told him of the conversation he had with Stern. Michel took care of Édouard on that one. Still, Mezzacappa, for one, had been impressed with the deal Stern negotiated with Crédit Agricole. "Stern negotiated a hell of a deal with Crédit Agricole," he told *Forbes*. "And he's gotten quite a lot of credit for that. He's been very successful doing what he's doing. But if he's ever going to run this firm, he's got to mellow out."

After two years in New York, Michel decided Édouard should move to Paris and have the experience of working at Lazard there. This was consistent with Michel's pattern of giving a number of his young talented partners the chance to work in different countries over time. But the fallout from that decision was immediate: the first casualty was a young, ambitious French partner named Jean-Marie Messier. In the late 1980s, Michel had recruited Messier, then all of thirty-two, as a partner at Lazard from his position as the senior privatization adviser to Édouard Balladur, the French prime minister. Messier's arrival signaled to the younger generation at Lazard in Paris that there was some hope of breaking into the very restricted ranks of the Paris partnership, which had long been dominated by a politburo of the old warhorses Bernheim, Guyot, and Bruno Roger. Messier spent some time in New York before moving back to Paris and was very successful, very quickly. There was talk inside Lazard that he could be the One. Some at Lazard in Paris saw him as the second coming of André Meyer, the kind of brilliant outsider that the David-Weills had always encouraged to become part of Lazard and whose immense talent could lead the firm into the future.

Messier was dubbed "le golden boy" and "a very smooth killer." Michel called him "the best merchant banker of his generation." When Messier returned to Paris from New York, he established a $300 million leveraged-buyout fund called Fonds Partenaires, with money from both Lazard partners and limited partners. It was the largest LBO fund in Europe at the time. The fund was successful, most notably with its 1992 investment in Neopost, the French equivalent of Pitney Bowes. Neopost went public in 1999 at €15 a share and now trades at around €82 per share. Over time, in addition to his principal investing work, Messier became one of the leading young M&A advisers in France. "On the advisory front, he was a genius," recalled Patrick Sayer, who worked for

Messier at Lazard on both principal deals and advisory deals. Sayer recalled Messier's brilliance in convincing the Neopost bank lenders to give the company more time to solve its financial problems early on—a decision that worked out marvelously. Messier's only flaw at the time, his former partners said, was his chronic inability to return phone calls. This, of course, was a violation of one of André's and Michel's cardinal rules of always being available. "Which really proves that he was very thorough and engaged in what he was doing, a little to the exclusion of the other things that he should be doing," Michel said. "Which for a banker is an inconvenience. Because a banker, again, is at the service of his clients and he cannot ignore his clients to the benefit of one client who he's working with at the moment. That was his mistake. If I have to say, professionally, his drawback was that one. Otherwise he was one of the best bankers that I've met." The Jean-Marie Messier Award is given annually to the Lazard partner deemed the worst at returning calls.

But within weeks of Stern's arrival at Lazard in Paris in 1994, Messier called it quits. Many partners are certain that Édouard's arrival convinced Messier the time had come to leave Lazard because his ambitions to run the firm one day could not be achieved in the presence of Michel's son-in-law. But Michel is not so sure. "One can debate," he said, "and I don't have the answer. And I would guess that Mr. Messier doesn't have the answer, either, whether the presence of Stern was very important, important, or not important in his decision to leave the firm. But clearly, again, it's the syndrome of succession. As soon as people have the feeling that there will be a succession, people who would normally cooperate nicely begin to distrust the other ones, saying, 'Ha, there is a chance it's him and not me.' "

Michel and Messier talked about Messier's decision to leave the firm for several weeks. It became clear to Michel that Messier had it in his mind to run the firm. "Which I should have known, but I didn't," he said. "But it didn't shock me, because he was bright enough and good enough." Michel suspected, though, that Messier may have been too French to be the one to run the firm globally. "It's important to have somebody Americans relate easily to, and Messier I didn't see as one which Americans related to easily," he said.

Just as Messier's arrival and success had been an inspiration to the younger bankers at Lazard, his abrupt departure broke their hearts. "At one point, Michel had to make a choice between Édouard Stern, who was the son-in-law, and Messier, who was a banker and a good one at that," recalled Jean-Michel Steg, a former Lazard partner who now runs Citigroup in France. "For me, that was the end, I knew I was going to leave. It's now clear I am working for a family. They're choosing the dynastic path rather than the best-qualified banker for establishing an advisory firm that will survive." Said another French partner about Lazard Paris after Messier's departure: "The partners there look like those old photographs of the aging Soviet leaders watching the May Day parades."

As predicted, Édouard was proving to be quite a handful. Nevertheless, despite his not being a traditional M&A adviser, his amazing intellect proved invaluable once he arrived in Paris. In the wake of Messier's departure, he helped resurrect the Paris franchise by bringing in a couple of big deals with important clients. He secured the mandate from the French government for Lazard to sell MGM, the movie studio, which Kirk Kerkorian then bought for $1.3 billion. And he advised L'Oréal on its $754 million acquisition of Maybelline from a buyout fund controlled by Bruce Wasserstein. He also had been the lead banker at Lazard in the privatization of Pechiney, a French aluminum company. "At first there was a lot of initial skepticism about Édouard just because he was Michel's son-in-law," one partner mused. "Then he had a huge amount of success in Paris commercially, so, generally speaking, people were very respectful because of that."

The firm started indulging Édouard—what choice did it have?—in his passions for private equity, the Far East, and Lazard's unsuccessful foray into derivatives. Michel appointed Stern to a three-man oversight committee responsible for investing no less than $15 million a year of the firm's and partners' money directly into private equity. Felix even nominated Édouard to be part of the firm's executive committee. Still, in the French press, Édouard was known as *"le gendre incontrôlable,"* the ungovernable son-in-law.

At the peak of his influence at the firm, in November 1995, Édouard was the subject of a profile in *Forbes* by the former Lazard financial analyst Kate Bohner Lewis. They had dinner together at the ultra-elegant Restaurant Laurent, near the presidential palace in Paris. When Bohner Lewis asked Stern about the incident with his father and the family's bank, Stern uttered his famous mantra, "I just detest incompetence," before adding for good measure, "My vice is I'm impatient—and my bad temper." He also told her that his ruthlessness was a key to his success. "It is not enough to be born with a good name," he said. "I have been sometimes brutal in my life. I regret that only because I have created an almost unchangeable image of myself to others. That is life. I have to live with it." Despite all the broken glass that Édouard's antics had created at Lazard, Michel defended him in the *Forbes* article. "I think everyone exaggerates the so-called animosity toward Édouard," he said. "I think Édouard is just the type of person who *enjoys* thinking he is disliked."

Although there was no mention of Stern being a successor to Felix during Felix's dalliance with the Fed—when there was much public speculation about what would happen if Felix finally left Lazard—the subject of Stern as a successor to Michel was part of Andrews's "Felix Loses It" piece. There was a picture of the menacing Stern seated in a conference room at Lazard in Paris, underneath a portrait of a Lazard founder. Felix, though, said he doubted Édouard would be the One. "I don't think Édouard will run the firm," he told Andrews. "Michel thinks it's important to have him around, as a continuum after Michel leaves, but I don't think he wants him to run the firm." Felix also added during his interview with Andrews: "Édouard is a nasty piece of work." An unnamed man said that Michel had asked the partners about Édouard and had received a blunter message: "If he elevates Stern, there are many, many partners in New York who would leave."

While it seemed certain to many at Lazard that Michel was positioning Édouard to be his successor, his impatience and impertinence were leading him down a path of self-destruction. First, it was around this time that his marriage to Beatrice started to crumble. He was said to have had numerous affairs. Although he denied it, Michel supposedly told one of his partners, "Beatrice would be better off if she divorced Édouard." While he was running Paris, a number of up-and-coming younger partners quit in his wake. A whole generation of younger future leaders in Paris left from a combination of Édouard's style and the ongoing refusal of the Parisian old guard to relinquish control or access to clients.

While Stern was running Paris, he hired Anne Lauvergeon, then thirty-seven and a former economic adviser to the French president, François Mitterrand. She spent a few months working in New York and became a partner in Paris in January 1995. She was the only woman partner in Paris and one of only four female partners in all of Lazard. A year later, the CEO of Pechiney, the newly privatized French aluminum giant, asked Lauvergeon to join the company's board of directors. Such a request to a banker is considered an honor, especially for such a young partner. Édouard, though, was incensed. He had been Pechiney's adviser, not Lauvergeon, and he thought he deserved the board seat.

Some believe that Michel was behind the selection of Lauvergeon as a Pechiney director, knowing full well that he had found his son-in-law's breaking point and the choice would infuriate Édouard. He was right. And the "Cobra," as Édouard's colleagues in Paris called him, was ready to strike. In his mercurial way, he fired Lauvergeon in November 1996, initiating a series of confrontations with Michel that led to Édouard's rapid downfall at the firm. Just after his blowup with Lauvergeon, news of the fight began to seep into the press in Paris. During an interview with *Le Monde,* Michel referred to the matter and praised Lauvergeon. "Ms. Lauvergeon's professional and personal qualities, since her arrival at the house of Lazard, have made an appreciable and appreciated contribution to the firm," he said. The *Times* picked up the story on November 13 and reported, to firm denials, that Édouard was on his way out of Lazard after "a furious dispute" with Michel in New York the previous week.

Accounts of what transpired between the two men differ, but the gist is that Michel was upset with Édouard for firing Lauvergeon unilaterally and blabbing about it throughout Paris for ten days before flying to New York to try to make amends with Michel. At that fateful meeting in Michel's New York office, Michel told Stern to "leave Lauvergeon alone." Stern then erupted. "Either I am going to be the boss or I am not," he reportedly said. "You picked me to run this firm, and if I don't, I am going to go." Another version of the meeting, one partner recalled, had Édouard telling Michel: "I want you to retire. I want to run the firm. I've got this position in Paris. You can't fire me, and I'm just not going to listen to you anymore. I'm going to keep running Paris." Michel remembered Édouard coming into his new office at 30 Rockefeller Plaza and attempting the Thanksgiving putsch. "I treated him like my son," Michel said. "He treated me like his father!"

Some Lazard partners have speculated that part of the impetus for Édouard's attempted overthrow was that at that time Michel was ill. He didn't look well. He wasn't around much. But Michel denied any illness. Still, Lazard partners wondered often about Michel's health. When he would come back from Paris after a few weeks away, partners in New York would go into one another's offices and chat: "Have you seen Michel? I just saw him. He really doesn't look well. What do you think?" He never looked particularly healthy. He often looked pale and blotchy. He put butter and salt on his baguettes. He inhaled his ubiquitous Cuban cigars. He never exercised. His tight-fitting shirts often revealed his stomach rolls. He once broke his arm after he slipped off a wood gangplank, covered with wet straw, leading from the yacht he was on traveling down the Nile. "Michel does know a lot about medicine," Loomis observed wryly. Once, when Loomis had a cold, Michel told him: "You know what you need to do? You need to smoke cigars." Loomis took his advice. But he still didn't feel much better. And he told that to Michel when he saw him the next day. "Oh, you have to do it for a week," Michel responded.

IT IS SAFE to say that every major article that has ever been written about Michel David-Weill—and there have been many over the years—at some point describes his passion for cigars. And each time, the description is nearly identical. Early in the conversation, the reporter observes Michel taking one of his signature Cuban cigars from his wood humidor, if at his office in New York, or from his silver-plated humidor, if at home on Fifth Avenue or in Paris. He chops off one end with his silver cigar-end chopper and, inhaling deeply, lights the stogie up, spewing smoke in every direction. Michel would take a few puffs to make sure the cigar was well lit, and then launch into a long, seemingly thoughtful answer to a question while the cigar slowly burned itself out. He relights it once or twice, before dropping it into an ashtray, three quarters unsmoked. Then, at some point, he reaches for another cigar and repeats the whole pas de deux. What never got mentioned was that these cigars cost around $20 each. Also, most people who smoke cigars really just *puff* cigars, taking the smoke into their mouth and letting it escape. Michel actually *inhaled.* "Michel is the only person I have known in my life who inhales cigars," said Kim Fennebresque. "And he puts salt on his butter. He has fucking balls that I don't have." Curiously, while Michel's love of cigars has been well documented over the years by the press, he declined to be interviewed for a lengthy 1995 *Cigar Aficionado* article about CEOs who smoke cigars. A spokesman for Michel noted that while he "enjoys cigars," he did not "feel comfortable" talking about smoking.

Cigar smoking was as much a part of the Lazard DNA as secrecy, ruthlessness, and money. The old Lazard offices at One Rockefeller Plaza may have been notoriously ratty, but they fairly reeked of the rich smell of cigar smoke. You could tell you were at Lazard with your eyes closed. André Meyer smoked cigars, a fact captured by a famous black-and-white photograph of him sitting behind his office desk with cigar smoke unfurling all around him. Michel favors Cuban cigars, which are not legally purchased in the United States, such as Hoyo de Monterrey Epicure No. 1. He buys them by the "fucking bushel," according to Fennebresque, at Gerard Père et Fils in Geneva and has them shipped to him at the office. Or, to be accurate, he used to have them shipped to him at the office until one day the U.S. Customs Service intercepted one of his bushels—of some fifteen hundred cigars—at the airport in New York. Instead of the cigars, Michel got an official letter from customs telling him what he needed to do, if he wished, to retrieve the stogies.

After a quick consultation with Marty Lipton at Wachtell, Michel decided to ignore the letter and let the cigars go unclaimed. "So some Puerto Rican is sitting in his apartment in Queens smoking some $25 heaters," Fennebresque said, with a smile.

Michel then had his cigars sent to Mel Heineman's attention. When Heineman left the firm, Michel took another tack. Now when his friends come to New York for a visit, they bring him some of his prized cigars. Customs seems to allow individuals to bring into the country a small number of Cuban cigars, although once Michel got caught doing this, too, and the cigars were confiscated. So he stopped trying to bring them in. "The law is very strange," he commented. "When I open some magazines, I've seen recently—as a matter of fact—an advertisement for Cuban cigars out of Canada in the U.S. press. And so I don't really know. . . . They have the list of the stores in Europe which send cigars, and if they see something sent by them, they stop them."

As with so many of the Lazard customs, what André and Michel did had a huge influence on their partners' behavior. "Lazard is like Wall Street was in the early 1980s" one insider said a few years ago. "Cigar smoke is thick on the floor by 10 in the morning, they're all smoking." (Felix, though, never smoked cigars; he smoked several packs of cigarettes a day when he was younger, and then smoked a pipe when he was trying to quit smoking altogether. Nowadays, he does not smoke.) As an indicative sample, Robert Agostinelli, Kim Fennebresque, Al Garner, Bill Loomis, Michael Price, Luis Rinaldini, and Dick Torykian all smoked cigars. (Steve Rattner, an occasional runner, does not smoke.) Naturally, the cigar-smoking habit trickled down to the ambitious vice president types. Kamal Tabet, now a big deal at Citigroup in London, used to chain-smoke cigars. Being a Big Swinging Dick in training, Tabet would, of course, ignore the pleas of his office mate to stop smoking in their small office, and so forced the overwrought guy to construct a stack of fans blowing constantly at Tabet to push the smoke back in his direction. Eventually, Tabet was moved to another floor (people were moved constantly, so this was not unusual), and he developed an ulcer. Tabet's doctor told him no more cigars. Another vice president cigar smoker was Tim Collins. Looking very much like an imitation of André, Collins used to puff away on a big cigar as early as eight-thirty in the morning. On the wall of his office was the infamous picture of André smoking a cigar. Collins is now a billionaire and the über-successful head of Ripplewood Holdings, a buyout fund. He is a regular at Herb Allen's Sun Valley conference.

For some partners, emulating Michel's cigar-smoking habit was such a preoccupation that it caused them to do strange things. Loomis, for one, took to heart Michel's odd advice that cigar smoking could help relieve his flu-like symptoms. So he amped up his consumption of them briefly to test the supposition.

KEN WILSON REMEMBERS a curious incident involving cigars and Robert Agostinelli. At the time, Wilson was head of banking and looked at his partners' expenses from time to time. In 1996, Ira Harris, through his friendship with Ron Gidwitz, the CEO of the beauty products company Helene Curtis Industries, brought into the firm the assignment to sell the company. Agostinelli was assigned to work on the deal and commuted regularly to Chicago to execute it. Explained Wilson: "Agostinelli had his girlfriend in Chicago, and his expenses were just unreal. He'd shack up for a weekend, and I'd see all these bills for limos. And the one thing that did catch my eye was that he bought several boxes of Cuban cigars for Ron Gidwitz. Well, it just so happened that I was out at the Grove"—the Bohemian Grove, a highly exclusive twenty-seven-hundred-acre compound in Monte Rio, California—"with Ron, [and I] was in his camp. He's a friend of a friend of mine, and we're talking. I said, 'You know, Ron, you must really love these Cuban cigars.' He said, 'What do you mean?' I said, 'Well, we're paying for 'em.' I said, 'I just approved the expenses for, you know, two boxes of Cohibas and another three boxes of something else.' He said, 'What do you mean? I never saw those goddamn cigars.' I said, 'Well, you know, we paid for 'em.' And then he went absolutely ballistic. It was Agostinelli and that lady." Agostinelli eventually made it up to Gidwitz by donating $15,000 to Gidwitz's unsuccessful 2006 campaign to become governor of Illinois.

Then there was the time Kim Fennebresque invited his friend the chairman of Beneficial Finance for lunch with Michel in the Lazard dining room in New York. At the end of a meal there, the tradition was that the waiters would pass around cigars to the clients and the bankers. But with Michel in attendance, he insisted that the waiter fetch his *own* cigars. "He had someone send for his stash because basically they put shit in the partners' dining room except when Michel was there," Fennebresque recalled. "I mean, it was just rolled camel turds. So when Michel came in, they brought the real stuff, right? So Michel offered one to the client, who said no. And I'm sitting there, smiling, like, 'I'll take one,' and you could just see as he handed it to me, the notion, the insubordination of one of his fucking domestic staff—*moi*—would deign to have one of his heaters was just too much to bear. It was a very funny moment, and I'll never forget it." Annik Percival would also have some fun with Michel's cigars. She would permit partners she liked—Fennebresque among them—to help themselves to Michel's cigars in his office humidor when Michel was off in Paris, London, or Sous-le-Vent. "She'd call me," Fennebresque said, "and I'd go fish some out of his humidor because they'd be stale by the time he'd get back."

But sometimes Fennebresque, now the CEO of the publicly-traded investment bank the Cowen Group, couldn't wait until Michel went out of town to get his Cuban cigar fix. At the partners' meetings on Monday mornings, he would watch in amazement as Michel went through his typical cigar-smoking ritual. "I used to watch Michel," he said. "And he'd smoke these things. He'd light them up and smoke them and literally smoke three-eighths of an inch and then put it in the ashtray and then light up another one. And I just thought this was fucking ridiculous. So I made sure I was the last guy to leave the partners' meeting. And I would clip both ends of his cigars in the ashtray, and I would fucking take them. So every Monday, I had two $15 cigars. And no one ever knew."

❦

Michel categorically denied being ill when the Cobra attempted his late-1996 strike. "You know, in life, sometimes you have people who create a problem for you because what they're saying makes sense," Michel said. "So you have to consider seriously what they say." But to Michel, Édouard's actions were unfathomable and did not fit any discernible logic. "It didn't make sense. It couldn't have happened even if I'd said yes." Had Michel acceded to Édouard's demands, the fallout in terms of partner objections would have been immediate and substantial. And for a man as logical as Michel, whose every move was designed for incremental, rather than radical, change, Édouard's behavior was simply unacceptable. "We do not like to make revolutions," he once said in 1993. "When you have to do that, it means you have somehow failed. We favor evolution." Asked once in Paris by his younger, incredulous partner Gilles Etrillard about his apparent lack of recollection about Lazard having forgiven a client's $50 million debt, Michel replied, "If I were not sure, I would be able to recall something; and as I cannot recall anything, I must therefore be sure." ("Brilliant," the witness to this display remarked to himself.)

"Édouard was very impatient," Michel continued, "and temperamental, and I'm not even sure he planned it, you know? I think he thought maybe he was losing ground, that I was getting a little discouraged with him, and he said, 'Okay, I'm going to call his bluff and say I leave if you don't.' And I said, 'You leave.' " And that was it. Édouard was swiftly removed from the two main operating committees in Paris and New York. He remained a partner of the firm, focusing on private-equity investments, while the details of his much-gossiped-about departure were being worked out. In New York, the Lazard partnership agreement allowed Michel to dismiss a partner in his sole judgment and authority. In Paris, it was not so simple—theoretically—for him to remove a partner; there, the partnership had to unanimously vote to remove a partner. In reality, though, Michel always got his way in both places. It took more time for partners in Paris to be removed, but "people basically respected my decisions," he said, although Édouard would retain his equity in Lazard in Paris, causing problems down the road for Michel.

Although the firm denied that anything like Édouard's attempted coup d'état had occurred, a story this juicy could not be contained for long, especially given its ability to upset the political dynamics inside the firm—a calculus already confounded by the likely departure of Felix, the apparent sidelining of Rattner and Loomis (who was by this time far away in self-imposed exile in San Francisco, where he had reestablished a Lazard office, the firm's first presence in the city in a hundred years), and Messier's quitting. Édouard's departure was bound to create a massive power vacuum. The details began leaking out in earnest during the first few weeks of January 1997. Although one partner familiar with the feud described Édouard as having "a kill-or-be-killed mentality," the firm still officially deflected the story, calling the falling-out "overblown." Finally, on January 11, 1997, the *Financial Times* published an on-the-record interview with Michel where the closest he came to admitting what happened was to say he was amused by the press reports about it. "What caught me by surprise was the idea in France that he was clearly and surely going to be my successor," he said. "It shows how royalist the French are at heart," before adding, "Mr. Stern is a man of many gifts but he reflected on what his career should be too publicly." He said turmoil in a successful investment bank is inevitable. "Any investment bank is by necessity full of people who are pretty highly strung because the talent needed to win customers is made up in equal parts of confidence in yourself and insecurity." Without conceding he was even contemplating leaving, he did allow that he was thinking about appointing a new management committee "of three or four or five, not more," Lazard partners to run an increasingly tighter-knit global firm.

As an additional move in that direction, in 1996 the three houses agreed to share some of their profits, although many of the bankers in London felt the tax consequences of this arrangement were most painful for them. "Sooner or later," Michel said, "Lazard is going to be the Holy Trinity. It will be three and it will be one." (The Holy Trinity concept, reflective of Michel's Catholic upbringing, became a mantra for him during the next few years.) Michel allowed that he had a plan for how this would work as well. To wit, Eurafrance, a private-equity firm controlled by Michel and some of his French partners, might be willing to swap its accumulated £360 million stake in Pearson for Pearson's stakes in Lazard Partners and the New York and Paris partnerships should Pearson's new CEO, the American Marjorie Scardino, decide to sell Pearson's Lazard stake as had been rumored. Michel, the longest-serving Pearson board member, would certainly have been in a position to know Scardino's thinking. He had always maintained that his stake in Pearson, accumulated over the years in the face of repeated takeover attempts by Rupert Murdoch, would be an insurance policy against an undesired outcome on the day Pearson decided to sell its Lazard stake. And that day appeared increasingly close at hand.

With the Lazard rumor mill now churning furiously with the speculation that Felix would soon be appointed ambassador to France and with the blowup between Michel and Édouard all but confirmed, the writer Suzanna Andrews struck again. In a lengthy profile, wittily titled "The Scion in Winter," in the March 1997 issue of *Vanity Fair*, Michel, "as charming as he is feared," sat for "an unprecedented interview" and talked about his growing set of problems. Also dredged up again was Michel's ongoing affair with Margo Walker. Essentially, Andrews blamed Michel for Lazard's many predicaments—among them, the altercation with Édouard, the horrific publicity about Felix and Steve, and Antoine Bernheim's desire to leave the Paris firm. "Michel is in a very tight spot," a "prominent" unnamed banker told Andrews. "He tends to minimize things, but this is very serious if he cares about his birthright." Another man offered a similar assessment: "Michel always tries to put the best face on things, but I think he's very worried that Édouard blew himself up on the launching pad, that Messier left, that Rattner is not committed. Michel made a mistake in allowing this culture to evolve where everyone is at everyone's throat every day, but I think that today he is trying to fix it."

Andrews described two Michels: the one seen most often, who is unfailingly gracious with his time—for instance, taking hours to meet with prospective new partners or clients to gab about art or politics—and the one who delights in pitting partner against partner to ensure his own importance and who relishes thwarting the efforts of onetime clients who dared not use Lazard for their M&A deals. The latter Michel was described as chilling, mean, and manipulative. "His joy is power and exercising power," said an executive who had known Michel for years. "Be careful with him," added another, "he is blindingly ruthless." But the revelation is that—in 1997 no less—this was any kind of revelation at all. The dirty little secret of the über-Darwinian world of investment banking has always been how charming, patient, and solicitous investment bankers are with their clients, the press, and attractive women and how petty, insecure, backstabbing, and, yes, ruthless they are with one another. The number of eviscerated colleagues an investment banker at the top of his profession has had to trample would make a marine wince. Leave it to the literary polymath Thomas Pynchon and one of his iconoclastic characters, in a cameo, to properly deride this behavior: "Those whose enduring object is power in the world are only too happy to use without remorse the others, whose aim is of course to transcend all questions of power. Each regards the other as a pack of deluded fools."

Michel told Andrews he intended to be running Lazard for a good while, no doubt tweaking those partners who believed his inability to relinquish power had held the firm back. They were together in Michel's sumptuous, art-filled Fifth Avenue apartment—the first time he had invited a member of the press there. "There is a fashion," he said, cigar smoke swirling around him, "that I think comes from the fact that people's minds are used to public-corporation people retiring. I have no intention of retiring. When I became a partner in 1961, André Meyer was 63. When I became co–senior partner in 1977, he was 79. OK? So I think that gives me a long time."

Not surprisingly, Michel tried to influence Andrews's article by letting her know from the outset, just as she was about to cross the threshold into the apartment, that he was not pleased with her *New York* magazine article. "He said it was a disappointment to have read it," she recalled. "He looked at me and his eyebrow went up. He told me he had expected so much better of me. 'It was all so beneath you' is what he said." Some of Michel's partners thought the *Vanity Fair* article was simply too much—too much exposure, too much confessing, too much Michel. "For some reason, he decided to do this article in *Vanity Fair*," said one partner. "And it talked all about Lazard, his personal life, his two wives—his wife and his girlfriend—all his homes, his relationship with his kids. All this stuff which we were shocked at. Here's this private guy, and it caused, I mean, you know, I just remember Felix saying this on so many different occasions that Michel had lost it. You could date the day that Michel lost it to that *Vanity Fair* article. It was the first time, I think, Michel had put himself above any of the other partners in the United States in terms of visibility. And that, I think, was something which really bothered Felix."

Regardless of what his partners thought, Michel was true to his word. Six weeks later, Édouard was gone. On the very same day that President Clinton announced Felix's nomination as ambassador to France, stories emerged in the French press that Stern would leave the firm to start his own investment company, with some of the money coming from Lazard. Official word of Édouard's departure came on May 1, 1997. He had been removed as a general partner and retained only a small, limited partnership stake in Lazard Paris. His new firm, based in Geneva with offices in Paris and New York, was awkwardly named Investments Real Returns, or IRR for short—a play on the basic private-equity concept of internal rate of return. IRR started with $600 million to invest, $300 million from what is now Eurazeo, the large publicly-traded private-equity fund in France controlled by Michel (and formed by the merger of Eurafrance with Azeo), and $300 million from Édouard and his friends. "Édouard has great and real talent as an investor," Michel explained at the time. In effect, though, the $300 million from Eurazeo was the price Lazard paid for having Édouard leave peacefully and not pursue a threatened lawsuit. "He always made money when he left places," Michel said. At this very moment, unbeknownst to all, Édouard and Beatrice had decided to divorce. Indeed, they kept news of the split quiet for "several months"—even from Michel—to avoid having it interfere with Édouard's arrangements to leave the firm. Beatrice remained living on Central Park West, in New York, with their three school-age children, Mathilde, Louis, and Henry. Édouard moved to Geneva, but he also owned an apartment in Paris and a château in the French countryside where he kept the taxidermic evidence of his big-game-hunting episodes.

As the news of their split slowly leaked out—although the news of their actual divorce remained very well hidden for years—the Lazard conspiracy theorists speculated that Édouard had married Beatrice only to get close to Michel and advance his professional aspirations. This speculation merely intensified after Édouard's unsuccessful Thanksgiving putsch and his split with Beatrice. But in truth, he remained a devoted father to his children, visiting them often in New York. He also spoke with them, as well as Beatrice, nearly every day, and they all took vacations together. After their divorce, he told his sister: "I love and respect Beatrice. She is raising my children. She brings a lot to me."

With regard to Felix's appointment as ambassador to France, Michel issued a statement to the press: "Felix Rohatyn has been my partner for over 35 years and it is with great emotion that I congratulate him on this important news. Felix has been a superb and important part of this firm and this news recognizes his leadership, insights and a great love of his country. We wish him every success."

CHAPTER 16

"ALL THE RESPONSIBILITY BUT NONE OF THE AUTHORITY"

With Édouard gone and Felix soon to be, there was the usual speculation in the press about who would fill Lazard's leadership vacuum. But inside the firm, surprisingly, a certain contentment reigned. Nineteen ninety-six had been the firm's best year ever, financially, with pretax net income worldwide of $379 million, up from $357 million the previous year. Édouard had not been particularly focused on being a banker anyway, and his presence was more disruptive than anything else. He would not be especially missed. Felix's departure, meanwhile, though a big loss for sure, was also no surprise.

Indeed, rather than everyone bemoaning the turn of events, there was a sense that now was the time for the younger generation of partners to shine. Soon after Clinton nominated Felix and it was clear he was going to leave the firm, many of the senior partners, led by Steve, demanded that Michel meet with them to begin to figure out a way to loosen his autocratic grip on Lazard. "We demanded that he attend," one partner told *Euromoney,* "and in effect dragged him into the room and said we wanted him to know what we thought. We said: 'This is no way to run a railroad—it cannot go on like this!' "

The collected partners had three points to make to Michel: First, he should explain what he intended for Lazard's future, as there had been numerous rumors about his trying to once again recruit Bruce Wasserstein, then CEO of Wasserstein Perella & Co., to Lazard. The opposition to Bruce was particularly intense. "You don't understand who Bruce is," one banker recalled Michel being told. "He's not at all consistent with our firm's culture." Second, the partners wanted to end Michel's secretive machinations, whether cutting separate deals with individual partners or bringing in his son-in-law Édouard Stern and acting as if he were the anointed successor. Third, the partners expressed doubts about Michel being able to continue to run the firm single-handedly, a tack that during the previous decade had led to lax controls and unprofessional behavior. (The firm still had to settle the two pieces of the municipal finance scandal, which promised to be costly.)

Michel had another plan, though, just as some of his partners feared. One day around this time, while having lunch at the "21" Club, he saw Wasserstein sitting across the dining room. Bruce's office at Wasserstein Perella was just a hundred yards west of "21," and the restaurant had become his cafeteria. For rainmakers like Felix, Steve, and Bruce a power lunch at the Four Seasons, "21," or that ilk was a chance to show off their plumage. They tended to pick a place, and then become regulars, to ensure appropriately fawning behavior. At these spots, one wag observed, "the pecking order is measured not by what you eat but rather with whom you eat and what direction you face." Another favorite lunch spot for the nonboldface Lazard partners was the secretive Rockefeller Center Club, founded in 1934 as part of the Rainbow Room complex on the sixty-fifth floor of 30 Rockefeller Center (now three floors above Lazard's offices). This was the ultimate—a scrumptious buffet of gourmet salads, fresh shrimp, and filet mignon, an uninterrupted view south of lower Manhattan, and the private companionship of numerous corporate CEOs and Wall Street bankers and attorneys. There was no bill or menu, just a warm greeting from the maître d' and the quiet comfort of exclusivity. Maybe the appeal of the Rockefeller Center Club was nothing more complicated than Fitzgerald's observation of the "consoling proximity of millionaires." But Michel rarely ate outside the firm. Not only was such theater not his style, but also he had the best French chef in New York on his premises, so why bother going out? Indeed, one of the best places to dine on the planet may have been the quiet wood-paneled dining room at Lazard's office in Paris, on the Boulevard Haussmann. There, white-jacketed waiters breathlessly served the finest French wines and cuisine to a very fortunate few. And besides, Michel's lunchtime appetite often ran to nothing more sophisticated than a baguette slathered in French butter and salt.

That rare day at "21"—so the story goes—Bruce came up to Michel, and the two men spoke briefly. Bruce had confirmed an idea Michel had been mulling. When Michel came back to Rockefeller Center, he walked into Felix's office and announced: "We're going to try to merge with Wasserstein Perella." Felix was stunned—and appalled. While he thought there may have been *some* logic to hiring Bruce Wasserstein, Gary Parr (a highly regarded financial institutions banker), and a few other talented Wasserstein Perella bankers, with Lazard still under the cloud of ongoing federal investigations into its municipal finance department, a merger between the two firms—even if it could be negotiated and announced—

would never close. There was also the concern that the majority of the Wasserstein Perella bankers weren't up to Lazard's standards, and that even Bruce himself was not cut from the traditional mold of a Lazard banker, to say nothing of the fact that a full-blown merger with Bruce's firm would be a total slap in the face to the aspirations of the younger Lazard partners who had been waiting patiently for the very moment, now at hand, when Felix's departure, like the felling of a mighty old-growth Douglas fir, would allow a little sunlight to hit the forest floor. Furthermore, the word was that Wasserstein Perella had not been making any money. Add to that the fact that Lazard had never, ever grown through acquisition, and there were any number of compelling reasons why Michel's brainstorm was stillborn. Felix told Michel, "You can't merge with Wasserstein Perella, you know. There's 120 people or something like that."

But Mr. 4.1 pushed ahead anyway. A small group comprising Mel Heineman, the general counsel; Steve Golub, a partner who had once been the deputy chief accountant at the SEC; and Steve Niemczyk, a young partner who worked for Wilson in the FIG group, were secretly dispatched to review the books and records of Wasserstein Perella & Co. Felix and Ken Wilson were kept abreast of their findings. Steve Rattner was kept in the dark. "Felix was deeply skeptical," Wilson remembered. "When you looked at the business that Wasserstein was doing, I think their average fee was like $250,000. I mean, it was a lot of tiny deals, marginal people and offices. Their capital markets unit was a joke." Wilson said the due diligence revealed that the firm was running out of money and had little in the way of backlog or receivables. "They were a bunch of turkeys," he said. As word of the potential merger started to circulate around the firm, Wilson recommended to Michel that a partners' meeting be held to "get this on the table." On a Friday afternoon, Michel invited only a subset of New York's most important partners to an impromptu meeting in a conference room on the sixty-second floor of 30 Rockefeller Center to discuss the possibility of a merger. "There was good attendance," Wilson remembered, a wry little smile forming on his face. Another partner at the meeting said of Michel, "It took a two-by-four piece of wood to gain his attention, but at some point he woke up. Like all of us, he tried to push things under the rug. But sooner or later he became a realist. He realized he could not avoid the fact that he had a problem."

Michel kicked off the meeting by talking about the potential merger and about the cost savings that could result. But mostly he spoke about Bruce as the next Great Man of Lazard. Michel explained that Bruce had always loved Lazard and had conceived of Wasserstein Perella in Lazard's image. This was a chance to get Bruce, Michel told his partners. Incredibly, Michel had been so utterly indifferent to his partners' hopes and dreams that he dashed them completely by proposing this combination. Ken Wilson recalled that Michel's "views were so far from reality that it was time to go around the table" to get input from the other partners. Jerry Rosenfeld, who had been seated next to Michel, spoke first.

Wilson remembered Rosenfeld's comments as being quite blunt. "So he turns to Jerry," Wilson said. "Jerry says, 'This is the dumbest fucking deal I've ever heard of. There isn't a single one of those people we would ever hire. We would never take them off the street. It makes no fucking sense.' And the comments went downhill all the way around." Steve Rattner recalled that "one by one, everybody just laid into Michel and just let him have it right between the eyes." All parties remembered that after the negative consensus had formed—a rare showing of unity of the partners against Michel—the Sun King backed down. "Then I will not go forward," Michel said quietly. And just like that, the Wasserstein deal was dead. But despite this victory, to some partners the Rubicon had been crossed. "In response to these comments that Michel had made at the outset about the fit and everything else, they were just so far from reality that his credibility was shot," Wilson said. "And Bill Kneisel, [a partner] who I recruited [from Morgan Stanley], a good guy—and at the end of the meeting, I walked out with Bill. He turned to me, he said, 'You know, Wils,' he said, 'this emperor has no fucking clothes.' He said, 'I'm gonna watch a lotta football games with my son this fall, and I'm out of here.' " (He left soon afterward and returned to Morgan Stanley.) Wilson recalled that Kneisel's reaction was typical. "The average foot soldier left that meeting saying, 'What the hell is going on?' There was no logic for it. And when Michel tried to articulate it, it just sounded awful."

Steve was furious with Michel about the Wasserstein gambit. Not only had Michel not explicitly told him about what was happening; Michel denied there was anything to the rumors Steve had heard even after he went into Michel's office to ask him. "The next thing I know, he's locked in meetings with him," Steve explained. Felix, who was leaving regardless of the outcome, remembered the meeting as initiating "a real revolution inside the firm." Independently, Steve used the exact same word to describe what happened as a result of the confluence of Felix and Édouard leaving, Bruce being approached secretly, and the mushrooming cost to the firm of the municipal finance scandal (eventually the firm paid a whopping $100 million to settle all aspects of the scandal).

"This was a revolution," he said. "This was not Michel's idea. Michel did not want this. He agreed to it grudgingly, but it was a revolution." The news of the Wasserstein discussions and their abandonment was leaked, without color, to the *Wall Street Journal,* which published the story on May 2, the day after Édouard left the firm.

For his part, Bruce found the schizophrenic discussions bizarre. One person who knows him well said, "Bruce describes it as like one of the most surreal experiences of his life. I mean, Michel comes to him. Michel proposes this to him. Bruce says, 'Well, what about all the partners in New York? I can work with Steve. I can work with Ken. I'll do whatever it takes to make it work with those guys.' Michel says to him, 'You don't need to. I don't care about those guys.' And this is one of the many times he says this. And, you know, Bruce is stunned when they all come back, after Michel saying it's all done, come back and say, 'No deal.' So it was kind of interesting."

Indeed, Mike Biondi, Bruce's longtime consigliere, doesn't even recognize the Lazard version of the brief courtship. Wasserstein Perella was doing fine financially, he said, and was growing faster than Lazard at this time. "The Lazard spin versus the reality of what happened there is 180 degrees different," Biondi explained in a conference room at Lazard, where, ironically, he is now a partner. According to Biondi, the process actually started with *Felix,* who, while leaving Lazard for Paris, wanted to have a hand in shaping the future of the firm. "Our perception was he didn't want the place turned over to any of the likely suspects who were here," Biondi said. "There was a lot of broken glass between him and Rattner and others, and in a very old Lazardian way. Felix preferred to turn Lazard over to somebody from the outside because, first, it would have been sort of his doing and, second, he had no confidence in the folks that he had lived with every day." With Michel's blessing, there were a series of negotiating sessions at the Manhattan offices of Wachtell, Lipton between Michel, Felix, Heineman, and Niemczyk (for Lazard) and Bruce, Biondi, and Clay Kingsbury (for Wasserstein Perella). Rather quickly, according to Biondi, there was a meeting of the minds among the executives that Lazard and Wasserstein Perella would combine in a no-premium "merger of equals" deal, where Bruce would become the CEO of the New York partnership. When the long-anticipated merger of the three houses of Lazard followed subsequently, Bruce would have a seat on the management committee of the merged global firm.

"The Lazard thing broke down in 1997 on one issue, as far as I'm concerned, and one issue alone," Biondi said.

> It broke down because when you got down to talking about what it really meant that Bruce would be chief executive—in Bruce's mind and my mind—it meant that we would have the ability to pay people and promote people, and do all that sort of stuff, without interference, other than obviously having to have a budget and being part of the firm. But that Bruce was going to be the final decision maker for that in New York. And we felt very strongly that if we were going to fix the difficult culture that existed at Lazard and make it more team-oriented and get the synergy out of doing the thing, people had to understand that Bruce was in charge and that he was serious about running it in a collegial, team-oriented way. But Michel said, "No, I'm going to have a veto, of course, over all this stuff." And I remember very clearly having a heart-to-heart with Bruce and with this fellow Clay Kingsbury and saying, "It won't work. It just won't work. People are going to run around us, keep going to him, and it'll be a nightmare. We're better off on our own." And Bruce is a smart guy. He understood that himself, and *that's* why the deal died.

Biondi and Bruce believed that Michel then—very cleverly—went back to his partners, announced that he was going to pursue a deal with Bruce anyway, and then when he retreated—following the easily anticipated firestorm—Michel would look like he had listened to the demands of his partners. The story of the Lazard partner revolt was then leaked to the press as the reason for the deal's demise. "You've been around Michel for a long time," Biondi concluded. "Do you think Michel gives a shit about what the Lazard partners say? The deal was dead before that ever happened because we killed it."

Regardless of what really happened, over the next few weeks Michel's massive office on the sixty-second floor of 30 Rockefeller Center became, if not quite the Bastille, then the epicenter of the revolutionary fervor surging through the New York partnership. In the wake of that Friday afternoon partnership meeting, Michel had learned firsthand about the dangers of the First Amendment's guarantee of freedom of speech and peaceful assembly. There would be no more group discussions with the partners about seminal matters. Instead, Michel met one by one with key partners to try to reach a consensus about how the firm should be managed in the post-Felix era. "Michel likes to do things one on one," a former partner said. "He hated big meetings because people could gang up on him." Out of these discussions emerged the evolving view that Michel could no longer run the firm unilaterally. The argument ran that Lazard's historically flat structure, where basically everyone—from banking to asset management to capital markets to real estate—reported to him, since he alone decided partner compensation and promotion, no longer worked. The firm was now too big and in too many business lines for Michel to manage alone. Left unsaid by most of the senior partners—but now painfully obvious since the firm seemed so out of control—was that they believed Michel no longer had the skills, either intellectually or temperamentally, to run Lazard day to day.

Out of these tortured discussions, a combination of Danton, Marat, and Robespierre emerged in the form of Steve Rattner. Since Ken Wilson had taken over as head of banking in 1995, Steve had returned to deal making almost exclusively. With Felix having retired on April 30, Steve was now the firm's largest producer. Steve recalled: "Everybody said to Michel, 'Michel, you've got to do something!' Michel said, 'What?' Out of it all came *me,* and frankly I was probably the last man standing. A lot of people said, 'Well, I don't know. He's never run anything. He ran banking once, and it didn't work out great for everybody, but who knows?' What happened was that a number of people who mattered, including the asset management guys, Damon, and some of the senior bankers, said, 'Steve may not be perfect, he may not have enough experience to do this'—which I surely didn't—'but there's nobody else. If you don't get him to do this, we're really heading toward a cliff.' "

Steve had also won the support of Loomis, then still in San Francisco but on his way back to live in New York, who wrote Michel a long letter on Steve's behalf. The problem, though, for Steve and Lazard in his being drafted to run the New York partnership was that at that very moment he was also considering whether to take a job in the second Clinton administration. Steve and Maureen had been ratcheting up to the stratosphere their interaction with and financial support for the Clintons. He raised millions for Clinton in 1996 as co-head of the Wall Street fund-raising effort. Soon after Clinton's second-term inauguration and as the revolutionary fervor inside Lazard was growing, Steve learned he was being considered for a "reasonably interesting job" in the second Clinton administration. He wouldn't say what job he had been offered, because he did not want the person who ended up with it thinking he or she had been second choice. "I wasn't going to be secretary of the Treasury" is all that he would allow. "It was a job that, but for this, I would have taken. Six months earlier, I was doing my banking thing, and the next thing I knew, I was thinking about either Washington, D.C., or being something at Lazard."

Having been nominated by his partners to run New York, Steve began a "long series of tortured negotiations" with Michel "over what I would do." He said he was not planning to accept the new Lazard job "without some authority" from Michel to actually run New York. At one point, in the middle of these negotiations, as a symbol of an emerging détente between the two men, Felix asked Steve if he wanted his office. Steve told him no—but what he really meant was "not yet." The negotiations between Michel and Steve produced a "kind of vague" agreement between them that was never formalized into a contract, although "we did actually write some stuff down and sign it," whereby Steve would participate in the meetings with Michel where individual partners received their annual profit percentage—a role Loomis had desperately wanted but Michel never before permitted. A new executive committee was set up, for which Steve both set the agenda and chaired. Steve also ran the weekly partners' meetings even if Michel attended. He decided to move into Felix's office. "The kinds of things that would cause people to say, 'Well, this guy probably does have some responsibility,' " Steve explained. The one quirk was what his title would be. Steve suggested to Michel that he be president and chief operating officer of New York, with Michel being chairman and CEO. But Michel objected. This was one of his "eccentricities," Steve explained. Michel told Steve, "You can't be president, because in France the president is the one who does all the work and my friends will all think I've retired and I can't have that." The two men agreed that Steve would be deputy CEO of New York, of all things, after Steve confessed that he cared more about what he would be able to accomplish than about his title. One partner at the time said that Michel viewed Steve as "a terrific rainmaker, very well organized, disciplined, and ambitious. He'll do some good things; he'll be a good leader. He's the most able of this whole group. And maybe I can control him, and if not, I can always get rid of him. Michel viewed Steve as a convenient person at the moment but certainly not with the potential of thinking that Steve could be somehow a successor in the long term."

On May 22, 1997, the firm held a rare press conference to announce the new management team. The night before the announcement, Michel hosted a cocktail party in the New York office in honor of Felix's retirement. Michel made a speech. Felix made a speech. "They gave me a vase or something like that," a still underwhelmed Felix recalled eight years later of that perfunctory event. "No, actually, they gave me a glass eagle, a U.S. eagle to take to France." Lazard also gave Felix a pension that paid him $1 million annually for life, the consideration for which was Felix's signature on a three-year noncompete agreement should he decide to return to investment banking after coming back from Paris. The *Times* reported on May 23 that Steve's appointment as deputy chief executive of Lazard Frères & Co. meant that he was "inheriting" Felix's "mantle as the firm's lead banker after several months of fierce internal squabbling." This observation, while a slight exaggeration, was a fair reflection of the turn of events. Steve would run the firm day to day and report directly to Michel. He would manage the New York partnership with the help of his four new vice chairmen, Ken Wilson, head of banking; Damon Mezzacappa, head of capital markets; and Norm Eig and Herb Gullquist, the co-heads of Lazard's $47 billion asset management business. Steve Golub was named chief financial officer—the first time that position existed. Michel, Steve, Wilson, Mezzacappa, Gullquist, Eig, Golub, and Mel Heineman, the firm's chief administrative officer and general counsel, formed the New York firm's new management committee.

"We wanted to both strengthen and broaden the base of management of the firm in New York," Michel said. At the press conference, Steve said of Michel, "Our goal is to take off his shoulders some of the things he has had to worry about." Michel explained that while the new management committee would strive for "very consensual" decision making, he retained his veto over any of its actions. Michel's personal ambition would be to continue to get the three houses working more closely together. And then, of course, he said, "The term 'Trinity' has been mentioned. We have to be one, and we have to be three. What is extremely gratifying in the three Lazard firms is how much the partners believe that our concept is not only viable but is going to make us even more successful."

After the press conference, Steve and Felix repaired to Felix's "usual conspicuous table" at the "21" Club for a very high-profile reconciliation lunch. *Newsweek* ran a short piece about Steve's promotion and wondered if the "fair-haired banker" was now in position to succeed Michel as well. Steve declined to make himself available to be interviewed. Instead, he issued a statement: "These changes are about the firm and not about me. We are moving forward as a team." Michel, though, as usual, felt the need to take his new deputy CEO down a peg. "Mr. Rattner is in an important position toward being part of the succession planning," he said. When asked by *BusinessWeek* if Steve was now heir apparent, Michel said, "Until things exist, they don't exist. He certainly is in line for that responsibility." Added another keen observer of the Lazard realpolitik, "Michel owns this firm. He runs the firm any way he wants." For *BusinessWeek,* Steve decided to comment about his hopes for democratizing the firm and Michel's role in that transformation: "Michel will be a little less the emperor and a little more the president." Felix also chimed in. "This isn't an industry that's appropriate for the superstar approach anymore," he said. "And the firm is a lot more diversified, a lot bigger, than when we ran a superstar business."

Despite Felix's view that the days of the Wall Street rainmaker were coming to a close—just as he seemed to be leaving the scene—Michel, incredibly, disagreed. He still longed for a superstar. The *Newsweek* article revealed that after the Wasserstein merger failed and as the negotiations with Steve were in full bloom, a group of senior Lazard partners, including Steve, approached the veteran deal maker Bob Greenhill about coming to Lazard as the firm's senior partner. Greenhill, who had spent thirty-one years at Morgan Stanley, including some time as Steve's boss there, had started his own eponymous firm in January 1996. The idea was for Greenhill to merge his small firm into Lazard and thereby bolster the senior ranks in the wake of Felix's departure.

Steve was fine with this. "I was the one who went to Greenhill, so it wasn't like I had any pride of place," he said. "I was willing to do almost anything to try to make it better for the firm." Greenhill turned down Lazard. In the *Newsweek* article, Michel defended his efforts to get Wasserstein and Greenhill, even though the efforts would have frustrated the aspirations of his younger partners. "As always, the difficulty is to get enough wind behind the sails," he said, adding in his convoluted logic that these efforts to recruit big-name outsiders had "helped provide the wind" to support Steve's ascension. Michel told *Institutional Investor* about the effort with Bruce, "The negotiations broke down because it proved impossible to combine the two firms without spending considerable money. If Mr. Wasserstein and a reasonable number of his colleagues had joined individually, we would have been very happy." He told *Fortune* about his effort to recruit Wasserstein, "Of course you can never have enough top talent." He stressed that Steve's selection was the result of a "collegial approach" where "certainly there have been no winners or losers."

But of course that wasn't true. Any power vacuum that is filled inevitably requires a wrenching political struggle among the possible contenders. Even though Michel didn't care to admit it, Steve's appointment as deputy CEO of Lazard Frères & Co. caused no fewer ripples. The most disaffected partners were those closest to Felix—Ken Wilson, Ira Harris, and Jerry Rosenfeld. All three had worked together at Salomon Brothers and had been heavily recruited to Lazard by Felix. And all three had been successful and productive at Lazard. With Felix gone and Steve, in effect, their new boss, there were many who felt it was just a matter of time before they followed their mentor out the door.

The bitter pill was probably toughest for Wilson to swallow. He had been running banking for two years, and at most other firms that would have meant he was Steve's boss. So with Steve's promotion he would now be reporting to someone who, theoretically, had been reporting to him. But the lines of authority at Lazard were never so clear. With Michel still making the compensation decisions alone, the job as head of banking was more titular and administrative than one with any real authority, especially when it came to the compensation of and authority over other partners.

For instance, without consulting Wilson, Michel asked Steve to do a study of the efficacy of Lazard's small capital markets business then, as ever, run by Damon Mezzacappa, Steve's ally and friend. Many Lazard partners believe Michel asked Steve to undertake the study as a way to help resurrect Steve's career at the firm. "Damon was in bed with Rattner, and so, not surprisingly, the study concluded that capital markets was pretty important when everyone except the brain-dead knew there was nothing there," said Wilson, who preferred to drastically curtail the department. "As Felix used to say about Lazard's capital markets business, 'Why don't we just stand on the street corner and sell cocaine?' " And while Wilson was himself an important producer of business, Steve was an even bigger producer, so in the Darwinian world of Lazard that gave him more overall leverage with Michel.

And Michel had decided for Steve. "It became clearer that there were two camps in the firm, two factions, two people, and Michel had to make a choice between either Rattner or myself," recalled Wilson, a former officer in the army special forces in Vietnam who used to walk up to the junior bankers at Lazard and ask them, "Is your shit tight?" "And, you know, I, to be honest, was losing a little bit of my ardor to want to have a dogfight, because, if anything, it was going to be a Pyrrhic victory. You know, Michel wasn't gonna go anywhere, and it dawned on me, as they used to say in the army, there's always the 10 percent that never gets the word." He remembered the jockeying being intense. "There was swirling, infighting, jostling," he continued, "and at a meeting in Paris that I went over for, Michel asked me to come by to see him. And I spent some hours at his house, and he was trying to work out a way that Rattner and I could work together, and, you know, to be honest, my heart was really at this stage not in it because I didn't see it leading to anything. Felix was gone. It was a personal kind of thing to me in terms of style and what he presented. Michel was gonna go nowhere, so that"—here he sounded very much like Bill Loomis—"you would have all the responsibility but none of the authority."

As one of the very top bankers worldwide who specialized in working with financial institutions, Wilson was acutely aware of Lazard's increasingly more difficult competitive position. He strongly advocated for significant strategic changes at the firm—among them folding the capital markets business, stopping the writing of equity research, terminating distressed-debt trading, and refocusing the M&A business on six or seven industries, eschewing the generalist Lazard bankers. "I felt Lazard really was getting a little too big for the space," he said. "It needed to be more crisp. Needed to be more focused. The quality needed to improve. I had tried to recruit some good people, and they would be turned off by what a deeply political place it was." Wilson argued that Michel and his family's annual take of the Lazard profits—then approaching 40 percent when all the various pieces were added together—made it nearly impossible to recruit the best bankers because there simply wasn't enough compensation left to go around when one nonproducer was taking so much out himself. He felt Michel's take should have been closer to 2 percent. He also would never have let Felix leave. Obviously, the kinds of changes Wilson was advocating were too revolutionary for Michel. "There was zero interest in this from Michel or the core group of partners loyal to him," he explained. "Michel was so wedded to the status quo because he felt it was a manifestation of his genius. Michel was definitely more comfortable with Rattner or someone more predictable."

There are partners who believe to this day that Michel's inability to find a way for Rattner and Wilson to coexist peacefully and productively was one of his larger mistakes. Wilson, many felt, had innate leadership qualities: intelligence, charisma, a ribald sense of humor, perspective, and a true understanding of Wall Street's competitive dynamics and Lazard's place in them. He had run banking very well for two years. "The fact that Ken Wilson and Rattner were under the tent and Michel didn't find some way to make it work, and basically chased them away, it's unbelievable, it's sinful," one partner said. Another partner chalked up Michel's refusal to let Rattner and Wilson run New York together as yet one more piece of irrefutable evidence of Michel's demented Machiavellianism. "I think he fundamentally decided that Ken was a good leader and that if he left it with Ken, it was gonna be pretty goddamn difficult to ever get it back again," he said. "If he chose Steve, Ken would leave. If Ken left, he'd have Steve. And Steve would burn out. And then he'd get it completely back again, full control. I think fundamentally that's what he did." Still, at the press conference announcing Steve's appointment, Wilson played the role of the loyal soldier. He agreed, for the time being, to continue to run banking and to report to Steve. He had also been appointed a vice chairman of the firm.

Jerry Rosenfeld, whom Wilson used to blow cigar smoke on when they shared an office at Salomon Brothers, was also more than a little irked by Steve's appointment. He had been having a good run—though some of his partners felt it to be greatly exaggerated—in the mid-1990s, most notably for his role in bringing in and executing the IBM-Lotus deal, among many others, and he had been an important and high-profile supporter of Wilson's in the race with Steve. But with Wilson having been bested, Rosenfeld began to think about what he might want to do next. He had always had an interest in private-equity investing. Indeed, when he decided to leave Salomon Brothers years earlier, he had tried to partner with Xerox, one of his clients, to set up a private-equity fund. But that did not work out. Instead, he went to Bankers Trust, now part of Deutsche Bank, to try to lead a private-equity and leveraged-finance effort there. With Bankers Trust more intent on becoming a powerhouse in derivatives rather than in private equity, Rosenfeld, with Felix's help, jumped to Lazard. He became very friendly with Édouard Stern, and their friendship blossomed. Theirs was an exceedingly odd match. On the one hand was Stern—the ruthless, flamboyant, smoldering, impulsive, bizarre demi-billionaire—and on the other Rosenfeld, the low-key, shaggy-haired, almost sheepish, cerebral Ph.D. in applied mathematics, former college professor, and McKinsey consultant. He nearly went to work with Stern at IRR but decided the strange dynamic between Michel and Édouard made it inadvisable.

Soon after Rosenfeld reached this difficult decision, Michel and Steve announced, in November 1997, his appointment as head of banking, replacing Ken Wilson immediately. Like all those before him, Wilson had grown tired of the administrative headaches of running banking without any commensurate authority. So in the wake of Steve's appointment, he told Michel he wanted to give up the position. He remained a vice chairman, a member of the management committee, and the leader of Lazard's Financial Institutions Group. Rosenfeld also was appointed to the firm's management committee, which may or may not have been a reward for not joining Édouard. But from the start his heart wasn't in the job. "And so I got to be head of investment banking, for whatever that was at Lazard," he said. "It was all right. It was fine. It was good. I tried to help people. It was a nice thing. Whatever."

The effort—such as it was—to appease the Felix loyalists in the wake of his departure was an utter failure, a fact that became painfully apparent after Lazard paid its partner bonuses at the end of 1997. Ira Harris, then fifty-nine, was the first to leave, in January 1998. "It was total frustration with Michel David-Weill and unhappiness with the way the firm was run," Harris told *Bloomberg Markets* in February 2005 about why he quit Lazard. Then, two months later, Ken Wilson left to become a partner at Goldman Sachs, one of Lazard's chief rivals, as head of its Financial Institutions Group. Goldman was in the throes of its massive internal debate about going public. When the Goldman IPO did happen, in November 1999, many of the longtime partners were worth, on paper, as much as $350 million. Wilson, who had been at Goldman all of eighteen months prior to the IPO, was said to have received stock worth around $50 million after the IPO. Several of his former partners thought the astute Wilson had made one of the best trades ever. (Wilson's Goldman stock is worth closer to $150 million today.) Two weeks after Wilson left, Rosenfeld announced his departure to run a new, $600 million private-equity fund with all the money coming from the newly merged Charlotte, North Carolina–based banking behemoth NationsBanc Montgomery Securities. He had been head of banking at Lazard for four months.

The loss of Felix, Ira Harris, Ken Wilson, and Jerry Rosenfeld in a twelve-month period was a major blow to Lazard's M&A business, from both a prestige and an economic standpoint. Even though these departures could have been anticipated, the actual loss of these highly productive bankers, from a firm where partners rarely, if ever, left voluntarily, was a major challenge for Rattner and Michel to confront. Steve spent several weeks after Rosenfeld left in one-on-one meetings with top partners reassigning his duties. "The beginning of a period of generational change is always a very difficult period," Michel said. "But change in itself is always pretty good." Instead of replacing Rosenfeld with one person, Michel and Steve decided to appoint a new committee to oversee banking at the firm. Along with Steve, who was its head, the new committee consisted of Bill Loomis—marking the start of yet another of his resurrections—and the newcomers Ken Jacobs, a young partner who had been recruited by Agostinelli from Goldman in 1988, and, even though he didn't get along with Loomis, Bob Lovejoy, a former M&A partner at Davis Polk, the Wall Street law firm.

The firm also announced it was ratcheting up its principal investing activities, both as a nod to its legacy under André Meyer and, more important, as a way to increase partner compensation at a time when other firms offered their senior bankers not only private equity but also stock options and restricted stock. Since it was not a public company, Lazard could not offer stock or options to its bankers and so had to figure out another way to increase compensation to prevent them from being lured by other firms and to attract new partners. In addition to

Jupiter Partners, which Édouard had started, there was now LF Capital Partners, $130 million of capital for minority stakes in smaller companies; a $500 million Singapore-based Asia fund; the $100 million Lazard Technology Partners fund; and a second $1.5 billion real estate fund, following the success of the first $810 million fund. Steve had arranged for the hiring of David Tanner, the son of a longtime friend, the investment banker Harold Tanner, to lead a new—still-to-be-raised—$750 million private-equity fund that would focus on bigger deals. Tanner was to work with Thomas Lynch, who came to Lazard from the Blackstone Group. As for selling the firm or taking it public, which would have been another way for the Lazard partners to get increased compensation, Michel told the *New York Times*, "I will never do it."

Not all the news on the personnel front after the 1997 bonus season was bad. The firm, at Michel's insistence, was able to make the very important hire, in February 1998, of Gerardo Braggiotti, the former second in command at Mediobanca, the influential and secretive Italian investment bank that Lazard had been close to since the 1950s, to head up the firm's investment banking business in Europe, outside of England and France. He also became one of the very few men to hold a partnership stake in each of the Paris, London, and New York firms. Along with Steve and David Verey, Braggiotti was named a vice chairman of Lazard Partners, the holding company with financial and ownership interests in the three firms. Braggiotti moved into Stern's old office at Lazard in Paris, next to Michel's. Even the furniture was the same. As he did with many Paris partners, Michel asked Braggiotti to sign an undated letter of resignation, so that it would be easier to fire him in the future. Understandably offended, Braggiotti signed the letter with that day's date on it, suggesting he was willing to resign before even starting at Lazard. He hand-delivered the letter to Michel. That was the last he ever heard from Michel on that topic. "I am starting to see the outlines of the next generation of the Lazard group," Michel said of Rattner, Verey, and Braggiotti, who were all in their forties.

HIGH-PROFILE HIRES and departures—and those still rumored—aside, Steve now had the responsibility of a lifetime running the New York partnership, which still accounted for nearly half of the profits of the Lazard entities worldwide. By all accounts, he could not have been less interested in whether he was Michel's anointed successor. There was simply too much to do to worry about that. He took as his immediate mandate the task of dragging the firm into the late twentieth century after decades of Kremlinesque ossification. Like Gorbachev in the Soviet Union, Steve was determined to initiate a period of glasnost. "His job right now is to lead an organization," his friend Arthur Sulzberger Jr. explained, "and you don't do that by putting yourself up front. The story is Lazard, not Steve Rattner."

There were many challenges at first, not least of which was dealing with another piece of the still-unfolding scandal in the firm's municipal department. On November 21, 1997, the SEC charged the former Lazard partner Richard Poirier with fraud in connection with secret payments, totaling $83,872, made by Lazard—at Poirier's direction—to a consultant, Nat Cole, who then gave half the payment to a banker from Stephens Inc. who was, theoretically, an independent adviser to Fulton County, Georgia. The Stephens banker, in turn, made sure that Lazard won mandates to underwrite both a 1992 bond offering for Fulton County and a 1993 bond offering for the Fulton-DeKalb Hospital Authority. The SEC also alleged that Poirier was reimbursed by Lazard for political contributions, totaling $62,500, that he made to the campaigns of two governors at the same time he was seeking underwriting business from their states. The government also charged that Poirier had been conducting business similarly in Florida. The SEC's charges were reminiscent of the malfeasance that Ferber committed. The SEC also charged James Eaton, a former vice president at Lazard, with having a role in the scam. Eaton settled with the government by paying a $15,000 fine and agreeing to never again work in the securities industry. A week later, the U.S. attorney in Atlanta indicted Poirier for wire fraud and conspiracy, among other crimes. That same day Lazard reached a settlement with both the SEC and the U.S. attorney's office in Atlanta with regard to the actions of Poirier and Eaton. Mel Heineman, Lazard's general counsel, explained that the settlement specifically recognized that the misbehavior was "limited to" Poirier and Eaton and "was hidden from the Firm." Heineman continued, "The settlements also make clear the Government's view that Messrs. Poirier and Eaton caused numerous false and misleading invoices to be submitted to us, thereby misappropriating the Firm's funds to further their improper activities." Notwithstanding the firm's apparent absolution, Lazard agreed to pay $11 million to the government plus "restitutionary payments of the profits earned on the transactions at issue."

With only the yield-burning piece of the municipal scandal left to be resolved, Rattner dispatched Steve Golub, the new CFO, to clarify, if possible, the firm's famously opaque accounting system. No one ever really knew, perhaps not even Michel, whether individual business lines made money or not. For some reason, the firm's accounting was done on a cash basis—recognizing revenue and expenses as actual cash either came in or went out—throughout the year, and then changed to an accrual basis—recognizing revenue and expenses when contracts were signed but before the cash associated with them had been received—at the end of the year. This worked to Michel's advantage for years since, under the cash basis, he paid partners based only on the cash received by year end, not on the engagement letters signed for deals not yet closed. Rattner and Golub sought to change the old accounting methods. "None of it made any sense," Rattner said. "It was beyond all description." Worse, the capital markets people thought they were carrying the firm. The bankers thought capital markets was a total wasteland. Asset management was said to be providing half the firm's profits. But no one really knew. With Michel deciding how much or how little his partners were paid each year, knowing where Lazard's profits came from was not all that important, but if you had in mind actually *managing* the firm, then having some idea which departments made money and how much was close to essential.

Steve asked Golub to figure out the accounting and to see if it was even remotely possible to get the firm to report based on generally accepted accounting principles, or GAAP, as required by the SEC for public companies. "The stuff that was going on was breathtaking," Rattner recalled. "Not crookedness, but stupidity." One "tiny" example Golub found of the "stupidity" was that Lazard's joint venture in Singapore with the two other houses was set up as a corporation, rather than a partnership, so that the annual million-dollar losses were trapped there and did not flow back to the United States to offset taxable gains. "We got no tax losses, and it was just $1 million or $2 million a year being pissed away for nothing," he said.

A far more egregious offense, according to Steve, was taking place in Lazard's storied real estate department. Since the days of André Meyer, real estate principal investing and real estate M&A advisory had always been important businesses for Lazard. Lazard and André also nurtured one of the smartest—and least known—real estate minds on Wall Street, Disque Deane, who under the careful watch of André set up in the 1960s Peerage Properties, Lazard's real estate company, and then founded Corporate Property Investors, or CPI, one of the nation's first real estate investment trusts. Over time many of Lazard's real estate investments were funneled into CPI, including Peerage, before it was established as its own entity, making Deane a very wealthy man. He also was, according to Felix, Felix's "blood enemy." He had once, in the 1970s, been considered as André's successor to run all of Lazard. "You may ask," Deane said in the late 1970s, "why I wasn't more interested in Lazard.

Why I didn't bow down to André Meyer and do his bidding and run the firm. The answer is *money.* When I came to Lazard in 1964 I had a cash net worth of $2 million. What do you think my net worth is today? Take a guess. *It's $70 million.* Felix's, I'd say, is $5 million." These days, Deane's net worth—he is still happy to convey—is closer to $1 billion, after having given away more than $150 million. He owns 80,000 hectares of land in Bolivia, some of which is mined for oil and some of which is agricultural. He also owns the six-thousand-unit Starrett City complex in Brooklyn, which was recently put up for sale at around $1 billion. Deane is also the man who ran into David Supino walking on Madison Avenue in the early 1990s, stopped, grabbed his former partner's lapels, inquired, "David, do you understand the power of compound interest?" and, without waiting for an answer, walked briskly down the sidewalk. In August 2004, though he is not an economist, Deane wrote a letter nominating himself for a Nobel Prize in Economics. He also still believes that Michel reneged on an ownership stake in Lazard he had promised to him.

After CPI was spun out of Lazard, Michel decided the firm needed to return to the real estate business. So he lured back to One Rock two of Deane's partners at CPI, Paul Taylor and Harvey Schulweis, a bearded former accountant who learned about real estate by auditing development companies. Taylor and Schulweis shared the responsibilities of running Lazard's real estate efforts, until the business was split, with Taylor taking charge of LF Property Investment Co., which invested in existing commercial properties, and with Schulweis running Lazard Realty, a riskier and more adventurous enterprise designed to develop empty lots or find downtrodden buildings and fix them up. The two men were not close, and that led to some spectacular real estate blunders.

In 1981, Schulweis masterminded the purchase of three old adjacent factory buildings in Long Island City, just over the Fifty-ninth Street Bridge from Manhattan's East Side. The original idea was to renovate the buildings and lease the space as offices. But with demand for office space sluggish, Schulweis came up with a new plan: the creation of the International Design Center, a massive redevelopment project, the idea being that interior designers and other businesses involved with home decorating would relocate from Manhattan to this new complex in nearby Queens. The cost to purchase and renovate the buildings was estimated at $150 million, with Lazard putting up $30 million. Schulweis's rival Taylor said of the IDC from the outset: "We should have put the key to the place in a desk." The project was a total disaster. Lazard fired Schulweis and lost a bundle on the IDC.

Art Solomon, who came to Lazard from Drexel in 1989, oversaw both the real estate advisory business and the billions of dollars in private-equity funds devoted exclusively to real estate. He had reported directly to Michel. Now, following Steve's appointment as deputy CEO, Solomon, a former CFO of Fannie Mae with a Ph.D. in economics from Harvard, reported to Steve. And he was in no mood to be brought into Rattner's fold. Solomon's first real estate fund, started in 1996 with $810 million, did well, earning annualized returns in excess of 25 percent. This led to the successful raising of the second fund, at $1.5 billion. Taking a page from Deane's book, Solomon attempted to engineer a spin-off of the Lazard real estate business in early 1999. He also wanted to recut his deal with the firm to get a bigger slice of the pie. Steve, not taking kindly to these moves, retaliated by telling Solomon he wouldn't consider it until he understood better how the real estate business at the firm had been operated.

As part of getting that understanding, Steve asked Golub to undertake an internal audit of the new real estate fund—the $1.5 billion LF Strategic Realty Investors II Fund. As an investor, Steve had received a notice from the fund stating that after the first nine months, the returns were 29.07 percent. He remembered thinking how odd it was that the number was so precise. His curiosity was piqued, and the audit revealed that Solomon had "revalued the portfolio based on his own whim of what he thought it was worth," Steve said. "It turned out to be a house of cards. The whole thing was jerry-rigged." Golub discovered that the fund had lost nearly $400 million—Solomon disputed this finding—after a number of investments in assisted-living centers had fallen precipitously in value.

Solomon was using the fund to buy control of *companies*—for instance, he invested $200 million in ARV Assisted Living Inc.—rather than just buying real property. ARV's stock plunged 80 percent at the time. He also used the fund to make a bid—as principal—for a large movie theater chain at the same time Steve was representing KKR, the buyout firm, in a bid for the same company. There had been no internal coordination. Steve struggled to imagine how he would have explained to Henry Kravis why Lazard's real estate fund had been bidding on the property at the same time as KKR, but fortunately it never came to that. Steve was not happy. As a result of these infractions, he fired two of Solomon's colleagues and demoted Solomon to nonexecutive chairman of the real estate group. Solomon was not one to go quietly. He organized a meeting in early April 1999 between Steve and several of the large investors in the Lazard real estate funds, but he neglected to tell Steve the investors were coming. Solomon had invited Tom Dobrowski of the GM

Investment Management Corporation; John Lane of the Pennsylvania Public School Employees Retirement System; and Barbara Cambon, an influential pension fund investment adviser.

Once the investors had assembled in a conference room, Solomon invited Steve to join. It was an ambush, and the investors demanded to know from Steve just what was going on with their money and the leadership of the funds, now that Solomon had been demoted and his two deputies fired. "We never would have invested had we known there were such troubles at Lazard," one of the investors said. Steve asked them to give him a few days to review the situation and invited Solomon to his office as the guests were leaving. Once there, Steve fired Solomon "for cause." Solomon responded by hiring Stanley Arkin, the white-collar litigator, and by filing a fiery arbitration suit "crafted in tabloid-ready prose" accusing Lazard of "breach of contract, defamation and other juicy charges." In legal papers filed with the New York Stock Exchange, Solomon said his "ouster from overseeing the funds that he has so carefully cultivated and groomed over the past decade is nothing short of a high-class hijacking." He also branded Steve a "journalist–cum–investment banker" whose "unbridled personal ambition and elbows-up demeanor" had resulted in a flood of senior-level departures from the firm.

A number of employees who worked for Solomon, though, wondered why he had been able to hang on for so long at Lazard. "We couldn't believe it didn't happen sooner," said a former member of Lazard's real estate department. Damon Mezzacappa applauded Steve for "cleaning up the whole real estate thing" because "these guys, these guys were just over the edge, in terms of ethics, over the edge." But he added that Steve had paid a price, too, because the Solomon firing really upset Michel. "Michel took great umbrage," he said. "But Michel was dead wrong. But he was really upset that we had basically fired these guys."

Lazard settled the suit with Solomon out of court in June 1999 for (once again) $11 million, one of the largest payments ever by a Wall Street firm to an employee. "It was really just awful," Steve said. "It was a consequence of there being no management." The immediate other consequence of the blowup of the real estate fund was that Lazard's effort to raise a separate, more generalized private-equity fund was totally derailed. The placement agent told Steve the real estate mess had badly damaged the firm's reputation for managing capital.

While he was grappling with the Art Solomon debacle, Steve got it in his head that all the so-called side deals that Michel had entered into with various partners had to be revealed, too. This would be part of the general thawing, even though both his own lucrative undisclosed arrangement with Michel about the firm's work for Providence Media (8.25 percent of the override in addition to his $900,000 annual salary and 4.75 percent of the firm's pretax profits) and that of his chief ally Damon Mezzacappa (3 percent of the pretax profits of capital markets plus his $900,000 annual salary and 3 percent of the firm's pretax profits) would all be disinfected by the sunlight, as the Supreme Court justice Louis Brandeis would say.

There were some startling revelations, especially among the nonbanking partners. For instance, Norm Eig and Herb Gullquist—who together ran the asset management business—had contracts with Michel and the firm that paid each 15 percent of the net profits of their department. They received $15.8 million *each* in 1998. The contract called for them to continue to receive 15 percent of the net profits for the three years after their retirement. Jack Doyle and Dave Tashjian, who together ran Lazard's fledgling high-yield debt business, each had 16.5 percent of the high-yield profit pool of $4.826 million in 1998—about $800,000—in addition to their salaries and their percentage stakes in the pretax profits of the firm. Harlan Batrus, who ran the lackluster but consistently profitable corporate bond desk, had a deal whereby he received 20.2 percent of the corporate bond profit pool of $5 million—just over $1 million—in addition to his salary and percentage stake in the firm's pretax profits. Even Art Solomon had a deal with Michel to receive 3 percent of the gross real estate advisory fees and 33.3 percent of the real estate fund department profit pool, net of bonuses paid to others, as well as a 15 percent share of the override from Lazard's first real estate investment fund. In 1998, this totaled, for Solomon, $8.235 million.

In sum, Rattner's investigations revealed some twenty of these side arrangements. Partners well below the radar, whose contributions were considered modest at best, had been paid millions and millions. "Steve made all that stuff transparent," a former partner said. "There were no more private deals." Ironically, as Michel had always maintained, the M&A bankers for the most part had no side deals with him. "The reality of the side deals was not as bad as the perception of the side deals," Steve said. "There were some but not as many as people feared. Part of the problem was the opaqueness. My approach was to be transparent. If I can't look you in the eye and tell you why banker X is getting a $20 million bonus, then he shouldn't be getting it. In other words, if he's entitled to it, then I should be able to defend it to you or any other partner who asks me." Steve also convinced Michel to reduce his personal take of the annual New York profits to 10 percent, from his traditional 15 percent, the idea being that in addition to the obvious symbolism, the extra five points could be used to recruit new partners or reward highly performing ones. He also convinced Michel to reduce the profit percentages for some of the other "capitalists" as well and established a policy for how to treat the older, limited partners whereby they would be paid a $75,000 salary, have an office and a secretary, and receive some small sliver of the profits. Steve said of Michel, "He didn't care that much about the money, up to a point. It was all about his pride, his place, and his power. Michel had many wonderful expressions. One of these great expressions was that 'all Americans care about is money; all the English care about is their lifestyle. And all the French care about is their pride.' "

Steve preached teamwork. He participated with Michel in determining partner compensation. He instituted weekly meetings of the management committee. He presided over substantive weekly partner meetings with reviews of actual deal pipelines and prospects. He instituted call reports to track whether bankers were making efforts to see their clients. He organized periodic dinners between bankers of specific industry groups and partners on the management committee. Steve insisted that partners have lunch together on a daily basis to try to warm the notoriously frosty partner relationships.

Previously, partners had had trays delivered to their offices, a lovely and simple Lazard tradition where one of the two full-time female French chefs whipped up an individually prepared meal of, say, *salade niçoise* with Dijon vinaigrette. Dressed in dark, conservative uniforms, the chefs, sequestered away in a cubby on the thirty-second floor (when the firm was at One Rock; the kitchen moved to its own *floor* at 30 Rock), would deliver the trays to each partner in his office at lunchtime, assuming he was not going out, a fact that would be ascertained sometime during the morning. It was not uncommon for partners to be chomping away on this little slice of a Parisian brasserie while vice presidents sat across from them without a morsel, taking down the latest deal directive. A rare treat indeed was to be invited into a partner's office to dine with him, and having one's *own* tray.

Steve also considerably dialed down his public persona as "a self-promoting guy in a hurry." Of that image of him in the mid-1990s, he said later, "There was some reality to it, and there was some perception. But the reality doesn't matter, because when it comes to image, perception is reality." He realized that to lead the generational succession at Lazard, he himself had to change. "It was very, very clear to me that I had to do two things," he said in 2001. "I had to really, to the best of my ability, lower my own profile way below the horizon, which I've tried my hardest to do for the last several years. Second, if I was going to succeed in making Lazard the kind of collegial environment that I wanted it to be, then I had to also lead by example. . . . The only way I had a chance of making all that work would be if I—to some considerable degree—changed my own style."

Steve's first year in charge in New York had been a whirlwind of activity, with many changes instituted and many more promised. The firm remained immensely profitable, making some $415 million worldwide in 1997. But Lazard's position in the closely watched M&A league tables had slipped to tenth worldwide in 1997, from sixth the year before, reflecting the double whammy of increasing competition from global banks and the loss of some of the firm's talent. In the press, Steve downplayed this development. "Our approach involves concentrating on high value-added business and doing quality work for our clients," he told *Fortune*. "In that context, market share is not the primary focus." Privately, though, he was more concerned. "I believed, and in retrospect I think I was completely right, the firm was living on borrowed time," he said. "It was trying to live in a new world using an old business model that didn't work anymore." He remembered seeing at that time an industry magazine ranking of Wall Street firms based on the value they provided to clients. There were a series of categories—what firm do you like for M&A, what firm do you like for financing, among others—but the only category in which Lazard placed in the top ten was for which firm do you think is most overrated. "And that's how I felt about it," he said. "That we were underinvesting in the business and living on borrowed time."

❋

THE JUNE 1998 150th anniversary of Lazard's founding provided a convenient backdrop to assess the firm's performance in the post-Felix era. Under Steve's direction, the firm threw a huge party for itself in and around the breathtaking Temple of Dendur at the Metropolitan Museum of Art (in stark contrast to André's decision to basically ignore the firm's one hundredth anniversary). Hundreds of tuxedoed guests, from corporate CEOs to political and cultural leaders, were invited to dine and to toast the firm along with its partners, who had come from all over the world to New York for the celebration. Felix came back from Paris. Michel gave a speech, as did Steve. In his speech, Michel failed to thank Felix and Antoine Bernheim, the longtime Paris partner, for their help in building the firm. "Investment bankers getting up and doing that sort of stuff is cringe-making," said one man who was there. The famous soprano Jessye Norman sang, and sang. "She was sort of prancing around the place and sang rather badly for too long," remembered a partner. Some partners thought the event was wholly inappropriate, from its pageantry to its history. "It was dear old Steve Rattner at his very worst," said one. "Because it was sort of in praise of Steve Rattner, really." Some partners objected to celebrating the 150th anniversary of the dry goods store as if it were the same as the founding of the investment banking firm, which did not get established until the late 1850s (accounts differ precisely as to its origin) in Paris. London opened its doors in 1870. The New York office was not started until 1880. When some of the partners deigned to point that out, Steve reportedly said, "Don't let the history interfere with a good story." Lazard continued to propagate its legends.

The firm published 750 copies of an expensive slim, leather-bound, and heavily abridged version of its story, titled *Lazard Frères & Co.: The First One Hundred Fifty Years.* The author is unknown but likely was someone in the public relations office. At the end, the author wrote of Michel's perception that the firm's 150th year marked a time for "contraction and recentralization" and that he was "optimistic" that could be achieved. "The job he sees for now is to prepare the Firm for the next generation," according to the book. "This has been achieved in London with David Verey and his partners. It is being achieved in New York with Steven Rattner and his forward-looking, collegial decision making. And the movement toward a fully coordinated approach with Paris and among and between the three Firms has, and is, progressing each and every month. 'I do believe there is a soul which is quite independent from whoever is presently here,' David-Weill said. 'With every passage of a generation, there is always the question: "Okay, you were lucky. You had good people. But what happens next?" I believe that as long as the spirit is there, the people get recreated.' "

Since most of the top partners worldwide were in New York for the celebration, Michel invited about twenty-four of them to a meeting atop 30 Rockefeller Center. The partners of Goldman Sachs had voted a few days earlier to end the firm's 129-year run as a private partnership. The agenda for the very unusual Lazard meeting had two momentous items: Should the firm's three houses be merged into one, as the written history suggested that steps toward that ultimate goal were "progressing each and every month"? And should partners be given, for the first time, an actual equity stake in the firm, which would carry with it not only an ownership interest but also an ability to vote on important matters, such as taking the firm public or seeking a merger? Both were items that the partners at Lazard, unlike at Goldman, had no say in whatsoever.

Several partners who were there said the meeting was "inconclusive." That was true, but that accounting omitted a material event that occurred—Steve's rather offhanded suggestion that the firm consider an

IPO. Michel's response was legendary. "We were up on the sixty-third-floor dining room with the management committee," Steve recalled. "There was one guy on the phone. We were struggling. I remember saying, 'One option is we go public.' Michel went nuts and said, 'Absolutely not.' He went around the room and said, 'I don't need you, and I don't need you, and I don't need you.' Then he pointed at the speakerphone and he said, 'I don't need you.' "

One thing was agreed, though. With Michel's blessing, and at Steve's urging, the firm hired McKinsey, the leading management consulting firm, to help sort through how the three houses could manage themselves in as closely a coordinated way as possible, as if they were one merged firm. There was also a desire to create a new set of management systems—regarding promotions, compensation, and accountability—that would reflect the best of what other Wall Street firms were doing.

Given Lazard's peculiar autocratic management history, the McKinsey agenda was radical stuff indeed. Calls went to McKinsey offices simultaneously in New York, Paris, and London to begin the assignment indigenously in each of the three locations. Forty-six managing directors were interviewed globally. Partner compensation was shared. Lazard's management practices were compared with the best practices in the industry. There seemed to be a high level of enthusiasm among the key partners in the various cities that the McKinsey study would be an important catalyst for making the governance changes needed to compete more effectively.

Steve was wholly supportive of combining the three firms but wary of the idea of providing actual equity in the firm to partners. "So many of the senior guys came from somewhere else," recalled the McKinsey partner Roger Kline, "so they didn't have to guess that there was another way to run the place. They just have to remember what it was like at Morgan Stanley or Goldman or whatever. And that made them less fearful of going in that direction because they knew it could be made to work. The firm was essentially operating on a model that other firms hadn't been operating on for twenty years."

Left unsaid, of course, was the fact that in the zero-sum world of power and control at Lazard, any McKinsey proposal for authority sharing was authority diluted from Michel, the Sun King. But at least at the outset, Michel seemed to be outwardly cordial and accepting that some changes needed to occur. For instance, at one point in the nine-month assignment, McKinsey suggested Lazard establish worldwide co-heads of its M&A business, as almost every major firm on Wall Street had already done. Lazard had never had a head of M&A. Over the years, Lazard had a head of banking—Loomis, Rattner, Wilson, and Rosenfeld—but since so much of the firm's banking business derived from M&A work, the idea of a separate head of M&A seemed redundant and needlessly bureaucratic. But McKinsey felt there was a need for Lazard to be able to deliver its product expertise—M&A advice—across industries and geographies. The new co-heads would be the ones to best coordinate the delivery of that service—again as most other firms had been doing for years. A conference call on the subject occurred in August 1998, with the Lazard team at their various summer retreats and the McKinsey guys in their offices. "Michel had previously been resisting that idea before we showed up," Kline recalled, after receiving permission from his client to recount the conversation. "On the phone he said, 'I don't think that will work.' I said, 'It works in a lot of other firms.' I gave him three examples of firms, and I named the guys. He said, 'Oh.' " The firm decided, for the first time, to make the appointments. Steve was very appreciative of McKinsey's help in getting Michel to accept this change.

As McKinsey was working on its research and recommendations, two somewhat existential articles—in *Institutional Investor* ("Lazard in Search of Self") and in *Fortune* ("Can Lazard Still Cut It?")—tried to grapple with all the changes taking place and determine whether Lazard was still relevant. As always, the articles broached the question of who would succeed Michel. Somewhat surprisingly, given his short tenure as deputy CEO of New York, these articles—obviously based on reporting—began to dismiss the possibility of Steve being the One. He was said to be too desirous of a top position in Washington, should Al Gore be elected in 2000. But *Fortune* also suggested that Steve's partners in London and Paris wouldn't abide him running the whole firm. *Institutional Investor* quoted an unnamed client saying, "As long as Michel is still running things, I'd emphasize the 'deputy' in Rattner's title." Both articles mentioned a rather shocking possibility that Michel still hadn't fully dismissed the idea that he would one day tap either Édouard Stern or Bruce Wasserstein to run the firm. "Not me," Stern told *Fortune* when asked if he would possibly return; Wasserstein did not respond to questions on the matter.

Lazard—and Steve in particular—suffered another blow in the fall of 1998 when Michael Price, then forty, who ran the firm's successful telecommunications practice, announced he was leaving to be co-CEO of FirstMark Communications, a much-hyped Madison Avenue–based start-up telecommunications company in Europe. He called on telecom companies at Lazard because no one else was doing it and "because they were big." While his unusual combination of zaniness, fearlessness, and intelligence had propelled his success at Lazard independent of Steve, he nonetheless benefited from Steve's rise. Steve paid Price well and allowed him to start and run Lazard Technology Partners, one of the firm's new private-equity funds. They were also quite friendly. But like so many bankers—and others—in the late 1990s who saw the rise of the Internet as a sure path to wealth and fame, Price couldn't resist the allure of Internet riches, despite living a rather modest lifestyle in Closter, New Jersey. "I spent my whole life advising the best and the brightest, and kept looking at these people and said, 'Why aren't I doing it?' " he told the *Wall Street Journal*. (FirstMark crashed and burned in the telecom meltdown; Price now works for Roger Altman's M&A boutique and owns Evercore stock worth around $40 million.)

Price's departure was not only a personal loss for Steve, given their friendship and professional success together; it was also emblematic of yet another, wider problem at Lazard: aside from them having drunk the Lazard Kool-Aid, there was no longer anything to bind the partners financially to the firm. In the Internet era, when competitors were easily matching and exceeding the compensation of Lazard partners and then sweetening the whole package with stock options, restricted stock, and investment opportunities in private equity and venture capital, the firm simply could not compete. Lazard used to pay the best on Wall Street, all in cash, because its costs were so low and its margins so high. No longer. In addition to Price's departure, the longtime partner Michael Solomon, a twenty-year veteran, left to form his own private-equity fund. At the same time a ten-person convertible bond team at Lazard left for ABN AMRO, a large Dutch bank. Then, in another huge blow, in January 1999 John Nelson, vice chairman of Lazard Brothers and a prolific deal maker, left for the rival Credit Suisse First Boston.

"There was nothing holding people together at Lazard," Steve explained. "There was no stock. Every other firm on Wall Street had these golden handcuffs. We had none. Everybody could leave for the next deal or for a signing bonus, and they did. So that made it all a lot more difficult." The impetus had never been clearer to take all necessary and immediate steps to restructure and merge the three houses into a single, global firm capable of providing its professionals competitive wealth creation opportunities, or what used to be called simply "more money."

In August 1998, just before hosting President Clinton—then in the midst of the worst of the Monica Lewinsky debacle—on Martha's Vineyard at his annual August bash, Steve convened the management committee to begin to outline some of his feelings about a potential three-house merger, "particularly coupled with initiatives to address concerns about ownership and wealth creation," he wrote in what amounted to a manifesto that revealed the extent of the firm's existential crisis. Steve argued that the "consequences" to "merging badly" were "enormous." He criticized a preliminary merger proposal, as outlined by McKinsey, as "not logical" in its governance provisions, and specifically blasted as "unjust" the "underrepresentation" on various management committees of partners "resident in New York, who have consistently contributed a majority of the Group's earnings." Steve was prepared to postpone the pursuit of a merger for a year and instead to continue to "concentrate on improving the relationships among the three houses." In closing, he reiterated the importance of addressing Lazard's competitive disadvantages during the Internet bubble: "It is critical to show substantial progress on the issues of ownership, wealth creation and governance by the end of the year, when many of our colleagues will be reassessing career options."

Throughout the fall of 1998, with McKinsey as their occasional sounding board, the senior Lazard partners thrashed around how best to combine the three houses. By all accounts, McKinsey had a rough time trying to craft a structure to satisfy the deeply entrenched partners in each of the three time zones. Some thought the McKinsey work had produced the equivalent of a camel—the "horse designed by a committee." "You ended up with this mishmash of a structure that wasn't any better than we already had, really," remembered one person familiar with the McKinsey work. Still, five versions of various proposals went back and forth across the Atlantic. Steve recalled: "It was all these things designed by committees, with this committee and that committee. Michel was still in charge of the whole thing, which was completely insane given what we had seen in New York. We understood how the place was running, and it would have been the exact opposite of how Jack Welch told us how to run something. The exact opposite. It made absolutely no sense." But, he continued, "some of the Europeans wanted it to stay as it was because they knew if we changed anything, they would end up further down the totem pole from New York." As these various drafts were circulating, Michel's posture with Steve was that he could live with the changes but he doubted whether the French or the English could. Michel said the proposal would fail not because of him but because of the Europeans. They were going around in circles.

During the first week of November 1998, there was a regularly scheduled meeting in Paris of Lazard Partners, the holding company for the three firms. The meeting kicked off with a dinner on November 5 at Michel's mansion on Rue Saint-Guillaume. Since wives were invited to these quarterly meetings, Maureen accompanied Steve to Paris for the dinner. She returned to New York the next morning just as the meeting commenced in an overheated conference room at the nondescript Lazard Paris office at 121 Boulevard Haussmann. Steve went into the 10:00 meeting the next morning, a Friday, feeling ambivalent about whether the fractious group would ever agree on something as complicated and momentous as a full-blown merger.

He was also rapidly coming to the conclusion that his career at Lazard was nearing its logical end, something he and Maureen had been talking about. The frustrations of the job—given Michel's iron grip and reluctance to change—were simply wearing him down. So he wasn't expecting much when Michel started the meeting off by going around the room eliciting comments about the draft proposal. While others were speaking about how they thought the merger should work, Steve made notes on the blotter in front of him. He wanted to talk last, and he sensed that Michel wanted that as well. When Michel called on him, at the very end, he had no prepared remarks but suddenly felt overwhelmed with emotion. By all accounts, he gave an impassioned "evangelical" plea for the merger, for doing the merger "right" and not getting "too cute" by succumbing to the various impractical compromises that McKinsey had fashioned. "We had to be one firm," Steve explained. "We had to have one direction, and we really couldn't fight this war with one hand tied behind our back. There was only one right way to do it, and we could all be respectful of each other." After he finished his comments, everyone looked at him and, according to one participant, said, "You're right, why don't you just do it? And we should get on with it."

Steve was more than a little giddy with this turn of events and the possibility of transforming the firm. Seconds later, as everyone was leaving the stuffy conference room, Michel pulled Steve aside and into his sparse office. There was a couch, the priceless Vuillard painting of his grandfather, and his desk, with nothing on it. Michel spoke. Imitating a French accent, Steve recalled his exact words: " 'Look, I have only two questions about this. One, what will you do with Mr. Verey?' Because there was nobody in Paris who could run it. Bruno [Roger] didn't want to run it; he was a little old, and the younger guys weren't quite ready. That was an advantage we had. Verey was the problem. So he said, 'You know, whatever you decide, you should think about Mr. Verey. He's a good guy. If you humiliate him, he will leave. You should find a place for him.' I said, 'I understand all that. What's the second thing?' And he said, 'Me! You know, I think I can be helpful,' and I said, 'Of course you can, and I want you to be helpful.' "

Despite the foreshadowing of this odd encounter with Michel, Steve was euphoric. He called Maureen and told her what had transpired and how it now looked like he might be finishing out his career at Lazard after all. With renewed vigor, he immediately set to drafting version six of the "Framework for Governance." "I said to myself, if I were starting from scratch and I wanted to do this right, what would I do?" He worked over the weekend, sending versions back and forth to Sally Wrennall-Montes, his assistant, indicating to her how the previous, unsatisfactory draft number five should be revamped and rewritten. In Steve's revolutionary blueprint, the old Lazard partnership agreement would be scrapped, along with Michel's absolute authority, and in its place would be established a more traditional corporate governance structure. This would be nothing less than the democratization of Lazard.

"I set it up so that the partners in effect elected a board and the board picked the CEO," Steve said. "The board could also fire the CEO, and the board was mostly working partners. I was always prepared to basically live or die by what the partners wanted. This proposal basically codified that commitment and said if the partners aren't happy, they can vote you off the island." Instead of a typical board of directors, though, the newly merged Lazard Group was to have a twelve-member supervisory board, to meet twice a year, consisting of three "capitalists" (the actual owners of Lazard's equity, for instance, Michel, his sister, and Pearson) and nine "working partners." Michel was to be the first chairman of the supervisory board for an initial five-year term. The board would enjoy a myriad of powers, among them the ability to hire and fire the CEO and to approve the sale, merger, or initial public offering of the firm. During the first five years of Michel's chairmanship, though, he would have the unilateral right to veto such an event.

Under Steve's construct, there was also to have been a nine-member management committee that would meet weekly and be chaired by the CEO. The management committee would make all compensation decisions as well as all decisions regarding promotion, hiring, and firing. The initial officers of the Lazard Group would be Michel, as chairman, Steve, as president and CEO, and Eig, Gullquist, Mezzacappa, Verey, and Braggiotti. Steve anticipated a formal announcement of the agreement to merge the three houses by Christmas 1998 and set the start of the new millennium as the "target date for full implementation." He circulated the revised term sheets to the relevant parties on Sunday.

To the existing New York management committee, he attached a cover memo with some of his thoughts about his new proposal. "The organization described in the attached term sheet is intended to address the present inadequacy of the Lazard Group to respond to the competitive threat that it faces," he wrote revealingly. The extent of the proposed dilution to Michel's historic authority was now abundantly clear.

❧

The betrayal was swift. So swift, in fact, that Steve never even saw it coming. On Monday morning, Michel had the Paris partner Bruno Roger call Steve in his New York office. Roger, whom Steve described as a "very talented banker who clearly saw Michel as his most important client," complained from the outset of the call about many aspects of the term sheet. Along with the call, Roger had faxed to Steve a list of objections. "Michel had read the proposal," Steve recalled, "and realized it marginalized him. He gave Bruno all these reasons why it was a bad idea and told Bruno to call me, kind of 'as Paris,' to tell me why it was a bad idea." Of course, Roger played it straight during the phone call with Steve. It was only later that Steve learned the truth of what had happened from Braggiotti, who told him that Michel had "torpedoed it" and enlisted Roger as his messenger.

Steve knew at that precise moment *les jeux sont faits* for him at Lazard as well. Both his clarity and his disappointment were total. "I think Michel was balancing two things," Steve said later. "What was right for the firm and what was right for him. The problem was that what was right for him consistently won out. While I think he knew that we had to do something like this, he was never willing. This moment finally exposed that, because until then he had been saying, 'I would appreciate this,' or 'This is fine with me, but the French will never live with it and the British will never live with it.' So we went into this meeting, and everybody with the possible exception of Verey, who was very quiet in the meeting, said, 'Great.' Now Michel had to come out of the closet in effect and say, 'Okay, it's about me. It's not about the English. It's not about the French. It's about me.' " A senior partner added that he believed Michel did not want Steve to have one more bit of authority. "That's why he had Bruno call," he said.

Another partner remembered, incredulously, "Michel dictated the fax to Bruno, and Bruno sent it. He doesn't even deny it. And that fundamentally killed that deal." Damon Mezzacappa, Steve's close ally, remembered how excited he and Steve were after the Paris meeting. Mezzacappa, who had informed a few people he was thinking of leaving the firm, told Steve he would reverse course and stay on under Steve's leadership. "We were excited because I think we could have put the firms together and run them very effectively," he said. "The potential was just enormous." But after he heard about the call from Roger, "the whole thing came apart and that was the end."

For his part, Verey was none too happy about the turn of events that Friday morning in Paris. He was every bit as ambitious as Steve. He had been head of Lazard Brothers for almost ten years and had helped resurrect the franchise by hiring a number of talented bankers and spurring them on to great achievements. He was not paid as well as Steve—due in part to the fact that London, in 1996, made half of what New York made, Verey got $3.5 million, whereas Steve was closer to $9 million—but he loved advising CEOs. He still proudly remembered the day, in October 1997, when the *New York Times* reported that Lazard Brothers was involved in five of the six large mergers announced in Europe that day. Verey and Steve were, according to Steve, "friendly rivals." Quite frankly, Verey wanted the job as Lazard CEO, too, even though he had no interest in moving to New York, the firm's locus of power since World War II. He held out some slight hope that Michel would consider allowing him to run the firm from London. Verey had a certain disdain for Steve's American-centric thinking, his apparent lack of appreciation of the firm's history, and his lack of understanding of the outside forces swirling around the two European houses.

In London, Pearson, the U.K. publishing conglomerate, had been considering selling its stake in Lazard at least since the Texan Marjorie Scardino became CEO in January 1997. The rumors heated up again in May 1998 after Pearson purchased Simon & Schuster's educational publishing business for $4.6 billion. Conversations between Michel and Scardino about the sale were well under way by the November 1998 Paris meeting. Verey, who was on the Pearson board, felt Steve had failed to factor in how Scardino would react to his merger proposal. Then there were the series of interlocking French holding companies—some public, some private—all with funny-sounding names, that held a portion of Michel's (and others') stake in Lazard. Verey believed Steve had no appreciation for how these holding companies had to be integrated into the mix as well. The Paris meeting and the consensus that formed around Steve that morning, though, dashed Verey's aspirations. But even before Verey himself could begin to try to rectify the "Rattner putsch," as he called it, Michel had already counterpunched.

Looking back on this unexpected turn of events, Steve fully comprehends Michel's convoluted, if crystalline, logic. "At that point, he wanted me gone," Steve said, "because that meeting—not to be immodest—but that meeting in that room in Paris was like the French Revolution.

Michel saw me for the first time as someone who could rally the troops, not only in New York, which he had seen, but globally, in a way that was dangerous to him. At that point, it didn't matter how much revenue I produced. Michel's control of the firm was more important than the firm's success. He didn't fire me, but he was terrified about what might happen with me still rattling around." With Felix gone, Michel was the only person at the firm who could have stopped Steve. And he did.

Steve didn't resign at that moment, or even step down as deputy CEO, because both he and Michel were concerned about how the professionals in New York would react. "He didn't want me to leave, because he knew I had a lot of support in New York," Steve said. "He was afraid that New York would unravel if I left." Also, while he knew his "democratic" proposal to merge the firms was dead, the need for the merger hadn't diminished one iota, and he thought he could have some impact, on the margins, on the eventual—and inevitable—merger by staying in his seat a while longer. "I felt that it was important for all concerned that I give it my best shot to effect a happy resolution," he said. But in truth, there was also a certain lame-duck quality to Steve's leadership during the next six or so months.

For instance, in March 1999, he organized one of the first dinners for the New York partners at the Four Seasons. The ostensible reason for the dinner was to honor the handful of new partners. But when Steve got up to speak "very much from the heart," his words, while inspirational, sounded like a swan song. "Nearly two years ago we set forth on a great adventure together to see if we could successfully navigate some pretty fundamental changes in our Firm," he said. The changes, he said, were not related to business strategy, to corporate structure, or to Michel ("to whom I am indebted for the willingness he has shown to allow this experiment to go forward, even though at times I'm sure he had doubts"). Rather, he told his partners, what he set out to do was to overhaul how partners related to one another and to the firm. "Our great adventure has been to begin to forge a true partnership among the people in this room," he said. "Having a true partnership does mean treating each other with collegiality and with respect. Having a true partnership does mean working closely together in the recognition that coordination and combination of effort, where appropriate, can make the whole greater than the sum of the parts."

He went on in this vein a bit longer, taking no credit personally for the firm's successes in the previous two years, giving special thanks to the members of the management committee, and lavishing compliments on the talented rank and file. "I am grateful to all of you," he said in conclusion, "and I know the many talented colleagues who are not part of this group but who will in turn inherit this Firm from us in the future should also be very grateful to you. Working together, all of us—the more than 1,000 men and women of Lazard Frères NY—can bring this Firm to even greater heights in the future." This was Steve at his best.

Throughout the early and late spring of 1999, Steve continued to contribute to the ongoing discussions about how to merge the firms. There was a spurt of inconclusive activity in April. And in the second week of May, a meeting was scheduled at the luxurious Bristol Hotel in Paris, near the American ambassador's residence. "My last shot to get something sensible done," Steve said. But "draft #9.2" was not all that different from what Steve had proposed the previous November, with the major exception that Michel, not Steve or Verey, would be the combined firm's chairman and CEO, for an initial period of six years.

But Michel would not endorse even this proposal, making it impossible for Steve to win support for it from either Verey or Roger during the meeting at the Bristol. "Michel had a plan to merge the firms as a headless monster," Steve said. "He wanted to do a lot of things that I thought were wrong. I said, 'Look, if you want to do that, that's fine, but I don't want to be part of it. I think I've done a reasonably good job in New York, and I think I can do this. I am happy to be part of something that makes sense, but this doesn't make any sense.' I was exhausted after two years of beating my head against the wall."

UNFORTUNATELY, IF ANYTHING, Steve's headache was about to get—potentially—much worse. At the behest of the SEC, the U.S. attorney's office in Atlanta was deciding at that very moment whether to indict Lazard for its role in the so-called yield-burning municipal finance scandals that the government had been investigating since December 1993, when news stories about Mark Ferber's behavior in Massachusetts had first prompted Michael Lissack, the Smith Barney banker, to call the U.S. attorney's office to describe the greater, hidden scandal. Had Lazard been indicted, the firm would likely have gone out of business, as Arthur Andersen quickly did after being indicted in March 2002 for shredding files related to the meltdown of Enron. Certainly Michel feared that this was a real possibility, and he conveyed that fear to his partners.

This was another of those extremely serious moments in Lazard's history. "It's like earthquakes in California," explained Loomis. The firm needed to convince the prosecutors in Atlanta that the actions of a few bankers in the municipal finance department were isolated incidents and not indicative of a pattern of behavior throughout the firm that might have resulted in the invocation of the RICO statute. To accomplish that crucial task, Steve, Michel, Loomis, and Norm Eig flew to Atlanta to meet with the U.S. attorneys. Prior to their meeting with the prosecutors, Michel stayed by himself in one suite while his partners remained in another. Then, at one point, Michel summoned Steve to his suite, leaving the others behind to collect their thoughts and try to stay calm. The full Lazard team met with the prosecutors for hours. "It was obviously difficult," Loomis recalled. "You're dealing with a cynical, understandably cynical, tough audience," he explained. Miraculously, by having Steve and Bill—mostly—talk to the prosecutors about the firm's history, its values, and how it conducted business, the prosecutors were slowly won over. Lazard avoided indictment and quickly agreed to another settlement—the fourth and final—in the decade-long scandal that plagued the firm and ended up costing its partners $100 million in fines and legal fees.

On April 22, 1999, the SEC announced a settlement with Lazard whereby it would pay another $11 million fine, with $7.5 million paid to the U.S. Treasury and $3.5 million paid to five municipal issuers, including the cities of Seattle, Pittsburgh, and Indianapolis, that had issued mispriced securities through Lazard. The settlement with Lazard was the "first comprehensive federal government resolution with a major Wall Street firm" involving "yield burning." In the end, the SEC settled with twenty-one Wall Street firms, for $171 million, in the yield-burning scandals. This was a very close call for the firm, as one former Lazard partner said that the Justice Department had been made aware that crucial documents relating to the scandal had been destroyed by a Lazard partner, a fact Justice chose to overlook in reaching the settlement. Loomis said Lazard was within a hairbreadth of being indicted. Steve was less sure how close the firm came to indictment. "The whole municipal episode reinforced my conviction that the traditional Lazard way of managing, or not managing, its businesses could not go on," Steve said.

Michel was extremely upset. In fact, of all the many scandals to beset the firm over the years, the municipal scandal hurt him most deeply, although he is much to blame, since the people who ran the department reported to him. "There I got really, really hurt because there was a group of people who thought it was the only way to conduct their business," he said. "And obviously it wasn't. It was just bad. And that in the name of the firm 'conduct unbecoming' was practiced, that I find very, very hurtful and disagreeable to me personally. . . . There were basically layers of people looking at it at the firm. It's not to excuse myself, because I feel responsible. But it was one area which I didn't look at very much, because for obvious reasons. Municipal is really very close to local political life in the United States. I'm not American; I'm not in it."

Michel listed the men, aside from Ferber and Poirier, who he believed were most directly responsible for what happened: Del Guidice—"hired by Felix"—Mezzacappa, who was "looking after that department," and the longtime municipal partners, thereby spreading around the blame for the fiasco. "This really got to me, that one," he said. "That one was serious. We could've been—I mean, if a firm is indicted, it's the end of the firm." He said when the scandal first broke, he wanted to take the approach of admitting the wrongdoing and handing over the responsible people from the firm—an idea very similar to what Loomis recommended in September 1993. "When I first learned about the municipal problem, I remember vividly calling up the lawyers we had chosen on Friday during the weekend and saying, 'Why don't we say we did wrong? Why don't we just say, "Look, some of the people working at the firm have done the wrong thing. And if you considered—Mr. Client—that you've been hurt, we are ready to settle with you." ' And this lawyer, he said, 'You must be dreaming. It's not done that way. You cannot do it that way.' Which is interesting. It's interesting, because it shows that it's a wholly artificial experience. They had to shut me up. I was all the time ready to say, 'We have been wrong.' "

BY NOW, NOT surprisingly, Steve was ready to abdicate his position as deputy CEO. He talked with Loomis, who despite his years in self-imposed exile was really the only logical person in New York to succeed Steve, given all the high-level partner departures during the previous two years. After a lunch together on April 23, the day after the firm settled the yield-burning scandal, Steve wrote Bill: "I could not have felt better after our lunch about the relationship between you and me. It gives me a great deal of pleasure to know that regardless of what else happens, we have established a strong feeling of mutual respect and affection. And regardless of where all this comes out, I will continue to do everything I can to support your efforts." Steve was thinking about when to resign. Somehow, Loomis prevailed on him to not give up the job yet.

Within weeks, though, Steve told Loomis, "Forget it." A mad scramble began around the Memorial Day holiday to once again solve a management crisis in New York. On June 7, the firm was ready to explain the changes. Michel announced that effective September 1, Steve had "decided to step back from his responsibilities" as deputy CEO in New York to become deputy chairman and that Bill Loomis, the phoenix, had replaced him. Michel also announced that the three Lazard houses intended to "combine as a global force in investment banking," a process that would take, he said, six to nine months. Effectively, the merger discussions would start, once again, from scratch but with Michel directing their content and with his partners' knowledge, never mentioned overtly, that exile in Siberia awaited anyone who tried to dilute Michel's authority. "David-Weill or the Highway," one magazine headline declared.

The press release contained all the usual masking tape, covering up what really happened in the delicious way that corporations do. "We would have preferred to have Steve remain as Deputy Chief Executive, but we understand and respect his desire to step back from his operating responsibilities as we begin the next phase of consolidating our worldwide operations," the firm announced. "This management change will afford Steve the opportunity to remain as one of the firm's most senior bankers and at the same time pursue his interests outside investment banking."

Steve's "step back" and the firms' intention to merge were big news. Throughout the 1990s, no investment banker, with the possible exception of Felix, had as calculatedly high a public profile in the United States as Steve. He was as tactical about promoting his own career as he was in advising a client about a big merger. For two decades, he had come to symbolize his generation's asymptotic move toward Wall Street. His career trajectory had been nearly vertical. Had he now suddenly flatlined? The *Economist,* half owned by Pearson, divulged that the merger announcement was "hastily publicized" by Michel on June 7 "after a leak" but acknowledged that Michel "has long dreamed of uniting the three firms." In a nifty bit of foreshadowing, the *Economist* also speculated—about its parent company—that Pearson's stake in Lazard Partners would be worth somewhere between £350 million and £400 million and could easily be swapped for Michel's 7 percent stake in Pearson, worth about £500 million. *BusinessWeek* reported that "once again" Michel had "lost a chosen successor."

But as usual, Michel was sanguine. "It is a very curious thing when a small internal decision provokes so much press," he said. "Lazard has an incredibly powerful brand. It is really quite magic. We have been a sort of irritant because we have never really changed. The question has [always] been, how can you compete?" Michel said, as usual, the perennial question of who would succeed him would be made easier by the merger and in the "coming years" would be clarified. "It's far easier with a unified structure to find a CEO in our midst, or a chairman," he said, "than it would be if we tried to replace me with somebody who has to run separate entities. I'm able to do it because I'm an owner."

For many of the younger Lazard partners, who had imbued in Steve their own ample ambitions for themselves and for the firm, his abdication was like a medicine ball thrown to the gut. "There [were] a tremendous number of people—not unlike Messier's in Paris a few years earlier—who thought that Steve's management was a complete breath of fresh air," observed a former partner. But there was also the belief that Steve failed as a leader because his mandate was to present, to Michel, by whatever means necessary, a united front for change. "All these people trying to do battle with Michel individually, trying to get Michel to change his ways, wasn't going to work," explained Luis Rinaldini, in comments representative of this point of view. "I don't think Michel was going to change voluntarily, because Michel was a very intelligent person and he had all the power under his senior partner designation in the partnership agreement. I think Michel's view was that 'it's kind of funny. If I'd wanted to change, I would have changed, so why are we having this discussion? I don't want to change. I want to do it this way.' I think that's pretty clear. And I think in that sense Michel was wrong but not necessarily deceitful.

"So to say," Rinaldini continued, "poor little Steve Rattner couldn't deal with it, I don't think is a fair assessment. . . . Michel knew what he wanted to do, he was doing what he wanted to do, he had all the power to do what he wanted to do under the partnership agreement. Especially the third or fourth time, you knew he wasn't going to do it on his own. It was like Charlie Brown and the football. By the time Michel pulled the football out the third time, you should have figured it out he was going to do it again the next time."

Steve conceded that aspects of this argument make sense. "The first time I ran banking, I had 25 percent of the tools you need to actually do the job. I didn't do it terribly well, but I don't think anybody could have done it at that point in time. I think by the time I was deputy CEO, I probably had 50 percent of the tools I needed to do the job."

Michel suggested that he and Steve didn't get along. "He didn't relate well with me," Michel said. "I don't think it was my fault. I'm not saying it was his fault. It's like that in life. I think I got on his nerves." But Michel could also clearly see that Steve's vision threatened his authority. He saw it when Steve suggested, perhaps offhandedly, in June 1998 that Lazard consider an IPO, and he saw it again, in spades, in November 1998 in the steamy Paris conference room. Michel believed Steve and his band wanted to eventually force a sale of the firm. A friend summed up Michel's thinking, in *Euromoney:* "Michel was right in knowing that was what Steve wanted. Once he saw that was what Steve was after, he decided Steve was his enemy and he had to kill him, and he did.

Steve picked a fight and he lost. Steve sensed an opportunity by getting the boys behind him to wrestle power from Michel. A number egged him on, seeing the possibility of making big money. I guess in the back of their minds was the thought: 'If we ever really want to make a bundle here, we need to be selling this thing.' It was in a way a kind of confusion because Michel was not motivated to do the most economically appropriate thing because he definitely wasn't and really isn't a purely economic man at all."

Steve agreed he could have done some things differently, but not many. He denied he was angling for an outright sale of the firm. His goal, he said, was simply to bring the firm into the modern age. And his supporters within the firm think he did just that before Michel eviscerated him. "In retrospect there are some things I probably could have done to get along with him better, but I'm not sure it ever would have really worked. As Loomis proved, you really only have two choices," he said. "You were either with the partners or you were with Michel. There was no way to be in the middle and survive. I chose to be with the partners."

CHAPTER 17

"He Lit Up a Humongous Cigar and Puffed It in Our Faces for Half an Hour"

Even though Steve's departure from Lazard was nine months away, on the evening of the June 7 press conference he delivered his "farewell remarks" to an impromptu gathering of the firm. He told his colleagues he was leaving "with a great deal of regret that I will not be in this chair to finish the journey together." He explained his reasons for exiting were "complex" and "not easy to describe," a mix of his desire to strike a more satisfying balance between work and family and his professional frustrations (although he never criticized Michel overtly; in fact he credited Michel with making possible the "successes of the past two years"). But there was no mistaking the slings and arrows directed at Michel. "As I hope you all feel," he said, "for the past two years my ambitions have been not for myself but entirely for this Firm. Since I took this job, I have asked for nothing for myself—not more compensation, not a grander title, not public recognition. . . . I have sought only the tools to make this Firm great again. In seeking those tools, I do not apologize for wanting us to win—this is not a business for people who are content to be second rate." He closed by expressing his deep gratitude for the new and prevailing spirit of partnership and made clear his desire that his legacy be judged by the successes the firm goes on to achieve rather than gloating should "chaos descend" after he departs. "You all have been of so much help to me that I hope you will never hesitate to call on me if I can reciprocate in any way," he concluded. "I am deeply, deeply grateful and wish you the very best in the years to come. I will never forget our time together and from the bottom of my heart, I thank each of you very, very much for the opportunity to serve you."

During the next few weeks, Steve sent a letter to "100 of his closest friends" explaining his "announcement and future intentions." Part of his motivation came from a desire to "repot." "Where my odyssey will take me, I honestly have no idea," he wrote, adding he had no deadlines in this process or preconceived notions. "But in just the past few days, I've had many interesting calls, including a number of intriguing ones from quarters that never would have occurred to me," he continued. "I may well end up doing something else in the commercial world, although perhaps in an entrepreneurial setting. And I am also tempted by the non-profit world (of which government life is by no means my only such interest or necessarily even the most compelling one)." In the meantime, Steve, now making more than $15 million a year, returned to doing deals with a vengeance. He again represented his friend Brian Roberts at Comcast, this time in its $9 billion consolation prize of selected cable assets from the MediaOne Group, which AT&T had recently bought, thwarting Comcast's initial efforts. Also, he worked for CMP Media in its $920 million sale to United News & Media. The year 1999 was shaping up to be one of his most productive.

STEVE WAS NOT surprised by Loomis's resurrection. "It was completely logical from Michel's point of view," he said. "He saw me as a threat, and he saw Bill as a friend. The last thing he wanted to do after watching what happened with me was to have someone else there who wasn't completely loyal to him. Bill viewed himself as having one client and that was Michel." Other Lazard veterans were far less pleased, though. One said he was "incredulous" when Michel named Loomis to succeed Steve because Loomis was just a "yes-man" for Michel who "wasn't successful at anything he did. He lived this kind of unexplainable charmed life." Steve's no-nonsense practicality gave way once again to Loomis's enigmatic and moralistic sermons, replete with references to Michel's long-held Gaullist view—now fully adopted by Loomis—that Lazard was more than just a special firm, it was a special idea.

The first one came at a partners' meeting that same June. "Lazard World is the continuation of an idea which I first saw myself in 1978," he opined. "Michel picked up the tatters of a Lazard franchise that year with a vision." Loomis said that vision had helped the firm grow net income from around $5 million in 1978 to more than $500 million globally in 1998. In closing, he thanked Steve and said, "It's up to us now. And it can be successful and fun, with the freedom to be different than the rest. We can do anything as partners of Lazard."

Michel tapped Loomis to complete the three-house merger *Michel's way* and to fulfill Michel's "dynastic ambitions," as one partner put it less than charitably. But not, nota bene, to be his successor or even the firm's

CEO. As a rainmaker, Loomis was certainly no replacement for either Felix or Steve, although he was their equal in inscrutability. He would without question, though, do Michel's bidding. Loomis told his partners he intended not only to spend time with clients but also to devote much of his energy to making the three-house merger a success.

The logical first step toward accomplishing the three-house merger to create what Michel liked to call a "one-firm firm" was to begin to aggregate, if possible, the various disparate ownership interests in Lazard not held by Michel or by the Lazard partners. There was no point in having a third party, in this case Pearson, in a position to thwart Michel's "dynastic" plans. The obvious—and long-expected—move was to buy back from Pearson its 50 percent stake in Lazard Partners, which translated into a 50 percent stake in Lazard Brothers, a 7.6 percent interest in Lazard Frères & Co. in New York, and an 8 percent stake in Lazard Frères & Cie in Paris. There was a time when many Lazard partners thought that Pearson would end up buying all of Lazard. But Scardino had the opposite view. She wanted to shed Pearson's extraneous collection of assets to focus the company almost exclusively on publishing. To the Lazard bankers, her calculus was simple. She told them Pearson wouldn't stand in the way of the three-house merger. She just wanted Pearson's stake in Lazard to be bought for a full price. "That was the moment when real money started to shift," Verey said.

In June 1999, without much fanfare and three days after Michel told *BusinessWeek* he hoped Pearson would "stay" as an owner of the Lazard partnerships, Lazard and Pearson announced a deal. After negotiating with Scardino in the elegant den of his Fifth Avenue apartment on a couch just below Picasso's 1932 masterpiece *Femme nue en dormie,* Michel—through his French private-equity fund, Eurazeo—agreed to buy Pearson's Lazard stakes for an initial price of £410 million, or $649 million, in cash (later reduced to £395 million, or about $625 million), plus a £15 million dividend. Pointing a few years later to the Picasso painting, which he believes is now worth well north of $10 million, he said of Scardino, "All the time she was saying, 'Look, if you give me this, my price changes entirely.' " The price paid to Pearson was considered high, implied a valuation for all of Lazard at some $3.785 billion, and would become known forever more as the "Pearson price," an important legal valuation benchmark to those managing directors, both active and limited, seeking to sell their ownership positions privately in Lazard, given the lack of a public market for the firm's stock. At the time, a Crédit Lyonnais analyst in Paris valued the firm at $5.1 billion based on comparing Lazard's earnings with those of its competitors. Verey called the Pearson negotiation "pretty good misery, frankly." He and Michel agreed to leave the Pearson board as part of the deal.

UNLIKE ANDRÉ, FOR whom art was part of a stage set, Michel had—and still has—an intense passion for art and art collecting. He unquestionably inherited his grandfather's love of art, if not his daily compulsion to buy—after all, art prices today are considerably higher, as a relative matter, than they were eighty years ago, and even a man with Michel's immense wealth has to be careful. "Dealers are very quick on the ball," he explained. "When they know you are less in the market, their solicitation of you decreases radically. When you are in the market, it increases radically." Michel fairly blossoms when the opportunity arises to explicate his world-class art collection, which is annually listed by *ARTnews* as among the two hundred best on the planet. "When you see Michel looking at a picture or talking about a picture, there is more than knowledge," the art dealer Guy Wildenstein explained. "He has incredible knowledge, yes, but there is more than knowledge. You can see how he's looking at it—probably like, I would say, the way Robert Parker sips wine, you know? And he's sort of enjoying every minute of it. . . . He is capable of buying something that is really expensive, or something that is not very expensive, but just because he loves it. But the one thing he has to do, he has to love the object. He doesn't buy for investments. He doesn't buy because he thinks it's in fashion. He doesn't buy because he thinks it's going to impress his visitors. He buys because he loves. That's really, really important."

Being in Michel's Fifth Avenue apartment, overlooking Central Park, is like being in a small, eclectic, and idiosyncratic private museum. There are sumptuous tapestries and lush carpets. Recessed lighting highlights the first-edition copies of the great works of French literature and the obscure antiquities. Everything is chosen with extraordinary care and attention to detail, as only the truly rich can do. Nothing is out of place, from the silver humidor where he keeps his stash of Cuban cigars to the family crest on the matchbook covers. Michel, of course, is modest about his lush surroundings. "What you have to understand is that I don't consider myself a collector," he said as we began a tour of the portion of his collection that is in his Fifth Avenue apartment. "I consider myself an amateur. The difference is that I have tried to surround myself with things I think are beautiful and I like which I think go one with another and which are of very diverse origins, very diverse expressions of art, mostly because they in a way elevate your thought process and your feelings. I have two key words, which are French words, and I don't know how they really translate to English: jubilation and grace. It's the joy of creation and grace, which is more religious in feeling, which is something given to you from outside. So that's what I've tried to do, and in part because of training, in part because of family, in part because of my work with museums, I have a very diversified taste, which makes it more fun but a lot more difficult in a way."

Not surprisingly, as with all his decision making, he rarely seeks outside counsel when making an art purchase. "Right or wrong, I am very solitary in my choosing," he explained. "It has to provoke an emotion in me, and I consult very little. . . . I may be completely wrong, but I've some confidence in my feeling for things. Sometimes I'm pretty glad. For example, at the Metropolitan"—where he joined the board in 1984—"there was a wonderful middle-aged virgin, and I said [to a curator], 'It's wonderful, but I don't know why the crown on its head disturbs me a little.' The guy said, 'Oh well, it was added in 1900.' I was very pleased that intuitively I felt there was something not completely right."

Michel's emotions are never more evoked than when he recalls the tragedies that befell his forebears' art collections, especially those of his father and his grandfather, both of which were looted by the Nazis. "I was always very impressed by my grandfather's taste," he said. "He was a great collector. So from time to time, I try to buy back things which belonged to him." There's a dazzling piece of Russian crystal from 1932 that he bought from a dealer who bought it after his grandmother's death. Then there are ancient pieces from the steppes of Asia: a horse bit from around 1500 B.C. from Luristan, what is now western Iran, and a Sumerian commemorative nail, from 2800 B.C., that was used to build a temple. The story of the place was written down on the nail. There is a drawing (once owned by his grandfather) of Fragonard's *White Bull*. The actual painting *White Bull* also belonged to his grandfather and then to his father. When Pierre died, Michel and his sister inherited the painting and donated it to the Louvre. "So when I saw the drawing," Michel explained, "I bought the drawing back." There is a Toulouse-Lautrec portrait of a Frenchman who was the first person in France who could decipher the markings on French silver. His grandfather, the avid collector of silver, liked the idea of a portrait of such a man, and so he bought the painting. Now Michel has it. He also has part of his grandfather's vast silver collection, specifically a very rare Louis XIV service set. Very few of these sets remain because much French silver was melted down to finance the country's many military campaigns. An English family saved this particular set from that fate. "Consequently, I think it's the only Louis XIV centerpiece silver service in existence," he said. Also in his dining room are two Monet paintings that were his grandfather's. In Michel's bedroom, there is a wonderfully cheerful Fragonard painting of a young girl reading a love letter. "I like optimistic things," Michel explained. "I don't like destructive art." Michel's grandfather owned the painting until Fritz Mannheimer bought it, probably around the same time that he bought Chardin's *Soap Bubbles.* At Mannheimer's death, the Fragonard passed to his wife. Michel politely kept after Jane Engelhard to sell him the painting if she so desired. And she did. As for *Soap Bubbles*, it now hangs in the Met.

While one clear direction in Michel's collecting is his ongoing efforts to reassemble part of his grandfather's collection, another theme, just as clearly, is his interest in the erotic. In his den, on the wall above his favorite caramel-colored suede couch, is Picasso's often coveted *Femme nue en dormie,* a Cubist rendering of a woman sleeping in the nude. The painting is subtle and elegant. He bought it for himself. "I added this, I think extraordinary, Picasso, which is pure jubilation," he said, "with the exultation of the love for the female body." Michel believes that the "loving of the human body" is one of the pillars upon which Western art has been built. "It's fantastic to have been able to present a body and all of its facets at the same time," he explained about the evolution of the presentation of the human body throughout art history. He then pointed out his latest acquisition—"because my purchases have drastically come down since I make no money," he said—a small Ingres painting of a naked woman, placed precisely on an end table in his den between the couch and a chair. "Very, very charming and also relatively very erotic," he said of the Ingres. "Every one of these objects, or many of them, have a history. This one was made probably for a Turkish fellow who lived in Paris who had a very erotic leaning. He's the one who had also *The Turkish Bath* by Ingres and a famous Courbet painting of a sex of a woman called *L'Origine du Monde,* which is now at the museum in Paris at Orsay. He commissioned this one, and then later it belonged to Degas, which is also interesting." *The Turkish Bath,* now in the Louvre, and which his grandfather once owned, and *L'Origine du Monde* are without question two of the most erotic paintings in nineteenth-century French art.

In Michel's bedroom and the changing room right behind it are more examples of his interest in the erotic. Near his bed is a Watteau. "Also terribly charming because you see that this fellow is relatively aggressively courting her with his hand on her breast and she is a little shy, but not that shy," he explained. "Not protesting, but a little shy. At the same time, Watteau has done the inverse in the background. It's the girl putting her hand on the fellow. It has this mysterious atmosphere of Watteau. One of the things which I adore about French paintings is that all the women look intelligent. In most other countries women painted look stupid. In France, especially in the eighteenth century, they always looked bright." In the changing room, where he also watches television, there is a large Balthus painting of an adolescent girl. "It is of a young girl, knowing she's becoming ugly, and that's the way I describe her," he said. "Certainly, it's not an erotic picture at all, huh? It's a poignant picture." Nearby is an obviously aroused male-nude painting. "That is an erotic one by a surrealist, a German," he said quickly as we turned back to the living room.

THE COMBINATION, IN a month's time, of Steve's ouster and Michel's successful negotiation with Scardino made it abundantly clear—in case anyone had any doubt—that Michel was firmly back in control of Lazard. Indeed, as part of the deal with Pearson, Michel for the first time laid out his retirement timetable: he would remain CEO of Lazard until 2005, when, at age seventy-three, he would become chairman and appoint an as-yet-unknown successor. "Once you start thinking about retiring, you might as well be retired," he told *Institutional Investor* at the time. "At a time when we are combining the three firms, it would be difficult to replace me because of my knowledge of how the pieces fit together."

Post-merger, he reiterated, finding a new leader would be easier. "It will be whoever is suitable in the eyes of the partners," he said. But despite the bravado about his own importance, he continued to flail around for the next Great Man, even at this time reportedly reaching out to Felix and asking him to return to the firm as the elder statesman. "Michel and I are old friends, and I wish him good fortune, but the subject has never come up," the ambassador told *Institutional Investor*. But that wasn't true. Michel and Felix *had* spoken on more than one occasion, in the ambassador's residence, about Felix returning to the firm. Michel kept suggesting Felix come back to serve on the contemplated supervisory board, a role that Felix found insulting. He declined to pursue Michel's entreaties.

Meanwhile, just how this merger was going to work was beginning to worry the firm's partners. In New York especially, the concern was mounting that the ten-page outline of the proposed merger failed to elucidate how the worldwide profits would be allocated. "There is absolutely abject terror regarding preservation of compensation in New York," explained one partner. But Michel said, "I don't think there is one partner who does not view this as a great step forward." And Loomis urged his partners to relax and let the details emerge in time. "Not to address this would be partnership suicide," he said.

FINALLY, AS THINGS happen in threes, came the most sustained threat of all—this one from outside Lazard and, seemingly, beyond even Michel's octopus-like control. Quietly and with the help of the longtime Lazard partner Antoine Bernheim—described as the "Felix of France"—the French entrepreneur and investor Vincent Bolloré, then forty-seven, began, in the late spring of 1999 (just as the deal with Pearson was being finalized and announced), to acquire a large stake in Rue Impériale de Lyon, one of the four publicly traded French holding companies that over the years Michel and some of his French partners had set up and that, in turn, owned stakes in Lazard. Bolloré's assault on Michel's cozy ownership scheme, which would not be disclosed publicly for more than a year, complicated matters terribly for him, and for his control of Lazard. "He's locked in his character and his legend," Bolloré said, in taking aim at his foe. "His group may have problems to solve in the future." A London newspaper described the battle as "rather like the Rome city council slapping a demolition order on the Vatican."

Bolloré was—and remains—the French equivalent of a 1980s-style corporate raider, but unlike most raiders, he also controls his own corporate empire. The indirect investment in Lazard was but one of several Bernheim had recommended Bolloré make in European private investment banks, the others being in Rothschild and Mediobanca. Apparently, Bernheim encouraged Bolloré in his activities because he felt slighted that Michel did not rise to his defense when Mediobanca deposed him as chairman of Generali, the Italian insurer, in April 1999, and because he did not appreciate that Michel failed to acknowledge his contributions to the firm at the 150th anniversary party at the Metropolitan Museum in June 1998. For his part, Michel denied any rift with Bernheim. "It is true that Monsieur Bernheim likes and is close to Monsieur Bolloré," he told a London newspaper in November 2000. "This being said, Antoine Bernheim has been totally faithful to the firm and me."

Bolloré's unprecedented bet on shaking up the Lazard holding companies in the summer of 1999 was, first, born of a desire to make a lot of money. He had figured the share price of the holding companies valued Lazard at an incredible 75 percent discount to its book value, an arbitrage opportunity par excellence. As a secondary matter, Bolloré had focused on Lazard's arcane corporate governance, just as he did with both the Mediobanca and the Rothschild investments: as the European

Common Market continued to evolve and mature, the rules relating to corporate ownership would begin to more closely resemble the far simpler paradigm in the United States. Few corporate structures were more convoluted than Lazard's, and by buying into a corporate stack that resembled nothing as much as wooden Russian *matryoshka* dolls, he intended to be a catalyst for change. His first desire—to make a huge profit on these shares—would be achieved in part, he hoped, by becoming such a nuisance to Michel that the older man, true to form, would have to figure out a way to have him go away.

These were smart bets, for that is precisely what occurred. For about €300 million, over time Bolloré accumulated a 31 percent stake in Rue Impériale, which indirectly owned a right to 15.8 percent of Lazard's profits. But as it turned out, several years before Bolloré made his investments in Rue Impériale, Jon Wood, an even cleverer Englishman responsible for proprietary trading at Union Bank of Switzerland, had the very same idea to buy into the publicly traded Lazard holding companies. "Michel David-Weill and his cronies have held back corporate France for years," Wood said. "They really are awful, egotistical people who wouldn't give money to a person to buy a loaf of bread." As a result, UBS, which had kept quiet about its Lazard investments until Bolloré came along, owned significant percentages of three of the Lazard holding companies as well. Wood said Bolloré was "a very interesting character and he certainly supports the concept behind what we're trying to do." Wood began pressing Michel very hard behind the scenes to do something to streamline the structure, by either merging some of the companies or buying back stock. He was on a crusade. "We have a mission, some might say, to see all of the anomalies you have in Europe just disappear, with shareholders getting a fair price," Wood told *Forbes*.

For his part, Bolloré started buying shares in Eurafrance, another holding company, to complement the ones he already owned in Rue Impériale. Feeling besieged, Michel invited Bolloré to Sous-le-Vent and told him to sell his position immediately as it was a bad investment. More than a little piqued, Michel also added ten years to a voting agreement between himself and the founding four families of Lazard through Société Civile Haussmann Percier, another, private holding company. "I'm not impressed by agreements," Bolloré said. "You can break an agreement." Rather than being intimidated by Michel, Bolloré sensed additional opportunity and bought more shares in Rue Impériale. He remarked that he was determined to "break up the Lazard empire and sell the parts to the highest bidder."

Michel met with some of the institutional investors during the summer of 2000. "He was unhelpful and incredibly arrogant," one who was there told *Forbes* in September 2000. "He lit up a humongous cigar and puffed it in our faces for half an hour. He really dismissed us as totally unimportant—and we had been large shareholders in his companies for years." Michel also wrote a personal letter to Marcel Ospel, the chairman of UBS, complaining about Wood and asking him to rein in the trader. Ospel declined to heed Michel's suggestion. Sophie L'Hélias, a well-known French shareholder activist with clients that owned shares in the Lazard holding companies, put it bluntly to *Forbes:* "The empire is not being ruled justly or fairly. David-Weill and his henchmen use holding companies to enrich the partners at the expense of the shareholders."

By November 2000, Michel, under pressure to resolve the Bolloré matter, summoned him again, this time to a breakfast in Paris. "He was not very happy," Bolloré said of the meeting with Michel. "The fact that I could dare buy those shares was unbelievable to him." At the breakfast, Michel discussed with Bolloré a plan to have Eurafrance merge with Azeo, yet another Lazard holding company, to create Eurazeo (as happened). Michel's view of the breakfast, which he attended at Bernheim's suggestion, was that "Bolloré bought shares, which was his right obviously. He bought quite a few shares and had no contact, while doing so, with me or the management of Rue Impériale."

Having taken the measure of Bolloré, and realizing his own weak position, Michel called in his friends from the French establishment to help him resolve the matter. First, Eurafrance offered to buy out Azeo at €90 a share, almost double the price Azeo had been trading for a year earlier. Second, Michel contacted the mammoth French bank Crédit Agricole, with which Lazard, through Édouard Stern, had established CALFP, the derivatives joint venture. In an act some described as "greenmail," at Michel's urging, Crédit Agricole bought the Rue Impériale stake from Bolloré, at the end of November 2000, for €595 million, a profit for the raider of nearly €290 million in eighteen months. By getting rid of Bolloré, "Michel has pulled off a remarkable coup," his partner Adrian Evans confessed. Others praised Bolloré's moxie. "A genius is someone who knows how to seize opportunity," Bernheim said of his client. Added Bolloré himself: "Let's say that no one had ever dared to behave so rudely to David-Weill until I came along." For his part, Wood, who had criticized the proposed valuation of the Eurafrance and Azeo merger, agreed to a truce with Michel after Michel agreed to have Eurafrance buy back some of its own shares in an effort to boost its share price. But UBS did not participate in the Crédit Agricole deal and reportedly was quite upset to have been abandoned by Bolloré.

"UBS now finds itself somewhat alone for going into battle because Michel David-Weill no longer has the pressure to simplify the structure," said one research analyst. Nevertheless, courtesy of Michel and Lazard, Wood and UBS had a pleasant Christmas bonus in 2000 of a gain of more than €250 million, representing, incredibly, one-third of UBS's pretax quarterly profits. "It is not often that investment banks give each other presents, but this is a nice bonus from Lazard," said one UBS observer. Added Wood: "Michel is only getting what he's been giving to other people for the past thirty or forty years." He continued, "We had to pinch ourselves. We couldn't believe how easy it was to knock Michel off his perch," and then in disgust he added, "I must admit that Michel is a very sad individual. He's very chippy. He's arrogant. He's dishonest. He's everything that is bad about French commerce. He's awful, just awful. He's thrown away a wonderful opportunity. It's ironic that Lazard, which had always given advice on how to look after all shareholders, now wouldn't do it." Wood has since left UBS to start his own hedge fund.

Ironically, just as Michel appeared to be tightening his iron grip on Lazard by casting out his internal opponents, the Bolloré-UBS gambit had shown just how vulnerable he and his carefully constructed empire were to outside attack. In truth, back down at ground level, Lazard—the investment bank—was still struggling in the aftermath of Steve's decision to relinquish the job of running New York. In September 1999, he became a vice chairman of the firm but also had one foot out the door. At the same moment, one of his chief allies throughout his two-year reign, Damon Mezzacappa, decided to make good on his sotto voce pledge to retire from the firm. On September 7, Lazard announced that Mezzacappa would retire at year end and turn over the reins of the New York capital markets group to David Tashjian, who had been head of Lazard's small high yield debt department. Tashjian would also become co-head, along with the Brit Jeremy Sillem, of the firm's worldwide capital markets effort. On some level, Mezzacappa believed, Michel blamed him for the scandal in the municipal finance business. "Michel kind of wanted me to take a hit, if someone had to go," he said. "I think Michel felt he was under some pressure. I think guys like Ken Wilson and Jerry Rosenfeld were pointing fingers at me, not directly because they wouldn't do that, but behind my back. And I was definitely on the defensive."

What further compounded Mezzacappa's political problems in the firm was the disclosure of the magnitude of his side deal with Michel, as part of Steve's campaign for clarity. In his last few years at the firm, Mezzacappa was making more than $12 million a year. To their astonishment, his partners discovered, his contract with Michel also called for him to continue to get the 3 percent partnership share for another three years, and if it was not extended beyond those three years, he would then automatically receive a 2 percent partnership share for five more years, after which his partnership share would be reduced by 0.5 percent per year for four *more* years. Mezzacappa had struck an unheard-of twelve-year deal with Michel. He was also to get a salary equal to that of other top managing directors, plus 2 percent of the override of the Corporate Partners fund. The extent of Mezzacappa's compensation agreement with Michel stunned his partners, many of whom thought, at best, he was making $6 million a year. Ira Harris, for one, was appalled. "When Ira found out about the Damon stuff, he went absolutely insane," said one partner. Another summed up his reaction upon reading the disclosure about Damon: "Damon was a fucking ganef. Damon was grabbing with both hands and both feet from everyone he could. He was just grabbing with both hands from everybody because he's a fucking ganef."

For his part, Mezzacappa explained, "What happened when all this transparency took place is that someone figured it out and went to Michel. And Michel, instead of saying, 'I organized that,' he didn't. He blamed it on me. And then one guy—Harlan Batrus—he resented it enormously because he thought I was stealing from him, which wasn't true at all because the money wasn't coming out of his profit pool at all. I really resented the fact that Michel didn't stand up. He let me take the blame for that. Now, of all the guys in capital markets, the only one who had a problem was Harlan, but Michel, instead of saying, 'I made this deal with Damon, it's not coming out of your profit pool,' didn't do that. He just sort of shrugged his shoulders." The final straw for Mezzacappa was, of course, his public support for Steve, which after the events of November 1998 became a liability with Michel. "My star had fallen somewhat," he conceded.

By October 1999, with the outlines still very sketchy of just how the firms were to be merged, Michel issued an unprecedented invitation to Lazard's two hundred top bankers worldwide to attend a retreat, near his Long Island estate, to discuss the firm's future. On the agenda for the meeting, which was held at a Nassau County conference center, was not only an update of the pending merger but also the important matter of just how Lazard, the small advisory firm, was going to compete in a financial world dominated by global behemoths with many products to offer clients. In the wake of the creation of Citigroup, from the merger of Citibank and Travelers, major consolidation was rocking Wall Street with the announcements of the combinations of Chase and J. P. Morgan, Credit Suisse First Boston and DLJ, and UBS and Paine Webber. In the face of these deals, Michel had always been consistent and stoic. "The more our clients turn to the big houses with large bureaucracies where the principal business is trading and raising capital, the more they are going to want an independent financial adviser," he told *Bloomberg Magazine*. Up for discussion as well was the perennial matter of who would one day succeed Michel. To help answer that question, the four likely internal candidates made presentations: Loomis, head of New York; David Verey, head of London; Bruno Roger, head of Paris; and Gerardo Braggiotti, head of the rest of Europe. But as usual, Michel decided to postpone any decisions.

The day concluded with champagne and dinner at Viking's Cove, Michel's three-story, 180-foot-long, brick Victorian mansion overlooking about seven hundred feet of Long Island Sound frontage, in the incorporated village of Lattingtown, near Locust Valley. Just off Peacock Lane, Viking's Cove sits on just more than twelve acres, with an assessed valuation of around $90 million inclusive of the land, and has been described as "so sumptuous that a Matisse hangs over a coatrack in the hall." (Michel is now selling the Matisse.) For a time, Michel allowed his assistant, Annik, to live in an apartment above the carriage house. He bought the home in October 1979 for $275,000.

Even as he had been constitutionally unable to maturely address the question of who would be his successor, Michel knew that without any Great Men to replace all the talented bankers who had left after Felix, Lazard would quickly become marginalized and risked no longer being relevant. "The idea of a small, private firm is very attractive to people," said one partner. "The only reason not to come to Lazard is because of the baggage." And there was plenty of baggage. The firm was trying to attract new partners in one of the most challenging recruiting environments ever. Not only were many bankers seduced by the seemingly limitless wealth of the Internet, but also the big Wall Street firms were able to offer huge pay packages, laden with restricted stock and options—something the private Lazard could not do. But it was at this juncture that Lazard, chiefly at Loomis's recommendation, began to violate the sanctity of its historical compact with its partners: for the first time, the firm started to hand out to newly hired partners both fixed-dollar-amount contracts, instead of simply a salary plus a profit percentage, and a percentage of their individual revenues. At Loomis's suggestion, in July 1999, Lazard hired Barry Ridings and Terry Savage from Deutsche Bank to resurrect Lazard's formerly world-class business of advising companies going through a financial restructuring or bankruptcy. The restructuring business at Lazard had lain dormant in the mid- to late 1990s after the retirement of David Supino following Michel's questionable decision to wind down the effort in the early 1990s. Ridings and Savage were given lucrative contracts that promised them a percentage of the restructuring revenues plus a percentage of the firm's profits. This was a new paradigm for Lazard's M&A bankers, for the first time driving a wedge between individual and collective interests. Still, the recruitment of Ridings and Savage proved brilliant, as Lazard was once again in a position to capture a large chunk of the lucrative restructuring business that followed in the wake of the bursting of the Internet and telecommunications bubbles. The firm also hired Paul Haigney and Robert Goodman from Wasserstein Perella & Co. to work, respectively, in the Internet and insurance sectors.

But the hire that made the biggest splash in 1999 was that of Vernon Jordan, the lawyer and ultimate Washington insider. "With so many senior people leaving, he was seen as one of the few who could get CEOs on the phone," one Lazard executive said. When Loomis approached Jordan about coming to Lazard, the idea was for Jordan, a principal figure in the Clinton-Lewinsky scandal and the ultimate FOB, to use his "platinum Rolodex" and vast corporate connections—at the time he served on ten corporate boards—to return Lazard to prominence with corporate CEOs during one of the most active M&A markets in history. The fact that Jordan had no investment banking experience was irrelevant to the decision to hire him. Jordan was the ultimate door opener, and that was what Michel and Loomis wanted him to do at Lazard. Loomis explained that, investment banking experience or not, "by virtue of how he is," Jordan would be a senior partner. "Vernon Jordan epitomizes the people we are looking for," Michel said in December 1999. "We want people who are strong individuals. That's the way this firm functions." At the time, he was the only black managing director at the firm. "But I don't walk into Lazard every day saying I'm going to be the only black fellow on my floor," he told the *New York Times*. "I walk into Lazard every day saying I've got a job to do."

Lazard desperately needed Jordan's help to restore morale in the wake of the numerous departures. "For the first two or three days, he was calling in associates and making them feel proud to be here," Loomis said of Jordan. "He will be as important at influencing the firm internally as he will be in getting new business." His positive attitude was infectious, even around the jaded confines of Lazard. Curiously, though, Michel and Loomis refused to share with their partners the details of the lucrative contract that Michel himself negotiated with Jordan, an infuriating reminder of the secretive ancien régime prior to the Rattner era. "This special treatment of Jordan was a huge symbol that they are returning to their old ways of doing business," a former, unnamed partner told the *Washington Post* in January 2000. Jordan, too, was mum. "Did you come all the way here in the cold to talk about rumor and innuendo?" he asked the *Post* reporter who had traveled to his corner office on the sixty-second floor of 30 Rock. "You know what I told [the gossip columnist] Lloyd Grove when he asked me, when I was hired, how much I was making? I said, 'It's none of your damn business.' " Indeed, the firm intentionally left the specifics of Jordan's compensation off the internal list disclosing all partner compensation for fear that the other partners and the press, if the information was leaked, would make a big deal of it. Which is of course exactly what happened anyway. Jordan, then sixty-four, reportedly signed a five-year contract for $5 million a year (a Lazard insider said he got $4 million a year), plus a 0.5 percent slug of the firm's profits and a generous housing allowance toward "an expensive suite" at the Regency Hotel, at 540 Park Avenue, where he spent four nights a week before returning to his principal home, Washington, for the weekend.

PERHAPS, GIVEN HIS unique stature, Jordan was a special case. But there was simply no getting around that, for the first time, a Lazard partner had a contract that paid him regardless of how the partnership itself performed. Some partners were left befuddled. At the very moment the merger of the three houses was supposed to herald a new beginning for the firm, things were looking a lot like déjà vu all over again.

The first order of business for Lazard in the new millennium was the long-awaited realization of Michel's "dynastic" ambition of the reunification of the three houses. The three firms had grown materially in partners (to 140), employees (to 2,745), and profits (to $500 million worldwide), but the interaction among professionals of the three houses on deals was surprisingly limited. There were no established rules for interaction and no financial incentive to interact. Cross-border advisory assignments, which should have been celebrated for playing to the firm's strengths, were instead an opportunity for political infighting over the allocation of fees. Lazard Partners, Michel's 1984 creation, established a framework for what would lead, some sixteen years later, to the combination of the firms. But it wasn't until 1997 that Michel took a first, tentative step toward actual unification by instituting a new bonus pool comprising 30 percent of each of the three houses' profits to be allocated based on cross-border interaction. At the same time, he also was able to combine the London and New York asset management businesses. Paris's asset management business was left on its own. Soon thereafter, Lazard cobbled together its capital markets businesses in New York and in London into a "global" effort. Then, of course, Michel started to refer divinely to the three houses as the Holy Trinity. Momentum for the merger accelerated into the late 1990s, only to be sidetracked in November 1998 by Steve's "democratic" vision, which proved far too radical for the hegemonic Michel.

Unlike Steve, Loomis eagerly complied with the directive to consummate the merger to Michel's precise specifications—with Michel as chairman and CEO. Some partners saw this as a disaster waiting to happen. "We did the merger with no management," recalled one. "We did it a little bit like the euro, you know, one common currency but no common management. Not even a central bank." Loomis wrote to all of the firm's managing directors on February 16, 2000, enclosing the documents, for their immediate signature, that would "formally unite the Houses of Lazard." The good soldier, Loomis displayed, with obvious literary flair, his unqualified support for the combination. "Lazard is unabashedly different in character and structure from the corporate cultures of any of our competitors," he wrote. "We rely on important individuals separated by nationality and united by belief in a business philosophy—Lazard."

Loomis explained that the combined firm would initially have more than twenty-five hundred employees and pretax profit, on a pro forma basis, in excess of $500 million. As with most other firms but for the first time ever at Lazard, the firm would now pay its managing directors from one global profit pool and would establish a "worldwide common system" of appraisal, promotion, and appointments. He also shared with his partners the crucial initial conversion ratio of their historic New York partnership percentage into a new, global partnership percentage: for instance, a partner in New York who previously had a 1 percent stake in the profits of New York would now have a 0.5 percent stake in the profits of the combined Lazard. A fifty-basis-point partner in the global Lazard, assuming $500 million in pretax profits, would have been paid $2.5 million in 2000. As their stake in the profits had been halved, New York partners would be indifferent as long as the size of the whole pie had doubled. Simple mathematics. Anything less meant trouble.

The agreements creating the new firm, now known as Lazard LLC, a Delaware limited liability company, were, no surprise, immensely complex. Exactly as had been feared by many partners, though, the documents were negotiated by a select few behind closed doors and drafted by Lazard's lawyers at Cravath, Swaine & Moore. The execution copies of the documents together with signature pages were dispatched by Cravath to partners worldwide with instructions to sign *immediately* so as not to hold up the merger. A number of partners, understandably upset, held the view that they had been presented with "a contract of adhesion," which they were being forced to sign or else risk losing their accumulated financial interests in the firm. Such contracts, typical of the language of an insurance policy, for instance, are drafted by one party and offered on a take-it-or-leave-it basis with little opportunity for the recipient to bargain or alter the provisions. No self-respecting M&A banker would ever allow his or her client to sign such a document without a proper vetting and negotiation.

No surprise, Michel retained the ability to set all salaries and profit percentages for partners, and bonuses for nonpartners. The board was given many of the typical powers boards have, including the authority to approve, or not, any material merger, acquisition, sale, or disposition; any public or private offering of securities; and the selection of the chairman of the board, the chairman of the executive committee, and the heads of the three houses. Some of the atypical powers included the authority to remove any chairman *other than Michel* and the ability to approve, or not, the transfer of nonworking partners' equity interests. There was also a poison pill of sorts, requiring that any person, other than Michel or his friends at Gaz et Eaux or Eurafrance, who acquires more than 20 percent of aggregate profit percentages also purchase the interests of all the partners at the same price said person acquired the 20 percent stake. As for individual partners trying to transfer or sell their stakes, the documents made that next to impossible. Working partners "generally" would not be permitted that right, while nonworking partners and investors would be permitted to make sales only after Lazard board approval and after "offering their interests to the other members on the same terms as those that apply to the proposed transfers," whatever that means.

After the merger, Michel—not including his family and affiliates—was to directly own just under 10 percent of Lazard LLC (9.9545 percent), which entitled him to about $22 million in current compensation if Lazard were to earn the $500 million that Loomis predicted it would in 2000. It is believed that Michel and his family took out about $100 million from Lazard in 1999. For his part, Loomis, as deputy CEO, would have to make do with a little more than $5.2 million. Unfortunately, the market had peaked—and the bubble burst—just as the ink was drying on the merger.

Still, Michel waxed rhapsodic about the possibility of cooperation among the three houses. He told the *Wall Street Journal,* "It became clear that it was a good idea, a necessity. For us, it's a refoundation. We want to act as one without losing the different national identities." Ken Jacobs, the new head of banking, waxed rhapsodic about the power of the Lazard franchise. "The one asset we have is the reputation and credibility in the boardroom," he told the *Journal*. Adrian Evans waxed rhapsodic about Michel. Without Michel's "astonishing good humour and determination" the merger would not have been possible. Like Madonna, the firm would henceforth be known simply as "Lazard."

In another, more ominous view of what the merger accomplished, Bruno Roger, the new head of the house in Paris and Michel's acknowledged consigliere, told a Paris press conference: "Lazard's is French again." Roger ruled the Paris office firmly, with a particularly Gallic combination of subtlety and complexity. "He's never straightforward and never where you expect him," according to one partner. "He has great insights and an extraordinary sense of minutiae, which is very helpful as an adviser. He's got a very black view of things but he also does infinitely detailed research. He thinks whatever can go wrong, will go wrong. . . . If you plan for bad news and the worst happens, the client is extremely thankful that you actually did plan for it. If that doesn't happen, then the client is happy anyway. Some people find him a bit peculiar—it is human nature that you want to grab on to some good news and you can't always live planning for the worst. He can." Jon Wood at UBS said Roger "was one of the most dishonest people you would meet in your whole life."

STEVE RATTNER SPENT the second half of 1999 casting about for the right thing to do next. His decision to leave, although not announced at the time of Loomis's taking over as deputy CEO, was clearly reflected in his 0.125 percent ownership percentage of Class A interests that was circulated at the time the merger was closing. This percentage was a mere kiss, and not even a wet one at that, and was far below what it had been. It was also below the compensation of many of the most junior managing directors, reflecting his lame-duck status. In a repeat of his departure strategy from the *New York Times* years earlier, he held a series of breakfasts and lunches with other "important" people, searching for the answer about what to do next.

Steve's decision came three months into the new millennium, days before the Nasdaq market peaked and at the same moment Lazard became one firm. Despite a distinct lack of principal investing experience, he announced he was leaving Lazard to form a $1 billion private-equity firm, to be called the Quadrangle Group, focused on making investments in the media and telecommunications industries. In an additional shock to the Lazard family, he was taking three Lazard partners with him: his protégés Peter Ezersky, then forty, and Josh Steiner, then thirty-five, as well as David Tanner, then forty-two, who had only recently joined Lazard to jump-start its principal investing business. (Steve also tried—unsuccessfully—to entice his former Lazard partner Jean-Marie Messier to join Quadrangle.) While having no experience in running a fund or even being a fiduciary for other investors, Steve had made a number of successful personal investments. The word around Lazard was that he had made a bundle investing in the distressed securities of his clients, for his personal portfolio, in the early 1990s.

Quadrangle's success as a private-equity investor remained to be seen, of course. But regardless of the fund's future performance, Steve was again front-page news. By setting up his own $1 billion fund, Steve—by then one of the Democratic Party's biggest fund-raisers—had taken himself out of the running to be in Gore's cabinet, should the vice president have won the presidency in 2000. With their shocking departure, all four partners' Class A percentage interests were thrown back into the pool for future reallocation.

The bursting of the market bubble on March 10, 2000, when the Nasdaq peaked intraday at 5,132, had a grave impact on Wall Street. Tens of thousands of investment bankers lost their jobs, and the compensation for those who remained was much diminished. Eliot Spitzer, the ambitious New York state attorney general (now governor), orchestrated the $1.4 billion Wall Street research settlement, and prosecutors began the steady stream of indictments of corporate executives from, among others, Enron, WorldCom, Adelphia, and HealthSouth.

Not surprisingly, Steve had no trouble raising his $1 billion buyout fund, despite his lack of an investing track record and the stock market's collapse. With the help of the Monument Group, a buyout fund-raising intermediary, he more or less corralled his former media clients and their friends and his friends and whipped the thing together. He and his three partners committed to invest a minimum of $20 million in the fund, and certain of their family members agreed to invest another $10 million. Although the investor list is private, *TALK* magazine speculated it included the likes of Steve Case, Mort Zuckerman, Arthur Sulzberger Jr., Michael Ovitz, Andrew Heyward, Alex Mandl, Steve Brill, Lorne Michaels, and Harvey Weinstein. The Quadrangle Group advisory board consists of Marc Andreessen, Barry Diller, Amos Hostetter, Craig McCaw, and Rob Glaser—all of whom have put money into the fund (as have I, in full disclosure). Like most other private-equity funds, Quadrangle investors pay to the general partners—Rattner et al.—a fee of 1.75 percent per year, payable quarterly in advance, of the money committed to the fund. Put simply, as is typical in the buyout industry, Steve's friends and investors are paying him and his colleagues close to $20 million per year to invest their money, and then paying even more if and when the profits on the investments roll in.

So many things went wrong so quickly for Lazard in the months after the consummation of the three-house merger that for many partners genuine fear quickly replaced whatever euphoria existed. That Steve intended to leave was well known, but by taking Ezersky, Steiner, and Tanner with him, he left a mortal wound in the firm's media and telecom business. The loss of Steve and his team was compounded almost immediately by the skidding U.S. public markets, which badly hurt Lazard's profitability in New York. New York had historically produced around 60 percent of the firm's total pretax profit, and at the time of the merger that fact resulted in New York being valued at around three times London and Paris. But as New York's business dropped precipitously during 2000, there was growing resentment in Europe at that original valuation and the partnership percentages that resulted for the Americans. Also, by the summer of 2000, word had begun to seep into the market of the sizable stakes that Bolloré and Wood had bought in the four public French holding companies that controlled Lazard. Michel, now the CEO of the combined Lazard, became preoccupied with the threats posed by these gentlemen instead of focusing on the Lazard operations.

Once again, several of the most important European partners started voting with their feet: in June, Nigel Turner went to the Dutch bank ABN AMRO; in Paris, Pierre Tattevin left for Rothschild, and David Dautresme, the newly appointed co-head of global M&A (with Ken Jacobs in New York), "retired." Coming on top of John Nelson's departure the year before, the loss of Turner "threatened Armageddon" for the M&A practice in London, according to one insider. There were also rumblings in the asset management business, which had been consistently generating $100 million in annual profit, that the co-heads, Eig and Gullquist, were restless and were pushing for the business to be spun off from Lazard.

What's more, it was increasingly obvious that the merger itself was not working. "Six months into it, there was no merger integration," said one partner. "There was no backroom technology. There were no common standards on underwriting committees. You had hard underwritings being done in Paris with capital that was in New York, and no one in

New York being told about it until after it was done, weeks after it was done. I mean things which—just commonsense kinds of things were not being done." And there was the ongoing problem of how to pay partners more competitively without the stock or options that public firms offered. Michel continued to resist calls for an IPO. "We may have to change our means of compensation," he told *Forbes* in September 2000. "Pay in money and also in hope." The senior partners quickly reached the conclusion that with ideas no better than that, Michel could no longer run the firm on a day-to-day basis. Just as Steve had foreseen two years earlier, the firm needed a real CEO.

IN JUNE 2000, David Verey first articulated this view to Michel, which obviously was not without professional risk, not least because the merger agreement guaranteed that Michel could remain CEO until 2005. "I said to Michel on a flight to Toronto that we have to have a chief executive," Verey recalled. "He said to me, 'He has to be American.' I said, 'Look, I'm past caring, just do it. We have to have somebody who is prepared to be CEO.' He said, 'Okay, it will have to be Loomis.' "

Another senior partner remembered hearing about Verey's conversation with Michel this way: "Look, I know I've always wanted this job, but I'm not going to be accepted by Braggiotti or Bruno or the guys in the States. The only one that can do it is Loomis. . . . You haven't run the firm, any of the firms, since the early 1990s. And now you're CEO, and you don't know the people. You don't know the business anymore. You haven't ever managed anything this complex before." This partner said that Verey's realization that he would not be accepted as the CEO of Lazard, while bittersweet, won him the respect of other partners. For a time thereafter, Verey had a tremendous influence on Michel.

Yet again, there was a leadership crisis at the firm, but now further compounded by the conflagration started in Europe by Bolloré and Wood. Although the formal announcement of his appointment as Lazard's first legitimate CEO would be months away (his appointment was announced in Paris on November 15), through the course of the summer and early fall of 2000 Loomis began assuming more and more of the day-to-day responsibility of the firm. As expected, he memorialized what he thought to be his mandate in a ten-page, single-spaced manifesto to the executive committee, drafted at its request, titled "Our Future Course" and dated October 24, 2000. Loomis began, "You each supported my appointment as Chief Executive Officer of Lazard. I am personally grateful. I am also professionally confident in our joint efforts on behalf of the firm. We will continue to benefit in our endeavors from Michel's participation as a strong Chairman who embodies the very essence of our partnership. Ultimately, however, I am also cognizant of my responsibility for the most difficult decisions and for the performance of the firm. The buck stops here."

Loomis then outlined a series of specific steps he planned to take to help achieve his vision for the firm, a vision—without having any authority to implement it—he had been refining off and on for some twenty years. To avoid the "easy" path of selling the firm, he proposed an ambitious slew of new measures: from hiring new partners "of prominence" while increasing pay for the best-performing partners to creating a seriously complex equity-like security as a way to bind partners economically to the firm for the long haul. He also wanted to reinvigorate the firm's private-equity investing program by creating a new, $800 million fund that partners could voluntarily invest in as a further way to increase their wealth. But, Loomis outlined, there needed to be some tough-love measures as well: he wanted to cull from the partnership ranks the weakest performers and also said he intended to fire 10 percent of the global Lazard workforce, or 275 people, within the first three months of 2001. He also said he needed to raise $100 million of new capital from the existing Lazard investors to pay off the firm's financial obligation, negotiated by Michel, to Eig and Gullquist.

Whether any of this reflected Michel's strategic thinking for the firm was unknown. But the one thing that was now crystal clear was that Loomis was simply Michel's puppet. "I remain chairman," Michel said at the Paris news conference after announcing Loomis's promotion. "The chairman, which I am, has relatively extended powers." He later summed up Loomis's prospects for succeeding him: "It would not be abnormal for Loomis to become the successor when I disappear," a comment one observer said was akin to "cutting off Loomis at the knees when he had only just started in the job." Loomis seemed to understand well what was expected of him. "We've been through a period of turmoil and now need stability," he told *BusinessWeek*. "Without Michel's 100% backing, I couldn't be successful. He truly embodies the perspective of the firm." Still, Marcus Agius, the London chief, told the *Wall Street Journal* the firm was still troubled. "The mood was ghastly," he said.

Just before the Loomis announcement, rumors circulated in Europe that Deutsche Bank was in talks to buy Lazard. Both firms denied the rumor, and the deal never happened. "We have no desire to sell," Michel said at the time. "We have no need to." Not surprisingly, in his first address to the firm as CEO, Loomis took up the boss's torch. "We are the independent and private alternative," he said. "It will remain so.

We are not going to sell the firm, take it public or sell a major business." As part of the work to reach accommodations with Bolloré and UBS, the accounting firm Ernst & Young valued Lazard at $4 billion, up slightly from the $3.785 billion "Pearson price." When *BusinessWeek* asked Michel whether the $4 billion represented a potential sale price for the whole firm, he reiterated that he had no intention to sell. But he added with a smile, "If we were to sell, let's say I'd be disappointed to only get that much."

Bruce Wasserstein, meanwhile, had just announced, in September 2000, the sale of his firm, Wasserstein Perella & Co., to Dresdner Bank in Germany for nearly $1.37 billion, plus $190 million for a retention pool, a price that certainly got the attention of the Lazard brass who had just a few years earlier rejected the combination with Wasserstein Perella because, among other reasons, it made no money. "The price was obscene," Alan Webborn, an independent research analyst, told *Bloomberg*.

Two weeks after Loomis became CEO, Michel announced that Crédit Agricole had agreed to buy the Bolloré position in Rue Impériale, securing Bolloré a €290 million profit. Inside the firm all this was viewed not only as a terrible diversion but also as devastating symbolism. "Bolloré caused just a huge distraction on the part of Michel and his French partners in 1999 and 2000," said one senior American partner. "And UBS as well. Just a huge distraction. And a distraction in a bunch of different ways. First is, I think it became obvious to these guys that they were no longer going to be able to run this place secretively with a relatively small ownership, both of Eurazeo and then all the chain companies and Lazard, forever. And second was, and probably the most important thing, is it created this chink in the armor of Lazard in continental Europe. And I think that hurt dramatically the firm's position in France. It shows you're vulnerable. I mean, when you have this mystique of power, this aura of power, and suddenly you are being attacked and the attackers are winning, it shows you're not as strong as you people think you are. And in France, that matters."

❋

The larger question for Lazard remained painfully unresolved: How was the firm going to be able to compete effectively against its historic rivals, Goldman Sachs and Morgan Stanley, which had remade themselves into hugely well capitalized global financial services firms able to attract the most talented bankers by offering the highest compensation and the best platform off of which to operate? The year 1999 was one of the rare instances when Lazard had fallen out of the top ten in the M&A league tables; Goldman and Morgan Stanley ranked one and two, respectively. The war for talent had reached the point where Bill Gates remarked that Microsoft's biggest competitor was not another software company but rather Goldman Sachs. "It's all about IQ," Gates said. "You win with IQ. Our only competition for IQ is the top investment banks." The *Economist* observed presciently about Lazard, "The crux for all investment banks is to be able to compete for the best talent. Ironically, says a senior banker with the firm, it might take a bear market to decide the issue for Lazard and to dictate whether the bank will have an independent future. If markets keep falling, the value of other investment bankers' share options will also fall. The gap between the rewards offered by Lazard and those of the rest of the pack would then narrow, extending the group's life expectancy as an independent entity. Now there's a good reason for a bank to be bearish."

Just as 2000 was closing, on December 11, the firm's executive committee was to meet for the first time with Loomis as CEO to review the firm-wide budget for 2001. Neither New York nor Paris had ever constructed a budget before, and as one partner observed, "The machinery, the culture to review it simply does not exist." That portion of the December executive committee meeting dedicated to reviewing the 2001 budget was postponed until mid-January, when the senior partners would have had time to review and vet the budget documents more thoroughly. The executive committee member Adrian Evans was further dismayed when he learned that while the firm had more revenue in 2000 than ever before, it was less profitable because expenses were out of control, especially in New York. "After an outstanding year, it is clear the economics don't work," he confided. "I wondered whether this is the Harvard Business School case that will be amusing future students on 'Lazard's decline.' If it is not to be so, we need to work now to redress our New York problems."

CHAPTER 18

"LAZARD MAY GO DOWN LIKE THE *TITANIC*!"

There was no question that by late 2000 or early 2001, Wall Street was in a full-fledged bear market, although economists wouldn't confirm it until later. Almost from the day he took over as Lazard's CEO, Loomis had to figure out a way to manage through its consequences. It was not easy for him, and nothing he or Michel did made it any easier. Just as Felix feared would happen to him if he accepted the job of running Lazard, some partners thought Loomis's power dissipated from the moment Michel introduced him as CEO. "That was the beginning of the end," one partner said.

Even if that was a slightly exaggerated rendition of events, it was not off by much. "Within weeks, Michel was undermining Bill every step of the way," said one partner then in a position to know. "He's undermining him with private conversations with Braggiotti before board meetings and all kinds of things which would be unfathomable with regard to how you would give a chief executive powers." But Loomis didn't help himself any, either, with his early decisions. From the outset, he had raised expectations among all the partners with his proposal to bestow upon them the funky "performance preferred" equity-like security, or if that proved impractical (which it soon did), some other incentive scheme.

To be fair, Michel knew that Loomis intended to get some form of equity security into the hands of partners, and by naming Loomis CEO, he seemed to be tacitly endorsing that idea. "Bill actually had come in on a platform of wanting to come up with something that provides long-term value to partners," one old Lazard hand recalled, "whether it was through private equity or it was going to be through some kind of partial ownerships that would then be recycled and bought back by the firm. So Michel kind of raised expectations a little bit."

To fulfill two other aspects of his manifesto—getting some points back from the capitalists to use to hire new partners and to pay some of the old ones better, and getting the capitalists to buy the new $100 million preferred—Loomis made a pilgrimage to Paris early on to speak to the non-David-Weill capitalists—the Meyer family, Jean Guyot, and Antoine Bernheim. He accomplished this twin mission successfully, but at a steep price. Said one partner: "He was told by them, 'Okay, we'll buy the preferred, but don't ever come back to see us again or ever ask for anything ever again,' on no uncertain terms. By these people who were no longer working here. And that got to be known by everybody in the firm." Although the working partners considered this a modest success, Loomis ended up tremendously upsetting the capitalists. "I mean, people thought that it wasn't nearly enough and it wasn't going to really sustain us going forward," a partner recalled, "but it was enough to get through the year end and make new partners."

Loomis's second challenge involved the technology banker Paul Haigney, hired from Wasserstein Perella as a partner in September 1999, to join the highly regarded partner Richard Emerson in the San Francisco office. In 2000, Haigney was a 0.625 percent partner, which put him in the middle of the pack (which still meant he was paid around $3 million). In February 2000, Haigney introduced Robert Davis, the CEO of Lycos (the Internet portal company), to the CEO of Terra Networks, an affiliate of Telefónica, the large Spanish telecom service provider and a Lazard client. In May 2000, Terra and Lycos announced a $12.5 billion combination. The deal closed in October.

By this time, Haigney knew that his close friend and partner Emerson was being wooed by Microsoft to become its senior vice president of corporate development and strategy. At the beginning of December 2000, just two weeks after Loomis became CEO, Microsoft announced that Emerson, then thirty-eight, would be leaving Lazard and joining the company. "Richard has been a gifted banker in the best traditions of Lazard," Loomis told the press. As Haigney no doubt suspected, Emerson's departure was another major blow to Lazard, even though the firm did become an occasional adviser to Microsoft afterward.

Haigney used the moment to demand an all-cash, three-year guaranteed contract, the first time a young working partner already at the firm had demanded such a deal. Either he would be given the contract or he would leave, he told Loomis. Lazard's executive committee debated the demand. Nobody wanted to lose Haigney, given his performance and how difficult it would be for Lazard to replace an accomplished technology banker at the top of the market. But the executive committee was firmly united against giving in to him for fear that it was completely antithetical to the historical Lazard compensation culture and because it would no doubt lead to other, similar requests, requests that Lazard would not be able to easily fulfill given its slumping performance. The executive committee voted it down. "But basically, Bill insisted that we do it, and that was it," remembered one partner. Haigney got his three-year guarantee, said to be some $4 million a year.

The executive committee minutes of January 31, 2001, confirm the approval of the Haigney contract but make no mention of the rancorous debate it ignited. Another member of the executive committee, while opposed to the decision, conceded there was at least some logic to it. "Now, you have to remember, this was against the backdrop of the TMT [telecommunications, media, and technology] boom," he explained. "Partner pay on Wall Street is out of control. We're trying to hire what's his name? Rob Kindler from Cravath, and he's getting a contract allegedly for $30 million from Chase instead. It's just all over. The numbers are astronomical. Wall Street is doing incredibly well. People are getting paid huge bonuses. The DLJ guys are walking around with a fortune from CSFB in the fall of 2000. Wasserstein's firm being sold for $1.6 billion in the fall of 2000 and then everybody finding out that this one partner at Lazard now has a guarantee and what about the rest of us?"

Loomis's decision was a watershed event. "All of us also knew that the instant he did this, the dam would break," a partner remembered. "We couldn't hire anybody, because we didn't have any currency to pay people with, so this whole thing was there and developed in 2000. But when this one partner got this guarantee and Bill came in, it just—the dam burst. Everybody here kind of felt like a huge dinosaur through this whole thing. And they felt like they were leaving their careers on the table versus going to other places."

Around the same time, just before Christmas 2000, there was a partners' meeting in London, presided over by Loomis, to discuss the firm's financial performance and talk about who did what during the year. This meeting was a disaster, too. There was tremendous anger among many of the partners. The Europeans felt they had carried the firm during 2000 and were on a growth trajectory, but under the terms of the three-house merger agreement their profit percentages were locked in for a couple of years. The Americans were also unhappy that their profit percentages had been halved just as the pie was shrinking. "Everybody in Europe wanted more points," remembered a senior partner. "Everybody in New York felt they were underpaid. So nothing worked." On January 2, 2001, Michel sent Loomis a handwritten fax from Cap d'Antibes on his Sous-le-Vent stationery. "Bill," he wrote, "on this first working day of 2001 I want you to know all the wishes I make for your success. All my life, since my early childhood, I have been proud of the firm and thanks to you it is with renewed belief that I think about our future. Your partner, Michel David-Weill." Michel's optimism—and that of the firm as a whole—would be sorely tested in 2001.

Indeed, within weeks, the stark reality of Lazard's financial difficulties became increasingly obvious to the firm's leaders. In preparation for an early January meeting in New York to discuss the 2001 budget, the senior partners in London came to the view that New York "has $50 million too much expense, provides 18% of the Lazard profit and receives around 40% of the Lazard profit share. Paris, London and the Rest of Europe were more or less the reciprocal: 40%-ish of the profit for 18% of the benefit in London and Paris and Rest of Europe approximately the same. This information is not yet before all partners but inevitably will be and it will cause a storm." The Brits were convinced "some sort of gesture needs to be made," for instance, a combination of all partners accepting a salary of $200,000, New York reducing expenses by $50 million or transferring a "significant number of partnership points" to Europe in 2001, or all of them together. "This would be a fine start," the London partner Adrian Evans wrote to Loomis.

Loomis explained to Evans, who recorded the exchange in his diary, that "Michel, with whom Bill had discussed the numbers, is of the view that to cut back now in New York is dangerous as there are no big hitters to depend upon, rather a lot of smaller hitters bringing in smaller deals." Evans further reported: "[Loomis's] belief is that any solution to the expense issue (which he also identifies as a $50 million overage) will demand the firing of a great many young, talented people and he clearly (and quite understandably) dreads it."

To get the French perspective on the firm's mounting problems, Evans and his longtime French partner Jean-Claude Haas had "our usual very frank conversation" over breakfast. The French just wanted to be left alone as their business continued to perform well, and partners there were of the view that they received little or no benefit from the three-house merger. Pondering this view, Evans swiftly concluded, "We will either work as one entity or die." He then reflected on how the firm found itself in such a tight box. "It is interesting to consider why we are where we are," he wrote. "Our great success has been largely due to Michel and his strange blend of pied piper and Louis XIV. Our problems—a chaotic, un-disciplined, un-run New York; an arrogant, uncommunicative Paris—are also due to him. London, of course, is not perfect and is viewed by other houses as isolationist, greedy, bureaucratic but I do know that London will change, indeed longs to change, but cannot do so until a Lazard strategy emerges that is credible and simple." The executive committee concluded that the performance in 2000 had been sufficient to hold the firm together, but 2001 would be the critical year.

The following week brought two more days of budget meetings in New York for the senior partners as part of the run-up to the much-anticipated executive committee meeting in Paris on January 31. As Evans sat in hour after hour of meetings, he began to make some observations about Loomis and his management style. "Loomis played an interesting, watchful game," he wrote, "and it became clear to me that what was happening in the room was a diversion. Loomis has clearly made up his mind to get a grip on the anarchic New York operation and will do so." What that meant, "all agree," is that New York "needs to take out a very large slug of costs and that to do so will mean partners having to go." In the further run-up to the January 31 meeting, word began to circulate among the European partners that Michel was "deeply and unusually depressed." It was not hard to see why. There was serious dissension among the troops. Many of them, if not all, had lost faith in their leader after the Haigney incident. The M&A market appeared to be in a serious slump. Michel added to the sense of despair when he told a French partner that he had decided unilaterally to add Georges Ralli to the executive committee as the result of "yet another threat to quit," this time for UBS Warburg (he had been offered $10 million a year for three years, guaranteed), in part because "everyone was unhappy." The stage was more than set for a divisive meeting in Paris.

For four hours, the committee debated the 2001 budget, which showed $17 million of expense cuts in banking (a $20 million decrease in the United States coupled with a $3 million increase in Europe outside of Paris and London), and eventually approved it with "big cuts" in New York "after quite a lot of self-justifications" from the New York partners. Loomis gave a little admonitory speech. "In a nutshell," Evans wrote, "he said that it was not possible for the firm to succeed if individual members of the Executive Committee behaved greedily, focusing on their own pockets. The insidious nature of one man telling another that Lazard could not make it would bring the firm down. . . ." Several partners observed that as Loomis spoke his hands were trembling more than usual. Then, with five minutes left in the meeting—Michel had called for its end—Loomis announced without discussion that he had decided, and Michel had approved, that Georges Ralli, Dave Tashjian, and William Rucker would join the executive committee. He also announced, again without discussion, that he had unilaterally put together a new "equity scheme," which Michel had also approved, whereby Loomis had selected the top twenty-three partners in the firm to be awarded equity in

Lazard equal to half their profit points, provided they stayed at the firm for at least five years and did not go work for a competitor. The objective of the plan was to retain "a core group of Managing Directors in the Firm."

This would have meant that about 20 percent of Lazard's equity would be put permanently in the hands of the top twenty-three partners—and no one else. That was it. No broad-based distribution of equity designed to energize the whole firm or give genuine authority to the firm's working partners. Obviously, this had been a compromise that Loomis had fashioned with his patron, Michel. Quite apart from the merits of the plan or of its philosophical underpinnings—which in any event weren't discussed, given the shortness of time—the reaction to Loomis's proposal was swift and visceral.

Obviously upset that Loomis had not consulted him and in "a rather excited voice," Ken Jacobs demanded to know how it would all work, and when the proposal could be discussed, since for the previous six months he had been "chasing abortive schemes and nothing had happened," and now this plan had been presented as a fait accompli. Jacobs's rebuke angered Loomis, whose hands were now trembling mightily. Evans recalled what happened next: "Bill appeared to lose his temper and said in a rising voice that this scheme was agreed, Michel had agreed it, and he had a list of the awardees. Reaching into his briefcase, he produced it and threw it on the table." The meeting broke up immediately. Evans bumped into Norm Eig, co-head of asset management, in front of Lazard's unmarked office on Boulevard Haussmann and asked him what he thought. "There will be trouble ahead," Eig predicted, his "eyes twinkling and with a big grin." "We're a $3 billion business and only one of my [guys'] names appears on that list."

Evans then went to the Gare du Nord, rode the train back to London with his partner William Rucker, and had "three hours to chew on this remarkable piece of theatre." They agreed the Loomis plan was a "pretty bizarre scheme" since all it did was lock up 20 percent of the firm and replace one group of capitalists with another one. There was also the problem, which "will cause comment," that thirteen of the twenty-three names on the list were American and only two were French.

The bigger problem, though, was Loomis's new demeanor. "Bill's behaviour is quite against the grain of the executive committee," Evans later wrote. "To date, it has been collegiate, deliberative, conservative (and, admittedly, pretty ineffectual). This new approach is Bill out in front giving instructions. It is quite hard to see how he handles his next move. I suspect that he will regret going quite so far." Verey's view was that to give "until death" equity to working partners would lead quickly and inevitably to either a sale or an IPO because to "monetize or to refresh" that 20 percent will require "outsiders" to come in. Verey was also depressed because, after leading Lazard Brothers successfully for ten years, he now had "no real focus in the new Lazard." He said he would rather resign "at whatever cost to himself" than watch Lazard be sold because of an ill-considered equity plan. Evans recalled: "He simply could not face all the people he had hired, had talked to and to whom he had expressed the Lazard ideal: an independent firm run by independent men." Evans cautioned him to spend some time in "calm reflection" and "leave the ball at Bill's feet." The firm seemed to be unraveling.

A few days later, after the members of the executive committee had had a chance to digest the events in Paris, the consensus was that the meeting was "unacceptable," "divisive," and "potentially destructive of the firm." The executive committee members, without consulting Loomis, decided to schedule a follow-up meeting before the next regularly scheduled one. This was done through Loomis's secretary as Loomis had gone on vacation after the meeting in Paris. With Evans as his editor, Verey sent a letter to Michel and Loomis, observing that the meeting in Paris was "unfortunate," that his loyalty to the firm after thirty years could not be "bought or sold," that the proposed equity plan was the "first step" to selling Lazard, and that therefore the firm should be sold "properly." He also said Loomis's unilateral appointment of the three new executive committee members was "unacceptable." The committee members were still reeling from Loomis's unilateral override of the negative Haigney vote. When Loomis found out about the unscheduled executive committee meeting, he was livid. He spoke with Michel, and together they made calls to the French partners, in a successful effort to divide the Europeans. Whatever they said or promised worked; the special session was canceled.

The executive committee reconvened for two days of meetings on February 20 in New York. Loomis kicked things off, in his understated manner, by admitting he had "received the impression" that the "unto death" equity scheme he had proposed in Paris was unpopular. The ensuing laughter helped break the tension that had been building for weeks. Michel then asked if anyone wished to speak in support of the proposed equity plan. Nobody spoke. Michel chaired a lengthy discussion, inviting dissension. Ralli got so upset at one point he threw his pen on the floor. Michel then delivered his version of an inspirational speech. In written form, the words seem incoherent and rambling. Perhaps it was better delivered live. "Our name in the world is excellent," he told his senior partners.

> We have valuable business and valuable talents. But there is doubt about our ability to survive. The doubt is pervasive among you, the top people at the firm. I am trying to give you the greatest opportunity any banker can hope for. The conduct of Lazard in the years to come: it seems obvious to me that this firm in five years can be at least twice as profitable. We can make $200 million net in money management, we can make a hundred million in capital markets; we can make $500 million net in M&A, which would result in $900 million of profit. I strongly believe these are realistic goals. In the meantime, it is evident that we can have poor years but you are in a position to do something about it. I have to admit that whether we adopt a lifetime ownership for some partners or some other form of incentives is secondary though important. What is needed now is full commitment. We all agree that Bill Loomis is decisive and courageous. He can lead the firm but needs a totally constructive attitude toward him.

Just before the end of this "commitment fest," as Evans called it, the partners discussed a new, two-pronged attack from Édouard Stern. He was threatening to sue the firm over his perception that LF Capital Partners, a small private-equity fund the firm owned, had been mismanaged. He had been one of the largest investors, and he had lost money. He was upset and wanted $10–$15 million to "keep quiet." (He sued the firm anyway, and the matter was settled.) He also wanted to disrupt the pending Eurafrance and Azeo merger. "Michel made it clear he had had it with Stern," Evans observed. "Bruno is clearly deeply concerned about all this and he is the most exposed," which explained Roger's subdued manner at the meeting. There was also concern that a disruptive Édouard Stern "could impact the timing of the commitment of any funds to Lazard's Alternative Investing activities," Evans observed.

Evans met privately with Michel after the executive committee meeting, and they agreed the meetings were better and people were now "bound in" to the firm. While they were together in Michel's office, Felix stopped in to say hello, having returned to New York from Paris. He and Michel were in the midst of a months-long discussion about whether Felix would return to Lazard. After Felix had left the office, Evans told Michel that his return would be like reliving the Stern fiasco. Michel appeared to agree with Evans's assessment.

Felix's tenure as ambassador to France ended a month after the November 2000 election. While sitting in the den of his Fifth Avenue apartment, surrounded by his Labrador retrievers, Noodles and Nobu, he told the *New York Times* in January 2001 that he had no intention of returning to Lazard. He reiterated his desire to write his memoirs—a "good book about what I have seen in my life"—and perhaps start a small advisory boutique with a few associates. He also said he would serve on the boards of Comcast, Fiat, and a few unnamed others. He also joined the Council on Foreign Relations. "I decided that I couldn't go back to Lazard in any full-time capacity," he told *Institutional Investor* in May 2001, "because it wouldn't be good for Lazard and it wouldn't be good for me." Yet, as Trollope might have said, in the "yellow leaf" of his career, he also said he thought about quietly retiring "not at all."

More than once during Felix's three years as ambassador, Michel had asked him to come back to Lazard, even though Felix had denied at the time that such conversations had taken place. A number of Michel's requests to Felix came early in his ambassadorship and so were dismissed by Felix as random musings. There was also his concern about whether Liz, his wife, would be able to successfully battle the breast cancer that had been diagnosed soon after the Rohatyns arrived in Paris. (Liz did win this fight.) On these occasions, Felix said he repeatedly told Michel, "No, you know I can't do this. I can't go back." This time Felix once again declined Michel's offer. But he also asked Michel for something: to release him from a provision of his noncompete agreement that prevented him for three years from working for a Lazard competitor. Felix had signed the noncompete when he left Lazard in April 1997 as consideration for his lifetime of pension payments totaling millions of dollars. He had been fielding a number of opportunities back in New York, and although, as he told Michel, he doubted he would accept any of them, he wanted to feel free to at least think about them without concern he might violate his noncompete. He also told Michel he doubted the noncompete provision was legally enforceable and that, in any event, he would be happy for Lazard to be the first place he negotiated with about returning on some basis.

Michel chose to torture Felix, instead telling him: "Well, we can't do that. I'll put it to a vote" of the executive committee. According to Felix, Michel went through this "extraordinary exercise" of soliciting the views of the other senior partners of Lazard to see if they would be willing to agree to let Felix—next to André Meyer the single most important person in the history of the firm—out of his noncompete provision. Felix told Michel, his anger rising, "I could go to court, and in five minutes

I would get a declaratory judgment. [But] I'm not going to do that. . . . Go ahead and vote, and then look me in the eye." Apparently unmoved and without a trace of irony, Michel reported back to Felix that the partners decided at the February executive committee meeting they could not vote on this request. Felix said Michel told him, "If they voted to release you, it would look as if they wanted to get rid of you, and they can't think of doing that." There was supposedly no vote. But there was agreement on the executive committee not to accede to Felix's request. Two points were communicated to Felix: there would be no "unilateral" rescinding of his noncompete, and he would be welcomed back to the firm even though only Michel held this latter view. "Another bizarre affair," Adrian Evans wrote in his diary, "is Felix Rohatyn who has asked us to release him from his non-compete clause so that he can decide where he is going to practice once he leaves Paris. Our view was that we should not release him (all agreed) and that we should not encourage him to come to Lazard (MDW disagreed). In any event, he is unlikely to come here. If he does, he will be massively disruptive." Felix was *not* released from his noncompete, nor did he rejoin Lazard.

Instead, in order to comply with his contractual obligation, he spent the three years beginning April 2001 in a suite of Lazard-paid-for offices on the fiftieth floor of 30 Rockefeller Center, ten floors below the firm's actual offices. He hung out his own shingle, Rohatyn Associates, to provide advice to corporations. A memo sent around inside the firm explained that Felix would be a "senior adviser" to Lazard. It said he would also run Rohatyn Associates and spend some of his time managing his family's money and his philanthropic activities. He elaborated on how this new arrangement actually worked. "The idea was that Lazard could use my name with clients that still had a relationship with me," Felix said. "And wherever possible I would still try to bring business to them if it was in my power to do that. I was totally independent to do business on my own in any way that I wanted, even with competitors of Lazard. And we did, and we did very well. I had my clients; I had my retainers. I was on three boards in France. I tried to put Lazard in a couple of deals. On one I think I succeeded, and on the others I think it didn't work. But that was it. My only obligation was in good faith to try to bring them business, and at the end of three years they paid me, and that was it." Lazard paid him $2.5 million in 2001, in addition to what he made from his own firm.

He was a controversial, if not particularly welcome, presence back at Lazard. Certainly, Loomis wanted nothing to do with Felix, as the memory of their early 1990s feuding was still fresh. The younger bankers, those partial to Internet chat rooms anyway, seemed indifferent to him. After the memo came around about Felix's new role at the firm, one anonymous author wrote, "So Felix is back. Has anyone seen him? Any guesses on what impact he will have? On the one hand, he seems to have hedged his bets re starting his own firm. On the other hand, this is one of the most renowned bankers of the last half-century. I think this can only be good for Lazard but I am interested to hear what others have to say."

A lot, as it turned out. "Isn't Felix in his early 70s?" someone asked. "I am curious about his motivations at this point. I doubt that he has the zeal to revive Lazard on his own. The departures of Rattner, Wilson, etc. might have been too much for even old Felix to overcome." This prompted the response: "Even with his return, that is not going to mean anything. Lazard is not the company it used to be. When Rattner left the firm, that's when the ship started to sink. The only way this firm will stay afloat is if it is sold. All the big guns are gone. Oh, that's right, there is Vernon Jordan who is bringing in tons of money. Right? Ha Ha Ha!!!" One wag wrote, "I think bringing Felix back won't help the firm at all. . . . It's like bringing grandpa back from the nursing home to run your business when all he talks about is how full his bladder feels." Another wise guy also failed to see how Felix would be useful. "Seems like Felix is taking over the 50th floor at 30 Rock," he wrote. "He's got a staff of around 10 waiting to drain some Lazard resources. I think they are going to be allocated like this: two to clean his thick glasses (1 per lens); one person to type out his rhetoric, as he can't use a PC; two for mistresses (one for him the other for MDW); and five hired thugs to stop him from strangling Vernon Jordan! Lazard's got its future in the right hands."

All this chatter evoked a blistering defense of Felix from his former partner Richard Emerson, then still at Microsoft: "Felix is truly the best banker that I have seen, from the details of the analysis through to the macro issues and on to the respect of the board. He is extremely diligent and motivated. Anyone who says less hasn't been around him and certainly hasn't earned his respect. And I was proud to be called his partner."

In addition to pursuing his deals, Felix worked on his memoir for a while, tentatively titled *Money Games: My Journey Through American Capitalism, 1950–2000*. Simon & Schuster, the book division of Viacom, was to have been the publisher, and Alice Mayhew, the respected editor of Bob Woodward and James Stewart, among others, was to have been Felix's editor. Felix, along with two ghostwriters, penned the book, and then stashed it in a drawer, where it remains unpublished, after he reread it and decided it was too deal-oriented and too much about himself. Vernon Jordan said Felix decided not to publish it because he had taken too many potshots at his fellow Lazard partners. He returned his advance to his publisher. James Atlas, the writer and founder of Atlas Books, has been after Felix to publish a slimmed-down version of his memoir. Instead, he is now writing a book about the important investments—such as the Louisiana Purchase and the transcontinental highway system—that America has made over its history. Rohatyn Associates, Felix's once thriving advisory firm, moved to a suite of offices at 280 Park Avenue that he shared with his son Nick, a former senior banker at J. P. Morgan, who now runs a $500-plus million hedge fund and who, in December 2000, paid $7.4 million for a forty-foot-wide mansion in Manhattan. In August 2006, Felix all but shuttered Rohatyn Associates and joined Lehman Brothers, of all places, as a senior adviser to CEO Dick Fuld and chairman of its international advisory committee. He keeps an office both at 280 Park and at Lehman on Seventh Avenue. Ironically, Felix had been poised to merge his small firm into Evercore, Roger Altman's boutique, just prior to the Evercore IPO, which would have netted Felix a financial windfall. But at the last moment, Felix decided against the merger because he was so aghast that Altman had allowed one of his partners, Jonathan Knee, to write a book about his experiences on Wall Street.

AT THE JANUARY 31 meeting, the executive committee decided that an immediate way to increase profitability was to fire people, something Lazard had never, *ever* done before in difficult times. When Michel arrived in 1977 to find the firm almost in shambles, he departnered seven men, but never before had across-the-board layoffs been necessary, in contrast to almost every other firm on Wall Street. But the situation was now increasingly desperate. Loomis's top objective at the time he became CEO was to reduce head count by at least 275 people globally in three to four months. The time had come to implement his plan. By early 2001, the dismissal process started with the seemingly odd decision to fire about fifty information technology employees, about one-third of the department, whose combined pay barely added up to that of one partner. The idea was to reduce the IT expenses by $9 million.

But even this relatively straightforward move set off a firestorm of protest inside the firm. Much of the frustration boiled over into Internet chat rooms, the new, albeit anonymous and sophomoric, outlet for mounting employee frustrations, regardless of industry. "We see the writing on the wall," one employee commented in March. "Is this the beginning of the end?????????? Lazard N.Y. MAY GO DOWN LIKE THE *TITANIC* !!!!!" "Lazard is being sold this year!!!" screamed the headline of another anonymous writer. "Due to the fact that MDW is now going to retire and no one in his family is willing to inherit Lazard's financial problems and managerial conflicts . . . This has been in the works for a long time; just look at the history of former well known MDs that left a while back, they knew and got the fuck out of here. For those of you stuck there like me run, run as fast as you can." Another warned a few days later, "In the next two weeks, all departments at Lazard will get hit: Trading, banking, asset management; specifically, departments like high yield, fixed income, accounts payable etc. Take it from me, no one is safe. Play it safe people and start getting those resumes out there and start loading up on the office supplies."

Morale at the firm, always low, dropped even further. "There are rumors of layoffs but no one has been laid off yet," another banker said. "That creates a level of panic that will not subside until they are made or it is made clear that they will not be made. This is coupled with markedly slower deal flow in M&A from a year ago across the Street. Furthermore, there are rumors that Lazard is being sold. . . . Right now, there is a level of group panic about something that could be very real and very ugly." Another disgruntled employee confided, "First of all for those support staff who have lost jobs and are supporting families, I am truly sorry. It is a shame that no managing director at Lazard has spine or soul enough to put down their martini and request a pay cut. I think it is about time that Lazard realizes where the true fat of the company lay. All the money in the world apparently can not buy common sense." A current employee, "getting his CV ready," wrote: "Lazard's reputation as an elite company has evaporated. Go in and talk to the employees. Take a look around. All that's left is a bunch of sheep headed for the slaughter. Lazard is like all the rest. No longer exclusive, simply common." Another wrote, "Imagine being in the middle of the ocean with a pair of cement shoes and an anchor around your waist. How would you feel? HOPELESS. That's what it feels like to be at Lazard." Another, fired employee was ecstatic. "I got a call from Bill Loomis last week and had to call friends to arrange a party before going down to his office," he wrote. "If they had been asking for volunteers to show up at Loomis' office I would have camped out all night to be first in line. While the poor people at Lazard go into their offices everyday and sit and pretend that Lazard has business, I will be in Africa for three months (still getting paid) before starting my new job in July." On a scale of one to ten, one banker claimed morale was minus ten. "It is shit," he wrote. "Imagine that every week you have to come into work wondering if the boss likes you or not (not based on any criteria but the closeness of your nose to his ass). On Tuesday everyone sweats, and no one is working. Why should we? Those wimps don't have the balls to do it at once. This has nothing to do with the market. They must have known for a while, but were too chicken to do it at one time. Typical."

Just as the reality of the first wave of firings started to register around the firm came the news that a European financial analyst, working in New York, died while sitting at his desk, of an apparent heart attack. "Everyone at the firm knows it," one colleague said, before adding that the firm was not particularly forthcoming about the incident. "They are just trying to hide stuff and lay blame elsewhere." Lazard also was said to demand that one Web site, Vault.com, that offered an online outlet for employees' thoughts shut down the Lazard forum.

Tensions were mounting inside the firm. "First, you had this level of expectations raised about, you know, we're partners, we're going to get something permanent in the firm," one partner explained. "Then you had a shift in the business occurring. The business environment turned very negative in 2001. Very negative. We went into the year with a projection that we were going to do $900 million in revenue. Michel said at the end of 2000 that his goal for Lazard for 2001—and he really believed it—was $900 million in revenue, up from seven-something in 2000. The backlog was disappearing by the minute going into 2001. Nothing was building. Everything was just closing stuff. It was pretty obvious by February or March to anybody that had been in the business for a while that we were going to be lucky to do $600 or $700 million in revenue that particular year." Michel seemed no more in touch with the reality of the situation as winter turned into spring. "By March," a partner recalled, "he was saying, 'Well, I've been in this business so long and we're going to have the exact same year as the year before.' And by March and April it was obvious that we were going to be lucky to have revenues of $550 million. At the end of the year, revenues were $435 million, by the way."

AGAINST THIS BACKDROP, there was an increasingly loud chorus inside Lazard calling for Michel to think seriously about selling the firm. For Michel, of course, just the thought of a public Lazard was anathema. This led him to deliver a lengthy speech against any scheme to sell shares on the market and for having the courage to try to rebuild the franchise. He also opposed the suggestion, dubbed Project S, that Lazard merge with Eurazeo as another way to go public. "The day we go public one way or another," he told the executive committee, "that is when trouble starts. Look at the way Warburg"—a reference to Jon Wood—"is blackmailing us. I don't anymore believe in the control of public companies."

At the March 15 executive committee meeting in Paris, the firm's leaders turned once again to the central question of "Who owns Lazard and for whom does its wealth operate?" Michel, Verey, and others took the rather restrictive view that whatever equity plan is pursued, it must maintain the status quo. This was no theoretical discussion, though. What quickly became apparent was that, once again, Loomis had been having one-off discussions about distributing equity. This time, it turned out, he had been negotiating with the leaders of Lazard Asset Management to give equity to its "key players" to prevent them from leaving. Eig and Gullquist told the committee they felt "shabbily dealt with" by Loomis, who was subjecting them to a "divide and rule programme."

Once again the stage was set for confrontation. "If Loomis goes ahead with a LAM equity offer," Evans wrote, "I suspect Verey will resign. If the Executive Committee prevents Loomis from going ahead, presumably he will resign (although I do not know him well enough to be sure of this). In any event, the withdrawal from LAM of what looks to be a pretty clear offer of equity will no doubt cause several or all of them to resign. So, the game is afoot." The discussion of the LAM equity plan was postponed to the April 24 meeting in London.

At that meeting, Loomis outlined a highly complex idea for providing an equity incentive plan to LAM that involved reducing the huge contractual payments to Eig and Gullquist and sheltering income on a tax-free basis using earnings from the firm's hedge funds. Loomis said he thought the incentive plan should be more fully developed in time for the June meeting. He also told his colleagues that the firm was negotiating to keep Eig and Gullquist since, Michel said, LAM would not be able to "cope with the 'rumours' of Eig and Gullquist leaving unhappily." Michel said that the LAM co-heads wanted to stay and run the business while preparing for an orderly succession.

Verey found himself disagreeing with Michel during much of the day. And Evans and Verey agreed "it had been a rotten day and that it was hard to feel involved." Before he left to go back home, Michel visited with Evans and Verey in London, in part, Evans believed, because he wanted to leave Verey "on a friendly basis after a day where they had repeatedly disagreed." The next morning Verey told Evans he had decided to resign. He had been approached by both Rothschild and Cazenove and felt that only by resigning could he "honorably consider alternatives."

Verey flew to New York on May 9—one day before the next executive committee meeting—to tell Michel and Loomis he was resigning. There was some speculation that Michel might resign as chairman and turn that position over to Verey, but that did not happen. Verey's resignation, on May 10, was yet another serious blow to the firm. Verey, then fifty and the longtime head of Lazard in London, had been with the firm for twenty-eight years. Despite his very public support for the three-house merger and for Loomis as its CEO, he no doubt felt diminished by the Loomis appointment, as it certainly was one he had hoped to get. A very proper British banker who had forgone deal execution for administration and had returned Lazard in London to respectability during his ten years at the helm, Verey had been described as "Dickensian" for his exacting behavior, which prompted one of his partners to refer to him as a "cheese parer." Michel said Verey left the firm because Michel didn't name him CEO. "The difficulty I had with David is that he wanted to run Lazard as a whole," Michel said. "And I didn't think he would fly in New York at all. And it's not my fault, it's a fact." Michel added that Verey is "a very nice man. I like him." It is an open question as to whether, in accepting the resignation, Michel recalled the day in 1996 when Verey was offered—and turned down—the job of chief executive officer of Pearson, preferring instead to stay at Lazard. "My first loyalty is to Michel David-Weill," Verey told Lord Blakenham at Pearson in turning down this attractive offer. Michel recalled years later that at the time, he was "very touched by that" display of loyalty.

No matter, life moves on, and Michel replaced Verey with Marcus Agius, who joined Lazard on the same day as Verey in 1972. Agius quickly made Michel look smart by advising the Halifax Group on its £28 billion merger with the Bank of Scotland, one of the largest European deals of the past five years. The day after Verey resigned, Bruno Roger sent a letter of support to Evans. "Your essential qualities—professional and human—are essential during these delicate moments," Roger wrote in his broken English. "I wish you to reassure my full and friendly support and the full and friendly support from all the team in Paris." Evans, touched and appreciative, wrote back, "It seems to me that the point of Lazard is the extraordinary team (almost extended family) spirit that exists among us. Your kind letter is confirmation of this." No mention of Verey's resignation appeared in the minutes of the May meeting.

Nor was there any mention of the other momentous decision made at that meeting: to *seriously* explore the sale of Lazard. But a problem loomed in that, per the terms of the three-house merger in 2000, the partners in London would not be entitled to any goodwill if the firm were sold. Only the New York and Paris partners, plus the capitalists, would be so entitled. No serious discussion of selling the firm could take place until the discrepancy with the London partners was resolved. There also needed to be a backup plan—in this case, a thorough, fully vetted internal restructuring—in the event that the sale process did not succeed.

Two weeks after Verey abruptly resigned, Loomis appeared before the Lazard supervisory board, where he made a somewhat opaque assessment of the increasingly acute problems: the firm's backlog was evaporating; Michel's unrealistic revenue goals were being missed, and badly; the firm's first layoffs had started; Verey had left, and there were rumblings that Braggiotti and Georges Ralli in Paris were not far behind; the co-heads of the asset management business were agitating for the unit's independence; the hiring outlook was bleak, Lazard could no longer pay people top dollar; and Loomis's initial two efforts to distribute equity to the top partners—first to the top twenty-three and then to LAM—were an embarrassment.

Furthermore, a consensus seemed to be building that Loomis may not have been up to the task of running the firm, which of course was not going to be easy for anyone with Michel still around. There were reports that he would get visibly angry when things did not go his way or when Michel did not support his initiatives. His temper was quick. He had taken to writing e-mails to other partners about how frustrated and angry he had become in the job, chiefly because of Michel. Some partners noticed that he would shake visibly in their presence. Had he started drinking more heavily? they wondered. "He lost control of the situation completely," one senior Lazard partner said. "He was nice to Michel, but for the rest he completely lost control. He never did anything. Anything. You should look at his speeches. He said all the right things, all the right words. He gets it all right, but then nothing happens. I don't know what he has in his mind. I mean he certainly has a problem, a psychiatric problem or something."

Loomis's May 25 speech to the supervisory board was yet another example of insight without execution. "We need to have more vibrant incentives to keep and attract outstanding partners here," he said. "There is nothing wrong with Lazard's business model, but the economic model needs rejuvenation. There is a need for us to better fit our business model by greater strength in retention and recruitment. Enhanced and longer-term incentives are necessary. We will accomplish this during the current year, or owe you an explanation of why not. We cannot have a convincing thesis if a working partner of excellence is remunerated less here than peers who work at boring banks."

He continued, building an impressive oratorical case for distributing *real* equity to the current and future partners or, if that was an unacceptable option, implementing a hugely divisive restructuring that would mean firing most partners and retrenching back to a very small core group of senior partners in New York—Loomis's target was said to be ten, a number he disputes—with a pared-down support staff to help them.

But, he noted, the radical restructuring concept wouldn't work, because the people the firm most wanted to keep were unlikely to stick around.

Loomis came to the conclusion at the end of June that the firm's only viable choice was to sell. Then he sought to round up support for his decision. Nothing was coming easily for him anymore. "A house divided against itself cannot stand," Loomis wrote Evans, quoting from the famous Lincoln speech from June 1858. Evans responded: "Yes, indeed, but you will recall that he had some pretty big 'restructuring' to undertake a year or two after he made that remark"—a not so subtle reference to his preference to pursue the "restructuring" rather than the sale. "It was only after that managerial tidy-up that the house became undivided and entered its golden era. Let us speak." Loomis either missed Evans's meaning or chose to ignore it. "Actually, Lincoln then had the bloodiest war in American history, a civil war," he responded. One London partner passed this exchange on to his senior colleagues with the thought: "Irony is always lost on Americans. I suggest this series of communications is deeply confidential."

After the July 4 holiday, Loomis continued to thrash over how the restructuring might work—at Michel's request—while having concluded himself that the firm should be sold. He spent two days working up an "economic analysis" of the restructuring. He then got a call from Michel, adding to his already immense anxiety. Michel had three messages for him: first, that Georges Ralli had spent five hours with Michel, at his house in Long Island, complaining relentlessly and specifically about Loomis's "failure" as CEO; second, that the "restructuring" should focus first on New York rather than on the firm as a whole ("which is impractical even in the simplest political terms," Loomis wrote later); and third, that since Braggiotti would not come to see Michel—implying he was well off the reservation—Michel would fly to see Braggiotti in London.

After hanging up, Loomis was fit to be tied. "With that, I went to bed seriously questioning why I had spent any effort for such a still dysfunctional place with so little concept of the otherwise universally accepted linkage between responsibility and authority," he wrote to Evans. Still, he soldiered on. "I got up this morning anyway and decided to change the paper back to about where I had it before, or five pages (instead of twenty-five of texts and charts). I am hurt, frustrated and furious. But I don't give up which is why I am still at Lazard. I can only promise you a lively meeting on Thursday. And courage." This gut-wrenching communication prompted Evans's genuine sympathy. As Loomis's leadership had now been openly called into question, Evans told him, for what it was worth, that the partners in London backed him as the CEO but that "if others wish to put themselves forward let them do so on Thursday and their claims will be considered. At the end of Thursday, however, we must have decided who is boss, that we back him, that we have an action plan, and that those who do not want to stay must go *whoever* they are." Evans pledged to Loomis to do whatever was necessary until these matters were resolved, even if it took all weekend. "We are close to being the team that put Lazard's future behind it and I do not wish to be part of that disgraceful brotherhood." With that, Evans was off to Tuscany for the weekend and urged Loomis to "have a wonderful weekend" and think of the meeting the following Thursday "as one of the best School Plays you are ever likely to be allowed to act in."

Evans kicked off the crucial July 12 executive committee session in London by reminding his partners of those—perhaps forgotten—moments in Lazard's history when the three houses stood together in times of crisis: in the early 1930s, when Paris and the Bank of England helped keep London afloat, and after the Nazis were defeated, when New York and London helped to resurrect Paris. Today, he told them, New York is in a difficult spot, with the loss of many productive partners and a high cost structure. "Perhaps it was an illusion that we could avoid a dangerous and difficult restructuring," he told them. "The danger facing us is that simply we disintegrate by people using their feet, taking the door and disappearing from sight."

Loomis then took the floor. He observed that there had been much discussion about him "both publicly and privately" but that he had been in charge only since November 2000 and had been asked by Michel "not to get too out in front too quickly." He became very emotional and started crying. He said that regardless of whether they decided to restructure or to sell, "we have to work together. If we are evidently in conflict, this will certainly complicate any sale. It is fundamental, too, in a restructuring." To that end, Loomis set a target of being able to tell the firm's partners "in early September" what "we are up to." He established two teams: Evans, Golub, Eig, Jacobs, and Ralli would focus on the restructuring (dubbed, appropriately, Project Darwin), and Michel and Loomis "alone" would focus on the sale of the firm.

The restructuring team went off to refine Project Darwin. But within a week, Loomis was already evidencing his frustration. He canceled one meeting, scheduled for July 19, and all but demanded that Evans come to New York in person in order to make real progress. As instructed, Evans flew to New York and continued to refine the Darwin analysis in preparation for a videoconference on July 24. On the prior Friday afternoon, July 20, while still in New York, he updated his senior colleagues in London about a series of disturbing phone calls Michel had made to Loomis and to him in New York.

Under the admonition "EAT BEFORE READING," Evans said that Michel had called on Thursday from Sous-le-Vent to report the following: that all the young partners in Paris "will go" and that "we" must give them cash bonuses, with the money perhaps coming from a shocking place—"capital retentions," the 10 percent annual holdback from partner pay given to retiring partners when they leave. Michel called again the next day, Friday, to report that Braggiotti had asked Ralli to go with him to Sous-le-Vent to see Michel to demand that the firm be sold. Ralli declined. Then, Evans reported, Loomis screeched when Michel told him he was disturbed by the firm's ongoing effort to integrate all the various management information systems under a new PeopleSoft platform. He then reported that Bruno Roger told him that the Paris office was between "secession and rebellion" and that he was "disturbed" ("evidently a catching phrase") that there is no one from Paris in New York helping on Project Darwin. Finally, Evans reported that he had been asked to join Loomis and Eig to try to "settle" the "LAM, Eig, Gullquist affair." He continued: "This will be colourful, if 'disturbing.' "

Michel set August 2 in Paris as the new day and place for the firm to figure out what to do. Meanwhile, the executives working on the restructuring had determined that to make the economics attractive, a partner with a 1 percent profit participation had to be paid $4 million. In other words, the firm needed to make $400 million pretax and prepartnership distributions for the calculus to work. As the firm was on track to make only about $140 million pretax in 2001, not only would forty partners need to be fired (freeing up fifteen partnership points to distribute to others), but also another $75 million to $100 million of either cost savings or revenue increases were required to make the math work. Evans wrote, "$70 million is unlikely to be achievable. Thus we will need to believe that a re-structured Lazard works well enough to deliver increased revenue."

Also that Saturday, Evans reported to his colleagues back in London, he and Loomis had received yet another call from Michel, who had Bruno Roger on the line with him. After delivering a fifteen-minute "lecture on Paris' feeling of isolation," Michel resurrected the idea of paying certain European managing directors fixed cash bonuses. Specifically, it seemed, the Lazard partner Jean-Jacques Guiony wanted a cash guarantee, and other Lazard Paris partners felt similarly. Years later, Roger said he believed that Michel's failure, by July 2001, to make good on his early 2001 promise of distributing goodwill to the partners had fomented nothing short of an insurrection in Paris. "When you say to partners, before the end of May, I give a gift to you, and then in September nothing arrives, in December nothing arrives, you create a revolt," Roger explained. "Because Michel is the king, and he has the power. And each person wished to have the goodwill. But Michel doesn't decide. Instead, he created a fantastic revolt. . . . It was not an individual revolt; it was a collective revolt. It's not necessary to read Machiavelli to know that we would have an automatic revolt. This is a case. A Harvard Business School case."

On the call with Loomis, Michel complained again that he was not involved in the PeopleSoft selection decision. This struck Evans as the height of absurdity. "To imagine Michel becoming involved is like contemplating Brigitte Bardot running NATO," he wrote his colleagues before signing off in his usual reference to Lazard as a theater of the absurd. "This amazing scene cannot possibly be repeated and I would not miss it for anything," he concluded.

Loomis was not even slightly joking when he wrote Michel the equivalent of a "Come to Jesus" letter on Monday morning, July 23. The purpose was to set the stage for the August 2 meeting and to let Michel know that Loomis had reluctantly, but unequivocally, decided the firm had to be sold. Coming as it did amid such protracted and unmitigated turmoil, the seven-paragraph missive from a beleaguered CEO to his chairman is nothing less than a cry of utter despair. "We need to be honest in our assessment of Lazard today, just as we need to keep our wits about us," he wrote. He described a perfect storm—"an accumulation of longstanding differences mixed with a recent merger in a very bad market environment"—coinciding with the near end of Michel's imperial reign. "We are under attack, internally and externally, on an exposed plain," he eloquently wrote. "We are without the protection of where we came from, or the sanctuary of our intended destination." He continued, "The restructuring numbers are not large enough to compensate for the lack of faith in our fragile constitution as one firm. There is no 'quick fix' for the reality of the 2001 results. The facts, however unattractive, remain stubborn things. We will continue to work diligently on the restructuring while preparing for a sale process. We will be in a position to start discussions with others immediately after the Paris meeting."

In a mere six hundred words, while excoriating his partners, Loomis had vitiated the restructuring and the efficacy of trying to placate the asset management team in one fell swoop. He had decided to sell the firm, ratifying the collective judgment first reached on May 10. "And that was the *only* future," one partner said of Loomis's thinking about this decision. "Who was going to follow him after that?" Another partner, who began to look for a new job at around this time, said: "I would say that I started to seriously question whether or not the firm could make it at that point in time because I felt that there was a recognition that we were not gathering enough revenue, that the asset management guys were angling for their own deal, that we didn't have a leader who could speak for the whole firm, and then frankly the economic substance of what kept you there was quickly coming to a close."

Michel's response to Loomis's extraordinary letter would take several months to play out fully. In the meantime, though, his initial reaction was filtering down through the partnership ranks. The French now appeared to believe it was "ridiculous to float or sell now" given the deteriorating performance of financial services companies in the market. "A sale is therefore very poorly timed," one French partner explained. "Therefore the restructuring becomes a necessity." There was also some discussion of having Michel come back as CEO, replacing Loomis—London's idea of the so-called MDW reinstitution—but this French partner rejected this as unlikely to be effective. "We might prefer restructuring but we do not have the people or the energy," he continued. But he predicted—absolutely correctly as it turned out—that Michel would manipulate the sale process because he did not want to sell the firm. "So nothing will happen," he said, adding that Michel wanted to give the firm "three months to find a rainmaker" to replace Loomis.

But there was also another indication of Michel's negative reaction to Loomis's letter: the fact they were now disagreeing aggressively about the firm's future direction. Michel had suggested that a number of partners be fired before the firm considered a sale and then, as part of a severance agreement with them, agree to pay them should a sale happen. One of the partners Michel wanted to fire was Tom Haack, whose father was the former head of the New York Stock Exchange. Haack had been a banking partner for about twenty-five years by that time, and a nicer person could not be found. Although not among the highly paid senior partners, he was well paid and worth every penny of it based on the fees he generated year after year. Still, Michel wanted to fire him. "You suggest that we 'fire' Tom in September but pay him in a sale within two years," Loomis wrote. "We then explore a sale. Thus, we create turmoil at no gain for anybody. Any prospective buyer would be aghast at the result of firings in New York, including your personal disloyalty to the ones loyal for so many years to you. It would be a complete mess and a forced sale because everyone would hate the management of the place. And then, we would pay Tom anyway by your terms, or because we would in arbitration. (We would also have to find someone to fire him; it will not be me in this scenario.)" Loomis signed off, "I will see you tomorrow. I am sadly pessimistic about the conversation and, more so, about the next day. With regret, Bill."

THE AUGUST 2 meeting was, according to Evans, an "angry, quarrelsome" one. Michel accepted Loomis's recommendation that Lazard explore the possibility of selling the firm. "The guy was the manager, he's the CEO, if he wanted to look at something, I might have said no after having decided I thought it was wrong, but I'm not going to limit his imagination," Michel said. "I've kept negative powers so I can say no to an idea—but I don't think it belongs to somebody who is really in the position of being a chairman, and then a relatively active chairman, to bar the management from looking at solutions."

The proposed sale was an extraordinary admission, by the firm's own executives, that either the firm could no longer be managed by the current leadership or its future and all its past—both its extraordinary accomplishments and its mythology—were better off in the hands of some other organization. "I think he was losing confidence in his ability to run the firm," Michel said of Loomis, "or for the firm to be run, other than him doing it. And I'm not sure it was personal; he just felt that we won't be able to manage." He added: "There's no doubt that the firm was in a state of disarray. Very frankly, it reminded me of when I arrived. It was full circle, exactly full circle. When I arrived in 1977, the firm was in total disarray. And 2001 was a little of the same atmosphere again, where basically, having given up authority, managerial authority, it was very difficult to take back managerial authority when Loomis didn't do the trick. So the place was in a feeling of flux."

Of course, some of the same factors that made 2001 an *annus horribilis* for Lazard made it an equally difficult time for other firms to seriously consider its acquisition, especially at a price—said to be around $4 billion to $5 billion—that would motivate Michel to sell. The big, global firms either saw no need for or had no interest in Lazard—Goldman Sachs, Morgan Stanley, and Merrill Lynch (although Merrill called Michel and expressed interest in taking a look at Lazard)—or were still digesting the major deals they had recently completed, Citigroup, JPMorgan Chase, and Credit Suisse First Boston. There were some potential candidates, though. Deutsche Bank had dabbled with the idea of helping the firm solve the Bolloré conundrum and needed to jump-start its global M&A business. Crédit Agricole was also an obvious choice since it already indirectly owned about a 10 percent stake in Lazard and had publicly announced in July that it wanted to buy another 20 percent. UBS, too, owned 15 percent of Eurazeo but was still working on the integration of Paine Webber.

For any number of reasons, though, the most obvious potential buyer was Lehman Brothers, which had been utterly reengineered during the past decade by its brilliant CEO, Dick Fuld. In August 2001, Lehman's market value was around $18 billion, thanks largely to its powerhouse fixed-income division, and was eager to consider deals. The firm was then not quite as strong in investment banking, and especially in M&A, as it would later become. So Lazard would have been an excellent complement, especially in Europe, where Lehman had not yet started building aggressively. Lehman also coveted Lazard's asset management business.

At the contentious August 2 executive committee meeting, two approaches were authorized: to ascertain whether either Crédit Agricole or Lehman had any interest in buying Lazard, Michel would contact Crédit Agricole and Loomis would approach Lehman. Michel, of course, had masterminded the Crédit Agricole purchase of the Bolloré stake. He was highly confident Crédit Agricole would be interested. Loomis, of course, had worked at Lehman before Lazard. And the two firms had a rich history together dating back to the days when André used to intimidate Bobbie Lehman. Crédit Agricole, while not as tony as Lehman, would be willing to give Lazard nearly complete autonomy and would be one of those *French* solutions that appealed greatly to Michel and his French partners. Michel had never been excited about selling Lazard to an American firm for fear the Americans would gut the firm's very Frenchness.

MICHEL AND LOOMIS were to take the month of August, make their inquiries, and report back at the August 29 executive committee meeting. Loomis called Fuld after August 2, without saying what he wanted to speak about; Fuld told him he would be away most of the month and they should meet in early September. Michel's Crédit Agricole report, therefore, would be the only update provided at the end of August. As a fallback position, in case the sale process did not work, Michel insisted that Loomis and Evans also pursue the separate "restructuring" exercise.

Michel had one other, supersecret strategy up his sleeve: unbeknownst to anyone except for Loomis, and perhaps Jean-Claude Haas, in August 2001, as part of his effort to see if a rainmaker could be found outside the firm, he had quietly rekindled his discussion with Bruce Wasserstein about becoming Lazard's CEO. By an odd and unexpected confluence of events, Wasserstein was once again free to discuss this possibility because in April 2001, three months after he had sold Wasserstein Perella to Dresdner Bank, Allianz, the large German insurer, bought the 80 percent of Dresdner it didn't already own for $20 billion in cash. Wasserstein was in the middle of a dispute with his new boss at Allianz, and was thinking of leaving his eponymous firm.

On August 29, Michel gave the executive committee an update on his discussions with Jean Laurent, then CEO of Crédit Agricole, about buying Lazard. Michel led off the discussion with the deliciously juxtaposed thought that while it was "unproductive and highly dangerous to open the firm to a sale process," there were "two possible, very interested parties": Crédit Agricole and Lehman (there was also mention of Merrill Lynch, so maybe there were three interested parties). As for Crédit Agricole, Michel reported, "we speak with them all the time and we know their minds." He said that he had two meetings with Laurent in Biarritz during August and that while "they are dying to do something with us," because Crédit Agricole had commenced the process of going public (completed in December 2001), the bank preferred taking a minority stake in Lazard that could be increased over time. The Lazard executives would be left in place to manage the firm. "Personally," Michel told his partners, "I am not against it." But as usual, he had concerns. "The only problem is that Crédit Agricole says, 'We do not want to manage.' Therefore, *we* have to manage." And Michel was not sure the leaders of the firm could manage it anymore. In sum, he said he had his doubts that Crédit Agricole would step up, especially given the asking price of around $5 billion.

Ralli offered his thought that Merrill and Lehman "were all the same" and that he would leave if these firms bought Lazard. To which Ken Jacobs replied, "You would be bribed to stay and work your butt off." The bribe would work, Jacobs argued, because "We are all the same, flesh and blood." To which Ralli responded, "I would not work hard."

At the beginning of September 2001, Loomis had lunch with Fuld at the Lehman Brothers dining room at the World Financial Center and brought up the idea of a merger. Fuld said that when Loomis had called him in August, he had figured that this was what he wanted to speak about. Fuld was interested enough in the idea to schedule a second meeting, with a wider group, for September 10. Obviously, Michel knew that Loomis had approached Fuld and even had a value in mind for Lazard at which he would consider selling.

"There was my knowledge but not my approval," Michel said three years later. "There is a difference. I told him, 'If you want to explore, explore.' " Debate rages about how serious the discussions became: some say Fuld offered Lazard one-third of Lehman's equity, then valued at around $6 billion; others say this is preposterous and Fuld would never have offered anywhere near that amount for Lazard. Some of his own partners didn't think Loomis knew how to sell the firm effectively and so tend to think the talks were never that serious. "I mean, even though they went to talk to Lehman to sell the firm, they didn't know what they were selling," one partner said. "They had no idea. I mean, so it was again talking about things but no one could actually take actions. Just out of control, totally out of control." This person thought Loomis should have given Felix—then still staked out on the fiftieth floor—the mandate to sell the firm. "Felix would've done it," he said.

Others, closer to Fuld, downplayed the level of Lehman's interest in a deal. "It's unclear how far the Lehman discussions got," explained Fuld's friend and former Lazard partner Ken Wilson, from his executive floor office at Goldman Sachs. "Some people would say quite far. Dick Fuld will not tell you that. Loomis really thought this thing had traction at one time. He was pushing hard. But I don't think Dick Fuld's recollection would be consistent with that." Michel recalled that Fuld called him at Sous-le-Vent in late August or early September to discuss the possibility of a combination. Michel remembered telling him that he would see him "with pleasure" but that perhaps it would be best if they waited "until the end of the year" for that get-together. Still, after that first lunch with Fuld at the World Financial Center, there was sufficient optimism in the air at Lazard about a deal with Lehman that, on September 4 anyway, detailed financial models were run divvying up the goodwill, according to section 7.03 of the operating agreement, among various groups of partners—New York, Paris, London, and the rest of the world. There was even a proposed name, Lazard Lehman, for the new firm.

Loomis pushed forward with Fuld, independent of Michel. The discussions between the two firms reached their apex on September 10, 2001, when Loomis and Golub met with Fuld and Brad Jack, then the head of investment banking at Lehman, and outlined the potential synergies of the combination. The Lazard team made a presentation about how it all might work, but no specific valuation was conveyed or discussed. They agreed to keep talking. Figuring he might soon be out of a job, Loomis that day—presciently—executed a two-paragraph agreement with Michel that called for him to receive, for one more year, a fixed percentage of the firm's profits plus some real equity in the event he was dismissed.

ALTHOUGH THE TWO firms planned to continue the discussions, the events of the next day derailed them, and then Loomis's banking career.

On September 11, Michel was in his palatial sixty-second-floor office on that pristine morning as the panorama of horrors unfolded outside his windows, three miles away. Many of his partners had a clear and unobstructed view south and saw everything, but Michel didn't see the two jets hit the Twin Towers. He couldn't miss the fireballs shooting out of them, though, and watched, alone and aghast, as the two 110-story buildings caught fire and collapsed. "Because I am an eternal optimist, my first thought was, what a crazy accident," he recalled. "The weather was absolutely beautiful. How could this happen?" Like the rest of us, he began slowly to comprehend the magnitude of the unfolding events. Unlike many others, though, he calmly completed his early morning business—presiding over a board meeting of the American Hospital of Paris. Finally, after nearly everybody else in the firm had left the building, Michel's longtime assistant, Annik Percival, insisted Michel leave, too. He eventually rode the elevator down to Rockefeller Plaza. With him were Loomis and Vernon Jordan. Walking together uptown, Michel borrowed Vernon's cell phone—since he himself did not have one—to see if he could reach his wife, Hélène. Unable to reach her since the attacks had interrupted cell phone service, he went to his apartment at 820 Fifth Avenue to await her return. Loomis went back to Greenwich.

Vernon continued on to his suite at the Regency. He had watched "horrified" with his secretary from his window at 30 Rockefeller Center as the second plane hit the South Tower. "I spent the rest of the day the same way many of you did—watching the disasters for hours on end," he said almost two weeks later in an incredibly moving sermon he gave to the First Congregational Church in Atlanta.

> Like you, I have seen interviews with the survivors, the lucky ones who escaped the burning towers in time. I have walked the streets where, on every corner, are sad homemade posters with names and pictures of the missing, pleading for information about them. Those survivors and the victims on the posters are Whites and Blacks, Asians, Latinos and Arabs. They are Christians, Jews, and Muslims. They are executives and janitors, bureaucrats and messengers. They are rich and they are poor. They are young, old and middle-aged. They are Republicans and Democrats. Politically, some are on the far right; some are on the far left, and some may even have sympathized with some of the terrorists' ideas. But they are all Americans. And in the eyes of the terrorists, they all stand for values that are central to the American fabric. And that was enough to make them targets, just as you and I and all our loved ones are targets now.

While the country struggled to grapple with the import of the single most devastating attack on American soil, Michel remained largely unfazed by it. He made a symbolic point of coming back to the office first thing the next morning to resume his routine. "The curious thing with me is because of the war in my childhood, catastrophe is normal," he explained. "Peace is relatively strange. But catastrophe! Ah, I think, back to normal!" In truth, Michel had little time to focus on the devastation downtown, for all around him at Lazard, his Cartesian order—so carefully constructed during the past twenty-five years of his absolute reign—was becoming completely unglued.

Following the attacks, Michel and Loomis held a telephone meeting of the executive committee, on September 13. The collapse of the World Trade Center had caused a tremendous amount of collateral damage to Lehman's headquarters in the World Financial Center, directly across West Street from the disaster. Lehman also had 618 employees working in the Twin Towers. All but one were safe. The Lehman headquarters building had to be evacuated and was no longer usable as an office. Lehman's employees were scattered around the city, many working from hotel rooms. Michel began to drop hints that any deal with Lehman, even if it was still interested, would be less desirable from his point of view for the very obvious reason that Lazard management would be utterly redundant. Michel wondered whether people in London, Paris, or Milan wished to work for a firm like Lehman. He wondered whether it made a difference if the name of the resulting firm was adjusted somehow. And what about value? Michel was greatly concerned that the price Lehman would have to pay for Lazard would so dilute Lehman's earnings that the stock would fall and the value of the Lehman stock Lazard would receive would fall, too.

"I was not totally against a deal with Lehman," he said. "You know I am very traditional, and Lehman was the second place I ever worked at. It's the same kind of firm, traditionally, as Lazard. So why not? But the truth is that you simply have to look at their price, and their P/E multiple, and their book value multiple. To do any deal is impossible. It's impossible. They would have been delighted at a third of the price, or let's say half the price, but they were completely unable to do more. I mean, because they would have been killed with dilution. Killed. So it couldn't work."

Taking the hint, Loomis wrote Fuld a letter suspending the discussions. Loomis was worried that, among other things, after the events of September 11, the relative valuations between the firms would have shifted unfavorably. Michel also called Fuld, whom he had never met in person. "Look," Michel said he told Fuld, "you know I never participated in the meetings you had with Loomis." Michel turned off the discussions. Not that Fuld had reason to care anymore, either. Lehman was in its own fight for survival.

Lazard had its share of problems, too, after September 11. Even though no Lazard employees were killed in the attack, many were traumatized by the horror they had witnessed downtown, thanks to the front-row seat their high perch in Rockefeller Center afforded them. For a time, half the firm didn't even bother showing up, because they "weren't even sure the sun was going to come up," one partner explained.

While not in any physical danger, five American Lazard partners were stuck in London during the days right after September 11 and were quite anxious to return to New York to see their families. But since the U.S. government grounded all commercial jets for three days, returning home would not be so easy. Using a little investment banker ingenuity—the kind with the unlimited checkbook—the bankers located a private Gulfstream jet in Switzerland that they could charter to take them home, at a cost of $75,000. One of the partners called up Ken Jacobs, his boss in New York, to arrange for Lazard to pay the bill. "There are five of us stuck here," he told Jacobs. "We're not sitting here anymore. I don't know when we'll be able to get on a commercial airline, but I can tell you, I found a plane, and we can get out of here, starting on Friday, I think we can leave on Friday. I'm gonna charter the plane." Jacobs hesitated. Given the expense pressure on the firm at that moment, a $75,000 bill for a seven-hour flight gave him pause. "He said, 'Well, I don't know,' " this partner continued. "I said, 'Ken, fuck you. I'm going to charter the plane, and you guys are going to pay the bill.' " Jacobs told him, though, there may be another way. "I said, 'What are you talking about?' and he says, 'Well, Michel's got a plane.' So then it starts unfolding."

After the July 2000 crash of the Concorde outside of Paris, where 113 people died—resulting in the suspension of Concorde travel and an unfounded rumor that Felix, then the ambassador, was on that flight—Michel had arranged to lease a Gulfstream jet, a G4. Michel, of course, needed to easily get back and forth from New York, Paris, and London, and with the Concorde no longer reliably available, he joined the ranks of the other billionaires with their own private jets. After September 11, in the same way that Osama bin Laden's family members were allowed to return on a private jet to Saudi Arabia from the United States, Michel's wife was permitted to fly on September 13 to Paris from New York on Michel's jet. Michel's plane would then be permitted to return to its home base in New York.

This partner continued: "I said, 'Well, Ken, that's a no-brainer. You just send his plane to London to pick us up. It's coming back anyway.' " He wouldn't do it.

> That really pissed me off. When Ken called, and he said, "Well, it's not going to work. Michel's not going to do it," I said, "Fuck all of you. We're chartering this plane." The long and short of it is that I had become friends with Annik, Michel's secretary, who is an institution. She thought Michel was behaving very badly. She knew this was all going on. She browbeat him into doing it.
>
> Ken called. He said, "Michel is going to let you guys come back on his plane. But you can't tell anyone," because Michel doesn't want anyone to know he's got this plane. But everyone knows he's got this stupid plane. Ken said, "But the plane's picking up someone in London." We go into the London Luton Airport, and sitting in the lounge is this guy I went to college with. His name is Tim Barakett. He runs a hedge fund here. One of the big investors in the hedge fund is the Rothschilds, who are of course good friends of Michel. So I said, "Tim, what are you doing here?" He says, "I'm taking this plane back." And I said, "Oh, we're taking the plane back, too. Where are you going?" He said, "Well, I'm just waiting for this group that this plane belongs to." It's Michel's plane. This fucker spent a day negotiating with us—his partners—about riding his plane back. It's coming back anyway. Not only was it going to Paris, it was going to London to pick up a guy who worked for a hedge fund where the big investors were the Rothschilds.

They all came back together on Michel's plane, and the Lazard partners were so angry at him, on the one hand, and so pleased to be returning home in luxury, on the other, that they helped themselves to Michel's stash of rare wines.

As life in New York slowly returned to the "new normal," and Lazard along with it, Loomis now seemed to feel even more pressure—even though several issues seemed resolved. For instance, after Evans sent around an e-mail to the executive committee on Friday afternoon, September 21, explaining that CALFP, the revived derivatives joint venture Édouard Stern created years before with Crédit Agricole, would lose as much as $15 million in 2001, Loomis sent a response (at 12:21 a.m. Sunday morning) to Evans, copying Michel, and laying into him. The controlled rage is palpable. "I have long been concerned and articulate about CALFP, including asking for (delayed) reviews," he wrote. "We have now late notice of a major problem there on a weekend, and you are just dumping this on the Executive Committee as a whole immediately by e-mail. Your conduct confuses me and shakes my confidence in you. I know that you are shooting some sort of birds on Monday. I would very much appreciate your finding a phone that day (and not calling me on Sunday)."

Loomis wasn't the only one whose behavior was mercurial. Michel, too, was having mood swings. Two weeks after September 11, he was in London, and London partners found him to be "joking" and "happy." When this assessment found its way to Paris, a partner there expressed his surprise. "Very interesting, very odd, very puzzling to have found *qui vous savez* full of beans etc. . . . I saw him today and found him resigned, quietly reconciled with the idea that sooner or later inescapably the end would come. Not tomorrow, but round the corner. Sure he may still enjoy a few days of artificial fun as if . . . But I feel he is somewhat like little boys playing at soldiers aware that at 5pm mummy will come to take them home, have their bath: game's up."

LOOMIS WAS NOW in a tough spot, as he was faced with having to make an argument about why Lazard should stay independent and private, after having pushed so hard for the sale. He was now adamant against this course of action—with Michel's support—because the valuations had dropped precipitously after the terrorist attacks and would no longer be appealing. But several members of the executive committee—Steve Golub, Ken Jacobs, and Dave Tashjian among them—were still pushing for a sale. Loomis, though, nixed it. He refocused the committee back on the increasingly controversial restructuring plan, which, among other things, would have meant deep cuts in New York and shuttering most of the capital markets operation. Closing capital markets would have meant firing many of the people involved, including Dave Tashjian, the head of the unit. On the evening of October 15, Loomis told Tashjian he was going to recommend closing the capital markets business the next day. Not only did he not want Tashjian to oppose him on this, but he also wanted Tashjian to resign and to think about not even showing up at the meeting. Loomis promised Tashjian a sizable retirement package if he went quietly.

Tashjian was not happy, nor was he one to go without a fight. He called Michel and told him what Loomis had said. Michel told him that as a member of the executive committee, he had every right to be at the meeting the next day. Tashjian also called Golub and Jacobs, and the three of them strategized overnight on how to counter Loomis's argument for closing capital markets. By the morning, they had their plan.

For starters, Tashjian attended the meeting. When Loomis recommended eliminating his group, he objected. Golub agreed with Tashjian and said the firm's capital markets effort, while small, was critical to the M&A effort because, among other things, it allowed the bankers intelligently to provide clients with a sense of how the market would react to their deals. He then reported that Pfizer—one of Golub's and the firm's most important clients—very much appreciated Lazard's ability to do stock buybacks for the company. Jacobs agreed and cited both Microsoft and Amazon as two more clients that appreciated the firm's capital markets work. "Fundamentally, if you shut down Capital Markets, you will have a meltdown of banking in New York," Jacobs said. Loomis and Jacobs started to argue.

At one point, Jacobs, speaking in a voice Evans described as a "menacing monotone," said, "To be perfectly frank, certain steps we take will drive away some of our best people and this is one. How will I explain this? The people who I have hired, say, to cover Pharma [the pharmaceutical industry], will go within a year." Loomis responded equally testily: "Every time we have this discussion, you go on to talk about a meltdown in Banking." The discussion of eliminating capital markets ended. Loomis had lost. At the lunch break, Tashjian approached Loomis, held out his hand, and hoped that despite the outcome, they could go on professionally with no hard feelings. While in the line to get food, off to one side, Loomis said there would be no hard feelings—and then he fired Tashjian. Nobody else on the executive committee heard what had happened. Tashjian was shocked.

When the meeting resumed in the afternoon, Loomis recommended implementing the massive restructuring plan that would have reduced New York to ten or fifteen partners. "Gratuitous violence" is how one senior partner put it. The opposition from the executive committee to this idea was equally fierce. Still, costs needed to be cut to accommodate the rapidly falling revenues. To that end, after the October 16 meeting, Lazard announced its intention to eliminate sixty, or 30 percent, of the New York office's two hundred investment bankers.

The firings were tangible evidence of how badly things at the firm—and across Wall Street—were spiraling out of control. At the time the cuts were made, the firm publicly announced that its full-year 2001 profit was to be about $150 million, a drop of about 75 percent from 2000. (In 1999, the New York office *alone* made $300 million.)

Finally, with cash running low and the prospects of year-end compensation greatly diminished, Loomis convinced Michel to distribute *real* equity to the working partners—"a watershed event" in the history of Lazard, Michel said, "and a mistake." He acceded to Loomis's request at the October 16 meeting only very reluctantly and because the internal and external pressures to do so were no longer bearable. "In a partnership," goes Michel's thinking, "the ownership of the partnership was virtual. It belonged to the partners, but who the partners were depended upon when you were speaking. It changed with the partners. Completely unfair system? Sure, but every system is unfair. Because if the firm were ever sold, the people who would get the percentage would be the people who worked there at the time it was sold." The details of how the equity would be distributed—and how much—remained to be determined. But the basic deal Loomis struck with Michel was that profit points would be turned into ownership points at a 70 percent conversion ratio. In other words, if you were a 1 percent profit partner, your ownership stake would be 0.7 percent. Since partners' cash compensation would be greatly diminished because of the firm's poor 2001 results, the distribution of real equity gave people a reason to stay around.

All of these events—the worsening financial performance, the failed talks with Lehman, September 11, the firing of bankers, the confrontation about closing capital markets, the palpable European dissatisfaction, Michel's begrudging decision to distribute real equity—took their toll on Loomis. He was no longer sleeping well, if at all. He explained: "I reached the conclusion that I was in an impossible position between the views of Michel, the views of various members of the executive committee, and my ability to reconcile people's views. . . . I felt two things. One is that I thought that I was in an impossible position to do a good job, and secondly I thought that if I continued, I would get progressively frustrated and unhappy and"—here he paused for some time—"Michel had already started to put strictures on what I could or couldn't do by way of restructuring the firm." And of course, Michel had already started talking to Bruce Wasserstein, which Loomis now knew.

Michel was a good poker player, though. He didn't let on to anyone, aside from his CEO (and perhaps Haas), that he was talking to Bruce. And Loomis wasn't telling anyone, not even his wife. So when his partner Ken Jacobs, then the head of M&A, who knew Bruce well socially—their wives, both French, were very friendly—asked Michel if he would like to speak again with Bruce, now that Bruce looked to be free from Allianz and Dresdner, Michel encouraged Jacobs to set up an appointment. "At that point I knew Bruce had left DKW," Jacobs explained, referring to Dresdner Kleinwort Wasserstein. "I asked Bruce if he thought he'd be interested in this. He clearly was. I said to Michel I thought that Bruce could be interested in this." But of course Michel already knew this information. As did Loomis. "So here I am in a situation where he's restricting what I can do to restructure," Loomis said. "The Europeans, particularly, are saying New York has to be restructured. The costs are too high. But my hands are tied in terms of making decisions, and he's holding conversations with Bruce Wasserstein."

Michel and Loomis agreed to meet at nine-thirty on Saturday morning, October 20, at Viking's Cove, Michel's mansion in Lattingtown. The afternoon before, Loomis had suggested a quotidian agenda for the discussion—including Braggiotti's compensation, what to do about new partner candidates where representations had been made previously, Lazard Asset Management, and clarifying his own role in banking. That morning Loomis drove from his house overlooking Long Island Sound in Greenwich to Lattingtown. As the crow flies, the distance between their two waterfront homes was roughly nine miles. The drive, that warm fall morning, some forty-five miles along some of the most heavily trafficked roads in the country, must have seemed like an eternity to Loomis. He had gone to see Michel to get his advice about the myriad of looming unresolved issues. He got that, and more: he got fired.

Michel eschewed Loomis's agenda and told him he was no longer being effective, had no base of support in either New York or Europe, and was unequivocally failing. "His advice was to hold on until Bruce could get there," Loomis said. "And also not to do anything to upset any of the partners—key partners, like people on the executive committee—who might then leave, and that I, essentially, had failed." Taken aback, Loomis told Michel, " 'Look, since I only took this job because of you and you don't have confidence in me, I don't have any interest in continuing the job, and it's very important in that I was and am very happy with my experience at Lazard.' I'd seen all these people who were bitter or walked away and I didn't want that." He remembered the conversation as being intense and emotional. But he did not cry.

On the ride back to Greenwich, he replayed the conversation over and over in his head. Michel had not only removed Loomis but also told him to sit on his hands, compromise with people, and wait to see if Michel could cut a deal with Bruce to replace him. There was also still a remote chance something could be done with Crédit Agricole. And oh, by the way, don't piss off anyone important in the interim, either, especially Braggiotti or Jacobs. Also, there appeared to no longer be a role of any sort for Loomis at the firm, not even as a banker. "Maybe you were once a banker, but others wouldn't regard you as one," Michel told him. Had his opportunity of a lifetime really dissipated in the span of eleven months? "This was an impossible situation," Loomis said. By the next day, he had thought even more about the conversation. And then it dawned on him: "I thought about it on Sunday, and then it's one of those things like, you know, how stupid can you be?"—and here he laughed at the memory. "You know, you've just been fired. You know, 'Oh. Now I get it.'" He decided the best thing to do would be to resign. "Otherwise, I just get tarred and kicked around after being judged a failure and having no leverage to make any decisions," he wrote. "Everyone ends up unhappy."

By the time Loomis returned to the office on Monday morning, he was confirmed in his decision to resign. His position was untenable. He knew it. His partners knew it, too. He had served at Michel's pleasure, and Michel had determined Loomis could no longer be effective. Furthermore, he was simply in the way of Michel's twelve-year unrequited infatuation with the Wall Street legend Bruce Wasserstein. He spent part of that Monday huddled, confidentially, with Scott Hoffman, the firm's youthful general counsel (Michel having pushed out Mel Heineman after Rattner's departure), drawing up the requisite resignation and severance documents. All agreed there had been a constructive dismissal, and the new compensation arrangement he had created six weeks before, on September 10, was now operative.

Whether Michel actually thought Loomis would resign at this moment is not clear. On the morning of the day he decided to resign, Loomis received an e-mail from Agius saying he had spoken to Michel, who had said that he didn't think the restructuring plan "goes far enough in NYC, that he wishes you"—Loomis—"would insist on more and that he would support you if you did!!! I asked him what Ken's reaction would be to your being more aggressive, and he said he thought 'it would hold.' I don't know what's going on, but it sure feels like there's a crossed wire somewhere. Go for it!"

That same afternoon, at the partners' meeting, Loomis made his announcement: he would be leaving the firm by year end. He also said, "I must also tell you what I'm not going to do. I'm not going to discuss my reasons for doing this, and I'm not going to gossip about it, so please don't come by my office and say, 'What's really going on here?' because I won't say anything. You'll just put me in an uncomfortable position." That night before leaving the office, he took the time to recommend to Michel that Evans be paid at least 1 percent and "probably 1.25 percent" of the firm's dwindling profits. ("You are a great partner at whatever percentage," he told Evans.)

A day after the Tuesday partners' meeting, on October 24, Lazard announced to the world that Loomis would resign as CEO, marking yet another failed effort by Michel to find—and stick with—a successor.

The firm said Loomis would become a limited partner, "work with clients and focus on other interests," and leave Lazard entirely two months later, at the end of 2001. In fact, he disappeared almost immediately after the announcement, rarely coming into the office, leaving others—particularly Ken Jacobs—to pick up the pieces of the year-end compensation process. Lazard made neither Loomis nor Michel available to the press to discuss this turn of events. Instead, Michel asked Jacobs to do that job. Jacobs told the world Loomis's decision to leave "was entirely his own." The firm also announced it was, for the time being, eliminating the CEO position, in favor of creating a chief operating officer, and named Adrian Evans, the London veteran, to that position; he was to run the firm in close conjunction with Michel and the rest of the executive committee.

The press pinned Loomis's departure on political infighting related to compensation and cost cutting and the fact that, for the first time, the European partners were generating a far greater share of the global M&A business (some 77 percent, compared with 59 percent in 2000) than their American counterparts and wanted a recalibration of the equity splits. Said a European partner, "If Michel had to offer them the olive branch in the form of Loomis's head, he would give it to them." Mostly, though, there was simply a crisis of confidence in Loomis's leadership exacerbated by the firm's financial meltdown. "He was so much in David-Weill's shadow, if Michel stopped, Loomis would bump into him," said one observer. "He was a Michel clone." Loomis had turned out to be the mirror image of Rattner. Whereas Steve had chosen to make his partners' happiness his main focus, at the expense of Michel, Bill had chosen to make Michel's happiness his main focus, at the expense of his partners. At Lazard, ironically, both strategies proved to be highly combustible recipes for disaster.

Looking back now, Michel is able to be completely rational about the decision to fire Loomis, despite his copious personal affection for him. (They still see each other socially in California, where Loomis is working on a Ph.D. in American history at the University of California, Santa Barbara, and in New York.) "People don't have a long time to be successful," Michel explained, in one of his favorite refrains, "because after six months it's usually pretty clear that it's not working." Michel said Loomis capitulated to the inevitable, which, as Loomis acknowledged, was that he was pushed off his perch.

With Evans at his side, Michel briefly attempted to once again run the firm after Loomis quit. He had not been involved in the day-to-day managing of New York since before he appointed Steve deputy CEO; in

Paris, his involvement dated to before 1992, when he appointed Édouard Stern to run the office, and he had never really been in charge in London. Predictably, Michel's return "was a catastrophe," one New York partner said. "It was a catastrophe here. It was a catastrophe in Europe. It was total chaos. There was no plan. There was no sense of where we were heading, no point about how we were getting out of the mess. No nothing." Michel acknowledged his return as Lazard's CEO was problematic. "Turning back the clock is very difficult to understand for some people. To tell them the sovereign returns is not a very good thing. . . . We had a problem. We had a problem, there's no doubt, because too many ideas had been put forward without a resolution. So we needed a watershed event of some kind."

LAZARD WAS ALSO slipping precipitously in the M&A league tables, especially in the United States. Through November 1, 2001, Lazard ranked seventeenth in advising on U.S. deals, down from tenth the previous year. Globally, the firm ranked twelfth, down from eighth the year before. Lazard has "never been able to keep anybody as CEO," explained Roy Smith, a former Goldman partner who is now a professor at New York University, because Michel "never retires." There were also reports that UBS had increased its ownership stake in the web of Lazard holding companies and that Jon Wood, the UBS proprietary trader, and his erstwhile ally, Bolloré, had met with Bruno Roger in Paris. They wanted Michel forced out. In an article titled "Men Overboard," the august *Economist* wondered what all "the high-profile departures" portended for the firm. "Are the rats leaving a sinking ship?"

At this moment, Michel decided to play his carefully constructed hand. He called an executive committee meeting for November 8 in Paris, which Golub and Jacobs joined by videoconference from New York. The agenda was full: 2001 performance, 2002 budget, proposed 2001 compensation, ongoing cost control efforts. They also spoke about how to allocate the goodwill points to the partners.

Then Michel announced that he had been having intense negotiations with Bruce Wasserstein, often at Michel's Paris home, about taking over the reins of the firm. He told his senior partners: "A change is required: Either hire Bruce Wasserstein or sell the firm." Michel explained that he had tried to hire Bruce before, in 1997, but that did not work out because Lazard would have had to buy all of Bruce's firm. "Now we just have to hire the guy," Michel said, before moving into sales mode. "He loves Lazard. He is quite international, lives in London, is proud of having gone to Oxford"—Cambridge, actually—"is close to Germany, and he understands the importance of the French to Lazard. He moves around. He will not be an absentee leader." Michel told his partners that he had had some rough negotiations with Bruce, who told him to his face "basically whatever we want, all is fine," and then through his attorneys "makes impossible demands." But now there was enough specificity around the idea—and certainty that it would happen—that he was informing the executive committee: the deal was that Bruce would be head of the firm for five years; Michel would be executive chairman and would appoint six board members; Bruce would be chairman of the executive committee and appoint five board members. Michel reported that Bruce had accepted a compensation arrangement that would vary between 4 and 7 percent, depending on the firm's profitability—if the firm made only $150 million, Bruce would be paid 4 percent (or $6 million), and if the firm made $400 million, he would be paid 7 percent (or $28 million).

Bruce also wanted 7 percent of Lazard's goodwill, or equity, immediately to give to his family trust. If, though, he were to leave the firm before one year, he would sell back two percentage points of the goodwill to the firm for nothing and keep the remaining five percentage points. "He argued that he increases [the value of] our goodwill by coming," Michel said, "and by not buying his outfit, we are getting him cheaply." Finally, Michel said that Bruce intended to buy (from Michel) a $50 million stake in Lazard, at a $3.5 billion valuation, giving him an additional 1.4 percent stake in the firm. He also said that Bruce intended to hire a bunch of new partners to help revitalize the firm.

Michel then asked his partners, "Is this better or worse than a sale? The question is not to be asked of Bruce Wasserstein. It is to be asked of us: Will we, here in this room, stay?" Michel told the executive committee, "I know I cannot do it [run the firm any longer]. I could have done it. It is a matter of how we are looking at the world. Are we winners or not?" With that, the executive committee began discussing the "most difficult clauses" of Bruce's proposal, deciding, for instance, he should only get half his goodwill now. But the committee concluded, "The deal is on." Looking back, Michel only regrets that because Bruce was his only viable option in November 2001—Crédit Agricole and Lehman having begged off for different reasons—Bruce had a disproportionately high amount of leverage in the situation. "Well, I've got to say it was my only choice," he said. Did that affect his ability to negotiate a better deal with Bruce? "Sure," he said, after a long pause. "Oh yeah. I'm pretty sure."

IT WAS A perfect storm, and a perfect vacuum, into which strolled Bruce Wasserstein. The timing of his rejuvenated negotiations with Michel could not have been more propitious for him; indeed, Bruce couldn't have scripted the events of 2001 any better had he tried.

At year's start, in rapid succession—and with no shame—the former yeshiva student from Brooklyn had sold his eponymous firm, for $1.37 billion in stock, to Germany's Dresdner Bank, which a mere half century before had financed, and owned a piece of, the construction company that built the Auschwitz concentration camp. Three months later, in April 2001, Dresdner was sold to Allianz, the huge German insurer, for $20 billion in cash. The improbable Allianz-Dresdner deal resulted in the immediate and unexpected conversion of Bruce's approximately $625 million equity stake in Dresdner into cash—years before it otherwise would have been. Suddenly, in April 2001, Bruce was faced with a not insignificant capital gain of $625 million, assuming that the basis in his Wasserstein Perella stock was at or near zero. Dresdner had expected Bruce to stay in the United States to expand the firm's investment banking presence here and to complement the efforts of Tim Shacklock, who was already well established in London.

But before anyone could figure out what he had done, or why, Bruce promptly moved to London after April 2001, and many people say he did this to change his residence to avoid paying the combined 12 percent in New York City and New York state capital gains taxes on his $625 million cash proceeds from Allianz. (There was no way for Bruce to avoid federal capital gains taxes, since U.S. citizens are taxed on their worldwide income no matter where they live.) Assuming Bruce had a very low basis in his original Wasserstein Perella stock, which is a fair assumption since the business was started from scratch, then 12 percent of $625 million is $75 million. Even if that is an inaccurate assumption because over the years Bruce had bought back stock from his partners as they left the firm—for instance, in the case of Perella's departure—and his basis in the stock was actually higher than zero, say, for the sake of argument, $100 million, his taxable gain would still be $525 million, and New York's cut of that would be $63 million, a sum the city and state would certainly have loved to have had during the fiscal year following the September 11 attacks.

Even Michel said he was struck by this maneuver on Bruce's part. Apparently, Bruce hired Harold Handler, a lawyer at Simpson Thacher, to find the specific, and quite legal, loophole in the New York state tax code that would allow him to avoid the sizable tax. "That's utter baloney," a Wasserstein spokesman told *Vanity Fair* in April 2005 when the matter first came up publicly. "If he'd wanted to evade New York State tax, he could have moved to New Jersey or Florida." But one of Bruce's former partners observed that he had the nasty habit of pushing his advantages to absolute limits—be they legal or financial—in a given situation. What he did to avoid paying New York state and New York City taxes on his windfall, in 2001, is but one example. "It's classic Bruce. When he's got the leverage, instead of taking a 51–49 win, he'll go for the 99–1 win," he said.

As part of the sale of his firm to Dresdner, Bruce also kept for himself and some of his partners Wasserstein & Co. Inc., Wasserstein Perella's $2 billion private-equity business, which he still owns and controls. But even here, he upset many of his former partners at Wasserstein Perella when, in their opinion, he more or less absconded with the buyout fund by forcing them to accept his terms or get a worthless piece of paper instead. Inevitably and almost immediately, the brash Wasserstein and the Germans clashed over strategic direction. They wanted him to spend more time in the United States building the firm's M&A business there, something he did only with great reluctance because he did not want to risk paying state and city taxes on his windfall or on his $25 million annual salary. On the rare occasions when he did come to the United States, he was said to direct his private jet to land and take off at precise moments—11:59 p.m.—to avoid spending an additional "day" in the country if possible, since being in New York more than 183 days a year would have made him a taxable resident. And the Germans were wavering on a supposed promise to him of becoming the CEO of a split-off, publicly traded investment bank, a responsibility he had long coveted. By the end of July 2001, the Germans nixed the IPO of DKW and announced the layoff of 17 percent of the workforce. Bruce was not only antsy; he was said to be "furious" with Allianz. At that point, news reports were saying he considered himself a "free agent," although, through a Lazard spokesman—being ever mindful of the legal implications—he denied having thought that at the time.

According to the *Wall Street Journal*, Bruce told Leonhard Fischer, the head of Dresdner's investment bank, that his contract had been violated and that "he should be free to leave the company." He reportedly reached out to Lazard, Morgan Stanley, and J. P. Morgan to see if any of them were interested in his services. A Lazard spokesperson said that Bruce's recollection was that after the late July announcement, Felix called him—not the other way around—on Michel's behalf to see if it made any sense to think about merging Lazard with DKW. (Felix has no recollection of this.) Word also began getting back to the firm that Felix was also pushing the idea that either Rothschild or HSBC consider a deal for Lazard. (Felix confirmed he did speak with John Bond at HSBC but he had no interest; he could not recall speaking to Rothschild.) Bruce's response was that there was nothing to talk about at the moment but there might well be a time in the near future when that kind of discussion would make sense. Bruce, the former Cravath lawyer, was being extra careful not to do anything to jeopardize his three-year contract with DKW, which gave him $25 million a year.

Michel and Bruce had danced for years, of course, but now the situation at Lazard had become so dire that Bruce started to look like a savior. True, his reputation as an M&A banker had been greatly diminished throughout the 1990s—Henry Kravis referred to him as "old news"—but he was still a well-recognized name, considered brilliant, and had run his own investment bank and sold it at a very high price. There was also no one around anymore who could stand up to Michel about whether or not Bruce was right for Lazard. Indeed, Michel would now show his partners how wrong they had been four years earlier by thwarting his efforts to hire Bruce.

The two men negotiated intensively for two months, mostly in Paris and often at Michel's Rue Saint-Guillaume mansion. The crafty Bruce used the lawyer Adam Chinn, from Wachtell, Lipton, a law firm extremely familiar with Lazard, to negotiate for him. Chinn had been involved with some of the largest financial mergers of all time and also advised Bruce on the sale of Wasserstein Perella. Chinn, who declined to be interviewed, knew many partners at Lazard—and former partners—and availed himself of their advice in the negotiations with Michel. It was as if Bruce had a spy inside Lazard continuously reminding him of Michel's hot buttons. Bruce also spoke extensively with the partners he knew at Lazard and with many ex-partners, including Steve Rattner. (At lunch one day at the Four Seasons, Bruce even asked Steve if he would return to Lazard; Steve declined but realized, for Bruce, Lazard was "unfinished business.")

Understandably, the partners' goal was to make sure Bruce got all the weapons he needed to run the place effectively, to prevent a repeat of the succession failures that had dogged the firm for years. "Before Bruce ever got into a discussion with Michel about economics or anything like that, he went out and spoke to everybody—including Steve and others who had all held this position before—and came to the conclusion that the only thing that mattered was the *'cause definition'* in his contract," explained one senior partner familiar with Bruce's negotiations with Michel, referring to what "termination for cause" meant. "And so that was the first and only thing they negotiated. And when Bruce was satisfied about that, then he did everything else. But that was it. Because without that, there's no power. One of the great ironies of everybody else who preceded him—here, in Europe, it doesn't matter where—is no one had any power. They all thought they did until they actually tried to do something that was different from what Michel ultimately wanted to have happen. And then they all lost it." For his part, Michel used a lawyer from Cravath, George Lowy, but mostly, as usual, kept his own counsel—and some said Michel had a fool for a client.

The head fakes continued, though, even as the negotiations were wrapping up. In a November 12 story, "Can Anyone Run Lazard?" *Business-Week* reported that Bruce declined Michel's offer. "Who would take this job?" the magazine quoted a "close ally" of Michel's as saying. "Bruce would demand absolute control, and I don't think Michel would give it." On November 14, Fischer had given Bruce a two-day deadline to decide whether he was going to Lazard or staying at DKW. If he were to remain, Fischer demanded he start "bringing in business" by spending more time in the States with clients and drop the request for a "guaranteed bonus." Bruce asked for a day to consider Fischer's requests. But in truth, he was awaiting the outcome of the difficult final negotiations with Michel about coming to Lazard. He wanted full executive powers and a significant ownership stake in the firm.

Michel was by now sufficiently confident about reaching an agreement with Bruce that he asked Loomis to call Dick Fuld at Lehman Brothers to tell him Bruce was about to be hired to replace him and that the suspended Lehman discussions were really off. Of course, if Lehman was interested in buying Lazard, this would be the moment to make that absolutely clear so that Michel could seriously consider that option alongside the Bruce option. But Fuld was no longer interested, and he told Loomis that Michel was making a big mistake hiring Bruce. But this was no longer Loomis's concern. The next day Bruce faxed a letter to Fischer. "Dear Lenny," he wrote, "with great regret I am resigning effective immediately." Somehow, just to make Bruce go away quietly—he had become a major irritant to them—the Germans paid him the balance of his contract, another $50 million. (Wasserstein's name has since been removed from DKW, which is now known as Dresdner Kleinwort, and the firm's New York office—the original Wasserstein, Perella—is being slowly dismantled.)

Within hours of sending the fax, Bruce appeared beside Michel in Paris to announce that Bruce, then fifty-three, had been named "head of Lazard," effective January 1, 2002, succeeding Michel, then sixty-nine, "in his executive capacities." Michel remained chairman of Lazard LLC and chairman of the Lazard board of directors. This announcement made it sound like Michel was finally giving up managerial control of the firm. "After 25 years of stewardship as head of Lazard, I am very glad to have a successor who will continue to lead Lazard as the preeminent independent bank," Michel said. "I've known Bruce for a very long time, and know that he is a fiercely independent and original adviser. These are qualities exemplified by Lazard bankers throughout the world, and what our clients have come to expect from our firm. Bruce has both my endorsement and the full support of our entire leadership team."

Bruce was equally effusive. "I am delighted to join Lazard," he said. "We've been discussing this possibility from time to time over 15 years. When I began my own firm, I aspired for it to become like Lazard. Lazard has an unmatched franchise with extraordinarily talented partners. I look forward to working with all my new colleagues." He added: "Since last August, a lot of [firms] have approached me. But the big event was that Michel decided he wanted someone to replace him as head." Reflecting on this moment some four years later, Bruce said his goal in taking over Lazard was a simple one: "To take a firm with potential to be a great firm and harness that potential and adapt it to any circumstances." He observed from afar that Lazard was a "great firm" with an "intergenerational transition" issue. "Classic small business problem," he summarized, unsympathetically.

In truth, Bruce had won more power from Michel than anyone else ever had, prima facie evidence of just how desperate Michel was for a well-known outsider with the ability to restore Lazard's luster. Confirmed one senior partner, "It was obviously a deal of desperation."

Wasserstein, "Bid-'Em-Up Bruce" to his enemies ("I could live without the name," he has said), the consummate deal tactician and the author of an 820-page tome (called *Big Deal: The Battle for Control of America's Leading Corporations*), had snookered his Lazard foe. "One of the most interesting things about this business is that you see people at their ultimate point of crisis," Bruce wrote in his 1998 book about the M&A world. When he got to Lazard, he gave every partner a copy of his book, which he had dedicated to his third wife, Claude, "my love and inspiration." (With that, he had now dedicated a book to each of this three wives.)

Bruce's big deal with Michel allowed him, for a contractual period of five years, ending in January 2007, to run the firm day to day without Michel's interference. He had absolute power to hire, fire, and set compensation. In investment banking, there are no more important motivational tools. In the end, Bruce bought from Michel, for about $30 million, a 1 percent stake in the firm, and Michel granted him another 7 percent stake, for free, by diluting the working partners—not the capitalists—bringing his total ownership to 8 percent, just below Michel's direct stake of 9 percent, and making Bruce the second-largest private shareholder in Lazard. (Michel owned other, indirect stakes as well.) The media misreported—or more likely were deceived about—the amount of Bruce's Lazard investment, claiming he had invested between $100 million and $200 million for his stake. This was a complete fiction that even Michel wondered about when he read it repeatedly in the press. "Well, I had two thoughts, not reactions, two thoughts," he said. "The first thought was that probably I did not negotiate with him enough, because it seems that it would be so normal that a guy like that *should* put in $100 million or $150 million, and remember that's huge, so maybe I should have forced him to put in $100 million or $150 million. That was my first reaction. And my second reaction or thought was I wonder if he is behind the story to make himself look more important."

Bruce also got Lazard to lease for him a Gulfstream jet, which he uses not only to fly to Lazard's twenty-nine offices worldwide but also for short jaunts to Boston or Washington. He remained chairman of Wasserstein & Co., his buyout and venture capital fund. Michel did appear to outnegotiate Bruce, though, with regard to certain governance provisions relating to the authority to take the firm public or to merge it. These rights Michel retained unilaterally. He also retained the right to renew, or not, Bruce's contract in 2007. Michel also held control of six of the eleven seats on the Lazard board of directors.

AT LAZARD IN Paris, which has remained more insular than New York or London, several of Michel's longtime partners told him the deal he had negotiated with Bruce was nothing short of *suicidal*. Michel listened to the other opinions but kept his own counsel. "I knew the accounts of the Wasserstein firm had never been very good," he said, "but I also knew the dream of his life was Lazard. Consequently, I believed that at Lazard he would care more because after all it was the dream of his life. It's not a job, I believe. It's a calling." He had tried Steve, the brash, young, energetic superstar who rightly prized independence from Michel above all; he had tried the courtier Loomis, the moralistic loyalist who seemed paralyzed with indecision from the start; and as Michel likes to say, he had sort of tried Édouard, his mercurial, erratic, temperamental—"cyclical" was Michel's word—son-in-law, who at least thought and acted like an owner. At Lazard, there is only one common denominator for all three of these men: Michel. The closest he comes to admitting his own role in their failure is to say, "It is very difficult to manage a private firm without being the owner."

How well Michel and Bruce would get along remained to be seen, of course. "Both are considered brilliant bankers who built businesses against the odds," the *Wall Street Journal* wrote. "But both are domineering personalities used to getting their own way, which could create conflict." From the start, the two men staked out their respective positions. In a joint telephone interview with the *Journal*, Bruce said he had "the same job that Michel had" and the "same executive functions." Michel jumped in and said that he was chairman of the board and retained "veto power." Bruce responded the board had veto power "only if I want to sell the company in an extraordinary transaction." Michel conceded he was finally ready to have Lazard managed by Bruce but added, "I won't become uninterested in Lazard, and I hope I can find a modest way of being some help in the coming months."

But in interviews Bruce gave to the American and British press after his appointment as head of Lazard, he left no doubt he was in charge and that the days of indecision, infighting, and drift were over. "People should worry about customers, not politics," he told the *Financial Times*. "Those days are ending at Lazard. Some people will come; some people will go, but the focus on politics—who's going to get what job—that's all over. . . . Clients, clients, clients are the top three priorities. The fourth priority is an end to politics." He said his vision for Lazard was one of husbanding intellectual capital. "My objective is to have it [be] not the biggest [firm] but certainly to aspire for the highest quality advice," he said. "The world is increasingly needing quality advice." As to whether the firm should one day be sold, he said he had not given it much thought. "I'm focused on developing the firm naturally," he said. "I'm not thinking about anything [else]." When asked by *BusinessWeek* if he would be sharing power with Michel, Bruce responded definitively but not entirely accurately, "There is no sharing. I have complete authority except that he's chairman of a board that has the right to veto a merger. Having said that, I look forward to his advice. I'm not threatened by it. And he wants to be helpful. [He knew] the only job I would be interested in is his job. He has known that for a while. It was just a decision on his part. . . . It was up to him, and that's why the offer was attractive."

The reaction within Lazard to Bruce's appointment was generally quite favorable, at least at the outset. There seemed to be a universal view that the Loomis era had been a total failure and the return of Michel had brought nothing but chaos. Anything different would have to be better—perhaps Bruce could stop the bleeding and attract new partners. Some partners hailed Wasserstein's arrival as the final chance to resurrect a moribund franchise. Wasserstein "inherited a ship with a mutinous crew," one observer said. Indeed Lazard partners had variously described the previous decade at the firm as an endless series of stabbings punctuated by the clear view that it would be unwise to send the Lazard partners "off on the same duck shoot . . . since they would probably have ended up shooting each other." Nicholas Jones, then vice chairman of the London office, said, "The benefit of someone who has come in from outside is that he has come in on his own terms." Paul Haigney, the partner in charge of the firm's small West Coast operations and a former partner of Bruce's at Wasserstein Perella, greatly appreciated that Bruce was an investment banker first and a CEO second. "It makes a huge difference to have a creative, practicing investment banker at the helm," he told the *Wall Street Journal*. "Let's face it. Bruce's name opens a lot of doors."

Other Lazard working partners were far less sanguine about Bruce's arrival. One partner compared Michel's capitulation to Bruce to that of the surrender of the emperor Hirohito at the end of World War II. Others were even more skeptical. "This is going to be a clash of egos on top of a clash of cultures," said one partner. Added another: "Bruce is great at doing deals for Bruce. But he's not the guy to save Lazard." But another partner understood perfectly what transpired between Michel and Bruce. "Clearly Michel knew what he had to do," he said. "Obviously Bruce had sold his firm. He'd always obviously cherished the Lazard name and worshipped the concept of being part of the firm and its culture. You know, as a teenager dreams about the chick in the centerfold of *Playboy*, I think this was his aspiration. I think the truth is that Michel probably did the only thing that he could do. . . . Half the firm wasn't even coming to work, because guys were freaked out. And Bruce jumped on it."

CHAPTER 19

BID-'EM-UP BRUCE

Bruce Wasserstein is the Harvey Weinstein of investment banking. Like Weinstein, the ample Wasserstein is arrogant, brash, boorish, and much feared. He's a creative and entrepreneurial genius, fabulously wealthy, notoriously strong-willed and short-tempered. He is also said to resemble, in both appearance and demeanor, the older André Meyer. He is an eccentric much loved by his small, rich coterie of bankers—who have followed him assiduously as he cut a wide swath across Wall Street in the 1980s and 1990s—and by few others, with the notable exception of the members of his gifted and quite devoted family. "Bruce is very creative," his sister Wendy, the Pulitzer Prize–winning playwright, once said. "He would tell you that what he and I do is not actually so different. Of course, I would tell you that he made up the three-tiered deal, but I couldn't tell you what it is."

Until Bruce went to high school, the Wassersteins lived in the predominantly Jewish section of Midwood, Brooklyn, right in the heart of the borough, south of Prospect Park. They lived in an eighteen-room, redbrick, stand-alone corner Dutch Colonial house on Avenue N. This was a family of serious achievers. Bruce was born on Christmas Day 1947 in Brooklyn, and a published report claimed he was the first Jewish baby born that Christmas. "His PR machine was working from the beginning," his first wife explained. Bruce was one of five siblings—with an older brother, Abner, and three sisters: Wendy, the youngest; Georgette, a Vermont innkeeper; and Sandra Meyer, referred to correctly by Wendy as a "female pioneer in corporate America." (A third son died a week after birth.)

Morris and Lola Wasserstein, Bruce's parents, were once described as a "little like Penn and Teller: One talks, the other doesn't." Someone who knew them said: "Morris was an extremely gentle, quiet, retiring person. By the time I met him, you just rarely heard him speak. He was very, very quiet. Lola was just a total pisser." They had a wonderful and long love affair. The quiet one, Morris Wasserstein, came to New York, through Ellis Island, in 1927 from Poland, according to the handwritten 1930 U.S. census records. Three of the Wasserstein brothers—Jerry, Teddy, and Morris—together started Wasserstein Brothers Ribbons on West Eighteenth Street. The company's clever slogan was "Ribbons Fit to Be Tied." Morris, a gifted businessman, also invested in real estate—he owned the building on Eighteenth Street where the ribbon business was, as well as buildings in what is now SoHo—and in the stock market. "They were in the ribbon business so they could be in the real estate business," explained Ivan Cohen, a cousin of Bruce's.

Around the mid-1940s, Morris's oldest brother George died. He had been married to a Lola Schleifer. They had two children, Abner, the oldest, and Sandra, who was born in 1937. After George died, in a variation of the once common Eastern European Jewish tradition, Morris married his widow. "We should all be as happy as they were together," remembered one family member, with approval. Morris then became the "father" to Sandra and Abner. Morris and Lola were the biological parents of Georgette, born on New Year's Day 1944 (named after her deceased uncle), Bruce, and Wendy, born in 1950. Bruce was not aware that Abner and Sandra were the son and daughter of his uncle George until he was in his twenties.

Abner was a bright and energetic child for the first five years of his life. But at five, he contracted meningitis from a cousin who was visiting Brooklyn from California. The disease ate away a large portion of his brain, leaving him mentally disabled and suffering from epilepsy. Abner's other physical characteristics developed normally as he got older, but he was frequently afflicted by seizures. Understandably, over time, Abner's problems overwhelmed Lola. When the Wassersteins moved from Brooklyn to Manhattan in the early 1960s, the family decided Abner would be better cared for through a program administered by the state of New York. Abner, who is now confined to a wheelchair and recently received an implanted device that warns him of imminent seizures, lives in a group home in upstate New York near Rochester.

Bruce is believed not to have seen Abner since he moved upstate. And the family's attitude toward Abner seems to be an ambiguous one. When Sandra died in December 1997, no mention was made of Abner in her obituaries. When Wendy died in January 2006, the Wasserstein family's paid notice in the *New York Times* about her death made no mention of Abner but did mention all of her other siblings.

No doubt his father's wheeling and dealing and his mother's independent streak rubbed off on Bruce. He had always been precocious, with a keen desire to be perceived as the smartest guy in the room, and he was eager to let you know it. Bruce attended the Orthodox Yeshiva of Flatbush, on Avenue J, not because the Wassersteins were particularly religious but rather because his parents believed the school offered the most rigorous and intellectual education. But his brilliance also set him apart and attracted the attention of those in search of raw talent. "Bruce was a genius, conveniently born on Christmas Eve with, according to my mother, Messiah potential," Wendy told *New York* magazine in 2002. Georgette recalled riding the subway with Bruce one day into Manhattan and hearing him declare, upon seeing the soaring skyline, "One day, this is going to be mine." Although Wendy made up characters in her plays based on every other member of her family, she never based a character on Bruce. When Bruce's oldest daughter, Pam, asked her about this, Wendy told her, "Sweetie, he's a play unto himself!"

He was also supposedly quite sensitive. During the economic downturn of 1954, both father and son, who was all of six years old, were worried about the consequences for the family's lifestyle. "It had a major effect on him," Sandra said of her brother. "We realized that we might lose our money and all of the things that represented." That was the year Bruce supposedly started reading *Forbes, BusinessWeek,* and *Barron's* cover to cover—although this may be an apocryphal story. Like his father, he started following the stock market closely and imagined himself trading stocks. "He was always the sort of kid who thought he'd run the world," Sandra said.

Bruce was very creative, even from a young age. This creativity extended to his reinterpretation of games. When he and Wendy played Monopoly, Bruce made up his own rules, transforming the game into a serious competition between mini real estate moguls. He started by dealing out all the property deeds, and then introduced serious financial leverage into the mix. Players could supplement the cash received at the start and from others throughout the game with money *borrowed* from the bank. Each property could then contain up to three hotels, rather than the one-per-property limit found in the conventional rules. He was pretending to be a *real* real estate mogul like the ones in Manhattan. His made-up Monopoly rules so infuriated his first wife she refused to play the game with Bruce and Wendy. He was also a chess champion. Wendy said later, "When I was a kid my life revolved around my brother."

Bruce stayed at the yeshiva until age twelve, and then for a year attended the Brooklyn Ethical Culture School. After the family moved to East Seventy-seventh Street in Manhattan, Bruce finished high school at

Felix's alma mater, the McBurney School. He became captain of the tennis team (just like Felix) and editor of the school newspaper. As editor, he instituted rhyming headlines. Among them: "Council's Coax: Give Up Smokes" and "Green and White Turns Black and Blue in Football Debut." There was also "Chicks to Cheerlead," which did not rhyme but Bruce conceded had "a certain sense of pzazz [*sic*]." The McBurney School administration didn't cotton to Bruce's humor, though, and removed him from the editorship during one Easter vacation. "The funny thing about the whole situation was that we won some type of award from Columbia which the headmaster kept on showing off," he later wrote.

Bruce graduated from high school at age sixteen, some two years ahead of his peers, and headed off to the University of Michigan in Ann Arbor. Although not a particularly enthusiastic student—he had no facility with languages, for instance—he marched through college in three years thanks to advanced placement credits and a heavy course load, graduating at age nineteen with an honors degree in political science. While in Ann Arbor, Bruce indulged his growing passion for journalism and a desire to change the world. He was not alone.

In January 1966, he became the second in command—executive editor—of the school's respected paper, the *Michigan Daily.* Though the position of executive editor had never before existed, Bruce, in typical fashion, convinced the previous year's editorial board (led by Larry Kirshbaum, his future publisher at Warner Books) to create it and give it to him. This was the eighteen-year-old's version of Bruceania, the fictional playland he had created as a child. He had a weekly column, Publick Occurrences—a reference to the first independent newspaper published in North America, in Boston, in 1690; the paper was shut down by the British after one four-page edition—and wrote occasional signed editorials and reported on subjects that interested him. He was on the editorial board. But he had no day-to-day responsibility for getting the paper out the door. "He had a tremendous intellect and an eccentric intellect that allowed him to think outside the box," remembered Harvey Wasserman, Bruce's former colleague on the paper. "So I was quite admiring of his ability to invent the executive editor position." The position gave Bruce a platform to pontificate on whatever subjects interested him. And pontificate he did, on subjects as diverse as the California governor Ronald Reagan's firing of Clark Kerr, the president of the University of California, and the need to resolve the 1966 New York City transit strike. He also advocated for having a meaningful student voice in faculty tenure decisions, for creating the opportunity for pass/fail classes, and for improving the oversight of the university's mammoth athletic department.

He also tackled such weighty issues as the racial, social, and economic inequities that motivated the civil rights movement.

The paper was the epicenter of the school's antiestablishment orthodoxy. Bruce was not shy about urging his fellow students to seek radical solutions to the changes he favored. In one column, "Raw Power Beats System Every Time," he was inspired by the Michigan political science professor Abramo Organski to wonder, in print, "How do you beat the system?" Bruce had been on the record for supporting a student voice on tenure committees, but what happens if the "faculty establishment" is opposed to the idea? What do you do? Bruce's rather straightforward solution, taken from the playbook of Saul Alinsky, considered the father of American radicalism:

> First, you pick a department in which a high percentage of students are liberals such as sociology. Then you get the students to boycott any class which is taught by a professor hired after a given date on which students demanded to be included in a tenure selection. Then you get people from Voice [a student antiwar organization] to picket the class so that wishy-washy students will be dissuaded from attending. Then you set up a picket line at the professor's house including all of the grubbiest students on campus. Assuming that the teacher lives in a nice, quiet middle class neighborhood he will begin to feel pressure from his neighbors. Of course, the home of the department chairman would also have to be picketed. Thus the sociology department would have hired a man who has no pupils to teach and is having one hell of a bad time in Ann Arbor. And, sure enough, he will take up that offer to teach at Berkeley. Although it is unfortunate that any individual has to suffer, that is the nature of politics. As Organski would be the first to point out, power is raw.

In addition to focusing on his writing duties at the *Michigan Daily*, Bruce turned his considerable attention to one particular assistant day editor, Lynne Killin. She was from a proper Presbyterian family in the Westchester County suburb of Larchmont, New York. Her father was an executive at Young & Rubicam, the advertising agency. Killin remembered one day walking into the offices of the campus newspaper and seeing Bruce. She was immediately attracted to his obvious intelligence and his total indifference to football, which made the pair an anomaly in Ann Arbor. Bruce was her first boyfriend. Much to the horror, though, of both sets of parents—the Scottish Killins and the Jewish Wassersteins—soon after her graduation from Michigan and his first year at Harvard Law School, on June 30, 1968, Bruce and Laura Lynelle Killin were married in Larchmont. Bruce was not yet twenty-one. Lola had always preached to him about the wisdom of marrying early, but Bruce had taken his mother's advice even further than she would have hoped. Both sets of parents were against this improbable union, although Bruce's parents softened toward Lynne somewhat upon discovering that she had converted to Judaism—a decision that made her parents insane. Lynne described Bruce as "slovenly" at that time, overweight, hair disheveled, and shirttails flapping. "Let's put it this way," she said, "he and I were kicked out of the lobby of a hotel once, in London, because we didn't look okay."

After the first year of law school, Bruce decided he had both the time and the inclination to pursue a joint graduate degree in law and business from Harvard. "Commuting by bicycle between the two schools in the winter was the real character-building part of the experience," he once said. He became one of the first people to enroll in the combined JD-MBA graduate school program. He graduated after four years, in 1971, from both the law school, cum laude, and the business school, where he was a Baker scholar with high distinction. One summer he worked as a poverty worker in two impoverished sections of his native Brooklyn, Bedford-Stuyvesant and Ocean Hill–Brownsville. But he didn't like the work because his co-workers thought he was just a rich Jewish kid who might give them money. At law school, Bruce joined the staff of the *Harvard Civil Rights–Civil Liberties Law Review* and was soon named its managing editor. In this role, he began to intersect with the consumer advocate, ITT nemesis—and future presidential candidate—Ralph Nader, and he was an active member of Nader's famous study groups. Improbably, Bruce was a Nader's Raider.

Bruce and Nader's top Raider, Mark J. Green, who had also been the editor of the *Civil Rights–Civil Liberties Law Review,* together edited *With Justice for Some: An Indictment of the Law by Young Advocates.* The book, a collection of thirteen essays by law students or recent law school graduates published in November 1970, was dedicated to "Laura Lynelle," Bruce's wife. "He damned well better have," she said. "I typed it." Nader met Bruce a few times that summer. "He always had a lot of fish to fry," Nader recalled. "He was clearly driven, and everything you would expect—very confident, very eclectic, nothing fazed him, and very ambitious. At the time, his ambition was to become chairman of the SEC." Killin remembered that Bruce was motivated not only by "winning" but also by a desire to create a dynastic legacy. "I remember him saying—back before we were even married, going to school—that he wanted to be remembered five hundred years from now," she said. "He wanted to set up a dynasty like the Rothschilds'."

Wasserstein and Green collaborated on another book, published in 1972, on antitrust law enforcement, titled *The Closed Enterprise System.* This book, also under Nader's auspices, argued that lax antitrust enforcement leads to inefficiencies in the system of supply and demand, which result in unnaturally high prices for goods and services. Part of the book took to task Felix, Geneen, and ITT for trying to evade the nation's antitrust laws. Felix especially was singled out for criticism.

After graduating from Harvard Law School and Harvard Business School, Bruce received a Knox Traveling Fellowship. He studied economics and British merger policy at Cambridge University, where, in 1972, he earned a graduate diploma in comparative legal studies in economic regulation. In 1973, the *Yale Law Journal* published his thirty-four-page "British Merger Policy from an American Perspective," based on the research he had done on the subject during his year abroad. Although this sort of writing tends to be convoluted and ambiguous, there are hints that Bruce favored greater regulation of mergers on both sides of the Atlantic. Regardless of what he was thinking by 1973 with regard to the economic and social benefits of the 1960s merger wave, it was unequivocal that he was one of the most knowledgeable twenty-five-year-olds on the planet on the subject of mergers and acquisitions at a time when most kids his age were worried about avoiding the draft and changing the world.

Upon his return with Lynne from England, he ruminated with his sister Sandra about what he should do. He passed the bar exam and considered practicing law in Alaska. And he thought about becoming the editor of a small-town newspaper. But driven by his ambition, his brilliance, and a preternatural bias toward the deal business, Bruce chose the far more conventional and lucrative route of becoming an associate at the elite New York City law firm Cravath, Swaine & Moore. The senior partner Sam Butler took Bruce under his wing and, after seeing him in action, supposedly promised he would become a partner in a few years' time. Nader saw Bruce's choice to go to Cravath more simply: despite all his raw talent and his desire for justice, he was driven by the "almighty lucre" to head to Wall Street. After Bruce became a banker, Nader wrote him a letter admonishing him for turning away from his public-service and regulatory-reform work to pursue Wall Street riches. Bruce keeps a framed copy of the letter at his palatial house in East Hampton.

Around this time, Bruce's marriage to Lynne began to deteriorate. "First of all, he was my first real boyfriend," she said. "I'm very attracted to brains and Bruce has brains. And when you put the brains to courting somebody, it's wonderful. And it was great for many years—well, not many years, for a long time, but what happens is, at least with Bruce, if you have a different point of view from him, then you're either stupid or ignored. He is not flexible. It's his way or, as someone said, the highway. You take it for a while, but then you say, 'Wait a minute. I'm a person in my own right. And I'm not competing, but you have to pay attention to me in a positive way.' He'll tell you himself that he's a very hard person to live with." There were two catalysts for their marital troubles. First, Lynne explained, even though she and Wendy were quite friendly for a time, she was not happy with the way Wendy depicted her in her play *Any Woman Can't,* which was produced off-Broadway in 1973. Lynne had been interested in rock collecting, and Wendy portrayed her as sitting on a carpet, playing with rocks as if they were marbles. "So she was making fun of my rocks, which I thought was stupid," she said.

Soon after watching the play, the couple had a fight while they were working on their tax forms. "We were doing taxes, and Bruce wanted me to be at home, like the wifey, you know, the at-home person," she said.

> But if we were out, he would introduce me as a jewelry designer, as someone who made jewelry, like I made rocks. I mean, we're not talking high-end here, okay? And Bruce would never balance his checkbook, and in fact he often wouldn't even write down the checks. He wanted me to do that. He wanted me to do a lot of work on the taxes. I exploded, saying, "You're the one with all the damn degrees. You do it." And one thing led to another. We'd had problems and he refused to go to counseling, and I didn't know enough to know that I could get a divorce without his permission. I wanted to get counseling. I wanted to get further therapy, and he said, basically, "I'm not going to do that. If you don't like it, leave." So I left. I didn't realize I could maybe negotiate. But Bruce was such a forceful person and I'm not. I have character and integrity and all that, and at some point you say, "Enough." We'd been unhappy. I'd been unhappy for a while. He wasn't, I was. But he didn't pay attention to it.

After being separated for eighteen months, they were divorced in August 1974.

There were no children. She got a total of $3,000 from him, which she used to help put herself through Columbia Business School. She worked for a long time at AT&T before being let go. She now earns extra money by selling used books on Amazon, using the moniker "Wasser-Kill." She has spoken to Bruce only once since they were divorced, as they were both approaching their fiftieth birthdays. Much to her disappointment, she never remarried.

IN THE FALL of 1976, Joseph Perella, a thirty-one-year-old accountant from Newark, New Jersey, was in charge of First Boston's fledgling M&A department, of which he was the only member. The same week First Boston announced Perella would be running the M&A department, Felix was on the cover of *BusinessWeek*, busy resurrecting his badly tarnished reputation. "I remember reading about all the fees he had collected working on deals," Perella said later. "I was so impressed. I said, 'God, this is really a great business to be in . . .' I was very impressed by seeing Felix Rohatyn on the cover of *BusinessWeek*, and I said to myself, 'Well, you know, someday if I work hard, I'll be on the cover of a magazine.'"

In the fall of 1976, Combustion Engineering hired First Boston to help it buy Gray Tool, then the subject of a hostile offer. Combustion was to be the white knight, the friendly suitor that would rescue Gray Tool. To help out, Perella called Sam Butler at Cravath. Cravath was available and took the assignment. At the first meeting with Combustion, Butler showed up with his associate Bruce Wasserstein. "I don't think I was at the meeting more than twenty minutes before Bruce had virtually taken charge," Perella recalled. "He was telling everyone the way the deal should be done from the lawyer's standpoint, and I said to myself, 'Holy mackerel, this guy is unreal.' It was one of those moments in life where I knew I had met a rare individual. Bruce had the ability to take what he knew about the law and translate it into action that was going to accomplish the client's objective." Combustion won Gray Tool. Within a year, Perella had offered Bruce a job doing M&A with him at First Boston. He doubled Bruce's salary to $100,000. By November 1977, the pair had completed two deals that combined brought in $3 million in fees, a fine haul in those days. They were on their way.

At Perella's urging, in April 1979 Wasserstein joined him as co-director of the M&A group. This was not the last time Perella would provide the grease for Bruce's career advancement. A few years later, Perella returned from a vacation and decided to turn over day-to-day management of the M&A group to Bruce.

At the time, First Boston was evolving into one of the most aggressive of the few Wall Street firms that provided merger advice to their clients (the others being principally Lazard, Goldman Sachs, and Morgan Stanley). First Boston's unprecedented success came from its guerrilla-like approach to deals. With very few establishment clients of its own, the firm became known for its ability to break up the deals of others using superior tactics (thanks in large part to Bruce) and, over time, to allow its balance sheet to be used by the LBO mafia to shake up corporate America. Leading the charge in this take-no-prisoners strategy was the powerful combination of Wasserstein and Perella, the Jewish bully with the studied rumpled appearance and the patrician Italian former accountant.

"When the M&A effort at First Boston seriously began in the late 1970s," Bruce later wrote, "we questioned how to crack the Lazard-Goldman-Morgan oligopoly. The solution was simple: Find the holes in the market, and then raise the stakes by outprofessionalizing the competition." Perella sought out and promoted Bruce because he knew he was brilliant and knew on some level that he needed Bruce's genius to succeed himself. By 1981, First Boston's nascent M&A department was on a major roll, having helped Bache & Co., the securities firm, elude a hostile takeover by finding the friendly suitor Prudential Insurance. The firm also helped keep St. Joe Minerals Corporation out of the hands of Seagram.

The breakthrough deal for the First Boston M&A department came in 1981, when Bruce and Joe advised DuPont on its successful $7.6 billion acquisition of Conoco, holding off in the process aggressive bids from both Mobil and Seagram, which Felix represented. "The structure of the deal was so complex that it earned the nickname 'Big Rube,' after the convoluted machinery drawn by the American cartoonist Rube Goldberg," the *New York Times* reported.

Although the idea was not new, Bruce's insight was to use a coercive two-part tender offer in the largest M&A deal in history. Bruce advised DuPont to offer cash at a premium to the Conoco shareholders tendering early, while leaving those who failed to tender with DuPont stock of undetermined value instead. The strategy, of course, was to get voting control of the company quickly by offering shareholders a high price in cash for their shares and penalizing those who did not tender. The tactic worked, and DuPont was able to win Conoco. The press coverage of DuPont's win was breathless, with Bruce as the genius and mastermind. In its own way, the canonization of Bruce as the tactical insurgent was the precise complement of the lionization of Felix as the ultimate insider.

Bruce had, literally, written the blueprint for the strategy some three years earlier. In *Corporate Finance Law: A Guide for the Executive*, published in 1978, he penned one of the first and most comprehensive handbooks on the arcane rules, regulations, and tactics of public financings, takeovers, and acquisitions. One section included a detailed overview of how to wage a takeover battle using tender offers. In another, Bruce wrote about the role of antitrust laws in mergers and took a dig at his former mentor Ralph Nader and the very observations he had himself made before he went to Wall Street.

Bruce was still only a *vice president* at First Boston when he wrote the book—on weekends and on vacations—and was thirty years old when it was published. Not only was the book—which he dedicated to his second wife, Chris, a tall, thin, red-haired psychotherapist—exactly what it set out to be, a useful guide for corporate executives, but it was also an exceedingly clever advertisement to them of the professional skills of its author: Bruce Wasserstein, experienced deal practitioner and former lawyer who understood the complex legal nuances of deal tactics. "Warning: In corporate financial transactions, ignorance of the law can be costly," the book's jacket proclaimed. "Whether you are working on deals as an executive, corporate director, banker, attorney, broker or accountant, you must understand the legal ramifications to be effective."

In his introduction, Bruce made the world of deals seem as exciting and as dangerous as war and a battleground not to enter unprotected. "The deal business is unfortunately replete with dangerous minefields," he wrote. "Hurtling roughshod over the intricate layers of governmental regulations is a prescription for disaster. The trick is to tiptoe lightly and not get blown up. Disciplined creativity, a very precious commodity, is required. It has sometimes been said that a bad lawyer is one who fails to spot problems, a good lawyer is one who perceives the difficulties, and the excellent lawyer is one who surmounts them. As J. P. Morgan is said to have remarked about his attorney, Elihu Root, 'I have had many lawyers who have told me what I cannot do. Mr. Root is the only lawyer who tells me how to do what I want to do.' " Bruce was both a lawyer and a banker who could tell his clients at First Boston how to do what they wanted to do. Furthermore, while younger than his colleagues, he was one of the first Wall Street lawyers to switch successfully to banking from law (leading a wave of other lawyers who followed suit) and thus ushered in the era of investment bankers skilled not only in valuation but also in legal nuance and tactics.

Bruce's skills were nearly the opposite of, say, Felix's. Felix was long on client relationships, reputation, and deal wisdom. He left the lawyering to the lawyers. Bruce, shorter on diplomacy, public profile, and deal experience, relied instead on his brilliance and encyclopedic knowledge of merger law. Sometimes he openly questioned the advice M&A lawyers were giving their clients. Although this rankled, he knew how to get things done in the context of the existing restraints, and he refused to be told something couldn't be done when he had an inkling it could.

In his physical demeanor, too, Bruce could not have been more different from the typical star investment banker. Somewhere along the way—some say as early as Cravath—he decided deliberately and with great skill to turn his bloated, disheveled, nerdy appearance into a distinguishing and memorable professional asset. "He has great ambition and great confidence," said someone who knows him well. "He knows how to cultivate his personal demeanor. That sort of studied sloppiness is very deliberate. He likes people thinking of him as Einstein or the Nutty Professor."

The Bruce brand got a boost in May 1980 when the *New York Times* economics columnist Robert Metz devoted his entire column to Bruce's views on whether the use of hostile tender offers was due for a renaissance. That anyone would care what a thirty-two-year-old, newly minted managing director at First Boston thought about this subject is a testament to Bruce's precociousness. But the Metz article also marked the beginning of Bruce's constructive and symbiotic relationship with the press, one of the most important assets of the late-twentieth-century investment banker. Felix had it. Steve had it. And Bruce Wasserstein, the former executive editor of the *Michigan Daily,* had it, too. They all used the media to advance their own interests.

In April 1982, the *Wall Street Journal* published a lengthy front-page article on Bruce and Joe. The article added to the studied mythology of Bruce as the disheveled, overweight Einstein—this time with *red* hair (a year before the *Times* described Bruce as "heavy-set and blond")—and Perella as his sartorially splendid foil. "Wasserstein is best at figuring out what a client should do and Perella is best at getting the client to do it," a competitor observed. The *Times* referred to them as the "Simon and Garfunkel of the merger and acquisition business. They are a poet and a one-man band; the abrasive but brilliant tactician and the immensely likable supersalesman with one major product on his shelf: Bruce Wasserstein." "I'm one of those people who needs a crisis to be at my best," Bruce told the paper, adding that conceptualizing a new takeover defense was "like playing chess where the rules change after every move." The reporter did allow a few anonymous digs into the piece. He described what "some say" was Bruce's "overweening ego." An unnamed competitor, though, seemed to be scratching his head in wonderment. "Bruce is a genius," the head of M&A at a competing firm said, "but when I see some of the companies he has put together, I wonder if he has even a shred of common sense."

Regardless, First Boston finished 1981 as the number-two adviser on M&A transactions worldwide, second only to Morgan Stanley, earning the firm huge bragging rights. Wasserstein and Perella, who by then were presiding over a thirty-six-member department, received identical seven-figure compensation packages and had identically sized corner offices on the forty-second floor of First Boston's midtown office tower on East Fifty-second Street. First Boston was the hot shop.

Bruce also began the time-honored Manhattan real estate and trophy-wife march of the nouveau riche. After the dissolution of his first marriage, he had been living at 240 East Eighty-second Street. He had become reacquainted with his *Michigan Daily* colleague Clarence Fanto, and the two of them would go barhopping on the Upper East Side. One night they went to a club together. "I spotted this tall, red-haired, rather very slim, willowy-looking woman across the room," Fanto said, "and I remember saying to Bruce, 'Oh, look at her. She's much too tall for me'—because I'm a very short guy. 'She's much too tall for me, but you might want to talk to her.' And Bruce was never shy about such things. As I recall, he went right over and spoke to her." Fanto left the club before Bruce, but Bruce called him later. "He sounded really excited and was thrilled to have met her, and it struck me that there had been an immediate connection there," he said. That night, Bruce got Chris Parrott's phone number. Their romance was swift. When he and Chris first married, they lived on East End Avenue. But as Bruce's wealth and family slowly started to grow, he moved up the East Side social ladder, too—first to 1087 Fifth Avenue and then to 1030 Fifth Avenue.

First Boston's M&A business continued to improve. In short order, Bruce advised Texaco on its controversial $10 billion acquisition of Getty Oil (breaking up a deal with Pennzoil), Cities Service on its $5 billion sale to Occidental Petroleum, and Marathon Oil on its $6.6 billion sale to U.S. Steel, eluding a hostile offer from Mobil Oil in the process. This unprecedented success landed Bruce a lengthy profile, "The Merger Maestro," in the May 1984 issue of *Esquire.* In the article Bruce made sure to point out to the reporter that he was the only investment banker to be involved in the four largest deals in American history to that time—a claim not even Felix could make in 1984. For the first time, the public got a rare and fawning glimpse of Bruce, in full. "Overweight and chronically rumpled, Bruce Wasserstein commands the same respect in a corporate boardroom as a general does before a major battle," the reporter,

Paul Cowan, wrote. No doubt captivated by *Esquire*'s attention and certain he could use the publicity to further his professional goals, Bruce let down his guard.

In case there was even the slightest shred of doubt left, Bruce showed Cowan that he had moved light-years away from the adolescent sympathy he once had for the common man. The men were discussing the fate of the thirty-five thousand residents of Findlay, Ohio, the home of Bruce's client Marathon Oil. Had it been successful in acquiring Marathon, Mobil had all but promised to close down Marathon's headquarters in Findlay. To "save" Marathon from Mobil, Bruce found U.S. Steel to buy the company. As part of the merger agreement, U.S. Steel agreed not to move "a substantial number of people" from Findlay. "Of course that is a good thing from the point of view of the town," Bruce said. "But from the corporate view there's no reason why one of the nation's leading oil companies should be located in Findlay rather than Houston." Would Bruce have supported a deal if it had meant moving people from Findlay? Cowan wondered. "Sure, I'd do that," he said, before letting out a nervous "whooping chuckle." "In fact, I think all those people should—" Bruce looked over to Cowan's tape recorder. "Oh, we're still on tape," Bruce continued. "Sorry. I believe in Findlay, Ohio. I really liked Findlay, Ohio." He whooped again.

IN RETROSPECT, BRUCE may have been at the peak of his M&A skills in the Orwellian year of 1984. On January 4, Getty Oil and Pennzoil publicly announced a roughly $9 billion deal whereby Pennzoil would buy Getty for $112.50 per share. At 8:00 p.m. that night, Texaco hired Bruce and First Boston to see if Texaco could break up the Pennzoil deal and win Getty for itself. Having anticipated this moment for at least six months, Bruce went into deal mode—a round-the-clock series of negotiating and strategy sessions—and advised Texaco it had to act quickly and pay up if it wanted to defeat the competition. Texaco took Bruce's advice and agreed to pay Getty $125 a share, a price that, not surprisingly, won the support of Gordon Getty, the largest Getty shareholder, despite his having just agreed to a deal with Pennzoil. Texaco's price was later increased to $128 per share, or around $10 billion, to accommodate the wishes of the Getty Museum, the other large Getty shareholder.

The Texaco-Getty deal was the largest takeover in American corporate history. As part of the new deal, Texaco had agreed to indemnify Getty against any legal fallout from breaking up the Pennzoil-Getty deal. Bad idea. Almost immediately, Pennzoil sued Getty to unwind the Texaco-Getty deal on the grounds that Pennzoil and Getty had an agreed-upon deal, even if the two sides had not executed a fully negotiated merger agreement before making their public announcement. A huge legal battle ensued, resulting in a jury trial in Houston, Pennzoil's home turf. On November 19, 1985, in one of the most shocking moments in American corporate history, the jury ordered Texaco to pay Pennzoil $10.53 billion, one of the largest such jury awards. The judge in the case later raised the award to $11.1 billion to include accrued interest. The legal battle continued until the spring of 1987, when the Supreme Court ruled that Texaco had to post a bond of $11 billion for the award. Soon thereafter, Texaco filed for bankruptcy protection, one of the largest bankruptcies in corporate history.

Whether a deal such as that between Texaco and Getty worked out for the principals involved was of little concern to most M&A bankers (Bruce among them), who were in the business of dispensing advice, banking their fee, getting publicity, and moving on to the next deal. Why bankers get paid millions for this Teflon-coated advice remains a mystery. But deals *do* have consequences for the stakeholders involved—for the employees of the companies, for the debt and equity investors, and for the management. Why should the investment bankers be the only ones to walk away with pockets overflowing and nothing at all at risk if their advice proves to be woefully wrong? Of course, bankers talk all day long about how their reputations are sacrosanct and how dispensing bad advice will inevitably damage those reputations, crushing their ability to win new business in the future. Bruce has said this himself. "What I'd like to think of as the hallmark of a Bruce Wasserstein deal is that the client got good advice, whether that is saying they should not do a deal or that they should do it and pay a dollar more," he said in 1987. "In the long run, they will appreciate that." But Wasserstein is living proof that there are very few consequences, other than a little negative publicity here and there, for delivering poor advice. In fact, in Bruce's case, he became a billionaire.

As would eventually become all too clear, the Texaco deal was a harbinger of serious troubles to come for Bruce's reputation. But this would take some time to become apparent. Bruce was certainly well respected for his tactical brilliance and for the increasing amount of fees he was generating for his firm. In February 1986, he and Perella were named co-heads of investment banking at First Boston, a major promotion that put the two men in charge of all the firm's corporate relationships while keeping them in control of the M&A group.

But by the mid-1980s, the M&A fraternity would be thoroughly dislodged once again by the emergence of Michael Milken and his firm,

Drexel Burnham Lambert. As has been well documented, Milken revolutionized corporate finance through the creation and use of high-yielding junk bonds. Not only did Drexel underwrite these bonds for corporations that could not get financing from more traditional sources—banks, insurance companies, and the public-equity markets—but also Milken pioneered the use of these securities to finance the huge financial ambitions of corporate raiders, like Carl Icahn and T. Boone Pickens, and of LBO firms, such as Kohlberg Kravis Roberts. Before long, the unknown firm of Drexel Lambert was both advising and financing these raiders and LBO firms in their acquisition sprees. Drexel was reaping *huge* fees as a result. Lazard's lackluster response to Milken was to have Felix protest loudly (and correctly) about his villainy and await his demise. Bruce and First Boston pioneered a different approach: together they decided to compete with Milken. It was a gutsy insurgent move that would later almost bankrupt First Boston and that certainly cost the firm its independence. Bruce, of course, walked away all but unscathed.

The unlikely conduit for Bruce's ambitions to compete with Milken was a man named Robert Campeau, an utterly obscure Canadian real estate entrepreneur in his early sixties. Although he had no discernible experience in retailing, Campeau was consumed by the idea of buying up the great names of American retailing and having them serve as anchor tenants in the American shopping malls he wanted to develop. In the early summer of 1986, with the help of the small investment banking division at Paine Webber, Campeau tried to reach a friendly deal to acquire Allied Stores Corporation, the United States' sixth-largest retailer at the time and the parent company for such admired stores as Ann Taylor, Brooks Brothers, Jordan Marsh, Bon Marché, and Stern's. Campeau was a minnow—with earnings of around $10 million—but like many a real estate developer he figured he could borrow the vast majority of the money he needed to buy the giant Allied, with earnings of around $300 million. He figured correctly. Thanks to Milken, the financing markets were heading into a period of excess. But by September 1986, Campeau had made little progress in his friendly pursuit of Allied and figured the time had come for both a hostile approach and a new M&A adviser with experience in hostile deals.

First Boston was hired. Bruce advised Campeau to launch a hostile tender offer at $66 a share for Allied, a 50 percent premium to where Allied had been trading two months before. But on October 24, Campeau dropped the tender offer and, on Bruce's advice, began to buy Allied shares in the open market at $67 per share. This brilliant tactic, known as a "street sweep," netted him 53 percent of the Allied stock in thirty minutes (and has since been forbidden by the SEC). He now had control of the company, thanks to Bruce and First Boston, which had agreed to make an unprecedented $1.8 billion bridge loan to Campeau to allow him to buy the Allied stock. (Campeau ended up using *only* $865 million of First Boston's money after Citibank stepped in and loaned him the balance.) Campeau and Allied signed a $3.6 billion merger agreement on Halloween. For tax reasons, Campeau needed to close the deal before the end of 1986, and to do so, he needed $300 million to invest as equity in the deal. But he did not have the money. In what became something of an infamous cliff-hanger, Campeau negotiated until December 31 to borrow another $150 million from Citibank that he could contribute as "equity" to the deal and the remaining $150 million from Edward DeBartolo, a San Francisco real estate developer who had first attempted to compete with Campeau for Allied.

The deal was done. Bruce had accomplished the unprecedented: enabling an obscure Canadian (with, it turned out, a history of mental illness and philandering) to buy, with none of his own money, a paragon of American retailing and saddle it with a huge amount of debt. Bruce had also introduced to the world of finance the idea of an M&A adviser using its own balance sheet to help a client win a deal—an idea, Bruce told the *Wall Street Journal,* that would "transform Wall Street." Bruce was quite pleased with himself and his Allied victory. "There was a swirl of controversy around this deal," he told *Institutional Investor* in June 1987. "Our competitors were passing around stories about all the difficulties we were having. But there *never* were any difficulties as regards the bridge loan. Things went according to plan."

Technically, as far as the narrow issue of First Boston recouping its huge loan, Bruce was correct. In March 1987, First Boston underwrote a successful $1.15 billion junk-bond financing for Campeau's Allied, the proceeds of which were used to pay off the First Boston bridge loan. Allied's successful refinancing of this loan was more or less the end of the good news for Allied Stores, with the denouement being the largest retail bankruptcy in history.

In the late summer of 1987, Campeau and Bruce began strategizing about having Campeau acquire the giant Cincinnati-based Federated Department Stores, parent company of Bloomingdale's, and merging it with Allied. This was another audacious idea, especially since Campeau had not yet made the Allied deal a success and did not have the money to buy Federated. But just as he did not have the money to buy Allied and he did it, by following a strategy mapped out by Bruce, on January 25, 1988, Campeau launched an all-cash $47-per-share bid for Federated, nearly a 50 percent premium to its trading price a month before. Campeau's bid for Federated set off an astonishing bidding war between the Canadian and Macy's, the icon of American retailing. On April Fools' Day 1988, Campeau won Federated with a bid of $73.50 a share in cash, for a total of $6.5 billion, most of which Campeau had once again borrowed, including another $2 billion bridge loan put up by First Boston and two unlikely small investment banks, Dillon Read and Paine Webber.

Less than two years later, on January 15, 1990, the entire Campeau retailing empire had filed for Chapter 11 bankruptcy in the U.S. Bankruptcy Court in Cincinnati, the largest bankruptcy in history to that time. First Boston was one of Federated's largest creditors, owed several hundred million dollars. "These collapses will be long and despairingly remembered," *Fortune* reported in a lengthy article six months later about the Campeau fiasco titled "The Biggest Looniest Deal Ever." *Forbes* observed: "Blood is everywhere." First Boston was left holding some $300 million, face amount, of Federated junk bonds and a $250 million Federated bridge loan. These securities were worth pennies on the dollar. The firm also faced numerous lawsuits about its role in the collapsed deals.

BY THIS TIME, Teflon Bruce had moved on, with a good chunk of the fees the Allied and Federated deals had generated in his pocket. And of course, he was no longer talking to the press about the deal. He told *Fortune* the only way he would comment for its treatise was on a not-for-attribution basis, an arrangement the magazine rejected. The combination of his promotion to co-head of investment banking in February 1986 and the improbable success of his strategy for Campeau in winning Allied that Halloween had convinced Bruce that he would be able to one day—soon—rise to the very top of First Boston. He was no politician, though, and some of his partners were far more skeptical about his career trajectory. One of them said later: "He didn't see that, while he was a great deal guy, he was not suited to running a business." Bruce had taken to going around the office wondering selfishly why First Boston management would allocate bonuses to anyone other than him. Naturally, this kind of talk at a full-service firm like First Boston—where the CEO, Peter Buchanan, had been a bond trader—started to grate on his partners' nerves. Said a friend at the time: "Bruce had incredible leverage within First Boston but the way he used it guaranteed that he would never get the influence he wanted. He had them by the throat and he flaunted it. And First Boston management resented it."

Frustrated with the increasingly low likelihood he would one day run First Boston, Bruce began, in the spring of 1987, seeing if he could scare up a bid in the marketplace for his own services. Dubbed "the Muppet Caper" inside First Boston, the idea was for Bruce to leave the firm with a handful of his fellow M&A bankers, including Perella. He spoke with Felix about coming to Lazard, as well as to Dillon Read. Bruce also considered starting his own firm. Word started to leak out that he was looking to leave First Boston. Buchanan called Perella to tell him he heard that Bruce was going to Lazard. "I thought Wasserstein was out of line and I told him so," Buchanan said. Perella then called Alvin Shoemaker, First Boston's chairman, and pleaded with him not to let Bruce leave. "If you shoot him, the bullet goes through me," Perella said he told Shoemaker. "I decided to marry Bruce in 1979 and I'll decide when to get a divorce." Bruce and the Muppets decided to stay at First Boston for the time being. As part of the agreement to stay, Bruce presented Buchanan with a list of his "personal goals" at First Boston that included taking over Buchanan's job as CEO in a year and then becoming First Boston's chairman in five years. He came away from his meeting with Buchanan thinking he had a deal for this aggressive career path. "It was smoke," a First Boston banker told *Fortune* at the time. "But Bruce acted the way people do when they're in a love affair. He heard what he wanted to hear."

Having passed on both starting his own firm and going to Lazard, Bruce went back to working on deals during the fall of 1987. One such deal brought him plenty of notoriety and, not for the first time, a seat at the table opposite Felix. Bruce agreed to advise Ron Perelman, the corporate raider, on his attempt in 1987 to buy Salomon Inc., the parent company of Salomon Brothers, the large Wall Street investment bank focused primarily on bond trading.

It was a given that if Perelman succeeded in buying control of Salomon, all of the firm's top management would be canned, in keeping with Perelman's typical behavior. Indeed, the rumor mill at Salomon had it that if he were successful in buying the firm, Perelman intended to install none other than Bruce Wasserstein at the top. Perelman denied the rumor, but the Salomon brass were worried nonetheless. This really was unprecedented stuff. Never in the annals of Wall Street had bankers from a couple of rival firms teamed up to attempt an unfriendly takeover of another Wall Street firm, let alone have one of the bankers—an M&A banker no less—act as the CEO of the target. When Michael Lewis, the author of *Liar's Poker* and a former Salomon bond trader, confronted Bruce about the rumor, Bruce "lowered both his eyes and the tone of his voice" in a most un-Bruce-like manner and responded: "I don't know how these rumors get started. How could it be true? I was in Japan at the time the bid was announced." In the end, Perelman failed when Warren Buffett stepped in to rescue Salomon. Bruce has maintained his relationship with Perelman, and the two men are equity partners in Nephros, a publicly traded renal-therapy company.

In the wake of the Muppet Caper, First Boston hired McKinsey & Company to analyze its businesses and make recommendations for changes, if appropriate. While awaiting the results of the McKinsey report, Bruce hunkered down again with Campeau to work on the hostile offer for Federated. But he was also monitoring the McKinsey work through a few M&A bankers who were on the committee that was working with the consultants. At that time, whenever the CEO of First Boston sent a memo around to the entire firm, it was printed on yellow paper. On the morning of January 22, 1988, Mike Biondi, who worked for Bruce, remembered, "The memo came in. It said, 'The report's in. The consultants agree. Our strategy is the right one. We're not changing anything. And by the way, we're putting Bruce and Joe [also] in charge of real estate and high yield origination because they're such great guys.' " Biondi was thunderstruck. He had just been promoted to vice president and attended his first officers' meeting the day the report came out. He remembered seeing both Bruce and Joe at the meeting. They didn't say a word. To make matters worse, the firm announced it would be laying off 10 percent of its fifty-five-hundred-person workforce. His wife had just given birth to their first child. "I was really pissed," Biondi said. "I mean, I had looked up to these guys. I couldn't believe they were just going to take this. This is bullshit."

The press reported the addition of high-yield and real estate finance to Bruce's portfolio as "a coup," but behind the scenes Bruce and Joe were seething. "Wasserstein was embarrassed," one of Bruce's friends told *Fortune*. They had wanted to run the firm. The next day Biondi got a phone call from his boss, Chuck Ward. "Chuck's obviously reading from a script the lawyer gave him. 'Hi, Mike. We've decided to resign. I'm over at Wachtell, Lipton. If you'd like to chat with us, we're in conference room so-and-so and so-and-so.' Click. That was basically the call."

This time there was no equivocation. Wasserstein and Perella had decided to start their own firm. Three days after the release of the McKinsey report, Campeau commenced his $47-per-share tender offer for Federated. In the middle of the management turmoil at First Boston, Bruce had found time to advise Campeau. But he had not told his client that he was seriously considering leaving the firm. On the morning of February 2, Bruce went to a board meeting at the Dalton School, which his son Ben Churchill Wasserstein attended. (At Bruce's insistence, all of his five children have short, punchy, monosyllabic—and supposedly memorable—first names and the middle names of historical figures.) After he joined up with Perella at Wachtell's offices, they walked over to see Buchanan. Reading from notes prepared by their Wachtell lawyers, Wasserstein, Perella, Ward, and Bill Lambert, Bruce's M&A idea guy, walked into Buchanan's office and resigned. Bruce was to be the president and CEO of the new firm; Perella would be the chairman.

Meanwhile, First Boston's $1 billion market value fell $127 million, or 13 percent, in the two days after Bruce's announcement. Such was Bruce's power and reputation at the time that even competitors acknowledged from the outset that the breakaway firm would be a success. "They can make a few phone calls and get $100 million in 10 minutes or $500 million in half an hour," a rival banker said. In a testament to the faith the First Boston M&A group had in Bruce and Joe, within a month twenty more bankers, including Biondi, had left for the ambitious start-up, Wasserstein Perella & Co. Naturally, a number of Bruce's friends from college were noting his progress with interest. "I'm in Boston at a journalism conference," his Michigan friend Dan Okrent recalled.

> And [the writer] Betsy Carter is there, and Betsy is a very good friend of mine and is a very good friend of Bruce's. I wake up in my hotel and I go get the newspaper from outside the door, and it's the announcement that Bruce has left First Boston and is starting Wasserstein Perella. So I see Betsy downstairs for breakfast. And I said, "Did you know about this, that this is happening?" She says, "Well, yeah, Bruce told me about it a few days ago." And I said, "Well, why would he want to do this?" And she said, "He said to me, 'I thought it was time to make some real money.' " Which, you know, to a journalist schlepper like me, and this is the late 1980s, you know, he made $7 million a year before. Not a lot of people were making that. It was before the big salary inflations in the executive suites in America. *And now he wants to make some real money.* And I realized that he lived in a very different world from the one that I lived in.

Wasserstein Perella & Co. set up shop in an office tower that had once been the home of the now defunct E. F. Hutton & Co., at 31 West Fifty-second Street. The business plan of the new firm was to provide M&A advice and to have $1 billion of private equity to use in leveraged buyouts. From the outset, it was clear to everybody that Bruce would be calling the shots, from the order of the names on the door to the color and shape of the firm's logo. "I didn't give a shit," Perella said about the name of the firm. "I didn't care if you called it Mickey Mouse. Bruce's personality required him to have his name first, to have his logo design [a cypress tree], to have his color [cranberry] be the color of the tree and on and on."

At first, everything clicked. The firm advised Philip Morris on its $13 billion acquisition of Kraft, and Time Inc. on its famous $15 billion acquisition of Warner, which Felix represented. The LBO mogul Henry Kravis hired the firm to sell Tropicana. Then Kravis hired Bruce for advice on KKR's legendary $25 billion LBO of RJR Nabisco. The firm earned a $25 million fee for that assignment, and Bruce's reputation as the king of the strategic leak to the press was confirmed. Campeau demanded that Bruce serve as his "tactical adviser" on the Federated deal. Even though, as a professional matter, First Boston did its best to prevent him from being too involved, Bruce remained a key adviser to Campeau on the deal every step of the way and got a $10 million fee.

From the outset, foreigners were eager to invest in Bruce's new firm. And in less than six months, the firm had negotiated a $100 million cash investment from Nomura Securities, in Tokyo, for 20 percent of Wasserstein Perella at a valuation of $500 million. Everything seemed to be going well. "For 18 months we were golden," Perella recalled. "Successful beyond our wildest dreams. At the end of 18 months, we had $200 million of cash in the bank, a billion-dollar unspent private equity fund, and we were ranked second in the M&A league tables, and we had no debt."

It is difficult to pinpoint the exact catalyst that caused the good times to end at Wasserstein Perella. The firm's reputation—especially Bruce's—was highly leveraged to the continuing boom in the public and private financing markets. The stock market crash of 1987 did not for a moment give Bruce pause as he and Perella devised the strategy for their new firm. Indeed, the crash merely served to hang a "30 percent off" sign on his clients' wish list of desired companies. But after Citibank failed to syndicate the financing for the $6 billion management buyout of United Airlines in the fall of 1989, the music stopped. And Bruce was left without a chair. Suddenly his high-profile, highly tactical, and highly leveraged deals came a cropper.

Bruce's reputation was also highly correlated to the mountains of favorable publicity he and Perella had garnered—and actively pursued. And Bruce received, justifiably, the lion's share of the blame for his years of aggressive tactics. Whereas for at least twelve years Bruce had been the focus of fawning publicity—publicity that he both sought out and encouraged—he was now being widely lampooned. At first, he waged his own counteroffensive against the criticism, claiming either that his advice was right at the time or, worse, that nobody had forced the clients to take his advice (a position that is surely the last refuge of a scoundrel). Soon enough, though, Bruce, the once notorious leaker, stopped talking to the press altogether, an irony richly noted by reporters.

The drumbeat of trouble began in July 1989. A *Newsweek* article noted that the Delaware Supreme Court had recently "chastised" Bruce for the advice he had given the year before to the board of directors of Macmillan Publishing, which had put itself up for sale. The court claimed Bruce perpetrated a "fraud upon the board" by "secretly giving more information to one bidder"—KKR—"for the publishing company than to another," Robert Maxwell. This "tip," in the words of the court, enabled KKR to know Maxwell's penultimate bid for Macmillan and helped KKR win the auction. Bruce was indifferent to the lashing he received. "Macmillan shareholders received a spectacular price," he said. But *Forbes* had another thought. "What advantage would Wasserstein get for tipping off the Macmillan-KKR group?" the magazine wondered. "We don't know. But we do know that about a month later Wasserstein Perella emerged as an investment banker on KKR's $25 billion RJR Nabisco buyout. Wasserstein Perella's take: a neat $25 million in investment banking fees."

Newsweek also reported on the ongoing battle that pitted the Time-Warner merger agreement against an unexpected and rich $200-a-share offer for Time from Paramount Communications. To fend off Paramount, Bruce restructured the Warner deal into a highly leveraged acquisition by Time of Warner from the debt-free original stock merger. At the time, Gerald Levin, Time's vice chairman, called Bruce "right up there with the best," adding, "Bruce was a good cheerleader for being bold." Fred Seegal, then a banker at Lehman Brothers, who worked with Bruce on the Time-Warner merger and whom Bruce later recruited to Wasserstein Perella, recalled the show Bruce put on in that deal. "It was the first time I'd ever really seen him in action," Seegal said. "Bruce would start getting on the soapbox, and he'd say, 'Well, you play this videotape, and you do this, and you do that.' It was all gobbledygook. And the Time guys, it was clear that they didn't understand. I didn't understand what he had said. But he had this mystique about him." Some seventeen years later, the combined Time Warner is still suffering from the crushing debt load Bruce advised management to take on. Levin, meanwhile, is long gone after becoming the CEO of Time Warner and engineering the disastrous 2000 merger with AOL.

The full-fledged media assault on Bruce began in earnest, though, three weeks later, in the first week of August, when *Forbes,* his old stomping ground, put a plump, well-dressed—now *dark-haired*—Bruce on its cover next to the devastating headline "Bid-'Em-Up Bruce." Like Nicholas von Hoffman's "Felix the Fixer," *Forbes*'s "Bid-'Em-Up Bruce" would stick. And like Felix, Bruce hated the moniker, especially since, as the CEO of his own firm, his profile in 1989 was far higher than Felix's was in 1972. Like the other publications that had profiled Bruce, *Forbes* could not ignore his prodigious and ongoing success. Not only had he masterminded the merger between Time and Warner, but there was also McCaw Cellular's $6.1 billion bid for LIN Broadcasting and three other large deals, totaling some $32 billion. "All at one time and all riding on Wasserstein's expertise," the magazine wrote.

What the article sought to answer was how Bruce was able to pull all this off. Its unflattering answer was that his "carefully cultivated image" had become his firm's "most powerful selling point," a conclusion Bruce actually agreed with. Whether he agreed with the next thought, that he was a master media manipulator, was not addressed. "In building this imposing image as a powerful friend and a dangerous enemy, Wasserstein has been positively brilliant in manipulating newspaper reporters," *Forbes* continued. The time had come, *Forbes* suggested, to call into question the wisdom of Bruce's standard "Dare to Be Great" speech that had time and again been successful in egging on his clients to pay the higher and higher prices necessary to win deals (it is binary after all, either a client wins or he loses). "Who will be to blame, then, if some of today's mega-billion-dollar mergers and acquisitions end in disaster?" the magazine asked rhetorically. "Wasserstein and his ilk? Or the corporate boards and corporate brass who let dreams of glory separate them from hardheaded reality?"

Although *Forbes* concluded that "the ultimate responsibility remains with the clients," Bruce's behavior at the end of the 1980s had prompted a rare—and unprecedented—attempt to determine why the well-paid bankers are not held accountable for their advice. In December 1989, the *Wall Street Journal* added to the debate. "Mr. Wasserstein has found himself under unaccustomed criticism—from courts, shareholders and even a few clients—for his conduct in several big takeover battles," the paper stated, damningly. "He has been accused of manipulating valuations; of encouraging clients to pay too much for companies, and of favoring the interests of corporate executives over the interests of shareholders." Even Bruce's old Harvard Business School professor Samuel Hayes chastised him for the Campeau debacles. Bruce "was the principal architect and was very proud of it at the time," Hayes said. "He can't escape the criticisms of the overpricing." Bruce refused to be interviewed for the article, in keeping with his new approach to the press.

By this time, any number of his deals had gone bust or were about to. Take, for instance, a company called Interco, formerly known as the International Shoe Company. Over time, Interco had transformed itself into a Fortune 500 conglomerate comprising the well-known brands Converse, London Fog, Florsheim, and Ethan Allen. In the summer of 1988, two brothers from Washington, D.C.—Steven and Mitchell Rales—launched a hostile, $64-a-share, $2.4 billion, all-cash takeover for Interco. The Raleses later raised their offer to $70 and then $74 a share, or $2.7 billion. After the brothers made their offer, Interco hired Wasserstein Perella.

Based on Bruce's advice that he thought Interco was worth first $68 to $80 a share and then $74 to $87 a share, the Interco board rejected the Raleses' deal. Bruce also devised a controversial counterstrategy—a complicated recapitalization, dubbed Project Imperial—whereby the company itself would borrow $2.9 billion and use that money to buy most of its outstanding shares in the market. Bruce valued the package at $76 per share, or $2 a share more than the Raleses' bid. Two other buyout firms—KKR and a Merrill Lynch fund—looked at Interco but decided they could not get close to Bruce's $76-per-share valuation. "I don't think the company is worth anything that starts with a seven," the KKR partner Paul Raether told Bruce. Although Bruce did not force the Interco board to take his advice, it did anyway, rejecting the Raleses' bid in favor of the Bruce-designed highly leveraged recapitalization. Bruce valued the stub equity at $5 per share, but it never traded above $4, and it was $2 at the time of the *Forbes* article. The newly issued high-yield debt also quickly traded down, causing those investors to lose money, too. Worse, 640 longtime Interco employees at two Florsheim shoes factories were fired from their jobs when Interco management decided to sell the facilities to raise money to try to service the new debt.

One of those who lost his job was Edwin Bohl. He was fifty-eight years old and had worked at the shoe factory for thirty-seven years. He had joined the company after graduating from high school. Over time, he rose to the level of supervisor. He lost his $19,000-a-year job two weeks before Christmas 1988. "The minute we came back from lunch," Bohl remembered, "they called us supervisors together. . . . The man read us the papers and said there were no jobs held for anybody. . . . They told us they had to close the plant because of the restructuring. . . . They had to raise money. . . . They told [us] it was not because of the quality. We were rated the top in quality and cost. . . . We had no idea this would happen." He opted for the lesser of the two evils Interco offered. In exchange for having Interco continue to pay his health insurance, he received a reduced pension. "We thought this would be the best time of our life," his wife said. "Now he doesn't know when he's going to get a day off. You either take a poor retirement and have your insurance, or have your retirement and pay for high insurance." Bohl took a job at a local Western Auto store. He was paid $4 an hour. At the time, Bruce was making "in the vicinity of $6 million annually," the *New York Times* reported. Perella was making around $5 million.

THE ALLIED AND Federated bankruptcies in January 1990 were the culmination of four months of rumors and financial distress for Campeau and his team. At the very least, there is no question that Bruce's architecture of the two deals proved way too complex for his client to execute successfully. Some people also charged that Bruce caused Campeau to overpay for Federated by $500 million. At the dinner celebrating the completion of the Federated deal, Campeau told the bankers and lawyers assembled at Le Cygne, a fancy East Side restaurant, "I'd like to thank all of you for your help. I couldn't have done this without you." Then he turned to Bruce and said, half joking, "Bruce, you cost me an extra $500 million," by encouraging Campeau to increase his winning, final bid to $73.50 per share, from $68. "The idea," Bruce later countered, "was to get the deal done."

But his nemeses at *Forbes* would have none of Bruce's justifications. "Wasserstein knowingly failed to stop his client from paying more than Wasserstein knew the company was worth," its reporters wrote two weeks after the bankruptcy filing. "Bid 'em up, Bruce." Meanwhile, in the bankruptcy proceeding, highly skilled, well-paid lawyers came to the conclusion that Bruce had orchestrated a "fraudulent conveyance" on the Allied Stores "estate" by encouraging Campeau to sell Brooks Brothers and Ann Taylor—two Allied assets—and then advising him to use all of the proceeds and a bit more ($693 million in total) to repay loans that Campeau had taken out from the Bank of Montreal and Bank Paribas as the equity for the Federated deal.

Even though he once eagerly took the credit for Campeau's successes—"It was like playing three-dimensional chess," Bruce told the *Times* in 1988—after the companies filed for bankruptcy protection, he sought to shift the blame for the fiasco away from himself and onto others. He now told *BusinessWeek* his post–First Boston arrangement with Campeau prevented him from orchestrating asset sales or refinancings. "The financing was not done on a timely basis" by First Boston, he told the magazine. "The asset values are there." But Campeau blamed Bruce. "Campeau is said to have raged through his Toronto headquarters like Lear on the heath, naming Wasserstein as the author of all his woes," the *New York Times Magazine* reported. In this forum, too, Bruce sought to deflect blame. "Robert Campeau failed to do three things," he said, "any one of which could have saved him. He did not float a new junk-bond issue when he could. He did not mortgage his properties, although Citicorp offered him one. And he did not sell assets. Anyway, I haven't been his adviser for a year and a half."

"People invent a simple, convenient fiction to account for our involvement in these deals," he told the *Times,* before articulating one of the inexplicable truisms of M&A advice. "Running something is not the job of investment bankers. Our job is to give people the options, to help them understand the risks and the rewards of what they're doing. But we don't make the ultimate decisions."

There was no question of the scheme's brilliance. The combination of Bruce's ideas and First Boston's balance sheet had enabled an unknown Canadian real estate developer to get control of the largest collection of retail stores ever assembled under one roof. And as far as could be determined, Campeau had put up virtually none of the money himself but still had control. But it was too clever by half, as they say. When all was said and done, the consensus seemed to be that if Campeau had only bought and run Allied, the deal could possibly have worked with enough time. While Campeau paid a full price for Allied, he did not overpay. He also received full prices in return for both Brooks Brothers and Ann Taylor. The problem developed when Campeau, with Bruce at his side, decided to reach for Federated. The bidding war with Macy's caused Campeau to overpay for sure. The two companies were never fully integrated to take advantage of the synergies on which the deal was based. When the economy slowed and they were stuffed to the gills with debt, the companies never had a chance.

But the true malfeasance came when Campeau took the proceeds of the Brooks Brothers and Ann Taylor asset sales and, instead of paying down the Allied debt, used the money as his equity to buy Federated. Thus, Campeau robbed the Allied estate to buy another overleveraged retail chain. This became the basis of a claim of "fraudulent conveyance" asserted by the Allied bondholders. This claim was sufficiently well documented and proven that, as part of the Allied-Federated plan of reorganization, the Allied bondholders received some $225 million of value beyond what they would otherwise have been entitled to. First Boston also made a multimillion-dollar contribution to the bankruptcy estate, as part of the plan of reorganization, in order to end the litigation that resulted from Bruce's advice.

It is simply not true to say, as Bruce did, that "people invent a simple, convenient fiction to account for our involvement in these deals." The inconvenient truth for Bruce was that he was directly responsible for what happened in the Allied and Federated bankruptcies, and he was not held even the slightest bit responsible. He had already banked his multimillion-dollar fees and moved on. The First Boston senior management could not even penalize him, because, of course, he no longer worked at First Boston when the bankruptcies occurred. This is the advice that supposedly savvy corporate CEOs pay millions for?

Despite Bruce's spin, this bankruptcy filing was unequivocal proof of the danger of horrific M&A advice. "What he was always best at," one investment banker said of Bruce at the time, "was getting boards of directors to take leave of their senses." But there was more. About two weeks before the Allied and Federated filing, the *Wall Street Journal* published a fifty-five-hundred-word excerpt from its reporters Bryan Burrough and John Helyar's *Barbarians at the Gate,* the soon-to-be-best-selling account of KKR's $25 billion LBO of RJR Nabisco, until November 2006 the largest leveraged buyout of all time. In the article—and the book—the authors reported that Henry Kravis accused Bruce (and Jeff Beck at Drexel) of leaking the news, to both the *Journal* and the *Times,* not only that Kravis's KKR intended to enter the fray for RJR Nabisco but how he planned to win. If true, this bizarre portrayal was an unconscionable breach of a client's confidence. Kravis was livid. *Barbarians at the Gate* also described, unflatteringly, how Kravis kept Bruce out of the most important meetings during the deal and how Kravis had hired him—and paid him $25 million—just to keep the other bidders from doing so.

Bruce fought back. He demanded the *Journal* print a retraction. But it would not. Instead, the paper printed Bruce's 242-word letter of denial. Bruce questioned the reporters' statement that the source of the leaks may never be known since Burrough and Helyar were the reporters on the RJR story. "Consequently, they do know for a fact who leaked to the *Journal,*" Bruce wrote. "They also know I wasn't the one. . . . I hereby release you and also any other paper from any pledge of confidentiality to reveal if I was the source of the alleged leak." Burrough, as he should, said he would go to his grave without revealing the source of the information. Some eighteen years after the fact, he said he found Bruce's reaction to Kravis's accusation that Bruce had leaked the story to be a somewhat halfhearted "show of fighting back" and nothing more "than an elaborate presentation to his existing clients and prospective clients" that he could still be trusted. But another reporter couldn't fathom how Bruce would recover from Kravis's accusations. "Kravis had to know the damage his portrayal of Wasserstein would inflict," wrote Joe Nocera (now a columnist at the *Times*) in a May 1991 profile of Bruce in *GQ*. "Investment banking is based on trust. Takeovers rely on secrecy. For Wasserstein, having the world see him as Wall Street had long seen him—as a loose cannon who couldn't be trusted—was bound to have devastating consequences."

Bruce's mug was now squarely in the media's crosshairs. Even when he found a friendly shoulder to cry on, the resulting story did him no favors. For instance, *New York* magazine's financial columnist Christopher Byron wrote sympathetically in February 1990 about how the rap against Bruce for the Campeau disaster may be "a bum one" but was wholly unsympathetic to the once-loquacious Bruce's refusal to consent to an interview. "Requests for interviews get shunted to an outside P.R. firm, and the stonewalling begins," Byron wrote. Still, Bruce allowed Byron up to his twenty-seventh-floor office for an *off-the-record* chat about the "exaggerations and distortions that have crept into the record regarding his deal-making activities." This didn't work out too well, either. "Get Wasserstein talking, even on background, about the potshots being taken at him, and, in frustration, he whips out page after page of documents justifying his actions," Byron observed. "Out come the lists, the tombstones, the internal memos and analyses. Poring over them, he can get so excited that he becomes a kind of mad professor, hunched over next to you, unaware that he has actually pulled off his shoe and begun picking eagerly at his toes." Byron's unalloyed conclusion: "A backlash is building against Wall Street's unrestrained decade of dealmaking, and Wasserstein has become a handy lightning rod for public frustrations." Even the reliably fawning *M, Inc.* trashed Bruce in its September 1990 annual New York power-broker article, claiming that he was "in a slump." (Felix and Michel were listed among the still powerful.)

THE ONSET OF the so-called credit crunch, following the collapse of the United Airlines buyout and the Allied-Federated bankruptcy, brought deal-making activity to a near standstill. Restructuring activity took center stage. There was a glimmer of hope for deal makers, though, toward the end of 1990, when the Japanese industrial giant Matsushita bought the Hollywood powerhouse MCA for $6.6 billion. From an investment banking standpoint, the deal was a testament to the growing importance of M&A boutiques after the dominance, during the 1980s, of the full-service, well-capitalized Wall Street firms. Felix and Lazard advised MCA. Allen & Co. and Michael Ovitz, the then-powerful chairman of Creative Artists Agency, advised the Japanese. The big firms were shut out of one of the biggest deals of 1990. At the end of November 1990, the *Wall Street Journal* reported that according to an unnamed source, and unbeknownst to both Allen & Co. and Ovitz, three Japanese bankers in the Japanese affiliate of Wasserstein Perella had secretly advised Matsushita's senior management by providing a "second opinion on price and structure" without attending any of the meetings for the deal. The Matsushita management "didn't want to disturb Ovitz" with Wasserstein Perella's involvement, the *Journal*'s source said, "but they really liked having a second opinion, someone who could be impartial." Wasserstein Perella's M&A ranking in 1990 stood at a dismal eleventh—down from the top echelons of previous years. The MCA deal would have doubled the dollar amount of the firm's merger activity in 1990 and raised its ranking to ninth.

But the story—and Wasserstein's involvement—were an embarrassing hoax. After further investigation, the contrite *Journal* discovered that it had been duped. Other bankers involved in the MCA deal openly questioned Wasserstein's role. Finally, when the required filings were made with the SEC, listing bankers and their fees, Wasserstein Perella was not cited. This fact the *Journal*—and others—conveyed with thinly disguised glee. "All in all, the incident made the once-fearsome Wasserstein look a little desperate: desperate to be connected to a big, sexy deal; desperate to recapture some of his old reputation; desperate to be seen as a player still," Nocera observed in his *GQ* profile. "Myself, I saw that story and thought, It's over for Bruce Wasserstein. It's amazing, when you stop to think about it, how dramatically the worm has turned on Wasserstein. It was once inconceivable that such a high-profile deal as Matsushita-MCA could go from start to finish without his getting his pudgy little fingers around it."

At this moment, many a Master of the Universe would succumb to the fire hose of criticism and, at the very least, begin to question his faith. Not Bruce. He saw himself as the ultimate Nietzschean *Übermensch*. He played by different rules from everyone else. He refused to give the naysayers the satisfaction of affecting him. He dug deep into Bruceania and set out to prove his critics wrong. "Neitzsche's whole posit was that there are certain superhumans who are above the fray, above normal constraints," a friend of Bruce's said. "He believes he is that. And so if you believe that, you're not bound by common morality, and you're just incredibly ambitious and impatient and not held back by that." He decided to make some changes.

Bruce separated from his second wife, Chris, and their three children. The family continued to live in their 1030 Fifth Avenue apartment, and he moved around the corner to the Westbury Hotel, off Madison Avenue. At a party in Bridgehampton a few months earlier, he had met Lorinda Ash, a lithe, dirty-blond beauty who was then working for Larry Gagosian, the über–art dealer. Eric Fischl had even painted her portrait for the billionaire art aficionado Eli Broad, whom she had dated (although the painting was snatched up by a New York collector before Broad could get it). Bruce fell for the much younger Ash hard and pursued her aggressively. "He was very decisive, even about leaving his wife," explained someone who knows both Bruce and Chris. "It wasn't this harangue about being back and forth and 'What do I do?' and 'What do I do?' He's just not a person who tolerates being unhappy." Soon after his divorce was finalized in 1992, he and Ash moved in together, first to East Sixty-first Street and then to 817 Fifth. Although his appetites remained robust, at Ash's suggestion Bruce started exercising, and lost fifty pounds. He took to wearing contact lenses instead of the preposterous eyeglasses that had been one of his goofy sartorial trademarks. Some of his studied schlumpiness appeared to recede. Ash introduced him to hip young artists and their work. But by all accounts, for Bruce art seems to be nothing more than another asset class with which to display his investment prowess. Under Ash's influence, he bought work by many of the artists in the Gagosian stable: Salle, Warhol, Serra, Halley, and Lichtenstein. Before he met Ash, he bought a few Impressionist paintings by Monet and Matisse. Art "is just another acquisition for Bruce," a friend observed. "It is totally the Charlie the Tuna syndrome—'I'm a rich guy, I gotta have class. I gotta have art.' " On the other hand, Bruce has always been enamored of creative people and enjoys spending time in the company of artists. He encouraged Ash to invite artists to dinner or to wrangle an invitation to an artist's studio. At one point in the doldrums of the art market in the early 1990s, Bruce, the lusty contrarian, paid $1 million for a painting by Mark Rothko. From an investment point of view, the purchase was a stroke of brilliance. (The painting is said to be worth at least $15 million today.)

PROFESSIONALLY, TOO, WASSERSTEIN Perella began to change. The firm's M&A advisory business had all but dried up, so Bruce focused on trying to resurrect the firm's struggling $1.1 billion LBO fund, which had in it $120 million of the firm's partners' own money. True, early on, Bruce had some signal successes, but the fund lost its $14 million investment in KDI, a swimming pool manufacturer, when the company filed for bankruptcy. Bruce's huge $350 million investment in a British supermarket group, Gateway, was a total loss after the renamed company, Isosceles, went bust. "He did this," a former partner told *Vanity Fair,* "against the advice of all the other partners in the room . . . all of whom subsequently left the firm." Its $100 million investment in Wickes, a homebuilding and auto-parts manufacturer, also ended up poorly. IMAX, the giant-screen movie theater chain, floundered. Another disaster was the $80 million or so Bruce lost in Red Ant, an independent record label, which he started from scratch, sold to Alliance Entertainment, and then bought back after Alliance filed for bankruptcy.

Someone who knows Bruce said that his tenure managing the Wasserstein Perella merchant banking fund shows his questionable ability as a fiduciary. "History has shown that when Bruce has been given a charter, he'll abuse it to whatever degree he can," he said. "He'll cross over fiduciary boundaries. He won't cross over legal boundaries." In a Nietzschean way, this makes sense. "Bruce on the investment side has what I would describe as smart man's disease," a former colleague said. "He can never believe he's wrong. And in this business you need to say, 'OK, I'm wrong,' and cut your losses . . . but he would continue to make larger and larger bets to prove he was right."

An even bigger problem loomed, though, with his longtime partner, Perella. Perella had long resented the rumors that Bruce had been badmouthing him behind his back in the corridors of power at First Boston and that somehow he had been forced to take a backseat to his more ambitious partner. Occasionally, he voiced these resentments. In the January 1990 *New York Times Magazine* article about the firm, Perella told the reporter that he was growing increasingly concerned that he was being "overshadowed" by Bruce and was being painted with the same brush of blame. He had his many accomplishments, too. "All of a sudden I read that I'm the sidekick," he said. "All of a sudden I'm Gabby Hayes. Look, I built that business up from nothing, from absolute scratch, by myself." Perella, said to be "mercurial" and more than a little bit odd, had repeatedly given serious thought to quitting the firm over the years, starting around December 1989. In 1992, his wife, Amy, was diagnosed with Hodgkin's disease (from which she recovered), and this development caused Perella to reflect on how he wanted to spend his time.

No doubt compounding his concern were the firm's ongoing problems: a precipitous drop to twentieth in the 1992 rankings of M&A advisers for completed deals; the demand by Gary Parr, the firm's insurance banker, for more money; and the biggest looming threat of all, the right held by Nomura to demand repayment of its $100 million investment sometime after 1995. There was a growing and serious concern that Wasserstein Perella could not repay the money if asked.

Finally, on July 23, 1993, Perella announced he would quit Wasserstein Perella on September 1, ending a nearly twenty-year relationship with Bruce that spanned all of Cravath, First Boston, their own firm, the highest highs, and the lowest lows. He had fulfilled his original five-year commitment to the firm, and that was it. "If you think I'm bitter," one of Bruce's former partners said. "I mean, he was even more bitter."

Meanwhile, after three years living with Ash, Bruce summarily announced to her that their relationship was over. Their separation was "brutal," *Vanity Fair* reported, with her clothes being packed up and moved out of Fifth Avenue and East Hampton. (She later married Peter Ezersky, who helped Steve Rattner start the Quadrangle Group.) Bruce had met, and fallen in love with, Claude Becker, a tall, dark-haired beauty fifteen years his junior. She was a successful producer at CBS News. They were married in 1995. "Claude is very charming, and very funny," one of their friends told *Vanity Fair.* "She knows that Bruce is socially awkward and makes jokes about how she has to go around cleaning up his 'little messes.' " They moved to their current duplex, at 927 Fifth Avenue, after unsuccessful attempts to buy apartments at both 834 Fifth and 2 East Sixty-seventh Street.

CHAPTER 20

CIVIL WAR

Needless to say, Bruce's approach to deal making could not have been more antithetical to that espoused and practiced by Lazard. Yet thanks to an unlikely confluence of events that could only have happened to Bruce Wasserstein, here he was, as of January 2002, in charge of Lazard and its second-largest individual shareholder.

Bruce wasted no time putting his imprint on the firm. Even before he technically took over—January 1, 2002—he was making authoritarian pronouncements: not only did he want the focus to be on clients, but he also insisted that working partners, such as Bruno Roger, relinquish their positions on the boards of the publicly traded Lazard holding companies. He wanted the partners to consciously choose between him and Michel.

He utterly dismissed the renewed assault on Lazard from Jon Wood at UBS. "I don't care about it," he told a British newspaper two days after his appointment. "If they owned all these companies together they would have only 40% of a company that has no power other than to block a sale. Even if they had 100% it wouldn't matter because I now have the blocking power within Lazard." Wood said of Bruce, "He's so pompous, he couldn't even bring himself to talk to me." As for the historic Lazard internecine warfare, Bruce declared: "The politics are over at Lazard. There is no point to them. The only point would be if anyone wanted to convince me they should make more money, and I'm not receptive to that approach." If partners choose to continue politicking? "They can leave," he said.

Bruce also addressed head-on the criticism that as a banker he was well past his expiration date. "Anyone who says that doesn't know very much about it," he said. "I worked on the Time Warner/AOL merger, the UBS/PaineWebber deal and the Morgan Stanley/Dean Witter merger. It's a sour grapes type of thing. In this business, youth is not an asset, since our principal product is advice." Of course, his former colleagues say he had nothing to do with the Time Warner–AOL deal, which in any case was considered a massive failure, and that Phil Purcell, the former CEO of Morgan Stanley, purposefully excluded Bruce from the negotiations when he sold Dean Witter, of which he was then the CEO, to Morgan Stanley. That deal is also considered to have worked out poorly and, in any event, cost Purcell his job as head of Morgan Stanley in 2005. As for his time at Dresdner and Allianz, after explaining that legally he was precluded from saying anything about it, he said, "What's that French song? Je ne regrette rien." After a round of press interviews in London, Bruce flew to New York to meet with the partners there and to announce that he had selected Ken Jacobs to run the North American business. "He introduces himself, and he says essentially that 'mediocrity is not going to be tolerated,'" one partner there recalled. "'We're going to do really well, and we've got a lot of rebuilding to do.' And he turns and says, 'Ken's in charge. He's my representative in New York.'" For the first year, Bruce ran the firm from London.

Right around Thanksgiving 2001 and in keeping with Adrian Evans's earlier statement, Lazard followed through on its promise to distribute actual equity ownership in the firm to its 147 partners worldwide. When Loomis and Michel had first negotiated the distribution of the goodwill points to partners during the late summer of 2001, the idea was that a partner with a 1 percent profit percentage would receive around 0.7 percent of the goodwill. But that was just an idea. When the goodwill points were *actually* distributed by Michel at the end of 2001, a partner with a 1 percent profit percentage actually received 0.44 percent of the goodwill. The balance of the working partners' goodwill was held in reserve for Bruce to use to hire new partners. "It was deflating," Ken Jacobs said of the last-minute change to the equity distribution plan. "But it wasn't destroyed. It was to be expected."

The distribution of the goodwill points, or equity, became incredibly important to retaining partners at the end of 2001. "It was a big deal because I don't think anybody would have stayed for Bruce if the points hadn't been distributed," Jacobs explained. "Let me put it this way: I'm positive it wouldn't have been successful if the points hadn't been distributed." The firm-wide pretax profits in 2001—some $145 million—were down two-thirds from the previous year. So even a partner such as Jacobs, who had negotiated an increase in his profit points in 2001—to 1.7 percent from 1.375 percent in 2000—received much less compensation in 2001 ($2.5 million) than he did in 2000 (close to $6 million). The goodwill points proved to be a tonic of sorts for the huge decrease in compensation. At least now, once the equity points were vested (half in early 2002, the other half a year later), the partners could potentially look forward to a payday if the firm was ever sold or went public.

A number of partners also received "top-ups" in cash in 2001, beyond what their actual percentage points would have given them, which further reduced the overall size of the compensation pool. "That was the collapse of the old compensation system," Jacobs explained. "People had lost complete confidence with the system as a result of that. That's why, when Bruce came, he just totally scrapped it. It was pay for performance now, that's what we call it." For the first time in the firm's history, longstanding partners no longer knew what their pay was likely to be from one year to the next. Michel's entire compensation system was junked. New partners joining the firm received multiyear contracts with compensation guarantees. Old partners were paid based solely on their annual production. No longer would there be even a perception of a partnership.

Lazard had overnight become just like every other firm on Wall Street, at least when it came to compensation. Furthermore, for the first time in some fifty years, one Lazard partner would no longer know what another partner made. The previous system was imperfect, too, since until Rattner pushed for complete disclosure the actual amounts paid to individual partners could never be certain—but at least one had a good directional sense of how one stacked up. No more. Bruce scrapped the whole thing. All compensation would be set at his total discretion; no one else would know what deals he cut.

The fallout was immediate, with the most acute pain felt by the two partners whose departures had been announced before Bruce's arrival—Loomis and Tashjian. Loomis had promised Tashjian a generous severance package as part of his departure, but it was a package based on the old system of profit points. The problem was—people were quickly figuring out—that despite Michel having given Bruce between 4 and 7 percent of the partnership profits, Bruce was likely to trash the short-term profitability of the firm in order to rebuild the depleted partnership ranks and to have a chance of creating long-term equity value. It was the exact same formula he had used at Wasserstein Perella, where the firm made very little money—some have said it was within days of not being able to meet payroll when it was sold—but Bruce was still able to create a tremendous amount of equity value.

When Tashjian figured out that his severance package was not going to be worth very much, if anything, he called up Loomis and yelled at him for deceiving him. But the truth was Loomis had no idea what

Tashjian was talking about. Nobody had told the increasingly invisible Loomis, either, that the old compensation system had been scrapped and profit points no longer had value. Now Loomis was upset because his own newly revised severance arrangement with Michel was also based on a profit that would no longer exist. After Loomis calmed Tashjian down, he called Michel at Sous-le-Vent. Loomis was not happy. He wondered why no one had told him the compensation system had changed. He went to bat for Tashjian and won for the man he had recently fired a better deal. Then he told Michel what *he* wanted: a nonnegotiable one-time cash payment based on the average of the past two years' profits times his average profit points. This worked out to be around $5 million. Within days, Michel had faxed to Loomis a signed agreement giving him exactly what he asked for.

More problems loomed, though. "The problem with Lazard is that it has always had a great-man strategy," the former Lazard partner Kim Fennebresque told the *New York Observer* (Fennebresque had also been Bruce's partner at First Boston):

> Because they don't offer capital; what they really offer is the advice of great men. They have always had an extraordinary stable of such men. With Felix at the top, Steve Rattner, Ken Wilson, Ira Harris—the list goes on and on. They have been able to sell themselves and their position in the commercial world, as well as the quality of their advice. When you lose all the great men, it becomes a problem. Bruce is a great man, a man of insuperable intellect, and he is extraordinarily commercial. But the problem is Wall Street has changed. If any man can bring back the great-man strategy at Lazard, it is Bruce—but the question is, are there any great men left out there? Because in the end, there really is nothing else to offer at Lazard than the intellectual capital of the partners themselves.

Needless to say, many Lazard partners found Fennebresque's comments objectionable, but in truth, his insights were on the mark.

Within weeks of these articles Bruce had to confront his first case of serious dissension in the ranks. Three of Lazard's leading bankers in Europe—Gerardo Braggiotti, Georges Ralli, and Jean-Jacques Guiony—were again threatening to leave, this time for senior positions with either UBS Warburg or Deutsche Bank. They were said to be unhappy with the swath of power Michel ceded to Bruce. They were furious at Michel for doing it. They were also irritated with the firm's failure to recalibrate the profit distribution between New York and Europe. They thought Bruce was rude. Braggiotti, at least, was probably disheartened that Michel had turned to Bruce instead of him. For Ralli, then fifty-three, this was easily his third or fourth threat to quit in a year.

Complicating matters significantly was that earlier in 2001, Michel had promised Ralli the opportunity to run the Paris office, and Michel's close ally Bruno Roger would have to be pushed aside to make that happen. When Bruce came in, he summarily dumped Roger, who now felt that he had been "publicly humiliated," and in Paris there was nothing worse than public humiliation. Jean-Claude Haas said Michel was "unhappy" about the way Bruno was treated, and "even people who detested Bruno were shocked." Roger was angry now with Ralli, Michel, and Bruce. Ralli was angry with Roger, Michel, and Bruce. While Ralli felt that people had grown tired of Roger, for Bruce to come along and publicly humiliate him was an attack on the honor of Lazard Paris. Haas told Adrian Evans that the possibility of Ralli leaving "is a disaster."

Braggiotti, then forty-nine, joined Lazard in 1998 from Italy's Mediobanca, where he worked for seventeen years, lastly as deputy chief executive officer. While at Lazard, he was the dominant M&A banker in Italy, completing twenty-two deals, with 60 percent market share, in 2001 alone. He was said to have the best Rolodex in Italy. He advised Pirelli on its €7 billion takeover of Telecom Italia despite Pirelli being an investor in Mediobanca. He also advised Italenergia on its €5 billion takeover of Montedison.

Bruce could not afford the loss of Braggiotti, Guiony, or Ralli, especially so soon after his own coronation. On behalf of the three men, Ralli presented a list of demands to his older partner Gilles Etrillard. Etrillard passed the list on to Evans. They wanted, among other things, for Paris to be governed by Parisians (not by Bruce).

In early December 2001, Bruce met with the partners in Paris and told them, "Okay, now I'm the boss." This went over poorly. Braggiotti, for one, considered Bruce's contract a "change of control" of the firm and therefore demanded a retention contract, or, he said, he would leave. He also convinced Ralli and Guiony that the three of them were better off joining forces—whether that meant leaving or staying. Braggiotti had one meeting with Ralli at UBS and one meeting with him at Deutsche Bank. But these were just tactics to force Bruce's hand. At that moment, Braggiotti had no intention of leaving Lazard. Ralli would have left but got most of what he wanted to stay. Bruce had blinked. He agreed contractually to cede all power in France to Ralli and all power in the rest of Europe (outside the U.K.) to Braggiotti, superseding what was in the new operating agreement. Guiony cut a new deal and remained head of M&A

in France. For three years, Bruce was not allowed in France or the rest of Europe. Braggiotti and Ralli could open offices, close offices, take on clients or not, and hire or fire professionals. Bruce was powerless. "He had no choice," one European partner said. "He couldn't announce in December, or whenever it was, that he was joining Lazard and the same day announce he had lost Europe. So he had no choice. He had to do it." From time to time thereafter, Bruce would try to direct events outside his sphere of influence in the United States and the U.K., but Braggiotti and Ralli all but ignored him. Braggiotti did make one concession to Bruce: when he complained about the "hold" music on the phones in the Milan office, Braggiotti agreed to change it.

ON JANUARY 3, Bruce took over as head of Lazard and announced his new management team, which effectively kept most of the existing senior managers in place and reflected his intention to delegate authority across geographies. But it also reflected the success of the Europeans' gambit weeks before. Braggiotti was named head of Europe outside of France and the U.K.; Ralli was promoted to head of France; Marcus Agius, then fifty-five, remained head of the U.K.; and Ken Jacobs, then forty-three, was promoted to head of the United States. All were named deputy chairmen of Lazard, a move that reflected Bruce's penchant for handing out highfalutin titles. All reported to Bruce and were to "act as a team to run the firm." Bruno Roger, then sixty-eight, was named chairman of Lazard Paris after Bruce expressed interest in having him as an adviser. The title also saved Roger from further public humiliation.

The *New York Times* reported that as of Bruce's arrival and "according to Lazard calculations," the firm was worth $3.8 billion, right in line with the "Pearson price." Bruce announced that "despite the recession," Lazard intended to hire twelve new partners in the United States in the first six months of 2002 and a "limited" number of new partners in France and the U.K. and was "launching a major expansion" in the rest of continental Europe under Braggiotti's direction. Bruce's contrarian view was that the severe downturn on Wall Street was the perfect time to be hiring bankers, just as others were firing them and compensation had fallen precipitously. He wasn't wrong. He had already spoken to seven of his former colleagues about coming to Lazard, among them Chuck Ward, then back at First Boston, and Jeff Rosen, then at DKW. The *Wall Street Journal* reported that he told them that a 1 percent ownership stake in Lazard was worth $38 million, a value consistent with the $3.8 billion valuation, and, according to Bruce, was consistent with other prices paid for stakes in Lazard, including his own. Bruce told the

Journal that the new financial supermarkets, such as Citigroup and JPMorgan Chase, were the "new fandangos" and said that he believed "good advice is the new, new thing."

The new year not only brought the announcement of Bruce's "new" management team but also revealed to all the partners the complexity of the deal Michel had cut with Bruce. A summary of the 116-page "Third Amended and Restated Operating Agreement of Lazard LLC, Dated as of January 1, 2002" bluntly stated the changes: "BW will take over from MDW as Chairman of the Executive Committee, will take on the positions of Head of Lazard (for an initial five-year term) and CEO of Lazard and will assume all of the powers of MDW and the Executive Committee. In these positions, BW will have all the powers with respect to Lazard LLC, subject to the approval rights of the Lazard Board described below." As for Michel, "MDW will become the non-executive Chairman of Lazard and Chairman of the Lazard Board. MDW will hold these positions until the earlier of his death, adjudicated incompetence or voluntary withdrawal or the date on which the MDW Group ceases to hold a Class B-1 Profit Percentage. The position of Chairman of Lazard will cease to exist after MDW ceases to hold this position."

While not then publicly revealed, the new Lazard board of directors consisted of Bruce and the four people who reported directly to him—Agius, Braggiotti, Jacobs, and Ralli—and Michel and his five close allies, François Voss, Didier Pfeiffer, Bruno Roger, Antoine Bernheim, and Alain Mérieux, the CEO of bioMérieux. By a majority vote, which Michel felt confident he could then easily obtain, the Lazard board had the right to approve, among other powers, a material acquisition of, merger with, or joint venture with another investment banking firm; the appointment or reappointment of Bruce; the removal of Bruce, only for cause (as "narrowly defined"); and the appointment or removal of a board chairman other than Michel.

As far as the day-to-day operations of the firm, though, it was clear Bruce had all the power. He alone could appoint or remove, with or without cause, all "Heads of House, Senior Managers and Global Heads." He could appoint or remove any managing director he wished "at any time with or without cause," with the notable, and interesting, exception of the managing directors in Paris, "where the existing system for nomination and removal of Managing Directors will be continued" (reflecting, no doubt, the deal he had to cut with Ralli and Braggiotti and longstanding practice). Bruce alone had the approval right over all other appointments at the firm and, of course, was given the sole right to determine the compensation of managing directors and the "aggregate compensation" of other employees of the houses, and retained the right "to determine the individual compensation of any particular employee of a House." For the working partners, Bruce would have the right to set and change at any time their Class A-1 profit percentage, their interest in the annual profits and losses of the firm. For the nonworking, limited partners and also for the so-called capitalists—Michel and the other founding families, plus Eurazeo, among others—their share of the annual profits and losses plus their share of the goodwill interests worked pretty much the same as that for the working partners except that the percentages were firmly set and not alterable by Bruce. The working partners were to get about 58 percent of Lazard's profits and the limited partners and the capitalists were to get 42 percent of the profits, although this split was subject to change, through dilution, as Bruce hired new partners.

Quite simply, the depth and breadth of Bruce's control of the firm were not only unprecedented for Lazard; they were unprecedented for almost any financial institution. His deal for a minority stake with full management control confirmed what many Lazard professionals had feared—that he stole the firm from Michel. Michel's deal with Bruce appeared to violate one of the cardinal rules of takeovers: never sell operational control of a company without being sure to fetch a "control premium," or an above-market price that attempts to value what selling management control is worth. But that is exactly what Michel did: in a decision rich with irony, he sold near-absolute control of Lazard—a firm worth roughly $4 billion—to Bruce for $30 million. What's more, the $30 million Bruce invested, it could be argued, came from the $75 million or so he saved by not paying state and local taxes in New York on his $625 million windfall from the sale of his former firm. In effect, it had not cost Bruce a dime to take control of Lazard.

Indeed for many Lazard partners, the January 1, 2002, documents conjured up a sense of another contract of adhesion forced down their gullets. Just as in 2000, the execution copies of contracts and "acknowledgment" forms started flying around the globe, with very little time to review them and no opportunity to negotiate. Scott Hoffman admonished the managing directors to sign the forms, without fail, by January 31, 2002, or "you will lose all the A-2 goodwill that has been allocated to you." Worse, the 2002 documents contained none of the vital schedules and annexes that were in the 2000 merger documents. The Lazard managing directors would no longer know, for instance, who was on the Lazard board of directors or how their fellow managing directors were to be paid. They also would not be given a copy of the crucial "BW Employment Agreement" that contained the details of Bruce's financial deal with Michel. Hoffman responded when asked for the addenda, "I have not included the schedules and annexes as they are not available." One longtime partner had his goodwill percentage diluted by 5.5 percent and his profit percentage diluted by 10.6 percent as a result of Bruce's appointment—all without his approval, consent, or ability to prevent or challenge the new arrangement. Another partner had his goodwill percentage diluted by 5.8 percent and his profit percentage diluted by 27.2 percent, again without notification or consent.

Such dilution was permitted by the third amended agreement. One infuriated longtime partner sent around a note to his colleagues: "In thinking about the end game, it occurred to me that Lazard is a corporation, a Delaware corporation, even though we call it a partnership, and that in corporate law, as I remember it, controlling shareholders have a duty not to self deal in a way that they profit to the harm of the minority." Even though Hoffman had warned the managing directors to sign their documents by January 31, 2002, or "forfeit all of your goodwill interest," and wrote that, "unfortunately, there cannot be any exceptions," the bickering between many of them and the firm went on through at least the end of March. These partners, smart men all, were struggling mightily to receive from Hoffman, Bruce's new consigliere, whatever tiny shreds of information they could to allow them to make an informed decision. Requests came into Hoffman for more information. Hoffman, as instructed, stuck to his guns and stonewalled. The changes were adopted and a new veil of secrecy descended on the house of Lazard.

KIM FENNEBRESQUE'S CONCERNS aside, Bruce clearly thought there were still Great Men available. Soon after taking over, he went into recruiting overdrive, ignoring the fact that other firms were madly cutting excess bankers to reduce costs. Hiring new bankers would, of course, further reduce Lazard's profitability, but Bruce did not care about that. He was determined to build Lazard's long-term equity value at the cost of its short-term profitability. Michel made the mistake of thinking that the short-term incentives he gave Bruce—an increasing percentage of higher profits—would be a bigger driver of his behavior than the 8 percent ownership he had. Instead, Bruce was determined to make Lazard relevant again by finding the next generation of Great Men; only, it turns out, the ones he ended up recruiting to Lazard bore an uncanny resemblance to his longtime band of banking brothers.

One week after taking over Lazard, Bruce recruited six bankers from DKW. Five of them—Neal Lerner, Michael Gottschalk, Douglas

Taylor, Steve Campbell, and Justin Milberg—had resigned, and Bruce rewarded them with fat, guaranteed pay packages. No firm was doing such things in January 2002, let alone one that had been on the brink of financial disaster the entire previous year. He also reportedly paid this group a total of $10 million to get them out of their existing DKW contracts. Campbell reportedly was to be paid $3 million per year plus "several million dollars in additional compensation" plus between 0.5 and 1 percent of the Lazard equity. The other bankers were to receive compensation packages of several million dollars per year plus equity. They were then sent on "gardening leave" and did not start at the firm until April. The sixth DKW banker, and the most senior—Jeff Rosen—was still negotiating with Bruce, as his existing pay package at DKW, where he was a vice chairman and head of investment banking in continental Europe, was more complicated. Those negotiations lasted but a few days longer. On January 14, Rosen, a founder of Wasserstein Perella, announced he, too, was joining Bruce at Lazard. The same day, Bruce also announced he was *rehiring* Dave Tashjian, the former head of capital markets who had been fired by Loomis two months before and remained a consultant to the firm. Tashjian had once worked at Wasserstein Perella, too, as the head high-yield trader. Ironically, had Loomis not fired him, Tashjian would have been at the firm when the goodwill points were distributed and would have fared far better than he did in his negotiations with the firm in mid-January. Alasdair Nisbet, also from DKW, was hired as managing director in London.

In February, Bruce was successful in recruiting Chuck Ward, the co-head of investment banking at First Boston, to Lazard as president. Ward, who had worked with Bruce at First Boston and then Wasserstein Perella (before returning to First Boston), got a pay package reported to be $7 million per year. Of these FOB hires, one Lazard banker wrote to a chat room: "With super rich contracts for the next few years and equity stakes in the company, what incentives do they have to do anything esp[ecially] since Lazard will most probably be sold within the next couple of years? Just sit back . . . get chilled . . . enjoy the expense accounts and wait for the acquiring firm to accelerate their guaranteed contracts. At best we cruise at current levels, but most probably the increased overhead and politics will mean tougher times."

Bruce's first unscripted challenge as the new head of Lazard came on the morning of February 28, when Michael Weinstock, Andrew Herenstein, and Chris Santana announced they were quitting the firm within hours to join Bruce's friend Steve Rattner at the Quadrangle Group, Steve's two-year-old private-equity firm. In October 2001, Weinstock and Herenstein, who had previously been Lazard's highly regarded distressed-debt research analysts, became the key professionals of Lazard's new Debt Recovery Fund. Weinstock and Herenstein not only had helped Lazard recruit outside investors but also were the ones primarily responsible for making the fund's investments in distressed securities. Santana was the fund's head of trading. By the time the trio split for Quadrangle, the fund had amassed some $280 million, most of which had come from outside investors. Lazard had spent $8 million on start-up costs to get the fund going.

On the day Weinstock and Herenstein quit, Steve called Lazard and told the firm that the men had signed employment contracts with Quadrangle and would be starting a distressed fund at his firm. He also said that Lazard had "little choice but to transfer the Fund and its assets to Quadrangle where they could be managed by Weinstock and Herenstein." If Lazard chose not to do this, Steve reasoned, the fund's "partners would suffer severe harm, and the Fund would likely be destroyed." Bruce ignored Steve's threat. Instead, he decided to wind up the fund in an orderly manner. He also decided to sue Weinstock and Herenstein. Lawyers for Lazard alleged, among other things, that the two men violated the "fiduciary and contractual duties" they owed the fund, "and their failure to disclose their consideration of their possible departure is alleged to have been fraudulent." In August 2004, Judge Leo Strine, vice chancellor of the Delaware Court of Chancery, threw the case out (except for a small dispute over the taking of supposed confidential information). "What [Weinstock and Herenstein] are alleged to have done wrong is to have plotted their departure from the Fund in order to seek what they perceived as a better opportunity elsewhere, and to have executed their departure in a manner that made it difficult for Lazard to continue to run the Fund itself and that therefore gave Lazard an incentive to accede to the suggestion that the Fund be transferred to Quadrangle," Strine wrote. "Candidly, I find this argument rather astounding."

Strine blamed Lazard for not "adequately" planning for the potential departure of Weinstock and Herenstein, who were not under contract and were therefore, of course, free to leave at any time without notice, just as Lazard was free to fire the two at any time without notice. The count that Strine allowed to proceed—on the question of confidential information—was later settled. Bruce also sued Steve in Bermuda, but Lazard lost there as well. Lazard was required to pay the legal fees of Weinstock and Herenstein since the firm had indemnified them. Bruce paid some, but not all, of what Lazard owed Quadrangle. Michel said that had he still been in day-to-day control of Lazard, he would not have pursued the legal option. "I've never sued anybody," he said. Still, he was not at all pleased with the way the former Lazard professionals handled their swift departure. Michel said the high-yield group that Weinstock and Herenstein were part of made about $30 million annually for the firm. When the two men urged the firm to set up the distressed fund, and to close the high-yield department, the firm agreed. The $30 million in profits turned into $15 million of losses as the fund was being established. The expectation was, of course, that the fees and profits from the fund would more than make up for the loss of the $30 million. "And then within minutes of them being ready to do a fund, they left," Michel said. "I found that, at the very least, inelegant frankly. Inelegant. In my way, this is a very severe condemnation, because in life you have to try to act decently."

The first outside hire who had not previously worked with Bruce came in March, when Bruce hired George Bilicic, then thirty-eight, from Merrill Lynch, to run Lazard's utility banking effort. Bilicic had been at Merrill for sixteen months after years at one of Bruce's other alma maters, Cravath, Swaine & Moore. Bruce also hired Perk Hixon, then forty-three, as a managing director from First Boston. In November 2002, he hired three "senior media bankers" from Merrill as new Lazard partners. In sum, he hired twenty-four new partners in eleven months. "People are cheap at the moment," he told the *Financial Times*. Along with his recruiting drive, Wasserstein called his first global meeting of all 150 Lazard partners, many of whom had never before met. "No more politics," Wasserstein declared again. "From now on we focus on clients." Of course, by reassembling his brood, Bruce had made Lazard as political as ever, much to the fear and frustration of the longtime Lazard partners, who felt very much alienated by his unilateral moves and the fact that the new hires were rewarded with large contracts and a disproportionate amount of the equity.

An eerie new dynamic was emerging inside the firm: there were all these new partners with explicit loyalty to Bruce who had been hired without their "teams," and so, in order to get anything done, they had to figure out a way to maneuver around the old Lazard partners, who by and large had no particular affinity for Bruce, to get access to the very limited resources. At the same time, the old partners and the new ones, many of whom were generalists, had to figure out who was going to call on which clients, all without upsetting the new partners who were close to Bruce, the absolute monarch.

In addition to upsetting the working partners, Bruce's hiring spree was also annoying the capitalists, such as Michel, Bernheim, and Guyot, who were beginning to figure out that the large guaranteed pay contracts were likely to mean Lazard would be hard-pressed to make money in 2002, a fact that was a serious threat to their normal annual dividend stream and something that had never happened in the post–World War II era of the firm—yet another example of how Bruce had outfoxed Michel.

One day in mid-April, in the midst of Bruce's manic hiring, Adrian Evans, the much-admired ten-year Lazard partner in London who briefly took over as Lazard's chief operating officer after Loomis's resignation and before Bruce took over, went out for an early-evening jog in the environs of his Eaton Square home in London. When he got back from his run, he collapsed on the stairs, and with his wife watching, he announced, "I'm gone." Evans had died of a heart attack, at age sixty, leaving his wife, two daughters, and two stepsons. At his memorial service in London, Verey, the former head of Lazard in London, remembered Evans—often described by his colleagues as "Verey's brain"—as a man who had the ability to make everyone feel as if he was your best friend. Michel did not attend the memorial service.

Soon thereafter, Bruce held a meeting at Paris's Bristol Hotel for about seventy managing directors to discuss ways to improve cross-border marketing and deal flow. "Historically, people had talked about the business in New York or the business in Paris," Chuck Ward said. "They never really talked about the telecom business or the media business." Now, he said, "we have industry groups really talking to each other on a global basis." After the meeting at the Bristol, Michel invited his partners to his fabulous *maison particulier* on Rue Saint-Guillaume for dinner, wine, and sumptuous surroundings. "He's the only guy that will serve '61 Petrus at the bar," said longtime partner Al Garner.

Bruce, meanwhile, who was still living in London during 2002, was not making many friends there. In July, he fired six managing directors in London, out of twenty-two, a move that caused one London securities lawyer to tell the *Financial News,* "After this, no corporate financier, however senior, can feel totally secure." The six were given a week to vacate their offices. The firings may have been harsh, but one European Lazard banker applauded them. "Recent layoffs of MDs were necessary and will encourage young and ambitious VPs and associates to push their way up," he wrote to a blog. "Deal flow improving after a difficult first half. Overall the franchise remains strong and confidence is pretty high that the firm will recover." But another banker, in London, was not so sure. "Morale is pretty low," he wrote. "And people are waiting when their turn will come to be sacked . . . There is no improvement in the situation in London."

Wasserstein also moved quickly, some say too quickly—two weeks, start to finish—in the summer of 2002 to lease, for Lazard's European headquarters in London, a brand-new seventy-thousand-square-foot modernist building on Stratton Street in the West End. It was the largest real estate transaction in the West End of London in ten years. The *Daily Telegraph* described the Mayfair offices as "some of the plushest used by any investment bank in London." Word is that Bruce spent close to $25 million outfitting the new offices (but that was apparently not enough to keep the telephone system from malfunctioning in the summer of 2003). Lazard agreed to pay £76 per square foot to lease the space for twenty years, or a total of about £5.3 million a year in rent (more than $9 million), a far distance indeed from the Dickensian ideal set by André Meyer both at the spartan 44 Wall Street and at One Rockefeller Plaza and from his pledge that Lazard would never pay more than $7.75 per square foot for office space. The problem was that Lazard still had about five years left on the lease at its *old* office building, at 21 Moorfields, a nondescript and ratty monster in the City of London. As a result of Bruce's move, Lazard had much more space in London than it needed. (Some of the old space was finally subleased in 2005.) Bruce also ordered the long-overdue renovation of the sacred *La Maison* on the Boulevard Haussmann. "Instead of a dimly lit waiting room with worn couches, the building now features marble floors, tall white columns, recessed lighting and beige furniture," *Bloomberg* reported. "Three blond female receptionists have replaced the aging male guards who used to greet visitors from behind a glass partition."

The combination of the pricey London lease, the aggressive recruiting effort, and the continued decline in the M&A business led to an almost immediate clash between Bruce and Michel over the way Bruce was running the firm. Michel knew—or certainly should have known—that Bruce intended to invest money in the hiring of new partners. What he may not have counted on, though, was how aggressively Bruce would do so, essentially by having the old partners and the capitalists pay for it. The leasing of the new London office was downright excessive in Michel's view. If nothing else, like André before him, Michel had always believed that the Lazard offices should be modest, if for no other reason than that clients would not get the impression that all of their fees were being spent on expensive furnishings. Profits should go into the partners' pockets, Michel believed, and then could be spent as they saw fit in multiple homes and priceless art collections. Michel subscribed to Descartes' dictum "He lives well who is well hidden." Bruce clearly felt money needed to be spent for elegant office space as well, especially when he could use the capitalists' money to pay for it all.

Not surprisingly, the two men fought over these money issues. "Michel was torn about that," one senior partner said.

> On one hand, he desperately knew that the only way the U.S. or any part of the firm was going to come back was to hire. In fact, we should have done much more in Europe than we did, in retrospect. On the other hand, he didn't like the idea that we were spending any money to do it. . . . The discussions were very antagonistic almost from the beginning. And it wasn't only Michel; it was all the old historical capitalists. They couldn't understand the concept that one had to reinvest to rebuild the firm. . . . I also think Michel was too clever by half when he cut his deal with Bruce. I think fundamentally he thought that putting Bruce on the same system he, Michel, was on—that is, he'd make more money if the firm made more money—would motivate Bruce. But it didn't. What motivated Bruce was making the firm successful, not short-term profits.

To help pay for his spending spree, Bruce hit upon a formula that had worked brilliantly at Wasserstein Perella: that of selling a minority stake in the firm to a foreign investor. In September 2002, he did it at Lazard when he came to Milan for the first time and Braggiotti introduced him to IntesaBci, Italy's largest commercial bank and the successor of Banca Commerciale Italiana, Braggiotti's father's bank. In return for Intesa's $300 million investment, Lazard set up an investment banking joint venture in Italy—with Braggiotti as chairman—combining Intesa's capital with Lazard's investment banking business in the country. The deal had two parts. First, Bruce agreed to contribute the sixty Lazard employees working in Italy to the joint venture with Intesa, which agreed to pay Lazard $150 million—$100 million in equity and $50 million in the form of a subordinated note. Lazard retained 60 percent ownership in the operation and day-to-day management control. Intesa owned 40 percent of the venture. In the second part of the deal, Intesa also agreed to invest an *additional* $150 million into Lazard itself, in exchange for a note convertible into 3 percent of the firm's equity.

The deal marked the end of Lazard's fifty-year association with Mediobanca in Italy. Still, Lazard partners were astounded at the price Intesa was willing to pay for this tiny piece of Lazard but were appreciative of the addition to the firm's capital at a time when the overall business was suffering and Bruce was luring new bankers with expensive guarantees. The Intesa price—$50 million for each 1 percent of Lazard—valued the equity of the entire firm at a nifty $5 billion, 25 percent higher than the Ernst & Young valuation of $4 billion that Michel had scoffed at earlier and 32 percent higher than the $3.8 billion valuation that Bruce had told new recruits the firm was worth (the premium, though, was in line with other convertible preferred financings at the time). Some partners saw the deal as the Italians throwing the firm a much-needed financial lifeline. "Bruce was on a spending spree and needed the money," one partner said. Another added, "Liquidity doesn't last forever. I mean, you just can't go on spending more than you make, you know, and that's why the Intesa sale was such a huge fucking deal because basically it was a lifeline to run the firm. There was a couple of hundred million bucks that they could continue to spend and spend and spend. And that's the best thing Bruce did." (By the summer of 2005 the Intesa deal was in shambles; the firms unwound the joint venture in the first quarter of 2006.)

The Intesa deal put a delightful and unexpected exclamation point on the end of Bruce's first year at the helm. He had reeled in $300 million of capital for Lazard at a very healthy price, especially given the firm's poor performance in the past two years. He was no doubt feeling ebullient when he gathered his seven lieutenants in his New York office for an orchestrated interview with the *Financial Times* in December 2002. And this led to a little blithering. "We have a spiritual ethos that creates a cohesion," Bruce served up. Even the New York CEO, Ken Jacobs, usually inscrutable and unemotional, explained that despite the decline in the M&A market, Lazard was winning mandates. He cited Lazard's role in Pfizer's $60 billion acquisition of Pharmacia, the largest deal of the year (Pfizer was a longtime client of the departed Felix and was one of the very few clients that he handed off to one of his partners, in this case Steve Golub), and made reference to Lazard advising Microsoft on a number of deals (the former Lazard partner Richard Emerson was head of M&A at Microsoft). Lazard was also benefiting from the surge in corporate bankruptcy filings; revenues in its financial restructuring business surged to $125 million in 2002, up from $55 million the year before (helping to offset the $100 million decline in M&A revenues to $393 million in 2002, from $492 million in 2001). The firm's leaders were trumpeting their success, though. "When you look across Wall Street, we are the hot investment bank," Jacobs boasted.

Bruce also sat down with the *Wall Street Journal* for an end-of-year interview. He defended his hiring binge. "Some people see talented people as difficult," he said. "I just see them as talented." He also said that a sale of the firm was not imminent. "Selling would be a pretty easy thing to do but that's not what's under contemplation," he said. "I'm more interested in implementing my plans and seeing how we develop."

Bruce's cheerleading masked the reality of the firm's financial picture at the end of 2002. By revamping Lazard's compensation structure to rely heavily on guaranteed contractual arrangements with the working partners rather than paying them a percentage of the profits, Bruce had effectively upended the firm's P&L statement. Whereas the firm had not lost money since the dark days of World War II, Lazard lost $100 million in its first year with Bruce as CEO. Of course, Bruce, the *Übermensch,* refused to look at it as a loss. He preferred to describe what happened as having "reinvested extensively in our future," according to a memo on the 2002 performance sent around to the partners by Michael Castellano, the firm's new CFO. But there was no getting around what was happening. Castellano's own writing proclaimed that the firm had a "good year" in 2002 "in a difficult environment" with revenues essentially flat from 2001, at $1.166 billion, and explained that the firm's "pre-tax operating profit before Managing Director compensation" was $337 million, which needed to be reduced by another $40 million due to minority rights of others to Lazard's profitability, leaving some $297 million of profit before making payments to the managing directors. The problem—ignored explicitly by Castellano in his memo—was that the payments made to Lazard's 160 worldwide managing directors in 2002 amounted to $395 million, leaving shareholders with a loss of roughly $100 million. Now, this was not much of a problem for the working partners, who still got their multimillion-dollar payouts and controlled some 60 percent of the firm's equity.

The problem instead arose for the nonworking partners, the capitalists, such as Michel, who controlled about 40 percent of the firm's equity and had nothing to show for 2002 but the losses Bruce had created. For the first time ever, Michel and his cronies received nothing from the firm aside from the $8 million in dividend payments on their $100 million preferred stock investment made at Loomis's behest in 2001. Bruce and Castellano knew the allocation of this $100 million loss to partners' capital accounts could be a problem, especially for those historical partners who had accumulated a fair amount of capital in these accounts. To try to assuage these partners' concerns, Bruce and Castellano created something called "memo capital," short for "memorandum capital deferred compensation," an accounting gimmick designed to create shadow equity for the increasingly disgruntled historical partners. The accounts would be credited with a fixed return of 6 percent per year. To get the allocation and the account, a partner had to execute an agreement with the firm.

The memo capital was to be paid out over three years after a partner left, so Bruce actually began making the argument that historical partners were better off from a tax point of view having their existing capital accounts depleted and the new accounts created that were akin to a deferred compensation scheme. "Bullshit capital" is how one partner referred to this idea. But there was a coherent explanation for it. "Michel wasn't going to watch his capital account get fucking wiped out," one partner said. "So they created a preferred level of capital. So as the capital gets rammed down, there was a preferred level of capital re-created so they paid you as if you still had your capital to make you indifferent. They would have had a riot because none of the partners had any say as to how the money was spent. That affected some guys differently than other guys. And frankly the guys who were getting all the money were stealing the money out of the other guys' capital accounts. Michel was furious."

David Verey described what Bruce accomplished as akin to a Communist revolution in the right ventricle of capitalism. The working partners at Lazard—the workers—with virtually no capital at risk in the business had picked clean the pockets of the nonworking partners with all the capital at risk—the capitalists—and there wasn't a thing the capitalists could do about it. The sheer brilliance of the workers' revolution that Bruce led inside Lazard—the blueprint of which Michel had directly negotiated with him—commanded admiration. And Bruce was only warming up.

Michel's fury continued into 2003, as did Bruce's prodigious hiring. Bruce's first move of the new year came as the dust was settling on the previous year's bonuses at Merrill Lynch. In February, Bruce airlifted a team of nine bankers—five of whom were managing directors—from Merrill to create a new business for Lazard in the blazingly hot area of raising capital, for a fee, for private-equity and hedge funds. (Eventually fourteen former Merrill employees from this area joined Lazard.) While Lazard had never before been in this business, the proliferation of buyout funds and hedge funds—and huge amounts of capital flowing to them—made the business of raising money for them extremely attractive.

But there were consequences to Bruce's aggressive move, namely the decimation of Merrill's market-share-leading fund-raising practice.

At first, Merrill tried to reach an amicable solution with Lazard. On February 14—a day after the resignations—a Merrill internal lawyer FedExed a letter to Charles Stonehill, the newly installed head of Global Capital Markets, asking Stonehill, "in order for Merrill Lynch to even consider forgoing litigation," to provide him with written assurance that Lazard would not hire any more Merrill bankers, would not "contact or solicit" any Merrill clients or prospective clients the former employees "knew of" while at Merrill, and would not further hinder Merrill's ability to do business in this area. Stonehill, with the help of Dave Tashjian, had recruited each of the former Merrill employees. He assured the Merrill lawyer the "Former Employees" would "respect their legal obligations" to Merrill and that Lazard had no further intention of hiring Merrill employees into the new "Private Equity Group." But Stonehill did not satisfy Merrill, which believed Lazard continued to ransack the Merrill business by hiring additional employees, by bad-mouthing the firm to clients, and by stealing confidential information.

On March 19, Merrill decided to sue Lazard and the nine bankers who left. In its amended statement of claim, as part of an NASD arbitration of the matter, Merrill stated that while all the facts were not then known, "the known facts compel the conclusion that the Former Employees breached their fiduciary obligations to Merrill Lynch and—aided and abetted by Lazard—conspired to destroy a Merrill Lynch business by misappropriating substantially all of its senior employees and clients and Merrill Lynch's Confidential Information." Merrill claimed that as they were walking out the door to go to Lazard, the bankers took with them many confidential investor profiles, which Merrill claimed had been painstakingly assembled over many years and contained valuable information about the leading investors in private-equity and hedge funds, how they made their investment decisions, and what funds they had invested in—in sum, the very essence of proprietary information.

"As part of their anticompetitive scheme," the suit alleged, "between about 6:28 a.m. and 6:46 a.m. on January 28, 2003, just days before resigning en masse, respondent [Robert] White [Jr., a Merrill vice president in London] sent eight e-mails containing numerous files in a compressed 'zip' format to respondent [Scott A.] Church [a sixteen-year Merrill managing director in London], to himself at an off-site e-mail address, and to Jessica White, who is White's wife. Those files that White downloaded and e-mailed to himself, his wife and to Church at off-site e-mail locations contained not less than 246 Investor Profiles" of investors globally who invest in such funds. Merrill claimed White would have had no reason to download these files but for "a scheme to steal the business" of the Merrill group they were leaving. The files were then copied to Lazard's computers. Merrill even claimed that Bruce himself had met with a potential client looking to hire a banker to raise a new fund and told the client that Merrill could no longer perform that function but Lazard could since it had recently hired the fourteen bankers from Merrill.

Resolution came swiftly enough, at the end of April. First, a New York state judge ordered that Lazard return to Merrill the computer files that the former employees had lifted, although the judge did not bar Lazard from using the information contained in them if that information could be remembered. To settle the arbitration case, Bruce was said to have gone to see Stan O'Neal, Merrill's CEO, to have apologized to him directly, and to have had Lazard pay Merrill a "seven-figure" dollar amount. Lazard viewed the settlement as the cost of doing business. "So what?" one Lazard partner said of the suit. "There are lawsuits all the time when you hire people." He said the business has been a good one for Lazard and the firm should have been in it far earlier.

Bruce kept on hiring. On the same day the judge ordered Lazard to return Merrill's electronic files, Bruce announced the hiring of another Wasserstein Perella alumnus, Gary Parr, then forty-six and a respected financial institutions banker at Morgan Stanley. Hiring Parr was a coup for Bruce. Parr was a true rainmaker in his industry and would help make up for the departure five years earlier of Ken Wilson to Goldman. Indeed, Lazard had been after Parr for years, but until Bruce gave him thirty-six million reasons to say yes to a Lazard offer, he had always said no.

He wasted little time in making Bruce look smart. In September, alongside his old firm Morgan Stanley, Parr advised John Hancock Financial Services on its $10 billion sale to Manulife Financial, one of the largest deals of 2003. Hancock insisted that Parr be added to the advisory team, regardless of where he happened to work. "I'm very appreciative that Hancock wanted my advice," Parr said at the time. Also in April, Bruce hired another old friend, Mike Biondi, to come to Lazard as chairman of investment banking. Just as he did at Wasserstein Perella, Bruce was handing out titles like straws. Lazard also hired Kevin McGrath from Deutsche Bank as a managing director in its new private fund advisory group. To help ensure that he got his side of the story out, Bruce hired, in September 2003, Rich Silverman as global head of corporate communications—another position Lazard never had before. Silverman reported directly to Bruce. (Bruce replaced Silverman with Judith Mackey in August 2006.)

Bloomberg Magazine, for one, decided that all of Bruce's hiring was merely a prelude to the sale of the company. In a February 2003 article, "Dressing Up Lazard," the magazine wondered if Bruce's aggressive efforts to reassemble his loyalists from First Boston and Wasserstein Perella—and then some—were just "to do one last deal: the sale of Lazard."

SINCE THE DAYS when Felix worked for Harold Geneen at ITT, Lazard has primarily been known for its M&A advisory prowess. Indeed, about 65 percent of its managing directors around the world today are M&A bankers. And M&A bankers have always run Lazard, whether when it was three separate firms or in its newly merged state. André, Felix, Steve, Loomis, David Verey, and Bruno Roger were all M&A bankers. Michel was not an M&A banker per se—he rarely worked on deals—but he thought of himself as a banker. Bruce and all of his deputy chairmen were M&A bankers. Bruce's focus—and much of the media attention, too—have been on whether he could restore the firm's luster by hiring a new breed of high-priced M&A bankers to replace the wave of talented ones that started leaving the firm in the wake of Felix's departure.

Despite the focus on M&A, Lazard has pursued other business opportunities over the years. Among them have been raising money for corporations and municipalities, investing capital in private companies for its own partners' accounts and those of other institutional investors, and managing the portfolios of individuals and institutions in public securities—the so-called asset management business. Indeed, aside from the M&A business, Lazard's asset management business has been its most important. At the end of 2002, Lazard managed $64 billion for institutions and wealthy individuals. And during 2001 and 2002, while the M&A business was suffering, the asset management business continued to produce a steady stream of profits, mostly from recurring management fees. The astounding declines in the troika of Lazard's other businesses—M&A, capital markets, and principal investing—during 2001 and 2002 made the importance of asset management disproportionate to the overall weal. In 2001, the money management business earned about $135 million, 93 percent of the firm's total profits of $145 million. In 2002, Lazard Asset Management, with its steady stream of annuities and fees, generated about $130 million, or about 65 percent of the entire firm's profits. Even before these difficult years for the firm as a whole, the asset management business steadily provided one-third to one-half of the firm's profits. "I wish I had Lazard's asset management franchise," said one former partner. "It kept Michel afloat. It is very well run—the hidden secret of Lazard." When Herb Gullquist and Norman Eig arrived at

Lazard in 1982 from Oppenheimer Capital to head Lazard Asset Management, the firm managed a modest $2 billion. As of November 2006, Lazard managed about $100 billion and was sixty-fourth on the 2004 *Institutional Investor* list of the three hundred largest money managers.

In 1997, Michel sought to merge the money management businesses of the three houses (as a prelude, one supposes, to the eventual merger of the houses themselves in 2000). He was able to merge the New York and London businesses under Eig and Gullquist's direction, but Paris balked. And Michel acquiesced. It remained a separate entity, under the name Lazard Frères Gestion, with around $17 billion of assets under management. As part of this quasi merger, Michel agreed, in yet another of his infamous side deals, to grant Eig and Gullquist an extraordinary 30 percent of Lazard Asset Management's profits, or 15 percent each. In 1998 alone, Lazard paid each man $15 million, which helps explain why Eig and Gullquist had among the largest capital accounts at the firm—more than $10 million each.

As, theoretically, a partner's capital account represents a 10 percent holdback of his accumulated paid compensation, a *$10 million* capital account would imply aggregate total compensation in excess of $100 million each for Eig and Gullquist. In 1998, Eig and Gullquist hired William von Mueffling to start a second hedge fund, called Lazard European Opportunities. (Lazard first offered investors a hedge fund in 1991.) In its first full year, von Mueffling's fund returned 182 percent for its investors. The fund stopped taking new investors after it had reached $1 billion in assets in August 2000. Von Mueffling began another hedge fund, Lazard Worldwide Opportunities, in 2001, and even though it lost 14.4 percent the first year—a difficult market for all—in 2002 it increased 20 percent. The importance of von Mueffling's hedge funds to the firm's overall profitability was quickly becoming apparent. In the summer of 2001, amid all the other turmoil at the firm, John Reinsberg, another partner in asset management, hatched a scheme where he would replace Eig and Gullquist as CEO of asset management and von Mueffling would become chief investment officer. Loomis reportedly took the idea to Michel, but Michel was busy with his own schemes—specifically working on jettisoning Loomis in favor of hiring Wasserstein. The idea died. But the dissatisfaction among the asset management team with how they were being compensated was one of the chronic problems in 2001.

When Bruce took over as CEO in January 2002, he immediately had to grapple with the ongoing demands of the asset management group for its own equity incentive plan. For years, Eig and Gullquist had conveyed the importance of having such a plan as a way to retain and reward portfolio managers, many of whom were fleeing the firm. In December 2002, Bruce floated a trial balloon with the *Financial Times* about his desire to take public the asset management business, which he valued at $2 billion. He viewed this partial IPO as a way to raise capital for Lazard and refocus its business on investment banking. As a prelude to any planned public offering, Bruce and Eig settled on the idea of granting the asset managers equity that would attain value upon a sale or IPO of the business. Eig doled out the packages, but von Mueffling, then thirty-five, and his hedge fund teams protested and demanded from Eig a greater serving of equity. When Eig refused, von Mueffling quit. Even Bruce's personal appeal to von Mueffling—"What can I do to get you to stay?" he asked—failed, and the star manager left to form his own hedge fund business along with most of his team.

"Norman Eig misread the whole situation," one insider said. "There was a huge amount of complacency. He thought nobody would leave because of the job market. It was a mistake." Another observer said, "These departures will be catastrophic for Lazard's revenue stream. These guys were rock stars and you replace them with people who will just push buttons." The possibility of a near-term IPO for asset management evaporated when von Mueffling and his team left the 30 Rock offices. Within eight months, 75 percent of the assets in Lazard's $4 billion hedge funds had flowed right out the door, too, most of it following von Mueffling.

In October 2003, Gullquist announced his intention to retire, setting off another round of political infighting to decide his successor. Bruce had previously—and very quietly—lured an old confidant, Ashish Bhutani, the former co-CEO of DKW North America, to be his adviser for "strategic planning" and quickly installed him in the asset management business, initially as part of an "oversight" committee. There was very little press coverage of his hiring. Word was that Bhutani would succeed Eig and Gullquist, but several of the senior asset managers objected vigorously to that appointment. A solution was promised for November. Finally, in March 2004, Bruce announced that along with a rash of new hires for LAM, Eig would move up to become chairman and Bhutani would be the new CEO. Soon after this announcement, in another "serious blow," Simon Roberts, LAM's head of U.K. equities, quit to join BlueCrest, a hedge fund. "What happened at LAM shows that even when a traditional money management firm is able to build a successful hedge fund business, the cultural and compensation issues can still come back to haunt you," one hedge fund consultant told *Institutional Investor.*

Around the time Bruce got the situation at Lazard Asset Management under his control and despite his many public denials on the matter, he made a preliminary foray into the market to sniff around to see if any firms on Wall Street had an interest in buying Lazard. His first visit, accompanied by Gary Parr, was to none other than Dick Fuld at Lehman Brothers. According to Goldman's Ken Wilson:

> Bruce came in and they started to talk, and Bruce said, "Look, the purpose of this meeting is we want to get together and have you know something more about our firm, so if we started to want to do anything, we've already done sort of the homework, this sort of thing." Dick, who hates Bruce, said, "Cut the shit, Bruce. You're here to sell your fucking firm. So how much do you think it's worth?" They go into this discussion of the amount of synergies that are going to come out as $500 million and you capitalize it and Lazard's worth $6 billion or $7 billion. And Dick says, "You know, I can see why you're such a shitty M&A banker. Why you give such bad fucking advice. If this is what you tell people, you gotta be out of your fucking mind." It went just downhill from there.

Two weeks later, according to Wilson, Michel called Fuld and said, " 'You know Bruce, he knows all along the right value for Lazard is $4 billion.' Dick says, 'Look, that could very well be the case. I know you have a lot of options, so what I think you should do is to explore all of your options. If nothing comes back, maybe we can talk, but it would be at a value well below $4 billion, and a good portion of the payments would be contingent.' [Fuld] never heard back." Bruce was also said to have spoken with Chuck Prince, the CEO of Citigroup. And with John Bond at HSBC, who reportedly said his meeting with Bruce was the "worst business meeting he ever had." And with Kenneth Lewis at Bank of America, who referred to Bruce as a "sleazoid." According to Wilson, Bruce had shopped Lazard around to such an extent that "it's just generally known it's a bid-wanted situation."

Perhaps the biggest news Bruce made in 2003 had nothing to do with Lazard at all, and illustrates how good he is at getting what he wants, repeatedly. Through Wasserstein & Co., his $2 billion private-equity firm that he kept for himself when he sold Wasserstein Perella to the Germans, Bruce owns a number of industry-focused publications, including the *New York Law Journal*, the *American Lawyer*, and the *Daily Deal* (an M&A industry publication). In August 2005, Wasserstein & Co. paid $385 million to buy seventy industry publications, such as *Beef* and *Tele-*

phony from Primedia, the struggling media company owned by the buyout mogul Henry Kravis. (In July 2007, Bruce sold *American Lawyer* and its parent company, American Lawyer Media, for about $630 million to a U.K. publisher, Incisive Media.)

But what got the media itself buzzing with amazement was Bruce's winning the auction for Kravis's *New York* magazine in December 2003. True, he agreed to pay more than anyone else—$55 million, a high price by any standard for a magazine then making about $1 million of profit. But he also emerged out of the auction's wings, using his long-standing and complicated relationship with Kravis, and snatched it out of the hands of the self-proclaimed winners—a high-powered investor group comprising such journalistic entrepreneurs as Mort Zuckerman, Harvey Weinstein, Nelson Peltz, Donny Deutsch, and Michael Wolff. Bruce made headlines and confirmed, yet again, his deal-making prowess. "It has to be considered brilliant that he managed to hide his interest so well," one media investment banker told Bruce's *Daily Deal*. "He lay low with the press, then came storming out of the shadows." No doubt his access to Kravis didn't hurt Bruce's ability to make sure he got the last look at the property. "What do you gain by having people know what you are doing before you do it?" Bruce said. He cited two reasons why he was able to win. First, he said, "We should be able to execute deals well, if nothing else." Without flinching, he then said his personal integrity was the key to his victory. "It basically goes to confidence," he said. "In other words, it's a funny business, but people trust certain other people because if they say something, they believe that they create a credibility over years, so I think partly that if I make a commitment, people know it will happen."

The *New York Times* found Bruce "maddeningly vague" about why he bought the magazine. John Huey, editorial director of Time Inc., said of the sale: "Certainly, if you look at it from a business point of view, it is insignificant. But because it is New York, with the New York media covering the sale of *New York* magazine, it takes on an aura that defies all logic." Curiously, Bruce bought *New York* not through Wasserstein & Co. but through a series of personal trusts set up for the benefit of his children, the same trusts perhaps that own the majority of his stake in Lazard.

People were left scratching their heads by the high price Bruce agreed to pay for the magazine, which some considered oceanfront property. "It's really weird," one private-equity investor commented. "I don't understand why he is doing it. This may be an interesting hobby but it is not an investment." Mark Edmiston, an investment banker specializing in media deals, thought Bruce's purchase of *New York* was symptomatic of what he perceives to be a growing phenomenon in the magazine business. "A lot of them are big ego trips," he said. "You know, you get to own a magazine about your friends and neighbors, and be the king of your universe. This is a little bit of what we call the *New York* magazine syndrome . . . meaning I don't think Bruce Wasserstein bought *New York* magazine to get richer. . . . Obviously, the price of the magazine is not justified by the facts."

The conventional wisdom on this point seems to be that even though Henry Kravis couldn't make *New York* work as a financial enterprise, Bruce believed that by focusing on more upscale stories about business and fashion, the magazine would be able to benefit from the improving metropolitan economy. He also intended to revamp the magazine's ineffectual Web site. "At best, the magazine is the embodiment of New York, a very exciting city," he told the *New York Times*. "All you have to do is be a good mirror of this city."

A question even more fundamental than whether Bruce overpaid for this one magazine is why the CEO of a Wall Street firm is permitted to make deals for his own private account, at his own personal and separate buyout shop, when he is running a twenty-five-hundred-person regulated securities firm. With a staff of about thirty in three offices (New York, Los Angeles, and Palo Alto), Wasserstein & Co. manages "approximately $2.0 billion of private equity and other assets" for individuals and institutions beyond just Bruce Wasserstein. The firm has been quite active in the past few years. Wasserstein & Co. bought the company that owns the Harry & David direct-mail fancy-food operation (a planned IPO is on hold) and Sportcraft, the maker of foosball and Ping-Pong tables. Along with Centre Partners, a buyout fund affiliated with Lazard, Wasserstein & Co. also owns American Seafoods, the largest harvester and at-sea processor of pollack and hake and the largest processor of catfish in the United States. In November 2006, one of Wasserstein & Co.'s portfolio companies announced the acquisition, for $530 million, of Penton Media, Inc., a portfolio of fifty trade magazines, eighty trade shows, and an array of online media sites.

Bruce is the firm's chairman, its principal owner, and its main beneficiary. His carefully crafted biography at the Wasserstein & Co. Web site makes no mention of his role at Lazard. Michel, who allowed Bruce a luxury no other Wall Street CEO would ever even contemplate, let alone be permitted by any self-respecting board of directors, said he didn't care whether Bruce had his own buyout firm as long as it didn't detract from his running Lazard. The third amended and restated operating agreement required Bruce to get Michel's "written consent" if he "desires to make available to Wasserstein & Co., Inc., any corporate opportunity of Lazard or any of its subsidiaries that arises from a relationship of Lazard or any of its subsidiaries or affiliates" other than any relationship Bruce may have had with Lazard prior to November 15, 2001. Of course, what is not clear is what is meant by "any corporate opportunity." Can Wasserstein & Co. look at an investment or buyout that Lazard is also looking at, or that one of Lazard's funds is looking at? And this document, of course, says nothing about why he is permitted this conflicting dual role. Bruce even permitted Lazard managing director John Chachas, with *his* own investment company, Sand Springs Holdings, to be one of the lead investors in the February 2005 $8.5 million acquisition of Gump's, the famous San Francisco department store. And he permitted the superstar Gary Parr to be a meaningful investor in the February 2006 buyout of Fox-Pitt, Kelton, an investment banking *competitor* of Lazard's, from the insurance giant Swiss Re. The question is, why?

Others have wondered about this, too. Although the *New York* magazine purchase appears to have been made through a company that controls his family trusts—by an entity called New York Magazine Holdings—for some reason the vice chairman of Wasserstein & Co., Anup Bagaria, helped to negotiate the deal and is the CEO of New York Magazine Holdings. "Mr. Wasserstein has stated that he wants to take the magazine up-market and increase its business reporting," the *New York Observer* editorialized. "But how can he avoid the conflict between *New York*'s coverage of corporate America and the city's high-profile C.E.O.'s and investment bankers, and the fact that he runs an investment-banking firm that does business with dozens of companies as well as dozens of investment and commercial banks? . . . What will happen the next time there's a $20 million M. and A. fee on the table for Lazard, and *New York* is about to cover the comings and goings of the corporate C.E.O. whose company is paying the fee?" The question of Bruce's objectivity as a publisher is even more interesting considering that the *American Lawyer*, the *Daily Deal,* and *New York* aggressively cover the M&A business (indeed that is *all* the *Daily Deal* covers). One of Bruce's "friends" suggested the *New York* purchase was about ego and social influence. "I think that Bruce was surprised by how little cachet there has been in owning *American Lawyer* and the *Deal,*" he said. "This purchase should fix that."

Only time will tell whether Bruce, the former journalist who is on the Board of Visitors of the Columbia University Graduate School of Journalism, commits the cardinal sin of journalism, imposing prior restraints on his reporters who dare tack too close to windward. And yet an overt act may not even be necessary to have the desired chilling effect, as Great Men work in a landscape of great subtlety and nuance. In her reporting on Bruce's tactical victory for *New York,* Yvette Kantrow, who writes a media column for the *Daily Deal,* allowed how, "just to be clear, Media Maneuvers has absolutely no inside information on any of this, and if we did, we probably wouldn't say. Which is the point. As fun as this collision of dealmaking and the media is, this will be one Media Maneuver you won't read about here." Exactly.

One clue to why Bruce bought *New York* became apparent during the summer of 2005, when it was revealed that his son Ben would, after Labor Day, become the magazine's associate editor, the only associate editor. There is nothing unusual or nefarious in any of this, of course. It is no different from the Murdoch children working at News Corporation or the Sulzberger children working at the New York Times Company. The company that owns the magazine is private and is likely controlled by a trust whose beneficiary is Ben Wasserstein (so he in effect already owns the magazine). What is amusing, though, was the need of the new editor Adam Moss (whom Bruce had plucked from the *Times* after summarily dismissing Caroline Miller, the previous editor) to justify the hiring to his staff. On July 14, 2005, Moss sent an e-mail to the magazine's editorial department, which said in part:

> everybody,
>
> i am happy to announce that ben wasserstein will soon be joining our staff. as many of you know, ben is now an associate editor of vitals, where he helps edit/assign all the text (there's more of it than you think).
>
> for obvious reasons, i have had the opportunity to get to know ben over the last year. he has impressed me as a smart and lovely guy, a talented editor who wants to work hard and to learn. i have remarked to some of you that he'd be a perfect candidate for a job here if he weren't a wasserstein—and then recently, it began to seem like his last name was a pretty dumb reason not to hire him.

If the past is any prelude to the future, what will not be covered by Bruce Wasserstein's *New York* is the topic of Bruce Wasserstein's Lazard. (In June 2007, Ben Wasserstein left *New York* to be online editor of the *New Republic.*)

⁂

By January 2004, in his two years running the firm, Bruce had hired fifty-five new partners at a guaranteed pay of a total of at least $180 million. And by April 2004, the number of new partner hires was up to fifty-nine. "There's a view at the big firms that you can put any guy in a suit and go out and sell products," Wasserstein told the *Wall Street Journal* in partial justification of his hiring spree. "I believe it matters who's in the suit." But did Lazard have anything to show for its expenditures? M&A revenue increased to $420 million in 2003, from $393 million in 2002, a 7 percent increase. The firm increased to twenty-nine, in 2003, from twenty-one, in 2002, the number of deals it worked on greater than $1 billion in value (flat with 2001 and down from forty-seven in 1999). The firm's real success in 2003, though, was its restructuring business, where revenues increased to $245 million, from $125 million in 2002. Restructuring advisory powered the financial advisory business to operating income of $311 million in 2003, up 54 percent from $202 million in 2002. But Bruce had nothing to do with Lazard's restructuring business; Loomis had hired those partners. In the closely watched M&A league tables, according to *Bloomberg*, Lazard ranked seventh worldwide in 2003, the same as 2002 and up from twelfth in 2001—commendable but modest progress to be sure.

Parr hit the jackpot for the firm in January 2004, when he advised his longtime client Jamie Dimon on the $53 billion merger between Bank One and JPMorgan Chase. Lazard received a $20 million advisory fee when the deal closed in July 2004 (JPMorgan paid itself a $40 million fee). Between his A-Rod-like compensation package and his Bank One coup, Parr has reached iconic status. Not unlike Felix or Steve, he began the obligatory Great Man campaign of writing "thought" pieces for respected journals. His essay "Europe's Banks Do Not Have Easy Options" appeared in the *Financial Times* in June 2004.

Anecdotally, though, the firm's performance after two years with Bruce at the helm was mixed. Lazard advised Pfizer on its $60 billion acquisition of Pharmacia in July 2002, although that had nothing to do with Bruce or someone he had hired, either. But the bulked-up Lazard had missed out on many of the largest deals of the past few years, including some of those that ended up being worked on by former Lazard bankers: Comcast's $72 billion acquisition of AT&T Broadband (worked on by Steve; Felix was then on Comcast's board), Comcast's attempted $60 billion takeover of Disney (worked on by Steve and Felix, who by then had left the Comcast board), Cingular's $41 billion acquisition of AT&T Wireless (worked on by Felix and Michael Price), SBC's $16 billion acquisition of AT&T and SBC's $89 billion acquisition of Bell South (worked on by Felix and Michael Price), and, most painful perhaps, Sanofi's $65 billion acquisition of Aventis. Lazard was excluded from the deal because of its close ties to Pfizer. Yet both Sanofi and Aventis are French, and Lazard long dominated the merger advisory business in

France; and Merrill Lynch advised Sanofi, even though Merrill was also an adviser to Pfizer. Even the difficult Édouard Stern had a role in the deal. *Tout Paris* was abuzz with the fact that for the first time in some forty years, Lazard would not have a role in an M&A deal of such import to the French economy.

At a meeting of about a hundred Lazard partners held in late January 2004 at London's Claridge's hotel, Bruce said he would focus in 2004 on boosting revenue after spending the past two years rebuilding the firm. Michel sat next to him, stone-faced, during the presentation and said nothing, according to people there. Of course, that is in part due to Michel's poor decision, "after twenty-five years of blowing cigar smoke into every corner of the firm," to cede to Bruce operational control of the firm, leaving him only the ability to veto Bruce's rehiring, in 2007, or to veto a sale or merger of the firm as a whole.

What had Bruce squarely in Michel's crosshairs, though, was the genuine dispute the two men were having about the firm's financial performance during Bruce's first two years. Bruce thought the firm was doing fine—great even—and he pointed to the 54 percent increase in operating profit as proof. Michel thought the firm was being totally mismanaged for the benefit of the working partners, who owned 64 percent of the firm, at the expense of the capitalists, such as Eurazeo, Michel, and his French cronies, who owned the remaining 36 percent. "The capital partners are concerned because the capital position has been eroded by losses," one Lazard banker said.

For Michel, who in some years received more than $100 million *himself* from Lazard, Bruce's destruction of short-term profitability was infuriating, especially when he thought he had given Bruce the necessary financial incentives to return the firm to the robust profitability of years past. "You can understand that the capitalists are not very happy about all this," one observer told *Financial News*. "If you have a big illiquid asset, like the stake in Lazard that is paying no income, would you be happy?" Added another: "Lazard is doing very well for Wasserstein, the equity partners and particularly the new partners but not for the external shareholders." Bruce was completely unsympathetic. "You'd go to a board meeting and it was entirely Michel's guys," he told *BusinessWeek* in November 2006, not entirely accurately. "They'd say, 'We don't like hiring new people.' I'd say, 'Well, thank you very much.' "

Michel and Bruce were locked in a tense stalemate. Outsiders began to wonder whether Lazard would be Wasserstein's Waterloo. Would Michel jettison him as he had all the others? It was now obvious to the world that Michel was nearly impossible to work for and to work with.

And it was equally clear that his Chinese water torture had already commenced its insufferable dripping on Bruce's forehead, as evidenced by the start of a well-orchestrated press campaign against him. In February 2004, British newspapers began to report the growing rift between the two men. In addition to all the new partners hired, Michel was upset with Bruce because of the new London headquarters building, the inexplicable purchase of Panmure Gordon, a venerable London broking firm (sold a little more than a year later at a small profit), and the establishment of a European private-equity business based in London at a time when other Wall Street firms were jettisoning their captive private-equity units (this has since been disbanded after all the partners who were recruited left). Relations between the two were said to be "cordial" but "not warm, let alone intimate." In truth, they were no longer speaking.

The *New York Post* reported the dispute a few days later. "Bruce has done a decent job by motivating people, building the firm's brand and leading by example," one Lazard banker said. "But he's wrecking the balance sheet and spending the shareholders' money, and it's not clear what the long-term future is for the firm." A columnist at *Bloomberg.com* wondered how Michel could have expected otherwise from Bruce. He described their argument as "absurd." "If you hire a brash, aggressive Wall Street banker, there's not much point in turning squeamish when he starts acting like a brash, aggressive Wall Street banker," Matthew Lynn wrote. "It's in his blood. He's only delivering what he has always delivered, and what he has always promised. . . . Wasserstein's path at Lazard may well be troubling for the older bankers, and for its complex network of shareholders. The dividends they used to rely on may be drying up. But the foundations of the firm are being rebuilt. It's being dragged into the modern financial world, where working bankers expect to make at least as much money as their shareholders. That must be the right thing to do." He also predicted, in February 2004, that the likely solution for both sides would be a face-saving IPO. "Don't expect either Wasserstein or David-Weill to leave quietly," he concluded. "But any row will accelerate a public offering of Lazard. Wasserstein needs to solidify his control of the firm. And the older shareholders need to be given a dignified, and lucrative, exit route. Only an IPO can achieve that."

In March 2004, Michel dismissed talk of a war between him and Bruce and told the *Financial Times*, "Mr. Wasserstein is head of Lazard on a five-year contract and we hope he will return it to a money-making position as he expects to this year," and added, comfortingly, "There is no war between us." He also said, though—in classic Michel fashion—that Bruce had enjoyed "some successes but had not yet become a success."

He said that the "firm's improved position"—particularly in the States and Italy—had come at a "high cost," and "by definition it is not satisfactory to lose money after expenses, nor can it continue forever." The *Financial Times* editorialized that the "ungentlemanly tussle" between Michel and Bruce "raises questions over what investment bankers really do to justify the money they are paid."

This rather straightforward warning shot from Michel came a day before the scheduled board meetings to approve the $3.2 billion merger between two of Lazard's cascade of holding companies, Eurazeo and Rue Impériale, which had been announced in November 2003. The merger was the final step in a four-year process designed to simplify Lazard's byzantine ownership structure and came about chiefly as a result of the ongoing efforts of Jon Wood at UBS, the activist shareholder. After the merger with Rue Impériale, Eurazeo would become, essentially, a large publicly traded private-equity fund. Together, Michel and the onetime Lazard suitor Crédit Agricole would control 54 percent of the voting rights of Eurazeo.

Michel had a huge influence on Patrick Sayer, the forty-seven-year-old Eurazeo CEO. He had handpicked the "hyperkinetic" Sayer to be CEO in 2001 after he presided over the withering away of Lazard's media and telecom business in New York, following the burst of the telecom bubble and Rattner's departure to form Quadrangle. Sayer was in a particularly difficult position. On the one hand, he was a creation of Michel's and existed, in this context anyway, solely as long as the Sun King wished. On the other hand, he was the CEO of a publicly traded company, which, even in France, meant he must occasionally pay some homage to his public shareholders, who controlled 61 percent of the ownership and 46 percent of the vote. Although the merger diluted its ownership stake to 8.9 percent of all shares outstanding, from 11 percent, UBS still controlled 4.2 million shares and was the largest single public shareholder. Inasmuch as its minority stake in Lazard was a huge percentage of Eurazeo's portfolio, Sayer had to be mindful—on behalf of all shareholders—of its lack of liquidity and the lack of dividends. Indeed, the puny—1 percent—return that Eurazeo had received on its Lazard investment in 2003 had pushed down its share price. Some analysts believed that for Eurazeo to be perceived as a "serious player" in private equity, the firm had no choice but to sell its stake in Lazard.

In an effort to play to his public audience, Sayer said, on occasion, that he would sell the Lazard stake if appropriate. Few believed it would be that simple. In his first "message" to Eurazeo shareholders as the chairman of its supervisory board, Michel wrote: "I am gratified by the relationship of complete trust which exists between myself and the Executive Board, in particular, its chairman, Patrick Sayer. Indeed, when the proposal to simplify our corporate structure"—the merger between Eurazeo and Rue Impériale—"was presented to the Executive Board, it immediately elicited their full and enthusiastic support, together with a recommendation that it should be implemented as quickly as possible." For his part, Sayer added some fuel on March 8 when he told the *Daily Telegraph,* "If Lazard goes back to delivering the kind of profits it has in the past, it might be a good idea to hold on to the stake. If and when there is a liquidity event, which is something Eurazeo will have a say in, then we will have to look at it." He declined to answer when asked whether his comments meant he was unhappy with Lazard's performance.

THE DISPUTE—it was quickly turning into a civil war—between the shareholders of Lazard and its management, while unfathomable prior to Michel's decision to cede power to Bruce, is certainly not without precedent. Private, family-owned companies often face generational clashes, as do public companies, as evidenced by the raucous fight between the large pension fund shareholders of Disney and the Disney board of directors about whether to keep Michael Eisner as CEO. What's extraordinary in this instance is that Michel did this to himself by cutting a secret deal with Bruce, without his partners' input and ignoring their voluble warnings. In an effort to salve these open wounds, Michael Castellano, Lazard's CFO, wrote a memo to the nonworking partner shareholders on March 12 suggesting that perhaps they had overlooked some accounting benefits in 2003—to the tune of $47 million—as a result of a positive currency translation that ended up in their illiquid capital accounts. In addition, he reminded them that they had also received $22 million in cash, or a total of $69 million in both cash and noncash benefits. He added they may have "overlooked" an illiquid $41 million currency translation in 2002 as well, along with $20 million of cash, or $61 million that year. "Because we have not highlighted this translation gain in 2002 or 2003, it is possible that [nonworking partners] may not have focused on the total benefits and proceeds they received," Castellano wrote.

The appeal fell flat, since these shareholders correctly pointed out that their illiquid capital accounts were frozen unless they sold their equity stakes in Lazard or died. "Lazard management is currently leading an investment policy which we will judge in 2006," Michel told the *Wall Street Journal.* He said, in a separate interview, that the Castellano letters were just "window dressing" and a complete fabrication since he received no dividends whatsoever from the firm in 2002, 2003, and 2004, only a small amount of contractual interest on his capital (all of which formed the basis for Michel's amusing comment that he could no longer afford to buy art because he was "so poor"). The same day that Castellano sent his letter, Greenhill & Co., the small advisory boutique founded in 1996 by Robert Greenhill, had filed an IPO registration statement with the SEC that valued his firm at around $500 million. This was a watershed event, and not lost on anyone at Lazard, least of all Bruce Wasserstein. In the wake of the recent myriad of Wall Street scandals, boutique firms offering impartial, independent advice had once again been garnering an increasing share of corporate advisory business.

The dispute between Bruce and Michel carried on into the spring. On April 3, after the contents of Castellano's March 12 letter were leaked to the press, Patrick Sayer told the *Financial Times* that "we have been told that this year the bank will be back to profit after all the working partner costs. We would be happy to keep an investment which has been very attractive in the past." Michel added that "all votes on issues such as the renewal of Bruce Wasserstein's contract as head of Lazard or a transformation of the Lazard business must be taken by the majority of the Lazard board." And here he pointed out that Bruce had nominated five of the board members, Eurazeo could nominate two, and "I, Michel David-Weill, have the right to name four representatives."

Despite his promises to Michel, Bruce kept on hiring in 2004. After all, if one of the legendary Great Men offered you the once-in-a-lifetime shot to remake one of the most storied franchises in all of investment banking history, complete with a huge guaranteed compensation and an equity stake for when the firm gets sold, how could you ever turn that down? In April, Bruce recruited William Lewis, forty-seven, as co-chair of investment banking. Lewis, who ranked thirteenth on the *Fortune* list of Most Powerful Black Executives (his new partner Vernon Jordan ranked ninth), spent his entire twenty-four-year investment banking career at Morgan Stanley, where he became the first black partner and achieved that milestone in seven years, faster than any other person in the firm's history. Lewis had been co-head of Morgan Stanley's global banking group.

The Lewis appointment, which should have been huge news, curiously received only the slightest publicity—the *Wall Street Journal* failed to mention it, to say nothing of Bruce's *Daily Deal*—and was another unkind cut in the long-simmering feud between Wasserstein and Perella (Perella had just been appointed head of the department to which Lewis belonged). But it revealed plenty about just how dictatorial and absolute

Bruce's reign at Lazard had become. When the internal press release went around inside Lazard announcing Lewis's arrival, partners discovered that the e-mail had been marked in such a way as to prevent its being printed out or forwarded to others.

On May 5 Sayer told the Eurazeo shareholders at the annual meeting that there was a definite disagreement between Lazard's management and its shareholders about Bruce's strategy of paying large contracts for new partners in the face of a market slowdown. Speaking to the shareholders, he said, "There were differences over the timing of a return to profit." And, he added, Bruce's "investment strategy" would not be tolerated for much longer. The hostilities between Michel and Bruce surfaced again a week later, despite Michel's earlier statement that "there is no war between us," when arch letters between the two men were sent to the firm's partners, each in a separate interoffice envelope. The two envelopes were stapled together. The letters appeared, in this fashion, on a Friday afternoon. By the next morning, their contents were in the *Financial Times.*

The background for this particular spat was the once-a-year meeting of the "Members of Lazard LLC" scheduled for June 3, 2004, at 30 Rockefeller Plaza, the sole purpose of which was to have the members approve the Lazard LLC consolidated financial statements for the year ended December 31, 2003. On May 11, Michel wrote, "According to the financial statements, the net income allocable to members in 2003 was down 13 per cent and covered only some 60% of distributions. As a result the firm had a financial loss of about $150 million in 2003. A loss of this magnitude may impair the value of Lazard's goodwill. Unfortunately, the financial statements that are being submitted to the General Meeting of Members do not show this loss. Therefore, the financial statements for 2003 cannot, in my opinion, be approved." Michel had also sent around a notice for the general meeting.

On May 14, Bruce issued a sharp rebuke to Michel's notice and to his letter. "With regard to the notice and/or letter that you may have received," he wrote, "1. The notice is moot. Just like last year, no meeting will be held, as working partners with a profit and loss percentage have unanimously given me their proxy not to attend the meeting. Therefore this approach is rejected. 2. The letter is wrong. Our audited financials, prepared in accordance with US GAAP"—generally accepted accounting principles—"show a profit before distributions. Our core operating businesses were profitable by any measure. 3. The letter omitted to state that the 'capitalists' actually received distributions and allocated increases to their capital accounts that exceeded any costs." The letter continued by urging those with further questions to speak with Mike Castellano and exhorted the recipients of Michel's letter to treat it "with grace, humor and tolerance."

Some observers believed the civil war had already started, and the public release of these letters was but the latest evidence. One astute Lazard veteran observed, "This is Michel's greatest nightmare. Michel, who fancies himself a person of enormous style and standing, has clearly handed over the keys to the ape-man and he's horrified. He got snookered. And he was cornered. As soon as it was handed over, he went from being"—and here he adopted a rich-guy, French accent—"the head of the mysterious three houses of Lazard, the scion, to being a guy who got duped by this guy from Brooklyn. I think there is a deep hurt and humiliation and shame because Michel is very invested in his family, his friends. His pride is hugely wounded."

Michel didn't know better than to make this deal with Bruce because of "muscle memory," this observer continued.

> People become creatures of habit, of an environment, and of a position. And when circumstances change, their muscles don't automatically adjust to the new reality. Or to think about it another way: if the lights go on in a darkened room, your eyes don't automatically adjust to the fact that the lights are on, or the lights are off. He was able for so long, because of the structural power he held, to manipulate people and have people ultimately bend to his will. And I don't think he really understood that it all wasn't coming from his personality and his charm. It came from his power. . . . Michel confused his effectiveness, which came from a whole host of factors that were independent of his own strength, and didn't realize that Bruce was going to ultimately use every resource he was handed.

The *Economist* deemed it all "a poisonous mix" and wondered whether "Mr. Wasserstein is more interested in pushing Lazard up the league tables in preparation for a sale than in stable, long-term profits for the bank from loyal clients. Some shareholders might not want to see a sale. The problem is that Mr. Wasserstein's contract does not expire until the end of 2006. That leaves a lot of time for fighting."

Slowly, Bruce started to reveal his hand. In its May 24, 2004, issue, *Investment Dealers' Digest* said that in the wake of Greenhill's very successful $87.5 million IPO on May 5—the first of a Wall Street firm since Goldman Sachs went public in 1999—Lazard had started interviewing underwriters for its IPO and had begun drafting a registration statement.

Although it was late to the IPO story, the *Financial Times* appeared to be emerging as the combatants' favorite boxing ring. First, in May 2004, came the release of the curt letters regarding the firm's accounting statements; then, on June 16, followed the leak—obviously from the Bruce camp—that Lazard was being "besieged" by bankers from other Wall Street firms pitching for the IPO of Lazard, which valued the firm at more than $3 billion. The pretext for these pitches was of course Greenhill's successful IPO. The *subtext*, though, reflected the tactics of the Wasserstein mind. It's as if he and Michel were engaging in a global, three-dimensional chess match. "Tactics are universal," he told an interviewer in 1998.

Bruce knew the Lazard shareholders had been griping about illiquidity and lack of dividends. He knew that Eurazeo alone among the shareholders had a fiduciary responsibility with regard to its 20 percent stake in Lazard and that Eurazeo's pain would ratchet up exponentially as Bruce continued to "invest" in the business and not pay dividends. He knew that the well-compensated working partners were increasingly loyal to him but now had equity in the firm that they would want to have the opportunity to sell. He knew that, at seventy-one, Michel would have less and less energy to think about once again re-creating the firm if Bruce's contract were not renewed. He knew that Michel was increasingly unhappy about his unfettered spending. And he knew that Michel had no heirs interested in running the firm. In this context, even though Michel actually had a veto over an IPO—such a move had to be approved by a majority of the Lazard board, including a specific positive vote by Michel, Bruce, and one of the Eurazeo board members—the IPO solution began to look more and more attractive, even to Michel. And what better way for Bruce to orchestrate that outcome than to leak to the *Financial Times* the very private fact that Goldman Sachs, Morgan Stanley, Citigroup, UBS, and Lehman Brothers had had meetings with Bruce and his team to offer their views on how an IPO would be structured and at what valuation?

Rich Silverman, the Lazard spokesman, had no comment on the IPO stories. Three *unnamed* sources within the firm cooperated further. From a "senior member": "We are listening and evaluating." Another indicated the information was "valuable," and a third said, "We do expect significantly improved performance over the next 12–24 months so I doubt we would do it now but it is a topic for debate." Another added: "If he doesn't come up with a plan within the next year or so, there could be an exodus of bankers. It's a question of realization."

The fact that the *Financial Times* and the *Wall Street Journal*, the next day, would give such prominent coverage to a story about bankers simply coming to talk about the *possibility* of Lazard going public—something that happens literally all the time, with no fanfare whatsoever—spoke volumes about the enduring interest of the financial press in the Lazard machinations. "An IPO could . . . solve one of the biggest problems for Lazard head Bruce Wasserstein," the *Journal* wrote, "by giving him the wherewithal to pay a new cadre of big-name banking talent and soothe a group of agitated retired partners. . . . But a public offering could also renew the rancorous fight in the firm's executive suite, while threatening the austere, private identity that Lazard so vigorously promotes." The truth was that Bruce had started having discussions about the possibility of a Lazard IPO with the longtime Goldman partner and FOB Tom Tuft, who organized a team to begin analyzing the many complexities that such an offering would entail.

In the pre-Bruce days of Lazard, Michel would have definitively snuffed out the mere thought of entertaining an IPO—let alone promoting it in such an obvious and public way—well before it had reached the stage of bankers making presentations. When asked by the *New York Times* in 1998 if he would ever consider an IPO, Michel answered firmly, "I will never do it"—this after Steve had floated the idea. This time, though, Michel knew all about the meetings Bruce had with the Wall Street firms. The *Financial Times* editorial on the subject conveyed wisdom: "Even if Lazard does one day plump for an IPO, however, Mr. Wasserstein's dealmaking reputation could be a two-edged sword. It might make Lazard a more palatable investment, assuming he and his senior lieutenants are tied in. But the last people who bought an investment bank from him are still licking their wounds."

The *Financial Times* articles were followed a week later by an article in *Le Monde,* the respected French daily, which essentially tossed a bucket of tepid water on the IPO idea. The article—an obvious plant by the French interests in Lazard—said that in the previous week Bruce and Michel had actually done something they had not done in almost two years: had a convivial conversation. Indeed, their differences were so profound at this point that in addition to not speaking, Michel had decided not to renew Bruce's contract at the end of 2006. By mid-2004, the matter of succession, supposedly solved by the hiring of Bruce, had returned to the forefront. But according to the newspaper, the two men "put aside" their "long-standing differences over the firm's strategy" and agreed to study a potential IPO, the consensus value of which, the paper said, was between $3.5 billion and $4.1 billion. This valuation range was still materially below the $4.8 billion at which Eurazeo carried its

Lazard investment on its books. Nevertheless, "the two men agreed that the listing was not urgent" and that "Wasserstein could face a tough challenge persuading Lazard's board to endorse the plan." Still, Bruce told Michel, an IPO of Lazard might be "the best way to solve their problems." Orchestrating the IPO of his own investment bank and then being the CEO of a public company were two of the only professional accomplishments that had consistently eluded Bruce in his long career. Bruce would be unlikely to give up this goal easily. "He yearns to be an industrialist and being sole chairman of Lazard would do that for him," said a former partner of his. "As it stands, he is still not part of the cultural or economic establishment."

He realized, of course, that Michel could snuff out his dream unilaterally at any moment. Tactical Bruce needed to win Michel over, and he realized after the *Le Monde* article that the French were lining up against him. He decided to appoint a special envoy to undertake a diplomatic mission to see if he could begin to bring Michel around to his thinking about the IPO. His choices were limited, though. He needed an American who had both longevity at the firm and Michel's trust. Here Bruce was brilliant. He picked for the assignment Steve Golub, the longtime partner who had been CFO of the firm during Rattner's brief reign and who had returned to deal making solely when Loomis took over from Steve. Along with Rattner, Golub had led the firm's brief period of glasnost in the late 1990s. He had also found Mike Castellano, the firm's first full-time CFO.

On the night before the June 2004 Lazard board meeting in Paris, Bruce asked Golub to come with him to Paris and deliver the presentation, even though he had had no role in its preparation. Thus began Golub's secret three-month mission to prove to Michel that the firm could develop a credible business plan around which an IPO could be achieved. From the outset, Bruce had been told by the underwriters to stick as closely to the Greenhill business model as practicable. As a result, he and Golub quickly concluded that as a public company, Lazard would have only the M&A and asset management businesses. The less profitable capital markets and private-equity businesses would be retained in a separate entity to be owned by the working partners and would not be sold to the public.

Golub then had to craft a business plan around M&A and asset management that was both believable and achievable. This meant figuring out how much cost could quickly be cut from these businesses to increase their profitability. Then he needed to convince Michel of its efficacy. "When we first started out, he saw there was no chance of it happening," Golub explained. "But the real key was getting him comfortable that there was a business plan to be executed that could deliver the value to the capitalists, that it wasn't just some pie-in-the-sky stuff."

When Lazard chopped ten of its nonpartner bankers in London in July 2004 as part of what it declared to be a routine weeding out of ineffective professionals, some observers viewed the unusual timing of the move (most Wall Street firms cut bankers after year-end bonuses are paid) as a cost-cutting effort consistent with a desire to improve profitability as a prelude to an IPO. But another prerequisite for an IPO was three years of audited financial statements, which, given the fundamental disagreement between Michel and Bruce about what those financial statements actually said, may have been the biggest obstacle of all. "Not good," snapped Jeffrey Sonnenfeld, the associate dean of the Yale School of Management, when asked about the prospect of Lazard solving its accounting problems. But Golub, the former SEC accountant, said the accounting dispute was just a red herring and was as simple as the difference between partnership accounting and corporate accounting—and, he said, both were accurate ways to look at the Lazard situation.

In the late summer doldrums of August 2004, the *Wall Street Journal* broke the unconfirmed news that Lazard had selected Goldman Sachs to lead an IPO. Goldman, of course, was the world's most highly respected investment bank and had just completed the successful offering of Greenhill. Still, the matter was far from decided. "No firm decision has been made on selling shares to the public . . . and Lazard also may be using talk of an IPO to flush out a takeover offer from a large commercial bank," the *Journal* reported. The paper suggested that a "base price" of $2 billion for Lazard had been established. As the story developed quickly over the following weeks, *BusinessWeek* reported that Michel would give his consent to Bruce to proceed with the IPO only if Bruce agreed to buy the combined 36 percent of Lazard owned by Michel and Eurazeo and the other shareholders based on the so-called Pearson price of $3.785 billion. The article added, though, that other Wall Street bankers valued Lazard closer to $3 billion, well below the Pearson price and well below the price at which Bruce sold a 3 percent stake in the firm, in the fall of 2002, to Intesa, the Italian bank. Both Eurazeo (which benchmarked at the Pearson price) and Intesa would be facing a meaningful write-down if Lazard went public at anywhere near the $3 billion level. Meanwhile, for Bruce to buy the 36 percent stake in Lazard at the Pearson price would cost the firm around $1.4 billion. Raising either sum, given the net losses the firm had been generating since Bruce took over, seemed like a monumental task in a still-shaky IPO market.

"David-Weill is one of the wiliest and most successful negotiators and financial intriguers in the world," Roy Smith, the New York University professor, told *Bloomberg News.* "Either Wasserstein meets his terms, or the IPO's put off." *Bloomberg* further reported that rather than buy the entire 36 percent stake, Bruce just had to buy Michel's 9 percent stake. Even if this were true, Bruce would still have to come up with around $375 million.

Regardless of the valuations being bandied about, the situation was "crazy," according to one partner, because "there is no turnaround plan in place" to return the firm to profitability—the ultimate determinant of the enterprise's value. He also noted that in addition to all the pricey contracts with the new hires, Lazard now had satellite offices all over the place—twenty-nine different investment banking offices worldwide, at last count—an expensive new building in London, and costs spiraling out of control. "It's a mess," he said. "And I still don't see a way out." François Voss, a Lazard board member, told some Lazard bankers that the losses in 2004 were running higher than those of 2003 and that he saw no profits for Lazard anywhere on the horizon. One partner said that Goldman Sachs, the IPO's lead underwriter, insisted that Lazard cut at least $60 million in operating expenses prior to launching the IPO.

And so, at the end of September 2004, the firm began once again to cut expenses, this time by reducing nonprofessional costs globally, which resulted in the firing of back-office workers in New York, London, and Paris. The *New York Post* also reported that Bruce had drawn up lists of professionals to cut and had insisted that those partners that remained take pay cuts of between 30 and 40 percent to allow the firm's compensation expense to fit within industry norms of between 50 and 60 percent of revenues. Lazard's compensation expense was between 70 and 80 percent of revenues. Also as part of the IPO, the working partners were insisting on changes to the governance provisions of Bruce's contract, as many felt he had too much power. "We don't want to go from having a king to having a dictator," one partner told the *Financial Times* at the end of September. Bruce and Michel were opponents in an intense battle.

But like the Terminator, Bruce kept pushing forward with his vision. At the end of September, he asked the banks under consideration to help Goldman underwrite the IPO to agree not to hire any bankers from Lazard for a period of two years after the IPO. They agreed. Interestingly, Lehman Brothers was never seriously considered as a potential underwriter, which fueled the ongoing speculation that it was still thinking about buying Lazard outright. But others believed that the exact opposite was the case: that Fuld had determined the $3 billion valuation of Lazard to be so excessive that he could not condone his firm being involved in the underwriting that would require the firm's institutional clients to pay a price for the stock far above what he thought it was worth.

"Rumpled, ruthless, Bid 'Em Up Bruce is right where he likes to be, in the midst of a hurricane of speculation," the *New York Observer* wrote on September 20. On Friday, September 24, Bruce gave a presentation to the firm's partners about how the IPO would work. Lazard's M&A and asset management business would be grouped together in a new company, to be called Lazard Ltd., and taken public at an enterprise value of $3.2 billion, comprising $2.5 billion of equity value and $700 million of new debt. The bulk of the IPO proceeds plus the debt offering, or a total of about $1.25 billion, would be used to buy out the nonworking partners' stock at a fixed price. The idea was to get rid of Michel and the legacy owners so that Bruce "can stabilize an environment so the deal-oriented guys feel comfortable" and, ironically, leave Bruce with the kind of absolute authority over Lazard that Michel enjoyed before January 1, 2002.

The fact that the vast majority of the money raised would be used to pay out existing shareholders and not be put into the company was the kind of "use of proceeds" that makes investors cringe. A "top New York banker" said that although institutional investors would likely buy the IPO because of Bruce's previous success selling Wasserstein Perella to Dresdner Bank, the public would be financing the buyout of Michel and his French partners. "The public is going to be along for the ride," he said. Some Lazard partners worried that the public filing of the IPO documents would show that the firm's vaunted M&A business was subsidized by the highly profitable restructuring and asset management businesses. Others worried that the proceeds from the offering would not be divided equitably among the historical partners.

Still, Michel had not yet blessed the IPO—far from it—despite Bruce's tactic of making it seem inevitable. "There are several issues—one is pride and ego and whatever," a former Lazard partner told the *Observer.* "Michel brought Bruce into the firm and expected to get some deference and respect, and got none. Michel has nothing to gain from an IPO. Michel's stake would be worth a lot of money, but he's interested in things other than money."

Meanwhile, Bruce kept the screws turning. Jeff Rosen, a deputy chairman and another staunch Bruce loyalist, sent a memo around to the firm's partners giving them until noon on October 4—a Monday—to sign a revised fifteen-page agreement endorsing the IPO filing and Bruce at the helm of the company with a new board of directors. Bruce wanted to get the Lazard board to approve the filing on Tuesday and then file the registration statement with the SEC on Wednesday. One longtime partner said he believed the partners who readily signed were the ones least confident of their ability to test the market for their services at other firms. Added another: "People fearful for their jobs and Bruce's boys will sign, but the core guys that bring in a lot of the revenues are not signing."

The dissidents—said to include Gary Parr, Gerardo Braggiotti, and the two heads of the restructuring group—accounted for a quarter of Lazard's total revenue and half of its advisory revenue. Their complaints continued to be about wanting to reduce Bruce's absolute authority and a concern that the firm's equity had not been fairly distributed. Others believed that once again—for the third time in four years—the Lazard partners were being presented with a contract of adhesion with no room for negotiation. "We are not going to sign under duress," one partner told the *Financial Times.* "The papers are very complex and some of us haven't even had time to read them all. This is a people business and the people need to be behind the plan. You don't have the consensus here, at least not yet." Of course, Bruce made clear that those who failed to sign the document would be forced to leave the firm. For his part, Michel said that while he was not for the IPO, as long as he got cashed out at the valuation he wanted and the firm's working partners "were happy" with the plan, he would not block the filing of the registration documents.

As Bruce's artificial deadline approached, the intensity of the backroom dealing ratcheted up, too. There were any number of complaints, from those about Bruce's "bullying tactics" to the belief of the old-time working partners that many of the partners Bruce brought in not only were underperforming but also had been paid far more than they and received more of the equity. None of the partners were happy with the lockup provisions that prevented them selling their stock for as long as five years. Partners had to agree to stay at the firm for three years and essentially give Bruce power of attorney over their shares and the creation of the company's bylaws. Not signing up for the IPO not only doomed your Lazard career but also meant that you could not sell stock for eight years. And because Bruce had given out more than 100 percent of the equity, nobody below partner received any, a shocking and extraordinarily demoralizing injustice.

There were also concerns that if Lazard became a public company, its culture and ethos would be forever changed. "I would completely agree with that," one former senior partner said. "I think the whole thing Wasserstein is up to is completely barking. Presumably he thinks he's going to make money from it but I think it is absolutely mad." And then there remained the fear that Bruce the dictator was just a younger version of Michel the dictator. "We're paying Michel out at a premium, and we're not getting the same," one Lazard professional observed. "All we're doing is saving Bruce's job." There was also the stark fact that if the 202 working partners didn't support Bruce, they might as well acknowledge that Michel would return to run the firm—and many considered that an even worse fate. Throughout the summer, Michel had been trying to figure out whether there was an internal alternative to Bruce, someone of stature who could run the firm. Would, say, some combination of Gary Parr in the States and Gerardo Braggiotti in Europe work? Or maybe just Braggiotti alone? This might fly, assuming, of course, he could figure out a way to get Bruce to leave before his contract ended in December 2006.

Braggiotti and Michel regularly discussed the possibility of Braggiotti replacing Bruce. And Braggiotti told Michel he could do it. His only requirement would be that Michel agree to many of the same governance terms that Bruce already had: Michel had to leave him alone and accept that he would receive no dividends for five years. After five years, they would reassess the firm's performance and go from there. Braggiotti refused to appease Michel by telling him he would again have a meaningful role in the firm or that the dividends would start flowing. Like Bruce, he knew the firm needed to be reengineered. The only good news for Michel in the Braggiotti scenario was that Lazard would remain a private partnership. One partner who was knowledgeable about their discussions said of Michel, "He was shocked and not very excited" by the Braggiotti alternative. "Michel doesn't need money. He's inherited Lazard and has contributed to its destruction. I think Michel should have been happy to see Lazard back doing what it should be." But he rejected the Braggiotti plan.

The four-hour October 5 board meeting in Paris, in an atmosphere of "serene ambience," did not go according to Bruce's plan. Michel told the board that "floating a company like Lazard is a move not to be taken lightly, which requires a significant amount of reflection and discussion." He said this was not the right moment to list the firm. Bruno Roger took exception to this argument; he said the time had come for the inevitable. Bruce interrupted Michel and for forty-five minutes defended his plan. He also said he knew that some of the Europeans, led by Braggiotti, had problems with the amount of Bruce's power, the inequitable financial distributions, and the tax consequences of the IPO. Michel fully expected Braggiotti to speak up at this moment, to lead a counterrevolution in effect.

But Braggiotti said nothing. "I remember being surprised that he was silent because I remember he told me, 'I will say something,' " Michel said. "Perhaps it's his nature. Some people love confrontation; others avoid it. Some people like to be on the outside looking in, taking shots from the outside. And it's no situation to announce that you are the would-be successor, especially with someone who has a contract until 2006." The moment passed. Braggiotti had become convinced his objections would not change the final vote. He also worried the Lazard board was utterly conflicted, chock-full as it was with both buyers and sellers. After lunch, the meeting reconvened, but the two board members from Eurazeo were now absent.

Although in the end no vote was taken, Michel had accomplished his goal of not yet allowing the IPO documents to be filed, ostensibly because Bruce had not been able to win the support of the most productive partners in the firm. One Lazard banker observed of Michel's coalition: "They are all at a canonical age. It's the Vatican, not a business." Another person close to the dissidents told the *Wall Street Journal* about Bruce: "Now he has to consult the most profitable partners in the group rather than trying to strong-arm them into doing things the Wasserstein way. We have sent him back to the drawing board to come up with new proposals."

After the setback, Bruce remained confident that ultimately he would win the support of the "heavy hitters" and the IPO would proceed. "Many of us are already rich as it is," one of the dissidents said, "and the real question is, where does an IPO lead the bank in the future?" Another dissident said of the IPO, "For Bruce it's a great deal because he buys control of Lazard without putting up a penny."

Bruce's relentless confidence caused Michel to remark, "Bruce seems very sure of himself. Maybe he will even get there eventually." Bruce reportedly agreed to reconsider some of the terms of the partner retention agreements and to begin to think about relinquishing some of his power. Still, "the firm is in a complete state of disarray," Kim Fennebresque told the *New York Times*. "Who wants to buy stock in a company where everybody is fighting with each other?" Taking a page from a humorous 2002 Charles Schwab advertisement, the *Times* likened Bruce's IPO march to "putting lipstick on a pig." "He successfully dressed up his firm, Wasserstein Perella & Company, before selling it to Dresdner Bank of Germany. . . . By the time the deal was completed and the lipstick had rubbed off—as Mr. Wasserstein and his bankers ran for the exits with their profits from the sale—Dresdner realized it was left with an overrated, underperforming boutique investment bank. Now, Mr. Wasserstein may be returning to the cosmetics counter."

The Bruce forces publicly disputed the accounts of the board meeting, and specifically the notion that he did not have the support he needed to go forward. So they leaked to the press a copy of a letter Bruce wrote to the partners after the meeting. "We have informed the capitalists that we have support of the majority of partners," he wrote. "In fact, the deputy chairmen were able to present the near unanimous support of the working partners for the project. At this point we still need to reach an agreement with the capitalists and we hope to move forward over the next few weeks." But the Michel confidants disputed Bruce's view, claiming that the "senior partners at Lazard, who are big revenue earners, are still against this plan." Vernon Jordan, for one, was long opposed to the IPO plan. "I'm wedded to history," he told *BusinessWeek*.

Indeed, once again, as with the dispute over the accounting of the firm's profitability, the two sides could not agree on the basic facts. They couldn't even agree on whether they had agreed to have a follow-up board meeting on Monday, October 11. Bruce ultimately canceled that meeting when it became clear he was having trouble winning the support of the dissident partners, said to number around twenty. Indeed, Bruce spent the weekend trying to woo them. "It is less a charm offensive than a cash offensive," one of them said. Donald Marron, the former CEO of Paine Webber, said of Bruce, "He draws energy from the situations like the one at Lazard—with its complexities and internal struggles." But one French client of Lazard was increasingly turned off by the public disputes. "When you hire an investment bank, you want it to be like a *femme de boudoir*: quiet and secretive," he said. "Not like a common whore off the street."

With the follow-up board meeting canceled, Michel, resigned to allowing the IPO documents to be filed soon, flew back to New York to see if the final details for the filing could be worked out between the intransigent few working partners and Bruce. He had decided not to oppose the filing if his conditions were met. But the signals still conflicted. Some partners said the filing was going "full steam ahead" and the lawyers and accountants were just putting the final touches on the complex documentation. Others, though, said the whole matter was, "one giant question mark." And the former Lazard Brothers chairman John Nott, whom Michel fired in December 1989, said, "As far as I'm concerned it's ferrets fighting in a sack." Gerardo Braggiotti emerged as the leading opponent of the filing. He was "opposed as a matter of principle," a friend said. The ongoing tug-of-war among the firm's leaders was starting to take its toll on the rank and file. "The people who are suffering are the partners," one said. "Here's this great firm and they're battling for control and we're caught in the middle."

As if all this squabbling weren't enough, Michel found a way to make it even worse. After a Eurazeo board meeting in Paris on October 21, he sent Bruce a message: "After having consulted with my partners who represent the majority of the Lazard board, we have decided not to oppose your I.P.O. project subject to your undertaking to resign from Lazard in case the I.P.O. is not completed before June 30, 2005." For Michel, the matter had become quite simple. He did not want to be part of a public Lazard. Nor did he want to be the one opposing Bruce's effort to take the firm public. That would make him the bad guy. "If I just say no, Wasserstein would have failed, but I would not have been able to come back with another solution," Michel explained, "because he would've said to everybody in the firm, 'Look, there was a perfectly good solution. Most of you were for it. This fellow is impossible. We all know he's impossible, but he proved it in spades. He is destroying the firm.' So what position does it leave me in?"

If Bruce succeeded in taking Lazard public, all Michel wanted was his money and a graceful exit. If the IPO failed, he wanted all vestiges of the failure removed, especially Bruce, whose contract he had already decided not to renew. For the first time, Michel put a fixed price on the stock to be sold and made achieving that price an inviolate condition of the IPO occurring. He told Bruce that Lazard had to buy the stock owned by the nonworking partners "with a strict, nonnegotiable total consideration in cash" of $1.616 billion, some $365 million higher than the $1.25 billion sum that had previously been bandied about. Since Michel and the other capitalists owned 36 percent of Lazard, the implied valuation for the whole firm was nearly $4.5 billion—some $1 billion higher than the value put on the firm by Bruce and the underwriters. This major discrepancy—selling stock at a price far below what you were paying someone else for the same stock—would add yet another degree of difficulty to Bruce's planned IPO.

Jean-Claude Haas explained Michel's logic for why it had to happen this way. "Michel tried to find a successor," he said. "As you know, failed with Rattner. Failed with his son-in-law. Failed with Loomis. And hired—put it like that—Bruce, and I think that two things happened. First of all, Bruce wanted to have control of the firm. In order to get control of the firm, he had to get rid of the historical partners one way or another. And the only legal way he had to get rid of them was to buy them out. Same thing with Eurazeo. How could he raise the money necessary to buy those guys who are not naturally sellers? The only way he could have chosen to buy them was to put on the table an irresistible sum of money." And that is exactly what Bruce did. The premium Michel et al. received would be described as the price he had to pay to get Michel's controlling stake in the firm and have him go away once and for all. And since public investors would be paying the price, who cared?

Should the IPO fail, Michel told Bruce, he maintained a "strong belief in the future of Lazard as a private firm fully dedicated to serving our clients." In that case, he wrote, he would not return as CEO, preferring instead that the firm's management be left with the "very credible and capable candidates within the senior partners group," out of which a leader would be found. He added that were the firm to remain private, he had no interest in selling but would not oppose a future "liquidity event proposed by the partners." In an interview following the Eurazeo board meeting, Michel told the *Financial Times* he was now "satisfied that enough of the partners support the IPO plan for me not to oppose it. Either we go public and I will not disapprove, but will leave, or we stay private and need a management that believes in that choice." He reiterated he would not return to run the firm in that case because "I have no will to come back and manage the firm myself. I don't believe in comebacks, they are generally brief and unhappy."

After Bruce had scraped himself off the ceiling and regained his composure—for Michel's conditions were clearly unacceptable and making them public was even worse—he replied to Michel's e-mail with one of his own. "I was very pleased to learn of your decision not to oppose an IPO on the financial terms we had previously agreed," he wrote, before proceeding to shred the conditions. "As you know, a decision to commence an underwriting will only be made under the then prevailing market conditions and will only be done if it is then in the best interests of the firm and its partners." Bruce deflected Michel's ultimatum requiring him to resign by reminding him of his "iron clad" contract. "Of course, as you know, I will continue as head of Lazard until Dec. 31, 2006, as you and I agreed almost three years ago." He added, "As we discussed, if there is no I.P.O. or an I.P.O. is inadvisable, we will all then decide what is the best plan in the interests of the firm and all its partners." June 30, 2005, was eight months away, which may have seemed like sufficient time to accomplish the IPO given that the lawyers had been drafting the requisite documents for months and were just awaiting board approval to file them with the SEC, and to begin the IPO process.

CHAPTER 21

"The End of a Dynasty"

But the matter was not that simple. Pricing an IPO, at least in the traditional, non-Google way, is a complex pas de deux between issuer, lead underwriters, and the institutional investors they persuade to buy the offering. The basic construct is for the Wall Street underwriter to buy stock at an agreed price from the corporate issuer and then immediately turn around and resell the stock to the preassembled, eager buyers. There is a split second at the end—when the actual stock is sold by the issuer and then purchased by the underwriter—where the underwriter and the issuer are adversaries and all the months of glad-handing and laughter evaporate. The issuer wants to sell its stock at the highest possible price, and the underwriter wants to buy it at the lowest possible price, knowing full well, of course, that it will turn around and sell it a split second later to the lined-up institutional and retail investors. But by fixing a precise deadline by which the IPO must be accomplished, the calculus of this arcane drama shifts decisively in favor of the underwriter and its investing clients. The holdup value of a fixed deadline would be enormous, a "poisoned chalice," some have said. The underwriter, no matter how chummy it had been with the issuer before, would figure out a way to stall the offering until the deadline loomed large, knowing the issuer would lose all leverage with the underwriter once the deadline passed and the deal did not happen. "Everyone then knew this was a stress sell," said one Lazard banker. "It was damaging."

Bruce was way too smart to allow the underwriters that kind of leverage. And so when Michel introduced the idea of the June 30 deadline, he and Golub went into overdrive to get him to relent and change his mind. Bruce wondered if he was dealing with a "Frenchman who was prepared to destroy his company and lose millions of dollars rather than cede control of it," one person close to him said, or would Michel blink? "In the end," Bruce's friend said, "he bet that David-Weill would blink."

First, Bruce continued his negotiations with the dissidents, who were becoming fewer in number daily as he succeeded in buying their support. Were these bribes? "Absolutely," the French partner Jean-Claude Haas responded. "But Wasserstein had the money to bribe them because he was head of the bank. Michel couldn't have done it. Michel didn't have the means to bribe them." Said an ally of Bruce's: "He was stacking the deck." Bruce was willing to relent on some of the more offensive terms for the dissidents. They didn't have to agree to stay for three years; rather, they could sign a nonbinding statement indicating a *willingness* to stay for two. They would also be exempted from the salary cuts. For instance, the star banker Gary Parr, who had a four-year, $36 million deal, agreed to support the IPO only after his contract was not impaired.

Golub, meanwhile, was working overtime trying to convince Michel to reverse his decision about the June 30 deadline. He worked closely with Haas to help convince Michel of his error. He also got Tuft, the Goldman partner, to sit down with Michel and get him comfortable with the idea that Goldman thought the deal would be a success, especially if the false deadline was removed. Golub was helped immeasurably in his tasks by improving market conditions for M&A and IPOs, which began to make more credible for Michel the business plan Golub created. In short order, the spinning began, and Michel's conditions seemed to melt away. "The conditions are not seen as that important," one Lazard source told the *Times* of London. "What is important is that David-Weill has agreed in principle to an IPO and that an agreement has been reached on a price for the capitalists' stakes." Some Eurazeo directors—in particular those representing Crédit Agricole—claimed Michel's comments about Bruce having to resign were made in "a personal capacity" and had not been endorsed by the Eurazeo board. Eurazeo itself released a statement confirming that its board had "authorized the pursuit of these negotiations" that could lead to the IPO, from which, if successful, Eurazeo would receive "a 100 per cent cash payment of $784 million," a huge development in its desire to transform itself into an active, independent private-equity fund.

Then came articles that reported the working partners were growing restless and angry. They had had enough of the disagreements between Michel and Bruce, which were beginning to hurt business. There were also reports that Bruce was close to reaching an agreement with a state-owned French savings bank, Caisse d'Epargne, to act as an "anchor tenant" for the IPO by buying a 5–10 percent stake in Lazard at the IPO price. In exchange, the bank would get a Lazard board seat and additional support for its joint venture between Lazard and CDC Ixis, Caisse d'Epargne's investment banking affiliate. Once again, Bruce had found a way to seduce a foreign bank; he also scored a public relations coup in his tug-of-war with Michel by getting a member of the French establishment to support *him*.

Momentum was building for the offering. Michel then told the *Financial Times* that he was "just trying to do what is best for the firm: to have it unified without me on a public project or unified with me on a private project." He added, with a breath of conciliation, that he *liked* Bruce. "In fact, I have a great deal of admiration for Bruce Wasserstein's intelligence and his dynamism," he said. "I actually like him, that is the funny part. The real problem is that we have a different conception of the future of Lazard. His conception is for it to become a public company, governed by the rules and duties pertaining to that status, while I am very attached to the concept of a private firm of partners at the service of clients." He said these "irreconcilable conceptions" were tearing the firm apart. "The gossip is like being asked 'Are you divorcing?' every day," he continued. "I am sure it is not good." But since he stood to reap hundreds of millions of dollars from a successful IPO, he took the opportunity to remark upon the firm's resilience. "If you look at the press coverage, you have to be impressed that the aura of the place is very great," he said. "It has carried us through tough times and may well carry us through to a public offering." Personally, he allowed that the potential sale of his birthright was "heartbreaking" and said, "I've lived every day for 45 years thinking, worrying and being elated by the successes of this firm," and then warned Bruce, "We could simply say 'no,' of course, which we have the right to do."

In the end, Michel's pragmatism overpowered whatever remaining shred of sentimentality he had for Lazard. The succession wars—which started in 1992 when Michel unilaterally brought Édouard Stern to Lazard and had come close to ripping the firm apart on any number of occasions during the ensuing twelve years—had reached their apex. Michel simply could not suit up for another battle. He was seventy-two. He was the father of four daughters who knew better than to pursue a role at the patriarchal Lazard. He had tried a procession of bright, ambitious men at the helm, but since Michel was unwilling to cede power to them, they quickly grew frustrated and left or melted down, or both. Braggiotti, it turned out, was not an appealing alternative, since he would not give Michel what he wanted, either. He had tried selling the firm, but when his preferred suitor, Crédit Agricole, unexpectedly balked, he thwarted the entire sale process. He finally consummated his decades-long infatuation with Bruce, only to find the affair one-sided. It turned out Bruce had no love for Michel; the younger man's passion was only for fulfilling his massive ambitions. Michel was simply a means to an end.

Michel's desperation had thrown him into the arms of the one person with the tactical ability and unrequited desire to outmaneuver him. The war was over. Of course, Michel could stop Bruce at any moment. All he had to do was vote no. But he couldn't do it. Even though he recognized his mistake in choosing Bruce. Even though he wanted the firm to remain private. Even though new leaders were available. Even though he was rich enough already. *Huis clos.* He had no exit, making the ultimate capitulation inevitable. Fortunately for Michel, he was "blessed with the psychological trait that I have no regrets."

On December 3, the *Wall Street Journal* reported that a compromise between the two men was imminent. Golub and Bruce had succeeded in negotiating a deal with Haas and Michel. In exchange for "undetermined concessions" by Bruce, Michel would relax the artificial June deadline. Finally, the two bucking rams signed their peace accord, however shaky, on December 6. In a joint statement issued simultaneously in Paris, London, and New York to the firm's partners, Michel green-lighted Bruce's pet project, at a price. "If the IPO or the buyout of the historical partners were not to be completed by the end of 2005, Lazard would continue as a private firm," the statement read. "In that case or in the event Mr. Wasserstein abandons the project earlier, over the ensuing three-month period we would work together with our partners and the Lazard Board to evaluate all strategic and governance alternatives that are in the best interests of the Firm and its partners. Mr. Wasserstein's current employment agreement would expire at the end of that three-month period. If during that three-month period Mr. Wasserstein and Mr. David-Weill so desire, they would negotiate a new employment agreement subject to the approval of the Lazard Board. We look forward to a continued vibrant future for Lazard. Whether public or private, Lazard will continue to provide outstanding advice and support to its clients."

Despite the accord and Michel's comment that he was a great admirer of Bruce, the palpable tension between the two men was on full display during an interview they gave to the *Wall Street Journal* at the Lazard Paris offices. As they sat together at a pear wood table in one of the firm's conference rooms, they acted very much like a warring married couple that had finally filed for divorce. "We have to be as unselfish as we know how to be," Michel said. Bruce compared the Lazard he found upon his arrival in 2001 to a house needing serious renovation. The firm needed "an extra steel beam and a cement support," Bruce said. "Once you have a strong foundation you're ready to go." Michel interjected to insist Bruce failed to consult him "about how the house was reconstructed. I received the bill, and I wasn't perfectly satisfied. I had one power and that was to be unhappy." (Michel later confessed to having one sole regret: not having forged a "better, more intimate relationship with Bruce.")

As to their May 2004 disagreement that led to the public release of their feisty letters about how to look at the firm's profitability, Michel said he felt "very good about the letters I wrote in May." To which Bruce snapped: "I feel good about my letters, too." He added that he intentionally had very little interaction with Michel during 2002 and 2003 so as to make clear that he had no interest in being mesmerized by Michel, as had previous partners. He sought to eschew "the history of ambiguity of authority between Michel and previous managers," he said. "I didn't want a system where we didn't have coherence."

There was no ambiguity, though, in the fact that Bruce had just put his career at Lazard on the line for the chance to get rid of Michel. Marty Lipton, the dean of Wachtell, Lipton and a longtime Lazard lawyer, believed the IPO was a brilliant compromise. "There are clearly two different points of view, and intelligent people sat down"—among them his partner Adam Chinn—"and worked out a resolution of it." But Jean-Claude Haas, Michel's consigliere through the tempestuous negotiations with Bruce, said that for potential investors the Lazard IPO was simply "an act of faith."

FRIDAY, DECEMBER 17, 2004, at 4:44 p.m. was a moment that few of the tens of thousands of people who had ever had anything to do with Lazard thought they would live to see. At that time, the Securities and Exchange Commission acknowledged receiving a Form S-1 registration statement, under the Securities Act of 1933, for the initial public offering of the investment banking firm now known as Lazard Ltd. By any measure—as originally filed or as subsequently amended over the next few months—the S-1 was a stunning document. For the first time in its 156-year history, Lazard's financial performance was revealed publicly—specifically for the years 2002, 2003, and 2004—as required by the SEC. Some of the data even went back five years. The information showed what many had come to believe of Lazard: until Bruce took over in 2002, the firm was obscenely profitable despite having—or using—little capital. And even under Bruce's command, the firm's operating income and margins were enviable, hovering around 30 percent year after year. What was also clear was the extent of the near meltdown in 2001, when operating income fell to $359 million, from $676 million in 2000, down 47 percent. M&A revenue in 2002 was $393 million, down 46 percent from $725 million in 2000. The effect of Bruce's spending spree throughout 2002 and 2003 could also be appreciated. The partners' capital, which had been built up to $705 million when Bruce took over—well beyond the $17.5 million in capital that André intentionally insisted was all that the firm had available—had plummeted to $385 million by the end of 2004, all as a result of absorbing the losses Bruce was racking up. (Goldman Sachs's total capital, meanwhile, both debt and equity, was closer to $60 billion.)

Financial disclosure aside—and truthfully, much of the key data had leaked out over the years—the S-1 filing had the feel of being part of some master plan Bruce had envisioned from the outset. He had continuously shown that he was willing to sacrifice short-term profitability for long-term equity value. He had done that at Wasserstein Perella, when, although the firm nearly ran out of cash, he was still able to sell it to the Germans for nearly $1.6 billion, including retention bonuses. To Michel's ongoing chagrin, he had done the exact same thing at Lazard. Cash dividends to the nonworking shareholders were eliminated as short-term expenses soared. In the fall of 2003, he repeatedly tried to sell the firm in an effort to replicate the Wasserstein Perella experience. He insisted on a high price, for sure, which the market rejected time and again. That was okay, too, for Bruce knew he was rapidly approaching his first window of opportunity to sell the firm publicly. The SEC requires new issuers to include three years of audited financial data in an IPO prospectus. So no matter what, the earliest moment that the filing could have been made to comply with that requirement and to coincide with Bruce's tenure as head of Lazard was December 2004, when he was ending his third year at the helm. Of course, the high tide of the improving M&A market and the performance of Greenhill & Co.'s IPO lifted Lazard's boat, too, and gave the underwriters the confidence a deal could happen, even with the discrepancy between the price the capitalists would receive and the price the public would pay.

Some of his partners have said that Bruce—the Genius—had even anticipated the rebound of the cycle in the fall of 2004; he's just that smart. He even more or less said so himself when speaking to a group of Yale MBA candidates in September 2005. "So we're at the beginning of a resurgence of M&A activity," he lectured. "Cyclically, this has been going on since the Civil War. It goes in spurts every decade or so. There's a five-year period where M&A accelerates, and then it slows down. Lots of things intervene. And right now, we're at the beginning of the surge.

That's my view. So, as it rebounds, of course the critics of M&A resurface, including many members of your faculty, I gather." One of Bruce's former partners at First Boston, Mike Koeneke, who was also once co-head of M&A at Merrill Lynch, agreed Lazard's filing was well conceived. "His timing as always is exquisite," Koeneke told *Bloomberg* of Bruce. "With all the merger news coming out, he's hitting it perfectly. I think it will be well received."

Others were immensely more skeptical. Upon learning that Lazard was attempting an IPO, Damon Mezzacappa, the former head of Lazard's capital markets business, expressed disbelief. "I'll be stunned if this company can go public, but stranger things have happened," he said, adding, presciently, that in his view the only way it *could* happen would be for Bruce to show Lazard's financials on a "pro forma" basis that backed out the hefty compensation guarantees he had been making to new partners.

Felix was more incredulous still, at least at the outset. "First of all, I think Bruce is very intelligent, and therefore whatever I say now, he knows, and therefore there must be something more to it," he began.

> It's hard for me to conceive that you can go to the public and sell stock in an enterprise which immediately will use that money to bail out the controlling shareholder at a price two or three times what the stock is worth. And leave behind an overleveraged, weak firm with a history of great internal factions. I don't know how you convince people to do that unless you've got it set up in some way with some institutions that for one reason or another are willing. But it's difficult. But is the firm viable once you've done that? That's why I'm still waiting for the other shoe to drop, [for] somebody to come and buy the firm. Because I think what Michel could have done, if he really wanted, [and] I think he really would like to have this firm back, is say to Bruce, "Look, I'll buy you out. And I'll keep my shares, and I will vote my shares in support of Ken Wilson or Gary Parr or whoever, you know, and I'll be there as the controlling shareholder, but I'll be there supporting the management." . . . I mean here he stands for the tradition of 150 years, for family ownership, for private ownership, all the things that he says he values, and if this deal happens—which I still don't believe it will—he will strip the firm of any future for the next *X* years.

As the IPO looked increasingly likely, Felix changed his mind and thought the deal would happen. "I was wrong," he said. Despite his blessing, even Michel was skeptical—in January 2005 anyway—that the IPO would happen because of the plethora of problems that needed to be solved.

"I'm very uncertain it will occur," he said. "In my opinion there are quite a few unresolved problems at this time and very few people working on it. I mean, working very hard, but very, very few."

But it was in the S-1's abundant details weaved throughout its 173 legalese-laced pages that Bruce's true genius—and that of his high-priced bankers at Goldman Sachs and lawyers at Wachtell and Cravath—became apparent. The Lazard IPO was nothing less than a testament to Bruce's creative brilliance and audacity. He had many problems to solve simultaneously. And one by one, he solved them. First, he had to focus the offering on those parts of Lazard that would appeal to investors. In this he had help from Goldman, which told him that Lazard Ltd. should look as much like Greenhill as possible and comprise only Lazard's M&A, restructuring, and asset management businesses. (Greenhill's stock had appreciated more than 50 percent between its IPO and Lazard's first filing.) M&A was growing well, and when that slowed, the restructuring business would kick in; the asset management business, meanwhile, provided a steady stream of profitability. That would be the public company, some $1 billion in worldwide revenue and 2,339 people. Left out of the IPO festivities would be Lazard's unprofitable capital markets business and its private-equity fund management business (but the French units in these areas would be part of the public company). Also left behind were "specified nonoperating assets and liabilities" that would detract from the profitability of the public company. These included an unfunded pension liability in the U.K. and the lease payments on Lazard's empty old building in London. The capital markets business, which would continue to be affiliated solely with Lazard, would be owned by all of the working partners, some of whom would be in the public company and some of whom would be at the capital markets business. About half the profits of the capital markets business would be transferred to the public company in recognition of the role the M&A bankers would have in generating financing deals. As for the private-equity business, Lazard would retain a nine-year, $10 million option to buy it, which will no doubt be exercised when the business starts becoming profitable in a few years after investments begin to pay off.

After solving which businesses would be part of the public company, Bruce had to figure out where the money would come from to pay off the inviolate $1.616 billion to Eurazeo, Michel, and his cronies. Actually, Bruce needed even more than the $1.616 billion. He needed to raise more than $1.9 billion in total because he also intended to leave the "separated" businesses—capital markets and private equity—with $150 million of operating capital to cover certain liabilities (mostly for the U.K. pension liabilities) and he wanted to refinance a preexisting $50 million Lazard debt obligation issued in May 2001. There were also $87 million in fees to be paid, to bankers, lawyers, and accountants. The IPO itself—the public sale of the firm's equity for the first time—would raise gross proceeds of $855 million (before a heavily negotiated 5 percent, or $42.7 million, fee to the underwriters; usually the underwriting fee on an IPO is 7 percent. Bruce also ended up capitulating to the demands of underwriters Morgan Stanley, Citigroup, and Merrill Lynch for a more equitable split of the fees with lead underwriter Goldman Sachs.) and net proceeds of $812 million. That left a balance of around $1.1 billion Bruce still needed. For this money, he turned to other sources of capital. His negotiations with Caisse d'Epargne were fruitful and yielded a $200 million investment—$50 million of common stock at the IPO price and $150 million of debt convertible into the Lazard common stock. Another $550 million came from the public sale of new unsecured senior debt.

To raise the remainder of the capital he needed, Bruce got a little creative. He raised $287.5 million through the public sale of "equity security units" that offered investors a combination of interest-paying debt and equity securities. What he was doing with Lazard is known in Wall Street argot as a "leveraged recap," a fairly common structure in the private-equity world. By adding nearly $900 million in new debt to Lazard's formerly pristine balance sheet and then taking that money plus the expected IPO proceeds of $812 million, Bruce was able to buy up all the stock of the existing shareholders and make himself the largest individual shareholder in the process. It wasn't an original structure, but as a way of getting control of Lazard with other people's money while at the same time getting rid of Michel, it was nothing short of brilliant.

More clever still was Bruce's decision to incorporate Lazard Ltd. in Hamilton, Bermuda, a well-known and controversial tax haven for American companies. Bruce is nothing if not creative when it comes to avoiding taxes. Lazard became the first large Wall Street investment bank to incorporate there, after first considering and then rejecting both Luxembourg and Delaware. Since the United States taxes corporations (and individuals) on their worldwide income, regardless of where it is earned, by incorporating in Bermuda, not only would Lazard not have to pay taxes there (there are no income or capital gains taxes on the island), but also its income from outside the States would not be subject to U.S. taxes. Income earned abroad would be subject only to the tax rates of those localities. Critics have called such tax avoidance "unpatriotic" and the "great tax evasion." Stanley Works, a 163-year-old Connecticut-based tool manufacturer, abandoned its plan to reincorporate there after intense criticism.

Bruce didn't care, though. Lazard acted as though Bermuda were simply a location neutral to its far-flung operations. The *Financial Times* chided Bruce: "The tax part was only a secondary consideration, of course. Who hadn't wanted to see Wasserstein's legs?" (a reference to the possibility that Bruce might soon be wearing Bermuda shorts).

Ironically, since Bruce was a historical shareholder—having bought some Lazard stock from Michel in 2001—he was entitled to be cashed out of this stock, just like Michel. But being a magnanimous sort and wanting to send a signal of support for the IPO to the market (he had also promised Caisse d'Epargne he would do this), Bruce converted his $32.9 million cash-out into Lazard stock at the $25 per share IPO price, for 1.317 million shares. These shares were in addition to the 9.958 million shares he was given by Michel as part of his original five-year contract. After a successful IPO, Bruce would own 11.275 million shares of Lazard, making him, by far, the largest single individual investor in the firm. (As far as can be deciphered, Ken Jacobs would be next, with 1.98 million shares.)

And Bruce would have paid absolutely nothing for those shares. At the IPO price of $25, all of his shares would be worth around $282 million. At that price, Lazard's 100 million shares of equity would be worth a total of $2.5 billion, and its market capitalization (equity plus debt less cash) would be around $3.5 billion, not far below what Michel, Loomis, and Bruce had attempted to sell the firm for previously, but a full $1 billion below the valuation at which Lazard would buy back Michel's stock. Still, for Bruce to have something for which he paid nothing be worth close to $300 million certainly qualifies, in capitalistic America anyway, as one of the leading definitions of "genius."

But Bruce was not done performing miracles. He still needed to show the market that *his* Lazard could be a profitable enterprise. While the businesses to be part of the public company had been consistently profitable on the operating line, Bruce's contractual obligations to his partners had eaten up all of that profit plus a good portion of the firm's historical capital. As a result of these contractual obligations, Lazard had been paying out between 70 and 80 percent of its revenue in the form of compensation—in 2002 and 2003, 74 and 73 percent of net revenues, respectively, were paid out as employee compensation—far above the industry average of around 50 percent. The underwriters knew this would not fly in the marketplace. Lazard's compensation expense needed to be brought more into line with industry norms.

To do this, Bruce and Golub resolved that after the IPO, Lazard's compensation expense as a percentage of net revenues would be fixed at 57.5 percent. In IPO parlance, this all-important change was called a "pro forma adjustment." And so even though Lazard in its history had never had a compensation expense equal to 57.5 percent of its revenues, by simple decree Bruce told investors it would be so—just as Mezzacappa predicted he would do from the outset. And that is how Bruce was able to show the market that on a pro forma basis for 2004, Lazard Ltd.—the public company to be—had net income of $32 million, even though in actuality Lazard had lost around $120 million in 2004. In other words, even though in 2004 Lazard's compensation expense as a percentage of net revenues was 74 percent (including payments made to people in the to-be-"separated" businesses), Bruce showed the market what the "new" Lazard would have looked like in 2004 had compensation expense been only 57.5 percent. Miraculously, Lazard was now profitable and could even pay a dividend to its new shareholders. Abracadabra! This must have been what Jean-Claude Haas meant when he said investing in the Lazard IPO was "an act of faith."

To be sure, in order to be able to reduce compensation expense by some $175 million annually (in the end, the reduction amounted to only $100 million), Bruce had some powerful weapons. First, he had the promise of the IPO itself as a way to create wealth for the partners. The Lazard goodwill that Loomis and Bruce had distributed in late 2001 and early 2002 was now going to have a public market and a public valuation—just as Bruce promised it would. Having that equity, most of which had vested but could not be sold, was key to getting the working partners to agree to reduce their current cash compensation. That was the carrot, a trade-off between reduced cash compensation and a higher firm equity value.

There was a stick, too. As part of the protracted negotiations leading up to the filing of the IPO documents, Bruce got nearly all of the firm's managing directors to sign so-called retention agreements that stipulated that "annual bonuses will be determined in the sole discretion of the Chief Executive Officer of Lazard Ltd."—in other words, Bruce *alone* could determine compensation. Since he had promised the market that compensation expense would be 57.5 percent, he had the sole power to make that happen. He just needed to convince investors he *would* do it. Warned one Lazard banker working late on Christmas Eve,

"I'd sure hate to be one of the many highly paid, non-rainmaking VPs and Directors . . . the axe is about to start falling." Of course, the "risk factors" section of the IPO prospectus gave Bruce all the legal wiggle room he needed in case he was unable to meet the new target compensation expense number. During the first three years under Bruce, "following the hiring of new senior management, we invested significant amounts in the recruitment and retention of senior professionals in an effort to reinvest in the intellectual capital of our business. We made distributions to our managing directors that exceeded our net income allocable to members in respect of 2002, 2003 and 2004"—this seemed to be a near admission that Michel's way of looking at the numbers was correct. The prospectus went on to say the firm intended to operate at the 57.5 percent target, even though compensation expense had been 74 percent in 2004. But "increased competition for senior professionals, changes in the financial markets generally or other factors could prevent us from reaching this objective," it said. "Failure to achieve this target ratio may materially adversely affect our results of operations and financial position."

Bruce was saying, in effect, "Look, we'll give it a try. I have the power to make it happen. If we make the 57.5 percent target, good enough, and if we don't, well, so be it—we warned you." Caveat emptor.

Bruce and the firm's other top four executives—the SEC requires all sorts of disclosure about a company's top five executives—also signed retention agreements with Lazard. Bruce's agreement guaranteed him an annual base salary of no less than $4.8 million for the subsequent three years. The Lazard board was left to decide what bonus, if any, he would get. If Bruce's employment were terminated without cause and without there being a "change of control," he would be paid twice his annual salary as severance and receive health care benefits for him and his family for life. If there were a change of control and Bruce lost his job, he would be paid severance equal to three times his annual salary—the standard over-the-top American CEO compensation package.

If a regular managing director were fired, he would receive no severance at all, other than his salary for a three-month period. By the terms of his retention agreement, Bruce was also permitted to remain chairman of Wasserstein & Co., even though that firm competed with Lazard's private-equity funds. If the IPO were to happen, Bruce would be the only CEO of a publicly traded Wall Street firm who was also the head of his own buyout firm. Nowhere in all of the reams and reams of revelatory paper Lazard filed with the SEC during the five months following the initial December 17 document was there a copy of Bruce's original employment agreement with Michel. Presumably that document was deemed irrelevant to the new Lazard.

THE FILING OF the S-1 in December was merely the first step of the official IPO process. There were many other formal steps along the journey. For instance, prior to starting the "road show," a two-week, multiple-city, worldwide tour where top executives meet with investors, make presentations, and answer questions, Lazard amended its original registration statement six times, each time peeling back another layer of the onion and revealing more and more about the Lazard *omertà*. But there was much for Bruce and his lieutenants to accomplish outside the realm of SEC filings. The first problem for Bruce came in Europe, where rival investment banks were heavily recruiting the Europeans who refused to sign Bruce's letter of support for the IPO. Firms such as HSBC, UBS, Lehman, and Deutsche Bank were said to have approached many of the dozen or so bankers in Europe who did not sign.

This was a mere sideshow compared to Bruce's need to extinguish the increasingly fractious skirmishes he was having with various groups of nonworking partners inside the firm—the aftershocks that followed the earthquake of the IPO filing. So little information had been conveyed to those partners about the IPO, and how they would be treated by it, that they devoured the document when it was filed. Many of them did not like what they read. What became quickly apparent was that the deal Bruce initially cut with Michel involved only the sale for cash of Michel's goodwill and that of the French founding partners. Left unaccounted for initially were the ten or so now "limited" partners who had been around since the creation of Lazard Partners in 1984 and thus had tiny slivers of goodwill, valued, in total, at around $20 million, a mere rounding error in the context of the overall deal but understandably extremely important to the partners involved.

When they discovered that Michel had essentially left them to fend for themselves—they would not get cashed out in the IPO—they were livid at both Michel and Bruce. They hired legal counsel to fight to be included in the cash-out. "These provisions [in the buyout agreement] are inappropriate except possibly in the context of a COMPLETE buy out of ALL our interests," one of these angered men wrote. "That complete buy out should be our prime goal. And Section 7 of the Operating Agreement seems our best negotiating weapon to get there." This group quickly got the attention of Steve Golub and Mike Biondi, and a measure of satisfaction. Soon enough, Bruce agreed to treat their goodwill like Michel's; they would get cash, too.

Another bunch of retired London partners presented Bruce with a thornier problem. Dubbed the London Group, these ten or so partners hired their own legal counsel to fight Bruce about their concern that their pension plan, which faced a $95 million shortfall, would not be fully funded at the time of the IPO, leaving them slighted and angry. "They believe in a strong attack not only on BW but also on MDW (breach of fiduciary duty, self dealing, front running etc.)," one partner wrote, adding this group's intention was to send "a stiff letter to both setting out their position, backed up with firm action to the SEC and if necessary recourse to the press." This battle would not be so easily resolved, and the London Group did resort to planting a number of negative stories in the press on the eve of the IPO. This tactic worked. Lazard agreed to set aside cash from the IPO to make sure the U.K. pensions were fully funded.

Bruce also needed to resolve a lingering dispute with Damon Mezzacappa, the longtime head of capital markets who retired at the end of 1999. Michel's gluttonous side deal with Damon called for him to get a large salary plus 3 percent of New York's profits from 2000 to 2002 at Michel's discretion. When Michel and Bruce allocated the goodwill at the end of 2001, Mezzacappa did not receive any despite still having his profit percentage. Soon after Bruce arrived and the profit percentage no longer had any value because there were no longer any profits, Mezzacappa was not happy. Like many others, he never imagined that the old Lazard way of paying partners based on a percentage of the profits could be turned on its head by Bruce, and junked. Damon sued, and the matter went to arbitration, per the Wall Street rules for settling bonus disputes. At the beginning of 2005, just as the arbitration was set to begin, Bruce and Damon settled (for stock worth at least $5 million at the IPO price). Then there was the battle with the so-called Walking Dead, those few Lazard partners who had received their goodwill in the firm when Loomis and Bruce distributed it at the end of 2001 but who were no longer at the firm at the time of the S-1 filing in December 2004. Ironically, Loomis himself was the former partner with the largest chunk of goodwill who had left the firm after the distribution and before the filing. But his "insurance" policy with Michel—negotiated on September 10, 2001—guaranteed him his goodwill (said to be more than a 1 percent stake in the firm, worth more than $25 million at the proposed IPO price) even though he was not at the firm. Together this loosely formed group, which also hired a lawyer, was said to have between 4.5 and 5 percent of the goodwill. Whereas Michel was getting cash at the IPO, and if they stayed at the firm, the working partners could convert their goodwill into equity in the public company in years three, four, and five, since they were no longer at Lazard, the goodwill of the Walking Dead would be trapped at a holding company for eight years before it could be converted into stock in the public company and sold. "Which is just not right, because we should be on par with everyone else," one member of the Walking Dead said. "We really should be on a par with the capitalists, because that's what we are effectively."

There were at least two parts to the Walking Dead strategy. First, with $1.616 billion in cash proceeds at a high valuation at stake, the thinking was that Michel and Eurazeo would not do anything to jeopardize that money—and thus the IPO—and so a bout of negative publicity and a lawsuit from former partners with 5 percent of the goodwill was to be avoided at all costs. Second, Bruce had actually allocated more than 100 percent of the firm's goodwill to the collective group of partners, and so he needed to get some of that goodwill back. (Bruce thought he would have plenty of time—at least three years—to get the overallocated goodwill back before it was convertible into the public stock.) The combination of these two points of leverage ended up working well. Bruce and his deputies negotiated one by one with the members of the Walking Dead, and in most cases settled with them—Loomis included—by buying their goodwill points back at around a 50 percent discount to the suggested IPO price.

JUST AS BRUCE was having increasing success solving all of these simultaneous equations came shocking Lazard news. Soon after lunch on March 2, Jerry Rosenfeld, the former Lazard partner and CEO of Rothschild North America, sent the following e-mail with the words "Tragic News Item" in the subject line: "It is being reported in the 'Lazard Loop' that Édouard Stern has been murdered in his apartment in Geneva." Rarely had a simple nineteen-word message screamed more emphatically, "Tell me more!" While on the surface, Stern, then fifty, appeared to have severed all ties with Lazard after Michel fired him in 1997, the truth was far more complicated, as with almost everything in Édouard's life. As his parting gift from Lazard, Michel arranged for Eurazeo to invest $300 million in Édouard's $600 million private-equity firm—Investments Real Returns—with Édouard and his friends contributing the rest. Édouard managed the fund out of Geneva without taking much input from Eurazeo, and IRR—as it was known—was not doing too well, and there was ongoing tension as a result. Édouard, who literally had teeth like a wolf, was also in the habit of making halfhearted attempts at getting Lazard involved in major M&A assignments where he had ongoing relationships. As a way to needle Michel, he had a nasty habit of suing Lazard (and lots of others) whenever he could. Even though Michel had fired him from Lazard, because of the French partnership rules, he retained a small stake in that partnership, and when in 2000 the three houses were merged, Édouard withheld his crucial vote for the merger until he was paid off, a sum said to be around $25 million.

The news of Stern's alleged death sent the Lazard legions to the Internet for any news about what had happened in his locked penthouse apartment above a police station at 17 Rue Adrien-Lachenal, in Geneva's fashionable Rive quarter. "He was found at his Geneva home on Tuesday afternoon," a spokesman for the Geneva police said on Wednesday, March 2, the first scrap of official word. "The death was the result of a crime."

Michel heard the news about Édouard from his wife. He was traveling in Africa with Margo Walker. They had just spoken when Hélène called Michel back ten minutes later to say that Beatrice had just heard the news of Édouard's death. "I called my daughter Beatrice," he said. "I didn't know he had been killed. I knew he had died. I told her what happened. At first, I thought he had committed suicide. Then she told me, 'I believe he received considerable help.' " *Le Figaro* reported that same day that Édouard had been assassinated. "He was rich, he got on people's nerves," the paper said. "His enemies could not find words strong enough to condemn his all-consuming ambition." Added Taki Theodoracopulos, the socialite columnist, "He was not only ruthless and a terrible bully, he was as close to being a monster as anyone can be and still be free to walk around in polite society."

After attending the press conference where the Geneva police confirmed that Édouard had been murdered—shot four times, in fact—and that an investigation had started, the *Tribune de Genève* spoke with "Tina" (not her real name), Édouard's Portuguese maid, who told the paper how events unfolded. Tina had just returned to Geneva from Portugal, where she had been visiting her ill father for a few months, with Édouard's blessing. He had not wanted to hire someone else while she was away. She worked at Édouard's apartment each day in the afternoon but had not seen him in a week. "He was a discreet man," she said. "I cleaned his linen, his apartment, I knew what kind of yogurt he liked but I didn't know anything about his private life. He never spoke to me about it." At around one-fifteen on Tuesday afternoon, she received a call from one of Stern's associates at IRR. "We have been looking for Mr. Stern everywhere," the man said. "Do you have the key to his apartment?"

A few minutes later, she arrived at 17 Rue Adrien-Lachenal and went to the fifth-floor apartment, where she met Sandy Koifman, Stern's former partner, and his two assistants. Koifman remained quite friendly with Stern, and his new office was but one floor away from Stern's. Koifman had been searching for Édouard since he had missed two morning appointments, one with a former Goldman Sachs partner and one with William Browder, the founder of the Hermitage Fund, one of the largest and most successful equity funds dedicated to investing in Russia. Despite Édouard's having missed these appointments, Koifman still was not particularly worried. He had seen Édouard's new Bentley in the parking garage that morning. Koifman went off to lunch at Hashimoto, the sushi restaurant the two of them frequented. When Édouard still had not shown up after lunch, Koifman headed to Stern's apartment. He also called the local hospital and ascertained that nobody with Stern's name or his description had shown up there. "I was thinking, maybe he slipped and fell in the bathroom," he said. "I had a friend who died of a heart attack at forty-five."

Tina put the key in the lock, and when the alarm did not sound, she told herself, "Good, Mr. Stern is home." Once inside the apartment, a weird feeling overtook her. "An intuition," she said. "I felt strange," especially when she saw a pair of his tennis sneakers in front of the bedroom door. Koifman and his assistants brushed past her into the bedroom. "They had a curious expression on their faces," she remembered. She walked toward the door to look in, but they told her to stop. "It is better that you not see what is in there," they told her. "Go call the police." In great anguish, Tina went down to the apartment building's street floor and into the police station there. By two-thirty, there were swarms of police in the apartment, including detectives investigating the crime scene. The police interviewed her. "But I had not seen the body or traces of blood," she said. "The less I knew about this matter, the better."

What Koifman found in Édouard's bedroom sent a shock wave not only through Lazard but also through much of the financial world. "I went to the door, pushed it with a finger," he told the *Vanity Fair* reporter Bryan Burrough.

> It opened. The bedroom is plain, a big bed—king-size, Americans would call it—nothing else. Very Zen. You see nothing laying about. Everything's in built-in closets. Just behind the door was a body on the floor, with a huge pool of blood behind the head. I have to admit, at first glance, I thought it was a piece of modern art. The French would call it Surrealist art. I thought it was something to step over, just a piece of art. I've seen weirder things in people's apartments. It took a moment—a

> minute, 30 seconds, five seconds, I don't know—for it to sink in that I was looking at a dead body in Édouard's apartment. It was covered head to toe in this, this flesh-colored suit—I later learned it was latex. There were no holes in the face. I don't know how someone could even breathe. You know when you walk past Macy's and they haven't dressed the mannequins yet? That was what it looked like. He was lying on his side. I couldn't see the face, the head. If I'd seen that same body in a Manhattan subway station, it would never have occurred to me it was Édouard Stern. You couldn't see anything.

According to Burrough's account of the murder, there was a thin white rope draped over the body and more ropes on a chair nearby. "It was really a nasty scene," Koifman continued. "You know that movie *Seven*? That kind of scene. It was just, you know, I don't mean to be dramatic, but it was . . . It was evil." Koifman spent the following six hours being interrogated by the police, and according to Burrough, he assumed that Stern had somehow died after hitting his head during rough sex.

He had no idea, though, that his friend and former partner had been heavily invested in the bizarre world of sadomasochism. It was not until two days after he found Stern's body, when the Swiss police held their press conference, that Koifman even realized Édouard had been shot.

Among former and current Lazard partners on both sides of the Atlantic, three theories quickly emerged about what had occurred. There was the Russian–eastern European Mafia theory, whereby Édouard was assassinated for trying to recover some of the money from soured investments he had made in that region. This theory was both complicated and enhanced by reports of his friendship with Alexander Lebed, a Russian army general who died in a helicopter accident in Siberia in 2002, and by Édouard's four-year affair with Julia Lemigova, a stunning former Miss Soviet Union. They had talked of marriage. In 1999, they also may have had a child together—Maximilien—who died suddenly six months later under the questionable care of an unnamed Bulgarian nanny. Had the nanny been hired to eliminate the evidence of their affair?

And of course, there was the S&M-gone-off-the-rails theory. Finally, there was concern that a series of lawsuits Stern had filed against Rhodia, a French chemical company in which he had invested—and nearly lost—$89 million, had upset many people, including the French finance minister, Thierry Breton à Bercy, who had been a director of Rhodia and a target of the suit. Koifman also discovered that a phone had been tapped in the New York office of IRR. Using the code name Operation Serrano, the DGSE, France's external intelligence agency, had Stern under regular telephone surveillance. "He was aware of men watching his apartment," a source close to Stern told the *Mail on Sunday.* "He said that powerful figures at Rhodia were trying to discredit him by investigating his private life." He told a friend the week before he died, "You will see, people will say that I am a homosexual but I don't care what people say."

Indeed, Édouard was sufficiently concerned about his own safety that he arranged in 2003 to obtain a permit to carry a gun for protection. Individuals are not permitted to carry a weapon in Switzerland, so Stern arranged for a permit in his native France, with the document being signed by Nicolas Sarkozy, who succeeded Jacques Chirac as the French president in April 2007.

But it was the mafioso-hit theory that gained currency rather quickly since, through IRR, Édouard had numerous connections to eastern Europe and had lost quite a bit of money there.

But Burrough, who started reporting the story for *Vanity Fair* after the murder occurred but before it was solved, suspected that the conspiracy theorists would be disappointed when the truth was known. His intuition proved accurate, if no less stunning, when police viewed the videotapes on the surveillance cameras that were all around the apartment building and discovered that a Frenchwoman, thirty-six-year-old Cécile Brossard, was the only person seen entering or leaving Stern's apartment the night of the murder. The tall, blond, and striking Brossard was said to be Édouard's long-term girlfriend, as well as a minor artist. "And she's some kind of artist, all right," Burrough wrote. "In addition to sculptures she creates in her spare time, her principal employment appears to have been as a very expensive call girl specializing in sadomasochistic sex." In 1996, she had married Xavier Gillet, an herbal-medicine therapist twenty years her senior, in Las Vegas. They lived an hour outside Geneva, but she apparently made frequent trips to the city as "Alice," a "leather-clad dominatrix," and appeared, for hire, at local hotels. It was supposedly in this kind of setting that Brossard and Stern met sometime around 2001. Her favorite movie was said to be *A Clockwork Orange*.

Oddly, until his murder on the night of February 28, very few people—even his closest friends, including Koifman—knew that Édouard and Beatrice had been officially divorced in 1998. The immediate family kept their divorce very quiet, even from Michel. When asked, Michel said only, "Édouard and Beatrice no longer sleep in the same bed," even though they had been divorced for years. They stayed in close touch, though, and Édouard was said to be an extraordinarily giving father to their three children. "He gave them both affection and energy," Michel said. "He was close to them. And for the children it was obviously a great blow. A great blow. And for my daughter, already separated, as you know, it is a blow, too, because he's been the person she has loved all of her life. She couldn't live with him, but she always loved him." Added Annik Percival, Michel's assistant: "It is very sad for the ex-wife and the three children."

Over time, by many accounts, Édouard's relationship with Brossard transcended its original—and ongoing—professional aspect. He seemed to be quite taken with her, and vice versa. He encouraged her artistic career and hired her to decorate his Zen palace in Geneva. He also reportedly took her on vacations to India and Africa. There is an extraordinary picture Brossard took of Édouard when they were on vacation together big-game hunting in Siberia. Édouard is holding a shotgun behind a freshly killed, massive brown bear. Blood from the bear's mouth appears on the snow. They once rented a game preserve—said to be the size of Belgium—near Lake Victoria in Tanzania. They would fly off for the weekend in his private jet to Venice, Florence, Bruges, and New York. Édouard pushed her to leave her husband and live with him. But she declined out of a fear that Édouard would lose interest in her, only to leave her forlorn and alone.

Much to Édouard's chagrin, they began to grow apart. She disappeared for a time in the fall of 2004 after they had vacationed together in Africa that summer. Édouard discovered she was in Las Vegas. He surprised her at the airport in Geneva when she returned. "Édouard was very upset at the time," a friend told *Vanity Fair.* "She didn't want to give up her life. She thought she would be left with nothing." He thought he had hit upon a solution in early January 2005, when he opened a bank account for Brossard at a Credit Suisse branch and put $1 million in it. He believed she could now leave her husband for him. Later reports, though, suggested Édouard had given her this money so she could buy a number of Chagall paintings for him, although how she would have access to such work is a mystery. They had also discussed getting married. In any event, once again, Brossard did not respond as Édouard had hoped. She stopped returning his calls and seemed to disappear once again.

On February 24, four days before his death, he confessed to his longtime lawyer Kristen van Riel, who had bailed him out of similar situations with other women, that he was in a bit of a fix. He told van Riel for the first time about Brossard and the $1 million bank account. The lawyer placed several calls to Brossard but, like Stern, had no luck. Then they decided to freeze her access to the account. "I'm never going to see her again," Stern told van Riel, who, on the contrary, predicted the scheme would get her attention and that she would call. "And—surprise, surprise—she did," said a Stern adviser. "She called Édouard on Friday," three days before his death. She was not pleased to have been "cut off," but in any event Édouard convinced her to fly that day to Geneva from Paris. They met three times over the next three days, including one final time on the evening of February 28. They were to meet at eight that night. Brossard arrived fifteen minutes early and let herself in with her key. "Only two people know what happened in that bedroom," Koifman told *Vanity Fair,* "and one is dead." It didn't take a great leap of faith, though, to believe that Édouard expected the Monday night visit to include some unconventional sex. Said Koifman: "I don't think you negotiate financial transactions wearing a latex suit."

Paris Match, the borderline racy French magazine, seemed to know exactly what happened that night in Édouard's apartment. "He presses a button concealed in the living room furniture, and two hidden drawers slide open," the magazine reported. "One contains sex toys for lovemaking sessions. The other holds four loaded firearms. Cécile Brossard continues to ask questions, but Stern doesn't answer her; he is elsewhere. He slips into the latex suit that she gave him, and begins to lead her on. She plays along. His hands are bound, and he's sitting on a 'pleasure accessory.' At this point, she reportedly heard him tell her, 'A million dollars is expensive for a whore.' At this, she grabs a gun and shoots four bullets in a row, two in the head, one in the chest, and one in the stomach. Stern falls to the ground." *L'Express,* another French magazine, confirmed in its own account that Édouard's final words were indeed "A million dollars is expensive for a whore." *L'Express* claimed Brossard then picked up a nine-millimeter pistol and fired one shot at Édouard's head from a distance of ten to fifteen centimeters, killing him instantly. She fired three more shots for good measure.

MICHEL BELIEVED THE simplest explanation for Édouard's murder was the most likely one. "Some people are always Machiavellian," he said, "and always believe things are more complicated than they appear. And I have the opposite tendency. I have the tendency that the explanation which is the stupidest is generally the right one and not the smartest. He had obviously just promised her money and then taken it back. What to me is unbelievable is then getting physically tied up, in front of somebody he had just done that to. It's a proof of either confidence or a wish to take risks, which is strictly unbelievable. But this is what occurred, and I believe it was in his nature to take this sort of risk. And so, it's not completely surprising that a person like him finishes in a tragedy like that. It's not totally surprising." He said he had not known of Édouard's unusual sexual interests, "but as my father used to say, 'In sexual matters, nothing is astonishing.' "

On March 15, the police showed up at Brossard's apartment, searched it, and took her away for questioning. She cracked. The records of her telephone conversations proved that what she originally told the police did not make sense. She told them everything. She took them to the shores of Lake Leman, where she had tossed the murder weapon and the two other guns she had taken from Édouard's apartment. A police diver found them all plus a key to his apartment she had also tossed. The police took from her the letter Édouard had written to her proposing marriage, but only after she had asked for—and received—a copy of it. At first Brossard was incarcerated in Champ-Dollon prison in Geneva. Suffering from severe depression, she was later admitted to a psychiatric hospital. "She is a desperate woman who cries a lot and has killed the man she loved," one of her lawyers said.

WHILE SHOCKING, AND an understandable diversion, Stern's murder had no discernible effect on Bruce's long march to the Lazard IPO. Édouard had been gone from the firm since 1997, and his needling lawsuits were immaterial at best. While the $300 million that Eurazeo invested in Stern's IRR seemed, over the years, like a poor investment—the original €264 million investment had been written down to €190 million at the end of December 2004—somehow even this was salvaged when, in October 2005, Eurazeo sold its IRR stake for €307.7 million back to IRR itself, for an improbable profit of €44 million after seven years. The combination of the cash sales of the IRR and Lazard stakes in 2005 completed Eurazeo's nearly decade-long transformation from Michel's personal investment vehicle into a full-fledged publicly traded private-equity firm, now one of Europe's largest. Eurazeo's stock price responded accordingly and now trades around its all-time high of €104 per share, up more than 100 percent since Bruce and Michel reached their truce. The rise in the Eurazeo share price, of course, greatly benefited its largest shareholders, including Michel and his sister; the proprietary traders at UBS, led by Jon Wood, who had been successfully fighting Michel for nearly ten years; and Crédit Agricole, which is close to making a profit on its investment after doing Michel a favor in 1999 and buying out the stake in Eurazeo held by the raider Vincent Bolloré.

On April 11, the IPO took another important step toward reality when Lazard filed with the SEC an amendment to the registration statement, including for the first time information that would allow investors to assess the price tag the firm had placed on itself. This filing revealed that Lazard and the underwriters were aiming for a price range for the equity of between $25 and $27 per share, valuing 100 percent of Lazard equity at between $2.5 billion and $2.7 billion. When the net debt of around $1.4 billion was added, the enterprise value of the firm was between $3.9 billion and $4.1 billion. Using the midpoint of $4 billion, Lazard would be valued at 11.8 times the 2005 estimated EBITDA (earnings before interest, taxes, depreciation, and amortization) of $339 million and a P/E ratio of 17 times the 2005 estimated earnings.

Both of these valuation metrics, by design, valued Lazard at a higher multiple than the global investment banks, such as Goldman Sachs, Morgan Stanley, and Merrill Lynch, which Lazard executives had taken to referring to as "hedge funds" and which tended to trade at a P/E multiple of 12. But the proposed Lazard valuation would be at a discount to Greenhill & Co., which in the year since it went public had become the gold standard of boutique investment banking at least as far as its public valuation was concerned. Many wondered who would invest in this offering that would leave Lazard with significant debt, largely dependent on the cyclical M&A business, when only a minimal amount of the capital raised would be retained in the business. Indeed, the money raised would be paid out to the historical shareholders at a materially higher price than the market believed the stock was worth. Also, for the first time, this value range indicated that Bruce's $30 million initial investment in Lazard, plus the shares Michel granted to him, were set to be worth around $290 million.

In the revised registration statement, Lazard finally admitted that if the compensation of its managing directors were included as an operating expense, "the firm lost money in each of the last three years," just as Michel had been saying. For some existing and former Lazard partners, this admission was confirmation that the financial statements in the S-1 were all but fraudulent because they failed to show the losses and then presented the profitability on a pro forma basis. One Lazard partner said he could not believe the SEC permitted the accounting to be presented in this way. He was even more astounded that this happened given that Steve Golub was a former deputy chief accountant at the SEC. "I am flabbergasted, I have to say," he continued. Ken Wilson, the former Lazard FIG partner now at Goldman Sachs—the lead underwriter of the Lazard IPO—shared the view that some top bankers on Wall Street were buzzing about the Lazard accounting. "There is a clear pattern of greed and deception" at Lazard, he said. "There is something in the culture that permitted it to happen."

The press was starting to hear these ruminations, too. "All this raises the question of why outside shareholders would want to get involved," the *Economist* stated. "Mr. Wasserstein has little option but to complete the IPO. But such are the uncertainties around this strange flotation that some observers are already wondering whether it is an opening move rather than an end game." *BusinessWeek* opined, "Add it all up and investors had better be real comfortable with Wasserstein's stewardship before they get involved in his next excellent adventure as the CEO of a public company. Eventually, the market will sort through the confusing details of the prospectus and value Lazard accordingly. Wasserstein has built a career by defying gravity. But this could be one rocky liftoff."

Finally, after four months of laborious legal filings and their revisions, the time had come for Bruce and his top executives to see if they could convince the market to buy the shares of what Robert Willens, a top tax and accounting analyst at Lehman Brothers, called "one of the most complicated things I've ever seen." While the S-1 and its amendments are the official documents the SEC requires of a private company seeking to become public, another key document—the prospectus—is used for marketing purposes with potential investors. The prospectus is a slightly jazzed-up version—color pictures are permitted—of the final amended S-1 and is prepared for use on the road show. (The Lazard IPO prospectus was one of the lengthiest ever written.) The culmination of the road show, assuming there is sufficient investor demand, is the pricing of the stock and its purchase by the underwriters.

Following the SEC's sign-off on the final amendment to the S-1, Lazard could print prospectuses and begin the road show. After a week or so of stops in major cities in western Europe—about halfway through the process—the Lazard IPO road show rolled into New York for lunch at the New York Palace hotel on April 27. The IPO pricing would be negotiated with Goldman Sachs after the market closed on May 4, allowing the new Lazard stock to trade—under the symbol LAZ—beginning at 9:30 a.m. on May 5.

The Goldman Sachs partner Tom Tuft kicked off the New York lunch, as would be expected, by lauding his client Bruce Wasserstein. "Bruce Wasserstein joined Lazard three years ago to take on the unique challenge of transforming an underdeveloped franchise with a tremendous history," he said. Much to the surprise of many of the approximately

250 listeners in the audience (some of whom were Lazard partners hearing the road show presentation for the first time), Bruce spoke for most of the forty-eight-minute session.

But as highly anticipated as the meeting was, investment bankers are not actors. Bruce was certainly no Henry V leading his men into the Battle of Agincourt on Saint Crispin's Day. Rather, he covered the saturnine marketing material in an uninspired, droning monotone. His presentation was disjointed and didn't seem to stick to any particular script, which most executives at these types of meetings have the good sense to do. Bruce's message, though, was clear. "The threshold issue when you're thinking about Lazard is, is the M&A market attractive?" he said. "If the M&A business is attractive, Lazard is an attractive investment." He then launched into one of his favorite history lessons about the cycles in the M&A market from 1861 to the present. His presentation was clinical and unemotional. And maybe that is the way Goldman recommended he deliver it. But he conveyed no sense of Lazard's rich and nuanced history on this, the eve of the most momentous event in the firm's 157 years. True, like a neutron bomb, in one fell swoop he intended to eliminate all human traces of the firm's aristocratic ancestry by buying out Michel and his allies. But for a man who seemed so taken with the firm for so many years and who fashioned his own firm after Lazard, his lack of passion was noticeably distressing. Whereas Michel described the firm as "a state of mind vis-à-vis the world" and had a palpable love for it, Bruce merely spouted some investment banking pabulum.

"Lazard is a very special place," he droned. "We've focused on the added value part of the business. We're particularly prominent in complex deals, international deals, and deals that require a high level of fiduciary responsibility. We feel that's a growing part of the M&A market." Indeed, the closest he came to anything resembling passion for Lazard—at least with this crowd anyway—was when he mentioned offhandedly just how much cash the firm would be able to generate because its two business units, M&A and asset management, required virtually no capital to operate. "In fact, this company spigots cash," he said. "It spigots cash because unlike, say, our friends, say, at Lehman Brothers, who need the capital to support their derivative portfolio or whatever, we don't need that. So we use cash in our minds, cash is for buying back shares, dividends, possible adjacent acquisitions, if we found them, and perhaps paying back debt, although not particularly a priority. So that explains sort of our position."

He also sought to anticipate some investors' questions about the offering's most unusual aspects. As for the $200 million reduction in compensation needed to achieve the 57.5 percent goal promised in the prospectus, he explained that $100 million of the savings would come from ending the huge payments to Eig and Gullquist. "So that's over, gone, done, nonrecurring," he said. The other $100 million of cuts would have to come, he said, from bankers' compensation, assuming no growth in revenue. But, he pointed out, if overall revenue were to grow at 13 percent in 2005, no compensation cuts would be required to achieve the 57.5 percent target. "We think this year we're going to make zero cuts, whatever that implies," he said. "We'll be at 57.5 percent." Without addressing the controversial decision to incorporate in Bermuda, he did explain why the firm's tax rate appeared to be 28 percent, lower than that of most U.S. companies. "It's 28 percent because we're a full U.S. taxpayer but we've got half of our businesses overseas," he said. "When you blend the two you are at 28 percent." As for ensuring that talented bankers stayed at the firm long enough to help it achieve the results that Bruce had promised to investors, he had a prepared answer for that, too. "So we have all these valuable employees, how do we keep them?" he asked rhetorically. "What everyone signed up to is a system where if they leave, they can't sell or borrow on their shares for eight years. So a pretty draconian methodology. If they stay, they can sell or convert on an average of four years. By the way, there is also a ninety-day notice and a ninety-day noncompete. And again, everyone signed up for this kind of provision. So we think that that's very powerful."

As the lunch wound down and Bruce's presentation ended, there were surprisingly few questions from the audience, and none of them delved anywhere near the controversial topic of how the firm found itself in this position after 157 years of privacy.

❦

BY ANY MEASURE, the Lazard public offering was a historic event. Not only would it spell the end of the firm's enigmatic secrecy, but it would also be the largest IPO—by far—of a Wall Street firm since that of Goldman Sachs in 1999. Yet the Lazard deal was merely *anticipated*—not *much* anticipated, not *wildly* anticipated, just *anticipated*—by institutional investors. The tepidness of their response could be felt at the New York Palace. Investors' thinking was that at a *price,* the Lazard deal would begin to look interesting. The problem was that Bruce had made the deal intensely complex by having to solve so many problems at once. Accordingly, he appeared to scare off many retail investors, putting more leverage than usual into the hands of institutions. "The more complicated the structure, the lower the price that can be achieved," one institutional investor told Reuters about the Lazard IPO.

Compounding the self-imposed problems were the external ones. In April 2005, five of the six IPO pricings were either at or below the low end of the range put on the prospectus cover—investor demand was weakening. Meanwhile, the Lazard IPO also suffered from the roiling debt markets, where the recent downgrading of the debt of bellwether GM had caused yields to rise—just as Lazard needed to price the debt part of its offering. Moody's didn't help Lazard's cause when it rated the debt Lazard would be issuing as Ba1, below investment grade. And then Duff & Phelps, another rating agency, gave the Lazard debt an unsolicited and unexpected below investment grade rating as well, giving the debt offerings the whiff of a junk-bond offering—itself utterly ironic given all of Felix's railings against the junk-bond market. Pricing pressure on the debt put pricing pressure on the equity.

Two days before the deal was to price, the high-profile professional stock picker and ranter Jim Cramer urged investors to stay away. "How awful is this Lazard IPO deal?" he wondered on his Web site (as opposed to in his financial column in Bruce's *New York*).

> I mean, has anyone looked at it? . . . This one's total hubris, especially in light of the downgrades of the real brokerages today. Sometimes I believe that Wall Street thinks we are the biggest bunch of morons. The more I read about this deal, the more I believe it's simply a very expensive buy-off of dissident partners and *nothing more than that*. . . . Moreover, its prospectus is the most confusing document that anyone I know has ever seen. Total lack of transparency. Sometimes this business cries out for a ref to throw a flag and say, "Nope, you guys can't do this." But there are no zebras, just guys like me saying, "Please stay away from this." And we have no clout or voice compared with the Street itself, which allows virtually anything to come public. What a crime.

Such was the backdrop when Lazard's management met with its Goldman Sachs bankers on the night of May 4 to price the IPO. According to Ken Wilson, that night there was the not unexpected wrangling between lead underwriter and issuer. "It was a complicated deal and a very hard deal to get done," he said a few weeks afterward. "There was resistance to Bruce. He has a lot of baggage." Wilson said there was a "weak list of investors" for the Lazard IPO and a "weak book" of demand thanks to "a lot" of selling pressure from "hedge funds that shorted into the syndicate bid." In the end, the demand was at $23 per share, he said, below the low end of the range, which was $25. "But," Wilson said, "Bruce was adamant. He said he had a gun to his head and he had to have $25 per share." According to the *New York Times,* some Goldman bankers pushed to price the IPO at $22 per share because of "weak demand." In the end, Goldman capitulated to Bruce and priced the IPO at $25 a share.

Furthermore, Lazard and Goldman increased by 3.7 million shares the amount of stock sold at $25 per share in order to raise another $93 million. Lazard needed to raise this extra money from the equity market because Citigroup was unable to sell the corresponding amount of subordinated debt in the increasingly choppy debt markets. "Given the change in the debt market, we thought it prudent to reduce the debt, which was possible given the demand for the equity," said Lazard's spokesman, Rich Silverman. Added Ken Jacobs: "Goldman priced right through the static. And we got it done. All power to Goldman. To be frank, Goldman did a superb job on this transaction, and you don't usually give competitors a lot of credit." After the pricing had been negotiated on the evening of May 4, Lazard put out a press release announcing the deal. "Lazard is the leading global independent advisor and a premier global asset manager," Bruce said in the release. "For more than 150 years, Lazard has served its clients under changing economic conditions, and we look forward to this exciting new era. We made the decision to become a public company after careful deliberation and with the best interests of our clients, our people and our investors in mind." The equity offering raised $854.6 million in gross proceeds, and $811.9 million after underwriting fees.

In total, on the evening of May 4, Lazard raised $1.964 billion, with all but $61 million going right back out the door. Of course, the bulk of the money—$1.616 billion—went to Michel, Eurazeo, and the other capitalists. Steve Rattner lauded Bruce's accomplishment. "Bruce had all the cards," he told the *New York Times.* "He outmaneuvered Michel at every turn." At a Eurazeo shareholders' meeting that day, Michel told the crowd, "I was associated with Lazard for 45 years, and was its head, and very honored to be, for 25 years, so it's a major turning point." The night of the pricing, the deal teams from Goldman and Lazard celebrated with a dinner at Per Se, one of the finest and most expensive restaurants in New York City.

FOLLOWING A TIME-HONORED tradition, at 9:30 the next morning, Bruce and a group of about seventeen FOBs appeared at the podium, high above the trading floor of the exchange and in front of a large banner with the word "LAZARD" on it. The group had assembled to ring the opening bell at the stock exchange and to watch the first trades of the

Lazard stock. After the bell ringing, Bruce and Steve Golub went down to the floor of the exchange, specifically to the trading post of Banc of America Specialist, the specialist firm Lazard had selected, to watch the shares trade for the first time. What they witnessed was not pretty.

In theory, IPOs are carefully priced so that the demand for the newly traded stock slightly outstrips the supply. When that happens correctly, good things result. The price of the shares trades higher, and investors are happy. Underwriters are happy, too, because they do not have to put their own capital at risk supporting the stock—hence the idea of an underwriting—and they can exercise an option on something called the green shoe, an additional overallotment of 15 percent of the Lazard stock (in this case 5.1 million shares) that allowed them to buy at $25 a share, sell into a robust market at a higher price under the guise of "stabilizing the market," and thus increase their profits. If an IPO trades below its offer price, it is said to be "broken." When an IPO breaks, almost nobody is happy. The original buyers of the stock watch as its value drops, despite their best effort to determine the right price before buying. And if the IPO breaks, the underwriters obviously will not exercise the "green shoe" but instead are obligated to actually *underwrite* the offering by using their own capital to create support for the stock in the market. If someone wants to sell in those early days, the underwriters have to buy, which puts them in a position to lose a lot of money very quickly—something Wall Street firms try very hard to avoid. In the case of a broken IPO the only happy people are investors who sold the stock short—they bet correctly the price would fall—and those people, such as Michel, who sold their stock to Lazard for a price far higher than it turned out to be worth initially in the market.

The Lazard stock traded flat—at $25 per share—for the first twenty minutes or so, and then actually traded up, to a high of $25.24, just before 10:00 a.m. The stock then returned to $25 a share until around 11:45 a.m., and then it went downhill. LAZ ended the day at $24 a share, off $1, or 4 percent, on volume of just under thirty-five million shares. "When you see it trading near the offer price like that it means the underwriters are supporting the stock," Steve Rattner told *Bloomberg* that first day. "You normally want to see it go up 10 percent." Added a trader about the $24 closing price: "That's where the demand is." *Bloomberg* pointed out that Lazard became the first IPO of an investment bank in some time to fall on its first day of trading—both Greenhill (up 17 percent) and Goldman (up 33 percent) rose on their first day of trading—and became one of only a dozen large IPOs since 1987 to do so. Some observers of the IPO market noted that Goldman could not afford to let the Lazard deal fail. "It's too high-profile of a deal," commented a trader at Cantor Fitzgerald. "It is disappointing. I am sure that they didn't anticipate that type of downward price movement." Renaissance Capital, which provides independent research on newly public companies, wrote in a May 5 report about the Lazard IPO that "it seems every last penny was squeezed out of the initial investors" and that "we believe the primary causes of the poor reception [for the IPO] were the company's convoluted corporate structure and the valuation premium on the original deal. We still believe the current valuation is too high, particularly with the mixed trading in investment banking stocks." *Red Herring* called the Lazard IPO a "belly flop" and added: "The moral of this story boils down to what Wall Street is all about: Look out for No. 1." *Financial News,* in London, applauded Bruce's tenacity in getting the deal done in the face of the many obstacles Michel laid in his path. "However," it concluded, "a deal that is so transparently designed purely to wrestle control of the firm from chairman Michel David-Weill for the individual enrichment of Wasserstein and his key cohorts at the expense of shareholders has no place in the public equity markets."

Over that first weekend after the IPO, *Barron's*, one of the bibles of Wall Street, roundly criticized the deal under the headline "King's Ransom for Lazard" with a caricature of Bruce striking a particularly Napoleonic pose. "There are numerous negatives associated with the Lazard deal," the magazine stated. "The company has the dubious distinction of being one of the few financial firms ever to come public with a massively negative book value and junk-grade bond ratings from two major credit-rating agencies. Other drawbacks include Lazard's home in Bermuda, whose laws provide less protection to public shareholders than those in the U.S." The article went on to catalog the flaws of the deal and its high price tag nonetheless. "The Lazard IPO shapes up as a great deal for Wasserstein, former Lazard partners and current managing directors," *Barron's* concluded. "But other investors probably should stay away. There are far better Street franchises available at much better prices, including Goldman, Lehman, Bear Stearns and even embattled Morgan Stanley." For his part, Goldman's Tuft said the Lazard IPO proved to be a tough sell, at least initially: there were too many hedge funds looking to short the stock or that got into the deal looking for a short-term pop, and when that didn't happen, they dumped the stock in the market.

Per the Wall Street settlement rules, even though Lazard received its nearly $2 billion in proceeds on the night of May 4, the firm did not have to pay the money it owed to Michel, Eurazeo, et al. until May 10. On that day, via wire transfers, the money flowed. Michel received a little bit more than $328 million. He also had a small interest in two trusts that he set up—Louisiana Corp. and Sociedad Recovia—that together received $70 million. A trust named after the first initials of his four daughters—B.C.N.A.—received $1.1 million. Michel's sister, Éliane, received $99.4 million. Eurazeo, in which both Michel and his sister were large shareholders, received $784 million, by far the largest chunk of the proceeds. Eurazeo's stock increased some 37 percent in the year after Lazard filed the original S-1 and now has a market value of close to €5.5 billion. Antoine Bernheim, the eighty-year-old Lazard Paris consigliere and éminence grise of French deal making whose parents died at Auschwitz, got $64.3 million. Jean Guyot, a few years older than Bernheim, the former associate of Jean Monnet and the man behind the merger of the carmakers Peugeot and Citroën, received $61.2 million.

Some of André Meyer's descendants also got windfalls. Philippe Meyer, André's son, who had recently retired as a physics professor in Paris and who never sold the Lazard stock his father had bequeathed him, received $18 million directly and another $57.4 million through the "PM" trust. Philippe's son, Vincent, received around $43.6 million. André's other grandchildren, the Gerschels, got nothing.

While in the aftermath of the IPO, champagne corks could be heard popping from Paris to New York, where Bruce threw a large private party for his partners at the Four Seasons restaurant to celebrate, Lazard's bankers down at the headquarters of Goldman Sachs, at 55 Broad Street, were left with a terrible hangover. As Lazard's stock dropped on the first day of trading, Goldman fulfilled its obligation to make a market for investors, eventually accumulating the unheard-of short-term position in Lazard's stock of more than 10 percent. "Goldman obviously went way out on a limb to protect the Lazard offering," observed John Coffee, a well-known securities law professor at Columbia University. "Very, very rarely do underwriters do enough to become 10 percent holders." During the ten days or so after the IPO, Goldman continued, in vain, to make a market in the Lazard stock as the price continued to fall, causing Goldman to suffer a loss estimated to have exceeded $15 million. Goldman also made a fee of about $25 million for agreeing to be lead underwriter. The Goldman partner Ken Wilson said his firm's financial support for his former firm "left us with a little bit of a black eye." Luis Rinaldini suggested that another part of Goldman's metaphorical face suffered, too. "Bruce got his $25 and Goldman is licking its wounds from paying to help support a stock that is $21," he said on May 23. "Goldman has the slightly more bloody nose than Lazard." A Goldman spokesman countered, "It is our obligation as a market maker to step up to the plate for our clients." The *New York Times* financial columnist Andrew Ross Sorkin likened Goldman's defense of its support for Lazard to a "doctor who botched a brain surgery but bragged about his skill in stitching the patient back together." Tuft had obviously hoped for better but insisted that Goldman did the right thing for both its client—Lazard—and for its reputation as a leading underwriter of IPOs. "I was just very gratified that we were able to take what could have been a very difficult, terrible situation, if it didn't get public, and to really make this a public company and to make it a better firm," he said. "And I think it is a better firm." As for the decision to act as a backstop for the IPO in the marketplace, Tuft said, "The trading decisions were made because we wanted to stand up and support the stock, and we probably supported it a little too long in retrospect. Because the selling kept coming in and we expected the selling to dry up, and it didn't dry up, and when you look back at it, you see that the short interest expanded, and basically there was a whole group of people coming in shorting it."

The broken IPO and Goldman's trading losses did nothing but further bolster Bruce's reputation as a too-clever-by-half self-interested wheeler-dealer. And the bad news kept coming. The same day the IPO started trading came word that Lazard's capital markets business—now part of the separated company and wholly owned by the firm's working partners—had become the target of a federal probe by the U.S. attorney in Massachusetts into whether executives in that business lavished inappropriate gifts and gratuities on traders at Fidelity Investments, the behemoth mutual fund company. This was in addition to the SEC's investigation into the matter. The U.S. attorney Michael Sullivan in Boston impaneled a grand jury to investigate reports that Wall Street firms, including Lazard, had offered "sex and drugs" to the Fidelity traders to try to win their lucrative trading business. One published report told of a wild bachelor party—including the requisite antics of a stripper and of dwarf tossing—for a Fidelity trader, held in South Beach, in Miami, with transportation on a private jet and a private yacht, all paid for by Wall Street. Lazard disclosed both that Sullivan's office had asked it for information and that several employees in the capital markets business had resigned, including Greg Rice, the partner in charge of the firm's equities desk.

Ironically, within days of the news that it was the target of a federal probe, Fidelity filed a report with the SEC announcing that it owned 5.5 million Lazard shares, or 5.5 percent of the firm. A few weeks later, JPMorgan Chase announced it was the beneficial owner of 5.8 million shares of Lazard, which made it then the largest single outside shareholder of the firm. Other institutions piled into the Lazard offering as well, including T. Rowe Price, Morgan Stanley, Prudential, and Jennison Associates.

As serious as the federal probe was, its likely consequences for Lazard—the newly public company—were immaterial. A far larger problem, though, emerged on May 30 when word started to trickle out of Lazard in Paris that the rainmaker Gerardo Braggiotti, then fifty-three, had submitted his letter of resignation because Bruce failed to follow through on his supposed written pledge that he would expand Braggiotti's authority, to include running all of Lazard's European operations, in return for Braggiotti's long-withheld support for the IPO. Braggiotti submitted his resignation after a number of French bankers—among them said to be both Bruno Roger and Georges Ralli—opposed his new appointment. One Lazard banker in Europe thought that naming Braggiotti to the European post "would give him almost unlimited power in Europe and reduce Bruce's own role." Said Bruce: "Gerardo is a really talented guy, but I'm obviously not going to go and put him in charge of the French."

Braggiotti had almost single-handedly made Lazard the number-one M&A adviser in Italy, and his current fiefdom—Europe outside of France and England—generated 20 percent of Lazard's M&A revenue in 2004. "The loss of Mr. Braggiotti would be highly embarrassing for Lazard so soon after the IPO last month," the *Financial Times* wrote. Even worse for Bruce than losing one of the firm's top bankers was that he had not only promised Braggiotti the promotion but also agreed to pay him in cash for his stock (unlike almost every other Lazard managing director) and allowed him not to sign a noncompete agreement. If he quit Lazard, Braggiotti would not only walk away with all his cash but also be able to set up—or join—a rival firm after a six-week "notice" period. The clock began ticking May 30; the notice period would end on July 11. At this same time, Michael Gottschalk, one of the partners Bruce brought with him in early 2002 from DKW, announced he was leaving Lazard to join its rival Rothschild in New York. Then the partner George Brokaw announced his departure for Perry Capital, a New York hedge fund. And then partner Eytan Tigay, who had taken the laboring oar internally on the S-1 filings, left to join Robert Agostinelli at the Rhone Group. Speculation soon emerged that Braggiotti would return to his former firm, Mediobanca, causing the Italian bank's stock to rise 4 percent on the news.

But on June 8, in his first public comments about his new feud with Bruce, Braggiotti told *Bloomberg* in Milan that he had just returned from meeting with Bruce in New York the day before. "I presented my resignation and it's being discussed," he said. "I am going on holiday, not to Mediobanca." Braggiotti added that there was a meeting of the new Lazard board—its first—on June 14 where the matter would be discussed. "Let's leave them to make any announcements," he said. A New York headhunter told *Crain's New York Business* about Lazard: "This firm is held together with Scotch tape and chewing gum."

After the June 14 board meeting, Lazard announced a major reorganization of its European operations. In a press release, Bruce said the European reorganization "confirms the emergence of a new generation of talented leaders, who, along with their U.S. counterparts, are the future of Lazard." Left unsaid was the fact that Lazard in Paris was having one of its worst years in more than a decade, having slipped to sixteenth among French merger advisers. As recently as 2000, Lazard had a 40 percent market share in France.

Also noticeably absent from the new structure was Braggiotti. Lazard announced not only that Braggiotti had resigned, effective July 15, but also that his departure would not cause a "material adverse effect" on the firm's "overall 2005 financial results." The firm added, cryptically: "Lazard has reiterated to Mr. Braggiotti that it has complied with, and will continue to comply with, the agreement that Lazard and Mr. Braggiotti had signed, and Lazard and Mr. Braggiotti are in discussions concerning their relationship." After he sold his Lazard shares in the IPO and resigned, Braggiotti opened G. B. Partners, his own Milan-based boutique advisory firm. At the end of November, he announced that he was buying, for €100 million, Banca Leonardo, a small Milan-based bank founded in 1999.

He said he intended to use the bank as a platform to build a pan-European advisory, private-equity, and money management firm. After Leonardo's transformation, Braggiotti would be a formidable competitor to Lazard and Mediobanca. He planned to advise on mergers in Italy, France, and Germany. To accomplish this, he intended to hire about twenty M&A bankers across the continent.

Braggiotti began seeking €500 million in new capital for the new Gruppo Banca Leonardo. He quickly announced his first investor: none other than Eurazeo, with a €100 million commitment, for a 20 percent stake. "He was the deal maker at Mediobanca," Patrick Sayer explained. "He left Mediobanca and became the Italian deal maker at Lazard. I don't see why he wouldn't be able to replicate the same record at Leonardo."

An analyst in Paris told *Bloomberg*: "This would effectively be rebuilding the links between Michel David-Weill and Braggiotti." There was much competition across Europe from equity investors to get in on the Braggiotti deal. Even Felix thought Braggiotti was onto something big. "He's putting together a powerful machine," he told *Bloomberg*. In the summer of 2006, Banca Leonardo acquired a large minority stake in a French asset management company and also bought Toulouse Partners in France to jump-start an advisory practice right under Lazard's nose. Plans for Leonardo to open an office in London were being drawn up. Even Michel's longtime consigliere, Jean-Claude Haas, announced he was joining forces with Braggiotti.

For his part, Michel was well aware of the irony of his involvement in Braggiotti's firm. He was also well aware that his noncompete agreement with Lazard did not expire until the end of 2007 and that Eurazeo's investment raised a few eyebrows at Lazard. The *Financial Times* had even taken to referring to it as *Michel's* investment in Braggiotti's bank, not Eurazeo's. "Look, I'm sure they're not happy," he said of his former Lazard partners. "There have been phone calls, not to me, but to others, saying, 'Are you sure Michel knows what he's doing? Does he remember he has a noncompetition clause?' " He paused and took a deep drag on his Cuban cigar. As the smoke escaped from his mouth and swirled around him in the rarefied, sweet air of his warm Lazard office, a wry smile crept onto his impish face. "I do remember," he continued. "I'm not an officer of Eurazeo. I'm the chairman of the board. I will not be an officer of Braggiotti. I will not be on the board of his company. I'm as removed as can be."

ALMOST AS AN afterthought to its June 14 board meeting, Lazard announced its financial results for the first quarter, ended March 31, 2005. Net revenue was $245 million, and net income was $31.3 million, or thirty-one cents a share. Compared with the first quarter of 2004, net revenue was up 21 percent, and net income nearly tripled. The consensus of the Wall Street analysts—who for the first time were covering the firm and publishing reports about it—was that Lazard would earn about twenty-five cents a share in the first quarter of 2005. Bruce had beaten the Street consensus by some 24 percent, but it was insufficient to counter the negative news about Braggiotti. After the stock rose ninety-five cents a share, to $23.10, on June 14, in anticipation of the earnings announcement, LAZ closed at $22.90, down twenty cents. The stock still had not closed above its $25 IPO price.

For Bruce, the IPO was not an anomalous event in the firm's history, but rather an inevitability. "For me, the IPO fits into the continuity of Lazard's history," he said. "What did we actually do? We reinforced the tradition of Lazard, which, for 150 years, has been giving its customers the best possible advice, relying on both sector specialists and locally grounded expertise." He said that Eurazeo's historical stake in Lazard made Lazard a quasi-public entity anyway, albeit accompanied by tremendous and ongoing confusion. "I am happier in the current configuration," he said, "and I have no doubt about Lazard's capacity to fulfill its obligations to the market and its investors." When asked if a sale of Lazard was in the offing, Bruce demurred. "No," he said. "We are an independent bank, and there is no reason why that should change."

*

ON AUGUST 10, Lazard reported its financial results for the second quarter of 2005. The all-important metric of M&A net revenues was $182 million, up 35 percent from the second quarter of 2004. For the first six months of 2005, M&A net revenues were $304.3 million, up 46 percent from the same period the year before. As Bruce had promised, Lazard's revenues were surging along with the buoyant M&A market worldwide. Still, Lazard missed by one cent the Wall Street consensus of thirty-three cents a share in net income for the second quarter. Instead, the firm reported net income of $32 million, or thirty-two cents a share. On the investor conference call, which Bruce announced would occur only twice a year, he proclaimed himself satisfied with the firm's results. As to why Lazard had dropped to twelfth in the global M&A league tables to date for completed deals, from fourth in 2004, Bruce said many of Lazard's most important transactions are either private and therefore not included in the league tables or the advice to the client had been not to do a deal—and that does not show up in the league tables, either. But Brad Hintz, a securities industry analyst at Sanford C. Bernstein, said of Lazard, "The real challenge that they face is that their disclosed fee share of M&A has been actually declining since 2001. . . . If we look at market share, the numbers aren't as impressive." Still, critics aside, Bruce put his money where his mouth was. As the Lazard stock was hovering near the IPO price of $25 and at his first legal window of opportunity, at the end of August, he bought 119,500 additional Lazard shares in the market, at a cost to him of nearly $3 million. The bulk of the shares—106,000—were bought at precisely $25. Bruce now owned 11,394,534 Lazard shares, which made him by a factor of two Lazard's largest individual shareholder.

❦

Reflecting on the denouement, Marianne Gerschel, André's granddaughter, said that "a certain phase in the history of Lazard" had now passed reminding her of "the famous remark of Hegel that 'the owl of Minerva takes flight at dusk' "—Hegel's view that wisdom comes only in hindsight.

On the last day of August 2005, Bernard Sainte-Marie, a thirty-two-year employee of Lazard in both London and Paris, announced his resignation in a bitter and ironic e-mail that he sent to *everyone* at the firm and then leaked instantly to the press. "I will be leaving Lazard effective tomorrow after more than 32 years with various firms of the Group around the world," he wrote.

> I will be pursuing my career in the general unemployment line, as I am neither old enough or wealthy enough to retire. I wish myself every good fortune in the future. I am leaving on the high note of the IPO of Lazard with the knowledge (i) that I will be contributing to the stated intent of reducing the employment costs at Lazard by a total of more than $180 million per year and (ii) that I will not have to comply with the non-disparagement provisions contained in the agreement between Lazard and the "Historical Partners." I wish to congratulate the Head of Lazard for his success in selling the Lazard IPO to the investment public and to most (!) of Lazard's "Working Members." This will probably be judged in years to come not only as an even bolder act of financial wizardry than the sale of Wasserstein Perella, but also as a gesture of extraordinary altruism, since it was essentially done—from a cash point of view—for the benefit of the Historical Partners. I wish every success to the Lazard Working Members in their task of working down Lazard's mountain of debt and hopefully ultimately returning to a situation where the tangible book value attributable to their own (still indirect) interests in Lazard Ltd. will again be positive. Finally, let me say how gratifying it is, as the only direct descendant of the founding Lazard brothers currently employed in the Group, to sever ties with Lazard around the same time as my distant uncle Michel David-Weill who was the last family member (albeit not a direct descendant of the founding brothers) to run the firm.

Other longtime Lazard employees were equally bitter about how the firm had been transformed during the first years of the twenty-first century. "It's obscene what's going on here," said Annik Percival, Michel's longtime assistant in New York. "It's a very sad end to things and very predictable. I could do a character assassination, but I assume others have already done that." Percival had also been André's assistant until his death. "When André Meyer died, it was, for me, the end of an era," she continued. "The end of a dynasty. And I think the same thing is happening here now."

Afterword

On the morning of November 9, 2005, Lazard reported blowout earnings of $51.7 million, or fifty-two cents a share, above the Wall Street consensus estimates of thirty-seven cents a share. Revenues for the first nine months of 2005 were up 57 percent from the same period in 2004. By any measure, Lazard's business model was working magnificently—just as Bruce had predicted it would. In the press release accompanying the earnings report, Bruce took a well-deserved victory lap. "It is now clear that we are effectively executing our plan," he said. "The Lazard franchise is vibrant, our professionals are enthusiastic and the outlook for our business remains positive. Our clients continue to value independent advice and our global strategy positions us to continue to take advantage of the strong M&A environment." Lazard's stock price reacted positively to the news, rocketing up nearly 15 percent on the day and closing at $29.60 per share.

Finally, after six months of Bruce being lambasted for mispricing the stock and for overengineering an immensely complex deal, the Lazard stock was now some 20 percent above the IPO price. As the mid-decade M&A boom continued, the stock hit its all-time high on December 6, 2006, of $49.28 per share, giving the firm a market capitalization of around $6 billion; Bruce's Lazard shares *alone* that day were worth some $560 million. This was less than a week after Lazard priced a $638 million secondary offering—at $45.42 per share—of its common stock, some $260 million of which went into the pockets of the Lazard partners, aside from Bruce, who chose not to sell any of his holdings. In 2005, Bruce also received total compensation from Lazard of $14.2 million, more than quadruple his $3 million in 2004, which made him—on a compensation-per-dollar-of-market-cap basis—the highest-paid CEO on Wall Street.

But he continued to struggle to gain the admiration of his peers.

His most notorious nickname—Bid-'Em-Up Bruce—derived from his reputation, in the late 1980s, of advising his clients to pay more than rival bidders for the companies they desired. Bruce was said to deliver the "Dare to Be Great" speech to clients before final bids were due, not unlike how Robert Duvall's character in *Apocalypse Now* played Wagner's "Ride of the Valkyries" before heading off into battle. Bruce hates the nickname, and in fairness, whatever its relevance twenty years ago, it is no longer germane today. Nowadays, people refer to Bruce as the "Wizard," as in *The Wizard of Oz,* and he is not shy about cultivating the image of an inaccessible and powerful genius.

Bruce's Lazard is, ironically, a far more secretive and enigmatic place than it ever was under Michel, the Sun King. The fact that Lazard is now a public company merely exacerbates this irony, for even though its financial performance is disclosed publicly, Bruce is now free to hide further behind the curtain of secrecy under the guise of the requirements of the Sarbanes-Oxley Act. In contrast, Michel's door was always open to his partners—and pretty much to anyone else—and he would happily while away the hours talking to them about, among other things, art, women, and cigars. He believed he had few secrets from his partners; after all, the partnership agreement was revised and circulated every year with the new partnership points. True, not all the side deals were disclosed until Steve Rattner forced the issue, but even after their disclosure, many partners have said, the details of the side deals were not all that surprising. And despite cultivating an aura of secrecy, Michel regularly made himself available for lengthy on-the-record interviews with reporters (as did, to be sure, both Felix and Steve). Michel also prided himself on answering any question asked of him, whether from a partner, from the personnel, or from a reporter.

Bruce, meanwhile, has made himself deliberately and tactically unavailable to the press. Not surprisingly, the tiny smattering of interviews he has condoned since coming to Lazard have been completely choreographed to put him in near-total control of the moment or have served a particular need. When the attention does not serve him, he can be ruthless. For instance, without bothering to inform the writer involved, Bruce refused in late 2005 to publish a finished manuscript Michel commissioned, and Lazard paid for, by the French writer Guy Rougemont about the histories of both the Lazard and the David-Weill families before World War II. Lazard had also paid a woman in Utah to translate the book into English so that it could be published in the United States and England. Michel, who had given Rougemont access to the Lazard archive, said he found Bruce's decision to be petty, especially since the history ended when Michel was still a child. "It hurt me a little," he said. "It shows an indication that he refuses the past of the firm, and for no good reason in my opinion." Nor, of course, has *New York* printed the words "Bruce Wasserstein" or "Lazard" once in its editorial pages since Bruce bought the magazine.

Bruce has become both a powerful and a wealthy man. Thanks to the run-up in the Lazard stock price, he is unequivocally a billionaire, far wealthier than either Felix or Steve and on a par with Michel. No one on Wall Street has made more money from investment banking in the past decade than Bruce Wasserstein. In addition to a much-coveted independence and an even more heightened aura of inscrutability, his wealth has bought for him and Claude, and their two children together, an eleven-thousand-square-foot duplex "palace" that combines the tenth and eleventh floors of 927 Fifth Avenue, one of the finest and most exclusive limestone-clad apartment houses on Fifth. The small but extremely elegant 927 Fifth was built in 1917 and designed by Warren & Wetmore, the main architects of Grand Central Terminal. The twelve-story building, which also housed the famous red-tailed hawk Pale Male and his family, has only ten apartments and the cooperative's board can be notoriously fickle about who is allowed in. Bruce bought the tenth floor in 1997 for $10.5 million, and for about another $15 million he bought the eleventh floor in 2001 from Richard Gilder just as Bruce "moved" to London to avoid paying New York City and New York state taxes on the $625 million in cash he received in the Allianz-Dresdner deal.

Bruce also owns an apartment in London and one in Paris. The London apartment is a mere holding pen until he completes the renovation of the massive 38 Belgrave Square as his new home in that city. Belgrave Square, a few blocks from Buckingham Palace, is London's equivalent of Embassy Row, where countries such as Germany, Portugal, and Turkey have their embassies. The square surrounds a 4.5-acre private garden designed by George Basevi in 1826.

Bruce also owns a large spread in Santa Barbara, California, and a twenty-six-acre Atlantic oceanfront estate—Cranberry Dune—on exclusive Further Lane in East Hampton, with a fourteen-thousand-square-foot home. He is said to have paid around $4 million for a house in 1984 and then knocked it down and, for another $4 million, built a new house, which, together with the land, is now said to be worth more than $75 million. Bruce's secluded house, with seven bedrooms, five fireplaces, a tennis court, and a pool, is his "favorite refuge," where he is said to conjure up ideas during long walks on the beach. In the summer, Claude and her neighbor Jessica Seinfeld—wife of Jerry—create Camp Seahorse on the beach for all of their young kids and others from the exclusive neighborhood. Camp counselors are hired—and put up for the summer—and an entire fantasyland is set up on the beach, complete with cabanas with refreshments, big umbrellas, and a huge heavy bag filled with beach toys to keep the kids busy. Naturally, Bruce shuttles between all of his expensive real estate and the twenty-nine Lazard offices worldwide by the private Gulfstream jet Lazard provides for him. He reimburses the firm for his personal use of the jet, although that amount is not made available publicly.

There seemed to be a consensus forming in the spring of 2006, with the Lazard stock reaching all-time highs amid the robust M&A market globally, that Bruce may be finally, at fifty-eight, getting some of the respect he had long sought. "His belief in his own ability to sort of make it up as he goes along and his own personal power fuels him," said a close friend. "You know how envy fuels some people and jealousy. Insecurity fuels different people. His kind of belief in his own power, in his own myth, is, I really believe, what fuels him and his real belief that he's kind of an *Übermensch* character." The corollary observation to Bruce the almighty, though, is Bruce the sower of the seeds of his own destruction. Along with some questionable business judgments, his Achilles' heel may turn out to be the one thing he seems reluctant to get control of: his own health. He pushes himself fairly hard, travels relentlessly, and rarely exercises. While he slimmed down in the early 1990s, he appeared in early 2006 to be chronically overweight. He is said to suffer from a heart condition, and a few years back had quadruple bypass heart surgery. In two interviews he gave in December 2005, he said he had just recovered from a bout of pneumonia and several of the flu. He was said to be out of the office, and ill, from February to May.

The questions about Bruce's health reached a fever pitch in the summer of 2006, when numerous people around New York observed that he no longer looked well. In July 2006, someone who spoke with him at a New York restaurant described him as looking "frail" and "shaky" from having lost "so much weight" and wearing a suit that was "multiple sizes too big." Another person who saw him that same evening said that he looked like a "sickly seventy-year-old" instead of the once-invincible conqueror, and added, "He is in bad shape." Felix and his wife saw Bruce at an East Side brasserie and remarked to themselves that he looked terrible. Felix had heard that Bruce had been out of the office for several months in the spring of 2006 and wondered why Lazard did not disclose that fact to the market. The *Financial Times* asked Steve Golub point blank about Bruce's health on August 2, 2006, after Lazard reported second-quarter earnings. "He's fine," Golub said of Bruce.

Indeed, in an "exclusive" November 6 *BusinessWeek* cover story about how Bruce successfully "seized control of Lazard" and was busy "remaking the granddaddy of M&A," he looked thinner, heavily made-up, and posed in his Savile Row suit. Asked about the rumors that he was "gravely ill," he told the reporter Anthony Bianco, "It's just silly" and added, "I'm exactly the same weight I was ten years ago. I go through these cycles. I am trying to be fit." Moments later, Bianco reported that Bruce was enjoying "an elaborate coffee-and-ice-cream concoction" he supposedly needed to "fortify" himself "for my first press interview." A few weeks later, the press noted that Bruce was enjoying a huge steak at Peter Luger's in Brooklyn. Sadly, though, the fates have not been kind to his generation of Wasserstein siblings. His sister Sandra died in her prime at the age of sixty, in 1997, after a long struggle with breast cancer. Equally tragic, after a secret and valiant battle with lymphoma, his younger sister, Wendy, the famous playwright, died on January 30, 2006. She was only fifty-five. Lucy Jane, Wendy's young daughter, who was born in 1999 with the help of fertility treatments and raised by Wendy alone, now lives with Bruce and his family at 927 Fifth Avenue.

THE BEGRUDGING ACCOLADES for Bruce keep coming despite the valid criticism he received in some circles for agreeing to represent, in late November 2005, the billionaire corporate raider Carl Icahn and a group of dissident Time Warner shareholders—who together owned some 3.3 percent of the company—in their very public battle to try to boost Time Warner's long-beleaguered stock price by either pushing out the CEO, Dick Parsons, or breaking up the company, or both. Lazard was hired to analyze various strategic alternatives, find a slate of candidates to run as replacement board members at Time Warner, and make recommendations to Icahn and his group. Atypically, Lazard's recommendations would be made public as part of the campaign. The firm's fee for the assignment was $5 million initially, plus another $6.5 million for each dollar the Time Warner stock moved above $18 per share during the following eighteen months.

The assignment was full of irony, of course, for not only had Bruce, when he was at Wasserstein Perella, been the architect, representing Time Inc., of the controversial 1989 deal creating the highly leveraged Tim Warner, but Bruce had also trumpeted his involvement in the landmark AOL acquisition of Time Warner in 2000 despite having had no role in the deal. When it suited Bruce and improved Wasserstein Perella's rankings in the M&A league tables—for instance, on the eve of the sale of his firm to the Germans—he claimed credit for the largest U.S. merger of all time. When it no longer suited him—for instance, when the deal proved to be an embarrassing disaster—Bruce ran, metaphorically, like the wind.

Indeed, many blame both the original Time-Warner merger and the ill-fated AOL–Time Warner merger for creating the situation the dissident shareholders—and now Bruce and Lazard—were fighting to improve. Some believed Bruce took the Icahn assignment because he had grown frustrated by not being hired by Time Warner for any assignment since the AOL deal. "He just wants to be in the center of the action," Parsons said of him. Was it really possible that Bruce had so little shame that he could, in good conscience, represent Icahn in deconstructing the very company he once supposedly took great pride in helping to create? Was there nothing he wouldn't do for a fee? "He leads his whole life in an immoral way," said someone who knows him well. "In the Time Warner deal and in his relationships with women and people. He's fundamentally dishonest, and he lies with greater conviction than he tells the truth. He does. He does. I've seen it. *That's* when he's trying. And he brings to bear all his wits and focus, and he's damn good at it."

Through the end of 2005, while Bruce was busy mounting a self-serving publicity campaign on Icahn's behalf, his team of Lazard bankers worked virtually nonstop for two months—including through the Christmas and New Year's holidays—crunching the Time Warner numbers, analyzing the company's business lines, and drafting a narrative to fit the preordained conclusion that Time Warner's stock was desperately undervalued and the company needed to be broken up in order for the stock price to rise. A centerpiece of the Icahn strategy was to mount a proxy fight at the annual meeting in May 2006 and to elect a new, Icahn-centric slate of directors. If elected, the new directors would be in a position to implement the changes Lazard recommended. A search firm was hired to find candidates to stand for election to the Time Warner board and also to find someone to serve as the chairman and CEO of the company to implement the changes Icahn and Bruce recommended. A Web site was also created, EnhanceTimeWarner.com, to publicize the dissidents' every move. But it was very slow going finding candidates for the dissident slate and for the position of CEO. Frank Biondi, a former Hollywood CEO at both Viacom and Time Warner's HBO, and the brother of Bruce's partner Mike, eventually agreed to take the slot. The $6 million he was paid, regardless of whether the proxy fight succeeded (and more if it did succeed), didn't hurt in his decision-making process.

Nevertheless, the betting was still running against the Icahn group. More important, Icahn was not getting much, if any, additional support from the fast-money hedge fund crowd that he needed to join his bandwagon if he were to be successful in forming a big enough bloc of Time Warner shareholders to leave Parsons little choice but to accede to their demands. To many of these investors, Time Warner was simply a slow-growth, stodgy "old media" giant unlikely to provide them with the desired return.

The stage was now set for the long-anticipated unveiling of "The Lazard Report," the firm's 343-page tome of analysis and recommendations about how Time Warner should proceed if it wanted to increase its stock price. As theater, the ballyhooed February 7 press conference in the penthouse of the luxurious St. Regis Hotel could not have been any more dramatic had it been a few blocks west, on Broadway. It was being streamed live over the Internet. Large projection screens flanked a dais at the front of the room, where Bruce, Icahn, and Biondi presented the report's conclusions before an overflowing crowd of some five hundred bankers, analysts, investors, and reporters. The report, dated February 1, had been embargoed until the meeting got under way, when Bruce's troops distributed it around the room, providing little opportunity for a substantive review before the show began. The highly anticipated document featured high production values, including a glossy white cover emblazoned with the words "Time Warner Inc." and "The Lazard Report" in large black type. Subtle it was not.

Nor were its conclusions anything but a strident—often gratuitously so—indictment of accumulated sins. "TWX"—Time Warner's stock symbol—"is at the center of the storm that has and will continue to jolt American industry," the report stated. "This is the TWX story. It is a difficult story to tell because the history and performance of the Company has been skillfully enshrouded in the fog of one of the largest public relations efforts in American industry. The spin is generated by scores of divisional people, over 30 corporate image executives and a series of outside public relations firms. Success is heralded as triumph; failures are trumpeted as success. A corporate mythology is spun and is largely accepted, unchallenged by the media. Some facts are simply obscured. . . . It is now time to begin to lift the fog." To raised eyebrows, Bruce blamed Time Warner management for creating a "corporate inferno" that immolated at least $40 billion in shareholder value through a combination of, among other things, "bloated overhead" (evidenced by the company's new corporate headquarters at Columbus Circle and its fleet of corporate aircraft) and a "history of ineffectual deal execution" (for instance, losing the acquisition of AT&T Broadband to Comcast and selling Warner Music to a private-equity consortium for far less than it later proved to be worth) that allowed competitors to "take advantage of TWX." "The Lazard Report" did betray Bruce's ongoing sensitivity about his role—or lack thereof—in the disastrous AOL–Time Warner merger when he directed the Lazard team to footnote the utterly irrelevant fact that Wasserstein Perella was not the only Wall Street firm to claim credit for the AOL–Time Warner merger without actually working on the deal.

At the St. Regis, Bruce spoke first and articulated the Lazard solution. "Time has not been friendly to Time Warner over the last three years," he said. "The time to implement change is urgent." In addition to initiating a $20 billion program of share repurchases and cutting costs, Bruce recommended—as scripted—that Time Warner break itself up into four separate publicly traded independent companies. "There are no compelling reasons today for these businesses to remain together," he said. Instead of promised synergies from the businesses all being under one roof, "dis-synergies" have resulted, with the market now "placing a substantial discount on the value of the underlying assets." "The Lazard Report" stated that the implementation of Bruce's plan would lead to an increase in the Time Warner stock price to between $23.30 and $26.60 per share, from around $18. If that proved to be true, at the midpoint—around $25 a share—Time Warner's stock would have increased nearly 40 percent, and Lazard's total fee would be in the vicinity of $55 million, right up there with the largest single M&A fee ever paid ($60 million to Citigroup for its advice in the AOL–Time Warner deal). "If Dick Parsons indeed has the secret super-spicy sauce to deliver and generate value, we all say, 'Hallelujah' and 'God Bless,' " Bruce said in conclusion, attempting humor.

The Lazard brethren in attendance were positively giddy after the presentation. "What do you think of the new Lazard?" Ken Jacobs crowed to a former Lazard banker in the audience.

Reaction to the report—and its theatrical presentation—was swift. It "landed with the deafening thud of a doomed Broadway play," opined the *Times*'s media columnist David Carr. Added a Wall Street analyst at Deutsche Bank: "We were disappointed that nothing really new came out of their presentation or their report." Some even suggested that the Lazard analysis was fundamentally flawed because it had ignored the tax consequences of splitting the company into four pieces and landed "in the equivalent of the remainder bin before it had a chance to reach store shelves." Naturally, Bruce denied that he or Lazard had made any analytical errors. "Taxes fully understood," he e-mailed Ken Auletta at *The New Yorker.*

Regardless, Time Warner's stock fell 1.1 percent after the report was released. For his part, Parsons—beginning to sense Icahn was quickly losing momentum—said he would take the time to study Lazard's recommendations and, to that end, announced the hiring of both Goldman Sachs and Bear Stearns to provide him with strategic advice in deciding how to respond to Icahn's salvo. The media started gearing up for "what may turn out to be the biggest proxy fight in history" and an "RJR-style fee fest," a reference to the hundreds of millions in fees Henry Kravis paid to bankers, including Wasserstein Perella and Lazard, in the 1989 battle for RJR Nabisco.

Ten days later, it was all over. By themselves, in the days following February 7, Icahn and Parsons reached a face-saving compromise. Icahn knew he was beaten, at least at this juncture. Time Warner would remain a conglomerate with Parsons as its leader. The company acceded to Icahn's desire for a timely $20 billion stock buyback and an additional $500 million cost-reduction program. Icahn would also be able to consult with Parsons on the appointment of two new independent directors but not be able to appoint any himself. The initial news of the settlement sent the Time Warner stock up to just over $18 a share, but then fell to less than $16 a share. "No one who really has been around this space for any period of time believed that Carl had any answers that were novel or likely to result in the stock moving up," Parsons told a reporter on the eve of Time Warner's May 2006 annual meeting. (By July 2007 TWX was trading close to $21 per share.)

Bruce's brief and embarrassing high-profile gambit on Icahn's behalf had revealed just how far the "new Lazard" had strayed from the subtle and powerful shadowy operator that had long comprised the firm's complex genome. "For reasons that remain inexplicable," Andrew Ross Sorkin wrote in the *Times* after the compromise had been reached, "Mr. Wasserstein assumed the role of activist investor himself." Sorkin then canvassed Wall Street opinion to see how much reputational damage Bruce and Lazard had suffered, especially since only a month before Bruce had told Sorkin he considered himself "the trustee for the future" of Lazard. "Had he won, it would have been a different story," Sorkin discovered. "Mr. Wasserstein would have again proved himself to be the smartest guy in the room and beaten the odds. But in an advisory business based on demonstrating good judgment, he proved in this case, he didn't have much."

Acknowledgments

I spent almost six years at Lazard Frères in New York, in the banking group—beginning just after Steve Rattner's arrival in April 1989—first as an associate and then, after a promotion, as a vice president. From the outset, I knew I was part of something very special, as the firm was then perhaps at the height of its substantial power. As lustrous as it was for Kim Fennebresque to tell people he was a partner at Lazard, it was equally lustrous, although far less lucrative, to be able to say you worked there at all—even as a mushroom in the banking group.

Still, I never once thought that I would one day write this book. After all, I was now an investment banker, and my journalism days were a thing of the past. Accordingly, I never made a single note about my impressions of Lazard, for the simple reason that I was kept far too busy on a quotidian basis to pause and reflect on what was transpiring around me. Nevertheless, the ethos of Lazard could not help but penetrate my inner recesses, as it had so many before me.

There are many, many people whose kindness and generosity helped to make possible a book of this scope and ambition. At the outset, I had a certain degree of trepidation regarding how my former colleagues—the most senior of whom were now my main characters—would react to my efforts to write this story. But I was more than a little bit surprised and a lot pleased to find them generally receptive to helping me. And so I extend a word of thanks to them—especially to Michel David-Weill, Felix Rohatyn, Steve Rattner, Bill Loomis, David Verey, Bruno Roger, Steve Golub, Ken Wilson, Damon Mezzacappa, Jerry Rosenfeld, Nat Gregory, Ken Jacobs, and Kim Fennebresque. Thanks are also due to Patrick Gerschel, Vernon Jordan, Arthur Sulzberger Jr., Pete Peterson, and Ralph Nader—for being so generous with their recollections, insights, and opinions. Of course, there were at least a hundred other people in England, France, and the United States who made themselves available to me during the past two years and whose contributions were no less essential. For any number of reasons, it is preferable not to thank them in this forum. You know who you are, and I am most grateful for your help. To spend so many hours with people of such intelligence, wit, and nuance was one of the singular pleasures of this project. As was his prerogative, Bruce Wasserstein turned down my repeated requests to be interviewed.

One of the enduring myths about Lazard is the firm's penchant for secrecy. While this may have been true during the André Meyer era, once Felix became an accomplished banker and public figure, the number of stories about him and the firm ratcheted up exponentially, providing a treasure trove of information. There are at least five published books about Lazard, from Cary Reich's trailblazing *Financier,* published in 1983, to Martine Orange's *Ces Messieurs de Lazard,* published in 2006. There is also Guy Rougemont's unpublished history, which one can only hope will see the light of day. It has been my good fortune to have access to a number of sources of information about Lazard and its top bankers that heretofore, for whatever reason, had lain fallow. Among these are the insightful and revealing diaries kept by Adrian Evans during his tenure on Lazard's executive committee. For access to Evans's invaluable musings during this crucial period, I want to thank both David Verey and Adrian's widow, Ingela. For access to the hundreds of letters Frank Altschul wrote on a regular basis before and after World War II to his partners all over the globe, I want to thank Tamar E. Dougherty, the curator of the Herbert H. Lehman Suite and Papers in the Rare Book and Manuscript Library at Columbia University. Simon Canick, the head of public services at the Arthur W. Diamond Law Library, also at Columbia, provided me with the essential direction needed to uncover numerous public records and congressional testimonies that proved so useful in understanding Lazard's involvement in the ITT-Hartford fiasco as well as Felix's ongoing role in trying to influence public policy. Also invaluable with regard to understanding what really happened between Lazard, Mediobanca, and ITT were the thirty-four boxes of unorganized, unindexed documents that the Securities and Exchange Commission agreed to let me have access to, thanks to the Freedom of Information Act. I am doubly indebted to the SEC in Washington for showing remarkable flexibility and sense by agreeing to ship the documents, at my expense, to New York, so that I could peruse them unfettered, and pressure-free, for many months in the SEC's downtown Manhattan office in the Woolworth Building.

John Gardner, the deputy inspector of companies at the U.K.'s

Department of Trade and Industry, helped me to understand just how close Édouard Stern came to the line in making his investment in the Minorco–Consolidated Gold deal. After my inquiries, Wendy Galvin at the Bank of England publicly released for the first time a cache of secret documents relating to how the Bank of England accomplished its bailout of Lazard in London and Paris during the 1930s. Laurie-Ann Paliotti at the *Brown Daily Herald* provided invaluable research assistance, as did both Breeshna Javed and Jonathan Dobberstein at the *Michigan Daily.* I also received invaluable research assistance from Nis Kildegaard.

As a professional matter, there were any number of people inside the confines of Doubleday without whom I would be *nowheres*, as the Lazard partner Steve Golub is wont to say. It would be impossible not to put at the very top of this list my friend Steve Rubin, the publisher of Doubleday, who from the outset has been the tireless champion not only of this book but also of the satisfaction that comes from reinventing oneself professionally. From there, in alphabetical order, I would like to thank Bette Alexander, Barb Burg, Maria Carella, Dianne Choie, Charlie Conrad, Stacy Creamer, Melissa Ann Danaczko, David Drake, Jackie Everly, John Fontana, Luisa Francavilla, Phyllis Grann, Kendra Harpster, Suzanne Herz, Meredith McGinnis, Christine Pride, Louise Quayle, Richard Sarnoff, Ingrid Sterner, and Kathy Trager. Quite simply, there would be no *The Last Tycoons* without my editor, Bill Thomas, who not only had a clear vision of the narrative from the outset but also managed to sustain that clairvoyance through hours and hours of tireless editing, including while on the Chunnel and in a London hotel room. As far as I can tell, his only respite came while watching his beloved Yankees lose to my beloved Red Sox.

Personally, I have been sustained throughout this monastic process by a peerless cast of friends and relatives, who were unparalleled purveyors of succor. Among them in close to alphabetical order were Kurt Anderson and Anne Kreamer, Jane Barnet and Paul Gottsegen, Charlie and Sue Bell, Clara Bingham, Bryce Birdsall and Malcolm Kirk, Brad and Mary Burnham, Bryan Burrough, Jerome and M. D. Buttrick, John Buttrick, BVD, Miles and Lillian Cahn, Mike and Elisabeth Cannell, Alan and Pat Cantor, Richard Casavechia, Peter Davidson and Drew McGhee, Tom Dyja and Suzanne Gluck, Don and Anne Edwards, Stuart and Randi Epstein, Esther B. Fein, John and Tracy Flannery, JDFe, Bob Frye and Diane Love, Ann Godoff and Annik LaFarge, Larry Hirschhorn and Melissa Posen, Ted Gup, Tod Jacobs, Stu and Barb Jones, Michael and Fran Kates, Jamie and Cynthia Kempner, Jeffrey

Leeds, Jeffrey Liddle, Tom and Amanda Lister, Frank and Katherine Martucci, Patty Marx, Steve and Leora Mechanic, Hamilton and Katherine Mehlman, David Michaelis, Gemma Nyack, Dan and Sally Plants, Dudley Price, David Resnick and Cathy Klema, Andy and Courtney Savin, Bob and Francine Shanfield, Jim and Sue Simpson, Jeff and Kerry Strong, David Supino and Linda Pohs, Kit White and Andrea Barnet, Jay and Louisa Winthrop, Mike and Shirley Wise, Tim and Nina Zagat, Rick Van Zijl—and not the least by far, my fellow Red Sox fan in exile Esther Newberg. I also want to thank my in-laws, the Futters, and especially my recently deceased father-in-law, Victor Futter, a saint of a man who loved the written word and would have passed many a happy hour, I believe, reading this book. My parents, Suzanne and Paul, as well as my brothers, Peter and Jamie, and their wives and families, all were immensely supportive of me through this sometimes perilous passage. I am eternally grateful to them. I would also be remiss if I failed to mention the wisdom of my legendary journalism professor, Mel Mencher, who taught me, some twenty-five years ago, "You can't write writing, you can only write reporting." And a special word of thanks and appreciation needs to go to my longtime mentor, Gil Sewall, who has been nourishing my intellect for thirty years and who took the time out from his precious summer to read and reflect on this book in manuscript form.

It turned out that my literary agent, Joy Harris, is both the dearest friend and my closest professional advocate. Like Bill Thomas, she saw early on what this book might be and worked tirelessly to make it so. My unending thanks and considerable love go out to her.

Finally, and most emphatically, neither this tome nor my life would have much meaning without the unalloyed, unyielding, and unequivocal love and support of my wife and muse, Deb Futter. In so many ways, over so many years, she has been there for me. She has also been the most dedicated and amazing mother to the other two loves of my life, my nearly perfect sons, Teddy and Quentin, whose only discernible flaw is that they are inveterate Yankees fans.

Needless to say, any errors in fact, of omission, or of commission are my responsibility alone.

Notes

Abbreviations

AE Diaries of Adrian Evans
BG *Boston Globe*
BOE Bank of England Archive
BW Bruce Wasserstein
CC Celler Commission
FAP Frank Altschul Papers. Herbert H. Lehman Suite and Papers, Columbia University, Rare Book and Manuscript Library, New York
FGR Felix George Rohatyn
MDW Michel David-Weill
NY *The New Yorker*
NYSE New York Stock Exchange Archive
NYT *New York Times*
SEC Securities and Exchange Commission Files
SJC Senate Judiciary Committee 1972 Hearings on Richard Kleindienst Nomination as Attorney General
SR Steven Rattner
WL William Loomis
WSJ *Wall Street Journal*

Chapter 1. "Great Men"

2. "It is a great honor": FGR testimony before the Senate Foreign Relations Committee, July 31, 1997.
4. Felix tries to parse: FGR interview, December 17, 2004.
5. In his memoir: Robert E. Rubin and Jacob Weisberg, *In an Uncertain World* (New York: Random House, 2003).
5. "I thought": Ibid., p. 88.
6. "a group of important": Ralph Nader and William Taylor, *The Big Boys: Power and Position in American Business* (New York: Pantheon, 1986); and Andy Serwer, "Can Lazard Still Cut It?" *Fortune*, July 20, 1998.
6. "the interstitial man": Ibid., p. 196.
6. "Felix is enveloping": Ibid., p. 198.
6. "Oh, because we are": Ibid.
6. "the Teflon investment banker": Ibid., p. 216.
6. "But he accomplished": *NYT*, April 21, 1981.
7. "Monnet played": Nader and Taylor, *Big Boys*, p. 198.
7. "Sure, absolutely": Ibid., p. 199.
7. "I think power": Nader and Taylor, *Big Boys*, p. 202.
8. utterly typical week: SEC, FGR's January 1969 calendar.
8. "the grand rabbi": Jeremy Bernstein, "Allocating Sacrifice," originally published in the January 24, 1983, issue of *The New Yorker*.
9. "who came from": Ibid.
9. "would take to a desert island": FGR interview, WNYC, January 5, 2003.
9. "rapidly lost": Bernstein, "Allocating Sacrifice."
9. "I mean, the Austrians": FGR interview, November 29, 2004.
9. "A very traumatic": Bernstein, "Allocating Sacrifice."

9. "I remember": Ibid.
10. The story of Felix's escape: Ibid. and FGR interview, November 29, 2004.
10. "the classic route": *WSJ,* October 10, 1975.
10. "We started driving": FGR interview, November 29, 2004.
11. "something I will never": FGR interview, November 29, 2004.
11. "And we thought, clearly": FGR interview, November 29, 2004.
11. "I have felt": Bernstein, "Allocating Sacrifice."
11. "It was a miracle": *NYT,* April 11, 2005.
11. "As the Germans": FGR interview, November 29, 2004.
12. "There were always": FGR interview, November 29, 2004.
12. "Securing these visas": *NYT,* April 11, 2005.
12. "looked very elegant": FGR interview, November 29, 2004.
13. "As a last step": FGR interview, November 29, 2004.
13. "There were not that many": FGR interview, November 29, 2004.
13. "I think that was": FGR interview, November 29, 2004.
13. "We went to": Bernstein, "Allocating Sacrifice."
14. "They thought this": FGR interview, November 29, 2004.
14. "I became enamored": FGR interview, WNYC, January 5, 2003, and July 6, 2003.
14. "My most basic feelings": Peter Hellman, "The Wizard of Lazard," *NYT Magazine,* March 21, 1976.
14. "That experience has left me": Bernstein: Allocating Sacrifice."
15. "because they had": FGR interview, November 29, 2004.
15. "to try to talk us out": FGR interview, November 29, 2004.
15. "And this guy": FGR interview, November 29, 2004.
16. "I just stank": FGR interview, November 29, 2004.
16. "It was about": Patrick Gerschel interview, June 21, 2005.

Chapter 2. "Tomorrow, the Lazard House Will Go Down"

17. "Entire business totally": Western Union Telegraph Company cable, April 20, 1906.
17. "It is hardly": Western Union Telegraph Company cable, April 25, 1906.
18. Together, on July 12, 1848: Partnership agreement.
19. "business was so brisk": *Lazard Frères & Co.: The First 150 Years* (New York: Lazard Frères & Co., 1998), p. 13.
19. "Gradually, the business": Ibid.
20. "The intellectual horizon": *Lazard Frères & Co.,* p. 15.
21. "already learning": *NYT,* February 25, 1898.
22. "to see what kind of man": FAP.
23. "There is a very real": FAP, Frank Altschul, Letter to George Blumenthal, October 21, 1918.
23. "This would involve": FAP, "Exchange Situation," January 24, 1924.
24. "As we do not desire": Ibid.
24. "Using a $100 million": Darryl McLeod, "Capital Flight," in David R. Henderson, ed., *The Fortune Encyclopedia of Economics* (New York: Warner Books, 1993).
24. "Things are looking better": FAP, Christian Lazard to Frank Altschul, February 26, 1924.
24. "My heartiest congratulations": FAP, Frank Altschul to Christian Lazard, March 13, 1924.
25. "You can imagine": FAP, Christian Lazard to Frank Altschul, March 19, 1924.
25. "All the time": Ibid.
25. *"a secret":* Ibid.
25. "sister firms . . . We have placed": FAP, Christian Lazard to Frank Altschul, March 27, 1924.
26. "at the disposal of the Trust": FAP, Christian Lazard to Frank Altschul, February 26, 1924.

26. "13 white, no black": NYSE, December 20, 1923.
26. "Picasso of banking": Cary Reich, *Financier: The Biography of André Meyer* (New York: Morrow, 1983), p. 18.
26. "weak heart": Ibid., p. 24.
26. "It called for a quick mind": Ibid., p. 25.
27. "So it is with a clear head": *NYT Magazine,* September 21, 1924.
27. "He just took everybody": Patrick Gerschel interview, January 20, 2005.
27. "acquire, hold, sell": General American Investors Company Web site and FAP.
28. "It seems to me": FAP, Albert Forsch to Frank Altschul, August 28, 1929.
29. "An immediate consequence": R. S. Sayers, *The Bank of England, 1891–1944* (Cambridge, U.K.: Cambridge University Press, 1976), vol. 2, p. 389.
29 "There'll be a terrible time": Interview with a Lazard partner.
30. "the irregularities to which": BOE minutes, July 17, 1931, released publicly for the first time in 2005 after my inquiry; *Times* (London), July 31, 2005.
30. "another member of the staff": BOE minutes, July 17, 1931.
31. "Tomorrow, the Lazard House": Interview with a Lazard partner.
31. "put matters straight": Sayers, *Bank of England,* p. 530.
31. "an Accepting House": BOE minutes, July 17, 1931.
31. "would probably give rise to a state of panic": Ibid.
31. "the matter should be kept secret": Ibid.
31. "might unduly weaken": BOE minutes, July 18, 1931.
32. "to find": Ibid.
32. "Mr. Pearson feared": Ibid.
32. "For a long time": MDW interview, April 12, 2005.
33. "then gave to the other": Bank of England documents, Committee of Treasury, April 27, 1932.
33. "The most remarkable part": Hugo Kindersley interview, May 4, 2005.
34. "fair valuation for probate": Deloittes's evaluation of Lazard Brothers for estate of Lord Cowdray II, October 5, 1933.
34. "And the people of New York": MDW interview, April 12, 2005.
34. cryptic cablegram: FAP, from London to Frank Altschul, August 10, 1931.
35. "In the development": *NYT,* September 25, 1934, p. 38.
35. "While investment bankers": *Newsweek,* October 6, 1934.
36. "As you remember": FAP, Pierre David-Weill to Frank Altschul, July 20, 1936.
37. "some of the questions": FAP, Frank Altschul to Pierre David-Weill, July 29, 1936.
37. "The method was employed": FAP, Albert Forsch to Frank Altschul, August 1936.
38. two-volume catalog: Gabriel Henriot, *Collection David-Weill* (Paris, 1926–27).
38. "In remembrance of our": Ibid., in Avery Library, Columbia University School of Architecture.
38. "David Weill was": Guy Wildenstein interview, October 28, 2005.
38. "a large part" and "one of the most important": *NYT,* February 20, 1937, p. 19.
39. "He had liberated his walls": Daniel Wildenstein, *Marchands d'art* (Paris: Plon, 1999), p. 30.
39. The truth: MDW interview, April 12, 2005.
39. "a logical development": *NYT,* December 22, 1937, p. 39.
39. "weighted with four telephones": *Newsweek,* October 6, 1934.
39. "We all agreed": FAP, Pierre David-Weill to Frank Altschul, November 10, 1938.
40. "The object of my trip": Ibid.

Chapter 3. Original Sin

41. The ostensible reason for the change: MDW interview, April 12, 2005.
42. "He wanted the power": MDW interview, April 12, 2005.

42. "I suppose by now": FAP, Frank Altschul to André Meyer, August 16, 1939.
42. "I dislike hearing": Ibid.
43. "I am wondering": FAP, Frank Altschul to André Meyer, December 20, 1939.
43. "friendly cable": FAP, David David-Weill to Frank Altschul, September 13, 1939.
43. "I therefore turn": Ibid.
44. "Supplementing my letter": FAP, David David-Weill to Frank Altschul, September 25, 1939.
44. "all the matters of common": FAP, Frank Altschul to André Meyer, September 27, 1939.
44. "I cannot tell you": FAP, Frank Altschul to David David-Weill, May 13, 1940.
44. Meyer sent his wife: Cary Reich, *Financier: The Biography of André Meyer* (New York: Morrow, 1983), p. 33.
45. "Meyer had no illusions": Ibid., p. 33.
45. "havoc": Philippe Meyer interview, as well as account of family's escape from Paris, February 1, 2005.
45. "Mr. Harrington": FAP, Frank Altschul to André Meyer, June 27, 1940.
45. "It is good to know": FAP, Frank Altschul to André Meyer, July 2, 1940.
46. "There are people": FGR interview.
46. At the outbreak of the war: MDW interview, April 12, 2005.
46. "We are very patriotic": Suzanna Andrews, "The Scion in Winter," *Vanity Fair,* March 1997, p. 275.
47. "When you have the run": Guy Wildenstein interview, October 28, 2005.
47. "I unfortunately": FAP, David David-Weill to Frank Altschul, August 14, 1940.
47. October 1940: *NYT,* October 30, 1940, p. 7.
48. "Aryan" control: *NYT,* February 23, 1941, p. 16.
48. They fled Lyon: MDW interview, November 30, 2005.
48. "When you are so busy": FAP, Frank Altschul to Wallace Phillips, October 6, 1941.
49. "Gordian knot" and "It is not only": FAP, Frank Altschul to Henry Styles Bridges, October 21, 1941.
50. "may not like his friends": FAP, Frank Altschul to Adolph A. Berle, Sr., October 21, 1941.
50. "Pierre Weil": FAP, Fletcher Warren to Frank Altschul, October 25, 1941.
50. "after careful consideration": FAP, A. M. Warren to Frank Altschul, November 1, 1941.
50. "Awaiting news from you": FAP, Pierre David-Weill to Frank Altschul, April 6, 1942.
51. "urgent business trips": FAP, Pierre David-Weill to Frank Altschul, April 9, 1942.
51. "Distressed at all these delays": FAP, Frank Altschul to Pierre David-Weill (date unknown).
51. "should merely try to": FAP, Frank Altschul to Herbert Lehman, July 23, 1942.
51. "has not resulted": FAP, H. K. Trevers to Pierre David-Weill, August 22, 1942.
52. Altschul shot off a letter: FAP, Frank Altschul to F. P. Keppel, October 14, 1942.
52. "in a huff": MDW interview, November 30, 2005.
52. "I was not completely foolish": MDW interview, November 30, 2005.
52. "It was wonderful": MDW interview, September 15, 2004.
52. "My father told me": MDW interview, November 30, 2005.
53. "It was perfectly ordinary": MDW interview, November 30, 2005.
53. "It was all a great shock": Reich, *Financier,* p. 36.
53. Simone Rosen: Simone Rosen interview, April 27, 2005.
54. "Getting the RCA account": Patrick Gerschel interview, June 21, 2005.
54. "Dear Friends": FAP, André Meyer to Frank Altschul, et al., December 9, 1941.
55. "On a practiced level": FAP, André Meyer to Frank Altschul, January 9, 1942.

56. "I hope that this time": Ibid.
56. wrote to the State Department: FAP, Frank Altschul to F. P. Keppel, January 29, 1943.
56. "have been treated": FAP, Robert Kindersley to Frank Altschul, February 13, 1942.
56. "very appropriate reproof": FAP, Frank Altschul to Robert Kindersley, March 26, 1942.
57. "Pierre used to refer": Reich, *Financier,* p. 39.
57. "In one year": Ibid., p. 39.
57. Altschul would be "retiring": *NYT,* December 16, 1943.
57. Altschul was voted out: Gerschel interview, June 21, 2005.
58. "that had become": *Lazard Frères & Co.: The First 150 Years* (New York: Lazard Frères & Co., 1998), p. 30.
58. "I don't think the control": Reich, *Financier,* p. 41.
58. "He looks at": Robert Agostinelli interview, May 31, 2005.
58. "Many thanks for": Frank Altschul to Robert Kindersley, December 20, 1943.
59. "You no doubt": FAP, Frank Altschul to David David-Weill, October 16, 1944.
59. He never received a reply: FAP, Frank Altschul to Ginette Lazard, May 23, 1945.
59. "The trip was abominable": FAP, Frank Altschul to André Meyer, May 16, 1945.
60. "deepest sympathy": FAP, Frank Altschul to Pierre David-Weill, June 22, 1945.
60. "Berthe deeply touched": FAP, Pierre David-Weill to Frank Altschul, July 27, 1945.
60. "It is such a long time": FAP, Frank Altschul to Ginette Lazard, July 17, 1952.
60. "What André Meyer": Reich, *Financier,* pp. 41–42.
61. "He wanted to make this": Ibid., p. 42.

Chapter 4. "You Are Dealing with Greed and Power"

62. "He wanted to be able": Reich, *Financier,* p. 21.
62. lived in hotels, too: Lazard Frères & Co. office directory, November 1, 1977.
62. "André was not a rich man": Cary Reich, *Financier: The Biography of André Meyer* (New York: Morrow, 1983), p. 33.
63. "You know, André": Ibid., p. 52.
63. "The Lazard offices": Peter Hellman, "The Wizard of Lazard," *NYT,* March 21, 1976.
64. "in some rarefied social circles": Michael Jensen, "The Lazard Frères Style," *NYT,* May 28, 1972.
64. "In many ways": Reich, *Financier,* p. 18.
64. "He had kind of a crazy": François Voss interview, January 31, 2005.
64. "He works at the top": Anthony Sampson, *The Sovereign State: The Secret History of ITT* (London: Coronet Books, 1974), p. 72.
64. "Behind that stern": Reich, *Financier,* p. 356.
64. "André carried with him": FGR interview, May 25, 2005.
65. Brooks Brothers shirts: Mel Heineman interview.
65. "chewed me out": Reich, *Financier,* p. 186.
65. "I wasn't dare gonna": Interview with Frank Zarb, April 27, 2005.
65. "André, you are the most": Interview with Zarb; and Ron Chernow, *The Warburgs* (New York: Random House, 1993), p. 554.
66. "a dangerous place to work": David Supino interview, June 21, 2004.
67. "In some sense": Interview with a Lazard partner, although this idea is mentioned in numerous articles about both Felix and André.
67. "the first two are really one": *NYT,* September 11, 1979, but first in T. A. Wise, "In Trinity There Is Strength," *Fortune,* August 1968.

68. "Oh yes, André had": Reich, *Financier,* p. 98.
68. "*very* common knowledge": Ibid., p. 100.
68. "She would get away": Ibid.
68. "I think my grandfather": Ibid., p. 101.
68. "It's very possible": MDW interview, November 30, 2005.
69. "Jackie opened up his life": Reich, *Financier,* p. 259.
69. "His name constantly": Ibid.
69. "These Kennedys": Ibid., p. 258.
69. "I think he was probably upset": Ibid., p. 262.
69. "she was very sad": Ibid., p. 356.
70. "It was a monster": Ibid., p. 58.
70. 20 percent of Les Fils Dreyfus: SEC documents
70. "I have this stepson": FGR interview, November 29, 2004.
70. "I said to myself": Ibid.
71. "André yanked me": Ibid.
71. "He made it crystal clear": Jeremy Bernstein, "Allocating Sacrifice," *NY,* January 24, 1983.
71. "André also had": FGR interview, November 29, 2004.
71. "André said to me": Ibid.
72. "This was summer": Ibid.
72. "Well, this was a time": Ibid.
72. "It was done": Ibid.
73. "Take the pay cut": Ibid.
73. "I went to work": Bernstein, "Allocating Sacrifice."
74. "Rohatyn is in total": Sampson, *Sovereign State,* p. 73.

Chapter 5. Felix the Fixer

76. "Get in the car": Cary Reich, *Financier: The Biography of André Meyer* (New York: Morrow, 1983), p. 109.
77. "I get a call one day": Ibid., p. 110.
77. "That is the top salary": Ibid., p. 112.
78. "These people felt": Ibid., p. 113.
78. "Townsend would torture Meyer": Ibid., p. 117.
78. "I'm ahead of your plan": Ibid.
78. "You insist on this?": Ibid., p. 118.
79. "I'm terribly allergic": Several press reports, among them *Washington Post,* September 11, 1979, and *NYT,* October 28, 1965.
79. For Felix, the Avis payoff: CC report contains a plethora of documentation about the Lazard-Avis deal produced in connection with the House Antitrust Subcomittee's hearings on conglomerates.
79. "You have been screwed": Reich, *Financier,* p. 119.
79. "Nobody ever got poor": Ibid.
80. "If you have a good company": Robert Townsend, *Up the Organization* (New York: Knopf, 1970).
80. "Even those who hate": *Forbes,* May 1, 1968.
80. "Gentlemen, I have been thinking": Jack Anderson, *The Anderson Papers* (New York: Ballantine Books, 1974), p. 48.
80. ITT acquired 110 companies: CC report.
80. "practically an employee": Reich, *Financier,* p. 233.
81. "the best man always to placate": SEC files about Lazard's relationship with ITT. The SEC has some thirty-four unindexed, unorganized boxes of documents from its two multiyear investigations. The file, made available under the Freedom of Information Act, is labeled HO–536.
81. "Geneen is a very difficult": Reich, *Financier,* p. 232.
81. "Actually, we were entitled": Ibid., p. 237.
82. "Apparently Levitt's forte": CC report.
82. "Mr. Levitt is apparently": Ibid.
82. "they are already active": Ibid.
83. "This is an internal": Ibid., FGR's testimony.
83. "The thing that strikes me": Interview with a Lazard banker.
84. "Working for Felix was very difficult": Interview with a Lazard banker.
84. "Working for Felix was a death sentence": Interview with a Lazard banker.

84. "No, David, you are wrong": Interview with David Supino, October 8, 2006.
84. "a small list of questions": CC report.
84. "L. is *unique*": Ibid.
84. "The Levitt stock": Ibid.
85. "This is probably just as well": Ibid.
85. "It may be that alternatives": Ibid.
87. "the assistance of a few advisers": Ibid.
88. "Our corporate clients": Ibid.
88. "Lazard will, from time to time": Ibid.
88. "In this connection": Ibid.
89. "Typically, we are asked": Ibid.
89. "As I tried to indicate": Ibid.
90. "I would say that": Ibid.
90. "No, sir": Ibid.
90. "We don't view ourselves": Ibid.
92. "While it is highly technical": Ibid.
92. "Yes, sir": Ibid.
94. "You should come": *NYT,* July 18, 2004.
95. "the worst of the paperwork": NYSE annual report, 1969.
95. "We were looking at the world": *NYT,* January 24, 1971.
96. "a bunch of blue bloods": Monica Langley, *Tearing Down the Walls* (New York: Free Press, 2003), p. 23.
96. "never heard of them": Ibid.
96. "At 9:15 that morning": *NYT,* January 24, 1971.
97. "The brokerage firm found": *NYT,* March 28, 1971.
97 "If you don't tell me the facts": *NYT,* March 24, 1971.
97. "If DuPont had failed": *NYT,* March 28, 1971.
98. "I'm sort of going through": FGR interview, December 17, 2004.
98. "We just threw money in": *NYT,* March 24, 1971.
99. "And nobody ever said": FGR interview, December 17, 2004.
99. "The questions raised": *NYT,* June 21, 1971; and FGR letter to Robert Haack, June 11, 1971.
100. "We had a house on fire": FGR congressional testimony, House of Representatives Subcommittee on Commerce and Finance, August 2 and 3, 1971, p. 144.
100. "Felix Rohatyn": CC report.
101. "Very shy but very clever": François Voss interview, January 31, 2005.
101. "If any banker": Reich, *Financier,* p. 295.
101. "The standard shot of him": Ibid.
101. "Their relationship was exceptional": Ibid.
101. "They were intimates": Voss interview, January 31, 2005.
102. "on top of everybody": SEC files, André Meyer SEC testimony.
102. Lazard's investment in Mediobanca: *NYT*, September 15, 1955.
102. "memorandum of understanding": SEC files.
103. Italian manufacturer, Necchi: Ibid.
103. "I refer to our meeting": Ibid.
103. "behind the back": Ibid.
103. "did have and do have": Ibid.
103. Tobacco Memorandum: Ibid.
104. "an excellent investment": Ibid.
104. "the long-range possibility": Ibid.
104. "Hartford—she's a blue-blooded lady": Ibid.
105. "I had an understanding with them": Ibid.
105. "the future vitality of our free economy": Ibid.
106. "full panoply" and "inexorable pressure": Ibid., Geneen memos.
106. "I think that during the ensuing": Ibid.
106. On his first day back in the office: Ibid., FGR's calendar.
107. "The course is scenic and exacting": SEC files.
107. "Now that it looks like": Ibid.
108. "he thought they had the size": Ibid., FGR's SEC testimony.
108. "Dr. Cuccia is a very cold": Ibid., André Meyer's SEC testimony.
108. "Have talked to both Geneen": Ibid., telex from FGR to André Meyer.
109. IRS ruling and John Seath's letters: Ibid.

109. "Mediobanca had the option": Ibid., FGR's SEC testimony.
109. October 7, 1969, version of the ITT deal: Ibid., SEC files.
112. "urging that the Department of Justice": SEC files, Walsh to Kleindienst.
112. "It was, I am afraid": SJC, Walsh testimony.
112. "it is our understanding": SEC files, Walsh letter.
113. "The door is open": SJC, Jack Ryan testimony.
113. "He is a rather quiet individual": Ibid.
113. "recognized financial figure": SJC, Richard Kleindienst testimony.
113. "at his invitation, to give him": SJC, FGR testimony.
113. "I thought he might have seemed": Ibid.
114. "I believe that for the record": Ibid., Kleindienst testimony.
114. "it might have additional repercussions": SEC files.
114. "I probably would have": SJC, Walsh testimony.
114. "Hi, Dick": From publicly available transcripts of Oval Office tapes of Richard M. Nixon.
115. "Immediately thereafter, I sent word": SJC, Kleindienst testimony.
115. FGR's April 29 meeting: SJC and SEC files.
116. Kleindienst's specific request: SEC files.
116. "amplify and augment": SEC files, FGR's May 3 letter.
116. FGR's May 10 meeting: SJC and SEC files.
116. "Rohatyn said it was a serious matter": SJC, Kleindienst testimony.
117. "They give us Grinnell": Nixon Oval Office tapes.
117. June 16 call to FGR: SEC files and SJC.
117. "negotiating memorandum": SEC files.
117. "within twelve seconds": SEC files and SJC.
118. FGR's June 18 call: SEC files.
118. FGR's June 29 meeting: SEC files and SJC.
118. "to complain about the rather rigid": SJC, Kleindienst testimony.
118. "Mr. Rohatyn indicated his belief": SJC, Peter Flanigan testimony; and Flanigan interview with author.
118. July 31 settlement agreement: SEC files.
119. "We wish to object": SEC files.
119. Geneen pledged some $400,000: SEC files and SJC.
120. "son-of-a-bitch" McLaren: Nixon Oval Office tapes.
120. "McLaren came in like a lion": I. F. Stone, "Behind the I.T.T. Scandal," *New York Review of Books,* April 6, 1972; also in SEC files.
120. Larry O'Brien letter to John Mitchell: SEC files.
120. "The settlement between the Department of Justice": SEC files.
121. the columnist Jack Anderson: Anderson's columns appeared on February 29, March 2, and March 3, 1972: Anderson, *Anderson Papers,* pp. 94–96.
121. "That was again totally stupid": Interview with FGR, December 17, 2004.
123. "the two persons with whom": SJC, Kleindienst testimony.
123. "No, sir," he told Kennedy: Ibid.
123. "In conclusion, I want to emphasize": SJC, McLaren testimony.
124. "I was thought qualified": Ibid.
124. "Every meeting was on the record": Ibid.
124. "The suggestion that discussions with Rohatyn": Anderson, *Anderson Papers,* p. 119.
124. "talking with my children": SJC, FGR testimony.
125. "Let me say now that I": Ibid.
125. "my influence and persuasiveness": Ibid.
125. "categorically false": SJC, Kleindienst testimony.
125. "I think those are terribly serious": SJC, McLaren testimony.

128. Colson memos: SEC files; and *NYT,* August 13, October 30, November 1, and November 19, 1973.
128. Colson and Nixon conversation: Nixon Oval Office tapes, March 30, 1972.
129. "Very occasionally": Nicholas von Hoffman, *Washington Post,* March 10, 1972.
130. "I am kind of a stubborn": SJC, Kleindienst testimony.
131. "One thing I learned": *WSJ,* October 10, 1975.
131. "I did something stupid" to "no clue what this was all about": Interview with FGR, December 17, 2004.

Chapter 6. The Savior of New York

134. "The world of investment banking": Michael Jensen, "The Lazard Frères Style," *NYT,* May 28, 1972.
135. "André was impressed": Interview with Robert Ellsworth.
135. "André didn't know": Cary Reich, *Financier: The Biography of André Meyer* (New York: Morrow, 1983), p. 189.
135. "I'd go over to his apartment": Ibid.
135. "trivial political gossip": Interview with Ellsworth.
136. "four or five hours": SEC files, Thomas Mullarkey testimony.
136. "had nothing to do with it": SEC files, FGR testimony.
136. "I just distanced myself": Interview with FGR, December 17, 2004.
137. On June 16, 1972: SEC files, SEC charge against Lazard.
137. "simple gold Tiffany clock": Cary Reich, "The Legacy of André Meyer," *Institutional Investor,* April 1979.
138. Kennedy told Casey: *WSJ,* June 28, 1973.
138. out-of-court settlement: SEC files.
138. "That was big, big stuff": Interview with Stanley Sporkin, October 22, 2004.
139. a rare public statement: SEC files.
139. lawsuits were filed against ITT: SEC files.
140. "Secret documents which escaped shredding": Jack Anderson columns from U.S. Senate investigations on the International Telephone and Telegraph Co. and Chile, 1970–71, March–April 1973.
143. "model of the new breed": "The Remarkable Felix G. Rohatyn," *BusinessWeek,* March 10, 1973.
145. "André didn't like it one bit": Interview with FGR, January 3, 2005.
146. "I am still far from satisfied": FGR "Dark Ages" memo, April 9, 1973.
146. IRS decided to revoke: *NYT,* March 7, 1974, and *WSJ,* April 15, 1974.
147. "In the unlikely event": SEC files.
147. FGR testimony November 16, 1973, and April 24, 1974: SEC files.
148. Mullarkey testimony November 16, 1973, and April 24, 1974: SEC files.
148. André Meyer testimony on four separate occasions: SEC files.
152. "merger mastermind": Michael Jensen, *NYT,* June 23, 1974.
152. "It's far and away": Ibid.
152. "If he pulls it off": *Time,* June 17, 1974.
153. FGR editorial about RFC: *NYT,* December 1, 1974.
153. Gus Levy and William McChesney Martin letters to the editor: *NYT,* December 22, 1974.
153. "If Lockheed is the kind": *Forbes,* January 15, 1975.
154. the SEC's *second* examination: SEC files.
155. "I got a call from David Burke" and the story of becoming head of MAC: Interview with FGR, January 20, 2005.
156. "For the last two weeks": *NYT,* June 5, 1975.
156. "They may be new to the problem": Ibid.
157. "I didn't tell the Republicans": *WSJ,* October 10, 1975.
157. "Congratulations. Sisyphus should have": *Fortune,* October 1975.
157. "Plays hob with my domestic life": *Washington Post,* November 11, 1956.
158. "Jeannette was very intelligent": Judith Ramsey Ehrlich and Barry Rehfeld,

The New Crowd (Boston: Little, Brown, 1989). p. 97.
158. "She was an extraordinarily bright": Ibid.
158. Description of FGR's years with Helene Gaillet: Interview with Helene Gaillet, February 3, 2006.
160. "stuffed with books, magazines": Peter Hellman, "The Wizard of Lazard," *NYT Magazine,* March 21, 1976; and *WSJ,* October 10, 1975. Felix even once described the Alrae as a "dump" and said that when he was dating his second wife, Elizabeth, she insisted he move out (Ehrlich and Rehfeld, *New Crowd,* p. 165).
165. "Look, I was living with a woman": Interview with FGR, May 25, 2005.
165. "In those days": Ehrlich and Rehfeld, *New Crowd,* p. 164.
166. "He is the Henry Kissinger": *Newsweek,* August 4, 1975.
166. "It was just a relatively small": SEC files, FGR testimony.
167. "There was no reason for me": Interview with Mel Heineman.
167. "The only recollection I have": SEC files, Heineman testimony.
168. "Mr. Heineman is a nice man": SEC files, Meyer testimony.
168. "To the best that I can": SEC files, Heineman testimony.
169. "were linked": SEC files, Mullarkey testimony.
170. "Mr. Sundick, are you": Ibid.
170. "It's my present impression": Ibid.
171. "André found some people": Interview with FGR, December 17, 2004.
171. Sam Harris's letter to Irwin Borowski: SEC files.
171. October 13, 1976, settlement between SEC and Lazard: SEC files.
172. "new light on one of the most complex": Judith Miller, *NYT,* October 14, 1976, p. 78.
172. the SEC's single-spaced compendium: *In the Matter of International Telephone and Telegraph Corporation, Lazard Frères,* release no. 14049, October 13, 1976.
174. criminal grand jury: Interviews with Robert Price, April 15, 2005; Disque Deane, August 17, 2005; Patrick Gerschel, June 21, 2005; and others.
176. Felix adamantly and repeatedly denied: Interviews with FGR among them, May 25, 2005, and January 17, 2006.
176. Sporkin denied: Interview with Sporkin, June 3, 2005.
176. "I swear on the Torah": Interview with Price, December 14, 2005.
177. "I will confirm that, yes": Interview with Deane, August 17, 2005.
177. "Felix would deny that he was walking": Interview with Gerschel, June 21, 2005.
178. "we are very pleased": *NYT,* May 9, 1981.
178. "was unable to push a paper clip": Reich, *Financier*, p. 311.
178. "It was brilliantly conceived": Ibid., p. 331.
179. wrapped in brown paper: Message from Disque Deane, August 22, 2005, and interview, September 13, 2005.
179. "It was not so much a sale": Ibid., p. 359.
179. "It was a typical rich man's": Ibid., p. 360.
179. "The prized André Meyer": Ibid.
180. "stand as an enduring": Douglas Dillon homage to André Meyer, *Congressional Record,* October 11, 1979.
180. "The Meyer Galleries were as crisp": Paul Goldberger, *NYT,* September 19, 1993.
180. "Timeliness, style and charm": Jacob Javits, *Congressional Record,* October 11, 1979.
180. "Rohatyn's voice cracked": Reich, *Financier,* p. 355.
180. "Sometimes I imagine": Ibid., p. 356.

Chapter 7. The Sun King

183. *"haute banque d'affaires"*: "The Making of Lazard's Michel David-Weill," *Euromoney,* March 1981.

183. "perhaps a little bit more": Interview with a Lazard partner.
184. "I guess the thinking of the 'early runners' ": Interview with a Lazard partner.
184. "Frank Zarb once told me": Interview with a Lazard partner.
184. "Objectively, Michel is the landowner": Jean-Claude Haas, "Assault on the House of Lazard," *Forbes,* September 4, 2000.
184. "This is not a partnership": Interview with Frank Pizzitola, April 18, 2005.
185. "You would need many advanced degrees": Interview with a Lazard partner.
185. "did things as a helper": *Fortune,* November 1977.
185. "If you don't see us getting back": Cary Reich, *Financier: The Biography of André Meyer* (New York: Morrow, 1983), p. 243.
185. "I had to persuade him": Ibid., p. 244.
186. "The president stepped down": *Fortune,* November 1977.
186. "the real significance of the Franco Wyoming deal": Reich, *Financier,* p. 246.
186. "Memorandum to Partners": André Meyer, December 26, 1974.
187. "So as to show who was in charge": Interview with a Lazard partner.
188. "Pierre was so smart": Interview with Robert Ellsworth.
188. "My father had, in my opinion": Interview with MDW, November 30, 2005.
189. "He was an immortal": Interview with Patrick Gerschel, June 21, 2005.
189. "I have a certain degree of influence": Robert J. Cole, "End of an Era at Lazard," *NYT,* January 30, 1977.
190. "Mr. Rohatyn is a very important man": Ibid.
190. "not something I yearn for": *NYT,* August 22, 1976.
190. "Suppose I was appointed": Peter Hellman, "The Wizard of Lazard," *NYT Magazine,* March 21, 1976.
190. July 2, 1976: Memorandum to partners from Donald Cook.
190. August 19: Memorandum to partners from Donald Cook.
191. "And it went from bad to worse": Interview with Gerschel, January 20, 2005.
192. September 1976: Memorandum to partners from André Meyer and MDW.
193. "strictly confidential": Cole, "End of an Era at Lazard."
194. "We saw them drifting downward": Cary Reich, "The Legacy of André Meyer," *Institutional Investor,* April 1979.
194. "The risk was not of losing business": "The Making of Lazard's Michel David-Weill."
195. "He was politicking": Interview with Gerschel, June 21, 2005.
195. "I told him it wouldn't be good": FGR, *Newsweek,* May 4, 1981.
195. "We were riding through": SEC files, Mullarkey testimony.
195. "The Lazard I knew": Interview with FGR, November 29, 2004.
195. "The firm was very lucky": Interview with MDW, January 31, 2005.
196. "I was born to great opportunity": Wyndham Robertson, "Passing the Baton at Lazard Frères," *Fortune,* November 1977.
197. "Too bad, you have come too late": Among others, *Institutional Investor,* May 1993.
197. low overhead, M&A focused: Robertson, "Passing the Baton at Lazard Frères."
198. Patrick Gerschel's background: Interview with Gerschel, January 12, 2005.
199. "You know a clerk is a clerk": Ibid.
199. "It was a very curious kind of place": Ibid.
199. "People who write memos": Ibid.
199. "This was cuckoo land": Ibid.
200. "To be number one at Lazard": Interview with François Voss, January 31, 2005.
200. "It was a shocking breach": Reich, *Financier,* p. 339.
200. "At first, Patrick was just": Ibid.
200. "Patrick was trying to become the senior partner": Interview with Disque Deane, August 17, 2005.

200. "since he never talked to Cook": Interview with Gerschel, January 12, 2005.
200. "wasn't very good": Ibid.
200. "I thought that was an asinine remark": Reich, "Legacy of André Meyer."
200. "André Meyer's view of life": Interview with Gerschel, January 12, 2005.
201. "He loved that firm": Ibid.
201. "He was just a young man": Interview with FGR, January 20, 2005.
201. "I was a special case": Interview with Gerschel, January 12, 2005.
201. "Don't be so silly": Ibid.
203. "In New York, if you had asked": "The Making of Lazard's Michel David-Weill."
203. "At that time and even seen": "The Last Emperor," *BusinessWeek,* May 30, 1988.
203. "the heir of a celebrated line": *Le Nouvel Économiste,* July 1978.
204. "After 183 years of doing business": *NYT,* May 1, 1975.
205."It was a Napoleonic first act": Interview with a Lazard partner.
205. no intention of promoting any internal candidates: Interview with WL, January 26, 2005.
205. "disappointed": Interview with Peter Lewis, March 8, 2005.
206. "We cut back quite a bit": *NYT,* September 11, 1979.
206. "Particularly during the years": Reich, "Legacy of André Meyer."
206."It was like looking in the mirror": Ibid.
206. "Mr. Meyer wanted to know": Reich, *Financier,* p. 348.
206. "It is a little different if you are a partner": Ibid.
206. "the relationships are getting closer": Reich, "Legacy of André Meyer."
207."Last month, four Lehman partners": *Fortune,* September 1978.
207."Before coming to Lehman Brothers": Ken Auletta, *Greed and Glory on Wall Street* (New York: Warner Books, 1986), p. 55.
207. \$5,000 bonus check: Ibid.
207. "So it is to be war": Ibid.
208. "Count me in, Jimmy": *Fortune,* September 25, 1978.
208. "I was very well impressed": Ibid.
208. "But my personal relationship with him": Reich, "Legacy of André Meyer."
208. "angry shouting, sealed desks": Ibid.
208. "Door locks were changed": Auletta, *Greed and Glory,* p. 58.
208. "With his big cigar": Interview with Pete Peterson, May 26, 2005.
208. "cancelled the bonus of my secretary": Auletta, *Greed and Glory,* p. 58.
208. attempting to buy a real estate asset: Ibid., pp. 56–58.
208. "Everybody was pretty appalled": Interview with Peterson, May 26, 2005.
208. "And I just sat there": Ibid.
209. "It is the sort of typecasting": Auletta, *Greed and Glory,* p. 56.
209. "People have said Jim Glanville": Ibid.
209. "Pete is a friend of mine": Interview with Ward Woods, February 16, 2005.
209. "I mean, Glanville was": Interview with FGR, January 3, 2005.
210. letter of "congratulations": FAP, Frank Altschul to Bobby Lehman, October 4, 1966.
210. "My view on U.S. relations with Israel": Auletta, *Greed and Glory,* p. 56.
210. "Glanville wrote one of the most": Interview with Peterson, May 26, 2005.
210. "And I recall saying": Ibid.
211. "That there was a place": Interview with Woods, February 16, 2005.
211. "We live in cramped quarters": *Fortune,* September 25, 1978.
212. "As is often the case": WL memorandum to Sidney Wolf, October 15, 1975.
212. "And he says to me": Interview with Mina Gerowin, January 6, 2005.
212. "The secretaries have to go": Reich, *Financier,* p. 349, and "Legacy of André Meyer."
212. "You don't have to say with whom": Reich, *Financier,* p. 349, and "Legacy of André Meyer."

212. "Do you want to know what I do": Reich, *Financier,* p. 349.
213. "I found a group": Interview with Woods, February 16, 2005.
213. "dark place": Interview with WL, January 26, 2005.
213. "He had a powerful grip": Interview with Damon Mezzacappa, August 2, 2004.
213. "We went to this meeting": Interview with Roger Briggs.
214. "created somewhat of a problem": "The Making of Lazard's Michel David-Weill."
214. "I remember Michel coming to see me": Interview with FGR, January 20, 2005.
214. "André Meyer treated Michel": Interview with a Lazard partner.
215. "He is a boy": Interview with Pizzitola, April 18, 2005.
215. "When he did ask me to come back": Interview with MDW, September 15, 2004.
215. "I was not sure I could": "The Making of Lazard's Michel David-Weill."
215. "Bobbie Lehman I can testify": Interview with MDW, January 12, 2005.
215. "There are just so many deals": *Newsweek,* May 4, 1981.
216. Oppenheimer approached Felix: FGR interview.
216. "I will always invent deals": *NYT,* July 23, 1978.
216. "Unlike most government officials": Ibid.
216. "My being able": Ibid.
216. "He is the Big Apple's Henry Kissinger": *WSJ,* September 22, 1978.
217. "Our economy is out of control": Felix G. Rohatyn, *The Twenty-Year Century* (New York: Random House, 1984), p. 170.
217. "Being in the public eye": *W,* February 2, 1979.

Chapter 8. Felix for President

218. "From my point of view": Interview with FGR.
218. "In the last couple of years": Cary Reich, "The Legacy of André Meyer," *Institutional Investor,* April 1979.
219. "broad tape": FGR's memorandum, January 24, 1979.
219. "The procedure outlined": Frank Pizzitola memorandum, February 28, 1979.
220. "One year, we paid": Interview with Frank Zarb, April 27, 2005.
220. "He has a European": Reich, "Legacy of André Meyer."
220. "today probably closest personal friend": Andy Logan, "Around City Hall," *NY,* April 30, 1979.
220. "Liz was getting very frustrated": Interview with Victor Gotbaum, February 28, 2006.
221. "Felix wanted him": Ibid.
221. "We had an extraordinarily enlightening": Logan, "Around City Hall."
221. "It didn't unwind": Interview with Gotbaum, February 28, 2006.
221. "Felix was very nervous": Ibid.
222. "propelled him to national prominence": *NYT,* October 16, 1983.
222. "I like big cities": *Newsweek,* May 4, 1981.
223. "felt that it was unfair," Logan, "Around City Hall."
223. "certainly a moral conflict of interest": *New York Post* and also *NYT,* March 7, 1979.
223. "The privilege of public service": Jack Tamagni letter of resignation, *NYT,* March 8, 1979.
223. "notable public service": *Economist,* March 17, 1979; and Logan, "Around City Hall."
224. "a pretty shabby episode": New York *Daily News;* and Logan, "Around City Hall."
224. "I don't accept that notion": Logan, "Around City Hall."
224. "If Guidry can pitch": *NYT*, May 18, 1979.
224. "I thought it was outrageous": Interview with FGR, May 25, 2005.
225. "the fact was that he did not": Interview with a Lazard partner.

225. "They are making a fortune": *NYT,* September 11, 1979.
225. "In any walk of life": *Euromoney* interview with MDW, March 1981.
226. "It would be a mistake": Interview with Damon Mezzacappa, August 2, 2004.
227. "for me it was all about the future": Ibid.
227. "That was Tom's job": Ibid.
227. "A nice man but": Ibid.
228. "became a bit of a sore point": Ibid.
228. "So for a while": Ibid.
228. "Really? Where is this computer?": Interview with WL, January 26, 2005.
229. "It was very controversial": Ibid.
229. "Then for the first time": Ibid.
229. "I mean, what are these guys up to?": Interview with Mina Gerowin, January 6, 2005.
229. "And I didn't want to be": Ibid.
229. "First of all, it was so": Ibid.
230. "Fred comes in and he lectures me": Ibid.
230. "I didn't have a clue": Interview with Luis Rinaldini, November 9, 2004.
230. "I must have called him ten to fifteen times": Ibid.
231. "Felix had a reputation at the time": Ibid.
232. "I think it really became the means": Interview with Jim Manzi, March 15, 2005.
233. "There are some incredibly smart people": Ibid.
233. "We explained to Jacques Attali": Interview with MDW, November 30, 2005.
234. "They understood before anyone else": Martine Orange, *Ces messieurs de Lazard* (Paris: Albin Michel, 2006), p. 196.
235. "I believe in the free market": William Serrin, *NYT,* April 21, 1981.
235. "demanding a fundamental change": Ibid.
235. "We have an educational system": Ibid.
236. "I am getting calls": Thomas Eagleton to FGR, November 29, 1982, used with permission of Sen. Eagleton and the *Thomas F. Eagleton Papers, 1944–1987,* Uniform Historical Manuscript Collection, Columbia, Mo.
236. "The war we are going to fight": In substantially the same form in Felix G. Rohatyn, *Twenty-Year Century* (New York: Random House, 1984), p. 36.
237. "For the handful of men": Leslie Wayne, "The Corporate Raiders," *NYT,* July 18, 1982.
238. "These fees don't come from widows and orphans": Ibid.
238. "The level of fees is so different": Ibid.
238. "There's a general perception": *NYT,* October 4, 1982.
239. "Anyone can win": Ibid.
239. "Rohatyn's progress": Michael Kinsley, "The Double Felix," *New Republic,* March 26, 1984.
240. "To me, this was an outrageous breach": Leon Levy and Eugene Linden, *The Mind of Wall Street* (New York: Public Affairs, 2002), pp. 131–32.
240. "We don't like you": *Institutional Investor,* February 12, 2004.

Chapter 9. "The Cancer Is Greed"

242. "calmly handed a co-worker": *New York Post,* December 11, 1984; and Dan Dorfman, "Probing a Mysterious Suicide at Lazard Frères," *New York,* February 11, 1985, p. 15.
243. "I think there were three people": Ralph Nader and William Taylor, *The Big Boys: Power and Position in American Business* (New York: Pantheon, 1986), p. 214.
243. John A. Grambling Jr.: The account of Grambling's illegal spree can be found in Brian Rosner, *Swindle* (Homewood, Ill.: Business One Irwin, 1990), and in Ed Cony's front-page *WSJ* article, March 23, 1987.
245. Forstmann Little closed the Dr Pepper deal on February 28, 1984: Tombstone advertisement, *WSJ,* March 7, 1984.

246. Continental Illinois Bank's contractual obligation: Bound volumes of closing of Dr Pepper deal from the offices of Forstmann Little & Co.
252. Robert Wilkis's role in the Dennis Levine insider trading scandal: James B. Stewart, *Den of Thieves* (New York: Simon & Schuster, 1991), and Douglas Frantz, *Levine & Co.* (New York: Holt, 1987).
255. "perhaps not the best person": Interview with John Grambling Jr.
256. "As the revelations of illegality": Felix Rohatyn, "The Blight on Wall Street," *New York Review of Books,* March 12, 1987.
256. "thunderstruck": Interview with FGR, February 25, 2005.
257. "And I just couldn't get over it": Ibid.
257. like Caesar's Gaul: Kate Bohner, *Forbes,* November 20, 1995.
258. the 1984 creation of Lazard Partners: This information comes from the May 1984 prospectus about the deal that Pearson was required to file publicly and from Ian Fraser, *The High Road to England* (London: Michael Russell, 1999).
259. "finally exorcising Meyer's ghost": *BusinessWeek,* June 18, 1984.
259. "It was Michel's doing": Ibid.
259. "Already I feel a fantastic current": *NYT,* May 28, 1984.
259. "I wouldn't be telling the truth": Ibid.
260. "You kiss Michel's ring": *WSJ,* September 6, 1984.
260. "I think very highly of him": Ibid.
260. "Michel goes anywhere": Ibid.
260. "no longer as influential": Ibid.
261. "was very reluctant": David McClintick, "Life at the Top," *NYT Magazine,* August 5, 1984.
263. "I am satisfied": Lenny Glynn and Elizabeth Peer, "Felix: The Making of a Celebrity," *Institutional Investor,* December 1984.
264. "Bankruptcy is like stepping into a tepid bath": Judith Ramsey Ehrlich and Barry Rehfeld, *The New Crowd* (Boston: Little, Brown, 1989), p. 133; and Peter Hellman, "The Wizard of Lazard," *NYT Magazine,* March 21, 1976.
264. tracked Felix's press notices: "The Felix Index," *Institutional Investor,* December 1984.
265. "I have compared him to a great fish": Glynn and Peer, "Felix."
265. "straight in the eye": Fraser, *High Road to England,* p. 356.

Chapter 10. The Vicar

266. "spent part of his youth": *Financial Times,* October 25, 2001.
266. "At the risk of intruding": WL to Chris Lacovara, January 20, 1988.
266. "the world's best associate": Interview with WL, January 26, 2005.
267. "I was concerned that I was ever more": Ibid.
267. "Anyone who does this job": WL memorandum, 1984.
268. "This damn thing turned into": *WSJ,* November 8, 1985.
269. "It's the deal of the century": Ibid.
269. "Today things are getting badly out of hand": "Merger Tango," *Time,* December 23, 1985.
269. "The integrity of our securities markets": FGR testimony before U.S. Senate, Banking, Finance, and Insurance Subcommittee, June 6, 1985.
269. "The way we are going will destroy": "Merger Tango."
270. Account of Marcel Katz's insider trading: *WSJ,* July 14 and August 8, 1986.
271. log cabin home: *Architectural Digest,* June 1997.
271. "while dazzling benefit dinners": Kathleen Teltsch, *NYT,* November 24, 1985.
272. "There is so much concentration": Kathleen Teltsch, *NYT,* January 5, 1986.
272. cover story: Ron Rosenbaum, "The Shame of the Super Rich," in *Manhattan Passions* (New York: Penguin Press, 1988), p. 25. Originally appeared in *Manhattan Inc.*

272. "Felix the Cat and Snow White vs. the Social Sisters": *W,* May 19, 1986.
273. "What we serve": *NYT,* June 8, 1986.
273. "It's just not something": *NYT,* March 13, 1986.
273. "Having followed your career": Ibid.
274. Felix's growing fame, though: *NYT,* April 12, 1990.
274. *W* feature article on MDW in Cap d'Antibes: August 11, 1986.
275. "This was just a terrible article": Interview with Damon Mezzacappa, August 2, 2004.
275. "Michel really started to love": Ibid.
275. "In *Euromoney* six years ago": WL memorandum, September 24, 1986.
277. "They were Pearson men": Interview with a Lazard partner.
277. "I don't think these people": Interview with MDW, January 31, 2005.
278. "In my judgment, we should": WL to MDW, November 6, 1986.
278. "Given the opportunity": Interview with Robert Agostinelli, April 21, 2005.
278. "I thought my career was over": Ibid.
000. "Bob is not normal": WL to MDW, November 6, 1986.
279. "You are Lazard": Interview with Agostinelli, April 21, 2005.
279. "There are, for example, more partners": WL memorandum to MDW, January 20, 1987.
280. "You people are the most ungrateful": Interviews with former Lazard analysts.
280. "There is a need to increase": WL memorandum to MDW, March 10, 1987.
281. "When I was an associate": WL memorandum to MDW, November 6, 1987.
281. "of paramount concern": WL memorandum to MDW, October 31, 1987.
283. "Fundamentally, the issues of concern": WL memorandum to MDW, April 10, 1988.
283. "This is the time to be commercially aggressive": Ibid.
285. "is a long-lasting boil": WL memorandum to MDW, May 9, 1988.
285. "The excellence of our partners": MDW and FGR memorandum, May 20, 1988.
287. "It's more than probable": "The Last Emperor," *BusinessWeek,* May 30, 1988.
288. "The intimacy between Felix and I": Ibid.
290. "Felix and Ira": Leslie Wayne, "In Search of a Richer Lazard," *NYT,* April 30, 1989.
291. "It's not bad having Babe Ruth": Ibid.
291. "None of your goddamn business": Interview with a Lazard partner.
291. "The Fortune 500 is our target" and "Lazard of the 90s": *WSJ,* February 3, 1988.
292. "The Wasserstein thing": *BusinessWeek,* May 30, 1988.
292. "Accountability for partners": WL memorandum to MDW, August 29, 1988.
293. "Bill Loomis has decided": MDW memorandum to the banking group, November 30, 1988.
293. "It was one of those moments": Interview with Nat Gregory, February 4, 2005.
294. "Running banking at Lazard": Ibid.

Chapter 11. The Boy Wonder

295. "special situations": *NYT,* April 30 and April 7, 1989.
295. "Lazard has been in the junk bond business": *NYT,* April 7, 1989.
296. "In two days the whole thing": Interview with SR, September 14, 2004.
296. "What I didn't really understand": Interview with Luis Rinaldini, November 9, 2004.
296. "It's tough competition": Ibid.
298. "Intelligence . . . spark . . . humor . . . wit": Partners' meeting minutes quoting MDW, February 21, 1990.
299. "soon after I got to Morgan Stanley": Ed Klein, "Paramount Player," *Vanity Fair,* January 1994.
299. "I used to develop sources": Philip Weiss, "The Rise of Steven Rattner," *Washington Monthly,* May 1, 1986.

299. "Hello Sweetheart, Get Me Mergers and Acquisitions": Ibid.
299. "Nothing good was going to come": Interview with SR, September 14, 2004.
300. In short order, she ran it into the ground: Summary of the lengthy May 31, 1995, "Decision and Order" of the National Labor Relations Board against Paragon Paint Corp. and its owner, Selma Rattner. The case is now used as part of a University of Texas at Dallas course, "Ethics, Culture, and Public Responsibility." Said the professor: "She inherited Paragon Paint from her father, and evidently was unable to deal with it and hated it. The workers were stuck."
300. "It's tough to be a first child": Weiss, "Hello Sweetheart."
301. "kind of 'Goodbye, Columbus' ": Peter Applebome, *NYT,* May 16, 2004.
301. 674 and counting: *Brown Daily Herald,* October 17, 1973.
301. "surpass Babe Ruth's mark": SR, *Brown Daily Herald,* November 5, 1973.
301. "those folks in University Hall": SR, *Brown Daily Herald,* January 11, 1974.
301. "the most honored job": Michael Wolff, "The Clark Kent Timesman," *New York,* November 10, 2003.
302. "Steve and I were both involved": Klein, "Paramount Player."
302. "I don't know how people": Weiss, "Hello Sweetheart."
302. "Something no one of my age": Interview with SR, September 14, 2004.
302. "He was very bright": Klein, "Paramount Player."
303. Blue Goose: Weiss, "Hello Sweetheart."
303. "There is no one": Ibid.
303. "No, but you're not": Ibid.
303. "What I like about Steve": Klein, "Paramount Player."
303. "For my part, I have tried": Weiss, "Hello Sweetheart."
304. "The thing I loved about reporting": Ibid.
304. "the world's best job": Ibid.
305. "a modern classic, the *Das Kapital*": Ibid.
305. "Steve and I talked about architecture": Klein, "Paramount Player."
305. "I once watched Apple": Ibid.
306. "I wasn't going to go": Interview with SR, September 14, 2004.
306. "It begins to get on you": Weiss, "Hello Sweetheart."
306. "week or two": Interview with SR, September 14, 2004.
306. "He could understand the interplay": Weiss, "Hello Sweetheart."
307. "it was like a match": Klein, "Paramount Player."
307. "Steve insisted that I reduce": *Newsweek,* June 9, 1997.
308. "This is the junk-bond market's": *WSJ,* October 16, 1989.
309. "Our clients want to have": *WSJ,* September 28, 1989.
309. "Michel was starting to exert control": Interview with Jeremy Sillem, January 27, 2005.
310. memoir: John Nott, *Here Today, Gone Tomorrow* (London: Politico's, 2002).
310. "David has been doing the job anyway": *WSJ,* September 20, 1991.
310. Steve had a side arrangement with Michel: Internal Lazard document and *NYT,* September 14, 2003.
311. "Paul, I just got a phone call": Interview with FGR.
311. "Which was typical of Lew": Interview with FGR, January 3, 2005.
312. "Market conditions may occur": FGR testimony, U.S. Senate Committee on Banking, Housing, and Urban Affairs, July 13, 1989.
313. "Lunch at the Four Seasons": In part *NYT,* July 7, 1976.
313. "By asking me to arrange a meeting": From interviews with FGR and his unpublished memoir, page 197, which he gave me a copy of.
314. "one of the oddest dinners": Ibid.
314. "This deal might be another feather": Ibid.
315. "After one year of some involve-

ment": WL memorandum, March 15, 1991.
316. "Today, Lazard is arguably": Suzanna Andrews, "It's Good to Be the Emperor," *M, Inc.*, October 1991.
318. "I am equidistant from people": Anne Sabouret, *MM Lazard Frères et Cie* (Paris: Olivier Orban, 1987), as quoted in Suzanna Andrews, "The Scion in Winter," *Vanity Fair,* March 1997, and Andrews, "It's Good to Be the Emperor."
318. "We pride ourselves": Andrews, "It's Good to Be the Emperor."
318. "Michel always says that you need": Ibid.
318. "She has a way of getting": Ibid.

Chapter 12. The Franchise

320. "Not a tree nor blade of grass": E. Cobham Brewer, *Dictionary of Phrase and Fable*, online edition.
320. "[Felix] has been cutting people off": Suzanna Andrews, "Felix Loses It," *New York,* March 11, 1996.
320. "He was my chief lieutenant": Geraldine Fabrikant, *NYT,* August 24, 2003.
321. "Mr. David-Weill apparently lacked the empathy": *New York Observer,* September 8, 2003, p. 4.
322. "this was illegal": Interview with David Supino, June 21, 2004.
322. "That's the way Felix liked": Ibid.
322. "very difficult because it was": Ibid.
322. "at best a dead end": Ibid.
322. "to engineer a way to get out": Ibid.
322. "David, I don't understand": Ibid.
322. "a very insecure person": Ibid.
322. "He wasn't interested in explaining things": Interview with Luis Rinaldini, November 9, 2004.
323. "I never really knew": Ibid.
323. "He could tell you the numbers": Ibid.
323. "CEOs are different": Ibid.
323. "What he really did": Ibid.
324. "He was Felix's butt boy": Interview with Ken Wilson, January 18, 2005, and February 3, 2005.
324. "I was really shocked": Ibid.
324. "The only issue I had": Interview with Rinaldini, November 9, 2004.
325. "I think Luis had one drink": Interview with Damon Mezzacappa, August 2, 2004.
325. "It was difficult for me": Interview with Rinaldini, November 9, 2004.
325. "I think for both Michel and Felix": Ibid.
326. "Felix's view would be": Interview with Jeffrey Leeds, July 29, 2004.
326. "What a Franchise!": Said especially by the former Lazard partner Michael Price.
326. "I think it was clear": Interview with Leeds, July 29, 2004.
327. "Kiss up, crush down": Interviews with Lazard junior bankers.
327. "As a generalist": WL memorandum to Peter Ezersky, March 10, 1992.
327. "The dilution of effort is greater": WL memorandum to MDW et al., April 23, 1992.
328. "But Felix was part of the problem": Interview with a Lazard partner.
328. "I have contributed to some of the progress": WL memorandum to MDW, April 23, 1992.
330. "He never would give an inch": Interview with WL, June 30, 2005.
330. "Bill wrote it down": Interview with a Lazard partner.
330. "I would always say": Interview with WL, June 30, 2005.
330. "cohesive plan or organization": WL memorandum to MDW, August 4, 1992.
330. "After some fearful hesitation": WL memorandum to MDW, August 13, 1992.
331. "Look, it's not important": Ibid.
331. "underlying causes" of the problems: Ibid.
332. "I am viewed by Damon": Ibid.
332. "in the wake of difficulties": *NYT,* October 2, 1992.
332. "Those responsible for the capital raising": Kim Fennebresque memorandum to WL, August 12, 1992.

332. "an empty suit": Interview with Mezzacappa, August 2, 2004.
333. "The purpose in telling you now": WL to MDW, August 12, 1992.
333. "As importantly, I want you to know": Ibid.
333. "There was a cabal": Interview with a Lazard partner.
333. "There absolutely was a cult": Interview with Kim Fennebresque, October 19, 2004.
333. "I think Bill does have qualities": Interview with Mezzacappa, August 2, 2004.
334. "Steve Rattner and Kim Fennebresque": MDW memorandum, September 22, 1992.
334. "What the fuck was that": Interview with Fennebresque, October 19, 2004.
335. "decided he was going to decapitate": Interview with SR, September 14, 2004.
335. "Someone told me Loomis": Interviews with Fennebresque, October 19 and 25, 2004.
335. "I didn't want to do it": Ibid.
335. "because I was a colorful": Ibid.
336. "I mean, what the fuck?": Ibid.
336. "I was unbelievably morose": Ibid.
336. "Steve Rattner was a luminary": Ibid.
336. "I thought managing the Lazard partners": Ibid.
337. "I had zero illusions": Ibid.
337. "Virtually every reporter": Interview with SR, September 14, 2004.
337. "Bruce was king": Interviews with Fennebresque, October 19 and 25, 2004.
337. "I got fired": Ibid.
337. "Everyone was dying": Ibid.
338. "The letter was unbelievably": Ibid.
338. "I wonder if you would": Ibid.
338. "I was raised Catholic": Ibid.
338. "talking about everything": Ibid.
338. "I went in and spent": Ibid.
339. "And it says such and such": Ibid.
339. "thirty seconds" . . . "If it takes longer": Ibid.
339. "Aah, it's not a good time": Ibid.
339. "Jeez, that's kind of low": Ibid.
339. "Can you take it": Ibid.
340. "Fiercely blunt": WL eulogy of Jim Glanville, September 1992.
341. "They asked us to consider": *WSJ*, January 3, 1989.
341. "You should view our investment": *WSJ*, June 28, 1991.
342. "clearly chose to work with us": Ibid.
342. "in a fraud-and-embezzlement scheme": *WSJ*, August 18, 1992.
342. "trying to shift the blame": *WSJ*, November 2, 1992.
342. Corporate Partners' performance: Interview with Jonathan Kagan, October 18, 2005, and Corporate Partners' returns documentation.
343. "Felix liked to walk the halls": Interview with SR, September 14, 2004.
343. first *New York Times* op-ed piece: Steve Rattner, "Short-Term Stimulus? Long-Term Error," *NYT*, November 17, 1992.
344. "Del Guidice was really more": Interview with a Lazard partner.
345. "a nice guy who was": Interview with Mezzacappa, August 2, 2004.
345. "Ferber and Poirier were two": Interview with a Lazard partner.
345. "Del Guidice had two guys": Interview with a Lazard partner.
345. "We had selected Prudential": *WSJ*, May 21, 1993, p. 1.
346. "lying, making unauthorized trades": Ibid.
346. "getting even with Poirier": Interview with a Lazard partner.
346. "We are dismayed by the article": *WSJ*, May 22, 1993.
347. "tinkering with tenths": Interviews with Fennebresque, October 19 and 25, 2004.
347. "If you go back in time": Interview with SR, September 14, 2004.
347. "You asked that I try to articulate": SR memorandum to MDW, May 24, 1993.
348. "summer evening" and "bullshitting": Interviews with Fennebresque. October 19 and 25, 2004.

348. "The problem is, you know": Ibid.
348. "I've got that message, pal": Ibid.
349. "And this guy didn't know": Ibid.
349. "Dumb idea? Okay": Author observation of Michael Price.

Chapter 13. "Felix Loses It"

351. "The clouds are parting just a bit": "Rattner's Star Rises as a Deal Maker at Lazard Frères," *WSJ,* November 10, 1993.
352. "did not obviously completely appreciate": Interview with a Lazard partner.
352. "Most other senior Lazard bankers": "Rattner's Star Rises."
352. "biggest rainmaker": "Felix Rohatyn in Autumn," *NY,* November 29, 1993.
352. "He said, 'You've worked very hard' ": Interview with SR, September 14, 2004.
353. "Among the financial wizards involved": Ed Klein, "Paramount Player," *Vanity Fair,* January 1994.
353. "Paramount was Ira's relationship": Interview with Damon Mezzacappa, August 2, 2004.
354. "Everybody in the firm knows": Interview with a Lazard partner.
354. "Today, when C.E.O.'s want": Klein, "Paramount Player."
354. "André Meyer used to say": Ibid.
354. "upright, self-depriving attitudes": Ibid.
354. "because we don't need": Ibid.
355. "At times, it crosses my mind": Ibid.
355. "Michael J. Fox of investment banking": Ibid.
355. "Felix has always been a problem": Ibid.
355. "Talking about an heir": Ibid.
355. "We're all worried for Steve": Ibid.
356. "Felix went berserk": Suzanna Andrews, "Felix Loses It," *New York,* March 11, 1996.
356. "Of *course* Felix was pissed": Ibid.
356. "Felix ran that deal": Ibid.
356. "He goes hot and cold": Interview with a Lazard partner.
356. "a real oh-shit moment": Andrews, "Felix Loses It."
356. "Marty went berserk": Interview with SR, September 14, 2004.
356. "Steve made it seem": Andrews, "Felix Loses It."
356. "That's bullshit": Ibid.
357. "horror" and "one of the most awful": Interview with FGR.
357. "Steve was almost fired": Andrews, "Felix Loses It."
357. "I have the utmost respect": Interview with Mezzacappa, August 2, 2004.
357. "But I really wasn't doing much": Interviews with Kim Fennebresque, October 19 and 25, 2004.
358. "I was unbelievably happy": Ibid.
358. "My guess is that in the end": Ibid.
358. "When I ran banking": Interview with SR, September 14, 2004.
359. "I didn't and I still don't": Ibid.
359. "When Steve arrived at the firm": Interview with Mezzacappa, August 2, 2004.
359. "The guy's a good guy": *BG,* February 5, 1993.
360. "In our view and in the view": *BG,* March 10, 1993.
360. "select Merrill Lynch": *BG,* June 21, 1993.
360. "while by no means illegal": Ibid.
361. "I'm not telling you it's pretty": Ibid.
361. "the investment banker who played": *BusinessWeek,* September 6, 1993.
362. "I believe that our best assets": WL memorandum to Mel Heineman and MDW, September 9, 1993.
362. "so extraordinary": Robert A. Cerasoli's report to Governor William Weld, "MWRA: Report on the Procurement of Financial Services," December 16, 1993.
364. "become the focus of federal and state": *BG,* December 17, 1993.
364. Thanks to Lissack's call: Numerous press accounts, but see especially Henry Scammell, *Giant Killers* (New York: Atlantic Monthly Press, 2004).
365. "Lazard was told by the feds": Interview with a Lazard partner.
365. thirty-four-hundred-word article: Leslie Wayne, "A Side Deal and a Wizard's Undoing," *NYT,* May 15, 1994.

365. "Many of you undoubtedly read": MDW memorandum, May 17, 1994.
365. "The New York partners": Ibid.
366. "Seldom do you see": Wayne, "Side Deal."
368. "I'm a bit worried that IBM": Interview with Jim Manzi, March 15, 2005.
368. " 'You know, Clinton really likes you' ": Interview with FGR, January 3, 2005.
368. "Running a big bureaucracy": Ibid.
369. "I didn't want the World Bank": Andrews, "Felix Loses It."
369. "The elevator opened into a massive": Michael Wolff, "The Clark Kent Timesman," *New York,* November 10, 2003.
371. "The subject is so provocative": *Broadcasting & Cable,* September 18 and 25, 1995.
371. "Why would you go to a video store": Ibid.
371. "Oh, Felix, go back to bed": Andrews, "Felix Loses It."
371. "There are lots of young": "The New Establishment," *Vanity Fair,* October 1995.
372. "That last article was bad": Andrews, "Felix Loses It."
372. SR's real estate transactions and activities in Martha's Vineyard: From public records and from ongoing press reports, from 1994 to 2006, in the *Vineyard Gazette.*
375. Account of Ferber's indictment and Lazard settlement: Leslie Wayne, *NYT,* October 27, 1995.
375. Lazard statement about its settlement with the SEC and the Commonwealth of Massachusetts: October 26, 1995.
375. "He was upset that his name": Interview with a Lazard partner.
376. "We're friends": Bob Woodward, *Maestro* (New York: Simon & Schuster, 2000), p. 155.
377. "We'll have a really interesting debate": Ibid. The analysis of the "politics" of the appointment also from ibid.
377. "That didn't make Michel happy": Andrews, "Felix Loses It."
377. "Why are you doing it": Woodward, *Maestro,* p. 156.
377. "squelch[ing] dissident thoughts": Ibid.
377. "You're crazy": Interview with FGR, January 3, 2005.
377. "Unlike some previous Fed vice chairmen": *WSJ,* January 19, 1996.
378. "R-O-H-A-T-Y-N spells stagflation": *Time,* February 26, 1996.
378. "What will happen if we send you": Woodward, *Maestro,* p. 162.
378. "financier-pundit Felix Rohatyn": Paul Krugman, "Stay on Their Backs," *NYT Magazine,* February 4, 1996.
379. "An example of what should not be done": Transcript of President Clinton's speech at the Sheraton New York, February 15, 1996, from Clinton Foundation.
379. Felix had already left: Interview with FGR, January 3, 2005.
379. "Michel has been buttressing himself": Andrews, "Felix Loses It."
379. "Felix is angry and bitter": Ibid.
380. "I don't believe Felix ever intended": Interview with Suzanna Andrews, November 9, 2005.
380. "Steve is so monomaniacal": Andrews, "Felix Loses It."
380. "I hope you throw away your notebook": Interviews with SR, September 14, 2004, and Suzanna Andrews, November 9, 2005.
381. "in the past few years": Andrews, "Felix Loses It."
381. "there is a perception": Ibid.
382. "You have to understand" and other quotations: Andrews, "Felix Loses It."
382. "The son is getting too successful": Ibid.
383. "It is almost a crime": Ibid.
383. "Culture change is hard": Interview with Arthur Sulzberger Jr., March 29, 2005.
384. "The success and the dysfunction of Lazard": Andrews, "Felix Loses It."

Chapter 14. "It's a White Man's World"

385. "And here they are at twenty-five thousand feet": Interview with a Lazard partner.
386. "I have never seen it to that extent": Interview with MDW, November 30, 2005.
387. "She has this house with birds": Suzanna Andrews, "The Scion in Winter," *Vanity Fair,* March 1997, p. 276.
387. "Fees for services rendered": Interview with a Lazard partner.
387. Interview with a Lazard partner, October 27, 2006.
388. "half of Michel is better": Interview with MDW, January 31, 2005.
388. "My wife, who is not terribly sensitive": Interview with MDW, November 15, 2006.
388. "He adored his girls": Interview with a longtime Lazard observer.
388. "Felix, why don't you go": Interviews with Lazard partners.
388. "No, it didn't happen": Interview with FGR, May 25, 2005.
389. "Getting into our building": Interview with Alan McFarland, April 5, 2005.
389. "moved from bachelor around town": Ibid.
389. two hookers: Interviews with Lazard partners.
389. "When I was there": Interview with a Lazard banker.
389. "Like all these beautiful young girls": Interview with a Lazard partner.
389. "And sure enough": Interview with a Lazard partner.
389. "Lazard being the way it is": Interview with a Lazard partner.
390. "I think the firm was small": Interview with WL, June 30, 2005.
390. "We were kind of": Ibid.
390. "She'd been there for a couple of months": Interview with a Lazard banker.
390. "It was a very small firm": Interview with Mina Gerowin, January 6, 2005.
391. "I told him to fuck off": Ibid.
391. "I'm so frosted at this": Ibid.
391. "He heard what was happening": Ibid.
391. "So did these things happen?": Ibid.
392. "You'd walk into their office": Ibid.
392. "I don't know why she's here": Ibid.
392. "Why are we firing Mina?": Ibid.
392. "It was so brutal": Ibid.
392. "You're not being very productive": Ibid.
392. "From the beginning": Interview with a Lazard partner.
393. "Why don't you just go home": Interview with a Lazard partner.
393. "And while we were one": Interview with Kathy Kelly, April 6, 2005.
393. "And it was the beginning": Ibid.
393. "utils," "cogs in the machine": Interview with a Lazard partner.
393. "Obviously that's where it becomes": Interview with a Lazard banker.
394. "It's a white man's world": Interview with a Lazard banker.
394. "I believe that Bill Loomis": Interview with Kelly, April 6, 2005.
394. "I remember Michel saying to me": Interview with Christina Mohr, January 6, 2005.
394. "I think that Christina Mohr": Interview with WL, June 30, 2005.
395. "Basically she came back": Interview with a Lazard partner.
395. "Michel sent us over there": Interview with a Lazard partner.
396. "And there were no walls": Interview with Kate Bohner, May 2, 2005.
396. "Remarkably, it wasn't as jarring": Kate Bohner, "Stiletto Feminists," *George,* August 2000.
396. "I was very naive": Interview with Bohner, May 2, 2005.
396. "still wouldn't have been": Ibid.
396. "Back then, if I was a client": Ibid.
396. "I lived at Claridge's": Ibid.
397. "I didn't understand": Ibid.
397. "I don't understand why a girl": Ibid.
397. "It was sort of just like constant": Ibid.
397. "She's getting killed": Ibid.
398. "When somebody confronted me": Ibid.

398. "The tally of people": Interview with a Lazard partner.
398. "I think that it is a remarkable": Interview with Kelly, April 6, 2005.
398. "blissfully unaware": Interview with FGR, May 25, 2005.
399. "Without going into personalities": Interview with a Lazard banker.
399. regular visitor to Bohner's office: Interview with Bohner, May 2, 2005.
399. Account of a senior vice president at Bohner's apartment: Interviews with Bohner (May 2, 2005), Mary Conwell (August 2006), and Lazard partners.
399. "throw me into a brick wall": Interview with Bohner, May 2, 2005.
399. "If I had gone to Bill Loomis": Ibid.
400. "I was embarrassed by the whole situation": Ibid.
400. Account of Kate Bohner's relationship with Ward Woods: Ibid.
400. "There were a series of very difficult": Interview with WL, June 30, 2005.
400. "I'd say, in 1980": Ibid.
401. "Kate came into my office": Interview with a Lazard partner.
401. "Then all of a sudden": Ibid.
401. "And of being a class act": Ibid.
401. Account of Robert Agostinelli incidents: Interviews with Lazard partners.
402. Account of Kate Bohner's post-Lazard activities: Interview with Bohner, May 2, 2005, and press accounts.

Chapter 15. The Heir Apparent

403. "We are at our very core": MDW memorandum, March 1, 1996.
403. "The article in *New York Magazine*": FGR memorandum, March 4, 1996.
404. "There's absolutely no excuse": Interview with FGR, January 3, 2005.
404. "Look, what happened, happened": Ibid.
404. "He's a complicated guy": Interview with SR, September 14, 2004.
405. "We were both viewed in the firm": Ibid.
405. "She was a dreadful woman": Interview with FGR, January 3, 2005.
405. "Which wasn't quite true": Ibid.
405. "They ought to have somebody": Ibid.
405. "And I said to Elizabeth": Ibid.
406. "You know, Mr. Rohatyn": Ibid.
407. "So I gave that to Vernon": Ibid.
407. "There is still no decision": Ibid.
408. "really, really terrible": Ibid.
409. Perella denied: Author's e-mail correspondence with Perella, March 17, 2006.
410. "He had immense charm": Bryan Burrough, "The Man in the Latex Suit," *Vanity Fair,* July 2005.
410. three facets of the Stern biography: From press accounts—especially Burrough, "Man in the Latex Suit"; Kate Bohner Lewis, "I Just Detest Incompetence," *Forbes,* November 20, 1995; and Suzanna Andrews, "The Scion in Winter," *Vanity Fair,* March 1997—and interviews with Jeffrey Keil on January 26, 2006, and March 8, 2006.
410. partridge, pheasant, and duck shoot: Interviews with Keil.
410. "I knew this was the way": Bohner Lewis, "I Just Detest Incompetence."
411. "True, it was the family bank": Ibid.
411. "Everyone said Édouard stole": Burrough, "Man in the Latex Suit."
411. "the person she had loved": Interview with MDW, April 12, 2005.
411. "Édouard was like a tornado": *Le Nouvel Observateur,* March 10, 2005.
412. "Beware of self-made men": Andrews, "Scion in Winter."
412. "The single most distinctive": Burrough, "Man in the Latex Suit"; and interviews with Keil.
413. "Those of you who trust me": "Stern: La mort enigmatique d'un homme presse," *Le Figaro,* March 12, 2005.
413. "Édouard sauntered onto the plane": Interview with Jon Wood, February 1, 2005.
413. "He always wanted to challenge": Burrough, "Man in the Latex Suit."

413. Account of investigation into Stern's purchase of Consolidated Gold shares: British Department of Trade and Industry, chap. 19, pp. 576–90, published in book form in 1994.
414. "were concerned to ascertain": Ibid.
414. "deliberately failed to ensure": Ibid.
414. "There is no evidence": Ibid.
414. "I see it as a learning experience": Bohner Lewis, "I Just Detest Incompetence."
414. "In Paris there were people": Interview with MDW, December 1, 2004.
415. crook: Interview with a Lazard partner.
415. "I think it had a huge impact": Interview with a Lazard partner.
415. "He can be absolutely": Andrews, "Scion in Winter."
415. "There was only one person": Interview with a Lazard partner.
415. "When things didn't go exactly": Burrough, "Man in the Latex Suit."
415. "If you had to choose, in France": Interview with MDW, December 1, 2004.
416. "Maybe I would have felt different": Ibid.
416. "there were a lot of questions": Interview with a Lazard partner.
416. "Jupiter turned out to be": Interview with a Lazard partner.
416. "This sent a clear message": Bohner Lewis, "I Just Detest Incompetence."
417. "I was not sure absolutely": Interview with MDW, April 12, 2005.
417. "I had to clean up Stern's mess": Bohner Lewis, "I Just Detest Incompetence."
417. Stern and the Chunnel bonds: Interview with a Lazard partner.
418. "Stern negotiated a hell of a deal": Bohner Lewis, "I Just Detest Incompetence."
418. "the best merchant banker": Interview with MDW, December 1, 2004.
418. "On the advisory front": Interview with Patrick Sayer, January 31, 2005.
419. "Which really proves": Interview with MDW, December 1, 2004.
419. "One can debate": Ibid.
419. "Which I should have known": Ibid.
419. "It's important to have somebody": Ibid.
419. "At one point, Michel had to": Interview with Jean-Michel Steg, February 1, 2005.
420. "The partners there look like": Andrews, "Scion in Winter."
420. "At first there was a lot of initial skepticism": Interview with a Lazard partner.
420. *"le gendre incontrôlable"*: *Evening Standard* (London), June 10, 2005.
420. "I just detest incompetence": Bohner Lewis, "I Just Detest Incompetence."
421. "I don't think Édouard": Andrews, "Scion in Winter."
421. "Beatrice would be better off": Ibid.
422. "Ms. Lauvergeon's professional": *Le Monde,* November 1996, and *NYT*, November 13, 1996.
422. "a furious dispute": *NYT*, November 13, 1996.
422. "Either I am going to be the boss": Andrews, "Scion in Winter."
422. "I want you to retire": Interview with a Lazard partner.
422. "I treated him like my son": Interview with MDW, December 1, 2004.
422. "Michel does know a lot about medicine": e-mail correspondence with WL.
423. "Michel is the only person": Interviews with Kim Fennebresque, October 19 and 25, 2004.
423. "enjoys cigars": "Cigars in the Boardroom," *Cigar Aficionado,* June 1, 1995.
423. "fucking bushel": Interviews with Fennebresque, October 19 and 25, 2004.
424. "So some Puerto Rican": Ibid.
424. "The law is very strange": Interview with MDW, April 12, 2005.
424. "Lazard is like Wall Street": Description of Lazard at iWon.com.
425. "Agostinelli had his girlfriend": Interview with Ken Wilson, January 18, 2005.
425. "He had someone send for his stash": Interviews with Fennebresque, October 19 and 25, 2004.

426. "She'd call me": Ibid.
426. "I used to watch Michel": Ibid.
426. "You know, in life": Interview with MDW, December 1, 2004.
426. "We do not like to make revolutions": Robert Teitelman, "Divided We Fall," *Institutional Investor*, May 1993.
426. "If I were not sane": AE, December 15, 2000.
426. "Édouard was very impatient": Interview with MDW, December 1, 2004.
427. "people basically respected my decisions": Ibid.
427. "What caught me by surprise": *Financial Times*, January 11, 1997.
427. "Sooner or later": Ibid.
427. "Any investment bank": John Gapper, *Financial Times*, October 6, 2004, and *Financial Times*, May 2, 1997.
428. "Michel is in a very tight spot": Andrews, "Scion in Winter."
428. "Michel always tries to put the best face": Ibid.
428. "His joy is power and exercising power": Ibid.
428. "Be careful with him": Ibid.
429. "Those whose enduring object is power": Thomas Pynchon, *Against the Day* (New York: Penguin Press, 2006).
429. "There is a fashion": Ibid.
429. "He said it was a disappointment": Interview with Suzanna Andrews, November 9, 2005.
429. "For some reason, he decided": Interview with a Lazard partner.
430. "Édouard has great and real talent": *NYT*, May 23, 1997.
430. "He always made money": Interview with MDW.
430. "I love and respect Beatrice": Burrough, "Man in the Latex Suit."
430. "Felix Rohatyn has been my partner": MDW memorandum, April 15, 1997.

Chapter 16. "All the Responsibility but None of the Authority"

431. "We demanded that he attend": *Euromoney*, January 2001.
431. "You don't understand who Bruce is": Ibid.
432. "We're going to try to merge": Interview with FGR, January 3, 2005.
433. "You can't merge with Wasserstein": Ibid.
433. "Felix was deeply skeptical": Interview with Ken Wilson, January 18, 2005.
433. "They were a bunch of turkeys": Ibid.
433. "get this on the table": Ibid.
433. "There was good attendance": Ibid.
434. "views were so far from reality": Ibid.
434. "So he turns to Jerry": Ibid.
434. "one by one, everybody": Interview with SR, September 14, 2004.
434. "Then I will not go forward": Interview with Wilson, January 18, 2005.
434. "In response to these comments": Ibid.
434. "The next thing I know": Interview with SR, September 14, 2004.
434. "a real revolution": Interview with FGR, January 3, 2005.
435. "This was a revolution": Interview with SR, September 14, 2004.
435. Wasserstein discussions: *WSJ*, May 2, 1997.
435. "Bruce describes it as like one": Interview with someone close to BW.
435. "The Lazard spin": Interview with Mike Biondi, December 12, 2005.
435. "Our perception was he didn't": Ibid.
435. "The Lazard thing broke down": Ibid.
436. "You've been around Michel for a long time": Ibid.
436. "Michel likes to do things": Interview with a Lazard partner.
437. "Everybody said to Michel": Interview with SR, September 14, 2004.
437. "reasonably interesting job": Ibid.
437. "I wasn't going to be": Ibid.
437. "long series of tortured negotiations": Ibid.
438. "we did actually write some stuff down": Ibid.

438. "The kinds of things": Ibid.
438. "You can't be president": Ibid.
438. "a terrific rainmaker, very well organized": *Euromoney*, January 2001.
438. "They gave me a vase": Interview with FGR, January 3, 2005.
439. "mantle as the firm's lead banker": *NYT*, May 23, 1997; and *Financial Times*, May 23, 1997.
439. "We wanted to both strengthen and broaden": *NYT*, May 23, 1997.
439. "Our goal is to take off": Ibid.
439. "The term 'Trinity' has been mentioned": Ibid.
439. "conspicuous table" and "fair-haired banker": *Newsweek*, June 9, 1997.
439. "These changes are about the firm": Ibid.
439. "Mr. Rattner is in an important": Ibid.
439. "Until things exist, they don't exist": *BusinessWeek*, June 9, 1997.
439. "Michel will be a little less": Ibid.
439. "This isn't an industry": *Newsweek*, June 9, 1997.
440. "I was the one who went to Greenhill": Interview with SR, September 14, 2004.
440. "As always, the difficulty is": *Newsweek*, June 9, 1997.
440. "The negotiations broke down": *Institutional Investor*, June 1998.
440. "Of course you can never": "Can Lazard Still Cut It?" *Fortune*, July 20, 1998.
441. "Damon was in bed with Rattner": Interview with Wilson, January 18, 2005.
441. "It became clearer": Ibid.
441. "Is your shit tight?": Interviews with Lazard bankers. Actually, the full quotation attributed to Wilson was "Is your shit tight? Because if your shit isn't tight, I'm not doing the hurt dance."
441. "There was swirling, infighting": Interview with Wilson, January 18, 2005.
442. "I felt Lazard really": Ibid.
442. "There was zero interest": Ibid.
442. "The fact that Ken Wilson": Interview with a Lazard partner.
442. "I think he fundamentally decided": Interview with a Lazard partner.
443. "And so I got to be head": Interview with Jerry Rosenfeld, March 1, 2005.
443. "It was total frustration": *Bloomberg Markets*, February 2005.
444. "The beginning of a period": *NYT*, April 9, 1998.
445. "I will never do it": Ibid.
445. "I am starting to see": *WSJ*, February 2, 1998.
446. "His job right now is to lead": "Lazard in Search of Self," *Institutional Investor*, June 1998.
446. "was hidden from the Firm": Mel Heineman memorandum, December 3, 1997.
447. "None of it made any sense": Interview with SR, March 16, 2005.
447. "The stuff that was going on": Ibid.
447. "We got no tax losses": Ibid.
447. "You may ask why I wasn't": Cary Reich, *Financier: The Biography of André Meyer* (New York: Morrow, 1983), p. 343.
448. "David, do you understand": Interview with David Supino, June 21, 2004.
448. "We should have put the key": *Institutional Investor*, October 1985.
449. "revalued the portfolio based": Interview with SR, September 14, 2004.
449. The account of Lazard's legal dispute with Art Solomon: Interviews with SR, WL, Damon Mezzacappa, and Steve Golub; and Devin Leonard, "Revenge of Solomon," *New York Observer*, June 21, 1999.
450. "We couldn't believe": *New York Observer*, June 21, 1999.
450. "cleaning up the whole real estate": Interview with Mezzacappa, August 2, 2004.
450. "Michel took great umbrage": Ibid.
450. "It was really just awful": Interview with SR, September 14, 2004.
450. Information about the historical side deals: Lazard memorandum.
451. "Steve made all that stuff transparent": *TALK*, April 2001.

451. "The reality of the side deals": Interview with SR, September 14, 2004.
452. "He didn't care that much about the money": Ibid.
452. "a self-promoting guy in a hurry": *TALK*, April 2001.
452. "There was some reality to it": Interview with SR, September 14, 2004.
452. "It was very, very clear to me": *TALK*, April 2001.
453. "Our approach involves concentrating": "Can Lazard Still Cut It?"
453. "I believed, and in retrospect": Interview with SR, March 16, 2005.
453. "And that's how I felt about it": Ibid.
453. "Investment bankers getting up": Interview with a Lazard partner.
453. "She was sort of prancing": Interview with a Lazard partner.
454. "It was dear old Steve Rattner": Interview with a Lazard partner.
454. "Don't let the history": Interview with a Lazard partner.
454. "This has been achieved": *Lazard Frères & Co.: The First 150 Years* (New York: Lazard Frères & Co., 1998).
455. "We were up on the sixty-third floor": Interview with SR, March 16, 2005.
455. "So many of the senior guys": Interview with Roger Klein, June 3, 2005.
456. "Michel had previously been resisting": Ibid.
456. "As long as Michel": "Lazard in Search of Self."
456. "Not me": "Can Lazard Still Cut It?"
457. "I spent my whole life advising": *WSJ*, December 14, 1999.
457. "There was nothing holding people": Interview with SR, September 14, 2004.
457. "particularly coupled with initiatives": SR memorandum, August 1998.
458. "You ended up with this mishmash": Interview with a Lazard partner.
458. "It was all these things": Interview with SR, September 14, 2004.
459. "We had to be one firm": Ibid.
459. "Look, I have only two questions": Ibid.
460. "I said to myself, if I were starting": Ibid.
460. "I set it up": Interview with SR, March 16, 2005.
460. "The organization described": SR memorandum, November 1998.
461. "very talented banker": Interview with SR, September 14, 2005.
461. "Michel had read the proposal": Ibid.
461. "torpedoed it": Ibid.
461. "I think Michel was balancing two things": Ibid.
461. "That's why he had Bruno call": Interview with a Lazard partner.
461. "Michel dictated the fax": Interview with a Lazard partner.
461. "We were excited": Interview with Mezzacappa, August 2, 2004.
462. "friendly rivals": Interview with SR, March 16, 2005.
462. "Rattner putsch": Interview with David Verey, May 31, 2005.
462. "At that point, he wanted": Interview with SR, September 14, 2004.
463. "He didn't want me to leave": Interview with SR, March 16, 2005.
463. "I felt that it was important": Interview with SR, September 14, 2004.
463. "Nearly two years ago": SR speech, March 2, 1999.
464. "My last shot to get something sensible done": Interview with SR, September 14, 2004.
464. "Michel had a plan to merge": Ibid.
464. "It's like earthquakes in California": Interview with WL, November 4, 2005.
465. "It was obviously difficult": Ibid.
465. "first comprehensive federal government": SEC press release and settlement agreement with Lazard, April 22, 1999.
465. "The whole municipal episode": Interview with SR, September 14, 2004.
465. "There I got really, really hurt": Interview with MDW, April 12, 2005.
466. "This really got to me": Ibid.
466. "I could not have felt better": SR e-mail to WL, April 23, 1999.

466. "Forget it": SR e-mail to WL, May 1999.
466. "decided to step back": Lazard press release, June 6, 1999.
467. "David-Weill or the Highway": *Institutional Investor*, July 1999.
467. "We would have preferred": Lazard press release, June 6, 1999.
467. "hastily publicized": *Economist*, June 10, 1999.
467. "lost a chosen successor": *BusinessWeek*, June 21, 1999.
467. "It is a very curious thing": Ibid.
468. "There [were] a tremendous number of people": Interview with a Lazard partner.
468. "All these people trying to do battle": Interview with Luis Rinaldini, November 18, 2004.
468. "The first time I ran banking": Interview with SR, March 16, 2005.
468. "He didn't relate well with me": Interview with MDW, September 15, 2004.
468. "Michel was right in knowing": *Euromoney*, January 2001.
469. "In retrospect there are some things": Interview with SR, March 16, 2005.

Chapter 17. "He Lit Up a Humongous Cigar and Puffed It in Our Faces for Half an Hour"

470. "with a great deal of regret": SR, "Farewell Remarks," June 7, 1999.
470. "As I hope you all feel": Ibid.
470. "100 of his closest friends": SR letter, June 17, 1999.
471. "It was completely logical": Interview with SR, September 14, 2004.
471. "incredulous": Interview with a Lazard partner.
471. "Lazard World is the continuation": WL speech to partners, June 1999.
471. "It's up to us now": Ibid.
472. "That was the moment": Interview with David Verey, May 31, 2005.
472. "All the time she was saying": Interview with MDW, September 15, 2004.
473. "pretty good misery, frankly": Interview with Verey, May 31, 2005.
473. "Dealers are very quick": Interview with MDW; also, MDW provided an annotated tour of his art collection in his Fifth Avenue apartment, September 15, 2004.
473. "When you see Michel looking": Interview with Guy Wildenstein, October 28, 2005.
473. "What you have to understand": Interview with MDW, September 15, 2004.
476. "Once you start thinking about retiring": *Institutional Investor*, July 1999.
476. "It will be whoever is suitable": Ibid.
476. "Michel and I are old friends": Ibid.
476. "There is absolutely abject terror": Ibid.
476. "I don't think there is one partner": Ibid.
477. "Not to address this": Ibid.
477. "He's locked in his character and his legend": Robert Lenzer, "Assault on the House of Lazard," *Forbes,* September 4, 2000.
477. "It is true that Monsieur Bernheim": *Sunday Business,* November 26, 2000.
478. "Michel David-Weill and his cronies": Interview with Jon Wood, February 1, 2005.
478. "a very interesting character": Lenzer, "Assault on the House of Lazard."
478. "We have a mission": Ibid.
478. "I'm not impressed by": Ibid.
478. "break up the Lazard empire": Ibid.
479. "He was unhelpful and incredibly arrogant": Ibid.
479. "The empire is not being ruled": Ibid.
479. "He was not very happy": "Vincent Bolloré, Banking Provocateur," *Bloomberg Markets,* November 2003.
479. "Bolloré bought shares": Ibid.
479. "Michel has pulled off a remarkable coup": AE. December 12, 2000.
479. "A genius is someone": "Vincent Bolloré, Banking Provocateur."
479. "Let's say that no one had ever": *BusinessWeek,* April 23, 2001.

480. "It is not often": *Financial News,* December 11, 2000.
480. "Michel is only getting": Interview with Wood, February 1, 2005.
480. "Michel kind of wanted me to take a hit": Interview with Damon Mezzacappa, August 2, 2004.
481. "When Ira found out": Interview with a Lazard partner.
481. "Damon was a fucking ganef": Interview with a Lazard partner.
481. "What happened when all this transparency": Interview with Mezzacappa, August 2, 2004.
482. "The more our clients turn": "The Last Emperor," *Bloomberg Magazine,* January 2001.
482. "so sumptuous that a Matisse": Ibid.
482. $275,000: Public records, Nassau County, New York.
482. "The idea of a small, private firm": *Institutional Investor,* July 1999.
483. "With so many senior people leaving": *NYT,* December 1, 1999.
483. "by virtue of how he is": Ibid.
483. "Vernon Jordan epitomizes": Ibid.
483. "But I don't walk into Lazard": "Questions for Vernon Jordan," *NYT,* July 16, 2000.
483. "For the first two or three days": WL memorandum, December 1999.
484. "This special treatment of Jordan": *Washington Post,* January 22, 2000.
484. "Did you come all the way": Ibid.
485. "We did the merger with no management": Interview with a Lazard partner.
485. "Lazard is unabashedly different": WL memorandum to managing directors, February 16, 2000.
486. "a contract of adhesion": Interviews with Lazard partners.
486. Details of the merger of the three houses: Lazard LLC merger documents.
487. "It became clear that": *WSJ,* March 7, 2000.
487. "The one asset we have": Ibid.
487. "astonishing good humour and determination": AE, December 10, 2000.
487. "Lazard's is French again": *Euromoney,* January 2001.
487. "He's never straightforward": Ibid.
487. "was one of the most dishonest": Interview with Wood, February 1, 2005.
487. SR's departure from Lazard: Numerous press reports.
488. Messier joining Quadrangle Group: *Financial News,* September 1, 2002.
489. "threatened Armageddon": *Euromoney,* January 2001.
489. "Six months into it": Interview with a Lazard partner.
490. "We may have to change our means": Lenzer, "Assault on the House of Lazard."
490. "I said to Michel": Interview with Verey, May 31, 2005.
490. "Look, I know I've always wanted": Interview with a Lazard partner.
490. "You each supported my appointment": WL memorandum, "Our Future Course," October 24, 2000.
491. "I remain chairman": *Euromoney,* January 2001.
491. "It would not be abnormal": Ibid.
491. "cutting off Loomis at the knees": *Euromoney,* November 2001.
491. "We've been through a period of turmoil": *BusinessWeek,* November 27, 2000.
491. "The mood was ghastly": *WSJ,* November 13, 2002.
492. "We are the independent and private": WL memorandum to the executive committee, October 24, 2000; WL speech, November 2000; and *Institutional Investor,* December 2000.
492. "If we were to sell": *BusinessWeek,* November 27, 2000.
492. "The price was obscene": "Dressing Up Lazard," *Bloomberg Magazine,* February 2003.
492. "Bolloré caused just a huge distraction": Interview with a Lazard partner.
493. "It's all about IQ": Rich Karlgaard, "Microsoft's IQ Dividend," *WSJ,* July 28, 2004.
493. "The crux for all investment banks": *Economist,* November 30, 2000.

493. "The machinery, the culture": AE, December 10, 2000.
493. "After an outstanding year": AE, December 22, 2000.

Chapter 18: "Lazard May Go Down Like the Titanic!*"*

494. "That was the beginning": Interview with a Lazard partner.
494. "Within weeks, Michel was undermining": Interview with a Lazard partner.
494. "Bill actually had come in on": Interview with a Lazard partner.
495. "He was told by them": Interview with a Lazard partner.
495. "I mean, people thought that it": Interview with a Lazard partner.
495. "Richard has been a gifted banker": Article/press release on Microsoft.com, November 30, 2000.
496. "But basically, Bill insisted": Interview with a Lazard partner.
496. "Now, you have to remember": Interview with a Lazard partner.
496. "All of us also knew": Interview with a Lazard partner.
496. "Everybody in Europe wanted more points": Interview with a Lazard partner.
496. "Bill, on this first working day of 2001": MDW to WL, January 2, 2001.
497. "has $50 million too much expense": AE, January 13, 2001.
497. "some sort of gesture": Ibid.
497. "This would be a fine start": Ibid.
497. "Michel, with whom Bill had discussed": Ibid.
497. "our usual very frank conversation"; Ibid.
497. "We will either work": Ibid.
497. "It is interesting to consider why": Ibid.
498. "to hold the firm together": Ibid.
498. "Loomis played an interesting, watchful game": AE, January 20, 2001.
498. "deeply and unusually depressed": AE, February 1, 2001.
498. "yet another threat to quit": Ibid.
498. "big cuts" in New York: Ibid.
498. "In a nutshell": Ibid.
498. "equity scheme": Ibid.
499. "a rather excited voice": Ibid.
499. "chasing abortive schemes": Ibid.
499. "Bill appeared to lose his temper": Ibid.
499. "There will be trouble ahead": Ibid.
499. "three hours to chew on": Ibid.
499. "pretty bizarre scheme": Ibid.
499. "Bill's behaviour is quite against the grain": Ibid.
499. The account of Verey's mood: Ibid.
500. "He simply could not face": Ibid.
500. "unacceptable": AE, February 4, 2001.
500. follow-up meeting: Interview with Lazard partners.
500. Verey sent a letter: AE, February 4, 2001.
500. "received the impression": AE, February 22, 2001.
501. "Our name in the world is excellent": MDW speech at February 20, 2001, executive committee meeting; speech dated February 12, 2001.
501. "commitment fest": AE, February 22, 2001.
501. "Michel made it clear": Ibid.
501. "could impact the timing": Ibid.
502. "good book about what I have seen": *NYT,* January 23, 2001.
502. "I decided that I couldn't go back": *Institutional Investor,* May 2001.
502. "No, you know I can't do this": Interview with FGR, January 3, 2005.
502. released him from a provision: Ibid.
502. "Well, we can't do that": AE, February 22, 2001.
502. "extraordinary exercise": Interview with FGR, January 3, 2005.
502. "I could go to court": Ibid.
503. "If they voted to release you": Ibid.
503. Two points were communicated: AE, February 22, 2001.
503. "Another bizarre affair": Ibid.
503. "The idea was that Lazard could use": Interview with FGR, January 3, 2005.
504. "So Felix is back": Lazard chat room on Vault.com, April 26, 2001.

504. "Isn't Felix in his early 70s?": Ibid., April 27, 2001.
504. "Even with his return": Ibid., April 27, 2001.
504. "I think bringing Felix back": Ibid., April 27, 2001.
504. "Seems like Felix is": Ibid., May 10, 2001.
504. "Felix is truly the best": Richard Emerson on Vault.com, June 21, 2001.
505. "We see the writing on the wall": Lazard chat room on Vault.com, March 15, 2001.
505. "Due to the fact that MDW": Ibid., March 16, 2001.
506. "In the next two weeks": Ibid., March 17, 2001.
506. "There are rumors of layoffs": Ibid., March 19, 2001.
506. "First of all": Ibid., March 20, 2001.
506. "Lazard's reputation": Ibid., March 31, 2001.
506. "Imagine being in the middle": Ibid., March 31, 2001.
506. "I got a call from Bill Loomis": Ibid., April 2, 2001.
506. "It is shit": Ibid., April 1, 2001.
507. "Everyone at the firm knows it": Ibid.
507. "First, you had this level of expectations": Interview with a Lazard partner.
507. "By March, he was saying": Interview with a Lazard partner.
507. Project S: AE; and interviews with Lazard partners.
507. "The day we go public one way or another": AE, around February 22, 2001 (undated entry).
507. "Who owns Lazard": AE, March 18, 2001.
508. "shabbily dealt with": Ibid.
508. "If Loomis goes ahead": Ibid.
508. "cope with the 'rumours' ": AE, April 24, 2001.
508. "it had been a rotten day": Ibid.
508. "on a friendly basis": Ibid.
508. "honorably consider alternatives": Ibid.
509. "The difficulty I had with David": Interview with MDW, January 31, 2005.
509. "My first loyalty is to Michel David-Weill": Interview with David Verey, May 31, 2005.
509. "very touched by that": Interview with MDW, November 30, 2005.
509. "Your essential qualities": Bruno Roger to Adrian Evans, May 11, 2001.
510. "He lost control of the situation completely": Interview with a Lazard partner.
510. "We need to have more vibrant incentives": WL speech, May 25, 2001.
511. "A house divided against itself": E-mail correspondence between WL and Adrian Evans, June 26, 2001.
511. Michel had three messages for him: E-mail correspondence between WL and Adrian Evans, July 6, 2001.
511. "With that, I went to bed": Ibid.
512. "if others wish to put themselves": Ibid.
512. "Perhaps it was an illusion": AE, July 12, 2001.
512. "both publicly and privately": Ibid.
512. "we have to work together": Ibid.
513. "EAT BEFORE READING": Adrian Evans e-mail, July 20, 2001.
513. "This will be colorful, if 'disturbing' ": Ibid.
513. "$70 million is unlikely to be": Lazard partner e-mail, July 21, 2001.
513. "lecture on Paris' feeling of isolation": Evans e-mail, July 21, 2001.
514. "When you say to partners": Interview with Bruno Roger.
514. "To imagine Michel becoming involved": Evans e-mail, July 21, 2001.
514. "We need to be honest in our assessment": WL to MDW, July 23, 2001.
514. "And that was the *only* future": Interview with a Lazard partner.
515. "I would say that I started": Interview with a Lazard partner.
515. "ridiculous to float or sell now": Interview with a Lazard partner.
515. "We might prefer restructuring": Ibid.

515. "So nothing will happen": Ibid.
515. "You suggest that we 'fire' Tom": WL e-mail to MDW, July 31, 2001.
516. "angry, quarrelsome" one: AE, August 2, 2001.
516. "The guy was the manager": Interview with MDW, December 1, 2004.
516. "I think he was losing confidence": Ibid.
517. Summer 2001 efforts to hire Bruce Wasserstein: Interviews with MDW, FGR, WL, and a spokesman for BW.
518. "unproductive and highly dangerous": AE, August 29, 2001.
518. "we speak with them all the time": Ibid.
518. Two meetings in Biarritz: Interview with MDW, November 30, 2005.
518. "they are dying to do something": AE, August 29, 2001.
518. "Personally, I am not against it": Ibid.
518. "were all the same": Ibid.
518. "You would be bribed to stay": Ibid.
518. "I would not work hard": Ibid.
518. "There was my knowledge": Interview with MDW, December 1, 2004.
519. "I mean, even though they went to talk": Interview with a Lazard partner.
519. "Felix would've done it": Ibid.
519. "It's unclear how far the Lehman discussions got": Interview with Ken Wilson, January 18, 2005.
519. "with pleasure": Interview with MDW, November 30, 2005.
519. discussions between the two firms: Interviews with Lazard bankers; and *WSJ*, November 7, 2001.
519. two-paragraph agreement: Interviews with MDW and WL.
520. "Because I am an eternal optimist": Interview with MDW, September 15, 2004.
520. "I spent the rest of the day": Vernon Jordan sermon to the First Congregational Church in Atlanta, September 23, 2001.
521. "The curious thing with me": Interview with MDW, September 15, 2004.
521. "I was not totally against a deal with Lehman": Interview with MDW, November 30, 2005.
522. "Look, you know I never participated": Ibid.
522. "There are five of us stuck here" and story of partners flying back to the United States in MDW's jet; Interview with a Lazard partner.
523. "I have long been concerned and articulate": WL e-mail to Adrian Evans, September 23, 2001.
524. "joking" and "happy": Interview with a Lazard partner.
524. "Very interesting, very odd, very puzzling": Interview with a Lazard partner.
525. "Fundamentally, if you shut down Capital Markets": AE, October 16, 2001.
525. "menacing monotone" and "To be perfectly frank": Ibid.
525. "Every time we have this discussion": Ibid.
525. he fired Tashjian: Interviews with Lazard partners.
525. "Gratuitous violence": Interview with a Lazard partner.
525. "a watershed event": Interview with MDW, December 1, 2004.
526. "In a partnership": Ibid.
526. "I reached the conclusion": Interview with WL, June 30, 2005.
526. "At that point I knew": Interview with Ken Jacobs, October 27, 2004.
527. "So here I am in a situation": Interview with WL, June 30, 2005; and WL e-mail to Scott Hoffman, October 21, 2001.
527. "His advice was to hold on": Interview with WL, June 30, 2005.
527. "Maybe you were once a banker": Ibid.
527. "This was an impossible situation": Ibid.
528. "I thought about it on Sunday": Ibid.
528. "Otherwise, I just get tarred": Ibid.; and WL e-mail, October 20, 2001.
528. "goes far enough in NYC": Marcus Agius e-mail to WL, October 22, 2001.
528. "I must also tell you": Interview with WL, June 30, 2005.

528. "You are a great partner": WL e-mail to Adrian Evans, October 23, 2001.
529. "work with clients and focus": Lazard press release, October 24, 2001; and *WSJ*, October 25, 2001.
529. "If Michel had to offer them the olive branch": *Daily Deal*, October 24, 2001.
529. "He was so much in David-Weill's shadow": *Euromoney*, November 2001.
529. "People don't have a long time": Interview with MDW, December 1, 2004.
530. "was a catastrophe": Interview with a Lazard partner.
530. "Turning back the clock": Interview with MDW, September 15, 2004.
530. "never been able to keep": *Bloomberg*, October 24, 2001.
530. "the high-profile departures": "Men Overboard," *Economist*, November 3, 2001.
530. "A change is required": AE, November 8, 2001.
531. "basically whatever we want": Ibid.
531. "He argued that he increases": Ibid.
531. "Is this better or worse": Ibid.
531. "The deal is on": Ibid.
531. "Well, I've got to say": Interview with MDW, November 30, 2005.
532. sold his eponymous firm: Numerous press reports.
532. "That's utter baloney": Vicky Ward, "Lazard's Clash of the Titans," *Vanity Fair*, April 2005.
533. "It's classic Bruce": Interview with a former Wasserstein Perella partner.
533. "he should be free to leave": *WSJ*, November 15, 2001.
534. "old news": Interview with a Lazard partner.
534. "unfinished business": Interview with SR, September 14, 2001.
534. "Before Bruce ever got into a discussion": Interview with a Lazard partner.
535. "Who would take this job?": *BusinessWeek*, November 12, 2001.
535. WL call to Fuld: Interview with WL; and WL letter to Fuld, November 8, 2001.
535. "Dear Lenny": *WSJ*, November 15, 2001.
536. "After 25 years of stewardship": MDW memorandum/press release, November 15, 2001.
536. "I am delighted to join Lazard:" Ibid.
536. "To take a firm with potential": BW on *The Charlie Rose Show*, January 4, 2006.
536. "great firm," "intergenerational transition," "Classic small business problem": Ibid.
536. "It was obviously a deal": Interview with a Lazard partner.
536. "One of the most interesting things": Bruce Wasserstein, *Big Deal* (New York: Warner Books, 1998), and *Harvard Business School Bulletin*, October 1996.
537. "Well, I had two thoughts, not reactions": Interview with MDW, November 30, 2005.
537. nothing short of *suicidal*: Interviews with François Voss (January 31, 2005) and other Lazard partners.
537. "I knew the accounts of the Wasserstein firm": Interview with MDW, January 12, 2005.
538. "It is very difficult to manage a private firm": Interview with MDW, September 15, 2004.
538. "Both are considered brilliant bankers": *WSJ*, November 16, 2001.
538. joint telephone interview: Ibid.
538. "People should worry about customers": *Financial Times*, November 16, 2001.
538. "There is no sharing": *BusinessWeek*, November 16, 2001.
538. reaction within Lazard: Various press reports.
539. "inherited a ship with a mutinous crew": *NYT*, January 4, 2002.
539. "off on the same duck shoot": *Economist*, December 5, 2002.
539. "Clearly Michel knew what he had to do": Interview with a Lazard partner.

Chapter 19. Bid-'Em-Up Bruce

540. "Bruce is very creative": *People,* June 25, 1990.
540. "His PR machine was working": Interview with Lynne Killin, March 2, 2006.
540. "female pioneer in corporate America": *New York,* November 18, 2002.
540. "little like Penn and Teller": Phoebe Hoban, "The Family Wasserstein," *New York,* January 4, 1993.
540. "Morris was an extremely gentle": Interview with a Wasserstein family friend.
541. "They were in the ribbon business": Interview with Ivan Cohen, January 23, 2006.
541. "We should all be as happy": Ibid.
541. Information about Abner Wasserstein: ARC of Monroe County Web site and other press reports.
542. "Bruce was a genius": *New York,* November 18, 2002; and Vicky Ward, "Lazard's Clash of the Titans," *Vanity Fair,* April 2005.
542. "One day, this is going to be mine": "Dressing Up Lazard," *Bloomberg Magazine,* February 2003.
542. "Sweetie, he's a play unto himself!": Pamela Wasserstein at Wendy Wasserstein's memorial service, March 13, 2006.
542. "It had a major effect on him": Paul Cowan, "The Merger Maestro," *Esquire,* May 1984.
542. "He was always the sort of kid": Ibid.
542. "When I was a kid": L. J. Davis, "Wall Street's Wonder Boys," *NYT Magazine,* January 28, 1990.
543. The headlines and "The funny thing about the whole situation": Bruce Wasserstein, "Never Trust a Naked Editor," Publick Occurrences, *Michigan Daily,* January 19, 1967.
543. "He had a tremendous intellect": Interview with Harvey Wasserman, December 22, 2005.
544. "First you pick a department": Bruce Wasserstein, "Raw Power Beats System Every Time," *Michigan Daily,* April 8, 1966.
545. "Let's put it this way": Interview with Killin, March 2, 2006.
545. "Commuting by bicycle between the two schools": *Harvard Business School Bulletin,* October 1996.
545. a collection of thirteen essays: Bruce Wasserstein and Mark J. Green, eds., *With Justice for Some* (Boston: Beacon Press, 1970).
545. "He damned well better have": Interview with Killin, March 2, 2006.
545. "He always had a lot of fish to fry": Interview with Ralph Nader, June 27, 2005.
545. "I remember him saying": Interview with Killin, March 2, 2006.
546. collaborated on another book: Mark J. Green with Beverly C. Moore Jr. and Bruce Wasserstein, *The Closed Enterprise System* (New York: Grossman, 1972).
546. his thirty-four-page: Bruce Wasserstein, "British Merger Policy from an American Perspective," *Yale Law Journal* 82, no. 4 (1973).
546. "almighty lucre": Interview with Nader, June 27, 2005.
546. Bruce keeps a framed copy: Interview with a friend of BW.
546. "First of all": Interview with Killin, March 2, 2006.
547. "So she was making fun of my rocks": Ibid.
547. "We were doing taxes": Ibid.
548. "I remember reading about all the fees": *Institutional Investor,* June 1987.
548. "I don't think I was at the meeting": Ibid.
549. "When the M&A effort at First Boston": Wasserstein, *Big Deal.*
549. "The structure of the deal was so complex": Davis, "Wall Street's Wonder Boys."
549. written the blueprint: Bruce Wasserstein, *Corporate Finance Law: A Guide for the Executive* (New York: McGraw-Hill, 1978).
550. "The deal business is unfortunately replete": Ibid., p. 4.
551. "He has great ambition and great confidence": Interview with a friend of BW.

551. The Bruce brand got a boost: Robert Metz, *NYT,* May 2, 1980.
551. "heavy-set and blond": *NYT,* April 21, 1981.
551. "Wasserstein is best at figuring out": Tim Metz, *WSJ,* April 21, 1982.
551. "Simon and Garfunkel": L. J. Davis, "Slightly Tarnished," *New York Times Magazine*, January 28, 1990.
552. "I spotted this tall": Interview with Clarence Fanto, February 4, 2006.
552. "Overweight and chronically rumpled": Cowan, "Merger Maestro."
553. "Of course that is a good thing": Ibid.
554. "What I'd like to think of as the hallmark": *Institutional Investor,* June 1987.
556. "transform Wall Street": *WSJ,* November 6, 1986.
556. "There was a swirl of controversy": *Institutional Investor,* June 1987.
557. "These collapses will be long": Carol Loomis, "The Biggest Looniest Deal Ever," *Fortune,* June 18, 1990.
557. "Blood is everywhere": *Forbes*, February 5, 1990.
557. "He didn't see that": Ward, "Lazard's Clash of the Titans."
557. "Bruce had incredible leverage": *Fortune,* March 14, 1988.
558. "I thought Wasserstein was out of line": Ibid.
558. "If you shoot him": Ward, "Lazard's Clash of the Titans."
558. "It was smoke": *Fortune,* March 14, 1988.
558. "lowered both his eyes": Michael Lewis, *Liar's Poker* (New York: W. W. Norton, 1989), p. 226n.
559. "The memo came in": Interview with Mike Biondi, December 2, 2005.
559. "I was really pissed": Ibid.
559. "Wasserstein was embarrassed": *Fortune,* March 14, 1988.
559. "Chuck's obviously reading from a script": Interview with Biondi, December 2, 2005.
560. "They can make a few phone calls": *Los Angeles Times,* February 3, 1988.
560. "I'm in Boston": Interview with Dan Okrent, January 7, 2006.
561. "I didn't give a shit": Ward, "Lazard's Clash of the Titans."
561. "For 18 months we were golden": Ibid.
562. "fraud upon the board": *Newsweek,* July 10, 1989; and *Forbes,* August 7, 1989.
562. "Macmillan shareholders received a spectacular price": *Newsweek,* July 10, 1989.
562. "What advantage would Wasserstein": "Bid-'Em-Up Bruce," *Forbes,* August 7, 1989.
562. "right up there with the best": *Newsweek,* July 10, 1989.
562. "It was the first time I'd ever really": Interview with Fred Seegal, April 18, 2005.
563. "All at one time": "Bid-'Em-Up Bruce."
563. "carefully cultivated image": Ibid.
563. "Mr. Wasserstein has found himself": *WSJ,* December 11, 1989.
564. "was the principal architect": Ibid.
564. "I don't think the company is worth": *WSJ,* July 11, 1990.
564. "The minute we came back from lunch" and the story of Edwin Bohl: Donald Barlett and James Steele, *America: What Went Wrong?* (New York: Andrews and McMeel, 1992), p. 29.
565. "I'd like to thank all of you": *WSJ,* January 11, 1990.
565. "The idea was to get the deal done": *WSJ,* February 11, 1991.
565. "Wasserstein knowingly failed to stop": *Forbes,* February 5, 1990.
565. "It was like playing three-dimensional chess": *NYT,* April 2, 1988.
566. "The financing was not done on a timely basis": *BusinessWeek,* October 2, 1989.
566. "Campeau is said to have raged": Davis, "Wall Street's Wonder Boys."
566. "People invent a simple, convenient fiction": Ibid.
567. "What he was always best at": Joe

Nocera, "Barbarian's End," *GQ*, May 1991.
567. fifty-five-hundred-word excerpt: Bryan Burrough and John Helyar, "Inside History's Biggest Takeover," *WSJ*, January 4, 1990.
567. "Consequently, they do know": Bruce Wasserstein, letter to the editor, *WSJ*, January 11, 1990.
568. "show of fighting back": Interview with Bryan Burrough.
568. "Kravis had to know the damage": Nocera, "Barbarian's End."
568. "Requests for interviews get shunted": Christopher Byron, *New York*, February 5, 1990.
568. "in a slump": *M, Inc.*, September 1990.
569. "second opinion on price and structure": *WSJ*, November 27, 1990.
569. "didn't want to disturb Ovitz": Ibid.
569. "All in all, the incident made": Nocera, "Barbarian's End."
569. "Nietzsche's whole posit": Interview with a friend of BW.
570. "He was very decisive": Interview with a friend of BW.
570. "is just another acquisition for Bruce": Interview with a friend of BW.
571. "He did this against the advice": Ward, "Lazard's Clash of the Titans."
571. "History has shown": Interview with a friend of BW.
571. "Bruce on the investment side": Ward, "Lazard's Clash of the Titans."
571. "All of a sudden, I read": Davis, "Wall Street's Wonder Boys."
572. "If you think I'm bitter": Interview with a former partner of BW.
572. "brutal": Ward, "Lazard's Clash of the Titans."
572. "Claude is very charming, and very funny": Ibid.

Chapter 20. Civil War

573. "I don't care about it": *Sunday Telegraph,* November 18, 2001.
573. "He's so pompous": Interview with Jon Wood, February 1, 2005.
573. "The politics are over at Lazard": Numerous press reports, including *WSJ,* November 13, 2002.
573. "Anyone who says that": *Sunday Telegraph,* November 18, 2001.
574. "What's that French song?": Ibid.
574. "He introduces himself": Interview with a Lazard partner.
574. "It was deflating": Interview with Ken Jacobs, October 31, 2005.
574. "It was a big deal": Ibid.
575. "That was the collapse": Ibid.
576. After Loomis calmed Tashjian down: Interview with WL, MDW, and other Lazard partners.
576. "The problem with Lazard": Landon Thomas Jr., "Will Lazard Make It?" *New York Observer,* December 10, 2001.
577. "publicly humiliated": AE, undated notes around December 2001.
577. "is a disaster": Ibid.
577. "Okay, now I'm the boss": Interview with a Lazard partner.
578. "He had no choice": Interview with a Lazard partner.
578. complained about the "hold" music: Interview with a Lazard partner.
578. new management team: Lazard press release, January 3, 2002.
578. "according to Lazard calculations": *NYT,* January 4, 2002.
579. "new fandangos": *WSJ,* January 3, 2002.
579. "BW will take over from MDW": Summary of "Lazard LLC Third Amended and Restated Operating Agreement."
579. "Heads of House": Ibid.
580. "you will lose all the A-2 goodwill": Scott Hoffman to recipients of the third amended agreements, January 10, 2002.
581. "In thinking about the end game": Memo circulating among Lazard partners.
581. six bankers from DKW: Numerous press reports, including *WSJ,* January 10, 2002.
582. "With super rich contracts": Lazard

chat room on Vault.com, February 17, 2002.

582. Details of Weinstock, Herenstein, and Santana's departure: *Lazard Debt Recovery GP et al., plaintiffs, vs. Michael A. Weinstock and Andrew J. Herenstein, defendants* (CA no. 19503), as filed and adjudicated in the Court of Chancery in the state of Delaware, and *Weinstock and Herenstein, plaintiffs, vs. Lazard Debt Recovery GP et al., defendants* (CA No. 20048), also in the Court of Chancery.

584. "I've never sued anybody": Interview with MDW, December 1, 2004.

584. "And then within minutes": Ibid.

584. "People are cheap at the moment": *Financial Times*, December 6, 2002.

584. "No more politics": *WSJ*, November 13, 2002, and numerous press reports.

585. "I'm gone": Interviews with Lazard partners.

585. "Historically, people had talked about the business": "Dressing Up Lazard," *Bloomberg Magazine*, February 2003.

585. "He's the only guy": Interview with Al Garner.

585. "After this, no corporate financier": *Financial News*, July 21, 2002.

585. "Recent layoffs of MDs were necessary": Lazard chat room on Vault.com, July 27, 2002.

586. "Morale is pretty low": Ibid., August 3, 2002.

586. "some of the plushest used by any investment bank": *Daily Telegraph*, May 3, 2004.

586. malfunctioning telephone system: *Financial News*, July 6, 2003.

586. "Instead of a dimly lit waiting room": "Dressing Up Lazard."

587. "Michel was torn about that": Interview with a Lazard partner.

588. "Bruce was on a spending spree": Interview with a Lazard partner.

588. "Liquidity doesn't last forever": Interview with a Lazard partner.

588. Details of Intesa's 2002 investment in Lazard and its unwinding in 2006: Numerous press reports, including *WSJ*, September 10, 2002, and Lazard public filings.

588. "We have a spiritual ethos": *Financial Times*, December 6, 2002.

588. "When you look across Wall Street": Ibid.

589. "Some people see talented people as difficult": *WSJ*, November 13, 2002.

589. "reinvested extensively in our future": Mike Castellano memorandum, January 30, 2003.

589. "good year" in 2002 "in a difficult environment": Ibid.

589. "memorandum capital deferred compensation": Ibid.

590. "Bullshit capital": Interview with a Lazard partner.

590. "Michel wasn't going to watch": Interview with a Lazard partner.

590. Communist revolution in the right ventricle: Interview with David Verey, November 10, 2005.

590. Details of Lazard's controversial hiring of the Merrill Lynch bankers and the lawsuit that followed: Supreme Court, State of New York, New York County, Merrill Lynch, petitioner, and Lazard Frères & Co. et al., respondents (index no. 600867/03), February–April 2003. Also Lazard's countersuit (index no. 601159/03). Also NASD arbitration no. 03–01–01484.

592. "So what? There are lawsuits all the time": Interview with a Lazard partner.

592. "I'm very appreciative that Hancock": *WSJ*, September 30, 1993.

593. "to do one last deal": "Dressing Up Lazard."

593. "I wish I had Lazard's asset management franchise": *Financial Times*, December 6, 2002.

595. Lazard Asset Management IPO idea: Numerous press reports, including *Financial Times*, February 6, 2003, and December 6 and 5, 2002.

595. "What can I do to get you to stay?": *Institutional Investor*, February 12, 2004.

595. "Norman Eig misread": *Financial Times*, February 6, 2003.

595. "What happened at LAM": *Institutional Investor,* February 12, 2004.
596. "Bruce came in and they started to talk": Interview with Ken Wilson, February 3, 2005.
596. "worst business meeting he ever had": Interview with a Lazard partner.
596. "sleazoid": Interview with Wilson, February 3, 2005.
596. "it's just generally known": Ibid.
597. "It has to be considered brilliant": *Daily Deal*, December 16, 2003.
597. "What do you gain": *Newsweek,* February 23, 2004.
597. "It basically goes to confidence": Ibid.
597. "maddeningly vague": *NYT,* December 18, 2003.
597. "Certainly, if you look at it": *NYT,* December 22, 2003.
597. "It's really weird": *New York Observer,* December 22, 2003.
598. "A lot of them are big ego trips": *NYT,* December 18, 2003.
598. "At best, the magazine": Ibid.
598. "approximately $2.0 billion": Wasserstein & Co. Web site.
599. "Mr. Wasserstein has stated": *New York Observer,* January 5, 2004, p. 4.
599. "I think that Bruce was surprised": *NYT,* December 18, 2003.
600. "just to be clear, Media Maneuvers": Yvette Kantrow, Media Maneuvers, *Daily Deal,* January 9, 2004.
600. "everybody, i am happy to announce": E-mail from Adam Moss to staff of *New York,* July 14, 2005.
600. "There's a view at the big firms": *WSJ,* November 13, 2002.
602. "after twenty-five years of blowing cigar smoke": *Financial Times,* February 20, 2004.
602. "The capital partners are concerned": Interview with a Lazard banker.
602. "You can understand that the capitalists": *Financial News,* January 2004.
602. "You'd go to a board meeting": "The Taking of Lazard," *BusinessWeek,* November 6, 2006.
603. "cordial": Interview with MDW, January 12, 2005.
603. "Bruce has done a decent job": *New York Post,* February 23, 2004.
603. "If you hire a brash": Matthew Lynn, Bloomberg.com, February 25, 2004.
603. "Mr. Wasserstein is head of Lazard": *Financial Times,* March 8, 2004.
604. "ungentlemanly tussle": *Financial Times,* March 5, 2004.
604. "hyperkinetic": *BusinessWeek,* February 24, 2003.
604. "I am gratified by the relationship": MDW in Eurazeo 2003 annual report.
605. "If Lazard goes back to delivering": *Daily Telegraph,* March 9, 2004.
605. "Because we have not highlighted": Mike Castellano memorandum, March 12, 2004.
605. "Lazard management is currently leading": *WSJ,* April 2, 2004.
605. "window dressing": Interview with MDW, November 30, 2005.
606. "we have been told that this year": *Financial Times,* April 3, 2004.
606. "all votes on issues": Ibid.
607. "There were differences over the timing": Press reports, including Dow Jones newswires, of the Eurazeo meeting, May 5, 2004.
607. "According to the financial statements": MDW memorandum, May 11, 2004.
607. "With regard to the notice": BW memorandum, May 14, 2004.
608. "This is Michel's greatest nightmare": Interview with a Lazard partner.
608. "muscle memory": Ibid.
608. "Mr. Wasserstein is more interested": *Economist,* February 26, 2004.
608. Lazard had started interviewing underwriters: *Investment Dealers' Digest,* May 24, 2004.
609. "besieged" by bankers: *Financial Times,* June 16, 2004.
609. "We are listening and evaluating": *Financial Times,* June 16, 2004.
609. "We do expect significantly": Ibid.

609. "If he doesn't come up with a plan": Ibid.
610. "An IPO could . . . solve one of": *WSJ,* June 17, 2004.
610. "Even if Lazard does one day plump": *Financial Times,* June 16, 2004.
610. "put aside" their "long-standing differences": *Le Monde,* June 25, 2004.
611. "the two men agreed": Ibid.
611. "He yearns to be an industrialist": *Financial Times,* October 9, 2004.
611. Steve Golub's role as intermediary: Interviews with Ken Jacobs (December 6, 2005) and Steve Golub (October 31 and December 2, 2005).
611. "When we first started out": Interview with Golub, October 31, 2005.
612. "Not good": Jeffrey Sonnenfeld, *WSJ,* July 14, 2004.
612. "No firm decision has been made": *WSJ,* August 20, 2004.
612. buy the combined 36 percent: Emily Thornton, "The End Game at Lazard," *BusinessWeek,* August 26, 2004.
613. "David-Weill is one of the wiliest": *Bloomberg News,* August 27, 2004.
613. "crazy": Interview with a Lazard partner.
613. "It's a mess": Ibid.
613. "We don't want to go from having a king": *Financial Times,* October 4, 2004.
614. "Rumpled, ruthless, Bid 'Em Up Bruce": *New York Observer,* September 20, 2004.
614. Bruce gave a presentation: Press reports (see *WSJ,* September 27, 2004) and interviews with Lazard partners.
614. "The public is going to be along": *WSJ,* September 27, 2004.
614. "There are several issues": *New York Observer,* September 20, 2004.
615. "People fearful for their jobs": Interview with a Lazard partner.
615. "We are not going to sign under duress": *Financial Times,* October 3, 2004.
616. "I would completely agree with that": *Sunday Telegraph,* October 10, 2004.
616. "We're paying Michel out at a premium": *WSJ,* October 4, 2004.
616. "He was shocked and not very excited": Interview with a Lazard partner.
616. "serene ambience": *Financial Times,* October 6, 2004.
616. "floating a company like Lazard": Ibid.
617. "I remember being surprised": Interview with MDW, January 31, 2005.
617. "They are all at a canonical age": *Le Nouvel Observateur,* October 14, 2004.
617. "Now he has to consult": *WSJ,* October 6, 2004.
617. "Many of us are already rich": October 6, 2004.
617. "For Bruce it's a great deal": Interview with a Lazard partner.
617. "Bruce seems very sure of himself": *Financial Times,* October 9, 2004.
617. "the firm is in a complete state of disarray": *NYT,* October 5, 2004.
617. "putting lipstick on a pig": *NYT,* October 3, 2004.
618. "We have informed the capitalists": BW to Lazard partners, October 5, 2004.
618. "I'm wedded to history": *BusinessWeek,* November 6, 2006.
618. "It is less a charm offensive": *Sunday Telegraph,* October 10, 2004.
618. "He draws energy": *Financial Times,* October 9, 2004.
618. "When you hire an investment bank": *Financial Times,* October 7, 2004.
618. "As far as I'm concerned": *Sunday Times,* October 17, 2004.
619. "The people who are suffering": *WSJ,* October 13, 2004.
619. "After having consulted with my partners": MDW e-mail to BW, October 22, 2004.
619. "If I just say no": Interview with MDW, January 12, 2005.
619. "Michel tried to find a successor": Interview with Jean-Claude Haas, February 1, 2005.
620. "strong belief in the future of Lazard": MDW e-mail to BW, October 21, 2004.
620. "satisfied that enough of the partners": *Financial Times,* October 21, 2004.

620. "I was very pleased to learn of your decision": BW e-mail to MDW, October 21, 2004.

Chapter 21. "The End of a Dynasty"

621. "Everyone then knew this was a stress sell": Interview with a Lazard banker.
621. "Frenchman who was prepared": Vicky Ward, "Lazard's Clash of the Titans," *Vanity Fair,* April 2005.
622. "Absolutely. But Wasserstein had the money": Interview with Jean-Claude Haas, February 1, 2005.
622. "The conditions are not seen as that important": *Times* (London), October 22, 2004.
623. "just trying to do what is best for the firm": *Financial Times,* October 23, 2004.
624. "blessed with the psychological trait": *WSJ,* December 7, 2004.
624. "We have to be as unselfish": Ibid.
624. "an extra steel beam and a cement support": Ibid.
625. "better, more intimate relationship": Interview with MDW, November 15, 2006.
625. "very good about the letters I wrote in May": Ibid.
625. "I feel good about my letters, too": Ibid.
625. "the history of ambiguity": Ibid.
625. "There are clearly two different points of view": Ward, "Lazard's Clash of the Titans."
625. "an act of faith": Interview with Jean-Claude Haas, February 1, 2005.
625. Lazard's financial performance: S-1 document, December 17, 2004.
626. "So we're at the beginning of a resurgence": BW lecture at Yale University School of Management, September 29, 2005.
627. "His timing as always is exquisite": *Bloomberg,* December 17, 2004.
627. "I'll be stunned": Interview with Damon Mezzacappa.
627. "First of all, I think Bruce": Interview with FGR, January 3, 2005.
627. "I was wrong": Interview with FGR, October 17, 2006.
628. "I'm very uncertain it will occur": Interview with MDW, January 12, 2005.
630. "The tax part was only": *Financial Times,* December 20, 2004.
631. managing directors to sign so-called retention agreements: Lazard Ltd. S-1.
632. "I'd sure hate to be": Lazard chat room on Vault.com, December 24, 2004.
633. "following the hiring of new senior management": Lazard Ltd. S-1.
633. "These provisions [in the buyout agreement] are inappropriate": Correspondence between various Lazard partners, January 14, 2005.
634. "They believe in a strong attack": Ibid.
635. "Which is just not right": Interview with a Lazard partner.
636. "He was found at his Geneva home": Swiss press reports, March 2, 2005.
636. "I called my daughter Beatrice": Interview with MDW, April 12, 2005.
636. "He was rich, he got on people's nerves": *Le Figaro,* March 2, 2005.
636. "He was not only ruthless": *Evening Standard* (London), June 10, 2005.
636. "He was a discreet man": *Tribune de Genève,* March 3, 2005.
637. "I was thinking, maybe he slipped and fell": Bryan Burrough, "The Man in the Latex Suit," *Vanity Fair,* July 2005.
637. "Good, Mr. Stern is home": *Tribune de Genève,* March 3, 2005.
637. "I went to the door": Burrough, "Man in the Latex Suit."
639. "He was aware of men watching": *Mail on Sunday*, April 24, 2005.
639. "And she's some kind of artist": Burrough, "Man in the Latex Suit."
639. "Édouard and Beatrice no longer sleep": Interview with MDW, January 12, 2005.
640. "He gave them both affection and energy": Interview with MDW, April 12, 2005.
640. "It is very sad": Conversation with Annik Percival, May 31, 2005.

640. "Édouard was very upset": Burrough, "Man in the Latex Suit."
640. They had also discussed: *Tribune de Genève,* October 18, 2006.
640. "I'm never going to see her again": Burrough, "Man in the Latex Suit."
641. "Only two people know what happened": Ibid.
641. "I don't think you negotiate": Ibid.
641. "He presses a button": *Paris Match,* March 24, 2005.
641. "A million dollars is expensive": *L'Express,* May 9, 2005.
641. "Some people are always Machiavellian": Interview with MDW, April 12, 2005.
642. "but as my father used to say": Ibid.
642. "She is a desperate woman": Press reports.
642. Eurazeo sold its IRR stake: Press reports and Eurazeo's 2005 annual report.
643. price range for the equity: Amended S-1, April 11, 2005.
643. "hedge funds": Interview with Steve Golub, December 2, 2005.
643. "the firm lost money in each of the last three years": Amended S-1.
643. "I am flabbergasted, I have to say": Interview with a Lazard partner.
644. "There is a clear pattern of greed": Interview with Ken Wilson, April 11, 2005.
644. "All this raises the question:" *Economist,* April 14, 2005.
644. "Add it all up": *BusinessWeek,* April 25, 2005.
644. "one of the most complicated things": Ibid.
644. "Bruce Wasserstein joined Lazard three years ago": Thomas Tuft, Lazard IPO road show, New York Palace, April 27, 2005.
645. "The threshold issue when you're thinking about Lazard": BW, ibid.
645. "Lazard is a very special place": Ibid.
646. "The more complicated the structure": Reuters, April 29, 2005.
647. "How awful is this Lazard IPO deal?": Jim Cramer, "Lazard IPO No More Than a Buy-Off," RealMoney.com, May 2, 2005.
647. "It was a complicated deal": Interview with Wilson, May 17, 2005.
648. "Given the change in the debt market": *Financial News,* May 5, 2005.
648. "Goldman priced right through the static": Interview with Ken Jacobs, December 6, 2005.
648. "Bruce had all the cards": *NYT,* May 5, 2005.
648. "I was associated with Lazard for 45 years": MDW press statement, May 4, 2005.
648. dinner at Per Se: Interview with Tom Tuft, February 6, 2006.
648. Lazard IPO first-day trading: From NYSE.com.
649. "When you see it trading near the offer price": *Bloomberg,* May 5, 2005.
650. "It's too high-profile of a deal": Ibid.
650. "belly flop": *Red Herring* research report, May 6, 2005.
650. "However, a deal that is so transparently": William Wright in *Financial News,* May 9, 2005.
650. "There are numerous negatives": "King's Ransom for Lazard," *Barron's,* May 9, 2005.
651. "Goldman obviously went way out on a limb": *Bloomberg,* May 25, 2005.
651. "left us with a little bit of a black eye": Interview with Wilson.
651. "Bruce got his $25": Luis Rinaldini, *Bloomberg,* May 23, 2005.
652. "doctor who botched a brain surgery": Andrew Ross Sorkin, *NYT,* May 29, 2005.
652. "I was just very gratified": Interview with Tom Tuft, February 6, 2006.
652. "The trading decisions were made": Ibid.
652. Lazard involvement in Fidelity probe: Numerous press reports, including *NYT,* May 5, 2005, and Lazard Ltd. public filings.
652. Details of institutional ownership of Lazard shares: Lazard Ltd. reports as filed with the SEC.

653. "would give him almost unlimited power": *Financial Times,* June 3, 2005.
653. "Gerardo is a really talented guy": "The Taking of Lazard," *BusinessWeek,* November 6, 2006.
653. "The loss of Mr. Braggiotti": Ibid.
654. "I presented my resignation": *Bloomberg,* June 8, 2005.
654. "This firm is held together with Scotch tape": *Crain's New York Business,* June 13, 2005.
654. "material adverse effect" to "Lazard has reiterated": Lazard Ltd. press release, June 14, 2005.
654. "He was the dealmaker at Mediobanca": Press reports.
655. "This would effectively be rebuilding the links": *Bloomberg,* November 8, 2005.
655. "He's putting together a powerful machine": Ibid.
655. "Look, I'm sure they're not happy": Interview with MDW, November 30, 2005.
656. "For me, the IPO fits into": *Le Figaro,* June 30, 2005.
656. "The real challenge that they face": Brad Hintz, research report, Sanford C. Bernstein, August 2005.
656. bought 119,500 additional Lazard shares: BW, Lazard Ltd., Form 4 filing, August 29, 2005.
657. "a certain phase in the history": e-mail correspondence with Marianne Gerschel, June 27, 2005.
657. "I will be leaving Lazard effective tomorrow": Bernard Sainte-Marie e-mail to Lazard employees, August 31, 2005, and from press reports.
657. "It's obscene what's going on here": Conversation with Annik Percival, January 14, 2005.

Afterword

659. "It is now clear that we are effectively": BW statement on Lazard Ltd. earnings call, November 9, 2005.
659. total compensation from Lazard of $14.2 million: Lazard Ltd. 2005 proxy statement as filed with the SEC.
659. Lazard priced a $638 million: Lazard Ltd. public filing with the SEC, December 6, 2006.
660. Bruce refused in late 2005 to publish: Interviews with MDW, Guy Rougemont, Ken Jacobs, and Scott Hoffman.
661. "It hurt me a little": Interview with MDW, November 30, 2005.
661. said to have paid around $4 million . . . and, for another $4 million: Interview with a friend of BW.
662. Camp Seahorse: Interview with a friend of BW.
662. Gulfstream jet: Lazard Ltd. public filings.
662. "His belief in his own ability": Interview with a friend of BW.
662. Felix and his wife: Interview with FGR, October 17, 2006.
663. "He's fine": *Financial Times,* August 3, 2006.
664. "He just wants to be in the center of the action": Ken Auletta, "The Raid," *NY,* March 20, 2006, p. 140.
664. "He leads his whole life": Interview with a friend of BW.
665. "The Lazard Report": February 1, 2006, released publicly February 7, 2006.
665. "TWX is at the center of the storm": Ibid., p. 1.
666. "Time has not been friendly to Time Warner": BW speech at St. Regis Hotel, February 7, 2006.
666. "There are no compelling reasons today": Ibid.
666. "If Dick Parsons indeed has the secret super-spicy sauce": Ibid.
666. "What do you think of the new Lazard?": Conversation with Ken Jacobs, February 7, 2006.
666. "landed with the deafening thud": David Carr, *NYT,* February 13, 2006.
666. "We were disappointed": Doug Mitchelson, Deutsche Bank analyst, in *Financial Times,* February 9, 2006.
667. "Taxes fully understood": Auletta, "Raid," p. 143.

667. "what may turn out to be the biggest proxy fight": *Bloomberg,* February 16, 2006.
667. Ten days later, it was all over: various press reports.
667. "No one who really has been around": Cox News Service, "Conversation with Dick Parsons," May 19, 2006.
667. "For reasons that remain inexplicable": Andrew Ross Sorkin, "The Adviser Who Became the Activist," *NYT,* February 26, 2006.
667. "the trustee for the future of Lazard": Andrew Ross Sorkin, *NYT,* January 15, 2006.
667. "Had he won": Sorkin, "Adviser Who Became the Activist."

Index

© DGF

William D. Cohan was an award-winning investigative journalist before embarking on a seventeen-year career as an investment banker on Wall Street. He spent six years at Lazard Frères in New York and later became a Managing Director at JPMorgan Chase & Co. He is a graduate of Duke University and received both an MS from Columbia University's Graduate School of Journalism and an MBA from its Graduate School of Business. He lives in New York City and Columbia County, New York.